THE REAL
AND THE ROMANTIC

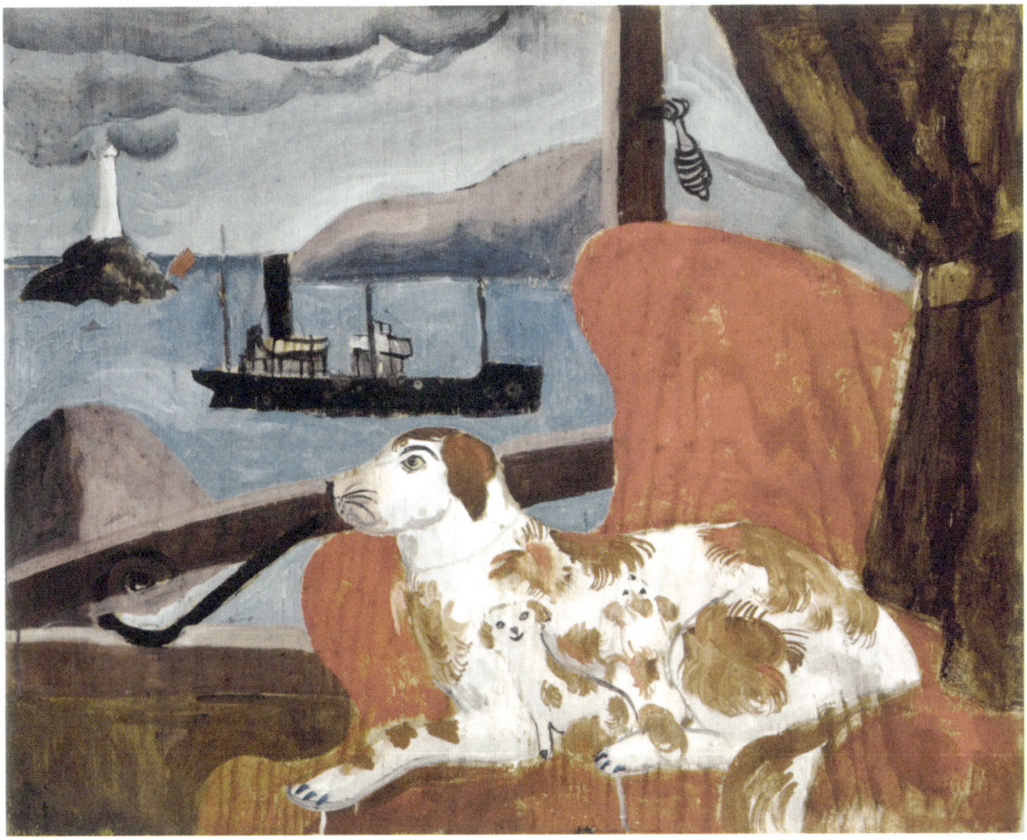

FRANCES SPALDING

THE REAL AND THE ROMANTIC

ENGLISH ART BETWEEN TWO WORLD WARS

Dedicated to Leanna Spalding, with love and thanks

FRONTISPIECE Christopher Wood,
China Dogs in a St Ives Window,
gouache on panel, *c.* 1926.

First published in the United Kingdom in 2022 by
Thames & Hudson Ltd, 181A High Holborn, London WC1V 7QX

Reprinted 2022

British Library Cataloguing-in-Publication Data
A catalogue record for this book is available from the British Library

ISBN 978-0-500-51864-9

Printed and bound in China by RR Donnelley

MIX
Paper from responsible sources
FSC® C144853
FSC www.fsc.org

CONTENTS

One could say that the time has come...honestly to enjoy the shine on the rump of a Munnings horse, the discretion of a Nicholson relief, the fresh-as-paint prettiness of a Susie Cooper teapot, the housewifely amateurishness of an Omega Workshops painted table, the wit of a Shell poster: to chuck exclusive theories overboard. The makers could not; perhaps historians now can. Fifty years should be about the time it takes for the intellectual scaffolding around art to decay, fall away, be dismantled.

Peter Campbell
London Review of Books, vol. 1, no. 4,
6 December 1979

INTRODUCTION

In the short, concentrated period between the two world wars, English art unfolded in diverse ways. Its nature is richly contrary. Staunch conservatism jostles with energetic revivalism; allusions to the classical past or the early Italian Renaissance become aligned with the pulse of the new; the pursuit of the modern and international is suddenly trumped by a return to native traditions, the local and vernacular. Major cities on the Continent continue to act as incubators of modernism, but London both attracts and repels, releasing a cohort of students from the Royal College of Art in the mid-1920s who favour rural life and its associated habits, including the making of gardens. The English countryside takes on a distinctive character in the public mind, inviting fresh and original responses to landscape. And the study of art from distant countries and cultures, which had begun before the First World War, encourages sculptors to expand the parameters of the Western European tradition. Liberating modernity slowly gains in appeal in a world increasingly dominated by glass and steel, by developments in science, engineering, new cinematic devices and photography's discovery of 35mm film. An increase in speed and movement is facilitated by the expansion of railway lines, the availability of cheap cars and the beginnings of a commercial aeronautical industry.

Nevertheless, with the Great War having cut right across cultural and artistic life, it is hardly surprising that this period begins with a decentred art world and a lack of direction. The Spanish flu pandemic, thought to have been brought to Britain by soldiers returning from the trenches, accounted for further loss of life, causing 228,000 deaths and more than fifty million worldwide. At a local level, it removed a founder member of the Camden Town Group – Harold Gilman, a much respected figure – from the presidency of the London Group, then the most significant artists' exhibiting society. It was partly the loss of Gilman that stirred Wyndham Lewis into action, and with the help of Edward McKnight Kauffer he attempted to revive the avant-garde with the 'Group X' exhibition. Held in the Mansard Gallery, inside the furniture shop Heal's in Tottenham Court Road, it ran from 27 March to 24 April 1920, but proved to be a damp squib. A disappointing start also accompanied the Seven and Five Society, formed in 1919 but which likewise held its first exhibition in 1920. Its lack of a clear vision troubled its identity during this period of retrenchment and recovery. Yet it did not fold after its first exhibition, like Group X, but instead rose to prominence in the late 1920s. Charles Harrison, in his landmark book *English Art and Modernism 1900–1939* (1981), regards the 1920s as 'an unpromising decade' but one which ended 'on a note of distinct and independent achievement', thereby preparing the way for the more progressive 1930s.[1]

Harrison was the first art historian to apply rigorous critique to this interwar period. His modernist lens brought clarity to his argument. It also excluded much, which may explain why Richard Morphet, also writing in 1981, noticed that the study of interwar art in England lacked balance. He regretted 'the perennial lack of curiosity in England as to what actually occurred in the art activity of the period'.[2] Since then, much that Harrison overlooked has been brought into focus. Taste has moved on, interests have broadened; interwar realism, instead of arousing mocking hostility, is enjoying popularity, and the art of the 1920s is now much admired for its diversity and imaginative vitality.

In the aftermath of war there were many reasons why a return to modernism felt inappropriate. The aggressive pursuit of the machine-age aesthetic in the pre-1914 period now seemed horribly predictive of industrial warfare, making further revolt against traditionalism undesirable in the wake of so much destruction. When sculptors began to refresh the language of art in the 1920s with modern ideas, they were inspired not by technological advances or the hectic attractions of the metropolis, but by objects from distant cultures found in dusty corners of the British Museum. A different kind of modernism simultaneously began to emerge in the art of painting. Gentler and more lyrical than its sculptural equivalent, it found a touchstone in the art of an untaught mariner, Alfred Wallis, whose instinct and intuition fashioned an art of such immediacy that it affirmed the need for a break with the past. Winifred Nicholson recognized this while looking at the seductive elegance of her father-in-law William Nicholson's still life paintings. His skilful handling of surface textures, highlights and shadows, in her view, shut out modern developments in art. Yet her own search for a more direct form of representation, like that of other artists within the Seven and Five Society, is not fiercely radical or oppositional. David Peters Corbett has argued that during the first fifteen years of peace, modernity in everyday life was rampant but overt or radical modernism in art was disavowed;[3] and that many of the attempts to confront modernity resulted in 'evasive formulations' that are 'nonetheless historically significant as signs of that very inability to speak clearly'.[4] This may be overly harsh, given that a wariness of modernity in the aftermath of war was widespread and understandable. 'To be modern', writes Marshall Berman, 'is to find ourselves in an environment that promises us adventure, power, joy, growth, transformation of ourselves and the world – and, at the same time, that threatens to destroy everything we have, everything we know, everything we are.'[5]

In recent years, retrospective and themed exhibitions have opened up new responses to the interwar period. Paul Liss and Sacha Llewellyn, under their working name Liss Llewellyn, have produced a long list of publications, mounted exhibitions and made loans to other art organizations that have made us look again at the work of less well-known artists. Dr Liv Gibbs, Richard Morris and others, communicating through social media, have further expanded awareness of the visual record associated with the period. Meanwhile the habit of building arguments around binary oppositions in art history, such as that between the city and the country, is no longer acceptable (in the latter example because an increase in public transport eased the transition between the two). Likewise, the former opposition between the romantic or traditional and the modern has been called into question by Alexandra Harris's promotion of *Romantic Moderns* in her book of this title. Over time, the questions asked about art inevitably change, and in the 21st century a more pluralist approach is required to acknowledge new perspectives and broader sympathies. This makes it necessary to look again, and to look differently, at select aspects of interwar art, especially those which offer a sudden intensification of purpose or meaning.

The title of this book, *The Real and the Romantic*, recognizes two recurrent tendencies within this period. Both words have been chosen to avoid the more prescriptive stylistic labels 'realism' and 'Romanticism'. 'The real' is a term often used by artists and, owing to their subjectivities, its meanings are diffuse; but the general underlying implication is that something actual, genuine, authentic and not merely imitative or artificial, has been discerned. 'To practice an art', Michael Ayrton wrote, 'is primarily to discover one's relationship with reality...an attempt to find what in essence is *real* [and to] communicate part of this experience to others and so enlarge their experience.' In the interwar years 'the real' never became a fashionable phrase, like 'significant form', which Clive Bell, influenced by Roger Fry's aesthetic theories, coined in his book *Art* (1914), as that which gives rise to aesthetic emotion. Yet the notion of 'the real' is closely related to this, implying that for a work of art to succeed it must go deeper than a mere visual record. For the artist, as well as for the viewer, it is often experienced as a sudden feeling, a gift or a challenge. Bridget Riley has explained that her paintings often begin with no particular associations or title in mind, and her criteria for judging the work only evolve when sensations begin to indicate its direction. 'They are not attached to anything particular, but when I recognise them in a painting, in certain abstract relationships there, then I feel that I have got something real, that I am on firm ground and can build.'[6]

A work of art can communicate a sense of the real without employing realism as its method of representation. Similarly, romantic feeling, during this period, is less related to a specific group of individuals or set of ideas than to a dominant mood or a shift in feeling. Raymond Williams identified 'structures of feeling' in relation to emergent art, using this seemingly paradoxical phrase to indicate the need for an artist to work through possibilities that are often felt before they are thought. Perception is critical to the expression of both the real and the romantic, and both are often grounded in observation, experience or the handling of materials. The romantic appeal of Winifred Nicholson's paintings or those of Christopher Wood lies in the vitality of their response to the subject *and* in the honesty of touch that is brought to their handling of paint. Both are partly shaped by the world in which the artist operates, for culture and society are inextricably imbricated.

This fact explains why, during the mid to late 1930s, as the international political climate worsened, Myfanwy Piper, then editing an art magazine with an international outlook, recognized the need for artists to turn to the 'reality of abstract art', to the 'most severe and the most stable elements, straight lines, curves, simple shapes and use them as a base', in order to express a 'new complexity which has an organic and spiritual force'.[7] The key ingredient, in her view, was that 'art to have any importance must be intimately related to life in its own time'.[8]

When brought together for the purposes of this book, the terms real and romantic may seem to sit at opposite ends of a scale; but in fact their relationship is more fluid than this, for each can tinge, colour or even merge with the other. The pursuit of the real is different to the pursuit of realism, but the latter is undeniably a dominant thread during these two decades. From a psychological point of view, it suggests a widespread desire to counter the shattering experience of industrial warfare with a return to wholeness and continuity. Art that imitates life, that has a certain mastery of the external world, gives the viewer a comforting sense that we too can map and manage the environment. After so much destruction, realism was initially the language of reconstruction. But realism is also a multi-purpose style: it can soothingly echo the style of Dutch old masters while simultaneously conveying a modern sense of female constriction, as it does in Isabel Codrington's *The Kitchen*; or it can create in Meredith Frampton's portraits an uncanny stillness, almost surreal in its effect. It also offered a conservative language useful for capturing modern pleasures, such as crowds at football matches, shoppers strolling down Oxford Street or travellers in the dining car of a train.

The word 'romantic' is admittedly here used as a loose, umbrella term, to suggest an emotional register that contrasts with the outwardly objective and dispassionate pursuit of realism. Romantic art traditionally seeks a convergence between the outer

Isabel Codrington,
The Kitchen,
oil on canvas,
1927.

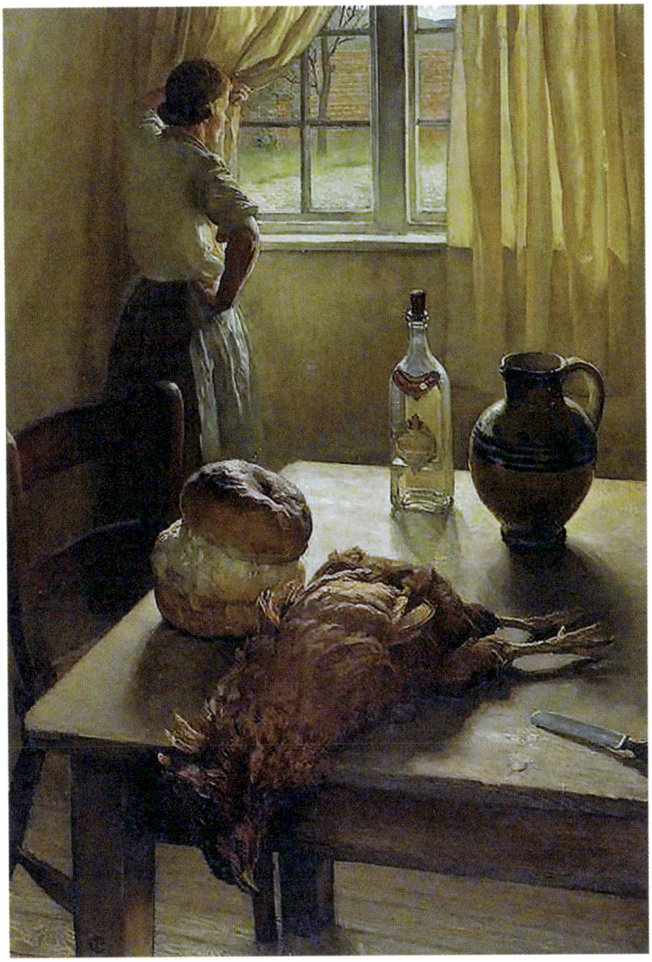

world of fact and the inner world of feeling, self and identity. Romanticism is often associated with a lyric vein in English art and poetry, but it can also be tough and chilly, as in the melancholy light found in Eric Ravilious's landscape watercolours. The romantic element in interwar art became visible long before Raymond Mortimer coined the term 'neo-romantics' in 1938, in connection with a group of artists united not by style, politics and ideology but more by a shared state of mind brought about by the threat and onset of war. John Piper showed how this new romantic movement had ancestral roots in English architecture, art, manuscript illumination and printing when he explored the romantic tradition and affirmed its visionary element in his book *British Romantic Artists*, published in 1942.

Whether real or romantic in outlook, art demands attention, not only to its visual language but also to the historical moment and the conditions in which the artist worked. The 'material turn', widely acknowledged across the humanities and social sciences, has encouraged a broader interpretation of the social construction of art. The interwar decades saw rapid social and economic changes, but the infrastructure within the art world remained very underdeveloped compared to the period after 1945. The Tate Gallery at Millbank (founded in 1897 and divided in 2000 into Tate Britain and Tate Modern) was a relatively young museum, its building gradually expanding but remaining under very conservative management until 1938, when John Rothenstein took over as its director. It lacked the stability of established precedent and was still struggling to assert its identity and purpose. During the interwar years, as a site of inspiration and encouragement, the Tate did little to support young artists. There was also scant help available to artists at this time in the way of state or corporate patronage. Admittedly funds were available for talented pupils wanting to take up art education, through County Council scholarships; Evelyn Dunbar, for example, obtained two, one for Rochester School of Art and the other for the Royal College of Art. These scholarships, with others from educational trusts, meant that art schools were not restricted to the wealthy. The difficulty for artists came later, when they tried to establish careers and make money. For women artists it was especially hard: in a male-dominated art world, teaching positions in art schools were mostly filled by men, while family responsibilities for women often extended to caring for both the very young and very old. The Arts Council did not yet exist and the British Council only came into existence as the cultural arm of the Foreign Office in 1938. As a result, private patronage once again came to the fore, but it was not encouraged by any system of tax relief. The interwar years were also innocent of the kind of celebrity culture that began in the 1960s. And the diasporic identity within the art world, which today forms a major contribution to contemporary British art, only began to establish a new foothold in the late 1930s.

One important advance made in this period was the move towards the democratization of art. The visual arts, and especially photography, had played a major role in communicating to the public understanding of the First World War. In its wake, art no longer seemed the possession of an educated elite. The influential Tudor Walters Report on social housing, published during the last year of the Great War, considered the social, educational and recreational needs of prospective tenants and decreed that not only should the living room be large enough to include an upright piano, but all rooms should have picture rails, thereby affirming that art was now regarded as an interest open to all.[9] A major contribution to this new audience for art was the collection of essays that Roger Fry published under the title *Vision and Design* in 1920, which, more than any other book, removed the notion that art was for the 'toffs'. Initially published in an expensive 'soberly grand' and 'larger than quarto format',[10] selling at 25 shillings, it had by 1923 been scaled down to a cheaper octavo publication to meet demand. Further reprints and cheaper editions followed until in 1937 it became one of the first Pelican paperbacks, published by Penguin and selling at sixpence. Fry's ability to talk about art in a way that could be easily understood was part of its appeal, but in addition he approached art in a way that broke down barriers of education, nationhood and class by insisting on the need to look at form. The limitations of this approach are today very apparent, but at the time it was radical advice, widening access to art by suggesting a new way of looking.

This broadening of the audience for art inspired a new confidence, not only in those looking at art but also in its makers. Katy Deepwell has drawn attention to the rise in membership of four leading women-only artists' groups in the interwar period.[11] Certain amateur groups gained renown. The East London Group is today the best-known example, partly because it attracted influential support and its pictures sold well. Its artists produced a range of subjects and were strongly drawn to the everyday environment and the poetry of urban life, especially in East London. Today these pictures have more appeal than the chocolate-box landscapes and still lifes shown in the interwar years at the Royal Academy's Summer Exhibitions. Similarly, the Ashington Group, a collective of miners in the north-east who set up a painting class on the advice of an art history lecturer, also focused on their environment, thereby creating a communal record of how they lived. They too were invited to exhibit in London's West End and they have returned to public attention in recent years thanks to William Feaver's book *Pitmen Painters*, which inspired Lee Hall's poignant and witty play of the same title.

The interwar period also saw the founding of educational societies 'for the Encouragement of Art', or similarly titled bodies, again instancing the widening appreciation of art. These were often linked to regional public art galleries, especially those in industrial cities that built up significant collections of contemporary British art, partly to enhance a sense of civic pride. These 'provincial' art galleries, as they were then called, had before this period often been regarded as bit players in the art world, too poor and too poorly administered to have any influential role. Many of them had opened with no collections at all. But this was to change in the interwar years as the provinces gained strength. Municipal art galleries were still very much led in their collecting habits by the standards of taste promulgated by the Royal Academy, but they gradually grew in confidence and sometimes paid surprisingly large sums for the acquisition of paintings showcased in the Academy's

Summer Exhibitions, where the popular vote chose the 'Picture of the Year'. In 1927 the *Daily Mail* acquired the Picture of the Year and gifted it to the Tate Gallery. Dod Procter's *Morning* shows a young woman enfolded in the light of early morning and heavily asleep. In real life, she was the daughter of a Newlyn fish merchant and had posed for Procter almost every day for five weeks. The degree of realism inspired by her solid physique challenged both the chic classical beauty associated with naked art deco figures and the mildly erotic nudes shown at the Royal Academy. But to admirers of Picasso and Matisse, such realism must have seemed regressive, and this painting was ignored by art historians while modernist art history was in the ascendant. The high status it has acquired in recent years owes much to a shift in cultural values, for it can now be recognized that Procter's 'realism', although it leans towards sentimentality, avoids banality. The chief danger of realism is that it can seem risible if its dependence on mimetic copying is not accompanied by recognition of art's need for multivalence, the capacity to hold more than one meaning, appeal or value.

Histories of modernism place much stress on the city as a generative environment for new art and avant-garde communities. Rightly so, as the facts about cubism, vorticism, German expressionism, dada and surrealism uphold. But much interwar art in England pursued a modern outlook in places far removed from the metropolis

Dod Procter, *Morning*,
oil on canvas, 1926.

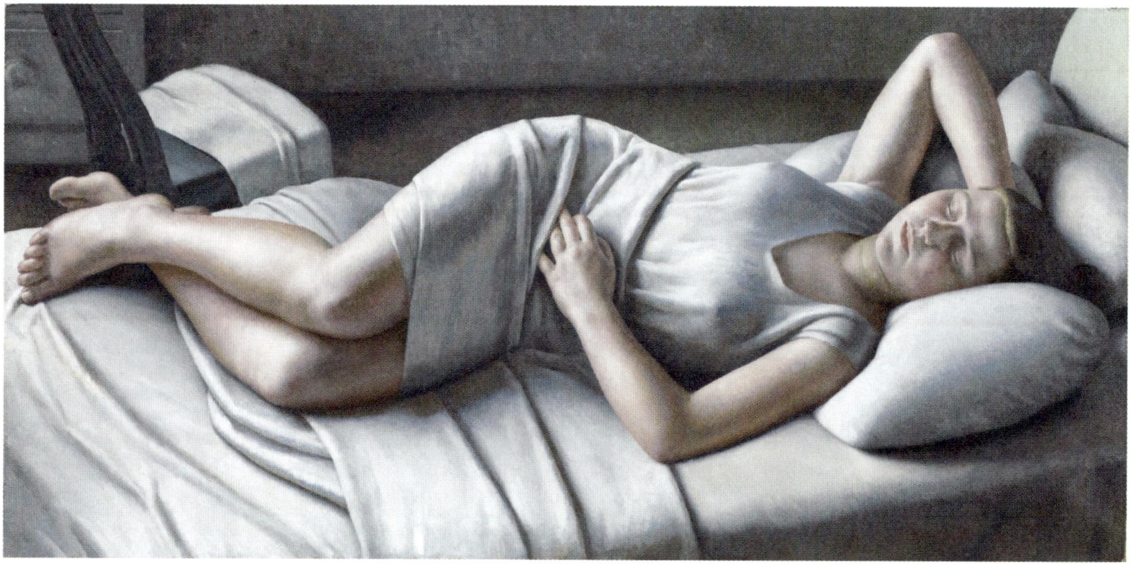

and the centre of the English art world: among the Cumbrian fells or in close proximity to downland, at coastal resorts or on a remote peninsula jutting out into the Atlantic in West Cornwall. Moreover, the most avant-garde English magazine of the 1930s, which introduced to its public some of the great names in 20th-century art, among them Kandinsky, Miró, Mondrian and Picasso, was edited and designed by a couple living in a sparsely furnished farmhouse with no gas, electricity or running water, in a small hamlet on the border of Buckinghamshire and Oxfordshire.

This book is neither a survey history of the period nor a deliberate alternative to mainstream history. It is a response to a need for a particular focus on key moments, sudden alliances and shifts in feeling that fed into the creativity of this period. Occasionally it touches on gaps, omissions and silences, where new evidence permits alterations to the received narrative. Readers may detect a recurrent interest in the interconnectedness of artistic networks and an interest in bringing to the fore women, be they artists, collectors, editors or curators, who were active agents in the history of mid-20th-century English art. If the shape of the book is partly driven by personal interests and enthusiasms, it is also responsive to shifts in cultural awareness and understanding. History is made up of large and small things and only momentarily stabilized when attention is given to a particular emphasis or perspective. The kind of art history I enjoy most consorts with ideas, networks, collectives, institutions as well as individual artists and their relation to the wider cultural, social and political field. My approach is therefore pragmatic, moving between art history, cultural history and social and political context as the topic under discussion requires. I have also, in places, mobilized biography as a critical tool that returns us to concrete particulars.

So much activity is packed into this short historic period that the need for selection has been inevitable. My intention, now and then, is to re-juggle hierarchies and to suggest in places new interpretations without necessarily offering definitive conclusions. The real and the romantic are my hammer points, but my underlying ambition is to enhance understanding of this disconcertingly wide field. As Wyndham Lewis said at the start of this period: 'Reality is what you want, and not Realism. And to find that, you must watch for some happy blending of the vitality of "Romance", the coldness of "science", and the moderation and cohesion of a "classical" mind.'[12]

Frances Spalding

CHAPTER 1

PITILESS REALISM

In 2014, the need to commemorate the centenary of the onset of the First World War gave rise to concerts, exhibitions, readings, ballets, documentaries and columns of light, among a great range of other cultural activities. But it was the poppy field that filled the moat of the Tower of London with 888,246 ceramic flowers – one for each of the British and British Empire servicemen who died in the Great War – which unforgettably caught the public imagination. Poppy fields reappeared again in significant numbers when it came to the centenary of the Armistice in 2018. Yet on both occasions, amidst all the calls upon our attention, silence continued to play its part. Silence neither justifies nor condemns; it does not tidy up, put away or seek to explain. Nevertheless, far from inert, it is mind-altering, opening up a fresh terrain for feeling and thought, as it did at 11 a.m. on the 11th of November 1918, when, in the wake of the Armistice, an uncanny quiet replaced the strafe of machine guns and the constant bombardment of trenches.

In the aftermath of this war, artists, who had witnessed or been involved in conflict and were sated with destruction, looked back with incredulity at some of the more extreme ambitions of the prewar avant-garde: at C. R. W. Nevinson's claim that 'there is no beauty except in strife, and no masterpiece without aggressiveness';[1] at the determination of Filippo Marinetti and the Italian futurists to shatter traditions and to destroy the past; and at the vorticists' praise of a machine-age aesthetic and its fierce economy of form, which, admirable from one perspective, now seemed tainted with a prefiguration of industrial warfare. Such ardent revolutionary stances, with hindsight, seemed misguided, the memory of them troubling. The past can be intractable, refusing to lie down, and often returns with powerful effect in the wake of injury, death and destruction. The fact that piles of the magazine *Blast*, in which Wyndham Lewis had published the Vorticist Manifesto, sat around his studio in the post-war period, unwanted, does not surprise. Even Lewis himself admitted: 'The geometrics which had interested me so exclusively before now felt bleak and empty. They wanted filling.'[2]

As the first anniversary of the Armistice approached, the idea took hold to employ silence as a form of remembrance. It proved to be a welcome alternative to the Peace Day victory parade held on 19 July 1919, a month after the signing of the Versailles Treaty, which was part of a whole programme of official celebrations. At a significant moment selected Allied troops marched past Sir Edwin Lutyens's *Cenotaph* in Whitehall and saluted as they did so, in memory of their fallen comrades. But to uphold the myth of a 'white war', no troops from the West Indies were permitted to march and neither were any Black African units represented.[3] Remembrance of the Armistice, however, extended to all. Initially a five-minute national silence was mooted, to be held, appropriately, on the eleventh hour of the eleventh day of the eleventh month of the year. Doubts as to its success were voiced by the King, who asked whether such a carefully timed event and the British people were compatible. (George V, a stickler for punctuality, was sometimes irritated by his own family's inability to appear at the dinner table on time.) But the event went ahead, although the five-minute silence was reduced to two. And at 11 a.m. on the 11th of November 1919, the famous 'Great Silence' descended on Britain: traffic, trains, the London tube – all came to a halt; factory production ceased; telephonists unplugged their wires.

Exactly a year later, a third silence unexpectedly fell over the crowds, some ten or twenty people deep, lining the streets of central London to watch the coffin of the Unknown Warrior, mounted on a gun carriage and drawn by six black horses, pass from Victoria Station to Whitehall. There it would pause for a short funeral ceremony in front of the *Cenotaph* before being taken to its resting place in Westminster

The funeral cortege of the Unknown Warrior, 1920.

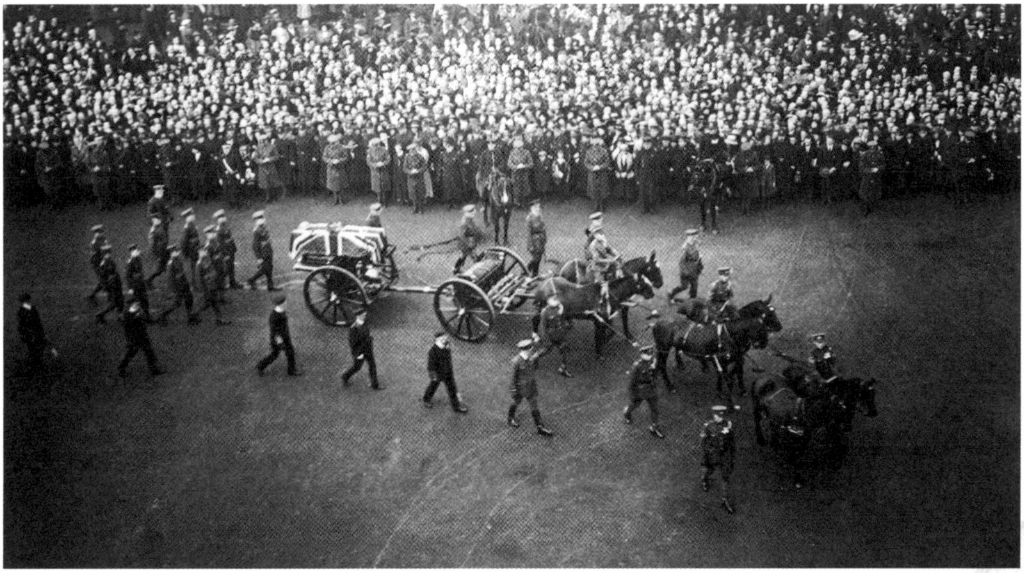

Abbey. Again, doubts had preceded this event. Those who felt it leant towards sentimentality dreaded a mawkish display of bad taste. But it proved not to be so. Because the bodies of those who had died fighting in the Great War had not been repatriated,[4] the Unknown Warrior provided a focus of attention for large numbers of people who had been denied a funeral for a relative, neighbour or friend; and at the Abbey the tomb of the Unknown Warrior became a welcome alternative to the *Cenotaph* as a site at which to mourn.

By then, the commemorative period was well under way. A great deal of funerary architecture was being commissioned in England, France and Flanders, and sculptors were hard at work producing war memorials commissioned by almost every village, town and city as well as by many institutions. Stanley Spencer's imaginative recreation of the unveiling of Cookham War Memorial exploits the flow and press of the village crowd in opposition to the stern vertical of white stone. Such intensity of remembrance seemed necessary to the continuation of life; it was not particular to Cookham, but repeated countless times as the nation sought to mourn the common man. Paul Gough takes this line of thought further by suggesting that the foreground crowd in Spencer's painting is not so much paying homage to the dead as acting out their missing townsmen, like a 'surrogate army of ghosts returned home'.[5]

This outpouring of funerary sculpture and war memorials took many forms. Some are workaday, mute and dreary. A great many simply take, as at Cookham, the familiar form of the cross. Others follow tradition and, by means of realism, try to evoke the heroism of the soldier. Edwin Lutyens offered something very different when in the immediate aftermath of war he created the *Cenotaph*. Its title looks back to the classical past and refers to a structure used to house an empty tomb, often associated with the notion of a missing warrior; hence the inscription 'The Glorious Dead'. It was commissioned as a temporary structure intended to ornament the Peace Day parade, but the memorial's dignified, abstract formality and its understated allusion to lost lives won considerable approval, and only four days after the parade it was agreed that it should be remade as a permanent fixture in Portland limestone. The remake enabled Lutyens to introduce entasis, as used by the ancient Greeks, by means of which straight lines are given a slight convex curve as they taper upwards, avoiding the distortion otherwise experienced when a rectangular monument or building is seen from below. The new *Cenotaph* was unveiled by the King on 11 November 1920, when the gun carriage carrying the Unknown Soldier en route to Westminster Abbey momentarily stopped alongside it.

Behind the approach adopted by Charles Sargeant Jagger for his Royal Artillery Monument on Hyde Park Corner lay the example not of the Hellenic past but of

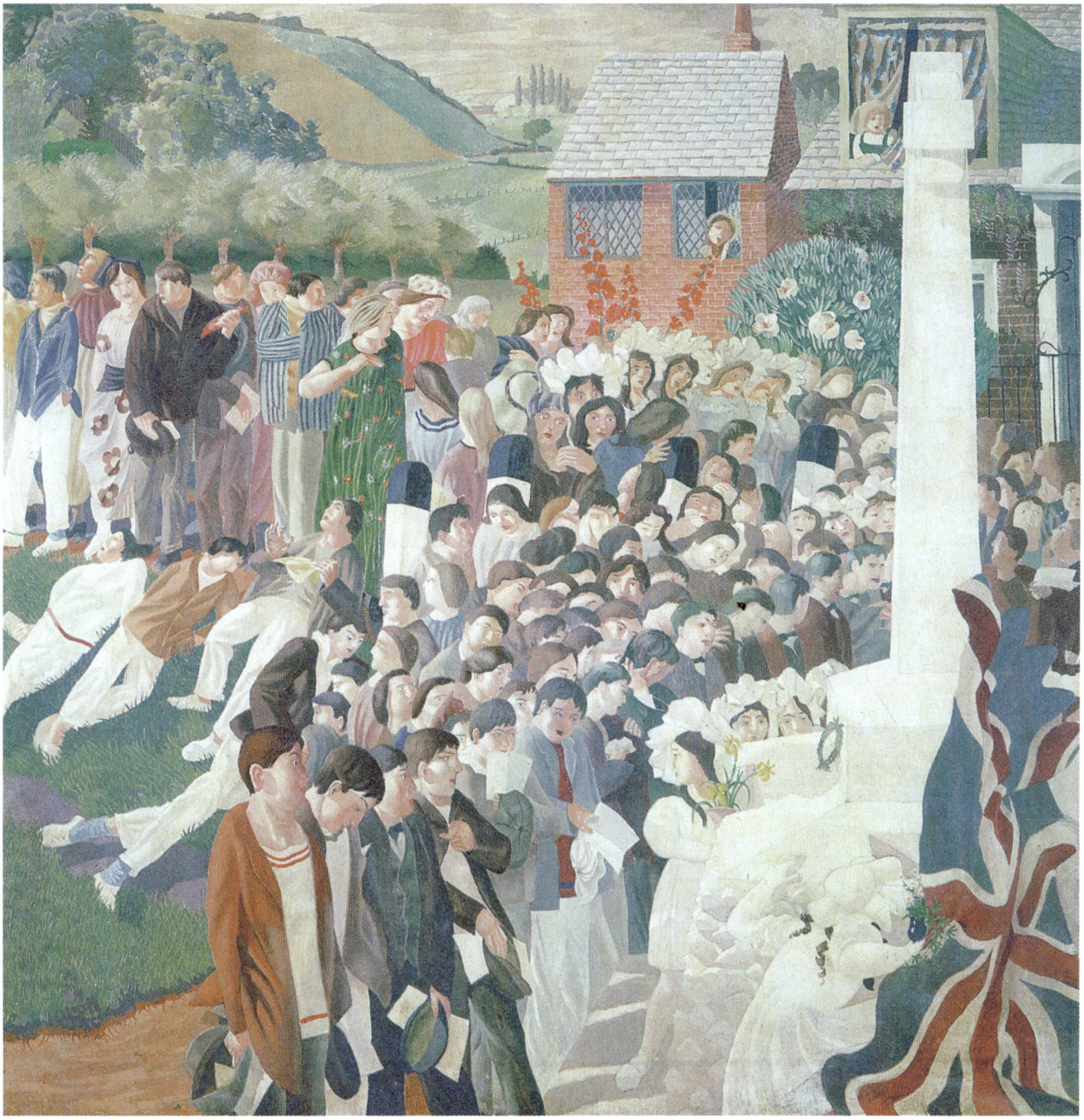

Stanley Spencer, *Unveiling Cookham War Memorial*,
oil on canvas, 1922.

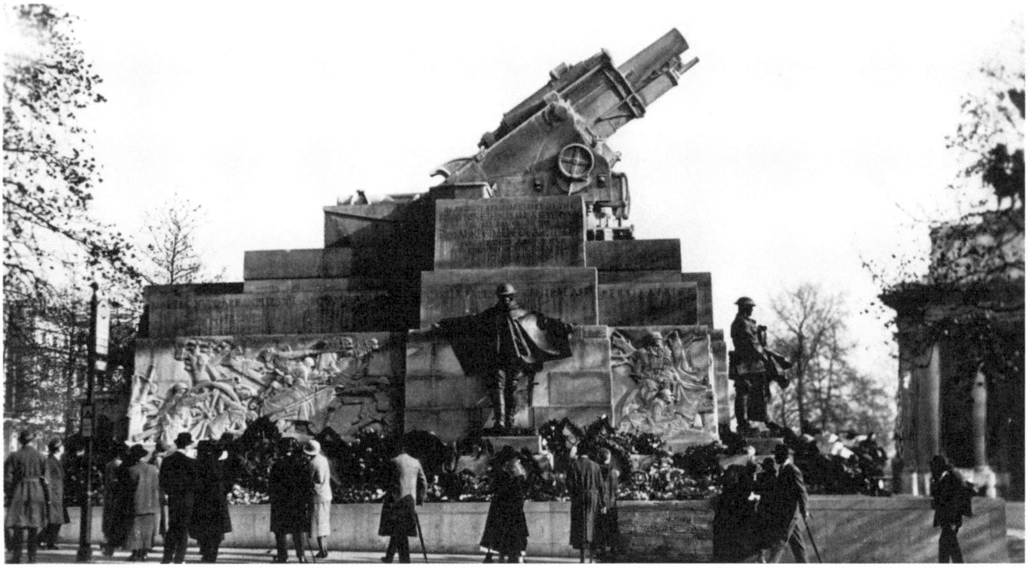

Charles Sargeant Jagger, Royal Artillery Monument, 1921–5.

Assyrian art. This was a major commission, commemorating the 49,076 soldiers from the Royal Artillery who had been killed in the war. An earlier attempt to get the project off the ground had failed; Jagger was then approached in 1921, and the unveiling finally took place on 18 October 1925.

The original commission had mentioned the need for a 'realistic thing' (implying a gun) and Jagger decided that the only gun with sculptural potential was a howitzer. He placed it, slightly exaggerated in size, on top of the main body of the memorial, which itself rests on a cruciform base with three soldiers standing guard on its east, west and south sides. On the north side lies a dead soldier, anonymized by the tarpaulin covering his body. These figures have a powerful presence.

For the scenes depicted in relief on the sides of the monument, Jagger drew inspiration from A. H. Layard's great cache of archaeological discoveries at Nimrud and Nineveh (now northern Iraq) and those of his assistant Hormuzd Rassam, later British Vice-Consul in Mosul, who, after Layard's departure, uncovered in 1853 reliefs based on the sporting exploits of the last great Assyrian king, Ashurbanipal (668–631 BC). Among these are the famous lion-hunt scenes, often regarded as the highest achievement of Assyrian art. Other scenes portray torture, massacre and battlefield execution as upheld by Ashurbanipal's murderously efficient reign, but the lion-hunt reliefs were intended to symbolize the king's ability to defeat the enemies of civilization and protect the land from dangerous or chaotic forces. When these large archaeological treasures arrived in London, they exceeded the space available for them in the British Museum.[6] Many arguments took place before sufficient room was created for the display of a reasonably logical sequence of Assyrian art. Although the existence of this art had been virtually unknown before the 1830s, once inside the British Museum it marked a turning point in the history of the institution. It has been credited with instigating 'the eventual shift away from the domination of narrow Hellenism towards the more open aesthetic and cultural pluralism of the modern Museum'.[7]

Jagger's side-reliefs on the Royal Artillery Monument forswear idealism and any form of allegorical figure in favour of a grounded, down-to-earth engagement with the activity, technology and equipment of modern warfare. What he admired in Assyrian art was its tensity and realism. These two qualities give a terse immediacy to his narrative scenes, which are best viewed at close quarters. Although the Monument is placed in a commanding position on Hyde Park Corner, it is today islanded by the daily grind of traffic; however, when seen close up or glimpsed from a passing car or bus, there is no doubting Gavin Stamp's remark: 'There is no idealisation here, no sentimentality; just truthful, brilliantly modelled realism about the brutal nature of conflict, though part of Jagger's genius was his ability to monumentalise the prosaic.'[8]

One of the chief lessons that had been learnt about art during the First World War was that it was no longer chiefly the possession of an educated elite. The public's understanding of the war had partly been gained through images: the government's propaganda unit, based at Wellington House, had made good use of photographs and had embarked on official pictorial publications. Its most successful publication was a monthly magazine, *War Pictorial*, which first appeared in 1916 and within a few months achieved a print run of 750,000. This same year, Wellington House decided to expand its brief and began to commission war art. Propagandist intent lay behind this patriotic endeavour, but as the war ground on, the overall result, in James Fox's words, was to be 'arguably the greatest act of state patronage in modern British history to date'. He rightly adds that the significance of this is hard to overestimate: the subjects given to artists had pressing national importance, the resulting works were widely disseminated through various communication channels and they reached 'an unprecedentedly large and receptive audience'.[9] Yet of all the various commissioning schemes which came to the fore in the course of the war, the most ambitious was the British War Memorials Committee.[10]

Founded early in 1918, the Committee held its first meeting in March. Although commissioning began well before the war ended, much of the work produced for the scheme was made after the return to peace; it looked back on the war from a point when the world was about to move forward. As with earlier schemes, one of its primary aims was to help forge a record of war and the activities associated with it, but this new scheme also aimed at enhanced resonance through grandeur of scale.

A number of artists was commissioned to produce paintings that matched in size Uccello's *Battle of San Romano* in the National Gallery. The hope was that the chosen artists would try to emulate the greatness associated with the old master tradition of grand narrative paintings and this in turn would reify the art produced. *The Battle of San Romano* had been chosen not only because it represents a battle scene but because it belonged to the early and not the High Renaissance – the former then gaining in popularity over the latter, so greatly admired by the Victorians. It was also assumed that if artists caught an echo of the greatness of the Italian Renaissance, they would be handing down a lasting witness of the Great War. Awareness of this led to the announcement that a Hall of Remembrance would be purpose-built to house these monumental paintings.

Together they form a curious achievement. Some are indeed epic monuments, offering searing indictments of war; others are gentler, more reflective and elegiac, capturing a mood which seeped in during the early months of peacetime, bringing with it a hint of critical distance as well as the need to say farewell to war.

Still today in Britain, on Armistice Day or the nearest Sunday, silence returns, and in some places it begins and ends with a bugle player sounding the Last Post. Whenever this happens, the past once again jams up against the present in an unsettling clash of memories, thoughts and feelings. Acts of memorialization are often contentious. And for some, in the 1920s, living under the long shadow cast by the

Paolo Uccello, *The Battle of San Romano*, egg tempera with walnut oil and linseed oil on poplar, 1438–40.

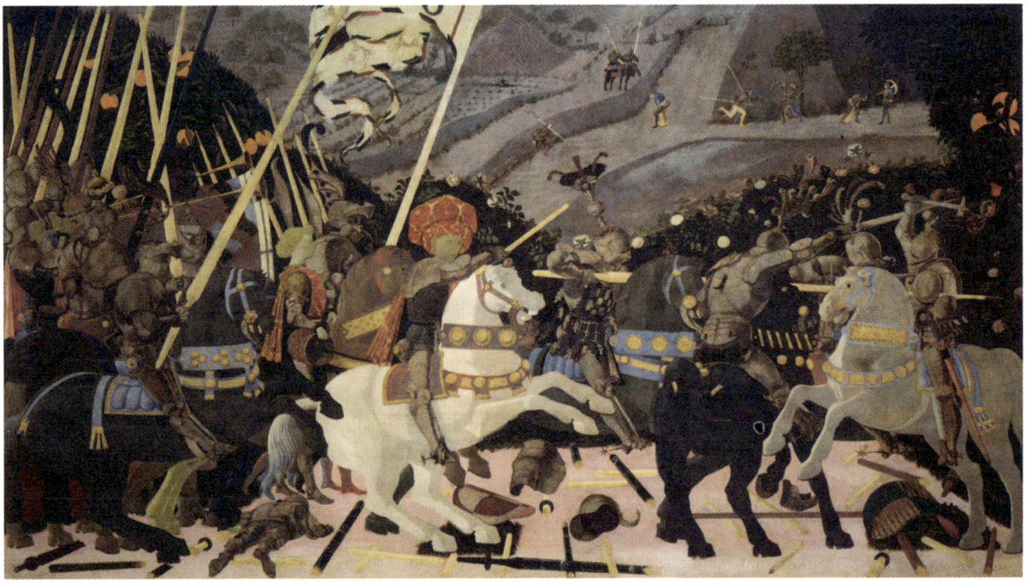

Great War, the annual two-minute silence was little more than a hateful reminder. Then, too, there was the business of starting again, amid uncertainty as to what the needs of a post-war era, dominated by an awareness of its 'lost generation', might be. Of the 5.7 million British men who had joined the armed forces, some three-quarters of a million had been killed and more than one and a half million seriously wounded. Many of those were maimed or shell-shocked, never recovering enough to work again. In this context it is understandable that artists in the 1920s were wary of fragmentation and instead leaned towards some form of realism that presented life as solid, whole and real, or at least, seemingly so. But, as we shall see, a recurrent pursuit of the real and the romantic surfaces repeatedly in the years following the return to peace, and in among the tangled motivations can be found some common roots.

By the time the British War Memorials Committee came into existence, Britain had acquired a national war museum. In 1917, Sir Alfred Mond, MP, responding to remarks made in the press, had proposed to the War Cabinet that such an institution was needed in relation to the ongoing war. This wealthy industrialist and collector, whose personal knowledge of art had enabled him between 1901 and 1904 to fulfil the distinguished role of Slade Professor of Art at Oxford, was tasked with forming, and eventually chairing, a committee that would establish the new museum. Before a year was out it had been founded by Britain's War Cabinet and named the Imperial War Museum: a title which took into account Britain's remaining empire and, later, the Commonwealth dominions.

Although it was formally established by an Act of Parliament in 1920, its collecting habits began three years earlier, and, in magpie fashion, it acquired works of art from earlier non-collecting commissioning schemes that had been initiated first by the Department of Information and then by its replacement, the Ministry of Information. These had emphasized the need to 'record' the Great War, as experienced at first hand, from the civilian as well as the military point of view. But the Imperial War Museum did not restrict itself to pictorial matter. Sir Martin Conway, its first director-general (an honorary post which he held until his death in 1937), toured the Western Front during 1917–18 on the Museum's behalf. He wanted the Museum to appeal to millions of individuals and therefore argued that it should be 'widely collected and arranged'.[11] Adopting a catholic approach, it acquired a range of objects: medals, uniforms, weaponry, posters, photographs, souvenirs, models, personal documents and diaries – in fact, any kind of curiosity that would help narrate the story of the Great War. As everything was treated with equal respect, the customary distinction between fine art and popular history became blurred. Nevertheless, around Christmas 1918 the Imperial War Museum gained in status when it took over responsibility for the series of large paintings commissioned by the British War Memorials Committee. This was an unexpected coup: the Museum would now have ownership of large-scale pictures that strove to revive the genre of history painting in modern terms.

Behind this development can be discerned the ambitious figure of Lord Beaverbrook, who had set up the War Memorials Committee in 1918 soon after David Lloyd George appointed him Minister of Information. A Canadian millionaire, he had settled in London in 1910 and swiftly moved into politics and newspapers, buying up the *Daily Express* in 1916. That same year, Sir Max Aitken, as he was then, set up the Canadian War Record Office in London, and a year later, as an offshoot of this, he created the Canadian War Memorials Fund to compile an artistic record of Canada's role in the war. Within a year it had acquired a significant collection of major canvases by Canadian and British artists, mostly the latter. When Beaverbrook established the British War Memorials Committee, his aim was to repeat his former success for the country of his adoption. He asked his friend, the writer Arnold Bennett, to chair the Committee. Bennett had seen Paul Nash's first exhibition of war art in 1917 and recognized the value of the avant-garde. He was not averse to academic art, but it was almost certainly he who prevented the Royal Academicians from moving in and taking control of the scheme.

Having first met on 6 March 1918, the Committee discovered by the summer of that year that it had to retrench: work not yet begun was cancelled and artists' salaries were reduced. Part of the problem was Sir Alfred Mond, who resented this government challenge to the collecting role performed by the Imperial War Museum. He persistently sniped at the British War Memorials Committee, asking questions in parliament about its commissioning. When he heard about its scheme to build a Hall of Remembrance on Richmond Hill, and that it had even gone as far as to approach the architect Charles Holden for designs, he went to the Treasury and ensured that the project was swiftly terminated. On 24 July 1918, the Committee lost its grand name and was retitled the Pictorial Propaganda Committee, and before the end of that year the entire administration of Britain's war memorials scheme had been taken over by the Imperial War Museum. All the works of art commissioned ended up joining the Museum's collection, where they remain to this day.

Before this takeover happened, the chief art adviser to the War Memorials Committee was the critic Robert Ross. It was he who recommended that a number of artists should be commissioned to paint major works on a similar scale to that of Uccello's *Battle of San Romano* – 182 × 320 centimetres or 6' × 10' – although if they wished, he suggested, they could employ a 'reduced Uccello' size of 6' × 7', which still ensured that these modern history paintings would be suitably monumental.

A similar desire for uniformity in size had earlier been applied to art commissioned by the Canadian War Memorials Fund, where the even more ambitious model had been Velázquez's *Surrender of Breda*, which is 10' × 12'. Both schemes wanted to align themselves with the ambitious patronage associated with the Renaissance period and aimed to attract works that would take their place within the old master tradition.

The term 'old masters' is gender-biased, as Griselda Pollock wittily showed when she used the title *Old Mistresses* for one of her books (subtitled *Women, Art and Ideology*). Invoking the old master tradition in 1918, especially in relation to war art, seemed likely to reinforce the existing obstacles to women artists being included in the War Memorials scheme. But in fact Muirhead Bone, an experienced war artist who sat on the Committee, drew up a list of nineteen women artists for consideration. Three were shortlisted – Anna Airy, Laura Knight and Tony Cyriax – but only Airy succeeded in gaining a commission, and that came from the Imperial War Museum's Munitions Committee rather than the British War Memorials scheme. In April 1918 she was asked to produce four large factory scenes, each representative of the munitions industry. She set out to paint a shell forge, a shell-filling department, a gun forge and an aircraft assembly shop, all of which offered challenging environments. While working at the shell forge at Hackney Marshes, she wrote to Robert Ross: 'They roll red hot shell cases in batches within four feet of me, to cool off! I can't describe the heat, but the general swelter and steam and the dust and the sweating are going to make a ripping picture I think.'[12] For *An Aircraft Assembly Shop, Hendon* (1918), she deliberately positioned herself high up so as to catch the full complexity of the working scene laid out before her. Both this and a further subject, *Women Working in a Gas Retort House: South Metropolitan Gas Company, London* (1918), are on the 'reduced Uccello' scale, but still large enough to catch the drama of their settings.

Anna Airy responded well to the task given her, but the demand for such large works placed an onus on artists more accustomed to working on a domestic scale. The Nash brothers had to go in search of a temporary studio to accommodate the canvases for their British War Memorials commissions; John Nash accepted a commission in May 1918 to paint *Oppy Wood, 1917. Evening* and Paul Nash undertook *The Menin Road*. Both were offered the opportunity to revisit the battlegrounds where they had served on the front line, but neither wished to do so, presumably because what they had seen and experienced remained indelibly impressed. Instead, 'a truck load of shards from the Western Front – metal fragments, sheets of corrugated roofing, concrete blocks and other detritus'[13] was delivered to their studio in the Chilterns.

John Nash's initial attempt to enlist in the army had failed, but as the slaughter continued and the age level and physical requirements for enlistment came down, he

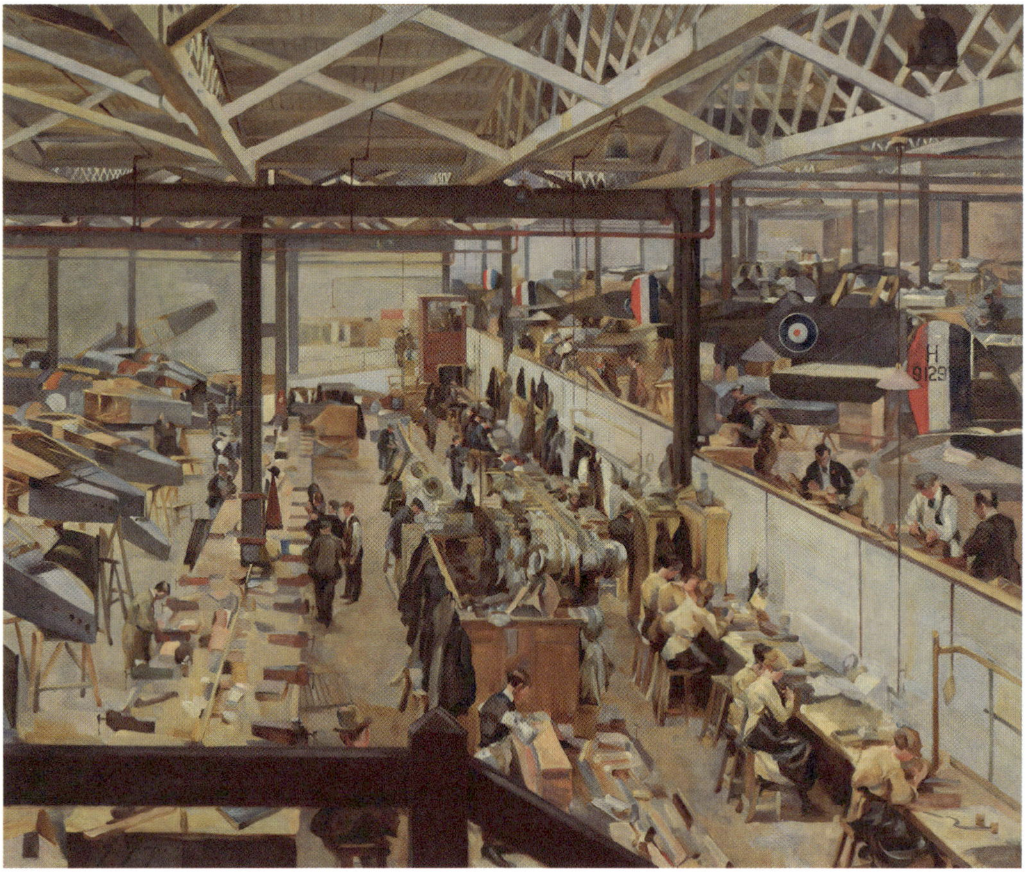

Anna Airy, *An Aircraft Assembly Shop, Hendon*, oil on canvas, 1918.

was able to enter the Artists' Rifles and join the 28th London Regiment. He served in France from November 1916 to January 1918, his initial training preparing him for the Battle of Passchendaele. Luckily for him, he became an expert in mortars and grenades and was kept back from the front line owing to his usefulness as an instructor, so that he could train replacements in the event of carnage – which was exactly what happened.

Later, he was commanded to lead a company of soldiers at Marcoing over the top, in an effort to divert attention from a nearby bombing raid. Sixty-eight of the eighty men were killed. After he had been officially demobilized from the army in February 1918, he relived this experience in his painting *Over the Top: 1st Artists' Rifles at Marcoing, 30th December 1917*, using pitiless realism to create a startlingly immediate reminder of an event he would later describe as 'in fact, pure murder'. In the case of *Oppy Wood*, he again knew his subject well. Not only had Oppy Wood

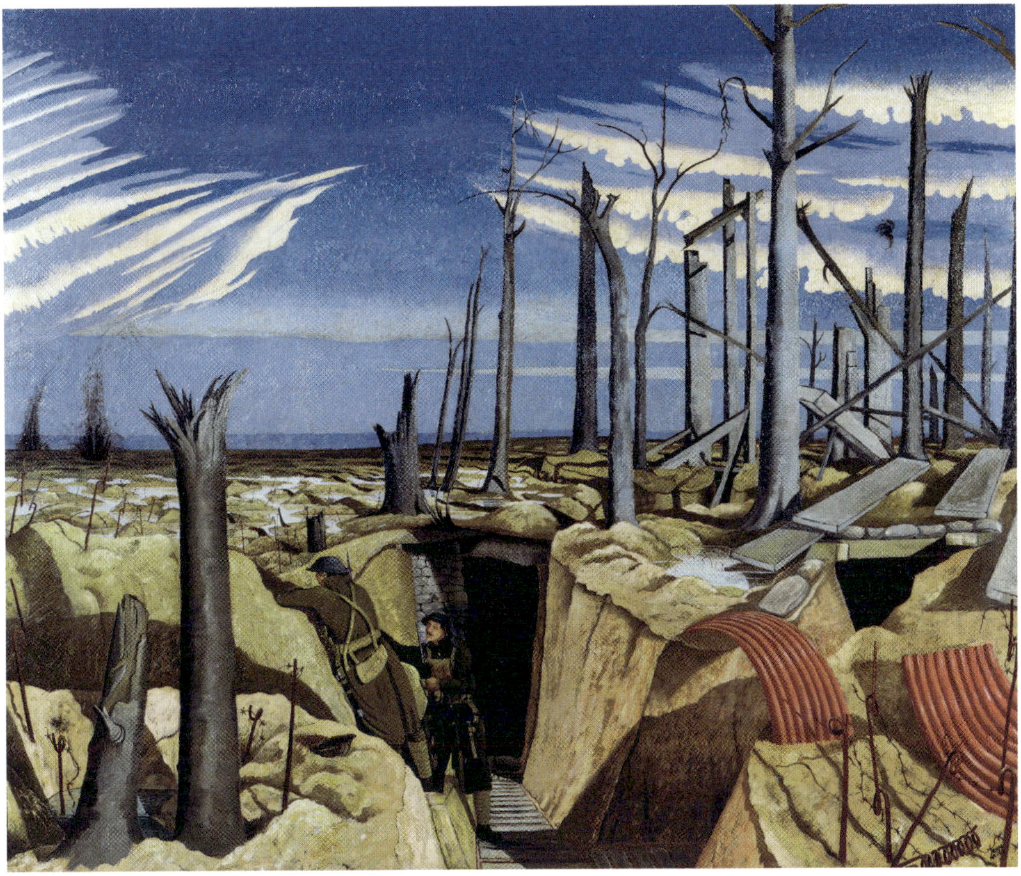

John Nash, *Oppy Wood, 1917. Evening*, oil on canvas, 1918.

more than once formed part of the No Man's Land between opposing armies, but John Nash had been sent there as part of his training, to study the ingenious trench system dug underneath the wood. In a tape-recorded interview now held in the Imperial War Museum archives, he recalls how explosions of any kind resounded eerily among the blasted beech trees. These create a Golgotha-like mood in *Oppy Wood*, partly because of the black coffin-like entrance into a tunnel at its centre and also because one part of a tree has fallen across another creating a cross-like formation, an image that is present in all the preparatory drawings for this painting.

Having had extensive experience of front-line fighting, John Nash knew what it was like to stand near the entrance of a dugout, viewing the terrain as the two men in this picture do, watching shells burst in the distance. Yet the picture feels emptied out, actionless. What is offered is not the urgency of military conflict but a recollection of war, made additionally poignant by the haunting meteorological effects in the sky. 'What skies!' wrote another artist, David Jones, of the Western Front's flat landscape, in his poetic memorial to the war, *In Parenthesis*. But John Nash, although haunted by the effects he had witnessed, painted this sky at Chalfont St Giles in Buckinghamshire, where he and Paul were now working at either end of a roomy seed shed with large windows down both sides, a space normally used for the drying of herbs. Here the two men and their young wives had lunch together, and, as there was a piano in the room, music was often played. 'France and the trenches', Paul wrote, while there in the summer of 1918, 'would be a mere dream if our minds were not perpetually bent on those scenes. And yet how difficult it is, folded as we are in a luxuriant green country, to put it aside and brood on those wastes of Flanders, the torments, the cruelty & terror of this war.' He concluded: 'Well it is on *these* I brood for it seems the only justification of what I do now – if I can help to rob war of the last shred of glory the last shine of glamour.'[14]

Both brothers had a deep love of the English landscape. John Nash became a great plantsman and intent observer of the rural scene. Paul Nash held dear a line from Tennyson's *Maud* – 'I have felt I am one with my native land' – finding its emotion satisfying when all his other feelings were bitter and dead. Yet he continued to find in landscape metaphors for human and spiritual predicaments, as well as echoes of the pastoral tradition. Paul had begun his career by drawing landscapes of the mind, inspired by his reading of the romantic poets, his admiration for Blake and D. G. Rossetti and his friendship with the poet Gordon Bottomley. To these he brought considerable imaginative power, but once he began to focus on the outer world he found himself able to transfer this depth of feeling to nature, notably in his drawings of trees and gardens. This was the beginning of his interest in the *genius loci*, something that is evanescent, difficult to pin down, resistant to over-neat design and sometimes simply the product of light. The strangeness of his landscapes often arises from a disturbing tension between his feeling for the spirit of place and his love of formal clarity.

What shook Paul to the core, and dramatically altered his art, was his experience of war. He had been sent as second lieutenant in the Hampshire Regiment to the Ypres Salient, but after only eight weeks he stumbled in the dark, found himself jammed in a narrow trench and suffered a back injury. As nearby hospitals were being cleared ahead of an offensive, he was sent back to London to recuperate. There he learnt that many in his unit had been killed in an attack on Hill 60 that presaged the Battle of Messines Ridge. When he returned for a six-week period in November–December 1917, he did so on different terms, having been given a temporary position as a war artist.

In the interceding period there had been an increase in artillery and munitions dumps. Concentrated bombardment meant that the intervals between explosions had disappeared, for war had become a matter of wholesale mechanical force. The flat, open landscape had been damaged beyond recognition, its trees reduced to jagged stumps and its drainage system smashed by constant shelling. The start of August brought the heaviest rainfall for thirty years, turning the already flooded ground into a quagmire of mud which clogged rifles, immobilized tanks, and was so deep in places that men and horses drowned in it. On his return to the front, Paul Nash quickly understood that if he were to communicate what he saw he would have to turn himself into the 'messenger' of a 'bitter truth'.[15] Profoundly anguished by this hellish landscape and seized with a sense of urgency, he worked furiously at drawings, mostly using ink, pencil, chalk and pastel on tinted paper and often portraying night scenes, yet bringing sharpness and clarity to a terrain that seemed to offer unending devastation.

Soon after his return to England his position as war artist was extended, giving him time to prepare an exhibition of his war work and accept a commission from the British War Memorials Committee. He never returned to the front, and by the time he embarked on *The Menin Road* (1919), a more dispassionate approach had replaced his earlier frenzy and despair. This large painting is a magisterial indictment of the devastation caused to landscape, and hence to the human spirit, by modern

Paul Nash, *The Menin Road*,
oil on canvas, 1919.

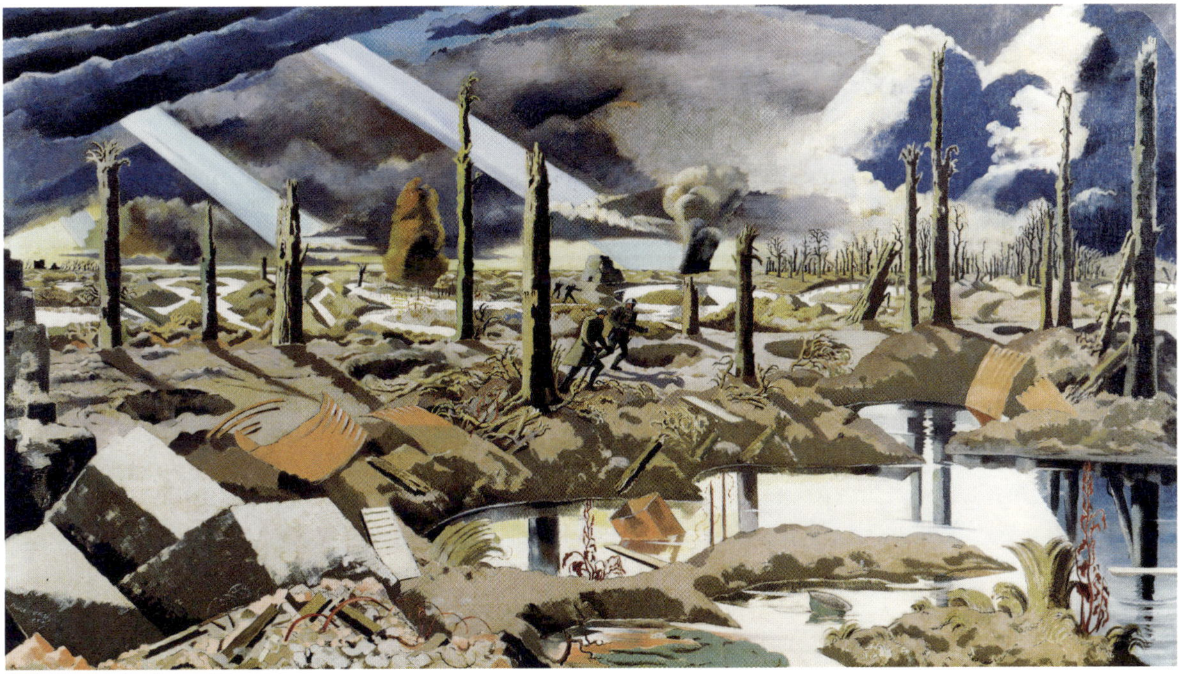

warfare. Nash lays out the facts of the scene like a surgeon with his scalpel, recreating a theatre of war that is true to the facts of his experience. The road and surrounding landscape have been potholed with craters by shells. The remaining trees provide the necessary verticals to link sky and land, and are echoed in the still pools of water that linger on owing to the smashed drainage. Nash's knowing handling of space enables the eye to travel in more than one direction: the main thrust, from left to right, is created by a road running parallel with the picture surface and is reinforced by the nearest line of trees. This horizontal thrust is challenged by tracks of water that catch the light and scissor their way into the far distance, conveying a sense of unending devastation, while further columns of light blast down diagonally from the sky and send the eye again across the landscape, searching for signs of life. The mood of the painting is calm, but it conveys a sadness and despair that echoes the sentiment of Wilfred Owen's famous phrase, 'the pity of war'.

Originally this work was to be called 'A Flanders Battlefield', but its more precise final title indicates that it was charged for Nash with specific memories of the aftermath of the Battle of Menin Road Ridge. This took place in an area known as 'Tower Hamlets' near the Belgian village of Gheluvelt, in one of the most battle-scarred areas of the Ypres Salient. The battle lasted five days, from 20 to 25 September 1917; in that short period, the British endured almost 2,000 casualties and 148 were killed. But this battle was merely part of a larger conflict – the Battle of Passchendaele – which lasted from 31 July to 6 November 1917. At the end of these three months the Allies had gained six miles of ground, at the cost of the lives of some 325,000 Allied soldiers and 260,000 Germans.

All the details in *The Menin Road* are recognizably authentic; but what gives the picture an epic status when viewed life-size is the way these details are woven into the artifice of art and made dramatic by Nash's assimilation of modernist tropes associated with vorticism. These had first been introduced into war art by C. R. W. Nevinson, whose successful exhibition at the Leicester Galleries in September 1916 Paul Nash had heard about while doing military training. He could not properly assimilate his understanding of Nevinson's achievement until his accident at the front returned him to England for some five months in 1917. He himself had an exhibition of war drawings at the Goupil Gallery, London, in June of that year which caught the attention of the critic and painter Roger Fry. 'I think you have a very special talent', Fry wrote to Nash, 'for recording a certain poetical aspect of such scene in a way that no other artist could.'[16] Although a much stronger exhibition of Nash's war work was to be shown at the Leicester Galleries, London, in May 1918, it was the 1917 exhibition that attracted the necessary support of influential people to gain him his appointment as an official war artist.

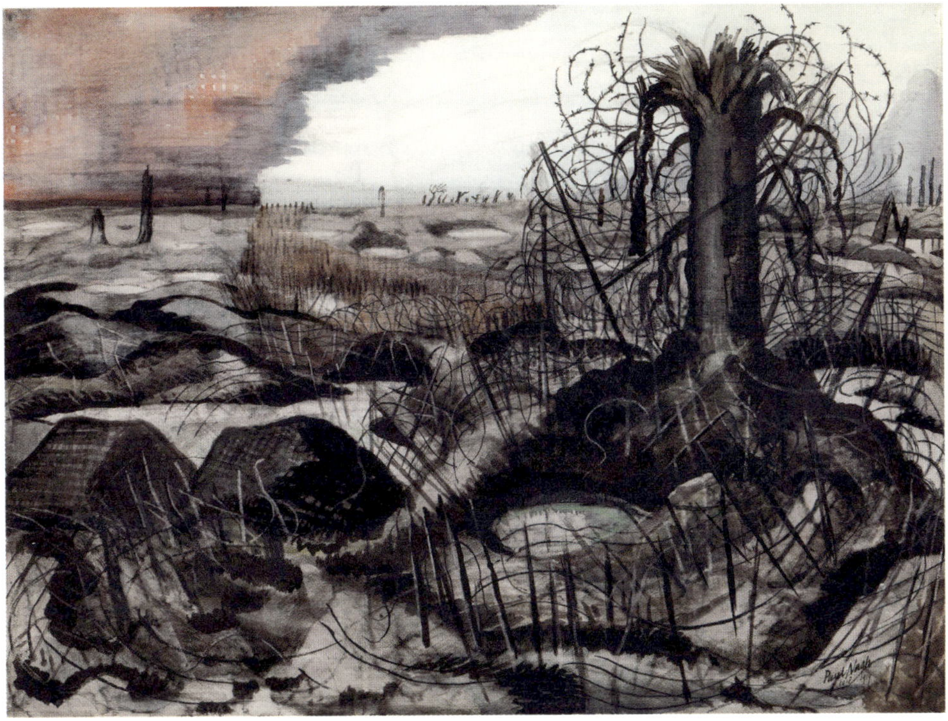

Paul Nash, *Wire*,
watercolour, chalk and ink on paper, 1918–19.

Wire is an elaborately worked drawing pushed to a high degree of finish over a period of several months, as is affirmed by the date – '1918–19' – inscribed by Nash in the lower right-hand corner. An exploded tree trunk with a few dripping remnants of branches has been raised into a symbolic position equivalent to that of a martyred saint; strands of barbed wire around its top suggest a halo or a crown of thorns. The almost demonic negativity of this work makes a telling contrast with *The Menin Road*, where evidence of destruction lies all around and yet there is no wounding or bitterness; instead, there is the critical distance brought by recognition and acceptance. As Andrew Causey, for many years the leading authority on Nash, puts it, '*The Menin Road* has an unexpected sobriety.'[17]

The British War Memorials Committee had been deliberately democratic in its commissioning of artists, recognizing the need for diversity if the scheme was, in time, to reach a wide audience. This approach was also in keeping with Sir Martin Conway's populist directorial style. Yet in 1917 C. R. W. Nevinson, who had won over the public with his use of an avant-garde style in relation to war art, caused an uproar when he resorted to a realist style in order to show two dead British soldiers face down in mud and titled it, bitterly, *Paths of Glory*. This contravened the Defence of the Realm Act, which did not permit imagery, such as dead soldiers, that could be regarded as unpatriotic. Delighted by the controversy, Nevinson exhibited the same picture again, now half obliterated by a strip of brown paper bearing the word 'Censored' scrawled across it in blue chalk. Yet if compared with the clipped semi-cubist style that had enabled him to convey, in images of troops marching or resting, the harsh anonymity, monotony and boredom of modern warfare, the half-hearted realism of *Paths of Glory* seems a retreat into painterly journalism.

Nevinson's reputation was strong enough to survive this and he was one of the select artists commissioned by the British War Memorials Committee to undertake an 'Uccello-size' picture. Having worked as an orderly, first for the Red Cross and then for the Royal Army Medical Service, he had been made a war artist in 1917. After being driven across a large area of France he was taken to Ypres, where he sketched the smashed and flooded landscape in preparation for the painting *Shell Holes* (also known as *After the Push)*. He returned to this scene in 1919 for his British War Memorials picture *The Harvest of Battle* (1919). By this point the earlier prohibition on the portrayal of dead soldiers had lost its relevance and disappeared, and unlike *Shell Holes*, the painting is crawling with figures: soldiers in retreat, some carrying the wounded, and women also fleeing. In the distance a village or small town is being razed to the ground, while in the foreground corpses litter the mud and craters of water. Nevinson took the opportunity offered him to revisit the actual landscape before beginning work on *The Harvest of Battle*. But whatever advantage this gave him, it did not prevent the painting, with its pitiful chain of figures in the middle distance, from falling into shallow melodrama.

Unlike Nevinson, William Roberts turned down the opportunity to revisit France before painting *The Shell Dump, France* (1918–19), his large-scale work for the War Memorials Committee, preferring instead to obtain the details he needed regarding a particular type of shell from Bramley Dump near Reading. This is one of the strangest paintings in the Uccello series. Preparations are being made for the loading of shells onto ammunition wagons, to be taken to the Gun Line. The picture shows three lines of soldiers in a narrow space, the foreground line twisting and turning as they form a human conveyor belt, passing shells from one man to the next. But every part of this canvas is busy and busily brought to our attention, for an unremitting evenness of focus brings out, with equal intensity, the shapes of the shells as well as the ribbed lines in the soldiers' puttees. The creases in the shirts, jackets and trousers also trip their way across the surface of the picture, while in the background, part of the raffia roof that obscured the dump from aerial

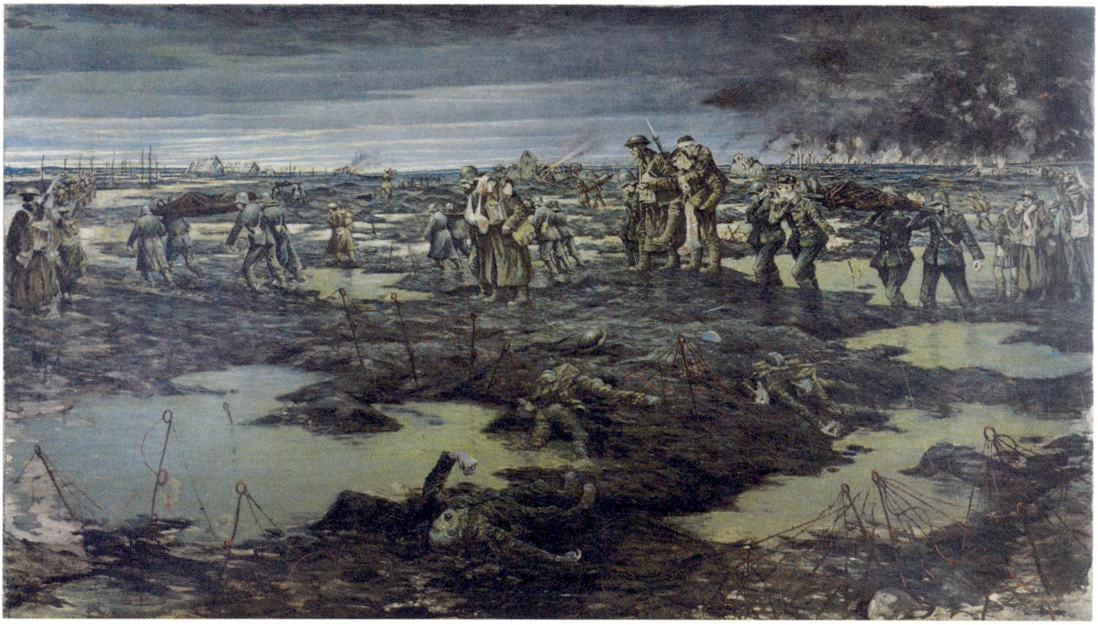

C. R. W. Nevinson, *The Harvest of Battle*,
oil on canvas, 1919.

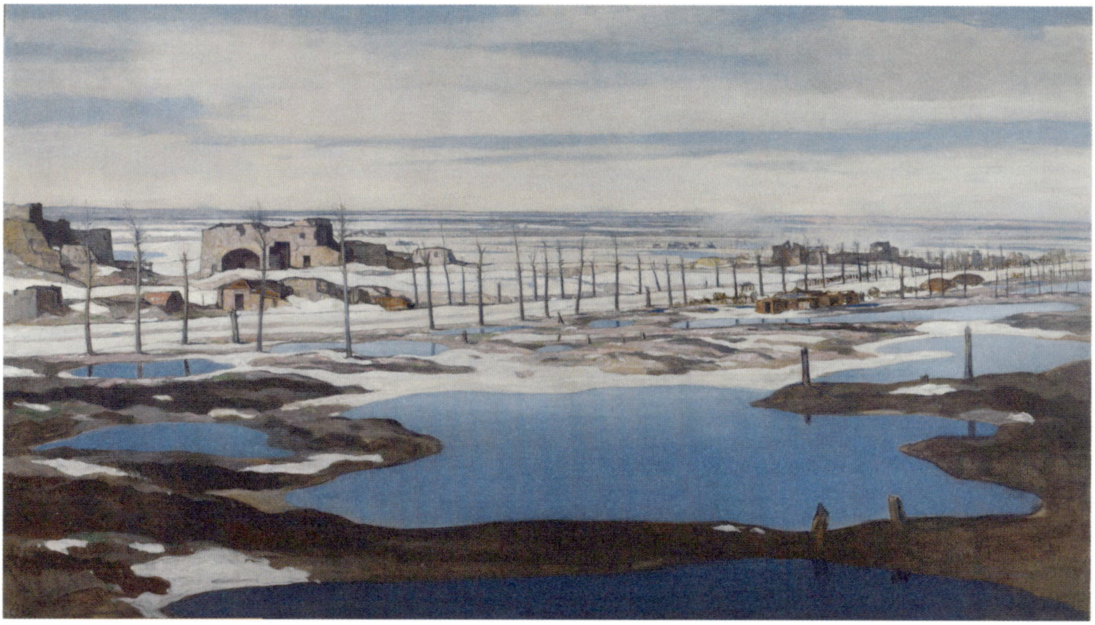

D. Y. Cameron, *The Battlefield of Ypres*,
oil on canvas, 1919.

observation closes in the scene. There is no relief, no escape from the visual urgency conveyed by the whole. A consistency of tone further adds to the claustrophobia, for it unites the hot, low-key colours and makes alteration in hue in places almost imperceptible. When first exhibited this picture baffled and annoyed viewers, and it remains difficult to read at any distance from the actual canvas.

Another 'Uccello-size' picture, D. Y. Cameron's *The Battlefield of Ypres* (1919), makes an interesting comparison with Nash's *The Menin Road.* A light snowfall partly covers the landscape, associated with the Battle of Ypres, with a forgiving softness, while a cold shadow in the foreground contrasts with the warm sunlight spreading across the valley. There is nothing harsh or mawkish about this deserted panorama, even though ruined buildings, blasted trees and the artificial lakes made by shell blasts are still visible. At the time the picture was painted, native populations in France and Belgium had begun the task of reconstruction and were revisiting battlefields in order to demarcate boundaries where there seemed to be little or nothing left to provide a sense of place. In some localities all physical markers had been obliterated and what remained was 'a space full of history yet void of obvious topography... the land overwritten with an invisible emotional geography'.[18] Cameron's landscape evokes this sorrowful emptiness, catching the scene on the cusp of a new beginning. This is a definite leave-taking, a farewell to war, its mood similar to that found in Emily Dickinson's poem 'There's a certain Slant of light'.

There's a certain Slant of light,
Winter Afternoons –
That oppresses, like the Heft
Of Cathedral Tunes –

Heavenly Hurt, it gives us –
We can find no scar,
But internal difference –
Where the Meanings, are –

None may teach it – Any –
'Tis the seal Despair –
An imperial affliction
Sent us of the Air –

When it comes, the Landscape listens –
Shadows – hold their breath –
When it goes, 'tis like the Distance
On the look of Death –

In December 1919, when 'The Nation's War Paintings and Other Records' opened at the Royal Academy, Nevinson was furious to discover that none of his work had been included in Gallery III, which showcased the best of the British War Memorials paintings and formed the climax of the show. His reputation as a leading war artist fully justified his annoyance, but it is perhaps not surprising that *The Harvest of Battle* had been cold-shouldered. He had, in addition, angered the authorities behind this show. This was the first time that a comprehensive selection of work from the Imperial War Museum had gone on public view and, in order not to dilute its impact, Nevinson had been told by Alfred Yockney, secretary to the British War Memorials Committee, that he was not permitted to exhibit *The Harvest of Battle* at the Royal Academy's annual Summer Exhibition (the 'Peace Show', as it was called that year). However, Nevinson discovered that John Singer Sargent's *Gassed* had not been subjected to the same restriction. In protest, therefore, Nevinson arranged a private viewing of his painting, sending out invitation cards along with information on bus and tube routes to his studio.

'The Nation's War Paintings' was undeniably a major event, with over 900 exhibits on show – almost a third of the Imperial War Museum's total collection. But visitor figures were slightly disappointing. Over 38,000 people attended the show between December 1919 and February 1920: a relatively low figure if compared with the 32,000 who had visited a smaller touring exhibition of trophies, pictures and photographs from the Imperial War Museum which had been shown at the Academy for just five weeks beginning in January 1918. It is possible that the public's interest in war art had begun to wane, assuaged, perhaps, by a recent showing of art commissioned by the Canadian War Memorials Fund and by 'Women's Work', a four-week exhibition of women's war work at the Whitechapel Art Gallery in 1918, which attracted 82,000 visitors. In December of that year, 36,000 people had gone to the Grosvenor Galleries to see naval paintings and other memorabilia, again all from the Imperial War Museum.

Yet, if 'The Nation's War Paintings' received fewer visitors than expected, it nevertheless occupies a significant position in the history of British art. It not only offered a record of the 'war to end wars', witnessed from many perspectives and in diverse styles, but it was also the first time that the full spectrum of contemporary art, from traditional or conventional styles through to avant-garde productions, hung side by side in the Royal Academy, one of the great bastions of the establishment. Momentarily it must have seemed as if hierarchies of taste had broken down and new freedoms had become possible. Here were images of the industries serving on the home front as well as a reminder of the immeasurable violence of the Western Front. Here was the bravery, the melancholy and bitterness of war. Here was art for all.

With hindsight, the exhibition highlighted not only the Imperial War Museum itself but also the unprecedented government sponsorship of the arts that lay behind the greater part of the Museum's collections. The British War Memorials Committee had been the most important of these schemes, and its faith in the endurance of art had produced large-scale paintings, seen for the first time at this show – all, that is, aside from Sargent's *Gassed* (1919), which, as mentioned, had been shown in the Summer Exhibition.

Sargent had been too old to fight in 1914 but, having been commissioned to paint the largest of all these works, he was encouraged to witness scenes of conflict or go to sites where conflict had taken place in order to gain the necessary experience of the landscape of war. In this way, he travelled to France in the spring of 1918 along with Professor Henry Tonks of the Slade School of Fine Art. Sargent had been invited by the British prime minister, Lloyd George, to produce 'a work of great and lasting service to the nation'; the subject, as was initially agreed, would be the uplifting theme of co-operation between the American and English armies. This was not an easy remit and Sargent wrote to Sir Evan Charteris: 'The Ministry of Information expects an epic – and how can one do an epic without masses of men? Except at night I have only seen three fine subjects with masses of men – one a harrowing sight, a field full of gassed and blindfolded men' (11 September 1918).[19]

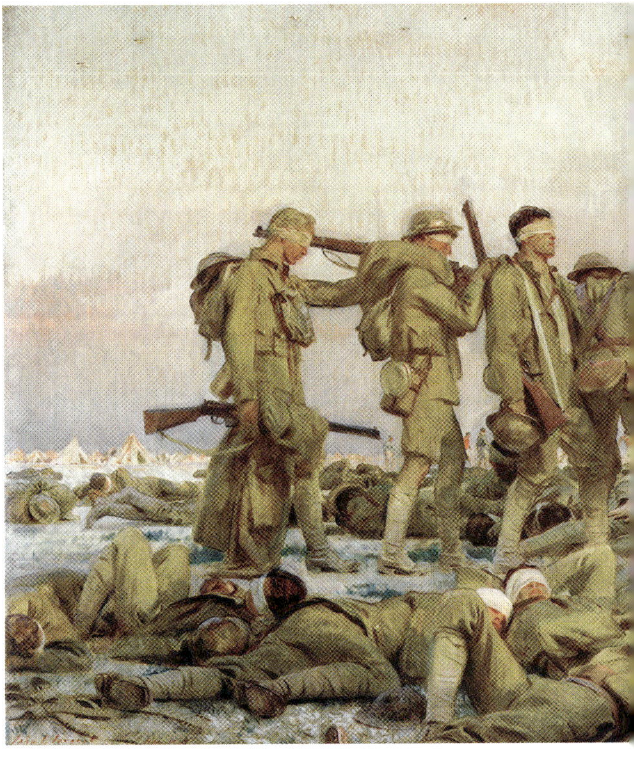

John Singer Sargent,
Gassed,
oil on canvas, 1919.

The scene he referred to was at Le Bac-du-Sud on the Arras–Doullens road, where a dressing station was striving to cope with the aftermath of a mustard gas attack. This new weapon of mass destruction, a chemical that savaged the skin, eyes and mucus membranes, caused excruciating pain and disorientation owing to injuries, burns and temporary blindness. In the immense painting which Sargent made of the scene he portrayed two chains of wounded soldiers, blindfolded by bandages, each soldier grasping the shoulder of the one in front as they are led by medical orderlies along a duckboard towards a dressing station, indicated by guy ropes on the far right-hand side of the composition. We view the scene from below, across a sea of wounded and possibly lifeless soldiers filling the foreground. Anonymity clings to these bodies, partly because of Sargent's impressionistic brushwork, which does not allow for too much detail.

Such warfare, although instigated by the Germans, was also adopted by the Allies, causing an enormous number of casualties and fatalities. In response to the public outcry that followed, an international agreement signed by the majority of world states was obtained in 1925, when, for the first time, weapons of mass destruction were banned by the Geneva Protocol.

It was envisaged that *Gassed* would form the centrepiece of the planned Hall of Remembrance. After hopes for this building collapsed, the painting joined the

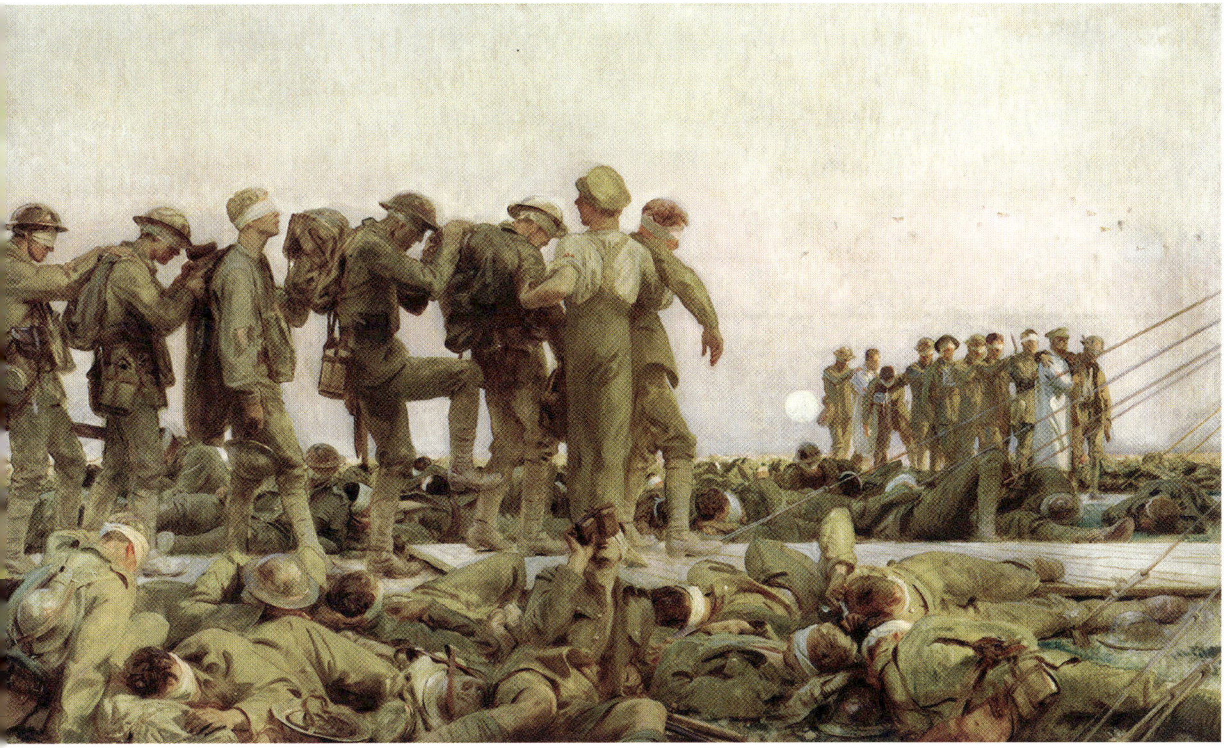

rest of the collection in the Imperial War Museum. Ninety-five years later, in the summer of 2013, it was chosen as one of the ten most popular pictures in Britain, and reproductions of it were mounted on billboards and shown on public slide displays as part of the 'Everywhere Art' scheme.

What makes *Gassed* so popular? And is it a critical success? Far from being triumphalist in tone, it belongs within a corpus of paintings and poems about the 1914–18 conflict that acknowledges the futility of war. What Sargent witnessed as observer, Wilfred Owen experienced on the ground; his famous poem 'Dulce et Decorum est' refers to 'the blood/Come gargling from the froth-corrupted lungs'. Rather than finding it sweet and proper to die for their country, Owen and countless others found themselves caught up in a system that seemed morally degenerate. Their unofficial view of war was the opposite of jingoism. It is this consensus that gives *Gassed* historical integrity and contextual relevance, a credibility that is still apposite today.

In *Gassed*, Sargent used a quiet, unaggressive form of soft realism, mediating the ghastliness of the scene he had witnessed. His choice of style makes this painting emotionally accessible to many. By dismissing avant-garde methods and embracing naturalism, he also painted a picture that has proved to be immune to changes in fashion. He adopts a low viewpoint in relation to the scene, elevating the line of wounded and temporarily blinded soldiers to the height at which we might view figures in an altarpiece. He also introduces a gentle late afternoon sunlight, which further softens the scene but adds to its plangency. It takes time to see the tiny figures in the far background playing football, their vigour in ironic contrast to the line of stumbling, blinded men. Yet these indistinct background figures only whisper to our attention, like a faint echo of another life. The overall mood is sorrowful, not harrowing or condemnatory.

At first sight, the style used by Sargent might seem stale and outmoded even by the standards that applied in 1918. But what is modern is the refusal to comment or prescribe, to be bombastic or to condemn. Sue Malvern has argued that 'to be truly modern, the spectator's imagination has to be freely exercised, never coerced'[20] – something that can only happen if, in the words of Wolfgang Kemp, 'spaces and surfaces...are open to the projective activity of the beholder'.[21] This may explain why the unexciting visual language used for this sombre elegy has proved so resilient and enduring.

The facts of war are very much to the fore in the catalogue to 'The Nation's War Paintings', which frequently expands on the title of an exhibit to name the regiment, battle, place, event, activity or task portrayed. A pictorial record of the exhibition was also published. These two documents would have satisfied the British liking for hard facts and helped them to ignore what wasn't there. Certainly the works on display placed more emphasis on the machinery of war, on howitzers, engines, battleships and hydroplanes, and on wireless operators, armaments manufacture and so on, than on injury and loss of life, although there was a number of allusions to medical services and dressing stations. Nevertheless, the human cost of this industrial war would have been to the fore in people's minds, and small details would have revived for many the grim nature of the conflict. Never again would war produce such a dramatic record: never again would it be fought at such close range.

The exhibition also had dull patches. The grand galleries of the Royal Academy encourage excess and a lack of discrimination. There were acres of competent portraits, many of them by Francis Dodd, whom the Ministry of Information had sent round France to draw all the British generals – after which, with Admiralty approval, he did all the admirals too.[22] And certain war artists were over-represented: there were fifty-two items by Sir John Lavery and sixty-nine by Muirhead Bone, despite the fact that the latter had a habit of viewing war scenes from a distance so that it was as if, as one critic observed, he had looked at them through the wrong end of a telescope. The select few, like Bone, Dodd and Lavery, who had been made full-time war artists had been well treated, given £500 a year as well as a chauffeur-driven car and an honorary commission. Yet the work they produced was often prosaic, or mere reportage. However, when literal description served a psychological narrative, as in Dodd's *Interrogation* (1919), the result was hugely popular. This cliff-hanger of a painting is set in an army camp. Two British officers are shown in urgent confrontation with a German prisoner of war, the bright daylight casting his face into shadow. Even in less theatrical paintings, such as Douglas Fox-Pitt's *Indian Army Wounded in Hospital in the Dome, Brighton* (1919), which records the makeshift convalescent ward created beneath the main dome of the Brighton Pavilion, there is an appeal to the English love of narrative and incongruity. It is still not adequately recognized that between 1914 and 1918, over a million men left India to fight Britain's war, many recruited from some of the poorest regions and most unable to write. Those needing to convalesce were sent to the Brighton Pavilion, a building from the Regency period inspired by India and boasting numerous onion domes. John Piper, when making an aquatint of the building for his book *Brighton Aquatints* in 1938, remarked in his commentary on the image that its Indian patients must have felt 'only vaguely at home'.[23]

Relatively little attention has been given to another hospital scene, Gilbert Spencer's *New Arrivals: F4 Ward, 36th Stationary Hospital, Mahemdia, Sinai* (1919), a painting on a 'reduced Uccello' scale which was added to the British War Memorials

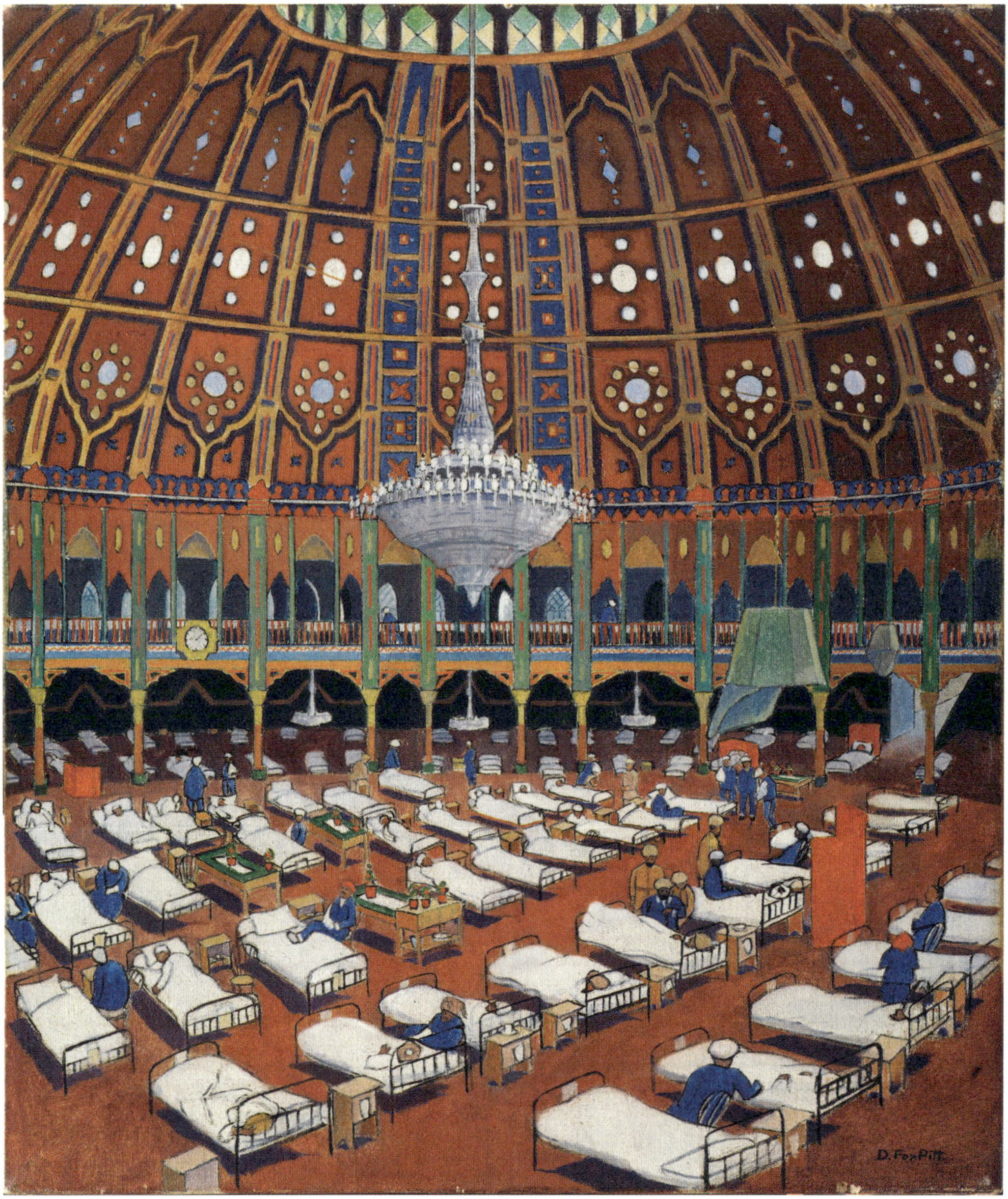

Douglas Fox-Pitt, *Indian Army Wounded in Hospital in the Dome, Brighton,*
oil on canvas, 1919.

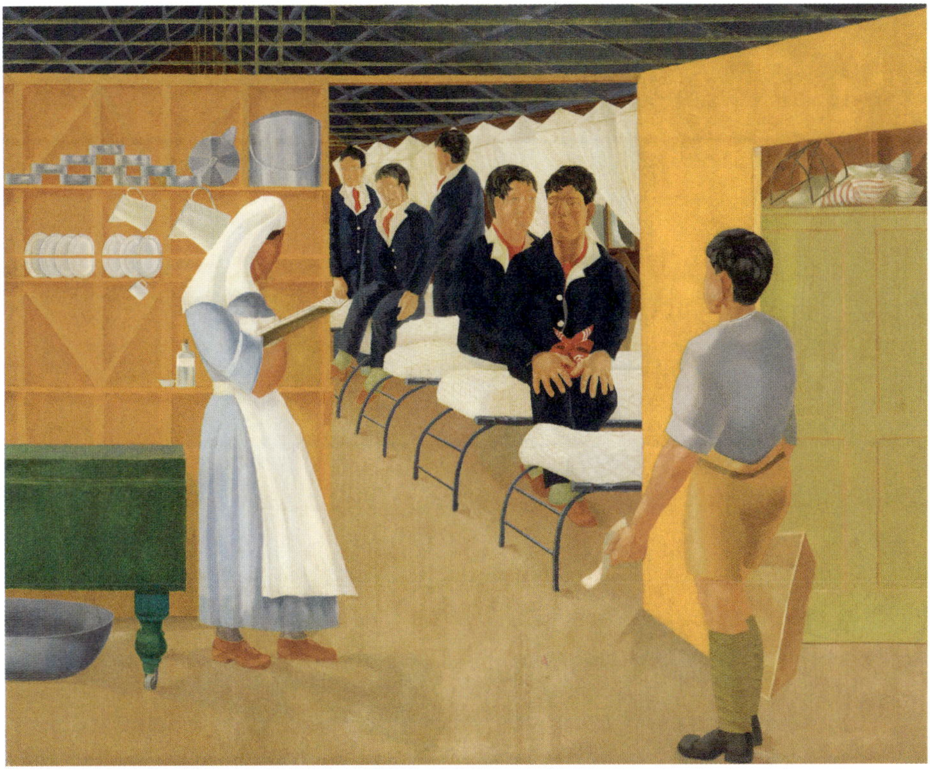

Gilbert Spencer, *New Arrivals: F4 Ward, 36th Stationary Hospital, Mahemdia, Sinai,* oil on canvas, 1919.

collection after the scheme itself had been closed.[24] A row of young men, in type very like the Spencer family, mostly sit waiting on their beds. Nearby are a nurse and an orderly. The scene has an awkwardness to it that conveys the unease of the new arrivals. The arrangement is therefore imaginative, but, again, every detail relates to actual experience, as the notes (presumably supplied by Gilbert Spencer) in 'The Nation's War Paintings' catalogue explain: 'The picture represents the interior of a Ward just after a Convoy has arrived. The patients are sitting on their beds, waiting for the Medical Officer, and the Sister is holding the Records book. Near her is the ice chest in which all the perishable food is kept. The orderly has in his hand the sheet and diet tray for rations. The study for this picture was made just previous to the first attack on Gaza in April, 1917.'[25] Such precise details heighten the narrative and reveal the artist's skill at holding the great and trivial in balance, here by focusing on the diurnal and nondescript while simultaneously hinting at the dangerous or sublime.

Much is achieved in these large war paintings through the handling of space, yet aerial views, which offered an exciting way forward, were largely ignored by artists commissioned to paint the air force. Partly because flying was still a new thing, the Imperial War Museum did not set up an Air Services section until 1917 and its art committee acted cautiously: Lieutenant-Colonel A. C. MacLean, who chaired this committee and who was also commander-in-chief of the Armaments School at Uxbridge, announced that he had no time for modern art. Yet he asked a twenty-one-year-old second lieutenant in the RAF, Richard Carline, who was also the youngest of the official war artists, to draw up a list of subjects and artists with a view to the formation of an RAF art collection. To this list MacLean added his own choice of artists, while also encouraging others on his committee to rate technical accuracy highly in the portrayal of aircraft and in images of reconstructed 'action'. He further ensured a conservative outlook by appointing as art adviser Harold Wyllie, a lieutenant-colonel in the RAF who was firmly committed to traditional forms of representation. Such was the conservatism surrounding the RAF art collection that by the end of the war it had more pictures of aircraft manufacture than of flight. The Carline brothers, Richard and Sydney, set out to rectify this situation.

One of Richard Carline's main objectives when making his list had been to obtain release for his brother Sydney from active service as a fighter pilot on the Italian front.[26] He was successful. Initially Richard flew over the battlefields of France while Sydney continued as an operation pilot, making flights in Italy, where he was supplied with a Sopwith Camel for sketching flights, though this cannot have been easy in an open cockpit, and at a certain height the paint froze on his brush. Then in August 1918 Sydney became, like his brother, an official war artist. Both Carlines were sent on a tour of the Middle East – partly on the ground, partly in the air – and tasked with recording scenes of RAF activity and reconstructing principal operations. The opportunities they were given were unique but, owing to money shortages, the initial request for twenty-five canvases had to be reduced to seven.

Aerial views lean towards a modernist use of space, especially when the horizon vanishes and the landscape flattens out like an abstract painting. Sydney Carline was one of the first artists to convey the disembodied lightness of flight. But the modernity in his and his brother's work created tensions between them and MacLean. The Carlines received fierce warnings that the RAF section was 'not prepared to exhibit, in the Museum, pictures showing any extreme forms of art'.[27]

When looking at paintings of aerial warfare, we occasionally find ourselves sharing vicariously in moments of extreme danger. This makes an aesthetic approach to these and other war pictures difficult to maintain, for they trigger a range of reactions, from patriotic pride in heroic action to recognition of the 'pity of war'. Because the initial scheme for commissioning war art had begun at Wellington House, where Charles F. G. Masterman directed a propaganda unit, it had, from the start, been linked to a propagandist intent. Tasked with making a 'record' of war, war artists often found themselves in a double bind, anxious to address their own response to a subject while also recognizing the need to satisfy the expectations of the commissioning body.

In February 1920, 'The Nation's War Paintings' came to an end. As intended, it had climaxed in Gallery III with a fine representation of many of the large paintings commissioned by the British War Memorials scheme. Sargent's *Gassed* was among them, as was Paul Nash's *The Menin Road*, Roberts's *A Shell Dump in France*, Cameron's *The Battle of Ypres*, Henry Lamb's *Irish Troops in the Judean Hills, surprised by a Turkish Bombardment*, Gilbert Spencer's hospital scene *New Arrivals* and his brother Stanley Spencer's *Travoys Arriving with Wounded at a Dressing Station at Smol, Macedonia, September 1916* – this last completed with difficulty and only after the artist had tried to resign from his commission. Further canvases associated with this commissioning body hung in adjacent rooms, which made it difficult to assess the collection as a whole. Of all these large-scale works it was *Gassed* that stood out, partly due to its size. Sargent, Augustus John and William Orpen had all been asked to work on an extra-large canvas – 8'6" high and 20' wide – but only Sargent fulfilled the task.

Alfred Yockney, the art critic turned civil servant who had overseen a great many war artist appointments, wrote a report on the British War Memorials paintings that had now joined the Museum's collection. He concluded that the scheme had differed from others in that the imperative to 'record' had not in every instance been requested, but had in most cases naturally occurred.[28] The subjects of these large-scale paintings had for the most part been mutually agreed, but in some instances had only been vaguely indicated, thereby permitting a degree of freedom which had let in unexpected things. The war had undeniably expanded the subject matter of art and the audience for it. It had undone the tense opposition between the establishment or status quo and the avant-garde, making it more difficult for a future avant-garde to establish an oppositional stance. It was unclear what direction artistic production would take next. But now that art occupied an expanded field, new opportunities were waiting in the wings to be explored.

CHAPTER 2

RESISTANCE AND INNOVATION

When peace was declared, Paul Nash and his wife were living in the countryside, at Chalfont St Peter in Buckinghamshire. Margaret Nash recollected they felt no excitement or even pleasure at the news: 'we were all so tired and exhausted by the struggle for existence; we just dumbly relaxed and then began to worry about the future.'[1]

The following morning the prime minister, David Lloyd George, announced that victory gave impetus to the need to reform and rebuild the country so as to bring 'light and beauty into the lives of the people'.[2] And ten days later he gave his famous electioneering speech in Wolverhampton, calling for 'a fit country for heroes to live in'. On both occasions he made it evident that he regarded the state of housing in Britain as a national concern. But Britain had borrowed hugely to pay for a brutal and expensive war, with only 26 per cent of its cost being met by taxation.[3] The hopes Lloyd George raised proved difficult to achieve. An immediate boom in the economy after the war, driven by pent-up consumer demand and a high volume of liquidity, brought with it inflation, which was followed by deflation, recession, unemployment and a prolonged economic downturn. The national debt in the late 1920s accounted for more than 40 per cent of government spending.[4] It is estimated that it took four years for the country to recover from war, but even then it did not return to its former status. Its position on the global stage had become less prominent. As a leading capital exporter, it had previously accounted for 27 per cent of the world's manufactured exports, but the war had allowed America and Japan to replace Britain in international markets and it had suffered a permanent loss of the world market share. In addition, America had superseded Britain as economic leader owing to the phenomenal growth of its economy, now the biggest in the world and bolstered by powerful industries – coal, the making of steel and railroads, as well as the new industries associated with electricity, chemicals and the automobile.[5]

In Britain, the major public housing and health schemes that had been drawn up by the Minister of Reconstruction in February 1918 as part of an ambitious programme of reform were to be undermined by debts and deflation. The shadow of war reached into many aspects of people's lives. Family outings were marked by the absence of those who had lost their lives in the war. Working women were forced to cede their jobs to returning soldiers. And a more general sense of loss was felt in relation to the past, with the realization that the way of life and values associated with the Victorian and Edwardian world had vanished. Radical change, if as yet inchoate, was to be the order of the day. Samuel Hynes, summing up C. E. Montague's *Disenchantment* (1922) – a book which makes a telling contrast between prewar and post-war life in England – comments that Montague's present was 'a negative space, emptied of everything good and secure that the past had held'.[6] This sense that certain things were not just ruined but irrecoverable explains why words like *loss*, *disenchantment*, *dislocation*, *discontinuity*, *futility* and *uncertainty* are often used of the immediate post-war period, a time veined with anxiety as to how modernity would affect everyday life and the power of the state.

A salary cut for war artists in December 1918 and new restrictions on 'painting necessities' indicated that the termination of state patronage was imminent. Paul Nash was fortunate in having received £150 from the British War Memorials Committee for *The Menin Road*, but the painting took him the better part of a year to complete.[7] Aware of the unstable financial conditions facing artists, Nash agreed to write an article in May 1919 in support of the newly founded Arts League of Service.

The Arts League of Service was the most influential of the many organizations that took root during the aftermath of war to encourage involvement with, and appreciation of, the arts. With hindsight, it set the model for the Council for the Encouragement of Music and the Arts, founded in 1940 and likewise driven by a desire to promote and sustain British culture. In 1919, the Arts League of Service announced its determination 'to bring the Arts into everyday life' and 'into reach of all', not just those in the metropolis but also in rural communities. It was going to promote the 'higher forms of entertainment' and pay particular attention to men returning from active service, as well as to artists struggling with soaring rents, unemployment and economic depression. It mounted talks on literature, dance, music and the crafts and set up high-profile lectures, as advertised in a programme of events that came out soon after the organization had been founded in 1919. It brought together a company of players that toured England, performing plays in towns and villages. It also set up a partnership with the XXI Gallery in the Adelphi, behind the Strand, where exhibitions were mounted. The overall ambition was to stir up civic pride in the nation's culture by making art accessible to all.

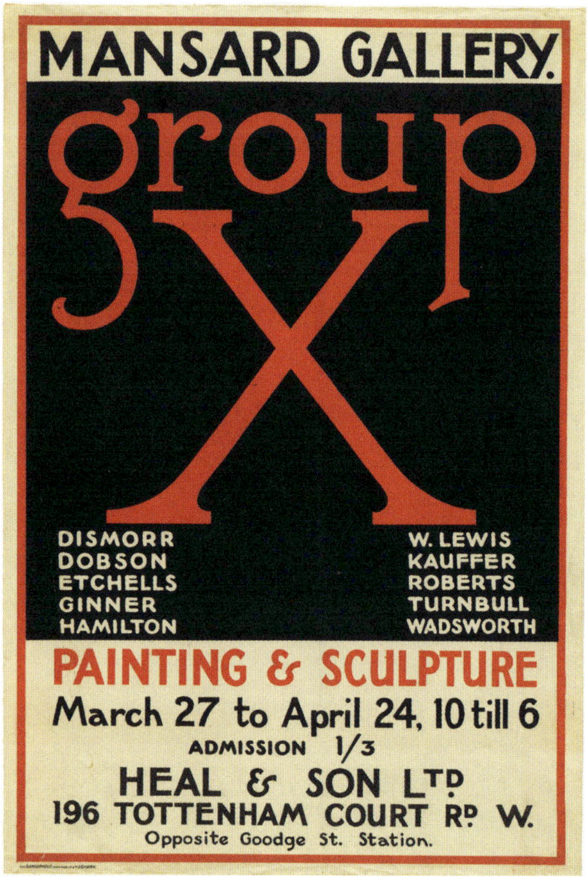

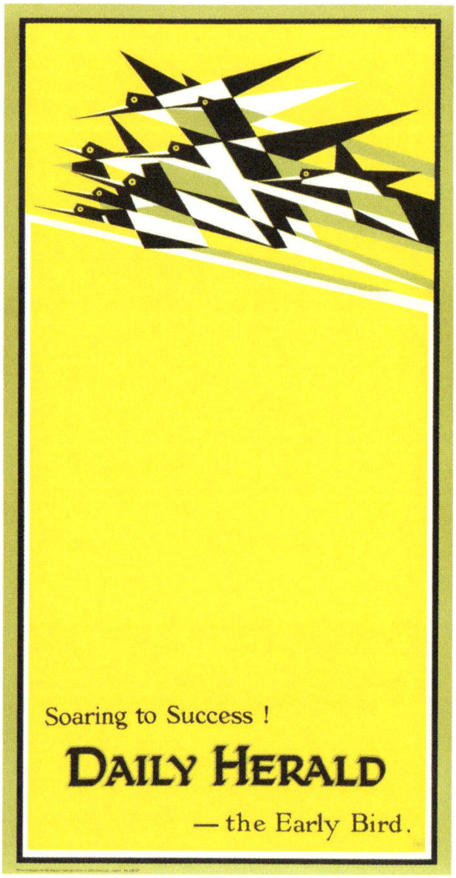

Nash's essay touched on the urgent need to strengthen the bond between artists and the public. 'The public should realize the artist is not merely an idle, eccentric figure practically dependent upon the patronage of the rich, but an intelligent man fighting for his living like the rest of us, only under more adverse and unstable conditions. And the artist in his turn must grasp the fact that if the public does appear a fool to him, it is not wholly the public's fault, but rather the misfortune of its education and its lack of opportunity to appreciate what he, the artist stands for....But times are changing....It is proposed to bring the Arts into everyday life.... it is unnecessary to be alarmed, the suggestion emanates from an apparently sound and serious movement, the roots of which, I hope, already grip the soil and strike down. I refer to the Arts League of Service.'[8]

One of the League's first exhibitions drew attention to experimental decorative art. It included work by Paul Nash, the former vorticist Edward Wadsworth and

OPPOSITE
Edward McKnight Kauffer, *Group X* poster, 1919.

Edward McKnight Kauffer, *Early Bird* poster for the *Daily Herald*, 1918–19.

RIGHT
Fred Taylor, LNER poster advertising Cambridge, using image of Erasmus.

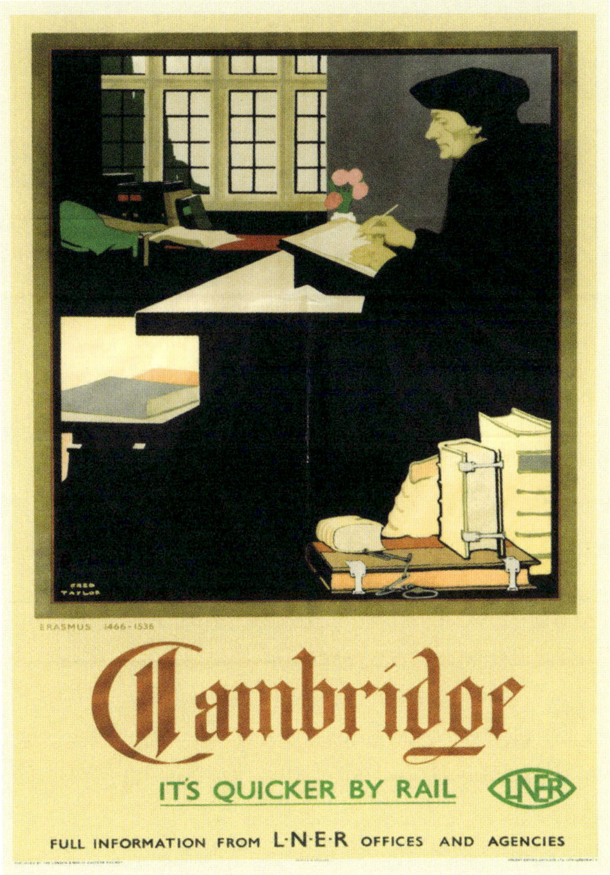

the American Edward McKnight Kauffer, who had arrived in Britain in 1914 after a stint in Paris and Munich. With remarkable alacrity McKnight Kauffer had embedded himself in the London art world as a painter and designer, exhibiting with the London Group, at Roger Fry's Omega Workshops and in the 'Group X' exhibition (held in March 1920), of which he was the principal organizer, though guided by Wyndham Lewis. He also designed the poster for this exhibition, creating a spare image around the letter X. At around this time he produced the famous *Early Bird* poster for the *Daily Herald*, in which he used sharp, clear-cut shapes to convey a flock of birds 'Soaring to Success', boldly leaving a large expanse of emptiness at the centre of the advertisement to convey height and space. The image has the edge over Fred Taylor's gentle merging of the historical with the modern in a poster showing Erasmus in his college rooms, which was used to promote a train journey to Cambridge by LNER railway. Taylor became one of Britain's foremost poster artists in the interwar years, his poster *Piccadilly Circus, West End, London* making a strong appeal to those within reach of a London and North Eastern line heading for London. But as a piece of commercial art it is again out of step with McKnight Kauffer's more sophisticated manner, which owed much to his early experience of Continental modernism. It is not surprising that in 1915 Frank Pick, publicity manager for the London Underground, began commissioning posters from Kauffer, as did the GPO and Jack Beddington at Shell. His signature style was to be characterized by succinct shapes, clear lettering and dynamic design, his fastidiousness enhancing the accessibility of the image and its message.

Generally, however, originality in art and design was in short supply after the war. By comparison with Paris, with its roster of leading collectors actively generating interest in modern art and design, new ideas in London seemed to gain little traction. It had no collectors to compare with the Steins or Jacques Doucet in Paris. It was not only the art that drew visitors to Gertrude and Leo Stein's regular salons (which continued when Leo moved out and Alice B. Toklas moved in), but also the discussion surrounding art and ideas. The same was true of Michael and Sarah Stein's decision to open their home on Saturday evenings, where it was evident that Sarah's unshakeable belief in Matisse matched Gertrude's commitment to Picasso. The Steins were also interested in architecture and friendly with Le Corbusier, who designed for them the Villa Stein at Garches, a Parisian suburb, where they lived until their return to New York in 1935. Jacques Doucet, owner of a couture house, had an enfilade of three rooms in his residence at 33 rue Saint-James, Neuilly-sur-Seine, which he referred to as his 'studio'. It was preceded by a staircase in which hung Picasso's *Les Demoiselles d'Avignon* – today regarded as the most seminal work in the history of modern art – and the 'studio' itself was chock full not just of modern art but also modern design, about which Doucet was equally passionate. He forged friendships with many designers and became one of Eileen Gray's earliest patrons. These collectors helped stimulate a climate of robust aesthetic and intellectual interest in contemporary art and design far stronger than anything that could be found in England.

Britain was further weakened by its lack of a robust economy. Admittedly the art market, having been in a depressed state during the Great War, benefited from the short-lived economic boom of 1919. There was a sudden flourishing of exhibitions and the number of dealers increased. Auction houses reported record sale prices for works of art by historic and well-known artists, while living artists also attracted larger sums for their work than ever before.[9] And at the top end of the market, significant transatlantic deals once again got under way. The Settled Land Act of 1882 had made it possible 'for life tenants to part with assets and heirlooms that had previously been virtually inalienable under the terms of strict family settlements'.[10] The new death duties, introduced in 1894, furthered the breaking up of large estates and brought more old master paintings, often spoils from Grand Tours as well as 18th-century British portraits, onto the market. Vast American fortunes were spent on these works of art. Wily dealers, notably Joseph Duveen (later Lord Duveen of Millbank), worked collaboratively with outstanding collectors to bring about transatlantic deals which, at another level, rested on an Anglo-American rapprochement that owed much to a shared language and a sense of shared historical lineage. David Cannadine astutely observes that the 'new American rich looked across the Atlantic to the tradition of the English aristocracy for inspiration, legitimation, reassurance and status'.[11] Duveen, on the other hand, noticed that Europe (by which he primarily meant the English and French aristocracy) had plenty of art and America had plenty of money, and, as his first biographer observed, 'his entire astonishing career was the product of that simple observation'.[12]

In 1921 he brokered the sale of Gainsborough's *The Blue Boy*, a painting that the American collector Isabella Stewart Gardner had earlier tried and failed to acquire. Duveen, on hearing that railroad magnate and collector Henry E. Huntington also wanted the picture, worked on its owner, the Duke of Westminster, with success. Huntington paid what was, at that time, the highest price a work of art had ever achieved.[13] After the painting had been cleaned, he agreed that it could be exhibited at the National Gallery in London for three weeks before it left Britain. News of its sale brought visitors flocking to see this immensely seductive picture, which drew on Gainsborough's admiration for the society portraits of Van Dyck. Newspapers ran daily reports on the exhibition, catching something of the wonder the painting aroused. But gradually the mood changed: as the date of its departure for the States drew closer, visitors began to realize that the nation was losing an icon of British culture. A protest began outside the National Gallery and 'mourning crowds' gathered in support. *The Blue Boy* went on public display again at the Duveen brothers' gallery in New York before travelling on to Southern California, where Henry Huntington was waiting on the station platform to meet it. Today it can be found in the Huntington Library, Art Museum, and Botanical Gardens in San Marino.

At the other end of the British art market, however, the situation was very different. Roberson's of Long Acre, a leading supplier of artists' materials since 1820, had opened a branch in Piccadilly in 1890 that included a gallery dedicated to the sale of small paintings. This aspect of its business failed badly during the 1920s, and its premises in the West End were abandoned in 1939. The firm's records state: 'Pictures today, unless of outstanding importance, fetch practically nothing in the sale room.'[14]

Thomas Gainsborough,
The Blue Boy,
oil on canvas, 1770.

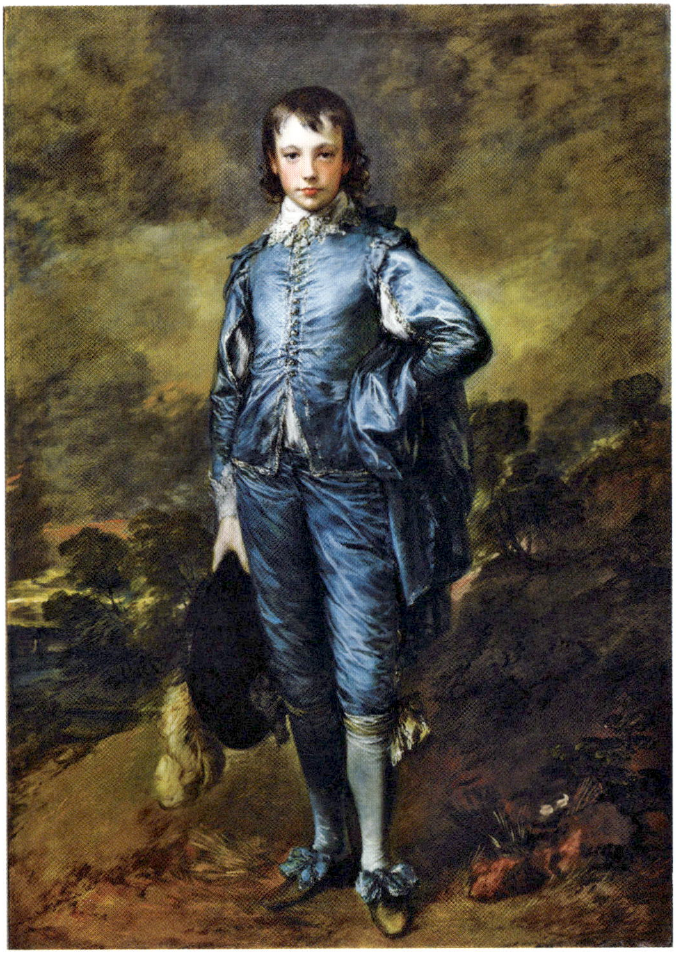

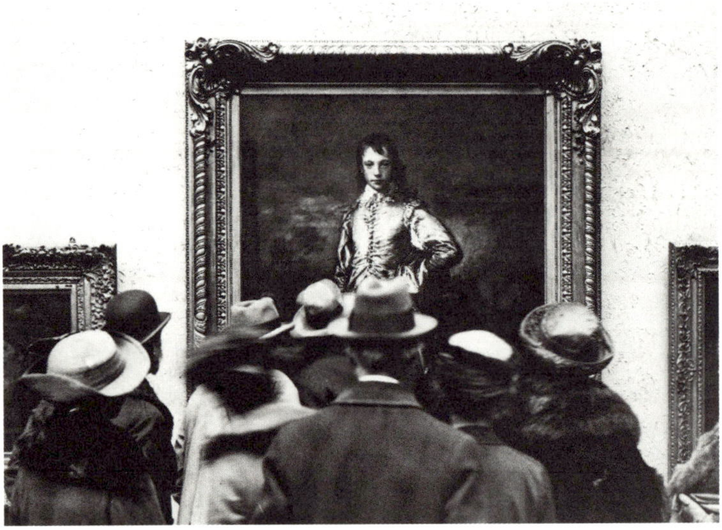

The Blue Boy on show at the National Gallery, London, 1922.

Financial hardship, post-war disillusionment and fear of change all combined to leave many artists uncertain of the way forward. Paul Nash, with his deep love of poetry and drama, landscape and its *genius loci*, must have welcomed the cessation of conflict, yet he felt disorientated when peace returned. In some notes made for his unfinished autobiography, he began this period with the melancholy remark: 'Struggles of a war artist without a war.'[15] After completing *The Menin Road* he was free to paint what he liked, but Nash was not alone in finding the 'responsibility of representation' burdensome, owing to the need to find new subjects and new approaches to the making of art.

While 'The Nation's War Paintings' ran at the Royal Academy during the winter of 1919–20, the issue of representation figured repeatedly in the press coverage. Critics recognized the difficulty of finding a visual language that would adequately convey the 'real' or 'authentic' in representations of war. The high visibility of photography in communicating and recording the Great War had enhanced the suspicion that technological advances achieved in photography and printing had overtaken fine art and that representation in painting was somehow inadequate, having lost something of its integrity, status and poetic power. At the same time, a loss of confidence in the move towards abstraction in prewar modernism, in both Britain and France, made it difficult to see a way forward.

In the absence of any other firm directive, the phrase *le rappel à l'ordre* (the return to order) took hold. Coined in France by the painter André Lhote in 1919 while writing about the recent work of Picasso and Braque, it was picked up at the time but only became a popular expression after Jean Cocteau used it as the title for a book of essays in 1926.

Lhote was both a painter and a teacher, as well as a leading voice in the French press. Two articles by him appeared in translation in the *Athenaeum* in the late summer of 1919, the first reflecting on the significance of the reopening of the Louvre and the second taking a revisionist look at 'Cubism and the Modern Artistic Sensibility'. Understandably, his conservative stance irritated Roger Fry, who had masterminded the two post-impressionist exhibitions of 1910 and 1912 that awakened the British public to modern art. It must have been painful enough to read Lhote's outburst against the modern movement; but still more infuriating, in Fry's mind, was his praise of the Le Nain brothers and the neoclassical Jacques-Louis David. 'For me that's almost a joke,' Fry wrote to his friend, the French artist Jean Marchand. 'The Le Nains are excellent people, but they have none of the great qualities of construction that all the Italians have, even the second rate, and as to David, Good Lord. I could find it in me to pardon his cold and chauvinistic rhetoric if he really had a great passion for form....But [with] David, it's no longer the passion for order but the love of authority – it's the schoolmaster. And then what a mistake to regard our movement as a kind of anarchy. Since Cézanne everything tends towards architectonic construction....It is very distressing for me who have always loved France, as if I belonged there, to see such a strong reactionary tendency taking hold of the young now, to see them tired of freedom and demanding discipline.'[16]

It was noticeable in England that the fearlessness behind much avant-garde art of the pre-1914 period had been driven out by the recent war. A reactionary impulse was now dominant and took the form of a search for continuity, a return to tradition and to pre-post-impressionist methods. There was a widespread desire for some form of realism. Yet among the more progressive artists there gradually unfolded a contrary awareness that the 'real' or the 'authentic' in art was neither straightforward nor secure, and that more dialectical ingenuity was needed.

The young Ben Nicholson, who had been kept out of the war by his asthma, was stung by a desire to 'bust up the sophistication all around me',[17] for it seemed to him that the reversion to realistic or naturalistic methods of representation amounted to little more than a final decadent gasp of the Greco-Roman and Renaissance tradition. In reaction to this, Nicholson began to give his allegiance to the 'modern movement' in England, which drew artists, designers and architects together, aware that the world around them increasingly glittered with steel and glass owing to advances in engineering, technology and science. Hence the recurrent tension in this period between a precarious stasis on the one hand and, on the other, a yearning for rapid change.

A shift in intent or change of mood had in fact begun before the return to peace. Two examples of this are Vanessa Bell's *A Conversation* and Jacob Epstein's *Torso in Metal from 'The Rock Drill'*. At the Second Post-Impressionist Exhibition at London's Grafton Gallery in 1912, an entire room had been devoted to the work of Matisse. It had a significant impact on Vanessa Bell and on Duncan Grant, both of whom produced some of their most experimental and chromatically brilliant work in the wake of this exhibition. In 1913 Bell began work on *A Conversation* (initially titled *Three Women*), in which three figures huddle together in front of a window with a view through into the garden beyond. Later, in 1916, by which time the number of deaths caused by war made bright colours in fashion or art unacceptable, she repainted this picture. By then, Bell and Grant had both begun to retreat from the use of strong, unmediated hues, turning instead to more sombre harmonies held together by tonal relationships and dense brushwork. As X-ray photography shows, Bell repainted the clothes of the three women in *A Conversation* so that muted shades of brown and ochre now predominate, but left the original colour scheme

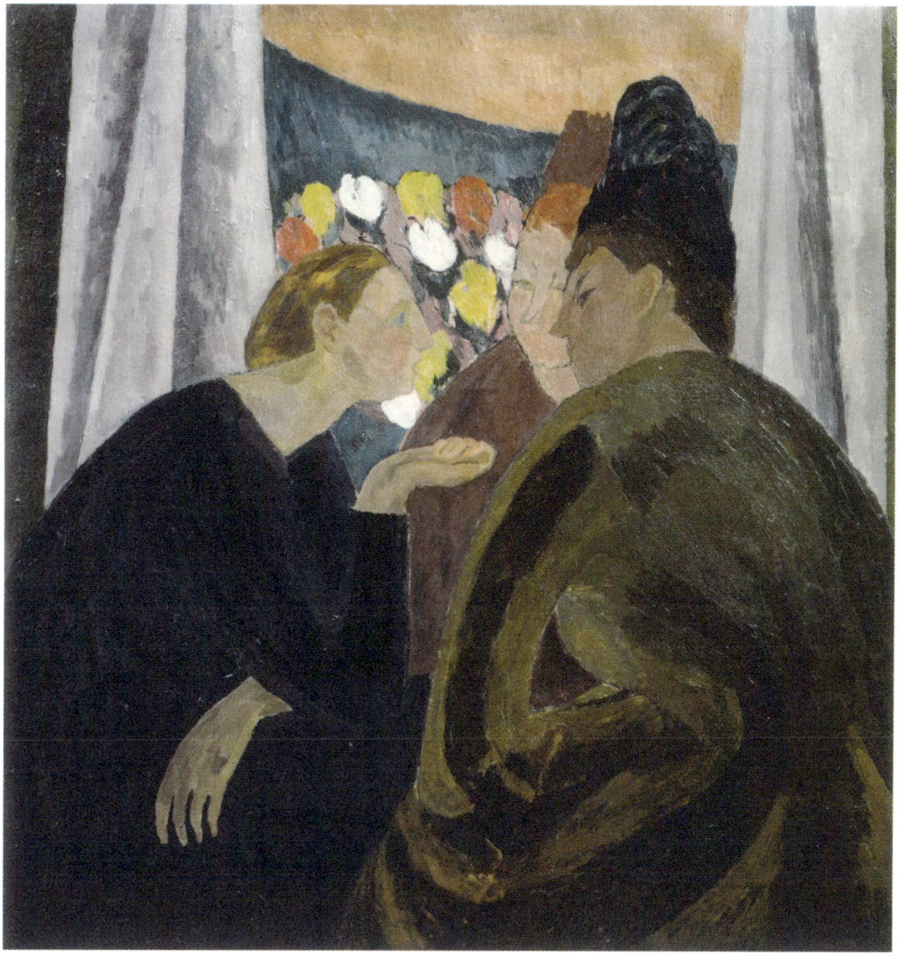

Vanessa Bell, *A Conversation*,
oil on canvas, 1913–16.

still visible in the view through the window of the garden, where blobs of bright colour against a flat area of green stand in for flowers while also metaphorically hinting at the exchange of animated gossip.

Similarly, as news of the Battle of the Somme and the Battle of Verdun came through in 1916, Jacob Epstein revisited his *Rock Drill*, which dated back to 1913. He now discarded the monstrous drill and truncated the white plaster robot which had straddled it, reducing the figure to a half-length; he also cut off one arm just above the elbow and the other at the wrist, thereby removing the hand that had once controlled the machine. What remained, he cast in bronze. This material alteration, from white plaster to dark bronze, further underscored a change in his attitude to

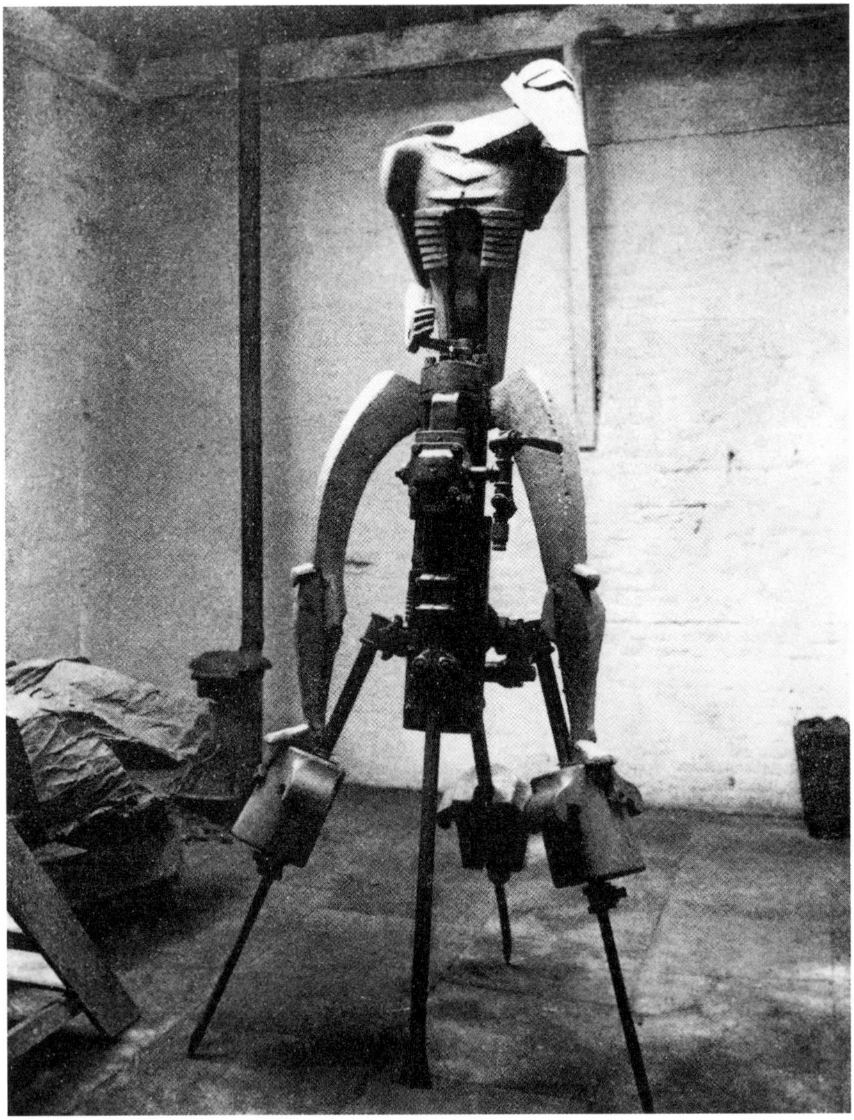

Jacob Epstein, *Rock Drill*
in its original form, c. 1913–15.

the work. Instead of a dramatic, menacing statement about the power and force of machinery and its relation to the modern world, the half-length figure exerts a melancholy air; the jutting head, with its visor fully obscuring the face, looks aside, as if haunted by the memory of recent slaughter.

In both these works we encounter a partial retreat from modernism. With the return of peace this retreat became more evident, even though C. R. W. Nevinson,

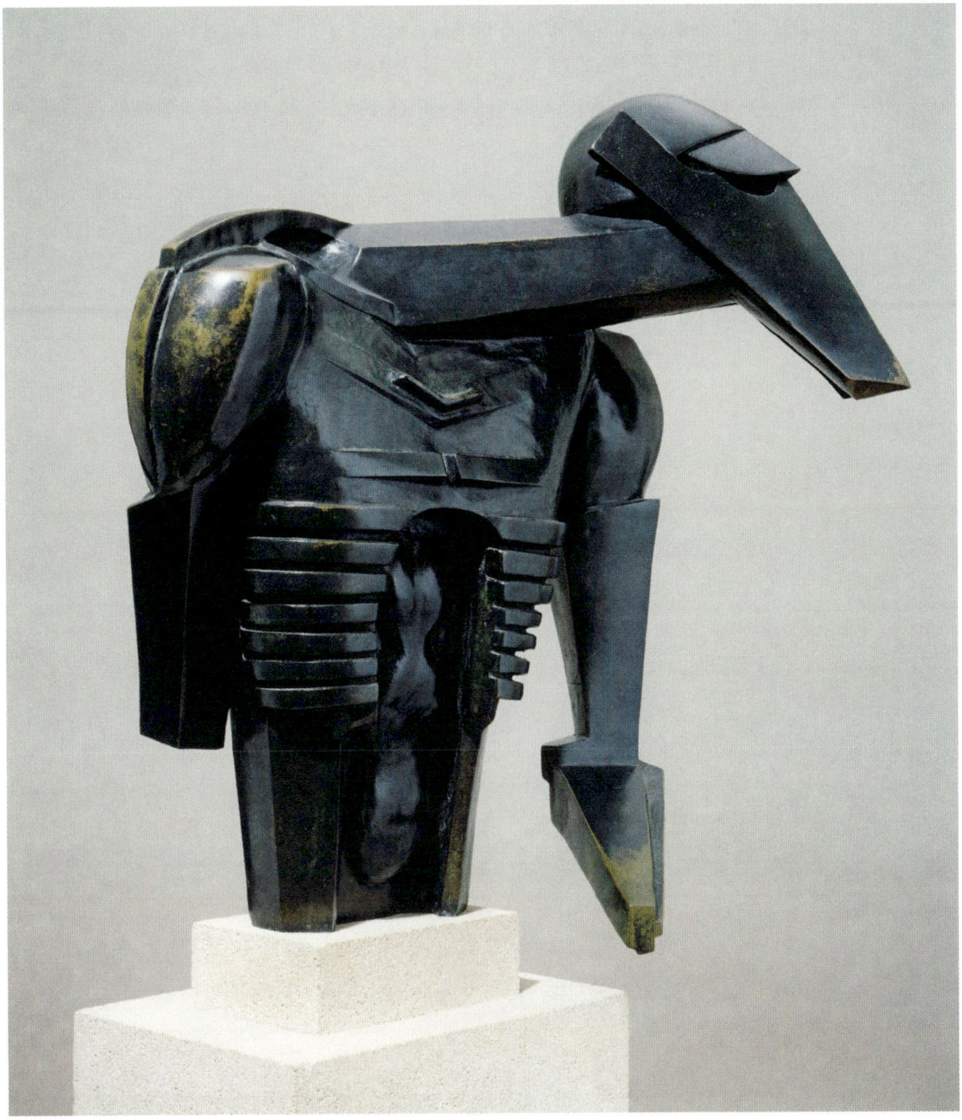

Jacob Epstein, *Torso in Metal from 'The Rock Drill'*,
bronze, c. 1913–16.

Paul Nash and William Roberts had made a modernist language of art acceptable by showing that it could apprehend and communicate the bitter truth of war. But this was part of the problem: modernism and war had become linked in people's minds. The more aggressive aspects of earlier modernism and its 'machine aesthetic' now seemed tainted with a prefiguration of industrial warfare. Hence the cold-shouldering of it by a public that had no stomach for further attacks on tradition in the aftermath of war.

One person with a broader view of art was Laurence Binyon, who, with his family, occupied a house in one wing of the British Museum, where he worked in the Department of Prints and Drawings. Sociable and well connected within both literary and artistic circles, he is a quietly ubiquitous figure within the history of British art. He had introduced Wyndham Lewis to the poet Ezra Pound, who associated the group of artists around Lewis with the whirl of energy around a still point created by the vortex, and thereby created the generic term 'vorticism'. Binyon had also spoken on behalf of Paul Nash when he was under consideration for a commission as a war artist. Binyon's encompassing breadth of appreciation rested on his knowledge of Chinese and Japanese art as well as European art. At weekends he took his youngest daughter, Nicolette, along with him to see exhibitions, opening her eyes to many things, including art outside the Western European tradition. Many years after she had married Basil Gray, also a specialist in the British Museum (and dropped a 't' from the spelling of her first name), Nicolete Gray put on record that if you wanted 'to see modern English art in the 1920s, the best place to go was the Imperial War Museum',[18] where could be found paintings by Nevinson, Wyndham Lewis, Paul Nash and Stanley Spencer.

This is interesting because at that time, the main depository for modern British art was generally thought to be the Tate Gallery. (Its official name in the early 1920s was the National Gallery, Millbank; but because it was associated in the public mind with Henry Tate, who had gifted his collection of modern British art to the nation and paid for the building of the Gallery in its early stages, everyone – even *The Times* and the *Burlington Magazine* – referred to it as the Tate Gallery.) To make way for this new palace of art, the vast Millbank Penitentiary had been pulled down, but a memory of its grim site lives on, as described by Charles Dickens in the seventh chapter of *David Copperfield*.

> There were neither wharves nor houses on the melancholy waste of road near the great blank prison. A sluggish ditch deposited its mud on the prison walls. Coarse grass and rank weeds straggled over all the marsh land. In one part, carcases of houses, inauspiciously begun and never finished, rotted away. In another, the ground was cumbered with rusty iron monsters of steam boilers, wheels, cranks, pipes, furnaces, paddles, anchors, diving-bells, windmill sails, and I know not what strange objects, accumulated by some speculator, and grovelling in the dust....Slimy gaps and causeways, winding among old wooden piles, with a sickly substance clinging to the latter, like green hair, and the rags of last year's handbills offering rewards for drowned men fluttering above the high-water mark, led down through

> the ooze and slush to the ebb-tide. There was a story that one of the pits dug for the dead in the time of the Great Plague was hereabout; and a blighting influence seemed to have proceeded from it over the whole place.

When the Tate Gallery opened in 1897, in a building about an eighth of the size that Tate Britain is today, it must have looked and felt precarious. Queen Victoria had declined the invitation to open it. But it evidently intrigued her, as on 11 May 1900 – during the last year of her life, when she mostly took her exercise in her garden chaise in the grounds of Buckingham Palace – she made a public drive in an open landau drawn by four horses. Normally on these outings, the Queen's entourage followed an accustomed route. But on this occasion, *The Times* reported, an alteration was made so that the Queen could be shown 'the Tate Gallery'. Crowds lined the main thoroughfares and cheered loudly as the sovereign approached. When the carriage reached the Embankment it slowed down so that a regal eye could be cast over a site previously associated with suffering, crime and disease. 'None who can remember the old Millbank prison', Balfour, then leader of the Conservative Party, remarked in his speech at the opening ceremony, 'could, in their wildest imaginations, have conjectured that in so short a period, by the generosity of one man, so vast a transformation could be effected.'[19]

It was initially titled the National Gallery of British Art, but despite this grand title, the Tate was then little more than an annexe of the National Gallery in Trafalgar Square. Its collection was vested in the trustees of the National Gallery and its administration was accountable to the senior institution's vote officer. Before the Tate officially opened, a decision had been taken at Trafalgar Square that the National Gallery would transfer from its collection to Millbank only 'modern' British paintings – by which they meant artists born after 1790, a date that conveniently kept Constable and Turner at the National Gallery. Other factors that constricted the Tate in its early years were minimal staffing and the absence of any purchase grant. Gifts came in each year through the Chantrey Bequest, but the Tate at this stage had no influence over the selection, as the bequest was administered by Royal Academicians who, in their choice, often pandered to their colleagues in need or chose sentimental or fourth-rate work. Complaints over the mishandling of the Chantrey Bequest were one reason why a committee was set up in 1912, under Lord Curzon, to review the scope and constitution of the Tate. H. M. Stationery Office published the Curzon Report in 1915, but the recent intervention of war temporarily stalled its recommendations.

Nevertheless, the Curzon Report succeeded in laying down the basis of the Tate's eventual charter. In 1917 it gained its own board of trustees and its keeper was advanced to the position of Director. The new board was responsible for management, administration and staff discipline, but the Tate's financial matters remained subject to the accounting officer at Trafalgar Square. The Report had looked not just at the Tate but at its relations to other national collections, in an attempt to rationalize collecting policies with regard to British art. It concluded that the Tate should become the national collection of historic as well as modern British art, and also the home for modern foreign painting. As a result of this recommendation, over 200 historic British pictures were transferred from the National Gallery to the Tate in 1919; but the National Gallery trustees, who had sat on Curzon's committee, were clearly troubled by the second decision. 'We have not in our mind', their report explains, 'any ideas of experimentalising by brash purchases in the occasionally ill-disciplined productions of some contemporaneous continental schools, whose work might exercise a disturbing and even deleterious influence upon our younger painters.'[20] Such xenophobic resistance to 'modern foreign art', as it was then called, instances the conservatism which troubled the collecting policies of both the National Gallery and the Tate during the interwar period. It is a subject that will be returned to in relation to modern French painting and especially to the work of Cézanne and Picasso.

The Tate had remained open when war began, but closed after the onset of Zeppelin attacks in 1916. By the end of the war, most of its collection was stored in the Post Office vault and Aldwych tube station. Although these works were returned in March 1919, the building did not reopen to the public until 1921 owing to the need of thorough redecoration. When it did reopen, the former wall coverings made out of heavy brocades had been replaced by modern fabrics using a broken texture but no patterns. Modern painting, either Whistlerian or impressionist in style, hung on pale neutral tones, while darker shades of fawn appeared in the 18th- and 19th-century rooms and the Pre-Raphaelites looked resplendent against a reddish-purple ground.

But where were the modernists? Admittedly the Contemporary Art Society had in 1917 gifted the Tate with C. R. W. Nevinson's *La Mitrailleuse* (1915), a picture in which, as the title suggests, the main protagonist is the 'death-scattering' machine gun.[21] It is a powerful image of trench warfare, showing soldiers who, acting as the gun's adjuncts and stripped of their humanity by the relentless destruction of war, ignore their compatriot slumped on the ground nearby. Walter Sickert pronounced this painting 'the most authoritative and concentrated utterance on the war in the history of painting' in 1916, in the pages of the *Burlington Magazine*. But for this very reason it must have sat uncomfortably alongside the other paintings in the collection, which mostly consisted of saccharine anecdotal subjects or mythological paintings from the late Victorian and Edwardian period. Most of Britain's outstanding modernist paintings at this time were war paintings and most had ended up not in the Tate, but in the Imperial War Museum. Nicolete Gray's claim that this was the Mecca of modern painting is therefore correct, but what is not clear is just how visible these paintings were, either in 1920, when the Museum acquired its first home at Crystal Palace, or after 1924, when it moved into the Imperial Institute in South Kensington.

At both venues the Imperial War Museum favoured sectional displays, each focusing on one of the armed forces or on 'Women's Work', the latter celebrating the contribution made by women to the First World War. Period photographs show that at both venues these displays were integrated, paintings, drawings and sculpture mingling with other forms of war memorabilia, including weaponry. These photographs also suggest that modernist war art was kept out of sight, perhaps because it was still difficult, in an era seeking a return to normality and the safety of conventions, to accept the subversiveness of modern art. The 'equation of radical art with destruction' had begun during the war, as David Peters Corbett reminds us; in its aftermath this belief, even when modernism had been modified by a return to figuration and realism, brought forward 'more traditional art as, by contrast, patriotically healthy and unsullied'.[22]

Further aggressive attacks in art were therefore unwanted. Yet the press cuttings on the 'The Nation's War Paintings', kept by the Imperial War Museum, reveal that the modernist tactics employed by Nevinson and Nash as war artists had largely been accepted: instead, as has been mentioned, it was the naturalism found in Sargent's *Gassed* that proved troubling in relation to the picture's subject matter. With hindsight, one of the most notable aspects of 'The Nation's War Paintings' is that, for the first time in its history, the Royal Academy had opened its galleries to the display of traditional *and* avant-garde artists in an equal, democratic fashion – something that would not occur again for several decades.

After this rare moment of accord, the Royal Academy appeared to sink back into the past and became a bastion of resistance to artistic innovation. In 1915, in the second issue of *Blast*, while conservatism was at its height, Wyndham Lewis had thrown out the remark that it seemed as if 'the splendid war army of England were fighting to reinstate the tradition of Sir Frederick Leighton'.[23] To some extent, this aperçu proved correct. Towards the end of his life Leighton had been made a baron, the first artist ever to rise to this rank, and as Lord Leighton and president of the Royal Academy of Arts he perfectly fulfilled the role of a great statesman and was rewarded with a state funeral at St Paul's Cathedral. The memory of this filled the academicians with pride. They also took pride in the fact that the Academy was (as it still is) an independent arts organization, funded by neither state nor crown, yet gifted with royal blessing in its 1768 foundation document through the signature of George III.

It certainly valued its connection with royalty. Each year, the president and secretary of the Academy had an audience at Buckingham Palace with the king, so that a report of the preceding year's business could be submitted for the monarch's signature. When the forthcoming marriage of Princess Mary, George V and Queen Mary's only daughter, to Lord Lascelles (later 6th earl of Harewood) was announced, careful thought was given as to what would make, in 1922, a suitable wedding gift. Predictably, the solution was a statuette version of Lord Leighton's *An Athlete Struggling with a Python*.

With such an imposing past, it is not surprising that the academicians took very good care of the dead. In the aftermath of war a suitable inscription was found for the gravestone of the recently departed president, Sir Edward J. Poynter, and the Leighton Fund was raided so as to repair Gainsborough's tomb in Kew churchyard and make a contribution to the cost of a war memorial tablet in St James's Church, across the road from the Royal Academy in Piccadilly. The academicians also welcomed the return of the past in the form of a ten-year loan of some relics of Sir Joshua Reynolds – a silver loving cup and cover, cake basket and eight teaspoons, as well as a box of card counters, a snuffbox, a pair of spectacles, a blue velvet coat and lace ruffle and an array of letters – all of which went on show in the Saloon (today one of the private rooms). This may have encouraged the gift, from one of Sir Lawrence Alma-Tadema's daughters, of her father's easel, paintbox, diploma and medals. Aware that much historical matter concerning the Royal Academy could be found in the 100 volumes of manuscript diary which the landscape painter Joseph Farington had filled with anecdotes and biographical detail in the late 18th and early 19th centuries, the Academy tried to bid for them at auction, but was outbid by the *Morning Post* newspaper, which promptly published extracts. (Eventually Farington's diaries ended up in the Royal Library at Windsor Castle.)

Amidst all this nostalgia, however, it is possible to discern a few nods towards modernity and innovation. Two oak frames appeared, in 1922, on the curved railings that led from Piccadilly into the quadrangle in front of Burlington House, the Royal Academy having requested permission from His Majesty's Office of Works for the right to display posters advertising exhibitions. The previous year, it had astonished Augustus John to learn that the Royal Academy wanted to make him Associate, or ARA – the first step to becoming a full academician. John later remarked that it seemed to him 'not a triumph but a surrender', for he had studied not at the Royal Academy Schools but at the Slade and afterwards had become an active member of the New English Art Club, which had been set up in opposition to the Academy's Summer Exhibition. Not once had John submitted a work to the Summer Exhibition's selection committee, nor shown any desire to do so. Yet, as he put it: 'Without even blowing my own trumpet the walls of Jericho had fallen!'[24]

John was an anti-establishment artist who had made his reputation as a portrait painter. His rival in this line of business was William Orpen, and both by the 1920s had become renowned as personalities within the art world. Orpen's audacity as a painter was somewhat obscured by his glittering success, his Rolls-Royces and his apparent absence of any intellectual curiosity; and talk of John's genius had given way to stories about his bohemianism, womanizing, and admiration for Gypsies and the freedoms he associated with their way of life. It was John who had set a new code for artistic behaviour, making it acceptable for an artist to be an amoral, free individual. Some of his uninhibited boldness inspired his most vital portraits, such as his unforgettable likeness of Lady Ottoline Morrell (1920), painted from memory in Ireland, in a house he rented in Galway City.

But despite his flair, his insouciant handling of paint and largeness of form, he held onto a tradition of painting that looked back to the old masters he had studied while at the Slade. 'We admired John', the critic Frank Rutter recalled, 'not because he was doing new things, but because he was doing old things superbly well.'[25] If a hint of danger still hung about his larger-than-life personality, his paintings were never seriously going to upset visitors to the RA's Summer Exhibition but might instead raise its standard of portrait painting. Six years later, in 1927, the Academy elected him RA, making him a full academician, which John accepted without any fuss. Yet ten years later he immediately resigned his RA on hearing that the Summer Exhibition's jury had rejected Wyndham Lewis's portrait of T. S. Eliot. The motivation behind this may have been his loyalty to Lewis, with whom he enjoyed a long-standing friendship. It was not prompted by admiration for the portrait, for he had not actually seen it when he publicly announced his departure and later, when he did see it, he felt inclined to agree with the Academy's dislike of it. But it seems that by then he needed an opportunity to escape, as the current regime displeased him. To Laura Knight, he wrote: 'It seemed pretty hopeless to oppose the predominant junta of deadly conservatism which rules. If by my beastly action I shall have brought some fresh air into Burlington House I shall feel justified.'[26] However, two years later, after a change of president, he accepted re-election and no bad feeling appeared to remain on either side: in 1944 he even came perilously close to being elected president of the Royal Academy himself.

John was not the only member of the New English Art Club to cross over to the Academy in the interwar years. If a degree of progressiveness crept into the Summer

Exhibitions during this time, it was largely due to the admission of work from members of this Club, which had existed since the 1880s and previously displayed a greater degree of interest in French art than the Academy. Now, however, there was little difference between the two bodies other than the undeniable attraction of the greater publicity given to the RA's Summer Exhibition, which was a recognized route to greater visibility and possible membership of the Academy.

The creeping progressiveness was made more noticeable when in 1922 Annie Swynnerton was elected, as John had been, an Associate Royal Academician.[27] This caused a degree of shock and surprise, as no women had been elected to membership of the Royal Academy for 154 years – not since Mary Moser and Angelica Kauffman slipped in as RAs in the year the Academy first began. There was a lot of uncertainty about how to address the new Associate and most mentions of her refer to 'Mrs Swynnerton', her marital status perhaps helping to mitigate the affront caused to many by her gender. She had, however, been endorsed by John Singer Sargent and George Clausen, and her paintings were respectably based not on the study of modern French art but on art associated with the Italian Renaissance or Continental symbolists. She lived in Manchester, where she had founded the Manchester Society of Women Painters and was a passionate supporter of women's rights. She was, however, already seventy-eight years old, and would never be made a full academician.

Growing pressure on institutions like the Royal Academy to allow women through their portals related to the ongoing demand for full suffrage for women. Women over the age of thirty, holding certain property rights, had been given the right to vote in 1918, but the argument in favour of the 'flapper's vote', which would extend this right to women aged between twenty-one and twenty-nine, did not happen until the Representation of the People Act was passed in 1928, affecting both men and women. In 1924 the press, referring to the 'Academy Flappers', had applauded the growing number of women artists in the Summer Exhibition. Laura Knight, Dod Procter and Ethel Walker were the three women artists most frequently noticed in the Summer Exhibitions of the 1920s. In 1927 Knight was made an ARA, and she became a full RA in 1936. Yet even though the numbers of women art students exceeded men at many art schools, including the Slade, the ratio of women artists to men in the Summer Exhibitions remained shockingly small. Andrew Stephenson has noted that in 1924 there were only 32 women artists among a total of 1,563 exhibitors.[28]

Liberalization, such as it was, niggled away within the Academy, but opposition to it was strong and often vitriolic. Ebenezer Wake Cook's book *Retrogression in Art and the Suicide of the Royal Academy*, published in 1924, berated the Academy for opening itself to French influence and women artists. At the heart of his farrago of bitter complaints was the belief that national traditions in art were being undermined by foreign influence and the barbarism of modernity. He feared that this degradation would spread to the Tate Gallery and elsewhere. In his view, the reputation of British art was already suffering under the impact of 'Bolshevism' and 'Anarchism'.[29]

Less obvious, but more worrying, was the fact that the Royal Academy had embarked on a long period of financial decline. Its most successful endeavour during the interwar years was the run of Winter Exhibitions showing art from different countries. These began in 1927, and the 1930 exhibition included the largest ever display of Italian art shown in this country. But this period also saw a drop in the number of visitors to the Summer Exhibitions. The Summer Exhibition not only showcased new art but also had symbolic importance, sitting as it did at the heart of the British establishment. It was preceded in April by the Royal Academy Banquet, which announced the start of the London Season and all its forthcoming pleasures, such as Henley, Ascot and Wimbledon. Attendance at the Summer Exhibition had first reached six figures (122,939) in 1851, and its high point came in 1882 when visitor numbers climbed to 377,814. This figure had dropped to 211,043 by 1910 and it fell further the next year, with still lower figures inevitably following during the First World War, when there was a collapse in the art market. The Academy never saw a return to anywhere near the high-water mark of the Victorian period, and during the 1930s the figures for attendance at the Summer Exhibition remained, for the most part, below 150,000.

Yet the Royal Academy sustained a dignified role within the London art world, even if it offered scant inspiration to young artists. The Diploma and Gibson Galleries on the second floor, where the Sackler Gallery and the Archives are today, were open to the public and it was here that some of the Academy's greatest treasures could be found: the Michelangelo *Taddei Tondo*, the Leonardo cartoon of St Anne and the Virgin (sold, for financial reasons, in 1962 to London's National Gallery) and a 16th-century copy of Leonardo's *Last Supper*, begun as early as 1515 and in Leonardo's lifetime. Many other works from the Academy's collection were also shown here in a display that changed annually, but the galleries are said, nonetheless, to have been very little visited.

Somewhat surprisingly, given the Royal Academy's conservatism, it is also associated with a sudden outburst of romanticism in the late 1920s. This took the form of a series of visionary paintings merging figuration with abstraction, seeming to address the feelings of the soul in relation to God and to the approach of death. These decidedly odd paintings were made by the former Keeper of the Royal Academy Schools, Charles Sims, but by the time they went on public view in the 1928 Summer Exhibition he had died. It was his son who named the series of pictures 'Spirituals'. They appeared to have little or no precedent in Sims's career, but they drew crowds and still retain a cult fascination today. One art historian has claimed that 'the paintings were among the most advanced, stylistically, that the Royal Academy had ever seen'.[30] If correct, then this bastion of conservatism momentarily became a promoter of the daring and the new.

The relationship between Charles Sims and the Royal Academy had begun well and ended badly. Sims had a habit of falling out with authority. As a young man he had been destined for the drapery trade, but escaped from his apprenticeship in Paris and began training as an artist. In both Paris and London, by means of winning prizes, he managed to keep penury at bay; but Luke Fildes, who was an influential member of the Royal Academy's council, threw Sims out of the Royal Academy Schools, possibly because he had picked up advice at French art schools that gave him a degree of arrogance.

He gained renown by wooing the British public with his landscapes, animated with striking effects of light and sometimes figures in classical dress or naked young women sporting in fountains, for he had a propensity for phantasy. He was also adept at anodyne society portraits. He suffered badly when his eldest son was killed fighting in the First World War, and he himself was traumatized by the conflict he witnessed in his role as an official war artist. After this, he appears to have undergone some kind of religious experience which led to an unorthodox series of pictures titled 'Seven Sacraments of Holy Church', painted in tempera during 1917–18 in a stark, awkward manner reminiscent of the early Italian Renaissance.

Towards the end of the war he received two prestigious commissions, one from the British War Memorials Committee and the other from the Canadian War Artists' scheme. For the latter he produced a large painting in which a crucifix plays a dominant role.[31] Its upright form rises the full height of the canvas and commands the scene beneath, showing a gentle gathering of mostly women and children in a snowy foreground landscape. But in the background, painted in a different register, as if in a ghostly dream, soldiers attend to the dead and wounded amid sharp threads of rain. Two smaller versions of this subject exist, in one of which the crucified Christ faces outwards, towards the viewer. However, in the large version for the Canadian War Artists' scheme, the Crucifixion is seen from behind so that the figure of Christ is largely obscured by the cross; while denying the viewer the more conventional view, it brings the Crucifixion into more direct relationship with both landscapes, that of the living and the dead. Running along the top of the canvas are nine coats of arms representing the nine provinces of Canada at that time, while the title of the work, *Sacrifice*, is found in large lettering across the back arms of the cross. In this picture Sims created a vast hymn to human suffering and sacrifice; but it did not appeal to Sir Robert Borden, the Canadian prime minister at the time. After being exhibited in 1919 and once again in 1924, the painting was put into storage and not brought out again by the Canadian War Museum until the millennium.

It was soon after the completion of this picture that Sims was appointed to the keepership of the Royal Academy Schools. This was a considerable honour, for the Schools had been part of the Royal Academy ever since its foundation in 1769; it was through them that the Academy sought to preserve and pass on the practices it regarded as the building stones of art. With the keepership came the keeper's house, situated inside Burlington House. During Sims's term of office, the students received lectures on 'Medieval Pigments and Mediums', 'Oils, Varnishes and Tempera' and 'Methods of Wall Painting', subjects mostly relating to their practical work. At the start of his keepership the number of students had been augmented by servicemen's grants, as mentioned in the Keeper's Report which he submitted for the Annual Report in 1922. In its entirety, it reads as follows:

> There are 86 painters on the books, more than can be accommodated, but many can only work intermittently, as they are under the necessity of earning a living.
>
> The maintenance grants for ex-soldiers have now ceased.
>
> To judge by this and other Schools the best brains are not at present attracted to the profession of the Fine Arts.
>
> The standard of work in the Painting School is not high: more time is given to Drawing, which therefore shows better results.[32]

It is hard not to conclude that the person who wrote this account was unhappy in his job. Further pain was caused to Sims when his portrait of George V, which the Royal Academy had commissioned for its monarchical collection, was rejected after the King expressed dislike of it. It was returned to Sims, who responded to this affront by arranging for the portrait to be shown for some months in America. On its return the Academy re-acquired it, to avoid further unwanted publicity, then cut it up and burned it – a slightly futile gesture, as a smaller version of the portrait had already been accepted and accessioned by the Scottish National Portrait Gallery. A good idea can be gained from this as to what was destroyed. The King is posed seated, dressed in full regalia, holding a sceptre and with his crown resting nearby on a velvet-covered stool. The composition is completed by a pillar on the left and a crimson swag hanging down from the top right. The monarch's face is

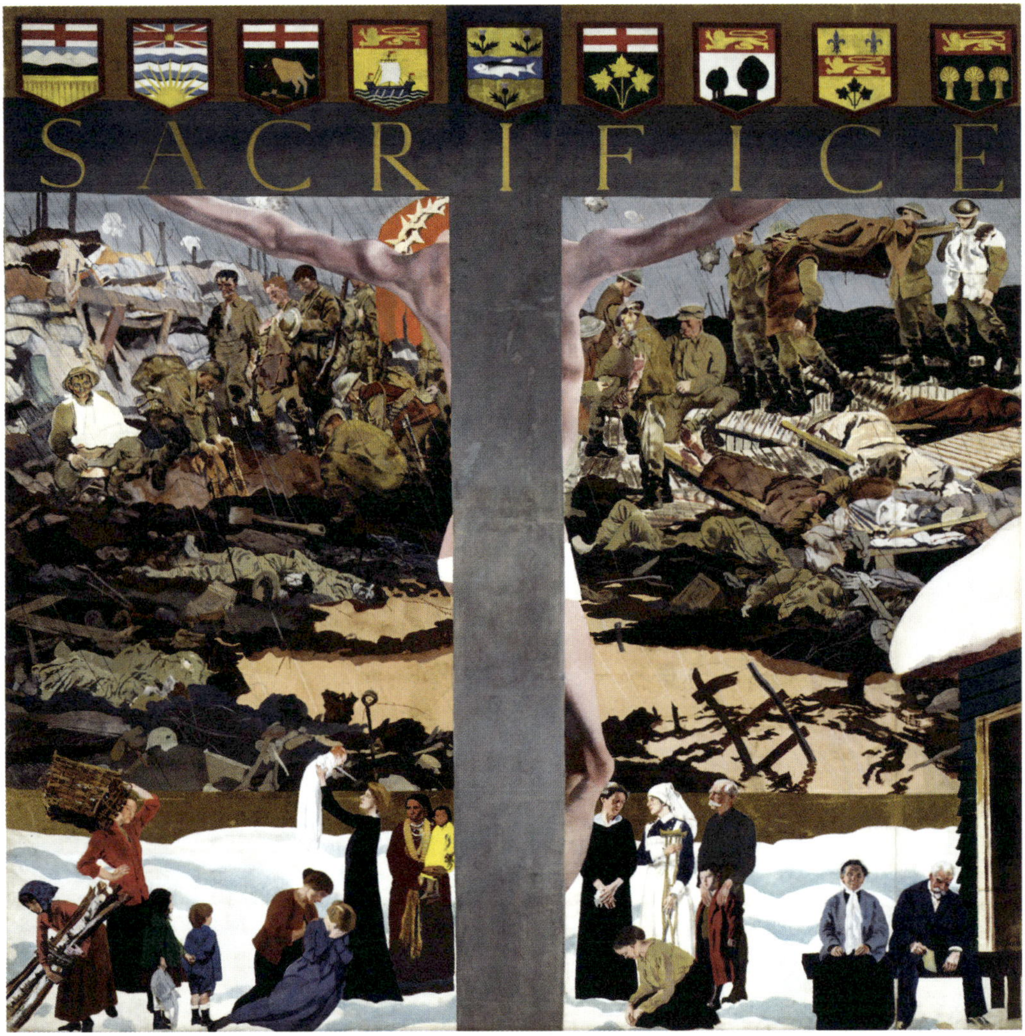

Charles Sims, *Sacrifice*,
oil on canvas, c. 1918.

studiously observed, but the drawing of his hands is flimsy and offhand. Unevenness of finish may also have troubled the original, given the grandeur of both sitter and setting. In the copy, the highlights and shadow in the folds of the monarch's cloak are imitative of John Singer Sargent's method, but Sims fails to achieve Sargent's nonchalant insouciance and the paintwork instead looks weak and unassertive. Sims had perhaps begun to tire of society portrait painting by 1924, the date of this commission. In response to the destruction of the original work, he took himself off to America in search of new society portraits; but he was unsuccessful in obtaining commissions, and returned disgusted with an aspect of society that he had formerly charmed. Back home, he discovered that he had annoyed the Academy by staying too long in America.

His inclination towards reclusivenesss had begun to attract notice. His relations with the Academy worsened, and he resigned in 1926. After a polite period of time, pressure was put on him to vacate the keeper's house. By this point he had already begun work on his 'Spirituals', producing many studies for these six paintings which, in their final form, are painted in tempera on linen.

The accepted view of the 'Spirituals' is that they were intended to convey God's mystic relationship to man. Yet further meanings can be inferred if attention is given not only to their imagery but also to their titles. The first, *Behold I have Graven Thee on the Palm of My Hand*, is Jehovah's reply to Zion's heartfelt cry, 'The Lord has forsaken me; my God has forgotten me,' and is found in Isaiah 4.19. The picture shows raised arms with open hands, a small naked figure floating between them. The second in the series is titled *My Pain beneath Thy Sheltering Hand*. This line can be found in the ballad 'Where the Long Shadow Falls', in which the speaker gives himself up to the 'Tempter', the 'rebel angels' who 'array' him with robes of water. An echo of these words is found in the title for the third picture, *The Rebel Powers that Thee Array*, which comes from a line in Shakespeare's Sonnet 146. Here the soul ('centre of my sinful earth') is advised by its owner to shake off 'rebel powers' in a gradual recognition of loss, of forthcoming death and the final consummation.

> Poor soul, the centre of my sinful earth,
> Pressed by these rebel powers that thee array,
> Why dost though pine within and suffer dearth,
> Painting thy outward walls so costly gay?
> Why so large cost, having so short a lease,
> Dost thou upon thy fading mansion spend?
> Shall worms, inheritors of this excess,
> Eat up thy charge? Is this thy body's end?

Then, soul, live thou upon thy servant's loss,
And let that pine to aggravate thy store;
Buy terms divine in selling hours of dross;
Within be fed, without be rich no more:
So shalt thou feed on Death, that feeds on men,
And, Death once dead, there's no more dying then.

By means of this reference to Shakespeare's sonnet, Sims seems to point directly to his intended suicide. But such a conclusion is not evident from the picture alone, in which a small crowd swarms around a Christlike figure on a cross, while above an indeterminate being reaches with open arms in a benign gesture, the whole displaying a sentimentality that repeatedly troubles this series.

The fourth picture is known chiefly through a study for it in the Ulster Museum, which may not be fully representative of the finished work. Here the small soul-figure rises from within the crossed arms of a larger figure, and at the same time turns away, as if rejecting the possibility of protection. The title is...*Man's Last Pretence of Consummation in Indifference*, for which no source has been found. It is quite possible that Sims invented it, in the same way that Turner's inscriptions, which he attached to his paintings, were sometimes invented. This is also in keeping with the practice found in 19th-century novels, where chapters often begin with a quotation, some authentic and others fictional; examples of this can be found in George Eliot's works as well as those by more popular novelists. But Sims, being a painter who thought poetically, needed this title for the fourth work in this series, and it can be interpreted as a further stage in his recognition of the limits of reason in keeping us untouched by the fear of death.

The fifth is titled *I Am the Abyss and I Am Light*. The Tate, which owns this work, admits that the title appears to have no identifiable source, or at least not one that has yet been found. Nevertheless it construes that the title and the image, which is almost completely abstract aside from the figure of the soul, affirm 'the absolute power of God over all creation and over the destiny of the universe'.[33] However, this overlooks a passage by Dryden, beginning in line 61 of his great poem 'The Hind and the Panther', written in 1887 after his conversion to Roman Catholicism:

Thy throne is darkness in th' abyss of light,
A blaze of glory that forbids the sight;
O teach me to believe Thee thus conceal'd,
And search no farther than thy self reveal'd;
[...]

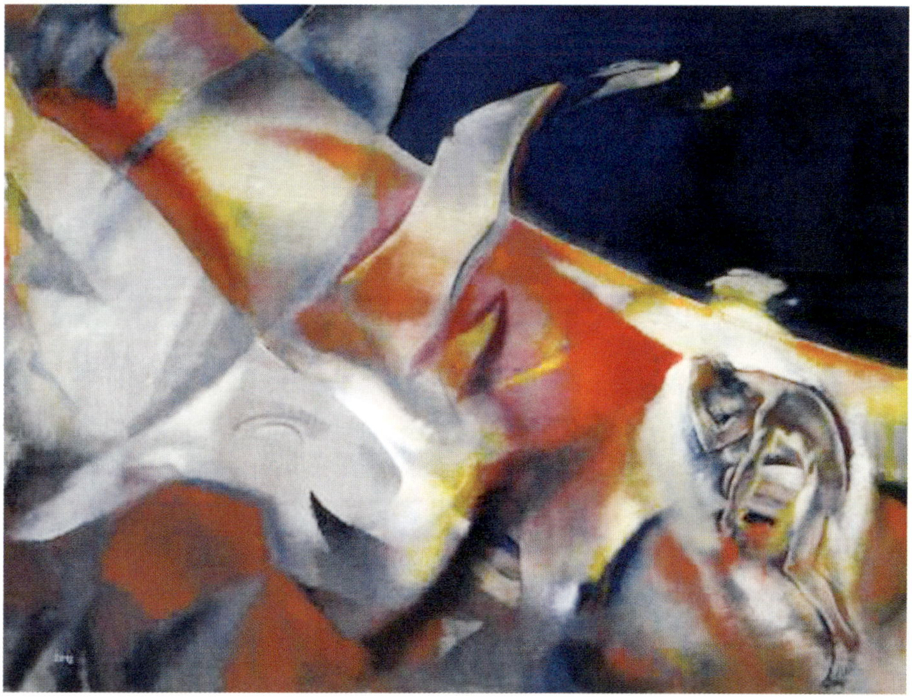

Charles Sims, *I Am the Abyss and I Am Light*, tempera on canvas, 1928.

My thoughtless youth was wing'd with vain desires,
My manhood, long misled by wand'ring fires,
Follow'd false lights; and when their glimpse was gone,
My pride struck out new sparkles of her own.
Such was I, such by nature still I am,
Be thine the glory, and be mine the shame.

The sixth and final picture, *Here Am I*, commits the soul to God, the title using words that appear several times in the Bible; in replies given, for example, in Genesis 21.1, when God calls Abraham before putting him to the test with his son Isaac, or in Exodus 3.4, when God calls to Moses from out of the burning bush and tells him that he must bring the people of Israel out of Eypyt.

It is hard to know what to make of Sims's 'Spirituals'. They need to be brought together as a series before any proper assessment can be made, but this may no longer be possible as some today are known only from studies or inadequate reproductions. *I Am the Abyss and I Am Light* appears to be the most complete and the most immersive. Its touches of strong colour have led Tim Wilcox to compare this work with Kandinsky's early abstracts. He also suggests that Sims may be battling in these works not so much with divine forces as with the institutional power of the Royal Academy,[34] but the cumulative understanding gained from the titles contradicts his argument. Among Sims's unpublished papers in the Academy's archive is a passage that affirms a larger vision: 'The use of mysticism', he writes, 'is for comfort. When the world grows dim in old age, our senses are dulled. It is the final truth....Perhaps it is only in a certain ripeness that one can enter this kingdom of abstractions, this epitome of Perfection, as far as we know it....More and more divorced from particulars. Persons become Types. Material becomes pattern. Incidents rhythm. Colour independent of the substance of decoration.'[35]

Sims had been suffering from insomnia, disillusionment and fear of old age in the period leading up to 13 April 1928, when, aged fifty-four, he drowned himself in the River Tweed in Roxburghshire, leaving a suicide note that stated he could not go on. His suicide momentarily troubled reception of the 'Spirituals', which he had submitted for the Summer Exhibition a few weeks earlier. A move was made to reject them on the grounds of mental instability, but letters of protest in defence of Sims's sanity were sent to the president of the Royal Academy, and all six went on display in the Summer Exhibition in Gallery X. Colour illustrations of them were shared between the *Sketch* and the *Illustrated London News*. A further display of all six, including the studies for them, took place in November 1928 at Barbazon House in London. It was then that *I Am the Abyss and I Am Light* was bought and gifted not to the Royal Academy, but to the Tate Gallery. However, Sims was honoured again by the Academy when a broader representation of his art went on show in the Summer Exhibition of 1933, as part of a posthumous display of work by late members.

CHAPTER 3

ON THE MOVE

The kindergarten class at Queen's College in London's Harley Street was in the middle of a singing lesson when a senior member of staff broke in with news that the Armistice had been signed. Present on this occasion were Myfanwy Evans and Penelope Chetwode, the future wives of John Piper and John Betjeman, then aged seven and eight. Myfanwy never forgot how, in the silence that followed the announcement, Penelope's upper-class Cockney voice rang out: 'Oooah! Naah we can all go to France!'.

Many artists thrive on travel, and the opportunity to do so was an obvious benefit of the return to peace. It meant that Paris, the focal centre of European developments in modern art and design, was once again in reach, and in the 1920s it was often cheaper for artists to live in France or Spain than in England. The appeal of the Mediterranean revived. The Bloomsbury artists Vanessa Bell and Duncan Grant, who had been living at Charleston near Firle in East Sussex during the last two years of the war, relocated to London a few months after the return of peace; but they kept their lease on the farmhouse and returned in holiday periods, regenerating a new English pastoralism with their French-inspired handling of paint and colour. They, too, were drawn to the Mediterranean. After a trial visit in 1921 to Saint-Tropez, they went regularly for some years to the south of France, where they rented a simple farm-worker's house on the Fontcreuse estate outside Cassis.

Roger Fry spent a large part of almost every year in the 1920s painting in France, exploring small towns and their surrounding views. He was impressed by the indigenous culture he experienced in Provence, initially by chance in 1919, while in Les Baux. A young schoolmistress, annoyed by a dull mountebank who tried to end a performance with some patriotic Breton songs, called upon the audience, consisting mostly of elderly peasants, to sing for the English stranger they had in their midst. Fry was astonished to hear the old peasants, in their black silk caps, singing like children: artless yet expressive, giving voice to a repertoire that was not

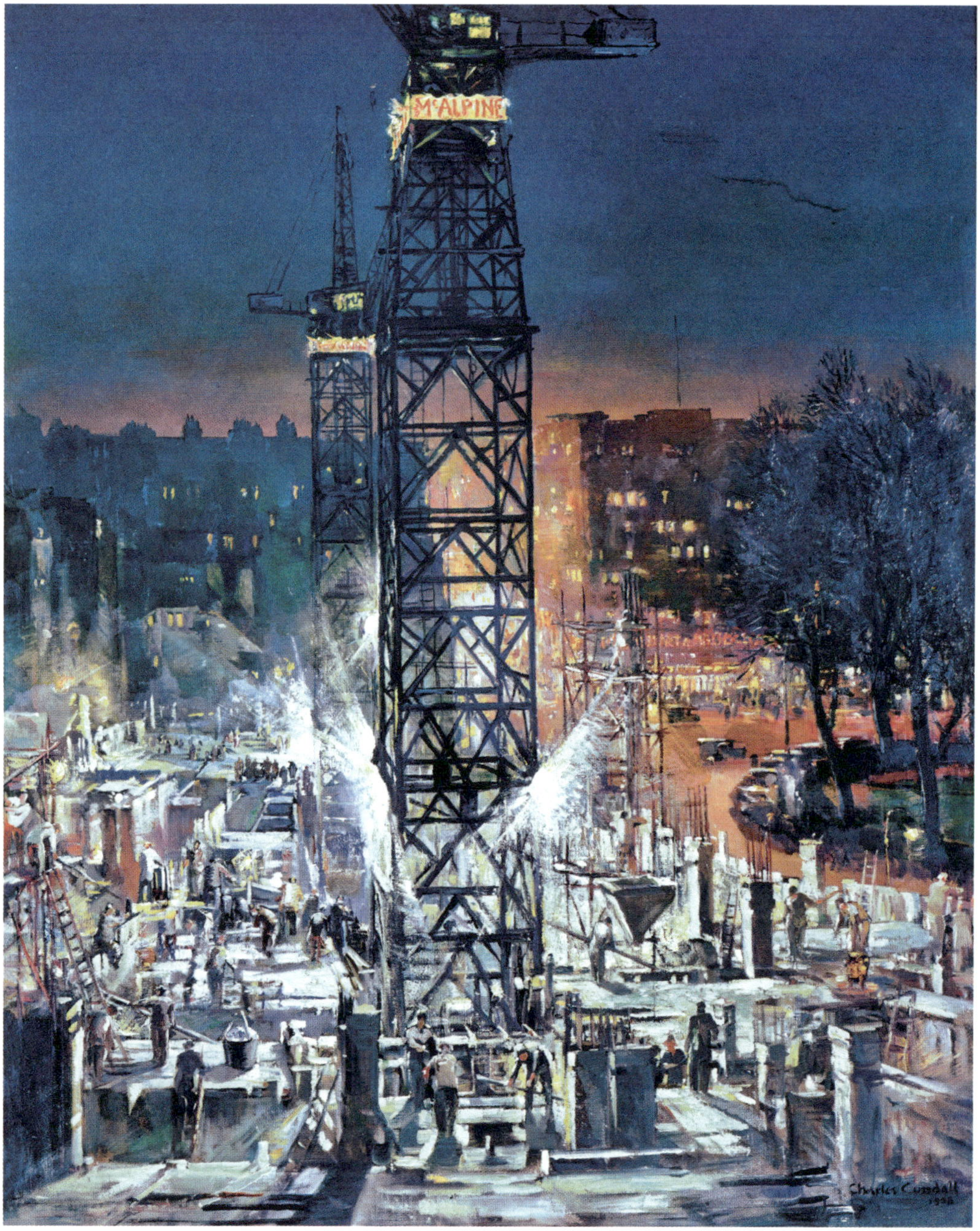

Charles Cundall, *Building in Berkeley Square*,
oil on canvas, 1938.

confined to folk songs but included ancient and modern songs and poems. Here, and at other moments while in Provence, Fry recognized the existence of a democratic culture which he greatly admired. He got to know the young teacher and her husband, Marie and Charles Mauron, and some years later acquired a *mas* outside Saint-Rémy-de-Provence, which he shared with them. It was surrounded by olive groves and from the upper floor looked across to Les Alpilles.

Aside from Frances Hodgkins, who appears later in this chapter, few landscape artists settled long enough to imbibe the spirit of a place, its local customs and way of life. Professional topographical painters, more efficient in their summary assessment of place, were mostly quick to move on. For Charles Cundall, for example, travel was the norm: a necessity rather than a cultural experience. His career began promisingly at the age of twenty-two with a scholarship to the Royal College of Art in 1912, but his studies ended abruptly when war began and he enlisted with the Royal Fusiliers. Wounded severely in his right arm, he learnt to paint with his left hand and returned to his studies at the RCA in 1918; he then did a year at the Slade before moving to Paris for further schooling. After this he travelled widely, developing a liking for panoramic views and displaying a catholicity in his choice of landscapes, cityscapes and seascapes, rural or industrial settings, mills and moors. He enjoyed crowd scenes, portraying the bustle and excitement of Derby Day or beach sauntering during a bank holiday at Brighton (1933), which he painted from a position close to the bandstand at the Kemp Town end of the promenade. He also had an eye for urban events such as the demolition of Waterloo Bridge or the building of Berkeley Square House on the corner of Berkeley Square and Bruton Street. This he painted twice in 1938, in daytime and at night, from a window in Bruton Street. If there is an element of painterly journalism here, Cundall nevertheless effectively registers the harsh white artificial light that made labouring at night-time possible, while two McAlpine cranes stand silhouetted against the deep blue of the night sky. The romance of the image caught the attention of the Chantrey Bequest, with the result that the picture entered the Tate collection the same year it was painted. Cundall mostly exhibited with the New English Art Club and ignored modernism, yet he occupies a definite place in the history of interwar art owing to his technical facility, demotic appeal and sensitivity to subtleties of light. He gained a weightier reputation later on, as a war artist during the Second World War.

For artists who moved out of London to recover or recuperate from the experience of war, their choice of destination often reflected inner needs or conflicts, and the chosen sites became places for the mind as well as for the eye. Both Paul Nash and Matthew Smith found themselves in a vulnerable state not long after the return to peace, needing to explore their past experiences and present states of mind. Nash, as will be seen in Chapter 4, chose Dymchurch as his point of focus. In Matthew Smith's case it was St Columb Major in Cornwall, where he moved after a family holiday at Porthcothan with his wife and two sons which had left him frustrated by his inability to paint. Both artists suffered breakdowns, but went on to pursue long and productive careers that earned them high regard. Nash became a crusader for modern art, and Smith the recipient of unlooked-for honours: a CBE in 1949 and a knighthood in 1954.

In his early years Matthew Smith had faced huge opposition from his father, a prosperous wire manufacturer who was determined his son should follow a career in business, not art. Patriarchy was very strong at this time, perhaps because the war had laid waste to so many sons that the line of descent became increasingly precious. John Piper, for instance, had caved in to his father's expectation that he would enter the family law firm rather than go to art school, because of the loss his family had suffered when their eldest son was killed in the war. All his life Piper regretted the five years that, in comparison with some of his peers, he had lost at the start of his career while working in a solicitor's office.

Smith, who did not arrive at the Slade until the age of twenty-six, may also have felt the pressure of lost time. As a mature student he was subjected to mockery by Professor Tonks in front of other students, perhaps prompted by the fact that (as John Russell has put on record) Smith was not only timorous by nature, but spoke like 'a highly intelligent moth'.[1] He was already struggling with some form of ill health and in 1908, on his doctor's advice, he left London for France and went to Pont-Aven in Brittany, where he caught an echo of Gauguin's influence and that of the Nabis. Still more important to his formation as an artist was the brief period of study he enjoyed in 1910 at the Atelier Matisse, shortly before the school closed. The custom was for students to leave work on their easels if they wanted criticism from the master. When Matisse did his rounds all the students followed, listening to his remarks. But by the time Smith joined Matisse had begun to lose interest in the school, and Smith recollected that he met Matisse on only three occasions. Yet this experience was nevertheless revelatory: Smith became familiar with Matisse's methods and bold use of colour and never forgot how, at one point, Matisse stopped by a Signorelli drawing of four figures pinned to the wall and ran his finger down it in several places, saying 'Voilà l'architecture.'[2]

After Smith's marriage in 1912 to Gwen Salmond, a former Slade student and close friend of Gwen John, they spent several idyllic months in the artists' colony at Grez-sur-Loing in the Fontainebleau district of the Île-de-France. The death of Smith's father returned them to England early in 1914 and once the estate had been divided between five children and other beneficiaries, Smith found himself relieved of financial worries. However, by 1915 his physical state was again fragile, as he reported to his friend John Lyman after a visit to a military doctor in Plymouth: 'He said I must put warfare out of my mind but still it is very difficult to settle down to painting when one's subconscious mind at least is *perpetually* thinking about war.'[3] He and Gwen had set up a house in Kensington, Smith also keeping a studio in Fitzroy Street, where in 1916 he painted two striking nudes, using extreme boldness in their colouring and design, building on the examples of Matisse and Van Gogh. He was perhaps fortified also by the cosmopolitan nature of Walter Sickert's open house meetings at his large Fitzroy Street studio, which Smith attended on Wednesday afternoons. These two paintings of a nude seated on a chair have scant before or after in Smith's oeuvre, and they appear like a sudden shout in the history of British art.

In November of 1916, after the Smiths' second son was born and the family had moved for safety to a Sussex cottage, he received a call to report as a private to the Inns of Court Officer Training Corps. The army at this time was staffing its Labour Corps with physically less fit or overaged men, and that winter Smith was sent for training at Berkhamsted. He was made a temporary second lieutenant and attached for duty to No. 25 Labour Company, Royal West Surrey Regiment.

The Labour Corps undertook salvage work behind the lines: cooking, cleaning and caring for soldiers, carrying the wounded and burying the dead, as well as helping to make roads and lay down railway lines so that supplies could reach the troops. Smith was to serve in the Battle of Passchendaele, and by May 1917 he had a hundred men under his command, tasked with clearing the battlefield of usable shells and abandoned equipment.[4] This was a time of heavy shelling and frequent gas attacks. On 17 September 1917, he suffered severe wounding when a large piece of shrapnel lodged in his thigh.

Authorities on Smith, including Alice Keene and Malcolm Yorke, agree that what happened next may be very close to the experience given to the character Dominique Prad in Alden Brooks's 1924 novel *The Enchanted Land*. Brooks, a diarist with a sharp eye for the observation of others, was a friend of Smith's and their lengthy conversations may have provided material for Brooks's portrayal of this fictional character. As Yorke points out, Prad's self-doubt and his use of hesitant, incomplete sentences echo Smith's own manner and habits of speech. Like Smith, Prad too is wounded in the war. While waiting for attention and half-unconscious with pain, he reviews his life, regretting how much time has been wasted and fearing he will never paint again. But then he hears a voice saying 'there's still some chance of saving this fellow; put him on the table'. While suffering 'wild spasms of pain' as they lift him, Prad swears that if he can be saved, he will 'never do anything else in future but live life, beautiful life, to the full, as it should be'.[5]

Yorke adds that if Smith himself made such an oath, it would explain 'some of [his] later, seemingly selfish decisions, such as his sacrifice of family life in order to paint'.[6] But the passage in question is clichéd, too obviously a fictional climax. And if Smith did have such an éclaircissement, there was no immediate visible impact on his approach to life. He was shipped back home to London Hospital and was sufficiently recovered to rejoin his family at Christmas, after which he returned to his London studio and attended monthly check-ups. In September 1918 he was made a full lieutenant and returned to work, running a prisoner-of-war camp full of German soldiers in Abbeville, northern France, which seems a melancholy way in which to end the war. By December he was in Paris waiting for demobilization, which did not come through until March 1919. It was here that he re-encountered Brooks, who introduced him to the Irish artist Roderic O'Conor, and the three men spent time in Paris together. O'Conor was a bold colourist and Smith would later refer to him as his mentor and guide.

Smith was so keen to return to painting that, once demobbed, he made only a brief return home, persuading Gwen to leave their children in the care of a nurse so that they could travel to Paris to see a Matisse exhibition in Paris. Afterwards they spent time painting at Grez, where his conversations with Brooks continued. But while in France, Smith's mental and physical health collapsed, and he and Gwen returned to London. She then took the two boys away, leaving Smith to recuperate in his Fitzroy Street studio. His sociability vanished. Shunning society, he made a set of watercolours based on Eugène Delacroix's lithographic illustrations to Goethe's famous poem, *Faust*.

Delacroix, while in England in 1825, had seen a romantic melodrama adapted from *Faust* and enjoyed its 'mixture of broad comedy and some extremely sinister effects'.[7] Thirty years later, he affirmed in his journal that it was this production that had 'inspired me with the idea of producing compositions in lithographs'.[8] Broad comedy and sinister effects may have been exactly what Smith needed when alone and ill, and they abound in Delacroix's lithographs, seventeen of which were published, in a large folio, in 1828 in Albert Stapfer's translation of *Faust*. Smith must have been fortunate to possess a copy of this book, now regarded as one of the finest illustrated books of the 19th century, for its rarity meant that the lithographs remained largely unknown until republished in 1932 by New York's Heritage Press. The previous year, while recovering from his war wound, Smith had gone in search of books on Delacroix. Almost certainly he had read Delacroix's *Journal*, which his painter friend Guy Maynard had recommended to him soon after the start of the

First World War; this book had become something of a bible to painters, not least because of its understanding of the tension between life and art. 'The things that are most real to me are the illusions which I create with my painting. Everything else is quicksand,' Delacroix wrote in February 1824.[9] That same year, the twenty-five-year-old artist asked himself: 'Why not take advantage of those antidotes to civilization, good books? They give strength and peace of mind.'[10]

Sadly, Smith's watercolours based on Delacroix's lithographs no longer exist and may have been destroyed. But they appear to have alleviated his nervous tension sufficiently for him to holiday at Porthcothan, a small village with sandy beach on the north-west coast of Cornwall, in the summer of 1920 with Gwen and their two sons. It was after they left that he moved to St Columb Major, a small inland town about eight miles east of Padstow, made austerely beautiful by the slate-hung houses and narrow streets in its oldest part. Smith, however, took a room looking directly onto the large medieval church, dedicated to the 5th-century Cornish saint Columba. The church sits on a grassy plateau at the head of the Vale of Lanherne. Here Smith spent the autumn and winter producing bold, original, haunting landscapes, using saturated colours and painting the sky and church windows a solid black in *Cornish Church* (1920). His searing reds, purples, blues and blacks were, he claimed, a faithful representation of the conditions created by the dour

Matthew Smith, *Cornish Church*, oil on canvas, 1920.

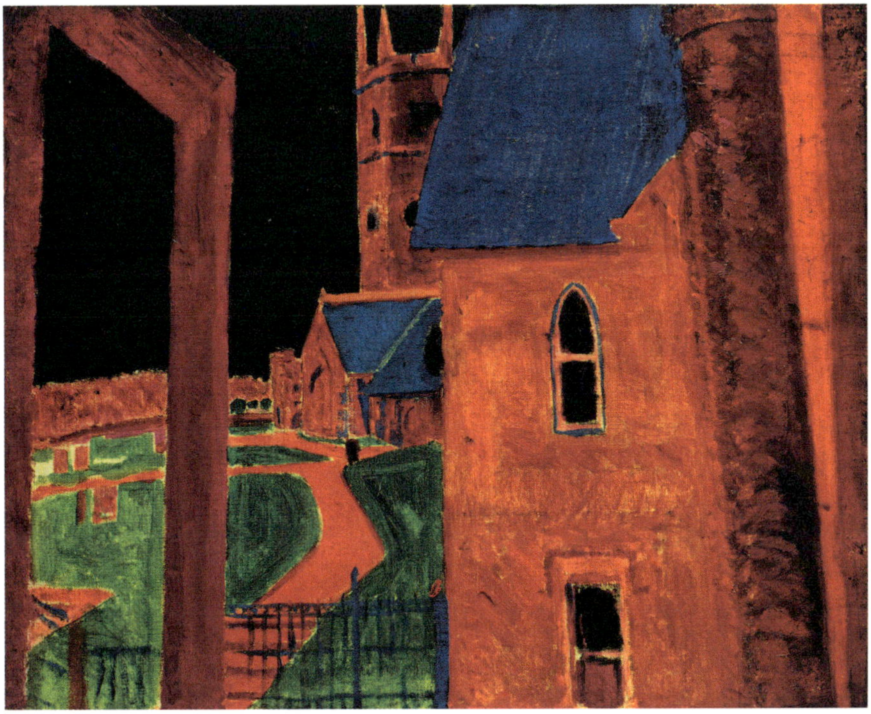

countryside and a wet summer and autumn. Yet there is no doubt that his work at this time also became an outlet for personal agony, compounded by his experience of war, his strained marriage and his chronic nervous depression. 'Painting is life itself,' Delacroix once claimed. 'It is nature transmitted to the soul without an intermediary, without a veil, without rules or conventions. Music is vague. Poetry is vague. Sculpture requires a convention. But painting, particularly landscape painting, is the thing itself.'[11]

For the rest of 1921, even at his much-loved Grez, where they now had a house, Smith remained in a turbulent state, troubled by problems with his eyes and his back and by recurrent melancholy. In March 1922, leaving his family at Grez, he booked himself into the Clinique Valmont at Lausanne to obtain treatment from the psychotherapist Dr Roger Vittoz, who had successfully treated T. S. Eliot the year before. According to Malcolm Yorke it was here, at this clinic, that he decided that 'family stifled his creativity'.[12]

The consequence of this was that he parted from his wife and family and subsequently took up with the artist Vera Cuningham. Story has it that in the winter of 1922 Smith called on the painter Bernard Meninsky, for whom twenty-five-year-old Vera had been posing as well as cooking for him and sharing his bed. Nevertheless, when the forty-three-year-old Smith left Meninsky's that day it was with Vera on his arm. There followed a passionate but short-lived affair, during which she acted as the model for many of his nudes. Cuningham was herself a painter and favoured the female nude, which may have encouraged the sudden emphasis on this theme in Smith's art. Not only did he now embark on what was to be his most productive period, but his method of painting changed again; it became more fluent and impulsive, Richard Cork observing that he 'handles his brush with such windblown freedom' that some pictures seem to still be in the process of change as we look at them.[13]

Although Smith never lost his timorous nature and continued to suffer from bouts of ill health, his blowsy nudes, flower pictures and succulent still lifes, painted at furious speed and with conviction and vivacity, earned him a major reputation, even if some forms, like the roses he painted, spill out, often overblown and dissolute. His admiration for Delacroix may have helped to light the fuse, but such strong, hot colours and fierce brushwork are only matched in this period by the exultant freedom found in David Bomberg's Spanish landscapes.

Throughout the various stages of his life and his relationships, Smith continued to arouse affection in others. He retained a lifelong friendship with his peer Augustus John, and among younger artists he had an admirer in Francis Bacon, in whose estimate Smith was 'one of the very few English painters since Constable and Turner to be concerned with painting – that is, with attempting to make idea and technique inseparable. Painting in this sense tends towards a complete interlocking of image and paint, so that the image is the paint and vice versa. Here the brush-stroke creates the form and does not merely fill it in. Consequently every movement of the brush on the canvas alters the shape and implications of the image.'[14]

Places of the mind do not always require an artist to travel, but can be discovered by staying still and re-evaluating familiar territory. Gwen John, for example, who reappears later in this book, decided after the war to stay in the flat she had taken in 1911 in Meudon, on the outskirts of Paris. It was on the top floor of an old house situated near a forest. When she took it, she had been having difficulty sleeping in her studio room at 6 rue de l'Ouest. Her initial intention was to sleep at Meudon but work in Paris most days, as she found she could get to the Gare Montparnasse in just half an hour. The flat pleased her, with its three rooms, small kitchen, many cupboards and its attic.[15] Throughout the war she had hung onto the studio in Paris, but now she abandoned it. Like a cat circling on the spot before dropping back for further rest, she used her settled state at Meudon to embark on *The Convalescent*, a subject she painted ten times. Whatever the need, be it for routine, release, refreshment or inspiration, for the seaside and salt air or the feeling of sanctuary offered by a garden, artists have an uncanny habit of finding places where their creative talents can flourish amid everyday life.

London could never be entirely cold-shouldered. In the 1920s and 1930s it inspired a spate of images, many specifically based on London life, that took the form of linocuts. These were made at the Grosvenor School of Modern Art under the tutorship of Claude Flight, who promoted this medium in the art press and in a textbook. Linoleum is more usually associated with floor covering, for which it was invented in England in 1860. Inexpensive and easy to handle, it attracted scant regard as a printing medium until the Grosvenor School began to make it the medium for light-hearted scenes conveying the 'machine aesthetic', a term first coined by the vorticists. Flight and his pupils, among whom were three remarkable talents, Sybil Andrews, Cyril Power and Lill Tschudi, depicted subjects such as competitive sports, industrial labour and the London Underground. What makes their work distinctive is a signature style dependent on rhythmic patterns that convey the speed and dynamism of modern life. Both are to the fore in Cyril Power's *The Tube Station* and *The Merry-Go-Round* and are treated with deft economy by Sybil Andrews in *Rush Hour* (1930), in which a few stylized forms suggest passing feet on an escalator. The print became a mnemonic for the constant journeying down into Underground trains and up again to street level, while also conveying the anonymity associated with city life.

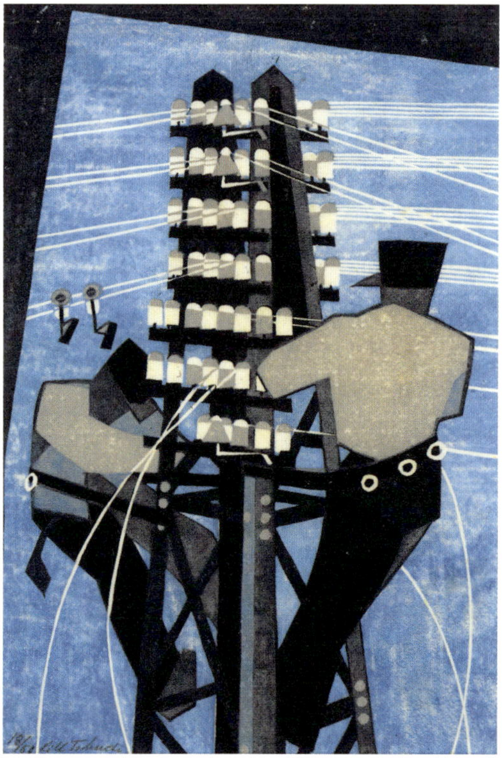

Lill Tschudi,
Fixing the Wires,
linocut on
oriental paper,
1932.

Cyril Power,
The Tube Station,
linocut, c. 1932.

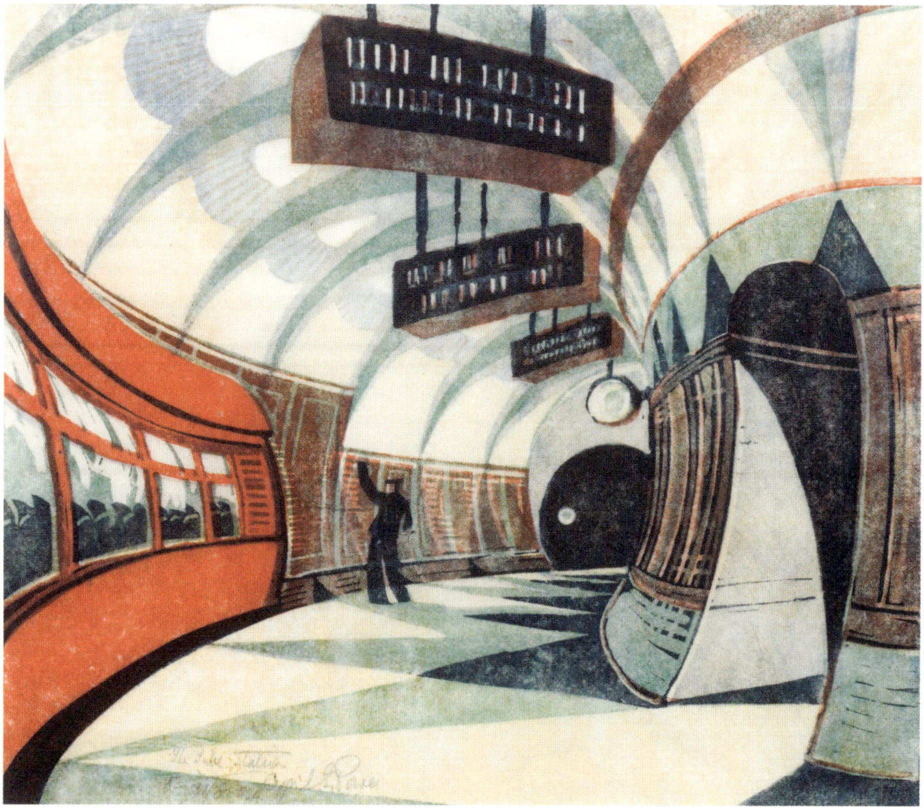

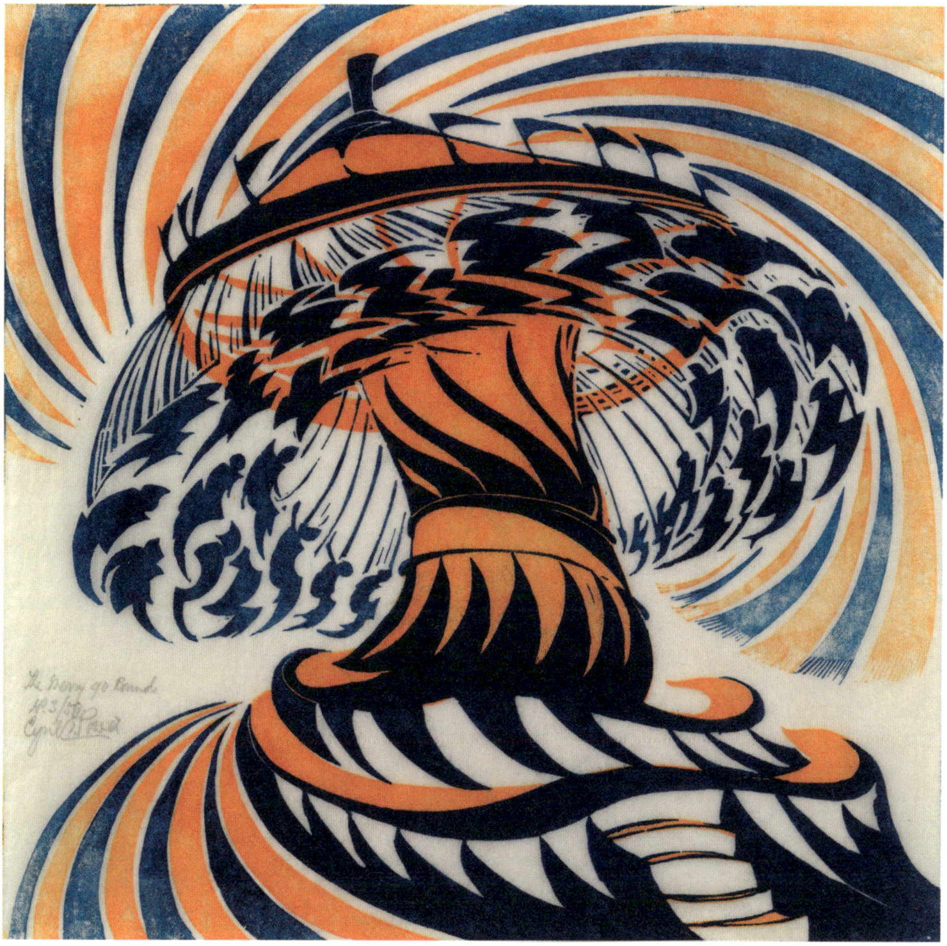

Cyril Power,
The Merry-Go-Round,
linocut, c. 1930.

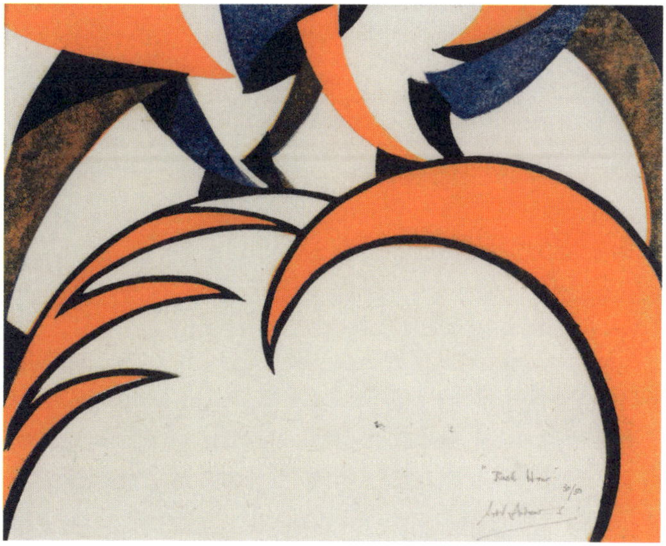

Sybil Andrews,
Rush Hour,
linocut, 1930.

Claude Flight was attracted into the ranks of the Seven and Five Society, exhibiting there between 1922 and 1927. Having been exposed to the Italian futurists' interest in speed and technology before the First World War, he is associated with a revival of interest in urban dynamism, an aspect of the modern age which he believed could best be expressed through the medium of colour linocuts. He raised the profile of this printing method through his teaching at the Grosvenor School, and work by his talented pupils was widely reproduced in art magazines. When references to modern technology appear in their work, they are always harnessed to witty, exuberant design. The figures may be whipped into distorted shapes by violent motion, but there is an absence of the kind of savagery associated with futurism and vorticism. Instead, the satire on modern urban life is light-hearted. As with much art deco, there is an element of the fashionably 'moderne' and a desire to please rather than to challenge. Linocuts did not need elaborate presses, but could be printed by hand with the help of a wooden spoon to transfer the design. They were relatively cheap to make and Flight wanted them to be sold at the same price that the man in the street paid for his pint of beer or his cinema ticket. They make a distinctive, democratic contribution to interwar art and are today fiercely collected. In 2020 they formed part of the new hang at New York's MoMA. If the artists had a shared belief it was that identified by Flight, that 'the art of to-day must be the expression of this collective spirit in terms of simplicity, of unity and of harmony'.[16]

The Grosvenor School linocuts reflect a willingness to regard art as fun, rather than anything more deeply challenging. Another example of this aspect of the cultural climate in the interwar period are the mosaic floor decorations in the National Gallery's vestibule opening out from the Portico entrance in Trafalgar Square. These were commissioned in 1928 from the Russian-born Boris Anrep, the foremost mosaicist in England at that time, and completed in 1933. Their overall title is *The Awakening of the Muses*, and they are all based on celebrities of the day: Greta Garbo as Melpomene, muse of Tragedy; Bertrand Russell as Lucidity; Margot Fonteyn as Delectation; Virginia Woolf as Clio, muse of History; Clive Bell as Bacchus. Owing to the durability of mosaic, countless feet have now walked over these well-known figures, the mosaics forming an engaging testament to a recurring need in the interwar years: the need to be amused.

For C. R. W. Nevinson and for Alfred Wolmark, however, urban attraction lay elsewhere – namely in Manhattan. In the prewar years, Nevinson had shared Wyndham Lewis's admiration for Filippo Marinetti, having heard him lecture in London, and been inspired to strike for independence. He began calling himself an 'English futurist' rather than a vorticist, thereby becoming the sole member of a self-invented group. Nevinson's success as a war artist meant that he had good reason to travel to New York in 1919: a firm of print publishers – Frederick Keppel & Co., run by father and son Frederick and David Keppel from within a four-storey gallery at 4 East 39th Street – was already selling his prints. Excited by the welcome he received and awed by Manhattan's skyscrapers, Nevinson gave an interview in which he stated that he loved the buildings so much, it was as if the city had been made especially for him. Alfred Wolmark must have been similarly smitten by the environment as he embarked on a series of cityscapes, seeking out the famous Flatiron Building (1919), so called because the site it filled was shaped like the base of an iron.

The following year, 1920, Wolmark was selling his cityscapes at an exhibition held at New York's Kevorkian Gallery; Nevinson, however, had begun to feel let down by the city's print world. His contacts had not achieved for him a similar success although his dynamic cityscapes, such as *Looking Down into Wall Street* and *Looking through Brooklyn Bridge* as well as other scenes made in Paris or London, would eventually earn him critical acclaim in this field. This reached its height just before the Wall Street crash of 1929 had a damaging effect on the print market. But in 1920, while back in England, Nevinson had worked up oil paintings of Manhattan from his prints and sketches and then returned to New York in the autumn for his second exhibition with Keppel & Co. He also exhibited at the Bourgeois Gallery, showing the painting *New York – An Abstraction*, in which a section of the elevated railway (now the High Line) carries the eye into the far distance, between skyscrapers rising above lines of washing and smoke. The painting did not sell and returned home with Nevinson to London. When exhibited again in 1925, it had been retitled *The Soul of a Soulless City*, now suggesting not the pleasure and excitement of modernity but its flipside, the associated pain and isolation.

London at this time continued to both attract and repel. It is perhaps inevitable that in a small country, the metropolis becomes a magnet for artists. John Sell Cotman, born in 1782, felt that London provided the air that artists must breathe. In 1834, having been appointed professor of drawing at London's King's College after years of working as a drawing master in Norwich, he famously wrote to his wife: 'My views are clear and splendid – never more so. I *must* come into contact with the first men in the country for talent, intellect and integrity. In all this I live, I breathe and feel a Man. This is what I have ever loved and tried to realize. It will now, with the blessings of God Almighty, be accomplished. No man can be more happy, even in prospect than I am now....Much as I have ever loved London I have never trod its gold-paved streets feeling so much a man of business, and so much *to belong to it*, as now.'[17] Another artist from this period for whom London meant much was Thomas Uwins (1782–1857). As librarian at the Royal Academy, he next

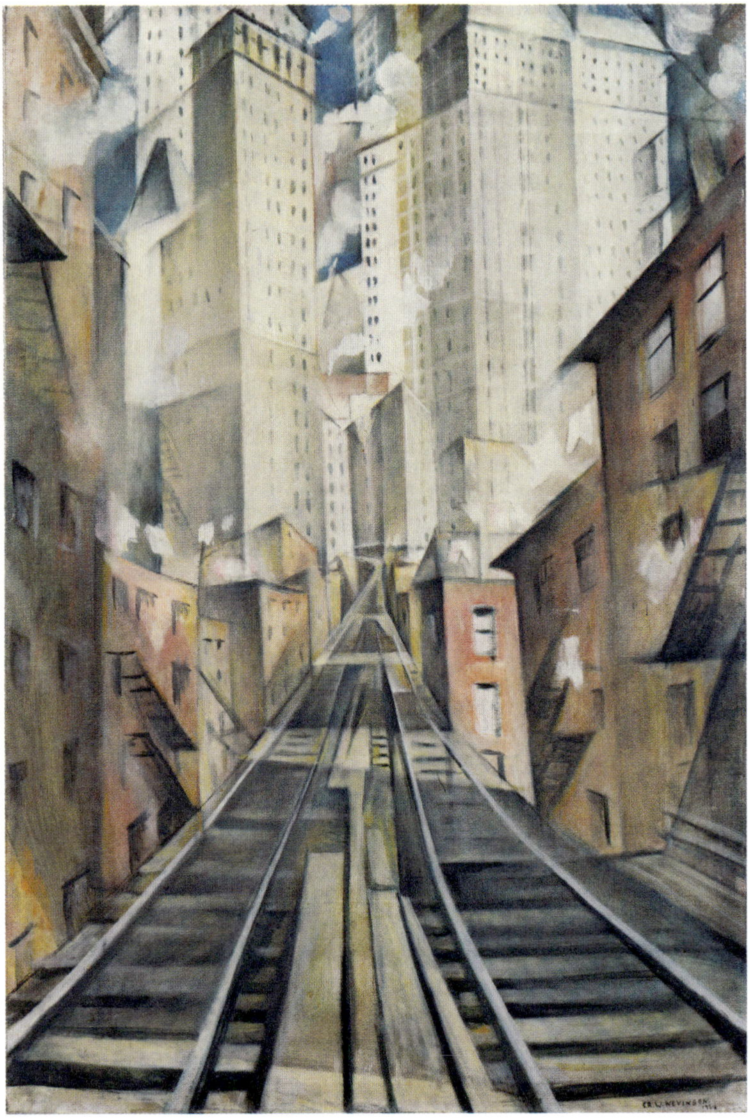

C. R. W. Nevinson, *The Soul of a Soulless City*, oil on canvas, 1920.

became Surveyor of the Queen's Pictures in 1844, and went on to succeed Charles Eastlake as Keeper of the National Gallery between 1847 and 1855. A letter written during the last year of his life suggests that the loss of London was like losing a dear friend: 'I am living in very humble retirement at Staines, near Windsor. London knows nothing of me, as I have abandoned every active employment in which I was once engaged.'[18]

Few would deny London's agency in the history of English art as a centre of commerce, culture and opportunity. Edward Burne-Jones, born and educated in Birmingham, was far from being the only artist in the 19th century who, having grown up in an industrial city or within reach of a mill or a mine, escaped to London as soon as he had the chance. It is perhaps hardly surprising that Birmingham, which by 1850 contained some of the worst industrial slums in Britain, spawned not realists or naturalists but artists who were mostly charmers and dreamers – David Cox, Thomas Creswick and Burne-Jones – while its only artistic development has been the revival of tempera painting, which looked back to the art and technique of 15th-century Italy. In the late 19th and early 20th centuries many artists also came to London from abroad, some fleeing pogroms, others seeking to advance their careers and wanting to benefit from London's art schools as well as the availability of high-quality artists' materials and opportunities to exhibit. Yet after the First World War, London's attraction for artists temporarily waned, many abandoning the metropolis for economic or health reasons or simply to avoid being sucked into its cultural hegemony.

Meanwhile, advances in transport and in moving images unsettled the conventions of landscape painting and drew to the fore unanticipated scenes, such as Eric Ravilious's *Train Landscape* (1940). Here the landscape is cut into a triptych by the train's windows. We look out at the natural scene from inside a third-class railway carriage, the detailed description of which establishes a sharp division between inner and outer. Viewing landscape through a pane of glass has often been interpreted as evidence of the modern urbanite's distanced position in relation to nature. But here the landscape offers release from the slightly claustrophobic nature of the railway carriage with its fixating detail. The climax of the scene is not the huge numeral indicating a third-class carriage, but the sudden shift in register created by the image of a white horse in the corner of the window on the far left. It is in fact an image of the Westbury Horse, which is carved into the chalky grassland of Bratton Downs in Wiltshire. The dating of these chalk figures is often uncertain, some being more recent than was originally thought. Nevertheless, they suggest a throwback to an earlier age, and in *Train Journey* the horse, which travels towards us through time, challenges the somewhat complacent factual certainty conveyed by the carriage interior. The horse is not painted but collaged onto the landscape, which might at first suggest that it was added as an afterthought. But, as has now been discovered, it covers up an earlier attempt to show the Long Man of Wilmington, proving that Ravilious was set on this conjunction of distant imagery with the commanding immediacy of everyday life.[19] The sharpness and tension of the composition and its originality would be considerably weakened if the horse were to be removed, for,

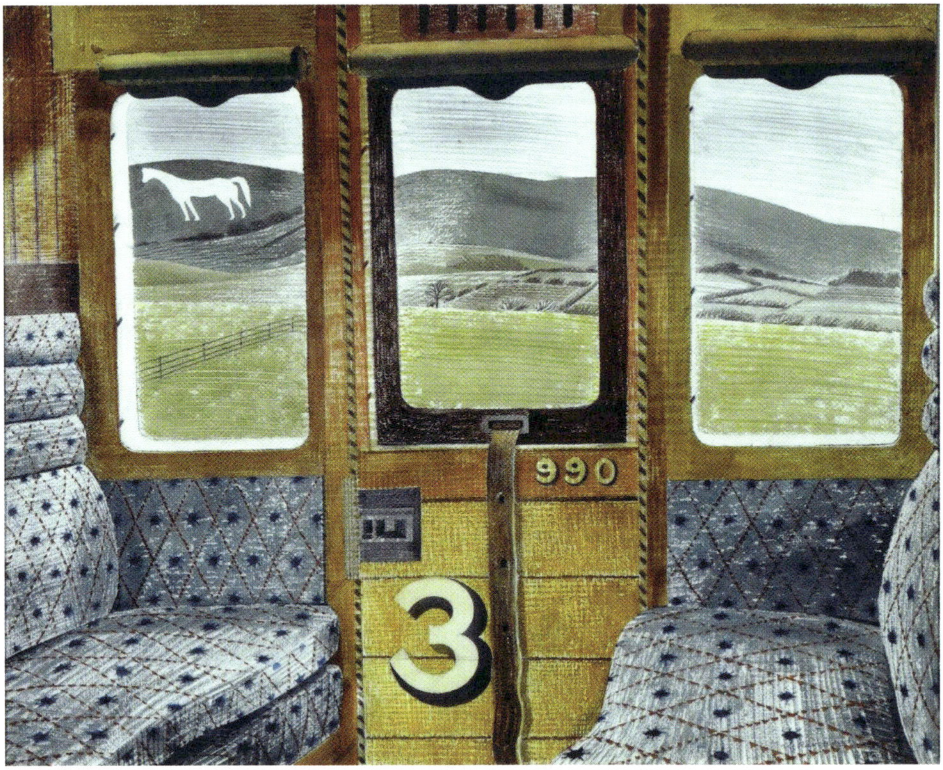

Eric Ravilious, *Train Landscape*,
watercolour, 1940.

paradoxically, its romantic associations simultaneously heighten and undermine the prosaic realism of the railway carriage.

Less startling and more urbane is Leonard Campbell Taylor's *Restaurant Car* (1935–6), where the passing slip of sky, distant hills, sea, beach and houses gives additional allure to activities inside the train's restaurant car, thereby again romancing the real. The scene is laid out to convey the pleasures of travel and the opportunity to read, eat and drink, smoke or chat, while the train's waiter executes his duties with ease and discretion. The viewer is positioned in the vantage point offered by the corner seat opposite the man with the newspaper, and is invited, by the tightly folded napkin and the cutlery setting laid out ready for use, to engage imaginatively in the sustenance on offer, an allusion that makes this painting additionally congenial. Various modes of travel, as well as the camerawork used in filmmaking or in aerial photography, opened up new ways of positioning the spectator in landscape during this period. Although landscape painting produced no new group style during the interwar years, it refreshed itself, becoming more singular and diverse, while also continuing to offer an emollient to the constant change and instability of modern urban life.

One artist who rushed back to London from Cornwall soon after the war ended, arriving early in December 1918 to rent a rickety studio in the garden of No. 1 Eldon Road, Kensington, was Frances Hodgkins. It could be argued that her entire career had been driven by a search for places that gave her subjects to paint and in which she could renew her vision; but this move reflected her realization that the war had severed her ties with France, where she had recently lived and taught. The focus of her professional life now necessarily shifted to London, its galleries and exhibiting societies.

Leonard Campbell Taylor, *Restaurant Car*, oil on canvas, 1935–6.

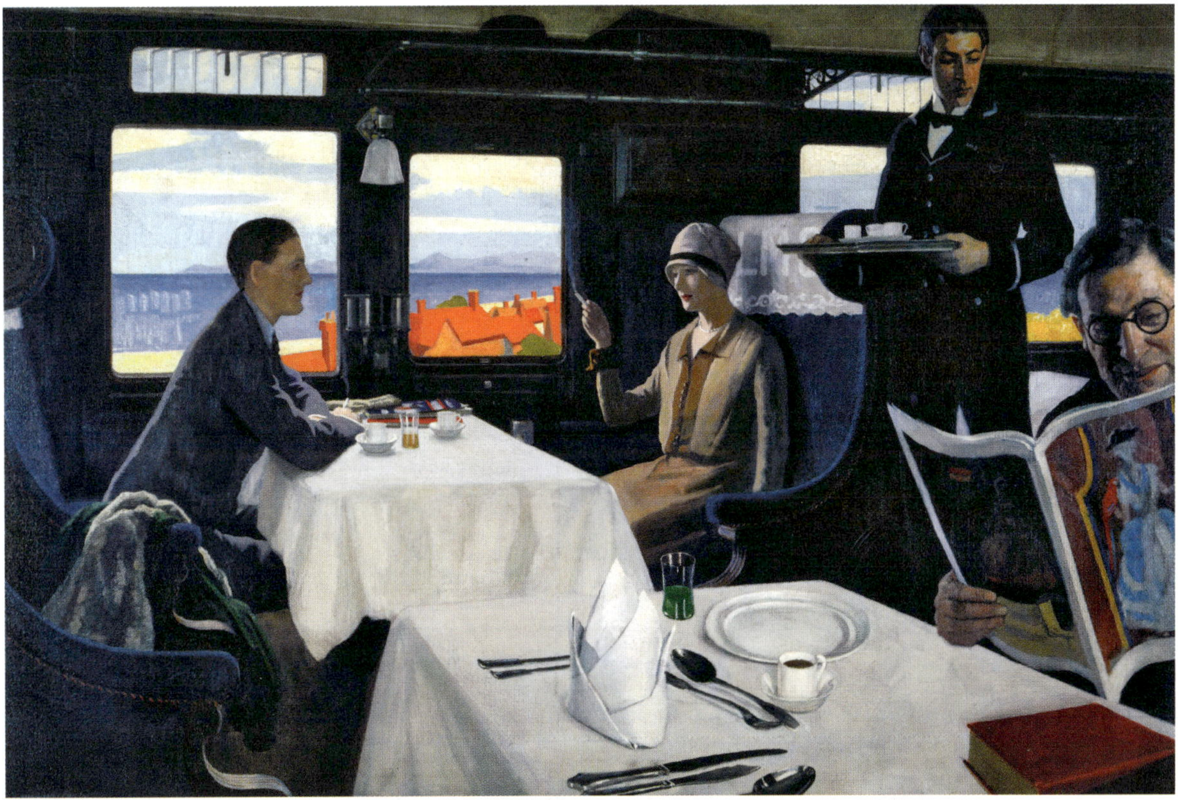

Throughout the war, Hodgkins's name had often appeared in reviews of group shows, and serious appraisal followed when the *Sunday Times* critic Frank Rutter singled her out for praise in 1916. He became a loyal supporter and in March 1919, reviewing the Women's International Art Club, called her 'one of the most richly gifted and personal painters of either sex we have today'.[20] This justified her recent move to London, undertaken in the hope of attracting exactly this type of attention.

A couple of weeks after her arrival she recounted to her mother, in New Zealand, the trials and tribulations she faced at a time when rationing was in place, milk and butter were hard to obtain, and no laundry would accept a new customer. 'I have been very overworked and weary I can tell you washing, charring, painting, teaching & going out to tea and dinner – too much altogether – I can't keep it up. In between the acts I get some painting done, but very little – you can't get any help at all – women ask £1 a week just to light yr. fire – the coal question is fierce. I have struggled along with a smoking stove & insufficient coal till I am desperate now I have decided to make a clean sweep of the stove & get a gas one instead and make my landlady go halves....I was warned of the great difficulties of life in London & I took it on with my eyes open so don't complain. There is lots of good food in the shops for the rich, but the price of everything is staggering to my modest purse.'[21]

Born in Dunedin, New Zealand in 1869, Hodgkins came from English stock mixed with some Scottish inheritance. She had been raised in a cultured and comfortable home, but her father, a lawyer and amateur painter, died relatively young in 1898, leaving her, the remaining unmarried daughter, and her mother with severely limited family resources. From then on, her need to earn her living remained imperative. But she held fast to her goal, which was to visit England and experience the wider horizons offered by Europe. She embarked on a fierce period of fundraising, giving piano lessons and teaching watercolour painting, for she had already made quite a name for herself as an artist in New Zealand. She finally left for England in 1901, aged almost thirty-one. When the boat reached Marseille early one morning, she responded immediately to the call of the Mediterranean and wandered around the town's ancient streets, marvelling at what she saw. But London disappointed her. Like many colonials, she had travelled with high expectations of her homeland, and she brought with her considerable knowledge of British art culled from books and magazines. 'On leaving New Zealand I went first to England – seeking schooling,' she told a journalist in 1913, 'but I did not find what I wanted. I was looking for colour and light, and I didn't find it.'[22] The Royal Academy of Arts had been one port of call, and she had also come across a New English Art Club exhibition by chance in Piccadilly. Both disappointed her, for she disliked the English habit that had evolved among watercolourists of making their watercolours look like oil paintings (this was done with an eye to pleasing the jury for the RA's Summer Exhibition, where oils were the favoured medium). After viewing one London exhibition, Hodgkins remarked: 'The best watercolour in the room was...a freshly painted coast scene vigorous and strong. Most of the modern watercolours are tremendously worked up...and it is quite a relief to see crisp, unworried-looking canvases.'[23]

Travel became her tactic for survival, then and for many years to come. After three months in London, she joined Norman Garstin's summer school at Caudebec-en-Caux in Normandy. There she discovered that £20 earned from the sale of some sketches would cover her expenses in France for two months. In this way, and with the help of portrait commissions, she embarked on a nomadic life. She developed an insatiable love of travel, made friends easily and often moved around in the company of other artists. She admitted to her mother: 'This kind of life quite unfits one for the colonial hereafter – everything is given up to painting we think and talk of nothing else which in itself is a tremendous stimulus....I feel as if I was possessed by a painting devil which is devouring me body and soul & claims all my brains and energy...& leaves me with no wish or inclination for anything else.'[24]

It is clear from one or two remarks dropped in her letters that, at this stage, she was intent on returning to New Zealand after obtaining what she needed from England and visits to other countries. And she did so in December 1903, spending two years mostly with her family in Wellington, but in an unsettled state. On the journey out she had been courted by Thomas Wilby, an English journalist. He left the ship at Cairo but continued to communicate by letter, with the result that they became engaged and agreed to marry in Europe in 1905. Hodgkins was on the point of leaving New Zealand in April 1905 when this slightly unreal relationship was called off, and she cancelled her passage to Europe. That experience was not the only reason why this was an unproductive period for Hodgkins; Wellington was less sympathetic to the visual arts than Dunedin had been and her sister, now that she was married to a prominent member of the House of Representatives, was much less companionable. Meanwhile in London, some of her paintings, as Hodgkins knew, were shown in the Royal Academy's Summer Exhibitions of 1904 and 1905 – and so, in January 1906, she returned to England. The following year she had her first solo exhibition in London, at the Paterson Gallery in Old Bond St.

Yet once back in England, Hodgkins soon resumed her nomadic lifestyle, with Paris, not London, gradually becoming her base. In 1909 she became the first woman to join the staff at the Académie Colarossi, where she tutored pupils in watercolour, eventually setting up a school of her own in Montparnasse. If anything weakened her position as an artist during these years, it was her long attachment to the technique of watercolour, which, although an excellent vehicle for her skilful portrayal of suffused light and atmosphere, did not enable her to stand out among the many other artists also working at this time in a vaguely impressionist style. Occasionally she introduced touches of strong colour which suggest awareness of more modern French art, but her handling of composition and perspective at this time showed scant understanding of post-impressionism. While living mostly in Paris, she missed the furore created in London by Roger Fry's 'Manet and the Post-Impressionists' exhibition in 1910; and when Fry mounted the Second Post-Impressionist Exhibition in 1912, now updated with greater emphasis on work by Matisse and Picasso, Hodgkins had just boarded the *Otranto* in order to make her second and last return visit to New Zealand.

However, earlier that year she had attended a major Italian futurist exhibition at the Bernheim-Jeune Gallery in Paris and listened to Marinetti expound his theories about art. She pocketed in her memory his valuable instruction that artists should 'represent the psychic cause and effect of things – the mental abstract, not the physical concrete',[25] and this may have strengthened her independence and originality. She never joined a group nor tried to imitate another's style but always worked in a manner entirely her own, remaining, in Myfanwy Piper's words, 'uncluttered by tradition or habit'.[26] To her former student Jane Saunders, she later admitted: 'I personally hate all rigid systems – but then I am a rebel.'[27] This, combined with her expatriate identity and her restlessness, made it difficult to know where exactly she belonged. She was aware of this, as another letter to her mother reveals: 'New Zealanders like myself cannot help becoming de-nationalized – they have no country – it is sad – but true....Art is like that – it absorbs your whole life and being. Few women can do it successfully. It requires enormous vitality. That is my conception of genius – vitality. One is fighting mental inertia *all* the time.'[28]

When the First World War forced her return to England Hodgkins settled, for economic reasons, not in London but St Ives, Cornwall. Some years before, she had joined the School of Painting in Newlyn and, while there, had visited St Ives on Show Day, when artists opened their studios in order to show pictures about to be sent to London for the attention of the Royal Academy's Summer Exhibition jury. This visit had made her aware that St Ives had many studios, 'huddled in the queerest places – down dark subterranean passages, up chicken ladders – on old boat houses up sail lofts – anywhere they could get a white-washed wall and a top light'.[29] These were a strong attraction and made her feel that St Ives was a place where an artist could flourish. But in other ways, this small town was lacking. Even in such a far-flung corner of England, the war remained a pressing reality. Hodgkins missed her friends in Paris and wrote to her mother: 'I find I am too modern for people down here and I am conscious of the cold eye of distrust and disapproval by the older members of St Ives. It is not an inspiring atmosphere tho' I love it for many other things. I will go a long way before I find another studio like the one I have now.'[30]

Her financial situation was still precarious after peace returned. An elderly magnate in New Zealand, Peter Waite, who bought her art, had sent her timely remittances during the war and now paid £100 to fund her move to London. Frank Rutter's critical support further emboldened her, for he had agreed to write a foreword to the solo exhibition offered her in 1919 by the recently opened Hampstead Art Gallery in London's Finchley Road. But despite financial help and Rutter's support, the difficulties Hodgkins faced in the studio at No. 1 Eldon Road proved insurmountable. She had replaced the malfunctioning stove with a gas fire, but it produced very little heat owing to a lack of pressure, and meanwhile the cost of gas had shot up 10 per cent. So cold was the studio that pupils for drawing and watercolour lessons fell away and models refused to pose. The plumber who had removed the stove was recalled and the old stove returned, but just then a serious coal and wood famine set in and obtaining fuel proved immensely time-consuming. For a person almost wholly dependent on sales for her living expenses, it was a deeply frustrating situation; Hodgkins found herself unable to paint for more than a few hours each week. Added to this was the misery of the cold and London's fog. To her mother she admitted: 'I nearly threw my demented self into the Thames. The agony of getting up in the morning & facing a dull cold world with a yellow sickly fog – it broke one's spirit. I saw trouble years ahead of me.'[31] After only four months, she was back in Cornwall recovering from a savage attack of flu. She apparently made three attempts to establish herself in the Kensington studio, but circumstances defeated her each time.[32]

She gained some respite by sub-letting the Eldon Road studio to two young men, and in this way met Cedric Morris and his lifelong companion, Arthur Lett-Haines.[33] On moving in they found the walls of her studio lined with her paintings of children, almost certainly leftovers from the twenty-two watercolours of young children she had exhibited at the International Society in London in October 1918.[34] She had begun painting Belgian refugee families during the war, and the painting she exhibited at the International Society in 1916, titled *Unshatterable*, is thought to be the same as *Belgian Refugees*, a painting which Cedric Morris at one point owned.[35] He certainly admired what he saw in the Eldon Road studio, especially the way Hodgkins juxtaposed textural effects with an emphasis on pattern. The more familiar he became with her vision and technique, the more he recognized her originality.

Hodgkins had hoped to let the Eldon Road studio for two years, and was disappointed when Morris and Lett-Haines decided to abandon London for Cornwall.

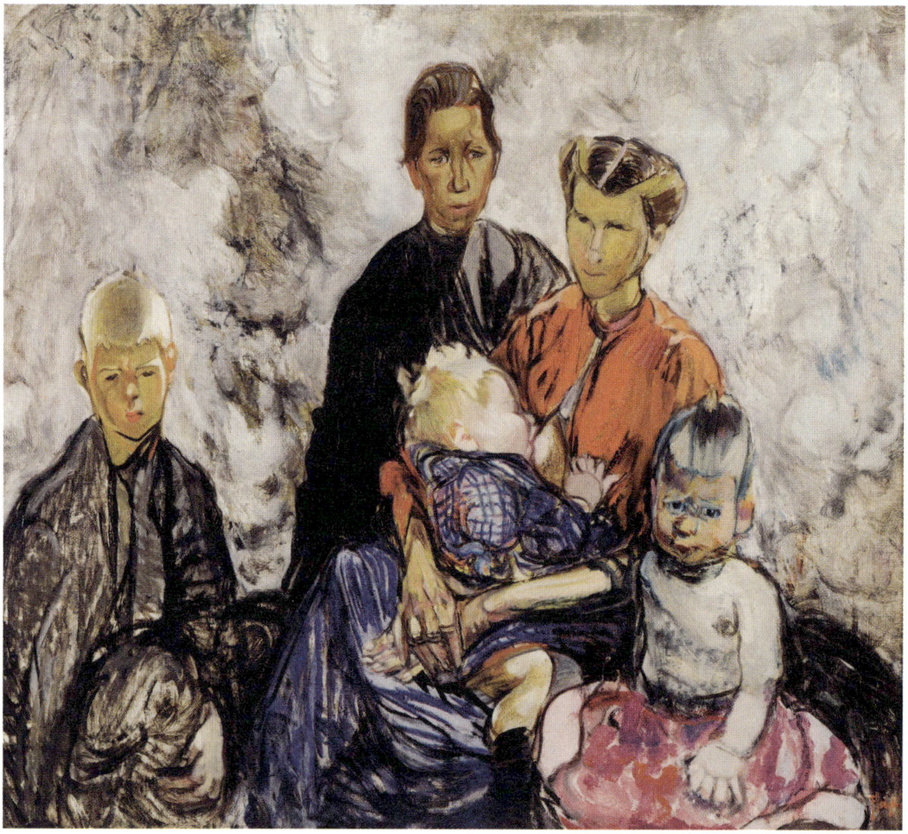

Frances Hodgkins, *Unshatterable (Belgian Refugees)*, oil on canvas, 1916.

But their friendship survived this, as well as the embarrassment of their discovering how much she had depended for her livelihood on the excess she charged them by sub-letting the studio. After they had established themselves in Newlyn, in a row of cottages overlooking the harbour which they converted into a house called The Bowgie, they invited her over from St Ives. They also held many parties for local artists.

Hodgkins, as a regular guest, spent much of the summer of 1920 in the company of Morris and Lett-Haines, whom she found stimulating. That summer also marked a turning point in her art. She had first tried painting in oils in 1907, and the following year had taken lessons in oil painting from Pierre Marcel-Béronneau in Paris. She had returned to this medium in 1915 but it was only now, in Newlyn, that she began to use it frequently. Lett-Haines thought that her work 'took on a new and decisive vitality, and her oils a more painterly quality'.[36] She also sold well. By October she had banked £200, enough savings for her to give up her St Ives studio and live economically in France for a year. Very different had been her situation earlier that year, when her niece from New Zealand, Lydia Pharazyn, had visited: Lett-Haines observed that Lydia had paid off the bill Frances had run up 'on tic' at Culleman's, an artist's colourman in St Ives, and 'remedied other embarrassments' elsewhere. There were to be more occasions during their friendship when Lett-Haines witnessed how dire Hodgkins's penury could be. Still more distressing, he said, 'were her efforts to disguise it, hindered by incapacity, impracticability and exaggerated pride'.[37]

The age gap between Hodgkins and these two young men did not inhibit their exchange. 'I always felt at ease with her,' Morris recollected: 'she was completely unconventional, rather comic especially to look at, was witty in a strange oblique way and was malicious, again obliquely, and covered up. And above all she was very gallant and of course a good painter and a completely original one.'[38] In turn, Hodgkins's admiration for Morris's art is expressed in a note to Lett-Haines: 'I hope Cedric is doing some shining work and both of you are well.'[39] Myfanwy Piper, almost certainly drawing on her conversations with Hodgkins, writes of the two men: 'Young, gay, and absolutely without prudence, they encouraged her in her independence and accepted her as a companion. During the next ten years they were necessary and undemanding friends.'[40] The only drawback to their friendship was that Morris enjoyed travelling as much as Hodgkins, and when summer ended he shot off to Paris and then to warmer countries around the Mediterranean. He and Lett-Haines left Cornwall that autumn before Hodgkins. She hoped to overlap with them at Cassis but just missed them, there and elsewhere, and although they kept in touch through correspondence it seems they did not properly reconnect as friends until 1927, when the two men moved into a large studio in London, at 32 Great Ormond Street.

By then, Cedric Morris had advanced considerably as an artist. Having begun to paint seriously in 1919 at the age of thirty, he had spent time in Paris, where he first met and made friends with Christopher Wood. Morris's work had found its way into group exhibitions in Rome, Germany and New York before Tooth's gave him his first solo exhibition in 1928, when thirty-one of his pictures sold during the private view. Success made him a prominent figure socially in London and Paris. His work always had character, but it was during the second half of the 1920s that he developed a distinctive method: he began painting by means of numerous small touches of a heavily loaded brush, thereby giving texture and depth to his work.

In 1930, he broke with his dealer and moved permanently to the country, and in 1937 he and Lett-Haines opened the East Anglian School of Painting and Drawing. From then on, both men would be closely involved with the school. Morris presumably had private means (he was the son of a prosperous industrialist and in

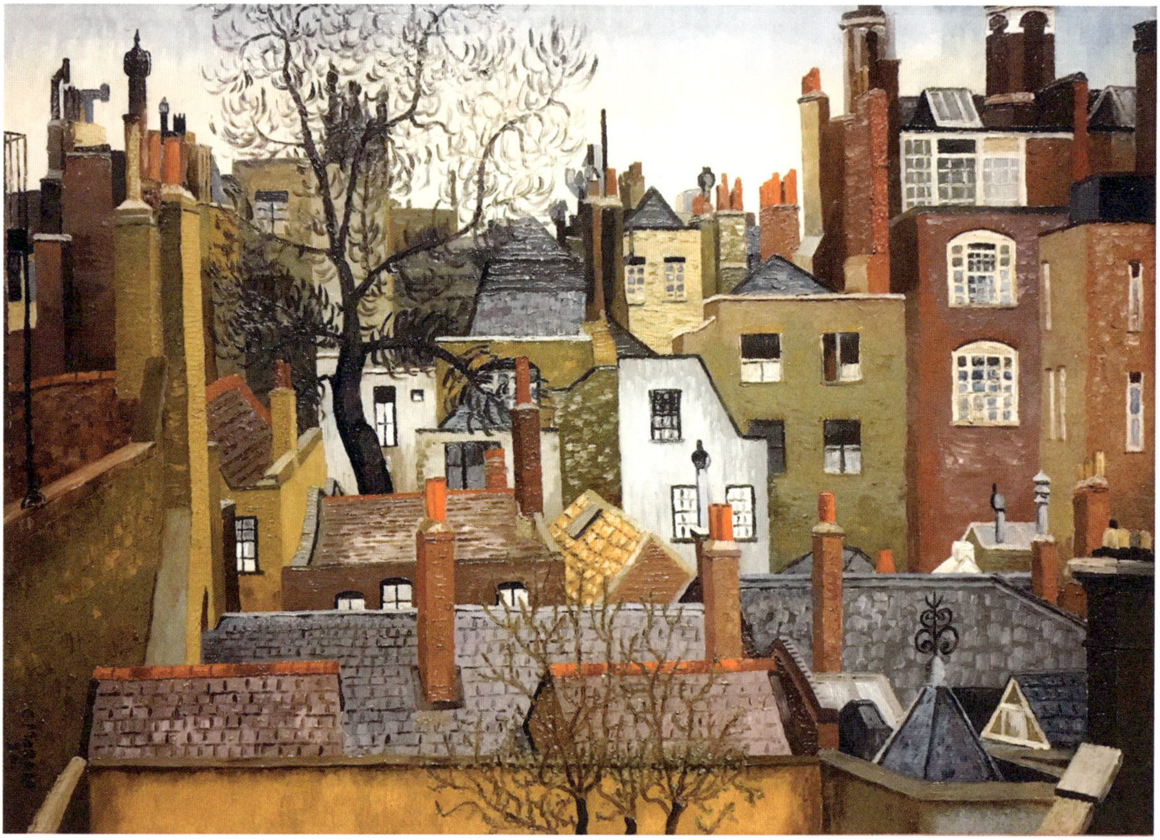

Cedric Morris, *From a Window at 45 Brook Street, London W.1*,
oil on plywood, 1926.

1947 inherited a baronetcy) and was a strange product of a society and class system he disliked. Passionately democratic in his approach to art, he for the most part despised art critics, dealers, stylistic fashions and the over-intellectual. Taste, he thought, was less debauched among the uneducated. All of which explains why this sophisticate flourished in the countryside, becoming a noted breeder of irises, and in his art practised a style that blurred the division between amateur and professional art, his paintings offering an affront to conventional artistic standards.

Morris's rejection of academic correctness was part of his search for expressive freedom, a freedom from the tyranny of appearances that enabled him to achieve a psychological acuity in his portraits, as can be seen in his 1928 portrait of Frances Hodgkins. When the East Anglian School opened, it was described in one prospectus as 'an oasis of decency for artists outside the system'.[41] Pupils were encouraged to express what they felt about appearances, suggesting that this mattered more than what they saw, and that drawing, dictated by feeling, licensed emotive distortion.

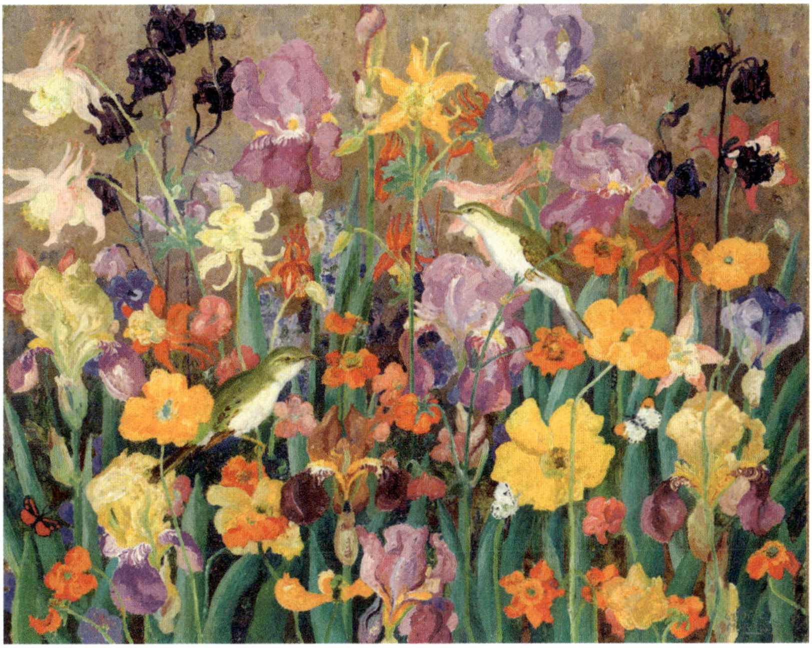

Cedric Morris, *July Flowers and Wood Warblers*, oil on canvas, 1929.

Hodgkins, who was herself something of an outsider, found Morris's anti-establishment stance sympathetic. Her own art in the late 1920s became more experimental and more definite. Much travelling had left her at ease with the new and unfamiliar, and she quite often moved things about in a scene to suit her pictorial needs. Marinetti's advice – 'represent the psychic cause and effect of things – the mental abstract, not the physical concrete'[42] – may have liberated her further, for objects in her pictures are never tethered by realism but seem to float into position like necessary props on a stage, so that the eye can move round them freely. Cedric Morris's frequent depiction of objects seen close up may have contributed to this development. But Frances Hodgkins's fascination with objects may also connect with her denationalized state: a love of objects often accompanies the exile's loss of home, and the loss of stability provided by family or personal relations. Melanie Klein, one of the first proponents of 'object relations', takes this further, arguing that the need for reconciliation with a fragmented or lost past underpins all creative

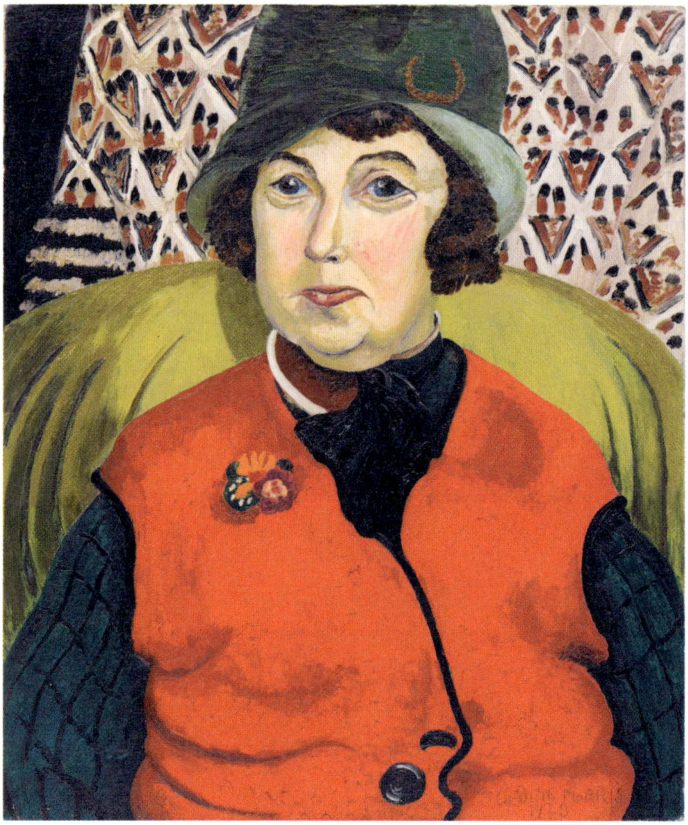

Cedric Morris, *Portrait of Frances Hodgkins,*
oil on canvas, 1928.

endeavour. If this premise is accepted, then Hodgkins in her still lifes is not just assembling objects to create formal relationships, but responding to an inner need to infuse life into objects so as to recreate life. It does not surprise that when she set out to paint a self-portrait, she did so entirely through the use of objects: a shoe, a belt, a scarf, a vase, a rose and other items (*c.* 1935).[43]

The isolation of ordinary objects in a still life for aesthetic and other purposes is one reason why it became a central component in the development of modernism. Hodgkins would have been aware, by the time she joined the Seven and Five Society in 1929, that a popular subject among the group was the view through a window, which, pictorially, requires the artist to unite the inside world with the outer. She also made use of this motif, but extended its parameters when she began situating her still life objects not in a room but in landscape, in closer conversation with nature, light and air. This new theme drew attention to her work within the Seven and Five Society, after Cedric Morris and the sculptor Betty Muntz nominated her

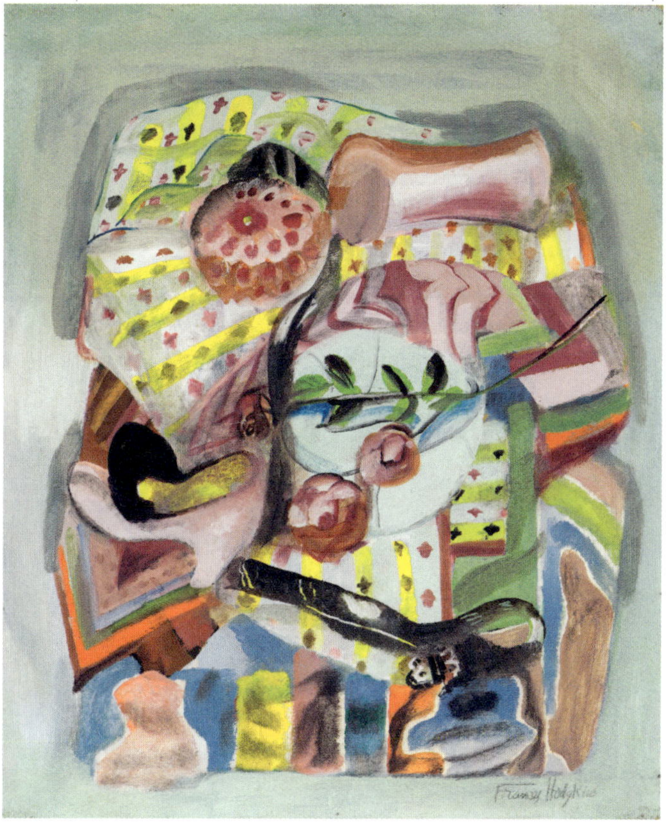

Frances Hodgkins, *Self-Portrait: Still Life*, oil on cardboard, c. 1935.

for membership. The Society had by this time become associated with a painterly lyricism, as found in the work of Winifred Nicholson, Ben Nicholson and Christopher Wood; Hodgkins's work was in keeping with this tendency, while also bringing to it a more earthy note.

Membership of the Seven and Five positioned her at the heart of the English avant-garde. It brought her friendship with a younger generation – the Nicholsons, John Piper, Barbara Hepworth, Henry Moore – all of whom treated her with affection and admiration. It is not therefore surprising that she produced some of her best paintings while a member of the Seven and Five Society, between 1929 and 1934. *Wings over Water* (1931–2), originally called *In Cornwall*, shows the view from a window in one of the rooms she rented at Bodinnick in Cornwall during the winter of 1931–2, looking over the River Fowey where it broadens out to meet the sea. Curtains frame the view, as in a theatre, and a slightly theatrical arrangement can be felt in the placing of objects, which has less to do with the actual scene than the

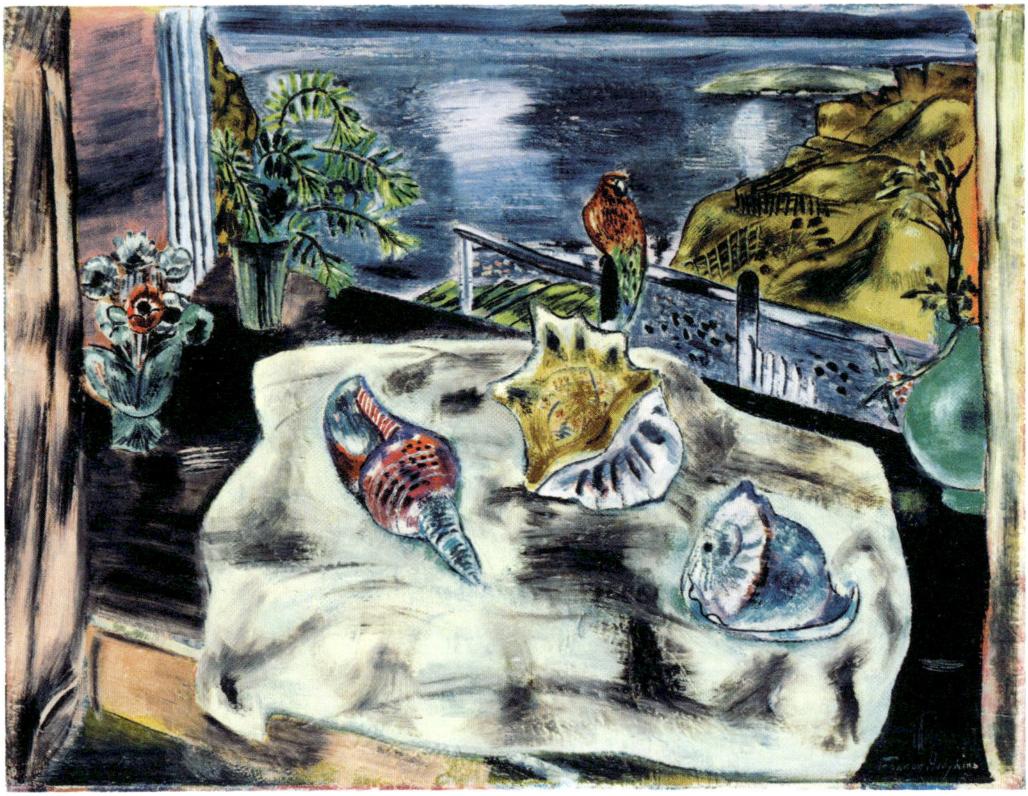

Frances Hodgkins, *Wings over Water*,
oil on canvas, 1931–2.

conception of it in the artist's mind. The vases of flowers, pushed into the corners of the windowsill, enable three shells, one a conch, to take centre stage on a piece of cloth. Just above the conch shell, but viewed outside, sitting on a wooden fence below, is a parrot that belonged to Hodgkins's landlady. It introduces an element of the exotic and is sufficiently interesting to offset the central arrangement of the shells while also introducing a strong red, found in small touches elsewhere in the composition. Hodgkins followed no set style or method but appears to have worked intuitively, applying paint thickly and allowing layers to build up where she made changes to her initial ideas. Texture is in places created by sgraffito, where she uses the wrong end of the brush or a palette knife to scratch through the top layer of paint so that underlying colour breaks through. A report on the picture by two conservationists discovered that Hodgkins may have added chalk to her lead white to thicken it and that, although she used paint from tubes, she then added dried pigment to the surface of the canvas, mixing it into the paint so as to achieve unusual effects of colour.[44] The most notable feature is her use of black. It is possible that this was the actual colour of the windowsill, and she used it as her starting point. But, often working wet on wet, Hodgkins introduces touches of black into many aspects of the picture – the central cloth, the shells, the fence, the landscape and the curtains at either side – with a powerful unifying effect. It has been observed that the dusky tones suggest an evening scene, but this ignores the theatrical construct behind the work and the fact that, as with a theatrical scene, a painting can create a world unto itself. This picture exists outside of everyday time and space, in a less literal and more imaginative world.

Hodgkins resigned from the Seven and Five Society in 1934, when she learnt that (under Ben Nicholson's leadership) it had been agreed that the following year, all works shown in its annual exhibition should be abstract. The 1935 exhibition was to be the Society's last show; an attempt to revive it in 1938 proved unsuccessful. By then Hodgkins had moved on once more, becoming an English neo-romantic, releasing more clearly the poetic element in her art and finding fresh harmonies of colour, as John Piper noticed, 'in Wiltshire farmyards, Welsh hills and Dorset coves'.[45] Her name was on the initial list of artists (and she was the only woman artist) to be included in the Penguin Modern Painters series of short monographs, conceived by the publisher Allen Lane and edited by Kenneth Clark. Myfanwy Piper was pleased to be informed that she and Hodgkins had been paired as author and subject.

The full trajectory of her long and prolific career was traced in 2019, when Auckland Art Gallery mounted 'Frances Hodgkins: European Journeys'. This exhibition was made possible by extensive scholarship on her work, mostly produced by scholars and dealers in New Zealand. Critical attention to Hodgkins was for a long time negligible in Britain: Charles Harrison dedicated little more than a paragraph to her in his *English Art and Modernism 1900–1939* (1981) and in 1987 two major exhibitions in London, 'British Art in the 20th Century' at the Royal Academy and 'A Paradise Lost: The Neo-Romantic Imagination in Britain 1935–55' at the Barbican, omitted any representations of her work. There is no mention of her work in David Peters Corbett's *The Modernity of English Art 1914–30* (1997), nor in Alexandra Harris's *Romantic Moderns: English Writers, Artists and the Imagination from Virginia Woolf to John Piper* (2010). More recently, several mentions of her occur in Katy Deepwell's social history *Women Artists between the Wars: 'A fair field and no favour'* (2010), and a small monograph on her by Samantha Niederman has appeared in a series on women artists published by Eiderdown Books.

The greatest testament to Francis Hodgkins so far is Linda Gill's editing of over 600 of her letters, published by Auckland University Press.[46] It is these that bring to the fore the way in which she pioneered independence and greater freedom for women artists, with fortitude, tenacity and a robust commitment to her work. Her art never stood still, but remained freshly surprising. Her handling of colour has been praised by many, including Myfanwy Piper, who found in it 'the same quality as some fine poetry....She has no formula, but the colour of each picture is as indicative of a mood as a blushing and sensitive skin.'[47]

In the immediate aftermath of war, many artists experienced an oscillation between hope and disillusion. The tension between resistance and innovation fostered unease. Very few artists managed to establish a method or style that would carry art forward and impact on other artists during the post-1945 period. The only member of the vorticist group who was able to achieve this was David Bomberg, who created a legacy that can be identified in the work of Frank Auerbach and Leon Kossoff.

Like many other artists, Bomberg found himself in an impecunious position after the return to peace in 1918. He had made his name, before 1914, predominantly with Yiddish subjects and the radical methods associated with vorticism. His best-known work is the Tate's *In the Hold* (*c*. 1913–14), where the shattered lives of figures emerging from the depths of a ship's hold are conveyed by glittering facets owing to the superimposition of two grids, one of which fractures the scene into sixty-four squares and the other, placed diagonally across the first, which further disrupts representational content.

Some months after the return to peace, still toying with modernism, Bomberg found himself labouring incessantly for insufficient reward. In need of additional income, he and his wife Alice abandoned London and moved to Beech, a village near Alton in Hampshire, to set up a chicken farm, with the hope that he could continue to pursue some form of avant-garde practice in his spare time. This proved disastrous as Bomberg, now stymied, found he missed the stimulation of London. He had, however, a friend and supporter in Muirhead Bone, whose past record as one of the full-time war artists gave him authority in official circles. Bone was aware that Bomberg needed a commission. At the same time, he knew that Bomberg's attempts to maintain an avant-garde style would not gain him the job Bone had in mind. He wrote to Bomberg in March 1922: 'I'm still sure that you should face the trouble and difficulty of realism and not take refuge in short cuts....we have all a tendency to put on a convenient uniform (which happens to be a kind of cubism today) instead of finding out what is personally at the bottom of our souls.'[48]

The outcome of this letter was that Bomberg agreed Bone should mediate between him and the Zionist Organization. This had been formed in the wake of the Balfour Agreement, which led to the establishment of a Jewish homeland in Palestine. Already a number of artists were engaged in the creation of propaganda for the Zionist cause. Bone, writing to the political secretary of the Zionist Organization, argued persuasively for the need not just for photography, but for an 'imaginative' artist painting on the spot. In this instance his letter failed. Bone, however, kept faith with his hunch that Bomberg with his Jewish identity, though not a Zionist, was well suited to this task; and finally Bone succeeded in securing for him a commission from the Palestine Foundation Fund, which was closely allied with the Zionist Organization. Bomberg's remit was to record 'Zionist reconstruction'.[49] He set out to witness the making of the Jewish homeland in April 1923.

On arriving in Jerusalem Bomberg was officially received by its chief architect and town planner, Clifford Holliday, who was closely involved with the restoration of the Old City. As has been remarked, Holliday could not have found a more sympathetic listener than Bomberg when expounding on the formal qualities of the city's architecture and its relation to the rolling landscape and the distant Judean hills.[50] In the words of Sarah MacDougall and Rachel Dickson: 'For the next four years the structure and colour of the cityscape (likewise in Petra and Jericho) became his abiding passion....And one can only imagine the extraordinary impact the dazzling light can have had on him[.]'[51]

Bomberg's work in the Middle East forms a distinct chapter in his career, but has come to be regarded as a transitional period. He discovered in Palestine his ability to create dynamism and flow through the aggregation of buildings and landscape, as found in Jerusalem looking towards Mount Scopus. But the excitement and dramatic awakening which the landscape first inspired in him diminished as the topographical requirements placed on him began to feel restrictive. Some years

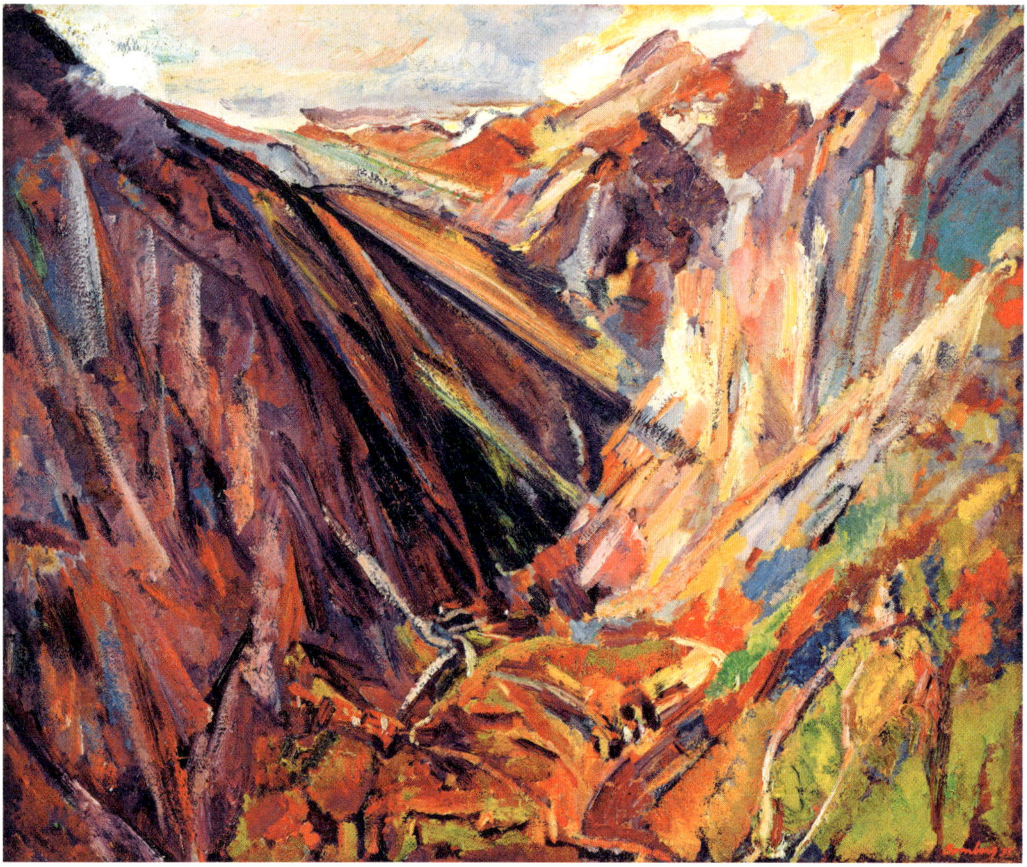

David Bomberg, *Valley of La Hermida: Picos de Europa, Asturias, Spain*,
oil on canvas, 1935.

later, looking back on this time in Palestine, he dismissively referred to the work he had done as 'painting postcards for government officials'.[52] Yet it was here that he developed the habit of working outdoors, in front of his subject, which stood him in good stead for the work he was to do in Spain, where he regained his power and originality. His first visit, in 1929, was to Toledo, a place Muirhead Bone had made the subject of a whole series of prints that Bomberg had recently seen. But it is more likely to have been the electrifying vitality of El Greco's paintings that drew Bomberg to Greco's home, giving him the opportunity to study this artist's work at first hand in the El Greco Museum. It was in Toledo that Bomberg began to develop what Richard Cork has called 'a more fiery and unfettered approach', using 'openly urgent brushmarks which no longer have time to deal with painstaking minutiae'.[53]

On his second visit, which began at the end of 1934, Bomberg developed a fascination with precipitous gorges; first at Ronda, where a huge ravine splits in two the great plateau on which the town is built. This evidently engaged his imagination and enhanced his desire to portray the pull of gravity and the fall of light. It was in Spain that he developed his understanding of what he called 'the spirit in the mass' – the identification of which became his central aim, and a part of his teaching when he gave drawing classes in the late 1940s at the Borough Polytechnic.

His largest and most important Spanish painting is *Valley of La Hermida: Picos de Europa, Asturias, Spain* (1935). Its rich impasto tells of a loaded brush, rapid handling and the use of strong colours, especially the pink and orange seen in the shafts of sunlight. Everything is brought together in a way that upholds structural rigour and a marvellous expressiveness. These Spanish landscapes did not fit into any English mainstream development of their day; they were ahead of their time. In recent years they have come to be recognized as a vital link within an English tradition, taking strength from Constable's passionate treatment of skies and clouds and, in turn, encouraging the intense physicality with which Frank Auerbach and Leon Kossoff have pursued their use of paint.

CHAPTER 4

LANDSCAPE AND PLACES OF THE MIND

In 1981 the Tate curator Richard Morphet, taking a broad view of English art between the wars, noted 'themes of permanence, of a settled and harmonious world, and of calm matter-of-fact observation'.[1] At the same time, a revival of interest in the achievements of Constable and Turner and in the golden age of English watercolours affirmed the genre of landscape painting as the most prominent tradition in English art. And as we shall see, a calm stillness frequently emerges in the views portrayed by the work of the East London Group. What made all this possible was the fact that Britain was spared the worst socio-political anxieties of this period, as experienced in France, Germany and Italy.

The attentive observation that the East London Group brought to their art was not intended to carry viewers back into the past but instead to intensify aspects of the everyday environment, mostly found in an area of London then identified as E3. In Harold Steggles's *Wharf Houses* (1930), for instance, the precise details, tonal relationships and steady grey light that give no hint of time of day, create an eerie stillness. Like his brother Walter Steggles, Harold began as a member of the East London Art Club, which, over four years, formed a cohesive identity – first at Bethnal Green Men's Institute and then in the Art Room at Bow and Bromley Evening Institute, where the Slade-trained John Cooper would provide criticism and advice on the pictures his pupils had painted in their spare time. Although some were unemployed, most of these men and women were in their thirties and had jobs. The Steggles brothers were clerks; Elwin Hawthorne was a casual labourer; Archibald Hattemore, the Club's secretary, was a Metropolitan Water Board inspector; Grace Oscroft sold wireless parts in a bicycle shop; Albert Turpin was a window cleaner; B. R. Swinnerton was a piano casemaker. In all, there were around thirty-five artists in the group, and in 1928 they held their first exhibition at the Whitechapel Art Gallery.

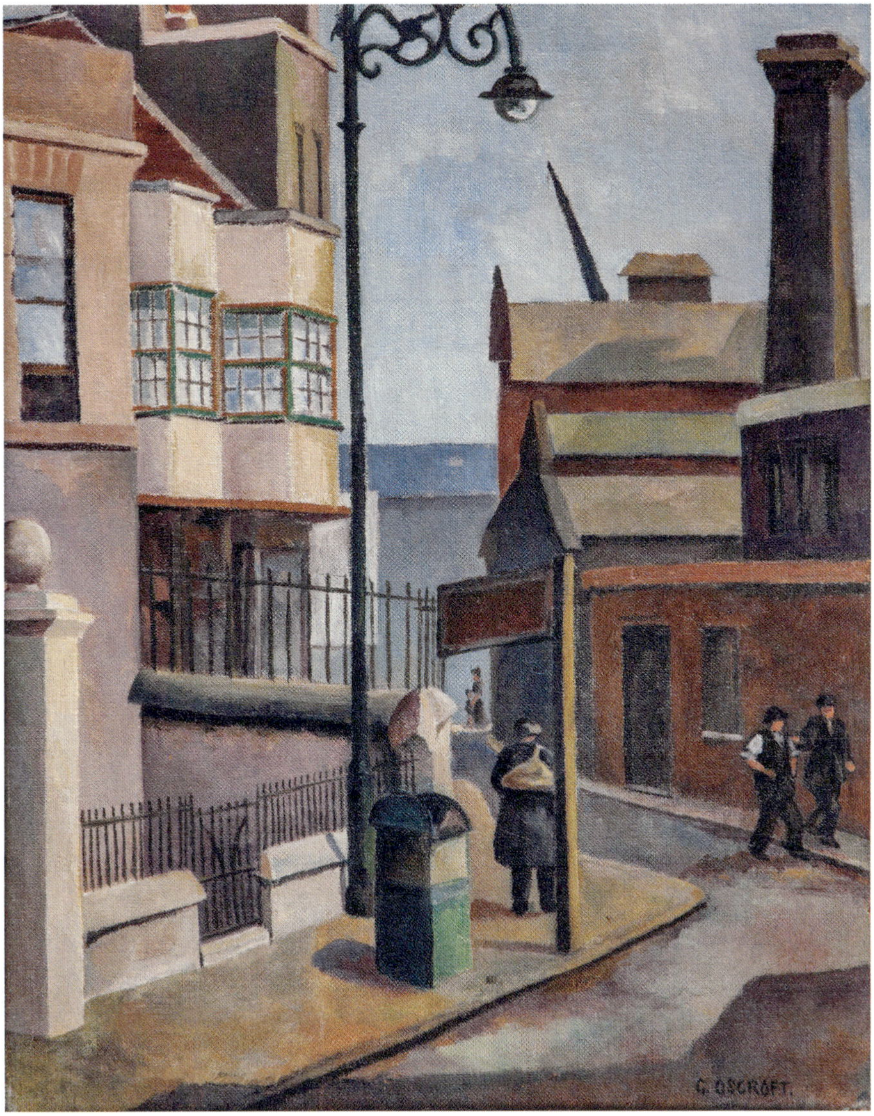

Grace Oscroft, *Old Houses in Bow Road*,
oil on canvas, 1934.

What is remarkable about this East End Group, as they came to be called, is the support it attracted and the professionalism with which its members promoted themselves. By the time the Whitechapel Art Gallery exhibition came about, they had decided this would be the first of regular annual exhibitions. They announced this in a dignified catalogue, sent out in advance with a map of the tube printed on the back to assist those who were unsure how to get to Whitechapel. They had already acquired as their patron the dealer and philanthropist Sir Joseph Duveen, who put up money to assist with their costs. In addition, Sir Charles Wakefield had set up a fund to help cover the cost of framing.

News of the exhibition attracted a degree of interest in the press, and among those who bought work was a number of celebrities. Other supporters, already in place, were the rayon manufacturer Samuel Courtauld, the writer Arnold Bennett, Lord Melchett and Lord Burnham. The catalogue boasted that 'every effort will be made to make [the exhibition] as representative as possible of what is best in East London Art'.[2] The East London Group went on to hold eight further annual exhibitions, all of which took place within the prestigious West End gallery of Alex. Reid & Lefevre, up until 1936.

One person who may have helped advance their visibility was the artist Walter Sickert – or Richard Sickert, as he, for a short period, preferred to be called. He gave a series of talks on painting technique to the Group and sometimes showed his own work alongside theirs in exhibitions. He had earlier warned his associates in the Camden Town Group to avoid in their art decorum and good taste. 'The more our art is serious,' he declared, 'the more it will tend to avoid the drawing-room and stick to the kitchen. The plastic arts are gross arts, dealing joyously with gross material facts...and while they will flourish in the scullery, or on the dunghill, they fade at a breath from the drawing-room.'[3]

One of the intentions of the East London Group was to continue the Camden Town Group's interest in urban realism, but there was no ideological or political intent behind this aim. As P. G. Konody, writing in the *Daily Mail* at the time of the first exhibition, realized: 'They paint what they see around them: the daily aspect of the East End of London, the week-end pleasures of the country, holiday impressions of Blackpool, the types they meet, the interiors they live in, or the concerts they attend.' He admired the absence of any straining after picturesqueness, and concluded that their charm lay in the simplicity and naturalness of their representations. But what may additionally explain the success of the group is Konody's admission that the pictures give the spectator 'a gratifying feeling of rest from the innumerable examples of artistic sophistications which confront him at innumerable shows'.[4]

A year later Virginia Woolf, in *A Room of One's Own*, was to advise her readers: 'Think of things in themselves.' In the middle section of her novel *To the Lighthouse*, which she titles 'Time Passes', she uses an empty house to good effect and tries to envisage a world without a self, a setting from which, in her words, 'life had parted'.[5] Elwin Hawthorne seems to aim at something similar in *Cumberland Market*, for as in many East London Group paintings, figures are absent here. As yet there is no sign of the market, for the time of day seems to be early morning, before any activity

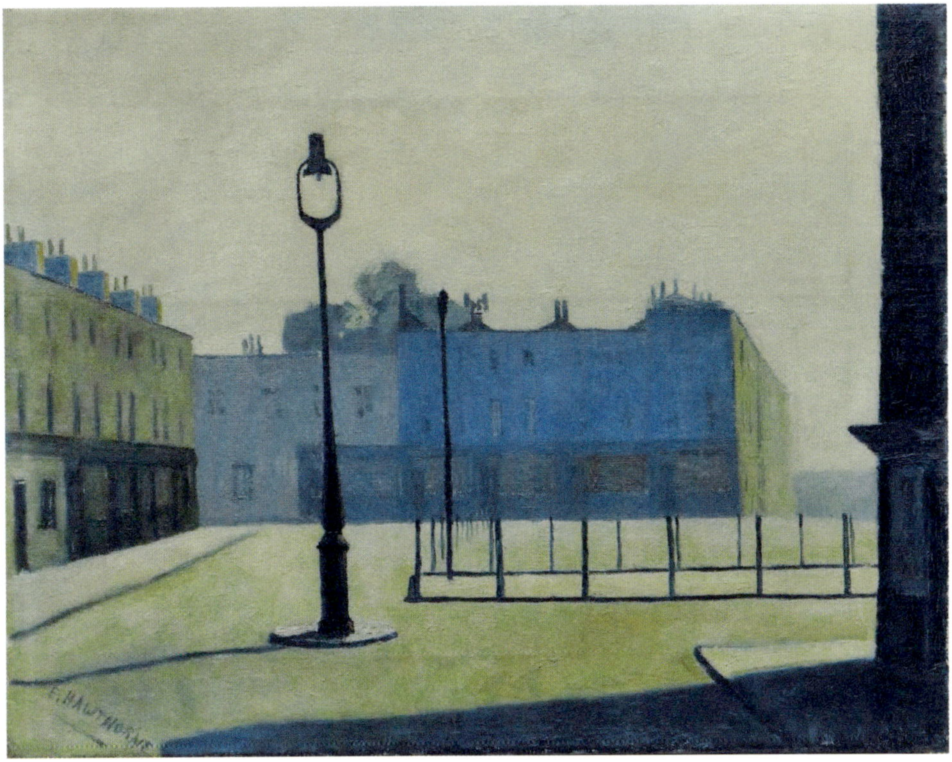

Elwin Hawthorne, *Cumberland Market*, oil on canvas, 1931.

begins. A hazy light, soft and tender, fills the air, while below a shadow, cast by a wall across the foreground, creates the necessary weight. Otherwise the scene is empty and still. Hawthorne had left school in 1919, aged fourteen, to work as an errand boy and then as a casual labourer. Walter Sickert took him on as his studio assistant for three years. Out of all this came a steady stream of quiet paintings, mostly of empty scenes in the East End, in a recognizable style, sure and enduring, if also gently melancholic.

Towards the end of the first exhibition Sir Joseph Duveen bought a handful of pictures. These joined a small number of paintings by the East London Group set aside by Charles Aitken, the director of the National Gallery, Millbank (still the official name of the Tate Gallery), which he intended to put temporarily on public display. While these paintings were on show at the Tate a press release went out explaining that they showed the practical interest in art among working people, 'which may lead to a wider appreciation of the National Collections'.[6]

The actual talent within the group was uneven. When in 2017 works by the East London Group were shown at Southampton Art Gallery alongside pictures in the Gallery's collection by Sickert and the Camden Town Group, the East Londoners suffered in comparison with the painterly skills and rigorous construction of the older group. Yet it can be argued that the East Londoners had arrived at a more modern grasp of urban space, bringing the work of Harold Steggles and Elwin Hawthorne closer to that of Edward Hopper than the Camden Towners. There is also a freshness and honesty in their approach to their subjects, alongside considerable skill and feeling. It does not surprise that Sir David Scott, a major collector of Victorian art, acquired a substantial holding of work by the East London Group. In recent years their work and reputation has been actively promoted on social media, thereby achieving recognition for the East London Group's legacy after years of neglect, when they seemed almost completely forgotten. The Group is now the subject of two books.[7]

As time passed and another war began to be felt on the distant horizon, landscape painting became less settled and harmonious and more layered. Awareness of the deep past was enhanced by the invention of aerial photography. This revealed aspects of the landscape that could not be observed at ground level by the human eye. It gave archaeologists a better understanding of the formation of landscape and its past use. Artists like John Piper, who took an interest in these developments, allowed an archaeological imagination to feed into neo-romanticism, which became a dominant vein in art during the Second World War. By then the whole tenor of landscape painting had changed. It can, however, be argued that a precedent for neo-romanticism is found in Paul Nash's drawings and paintings of Dymchurch, through which, as discussed later in this chapter, he explored a complex set of responses.

Between the two world wars, travel books proliferated and helped to deepen public appreciation of the English countryside and its associations with national identity. Familiarity with the countryside as a source of health-giving pleasure was further enhanced by developments in public and private transport. A map of the railways available to Londoners wanting to gain access to the countryside, within a radius of twenty-five miles from St Paul's Cathedral, can be found in Edric Holmes's *London's Countryside*, published in the late 1920s.[8] 'Upon the Northern and Western lines', he writes, 'certain days are set apart for the purpose of cheap trips, though "walker's tickets" at slightly higher fares, available nearly every day and which enable the wayfarer to return from a different station, are a great convenience.'[9] The bicycle was another means of getting around the countryside, enabling John Piper to complete his tour of every church in Surrey by the age of fourteen, and the development of the cheap motor car encouraged the growth of car ownership. While the housing problem in the inner urban ring of London remained acute, the Home Counties gained in popularity in the first quarter of the 20th century and became more residential. New houses met population needs and made possible second homes for the more fortunate. The rapid spread of housing led Edric Holmes to remark that 'the once charming series of landscapes between the Chiltern Hills and the North Downs, and for some distance beyond those natural frontiers of the Thames Valley, is in serious danger of being utterly ruined by indiscriminate building'.[10] Although writing for the motorist or rambler, he was also addressing those who recognized that the pleasures of the Home Counties were under threat.

Holmes's book was part of a series titled 'England's Countryside'. These volumes differed from other county guides in that their content was shaped by natural divisions within the landscape rather than 'the arbitrary political boundaries of the shires'. There was also a readiness to accept the limits associated with ancient kingdoms of the first millennium; Holmes himself wrote one titled *Wessex: An Exploration of the Southern Realm from Itchen to Otter*, as well as a third volume in the same series titled *Seaward Sussex*. Writers of guidebooks did much to proselytize for the countryside in a style often reminiscent of the model laid down by *Highways and Byways*, a late Victorian and Edwardian series of guidebooks that were conversational in tone, attentive to legend and folk history, and nostalgic in relation to the past. The bestselling guidebook of this period was H. V. Morton's *In Search of England* (1927), a record of a motor-car journey around England, which went through twenty-six editions in twelve years. His jocular description of Bath – 'the dear old lady of Somerset: grey-haired, mittened, smelling faintly of lavender; one of those old ladies that have outlived a much discussed past, and are now as obviously respectable as only old ladies with crowded pasts can be' – as Sarah Fill has argued, assisted the personification of the English landscape as gentle and feminine.[11] But when John Betjeman went to Jack Beddington, then head of publicity at Shell, with the idea for a set of county guides that would favour great brevity and more arresting presentation, Beddington immediately recognized the need for a fresh approach, not least for car drivers whose consumption of petrol would benefit Shell. He commissioned Betjeman to produce a guide to Cornwall, a part of the country he knew well. It came out in 1934; Betjeman initially proposed an over-long title, *Cornwall Illustrated in a series of views of Castles, Seats of the Nobility, Mines, Picturesque Scenery, Towns, Public Buildings, Antiquities*, as a mocking reproach to the 19th-century approach.

Two years later Betjeman, now editor of the Shell Guides, commissioned Paul Nash to write a Shell Guide to Dorset. Nash deliberately set out to abandon the *Highways and Byways* tradition, announcing that he wanted to give 'the most straightforward view of the county's resources *as they are* today'. For reasons of space, he explained, 'historical references, anecdotes and legends have been ruthlessly curtailed'.[12] This, combined with his emphasis on the Iron Age hillfort Maiden Castle and other prehistoric sites, presented 'a landscape that was fundamentally at odds with conventional perceptions of quaint England'.[13]

Opportunities to visit the countryside were further encouraged by the establishment of the Youth Hostels Association (1929), the formation of the Ramblers' Association (1932) and the passing of the Footpaths Act (1934), which not only established new footpaths but also reopened many that had become closed or overgrown. Meanwhile, the ordinary person's leisure time had increased owing to the reduction early in the interwar period of the average working week from fifty-six to forty-eight hours, while in 1938 the Holidays with Pay Act further encouraged the wider public to make use of the countryside as a place for refreshment.

Reporting in art on this development, James Walker Tucker may have surprised viewers in 1936 with his suggestion that women had as much right as men to experience the freedoms associated with hiking. His *Hiking* (1936) has a startling immediacy and a sociological realism, even though the picture is highly contrived. His three young women are well kitted out, though their prim footwear seems a long way behind the later preference for walking boots or trainers, and the strong light appears to be sunlight but has none of its radiant power. All paintings make use of artifice, but here the landscape seems counterfeit. A drystone wall creates the setting and in the background a manor house is dropped in, improbably without garden, behind the figure on the left. The expected church is found on her right, and on the other side of the picture is glimpsed a stone-built village. The landscape information is sufficient for the viewer to imagine that these women are hiking in the Peak District, or the Yorkshire Dales, or Northumberland. Interestingly, the three hikers are not looking at the landscape but at a map, to check their whereabouts or ascertain their route. The centrality of the map helps create another sociological marker. It is very obviously a one-inch-to-the-mile Ordnance Survey map, a product of the Ordnance Survey Office, Britain's national mapping agency. This size of map first appeared in 1805 and went through many editions. A circular in 1909 defined it as a 'touring, cycling and small-scale manoeuvre map, [with] the primary object being that the average man should be able to find his way about unfamiliar country with ease'.[14] But Edric Holmes, in *London's Countryside*, had no specific gender in mind when he told his readers that 'the popular Ordnance "one inch map" will be found indispensable in any systematic exploration of the Home Counties'.[15]

The Ordnance Survey Office was extremely busy in the twenties and thirties,[16] devising maps in different scales and formats – all of which appeared under the royal crest and the proud heading 'Ordnance Survey of Great Britain', further

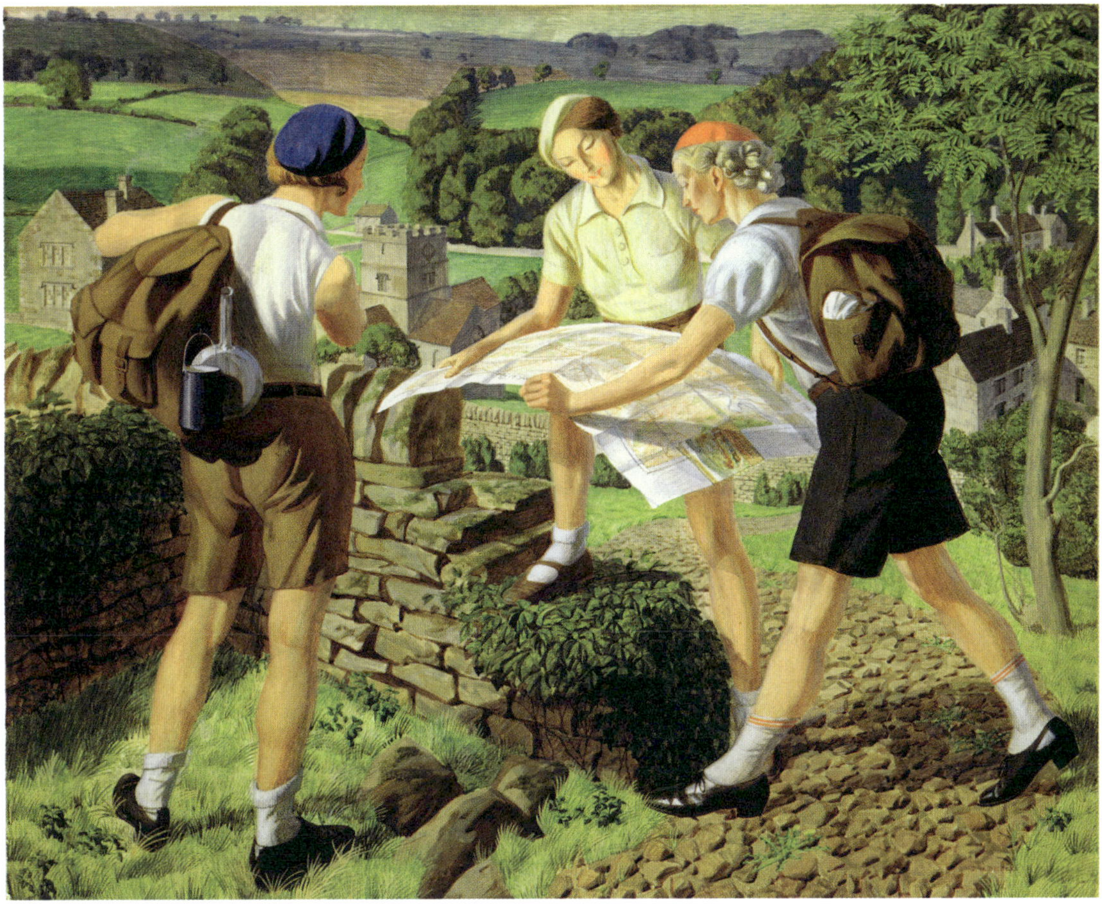

James Walker Tucker, *Hiking*,
oil on canvas, 1936.

upholding their topographic authority. Their use of symbols, colours, lines and shapes to represent roads, footpaths, urban areas, railways, woods, orchards and formal parkland, as well as areas of rough pasture, rivers, streams and much more, made them readily understandable, and much pleasure was to be had by those who enjoyed roving over the landscape from the comfort of an armchair. These maps fed into a growing leisure market, made the countryside more accessible and understandable, and established in the public imagination the characteristics of England's landscape in a new and more definite way.

Yet simultaneously the English countryside had begun to give rise to a sense of loss. This underlay Holmes's remark about the vanished landscapes between the Chiltern Hills and the North Downs caused by development. While the more patriotic guidebooks, celebrating the British or English landscape, tried to suggest a timelessness associated with long-standing traditions and values, the reality was that England's landscape was vulnerable to change, decay, agriculture development and destruction. Its productivity was damaged when the Agriculture Act, guaranteeing minimum wages and minimum product prices, was repealed in 1921, at a time when the government faced a potential subsidy bill of £20 million – a sum that far exceeded the subsidy given to any other industry. The savage reduction in wages caused by this loss of subsidy, together with a further blow caused by the removal of restrictions on Canadian grain, started an agricultural depression that increased rural poverty, left some land lying waste and brought about further emigration to towns. In 1931, the onset of the Depression cancelled out what minor recoveries had been made in the 1920s.

Help came in the 1930s with the creation of marketing boards for various subsectors of the farming industry, which enhanced production while government-imposed tariffs restricted some imports. But it was wartime subsidies and tariffs that brought full recovery, and farmers temporarily experienced unprecedented wealth. Memory of the preceding period was not easily forgotten, however, and is best described by the author and farmer Adrian Bell in his *Men and the Fields* (1939), where one farmer says: 'If I had my time over again, I wouldn't be a farmer, though I love it. There's no living in it now.'[17] The book was illustrated with drawings and colour lithographs by John Nash, a great celebrant not of beauty spots but of ordinary, unromantic working landscape. His illustrations for *Men and the Fields* have an immediate sympathy with the text; Nash and Bell enjoyed a working friendship and shared a deep love of nature, and of East Anglia and the Stour Valley in particular.

Another threat to landscape was the quickening pace of development between the wars. Four million new homes were built in England during this period, contributing to the growth of suburbia, the rapid building of new arterial roads and bypasses, and the hideous spread of ribbon development. One prominent voice among those protestors who felt development had got out of hand was Clough Williams-Ellis, whose *Britain and the Beast* (1937) contained a collection of essays examining the threat to England's countryside made by modern industrial society. 'We are all now apprehensively aware', he wrote, 'that a mere handful of active speculators of only average barbarity can quite easily destroy the virginity of a whole territory in no more than a year or two.'[18] This realization of the speed at which beauty could be destroyed had earlier been communicated by Gerard Manley Hopkins in his 1879 poem 'Binsley Poplars', about the felling of the eponymous trees:

> After-comers cannot guess the beauty been.
> Ten or twelve, only ten or twelve
> Strokes of havoc unselve
> The sweet especial scene
> Rural scene, a rural scene,
> Sweet especial rural scene.[19]

To protect the landscape and to conserve English heritage, the Council for the Preservation of Rural England (now the Campaign to Protect Rural England) was formed in 1926. Ten years later, the National Trust was enhanced by the creation of its Historic Country Houses Scheme. But 1936 was also the year in which Hitler sent his army into the Rhineland, a sign to many that a second world war had become a possibility, and with it the likelihood of attack and invasion. A threat to England's architectural heritage and to its landscape was now felt from without as well as within. It does not surprise that an undertow of melancholy begins to enter landscapes and architectural scenes of the late 1930s. Readers of Paul Nash's *Shell Guide to Dorset*, published in 1936, found it dedicated to 'the landowners of Dorset, the Council for the Preservation of Rural England, the Society for the Protection of Ancient Buildings, and all those courageous enemies of "Development" to whom we owe what is left of England'.[20]

Dymchurch, on the Kent coast, with its vast expanses of flat sand, is dominated by its sea wall. Originally built by the Romans, it runs today for almost four miles in length in order to protect Romney Marsh, a good part of which is below the mean high tide level. It was here, in the wake of the First World War, that Paul Nash went through an intensely romantic period.

Romantic art often expresses a charged relationship between the artist and nature, triggered by a sense of drama to be found, say, in mysterious woods or a rocky landscape, or in atmosphere, the weather or the seasons. But if nature is the catalyst, an inner responsiveness on the part of the artist is needed to bring about a romantic vision; in John Piper's words, this is 'a vision that can see in these things something significant beyond ordinary significance: something that for a moment seems to contain the whole world; and, when the moment is past, carries over some comment on life and experience besides the comment on appearances'.[21]

'First sight of Dymchurch-under-the-wall', Paul Nash wrote, when making notes in 1919 for an autobiography that he would never finish.[22] These words signal the importance to him of a place he had visited at the invitation of Raymonde Collignon, a French singer and *diseuse* who wanted to discuss with him a design for the cover of a songbook. The outcome must have pleased her as she afterwards gave a concert in Nash's studio, almost certainly at 9 Fitzroy Street, the studio briefly lent to the Nashes by the artist William Tryon in November 1919 and where Nash held a private show of his drawings. Early in 1920, he and Margaret returned to their small flat in Judd Street, which looked onto the St Pancras Hotel.

Paul Nash's Dymchurch period began in the summer of 1920. The previous summer he and his wife had spent some weeks living at the Red Lion at Whiteleaf, in the Chilterns, so that Paul could paint the countryside and be in easy reach of his brother John and his wife Christine, a former Slade student. While there, they realized that they no longer wanted to live in London. Then in December 1919 Paul received terrific acclaim when 'The Nation's War Paintings' opened at the Royal Academy and ran through to February 1920. 'Triumph of "The Menin Road"' is the phrase he noted down in preparation for his autobiography.[23] Yet simultaneously he experienced a humiliating public reprimand. Back in April 1919, to bring in some earnings, he had begun writing art criticism for *New Witness* magazine under the pseudonym Robert Derriman. Using this as a cover, he had praised his brother's work in print as well as that of his friends, and even penned a few phrases in favour of his own. This lack of integrity was exposed by the critic Frank Rutter in the *Arts Gazette* in December 1919, and in January Nash had to write a shaming apology.

The friendship Nash established around this time with artist and designer Claud Lovat Fraser and his wife Grace led to their sharing his interest in Dymchurch, and they too began to visit it. In the summer of 1920 the Nashes rented 2 Rose Cottages, behind the sea wall at Dymchurch, and for a while the Lovat Frasers shared it with them. Together Paul and Lovat (as his friends called him) explored the Marsh,[24] and by May 1921 Paul was describing this coastal town as a 'delightful place with much inspiring material for work'.[25] However, his equanimity was shortly to be destroyed. At the age of thirty-one, Lovat Fraser fell seriously ill with a duodenal ulcer in the house at Dymchurch. He was taken into hospital and operated on, but

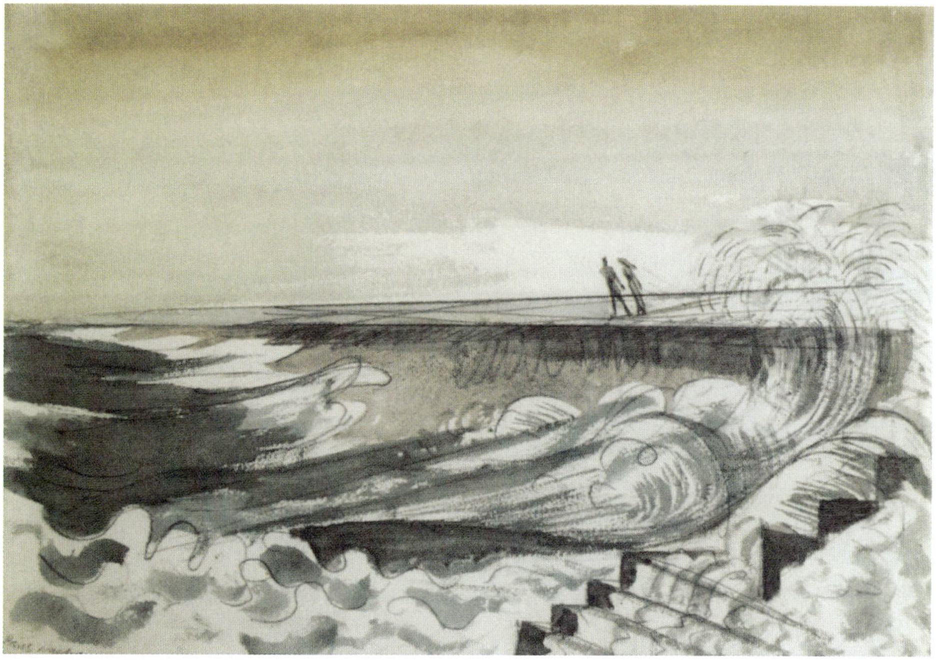

Paul Nash, *The Sea Wall, Dymchurch 1919*,
ink, chalk and watercolour on paper, 1919.

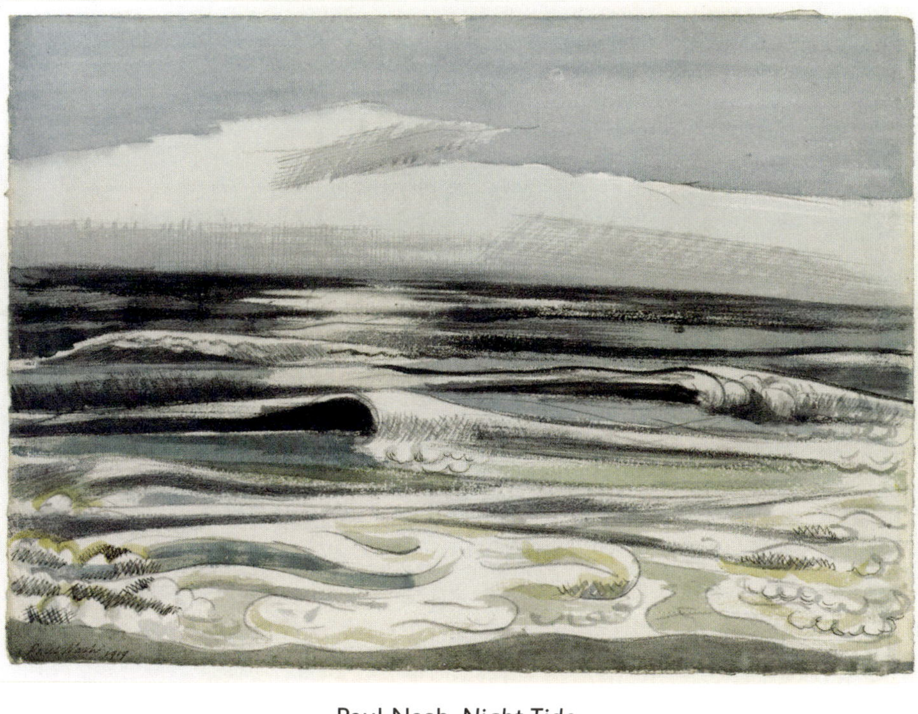

Paul Nash, *Night Tide*,
ink, chalk and watercolour on paper, 1919.

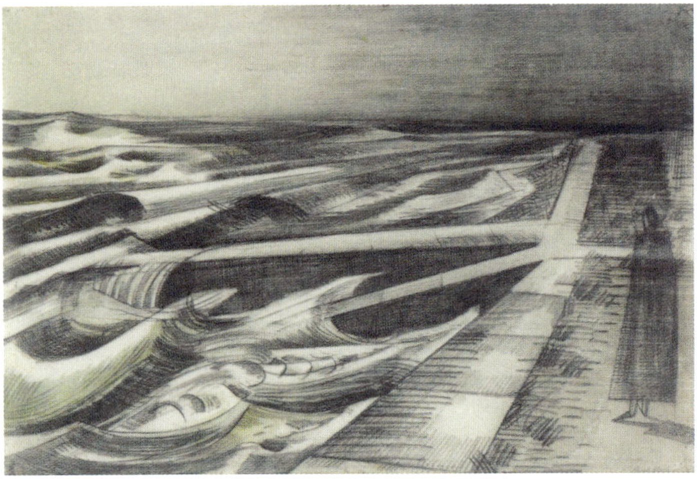

Paul Nash,
Night Tide, Dymchurch,
pencil and wash
on paper, 1922.

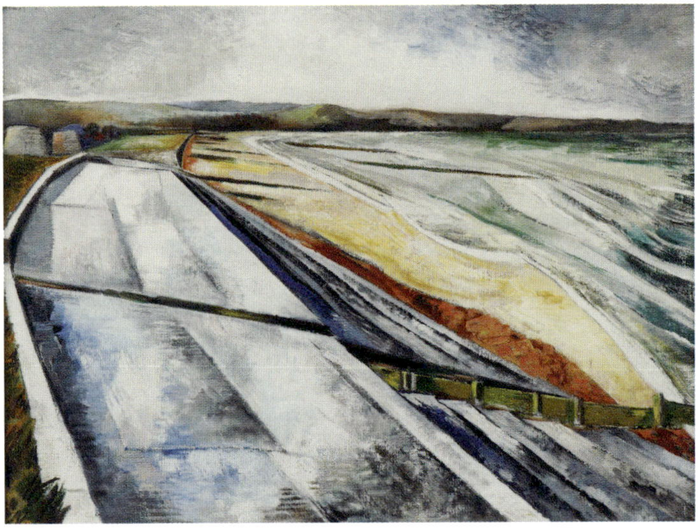

Paul Nash,
Dymchurch, Kent,
oil on canvas,
c. 1921–2.

soon after died. Nash was deeply disturbed by the sudden loss of his friend and went with Grace Lovat Fraser to visit her parents-in-law so that she could break the news about their son. Then in September 1921, while staying with his own parents-in-law in Hillingdon, Nash visited his father at Iver Heath in Buckinghamshire and found him lying on the floor, seemingly dead. (In fact, he had suffered a minor heart attack brought on by influenza.) Coming relatively soon after the prolonged strain of reliving his wartime experiences for the sake of his war paintings, these two shocks may have triggered the breakdown that subsequently left Nash unconscious for a week. 'I get up in the night and fall down. Black out,' so his notes record.

Equally dramatic is his next revelation that his wife took charge and 'defied five doctors',[26] with the result that he was taken, still unconscious, to the Hospital for Nervous Disease in London's Queen's Square, where he was diagnosed with encephalitis, a form of meningitis. His biographer, Anthony Bertram, voices the accepted view that 'suppressed war strain aggravated by his recent strain and shock' was the underlying cause.[27]

Nash was forbidden to work, and quickly recovered. After only four weeks he was back in Dymchurch, where initially he confined his attention to the making of theatre models for two plays by Gordon Bottomley. Later on, his perceptions of Dymchurch were to filter into his theatre designs. But of more immediate urgency were three large things: 'I begin painting again,' his notes reveal. 'The Sea. The Shore. The Wall.'[28]

Although the Nashes made frequent visits elsewhere and kept the Judd Street flat as a pied-à-terre, Dymchurch remained their base for four years. In 1923 they moved from 2 Rose Cottages to Pantile Cottage on the road to Lydd, which gave Nash a broad view of Romney Marsh, an ancient landscape with associations going back to Roman times. But his chief obsession had become the sea wall. 'The architecture of the Dymchurch Wall', writes Margaret Nash, 'with its majestic sweep facing the approaching and receding sea: this provided him with endless designs and ideas for pictures.'[29] These were executed in a variety of media – oils, watercolours, pen-and-ink or pencil drawings, etchings, lithographs and wood engravings – and they express a range of emotional energies, at moments tender and enquiring, at other times harsh and austere.

The repetitiveness of the imagery suggests that Nash had something he needed to tackle and allay. It is generally accepted that at Dymchurch he continued to work through his memories of the war. Having done this in relation to the major public statement that *The Menin Road* represents, he now needed an outlet for less comprehensible feelings. Emma Chambers, the lead curator behind a 2016 Paul Nash exhibition at Tate Britain, finds two of his Dymchurch oil paintings, *Wall Against the Sea* (1922) and *The Shore* (1923), 'resonant with his war experiences in their exploration of threat and defence, the geometric forms of the sea wall echoing the zig-zag rhythm of the trenches'.[30] The coastal defences that protect Romney Marsh may also have resonated with Nash's need to protect his own sanity from a returning flood of memories of the war. The late Andrew Causey, who remains a leading authority on Nash, described the sea wall as 'a bastion of certainty against the uncertain moods and motions of the water' and claimed that Nash identified it in his mind with himself.[31]

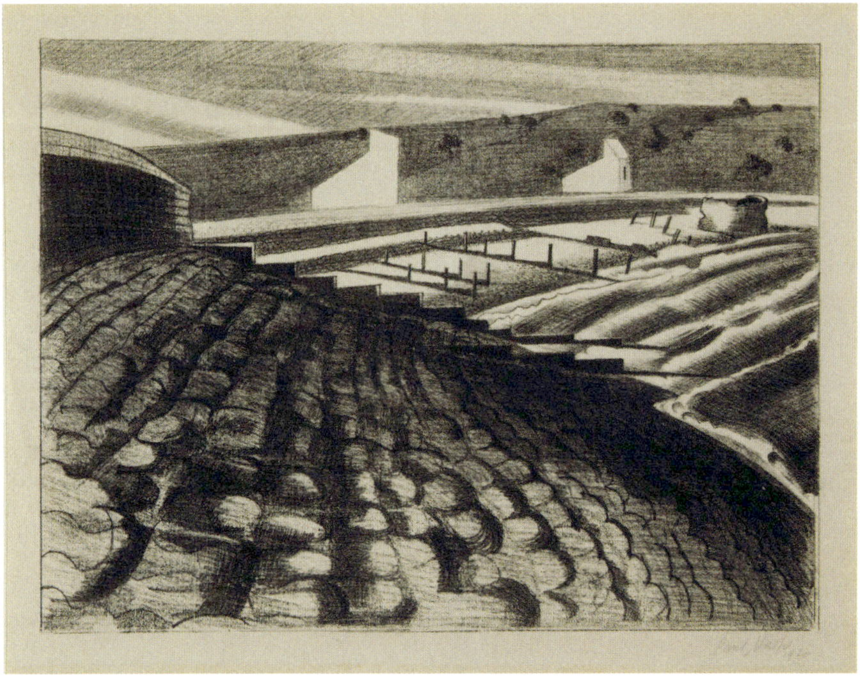

Paul Nash, *Strange Coast*,
lithograph, 1920.

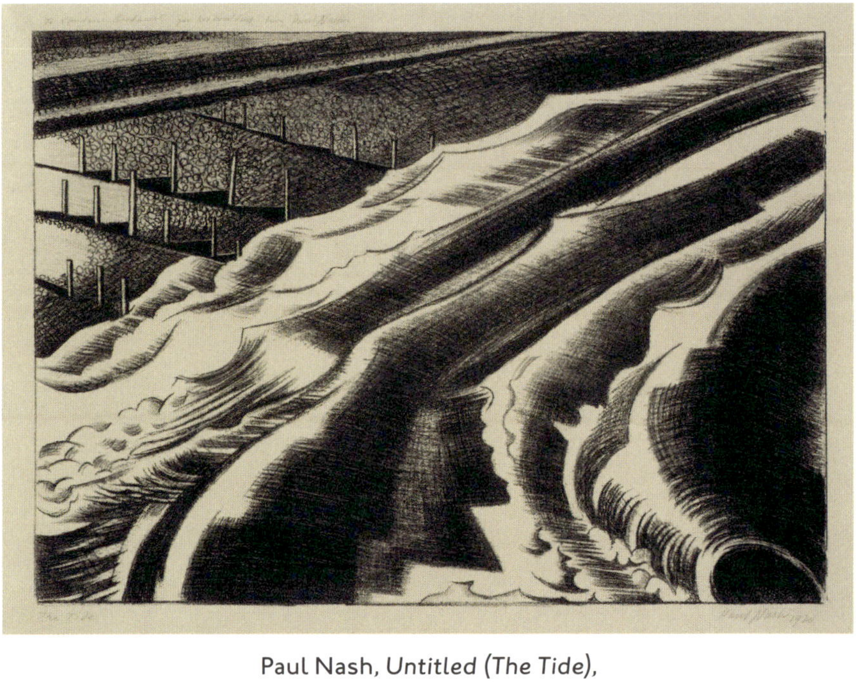

Paul Nash, *Untitled (The Tide)*,
lithograph, 1920.

It is possible that he may also have identified himself with the sea, in all its changing moods. One of his earliest watercolours of Dymchurch, dating from 1919, shows waves beating up against a corner of the wall where it meets some steps, while two small figures, identifiable as a man and a woman, cast a late afternoon shadow as they take a brisk walk along the top of the wall. Using mostly pencil and watercolour, Nash has worked at speed and with brio. The overall mood of the picture is one of happiness, the sea, if anything, being a cause for gaiety. Another early drawing of the sea, *Night Tide*, signed and dated '1919', was bought by Campbell Dodgson, then Keeper of Prints and Drawings at the British Museum,[32] from a private show of his drawings which Nash held in his studio in late 1919. Again, it is a predominantly naturalistic study, depicting gently lapping waves and encroaching darkness. Nash made another drawing titled *Night Tide* in 1922, by which time he was honing the patterns created by the waves into stylized shapes that have a sharper rhythm. The romantic nature of this image is heightened by the late addition of a tall, cloaked female figure on the far right, made spectral by the fact that the path in the background shows through her body. Interestingly, in an interview with William Gaunt in 1926, Nash shied off discussion of this work because he thought it too romantic. In 1931, when the work came up for sale at Sotheby's, he asked a friend to buy it back for him, after which it remained in his possession.[33]

By 1920 Nash was experimenting with lithography, and two very striking images of Dymchurch exist in this medium. One, called *Strange Coast*, offers a more conventional view, in that we look down and across at the sea and wall from a hill, possibly part of the wall, covered in cobbles. The second is *Untitled (The Tide)*, the additional subtitle probably added for cataloguing purposes. The parts are still recognizable, in that a glimpse of the sea wall and rows of wooden piles appear in the top left corner, but a flood of water covers the greater part of the image from top to bottom, giving the overall picture an almost abstract quality. Together the images hint at how disturbing Nash found Dymchurch.

Nash's seas are varied and unfathomable. As with his earlier representation of trees, the repetitive focus on this subject suggests a possible symbolism; but Nash never systematized his symbolical references, nor did he see himself as the inheritor of any stable iconographic tradition. His love of Romantic poetry would have left him familiar with the association of the sea with eternity and the horror of death. And Causey, in more than one place, when writing about Nash's work at Dymchurch, draws our attention to Shelley's poem 'Time' and these lines:

> Unfathomable Sea! Whose waves are years,
> Oceans of Time, whose waters of deep woe
> Are brackish with the salt of human tears![34]

Nash's awareness of the ancient terror of the sea may have helped exorcise the terror that war had etched into his memory. The wall, together with the repeated beat set up by receding groynes and the wide open beach, conveys an enormous stretch of space disappearing into the horizon. But in this harsh setting, the mood more usually found in Nash's art is not one of release or elation but of tension, struggle and alienation.

A striking contrast is presented by Ben Nicholson's *1923 (Dymchurch)*. He and Nash had been companions at the Slade, and that year Ben and his wife Winifred arrived at Dymchurch to spend a few days with the Nashes. For this painting, Nicholson turned his back on the omnipresent wall and looked directly at the sea, dividing the painting into beach, sea and sky. Patches of light and shade on sand and sea, with its incipient waves, are translated into unfussed horizontal strips and patches of colour held together by subtle alterations in tone and hue as well as warm/cool colour contrasts. The picture is more compact, sensuous and painterly than most of Nash's Dymchurch works. Although Nicholson moves the eye across sand, sea and sky, the painting does not convey the same sense of journeying through landscape that is found so repeatedly in Nash's images of Dymchurch. Nor does Nicholson attend to weather sensations such as the lashing of waves, wind and rain, which Nash sometimes employs.

An additional poignancy is created when Nash shows a single figure or a couple walking along the wall. The solitary figure alone within nature is a familiar romantic trope. Causey, however, reminds us that Nash 'was distressed by the memory of the lonely figures living and dying in the great waste' of Passchendaele, and therefore suggests that these ghostlike figures, haunting the largely featureless space of Dymchurch, became in Nash's mind revenants returning from the mass death that he had earlier witnessed, to this other barren and threatened corner of the world.[35] Christopher Neve, on the other hand, refers to the 'vacant stare' of Nash's Dymchurch pictures, arguing that 'vacancy' was now Nash's preoccupation, his mind having been 'emptied by the horrors of war'. He continues: 'He showed how concrete ramps and army-grey shingle sloped into the grey sea towards France. It was a landscape that replaced the urgency of suffering with the vacant afternoon of no feeling at all.'[36]

First-time visitors to Dymchurch often need to readjust their sense of scale. Conventional understanding of the meeting between land, sea and sky falls away and a sense of strangeness takes hold. Time withdraws, as it does in a theatre when we sit looking at an empty stage, waiting for the drama to begin. Nash himself was intensely responsive to the poetry of the theatre, and at Dymchurch he reimagined its sea wall as taking part in an ongoing drama.

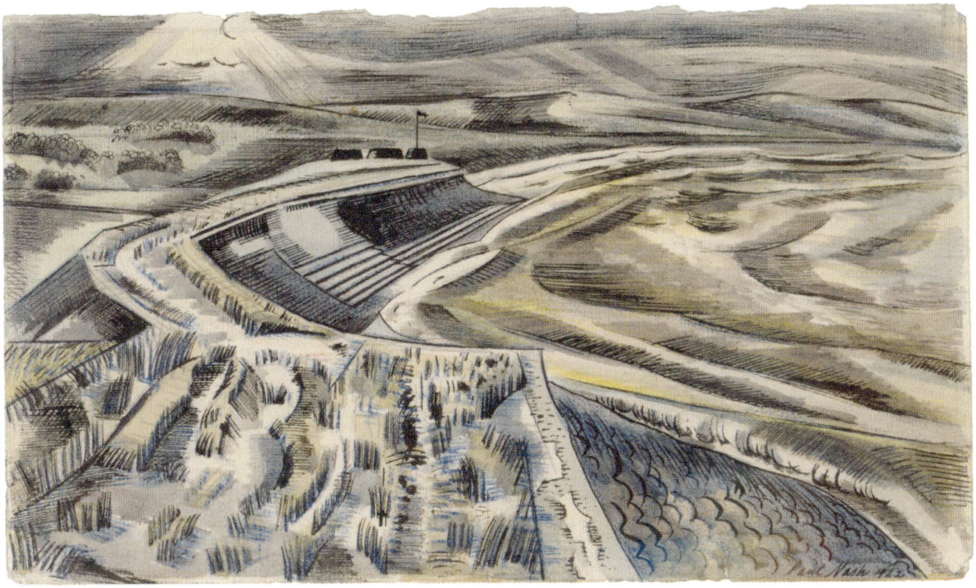

Paul Nash, *Dymchurch, Kent*,
watercolour and ink on paper, 1922.

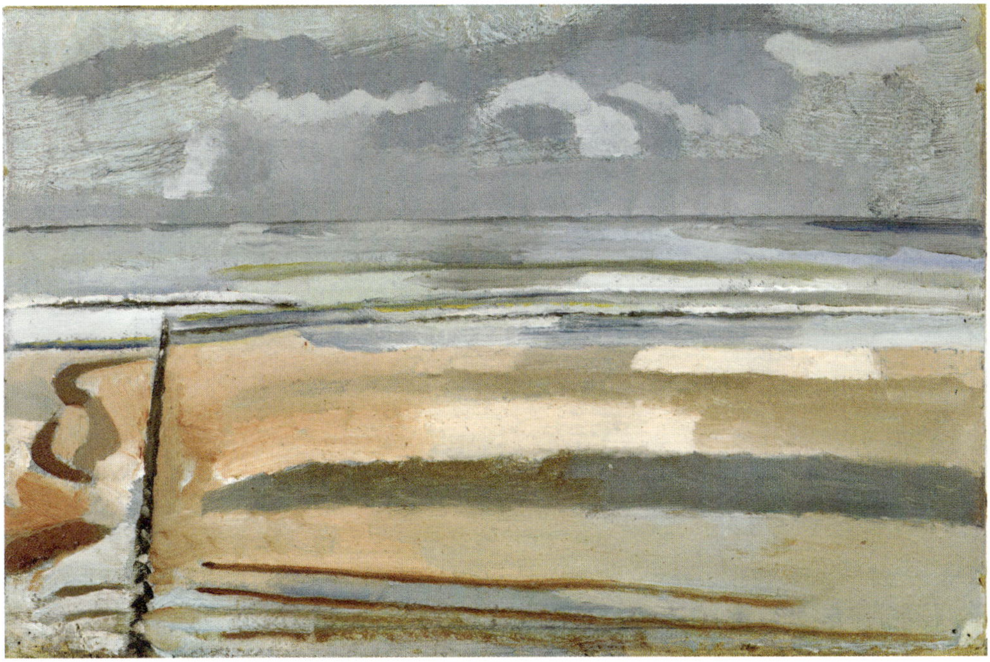

Ben Nicholson, *1923 (Dymchurch)*,
oil on canvas mounted on board, 1923.

Paul Nash had been interested in theatre from the age of twenty. In 1910 he had borrowed the script of Gordon Bottomley's play *The Crier by Night* from a neighbour. When the thirty-two-page quarto was returned, the owner noticed that two drawings had been added. They were shown to Bottomley, who was so impressed by their originality of technique and imaginative power that he wrote to Nash. In turn, Nash was delighted by Bottomley's discriminating praise. Despite a difference in age of some fifteen years, the two men became friends, sharing interests in art, the theatre and literature, with Bottomley acting as a mentor to the younger man.

Although around thirty-five when they met, Bottomley was already leading the life of an invalid owing to severe haemorrhages. But if his physical life was constrained, he nevertheless led 'a life of passionate intense meditation and contemplation' owing to his deep love of literature and art and ability to write poems and plays.[37] His belief that art was 'a distillation of life and nature',[38] not a record or a commentary, chimed with Nash's stance as a painter. Bottomley and his wife Emily were avid collectors of art, especially the work of the Pre-Raphaelites, and eventually gave their entire collection, numbering some 600 works, to Tullie House Museum and Art Gallery in Carlisle. Owing to the benign atmosphere that Bottomley created around himself, he reminded Nash of 'a kindly unwarlike old Northern God who in happier times might have lived in a grove and dispensed oracle'.[39]

Nash evidently felt at home with the Bottomleys and wrote regularly to them about his work and his unfolding career.[40] But their shared interest in theatre was a central ingredient in their friendship. Nash undertook designs for two of Bottomley's plays, *King Lear's Wife* and *Gruach*, first performed in 1920 and 1921 respectively. Although the designs did not go into production, they found their way into exhibitions and were also published as illustrations in magazines. In his understanding of the theatre Nash had been greatly stimulated by reading Edward Gordon Craig's *On the Art of the Theatre*, although when he met Craig he was disappointed to encounter a man who, he felt, had 'shot his bolt'.[41] This did not diminish Nash's interest in the theatre and work by him was included in the 1922 International Theatre Exhibition, which opened in Amsterdam and then came to London's Victoria and Albert Museum between 2 June and 21 July 1922. Nash visited the exhibition as often as he could. It included his designs for Bottomley's plays as well as a drop curtain design for J. M. Barrie's *The Truth about the Russian Dancers* and a drawing titled 'A Platform facing the Sea'. This last relates to no known play, but mention of it recurs two years later in a letter from Nash to Bottomley: Nash states that he looks forward to carrying on 'the Dymchurch drama of The Platform facing the Sea.'[42]

Two drawings with this title were reproduced by Andrew Causey in 1980. They are also shown here, as a reminder that both affirm their connection with Dymchurch through the sea wall. One is subtitled 'Dawn', which explains the long shadows cast by the two tiny figures, one standing on the sea wall facing the sea with his arms raised above his head, the other standing watching from behind at a lower level. The figure with raised arms is framed by two thin vertical lines, possibly reminiscent of flagpoles or suggestive of a sheet of glass between the figure and the actual sea. Around the edge of the drawing is a framing device that affirms the stage-like setting. It is and is not Dymchurch, for it has been distanced and made strange by the influence of German expressionist theatre or film. Herman Ould, writing about the other of these two drawings, shown in the International Theatre Exhibition, pointed to 'the rhythmic dynamism characteristic of the best Continental work'.[43] Causey concludes that the 'cold clarity' of the drawings is intended to convey a 'charged and threatening' atmosphere.[44]

'The Platform facing the Sea' drawings affirm Nash's association of Dymchurch with psychological drama. The setting has become a theatre for memory and existential identity. Frances Yates, who wrote the first modern book on the history of the art of memory, reminds us that St Augustine of Hippo pondered deeply on this subject. Still today we know little about memory or where it is, but it is thought to be not a single faculty but a set of processes or the product of multiple systems. To some extent this notion chimes with Augustine's belief that memory is activated by space and its behaviour is versatile. His famous meditation on memory begins:

> I come to the fields and spacious palaces of memory (*campos et lata praetoria memoriae*), where are the treasures (*thesauri*) of innumerable images, brought into it from things of all sorts perceived by the senses. There is stored up, whatever beside we think, either by enlarging or diminishing, or any other way varying those things which the sense has come to; and whatever else hath been committed and laid up, which forgetfulness hath not yet swallowed and buried. When I enter there, I require instantly what I will to be brought forth, and something instantly comes; others must be longer sought after, which are fetched, as it were out of some inner receptacle; others rush out in troops, and while one thing is desired and required, they start forth, as who should say 'Is it perchance I?'[45]

In addition to fields and spacious palaces of memory, Augustine also refers to the 'vast court' of memory (*in aula ingeni memoriae*) and its large and boundless chamber (*penetrale amplum et infinitum*). These metaphorical large empty spaces and caverns are, in Augustine's words, 'innumerable and innumerably full of innumerable kinds of things'. Yates argues that sensory images of this kind are used by

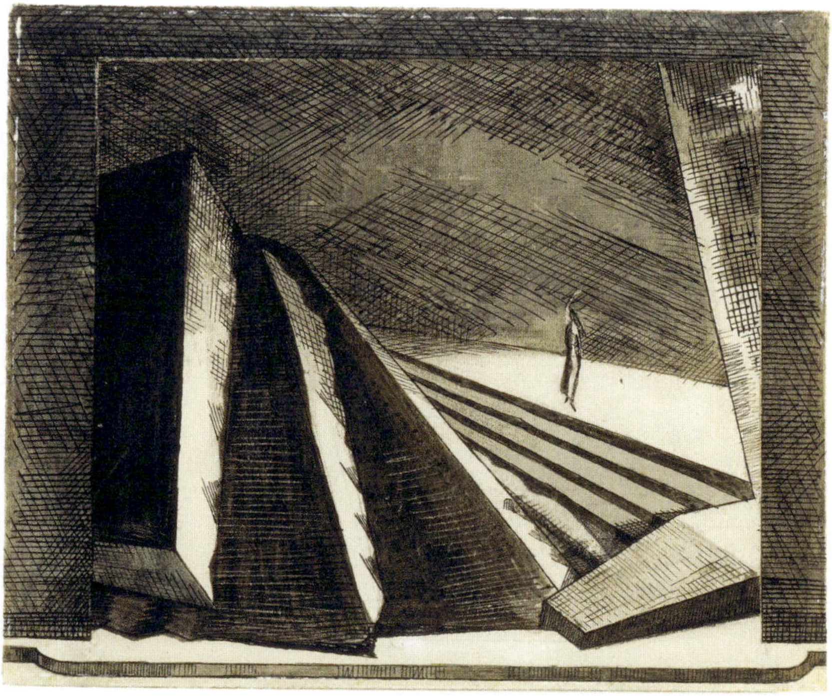

Paul Nash, Design for The Platform Facing the Sea,
gouache and ink on paper, 1922.

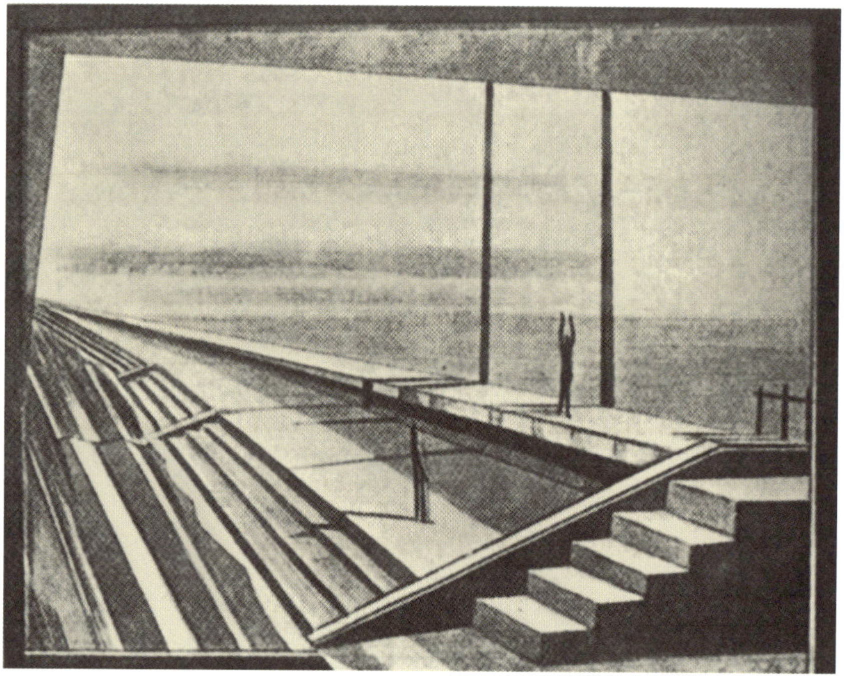

Paul Nash, *A Platform Facing the Sea (Dawn)*,
ink, pencil and watercolour, 1922.

Augustine because much memory comes to us through the eyes and through our experience of space, as is also suggested by Augustine's linking of the architecture of the mind with memory's vast, echoing chamber. Awareness of this makes it unlikely that Dymchurch induced in Nash 'the vacant afternoon of no feeling at all'. Memories, called or uncalled, came and went. It was a site where past, present and future could be revisited, weighed up and worked through, with the sea, shore, steps and wall serving as mnemonics.

Photography was to play an important role in Paul Nash's art. It helped bring out the extraordinary breadth and originality of his imagery. In an article for the *Listener*, he drew attention to the 'peculiar power of the camera to discover formal beauty which ordinarily is hidden from the human eye'.[46] The single mechanical eye of the camera, with its cold impersonality, can uncover patterns normally obscured by the human eye's habitual tendency to interpret much of what we see in terms of function and use. If Nash employed the camera's depersonalized objectivity to bring

Black and white photograph of Dymchurch taken by Paul Nash.

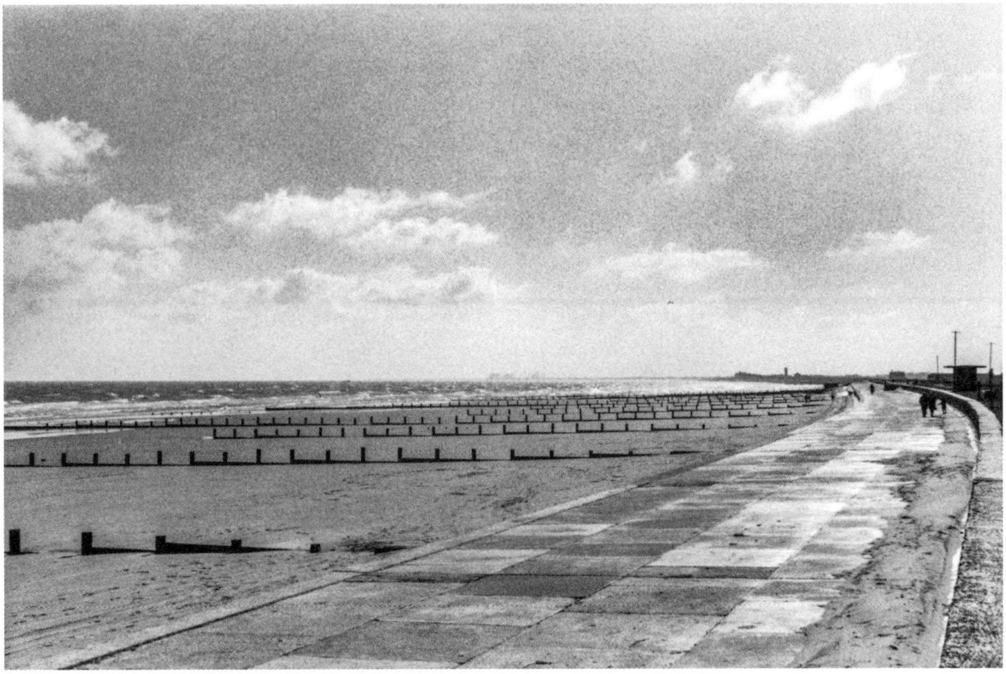

out the design element in art, it also opened his mind in the 1930s to the strange or uncanny, which became a mode valued by the surrealists. This was an interest he shared with Eileen Agar, as will be mentioned in Chapter 11.

Equally telling is the sense of melancholy loss that accompanies awareness of death which he embedded in one of his still lifes, *Dead Spring*. This can be felt even before we acquire the information that Nash painted the picture soon after the death of his father in 1929. The withered plant positioned on the windowsill of Nash's flat in Judd Street reminds the viewer how damaging a sudden, harsh overnight frost in early spring can be. But the complexity of this picture owes much to Nash's insistence on merging the central image of the plant with a set of architect's or draughtsman's tools, including a ruler resting against the window divide and a set square leaning against the plant pot. This last, although transparent, alters the colour of the pot, dividing it into light and dark. The opening in the middle of the set square not only echoes its triangular shape but also repeats the light/dark contrast in inverted form. The abstract shape of the triangle, initially observed in the set square, appears repeatedly in the picture, even in the outline created by the string wound round the three wooden rods that hold the plant in position. This use of geometry stiffens the image and throws into contrast the collapse of the plant, while further play with abstraction can be observed in the geometric structure that appears outside the window and leads the eye towards a section of roof, beneath which is an area of such dense black that it has a tomblike finality. The matrix of geometrical shapes in this picture led Causey to suggest that Nash is here thinking about the 'artist as geometer', as a person who can gain some control over organic life.[47]

Much of the literature on Paul Nash emphasizes the formalist aspect of his art, and rightly so. His writings reveal that his interest in art was underpinned by a belief in the importance of design. When he wrote to *The Times* on 2 June 1933 to announce the creation of a new artists' group called Unit One – a group of eleven artists committed to 'the expression of a truly contemporary spirit' – it was because he himself felt the recurrent weakness in English art to be a 'lack of structural purpose'. His letter states: 'This immunity from the responsibility of design has become a tradition....Nature we need not deny, but art, we are inclined to feel, should control.'[48]

His love of firm design is clearly expressed in *The Rye Marshes* (1932), a painting made specifically for reproduction as a Shell poster. Here an inlet zig-zags out to sea, styled with vorticist precision. Nash's need for aesthetic control did not end with the canvas: he was equally concerned with the niceties of presentation, framing his pictures beautifully and keeping his drawings ready mounted. Visitors to his studio always found it tidy and well ordered. His correctness gave him the air of a trim naval officer. His mother's family had served in the navy, and only his weakness at mathematics and his failure of some exams had prevented the young Paul from following in the same profession.

More than any other artist, Paul Nash reinvigorated the English landscape tradition in modern terms. Initially his drawings and watercolours owed much to literature, especially his reading of poetry, for early on he developed an admiration for Keats, Coleridge and Blake and an overriding interest in Dante Gabriel Rossetti, both as artist and poet. Some of his earliest drawings were inspired by George Borrow's *Lavengro*. Later, in 1916, as part of his military training, he was sent to Hare Hall in Essex, where his map-reading instructor turned out to be the poet Edward Thomas, whom he also admired; and for much of his life he maintained his lengthy correspondence with Bottomley, who remained a loyal friend. But if

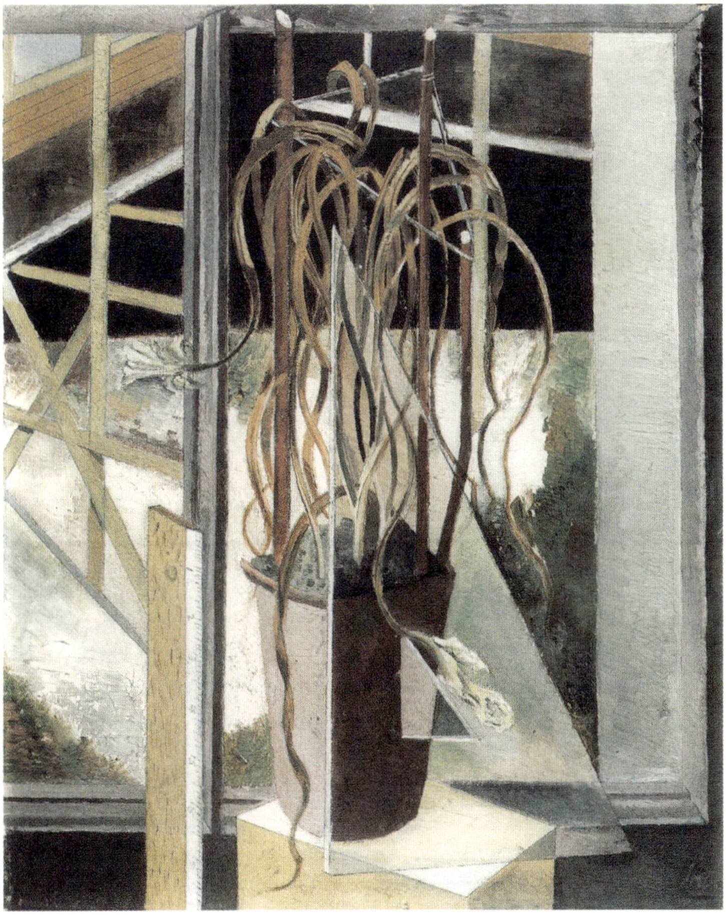

Paul Nash, *Dead Spring*, oil on canvas, 1929.

the imaginative power in his early drawings and watercolours owes much to the influence of literature, once he began to focus on the outer world he found himself able to transfer a similar depth of feeling to his drawings of nature; this was the beginning of his interest in the *genius loci*.

When Nash tired of the coastline at Dymchurch, he went inland and painted, among other things, *Sandling Park* (1924) near Hythe, returning again to his love of trees and bringing an understanding of Cézanne to his search for a satisfying compositional design, in calmer vein. In 1925, he put Dymchurch behind him. 'I shall never work there anymore,' he wrote to a friend, adding: '...a place like that and its effect on me – one's effect on it. It's a curious record formally and psychologically when you see the whole set of designs together.'[49] Although he returned to an unfinished picture, *Winter Sea*, in later years, he never painted again in Dymchurch after 1925. In 1932 he returned to photograph it, for reasons unknown.

Having a more cerebral, hugely talented and restlessly ambitious elder brother cannot have been easy for John Nash. It was a position that Gilbert Spencer suffered in relation to his brother Stanley, and it is perhaps not surprising that John and Gilbert became close friends; John, wearing tweeds and looking nervous, was best man at Gilbert's wedding.[50]

Although he began his career on an equal footing with his brother, John gradually became overshadowed by Paul's vaulting reputation. Only recently has he come more fully into view, owing to the publication of a substantial monograph and a full biography.[51]

John Nash readily admitted his debt to Paul. He doubted that he would have started making pictures had not his elder brother spent his childhood endlessly drawing. Other aspects of their childhood bonded them further. Both received their earliest experience of landscape from Kensington Gardens, owing to its proximity to their first family home. The family moved out of London in 1901, when Paul was twelve and John eight, to Iver Heath, Buckinghamshire; their father hoped that this rural setting would cure his wife, Caroline, of her mental problems, for she had developed a habit of sitting motionless for long periods of time and staring vacantly into space. His hopes were not fulfilled. During one disturbed bout in 1904 she attacked John with a butcher's knife, after which she mostly lived apart from her children. The house at Iver Heath was eventually let and the family decanted into a boarding house so that enough money could be found to pay for a private sanatorium for Caroline; but even in 1901 it would seem she could not properly be part of the family. When the three children, Paul, Barbara and John, posed for a family photograph taken by a professional photographer, their mother was absent;

the woman in the centre of the picture is their nurse, Harriet Luckett. Caroline Nash died in 1910, just as her two sons were setting out on their careers. Her illness and death may explain why the relationship between the two brothers remained close.

Although Paul showed some of his younger brother's drawings to William Rothenstein, then principal of the Royal College of Art, John, then still a schoolboy, had no intention of becoming an artist. However, neither he nor anyone else seemed to know what he should do or be instead. It was suggested that he try for a place at Oxford, as he took a scholarly interest in things.

A formative influence on John Nash at the age of ten, as he recalled towards the end of his life, had been a short story called 'Eyes, and No Eyes', which stirred his interest in observation – as it did also in the young John Ruskin. It had initially been part of *Evenings at Home*, a collection of stories by Dr John Aikin and his sister Mrs Barbauld, first published in 1817. Its full title – *Evenings at Home, or The Juvenile budget opened. Consisting of a Variety of miscellaneous pieces for the instruction and amusement of young persons* – explains its purpose, for it upholds the educational methods pioneered by dissenters in pedagogical programmes for independent academies, when their children were excluded from mainstream Anglican schools.[52] Although prim and didactic, it is nevertheless very engaging, taking the form of a dialogue between a tutor and two pupils, both of whom have been asked to report on country walks taken that afternoon. The first, Robert, admits that the route he took seemed dull as he did not meet a single person. The other boy, William, who has taken much the same route, is bursting with information about things observed in nature, animals seen and incidents encountered, also bringing out a handkerchief filled with some of the curiosities he has collected en route. At regular intervals, the tutor intersperses William's account with natural history information to enrich the boy's knowledge and understanding. The moral of the tale is clearly spelt out at the end. 'But so it is – one man walks through the world with his eyes open, and another with them shut; and upon this difference depends all the superiority of knowledge the one acquires above another.'[53] Ronald Blythe was the first to link 'Eyes, and No Eyes' with one of John Nash's own sayings: 'The artist's main business is to train his eye to see, then to probe, and then to train his hand to work in sympathy with his eye. I have made a habit of really seeing.'[54] And Andy Friend sees the intensity of this habit as 'the wellspring of all that followed'.[55]

It was perhaps just as well that the young Nash failed to get into Oxford. He also gave up an attempt at journalism after spending the summer of 1912 as an unpaid apprentice on the *Middlesex and Buckinghamshire Advertiser*. He continued to draw, paint and write, showing more interest than his brother in the work of Edward Lear, who had been a close friend of one of their aunts. It is said that Lear wanted to propose marriage, but thought himself too old and ugly to do so. More definite is the fact that Lear gave the boys' aunt a collection of his work, and they were shown it and given copies of his books. His comic drawings and illustrations for his nonsense verses left their mark on John, whose own gift in this field later led to occasional work as an illustrator for *Punch*. Further inspiration came from his visits to the Victoria and Albert Museum's Prints and Drawings Department, where he studied watercolours by Cotman and de Wint at a time when the revival of interest in the golden age of English watercolour painting was just beginning.

Paul noticed that when his brother set his comic drawings in landscapes, they showed 'an intrinsic sense of plan and decoration'.[56] Then he chanced on a watercolour painting of flooded meadows under a night sky by John, and promptly told his father that John should be given every possible chance to fulfil his talent as an artist. Because the naivety of John's work reminded Paul of the French primitive, the Douanier Rousseau, he advised him not to go to art school, as it might undermine his artistic identity. Paul himself had undergone instruction at the Slade under Professor Henry Tonks, and although John often hung around the Slade while his brother was there, he followed Paul's advice and never had any art training other than that given him by Paul's Slade-trained friend, Claughton Pellew-Harvey, during a painting holiday to Norfolk.

As young men, the two brothers were often seen out and about together dressed in identical clothing. They held their first exhibition together, Paul persuading the owners of the Dorien Leigh Gallery in Pelham Street, South Kensington (which primarily sold lampshades) to let them hire the space for an eight-day exhibition titled 'Drawings by Paul and John Nash'. This was in November 1913. John sold seven pictures and Paul four, but as Paul's were more expensive, the amount earned by each brother was probably similar. Their success owed much to Walter Sickert, who encouraged influential people to visit the exhibition, among them Sir Michael Sadler (the vice-chancellor of Leeds University and a percipient collector) and Roger Fry. With the money earned from this exhibition John took himself off to Italy, where he would develop a more mature sense of both art and landscape.

His pre-1914 career then took off with astonishing speed. He received invitations to join the Friday Club and to exhibit with the Camden Town Group; and when this latter group merged in 1914 with Wyndham Lewis and the vorticists, John found himself a founder member of the London Group, whereas Paul was not elected until a few months later. At this stage it was Harold Gilman who played an important role in John's development. A key figure in the Camden Town Group and afterwards the first president of the London Group, Gilman encouraged the younger man's move into the use of oils, a medium he had only recently adopted. It caused a radical alteration in his working methods. Gilman advised against painting direct from nature, instead encouraging John to make drawings and watercolours that could be squared up and then transferred to canvases, which would be worked up entirely in the studio. He also advised using oil paint straight from the tube, pointing out that there was enough oil in the paint to make a thinning ingredient unnecessary. The result was that John Nash from then on mostly painted in oils, with opaque rather than transparent colours. Later, in the 1920s, he and Paul evolved a watercolour style that owed much to Cézanne.

Despite their strong alliance, the differences between the Nash brothers began to interest Sickert. Reviewing a London Group exhibition in 1914, he wrote: 'The brothers Nash are always interesting, Paul with his head where a poet's should be, and John, like the child that a painter should be, putting his hand in his mouth to tell us what he has seen in the field or on the farm that afternoon.'[57] The civil servant and collector Edward Marsh made a similar observation: 'These two have, or at any rate had then, much in common; but there is a difference between them which may roughly be conveyed by saying that when Jack [John] sits down before a landscape, his only desire is to do his best for it, whereas Paul, who likes to order nature about, uses it as a spring-board for some constructions of his own.'[58] Marsh had been appointed private secretary to Winston Churchill during his role as private under-secretary of state for the Colonies in 1905. He had taken rooms at Gray's Inn and offered overnight hospitality to young artists who, like John, lived outside London. He became a major collector of Stanley Spencer and his brother Gilbert, also a significant supporter of John Nash. 'Under the influence of these boys', he recollected, referring to Stanley Spencer, the Nash brothers, Mark Gertler and John Currie, '...I experienced Conversion' – meaning that he gave up collecting old masters and switched his attention to contemporary art. 'How much more exciting to back what might be roughly called one's own judgement...to go to the studios and the little galleries, and purchase, wet from the brush, the possible masterpieces of the possible Masters of the future!'[59] He also claimed that he had followed the Nash brothers 'from their beginnings'. At least one John Nash watercolour he owned was bought from the Dorien Leigh exhibition, and an oil soon afterwards.

Over time, Marsh came to believe that his two best paintings by John Nash were the watercolour *The Vale of Aylesbury* (1924) and *The Cornfield* (1918). The second of these had been carried out in the late afternoon and evening, after John had been working most of the day on his official war paintings. The absolute firmness and solidity of the design in *The Cornfield* serves as a deliberate riposte to the shattering negativity of the war. It held its place on the walls of Marsh's rooms at 5 Raymond Buildings with – in John Rothenstein's words – 'glowing dignity',[60] and in Andy

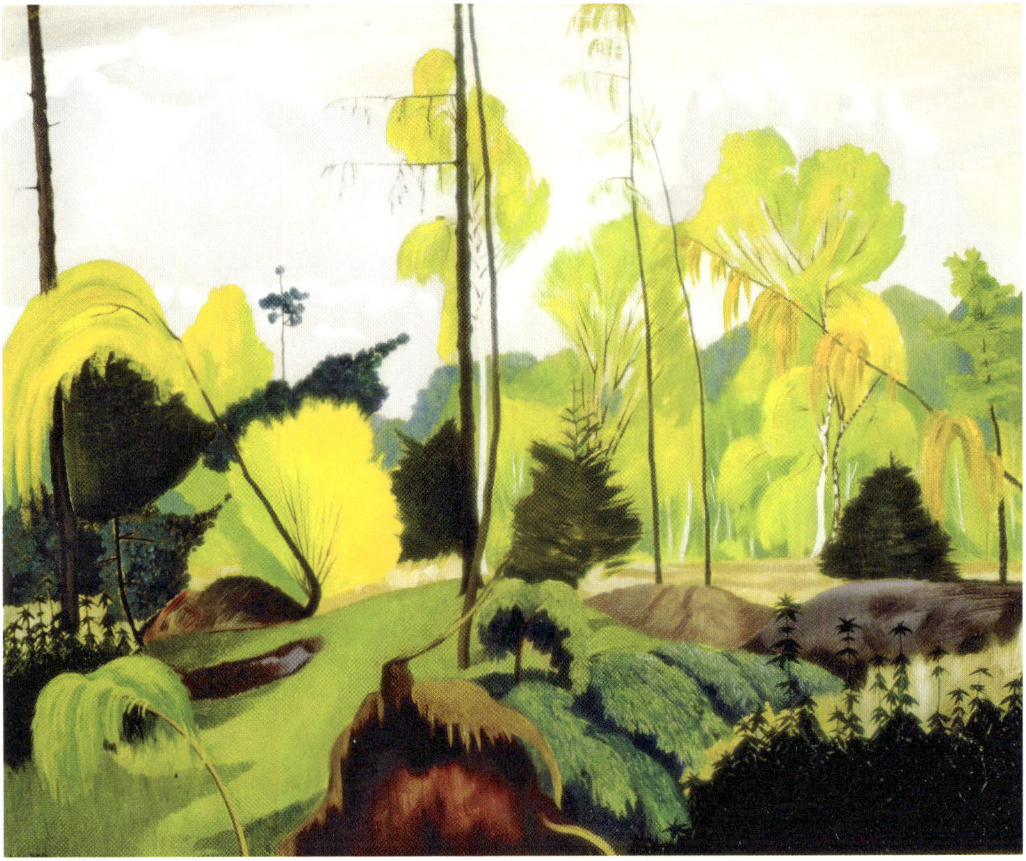

John Nash, *Dismantled Wood*,
oil on canvas, undated (c. 1920).

Friend's view it is 'redolent of peace and plenitude'.[61] A couple of years later, around 1920, Nash painted a spring landscape in a work titled *Dismantled Wood*. The fresh greens are given a luminous intensity and the landscape at first sight seems almost hallucinatory. Again, this may be a riposte to his wartime memories of Oppy Wood, which, in his painting of the same name, shows a brutally destroyed landscape in which trees have been reduced to torn husks. In contrast, *Dismantled Wood* portrays a furious affirmation of nature's return to life.

The war had interrupted John's development as an artist and after witnessing the slaughter at Marcoing on 30 December 1917, he had been relieved to be lifted out of the conflict and made a war artist. Again it was Paul who helped achieve this, pressing John's case to Edward Marsh and visiting Campbell Dodgson, the much respected Head of Prints and Drawings at the British Museum. He asked Dodgson to write on John's behalf to C. F. G. Masterman, Director of Propaganda at the Ministry of Information. Paul himself also wrote to Masterman about John: 'He is a very good artist and has an entirely personal vision. I am sure you will get good work out of him.'[62]

Only after he had been demobilized and finished his paintings for the British War Memorials Committee was John, like Paul, able to begin painting for himself again. In 1918 he had married Christine Kühlenthal. They moved into a small flat above a chemist's shop in Gerrards Cross, after which they began their habit of making long summer painting expeditions, Christine often making forays in advance to find places with good subjects to paint. It was also at Gerrards Cross that John's fertile career as an illustrator began, and during his lifetime he is said to have illustrated forty-seven books in all.

In 1922 he and Christine moved into a house at Meadle in Buckinghamshire, where he enjoyed living in the shadow of the Chiltern Hills. For the first time, he now had a garden in which he could develop his knowledge and understanding of plants. Having been sent to Wellington College, an army school, John had avoided cricket by working towards a botany prize, unaware that this would begin his lifelong interest in plants. He was greatly helped by friendship with the famous botanist Clarence Elliott, who had accompanied Frank Kingdon-Ward on his East Himalayan plant-hunting journeys and who ran the Six Hills Nursery in Stevenage. At one point one of Elliott's sales catalogues bore nine illustrations by John. In turn, Elliott's knowledge about plants benefited John's understanding and enabled him to develop in his drawings and illustrations an especial feeling for the architectural and structural qualities of plants.

One of Nash's most remarkable books of plant illustrations is *Poisonous Plants*, produced in 1927 by the Curwen Press in an edition of 350. Its introduction is written by him and powerful use is made of wood engraving, a medium which, in John Nash's own words, demands 'tight control and respectful deliberation'.[63] These wood engravings were widely reproduced after the book was published. Both he and Paul had begun to explore the medium after the war, John becoming a founder member of the Bewick Club, which evolved into the Society of Wood Engravers in 1921. Paul, trailing a little after him, joined as a member in 1922. John thereafter produced a great flow of illustrated books using this medium. Although he became a leading practitioner in the field, he abandoned wood engraving in 1935, perhaps because the painstaking work and concentration it required diminished the time and attention he could give to his paintings.

Living in the Chilterns, John painted woodland throughout the year's cycle. In spring he noticed more movement, the trees suddenly appearing in sweeping dress, trailing flounces and carrying parasols of shrill acid green. The play of light could seem bewildering. He often chose low-key subjects, preferring the colour of snow, not sunlit, but as it is found under an overcast sky. When asked about the formation of his vision, he replied: '...if I have a private vision...then it is so private that I hardly know what it is myself! You know, I never look for more than the reality, the farming, the trees, the river. I suppose the poetry gets into the reality.'[64]

His interwar landscapes are varied in mood, style and approach, but all share a recognizable underlying simplicity in their handling of nature which is modern. The mood can vary from brooding introspection to quiet wonder at the light of summer inhabiting a scene, or, in the case of his paintings of Bath, a desire to reflect the grandeur of the city and compete with the Georgian influence found in some of Rex Whistler's landscapes. But the chief motivation behind Nash's landscapes is his respect for nature, for the look and feel of the actual scene. Here the training in observation stimulated by 'Eyes, and No Eyes' played its part, as did his association with the Camden Town Group. He had joined the Group at a time when Harold Gilman and Charles Ginner were promoting a return to realism, partly in protest against Matisse and cubism. Ginner's manifesto 'Neo-Realism' had appeared in the January 1914 issue of *New Age* and was reprinted in early summer as a catalogue foreword to a Gilman and Ginner exhibition at the Goupil Gallery. 'Neo-Realism meets intimate study of nature, deliberate objective transposition, good craftsmanship and a love of the medium....All great painters by direct intercourse with Nature have extracted from her facts which others have not observed before, and interpreted them by methods which are personal and expressive of themselves – this is the great tradition of Realism.'[65]

John Nash's landscape realism further unfolded in the Essex–Suffolk border countryside. In 1929, he and Christine rented a clapboard bungalow belonging to the nearby mill at Wormingford. On the final evening of their stay, the engine room in the mill caught fire, and the conflagration was so great that John only just managed to save his pictures by removing them to the far edge of a nearby field before the bungalow was also burnt down. This alarming event in no way dimmed their love of Wormingford, which they continued to visit and where eventually, in the mid-1940s, they bought Bottengoms, a house sitting at the end of a long farm track, where they lived for the rest of their lives.

At Wormingford they were only eleven miles downriver from East Bergholt and the Stour estuary, in 'Constable country'. Ronald Blythe, who became very close to the Nashes in the last part of their lives, claimed that John took no interest in

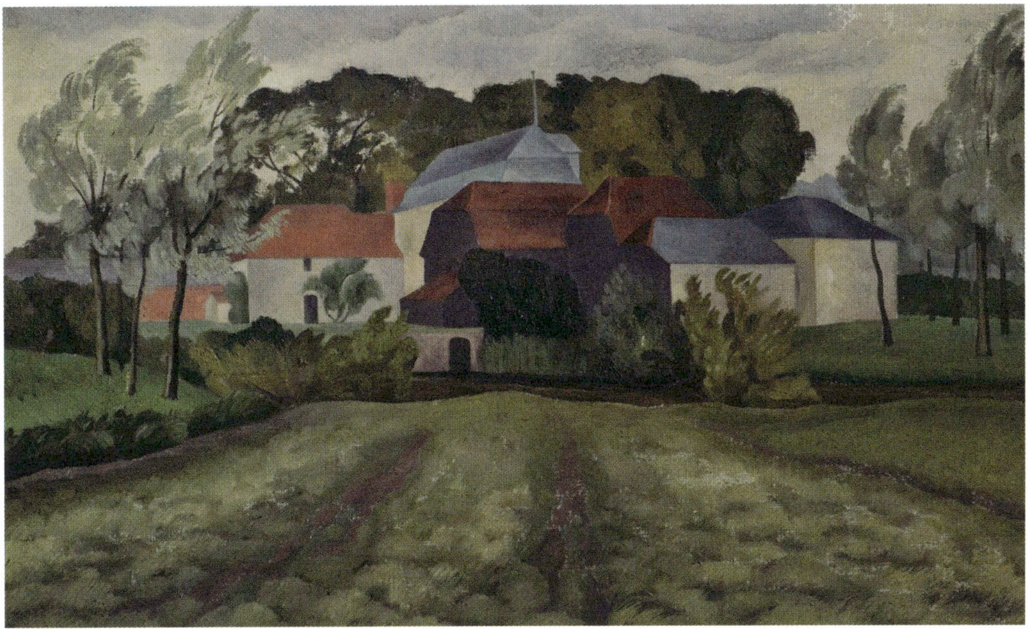

John Nash, *Wakes Colne Mill, Colchester, Essex,*
oil on canvas, 1931.

other artists and was indifferent to Constable's connection with the area. Andy Friend contradicts Blythe by pointing out that in 1915 John had read C. R. Leslie's *Memoirs of the Life of Constable* and had been pleased at Christmas 1918 to receive a book on Constable with very good illustrations; and that the title of his painting *The Cornfield* (1918) could be interpreted as an explicit homage to Constable. It is almost certain, too, that John would have admired the atmospherics of place in Constable's art and been stimulated by his achievement. Nevertheless, it is Blythe who neatly articulates John Nash's achievement, claiming that he produced 'a whole series of landscapes whose subtle mixture of agricultural realism and underlying poetry established him as an artist in the classic English tradition of Cotman and Girtin'.[66]

When Dora Carrington arrived at the Slade School of Art in 1910, she found herself in the same cohort as Paul Nash. It was through him and the Slade that she met John Nash in 1912. They had much in common, sharing a love of the countryside, gardens and flowers. It was to him she admitted her dislike of 'this city

London, with its ugly faces & hard pavements'.[67] He taught her wood engraving and she shared with him her enjoyment of such authors as Gilbert White, William Cobbett and Richard Jefferies. She also admired John's paintings, and, at a time when mural painting was all the rage, expressed the desire to have on her wall a big landscape by John and, if possible, Paul. 'Your pictures were good,' she wrote to John in 1913,[68] possibly after seeing his and Paul's exhibition at the Dorien Leigh Gallery that same year.

John's early landscapes may have encouraged Carrington's search for a 'natural' style. Like another Slade student, Mark Gertler, she had been somewhat confused by the explosion of new ideas following Roger Fry's two post-impressionist exhibitions in 1910 and 1912. This sudden opportunity to see considerable numbers of paintings by Cézanne, Van Gogh and Gauguin in the first exhibition, and by Matisse and Picasso in the second, had challenged existing methods and ideas about beauty in British art. John Nash, however, had visited neither of the exhibitions and therefore was able to maintain a straightforward approach to landscape painting, which heartened Carrington and gave her the confidence to hold onto a style of her own making.

John Nash was always proud of the fact that through the Slade he had met the two most important women in his life, Carrington and his wife, who had been good friends since their student days. But even after he began to court Christine he remained for some years obsessed with Carrington, until her passion for the homosexual Lytton Strachey became an unalterable element in her life. One of Carrington's watercolours, *Hills in Snow at Hurstbourne Tarrant*, was at one point attributed to John, even though its fine detail reflects Carrington's interest in Pre-Raphaelitism. This may seem surprising, owing to her close involvement from 1915 onwards with Bloomsbury and her awareness of the impact of French post-impressionism on the art of Vanessa Bell and Duncan Grant. But art historians have tended to overlook the fact that the pre-1914 period not only included two influential post-impressionist shows at the Grafton Galleries, but also two exhibitions of Pre-Raphaelite paintings at the Tate Gallery. A letter from Carrington to John Nash, dated 2 August 1913, reads: 'How exciting the Pre-Raphaelites being back again, I shall go and see them immediately I get back. Oh isn't *The Hireling Shepherd* [by Holman Hunt] amazing!....Wouldn't you like to do a real painting like that?' Her love of the Pre-Raphaelites informs her visionary painting of Tidmarsh Mill, the house she rented for herself and Strachey in late 1917, but equally memorable is *Farm at Watendlath*, painted on a visit to the Lake District in 1921 and later given to the Tate collection by her brother, Noel Carrington. In both pictures, the careful observation of an actual scene is shaped by the artist's personal vision, with the result that in *Farm at Watendlath* the weighting of every tone and detail is finely judged in relation to the square format. The hills behind the house rise abruptly, as they do in the Lake District, and this makes the positioning of the woman and child on the foreground path significant to the whole, for they turn back to look at the farmhouse, thereby helping to reinforce the sense of pictorial space. Both are dressed in white, striking a note that is echoed in the whites of the sheets drying on the washing line and in the walls of the house. This sets up a circular movement around the picture that conveys a sense of nestling in the landscape, in a painting that is compact and whole.

Carrington might have achieved further success with the painting of landscape had her personal life been less fraught and her artistic interests less diverse. Shortly before arriving at Watendlath she had married Ralph Partridge, 'which some old gentleman at St Pancras [Register Office] tells me is my husband', she wrote offhandedly to her brother Noel.[69] Partridge had initially been brought to Tidmarsh Mill by Noel at a time when, as a soldier, he was about to return to the Italian front. On later return visits to Tidmarsh this tall, strapping, blue-eyed young officer made himself a welcome visitor by helping with physical tasks, while also revealing a good brain and a well-educated mind. Lytton Strachey, who had begun spending much of the week in London following the success of his book *Eminent Victorians* in 1918, found him very attractive. Carrington also found him attractive, but when he began pressing her to marry him she at first resisted. By the time she gave in, in May 1921, she had begun to realize that if Ralph went elsewhere it would damage the security of the domestic arrangement she enjoyed with Lytton. Soon after marrying Partridge she embarked on a passionate, secret affair with his friend Gerald Brenan, as if in protest at her own marriage.

But another reason why Carrington's paintings began to lessen in intensity was her interest in the popular arts. Shortly before the 1921 visit to Watendlath she had painted her first signboard for the Tidmarsh Inn, and promptly received commissions for three more. She also became fascinated by craft and folk traditions such as painting on glass lined with foil, herself producing several works in this vein. She was not alone in this shift of attention away from the avant-garde or mainstream painting: there was a growing interest among artists in indigenous art and native traditions such as Staffordshire decorative and ornamental pottery, as well as in Victoriana. Carrington's admiration for such work was shared with Noel, who in 1945 published *Popular Art in Britain* in the King Penguin series, which preceded Barbara Jones's *The Unsophisticated Arts* (1951). Carrington, therefore, in her own vein, was ahead of her times, at the start of a new wave of taste that depended on 'the magpie eye'.[70]

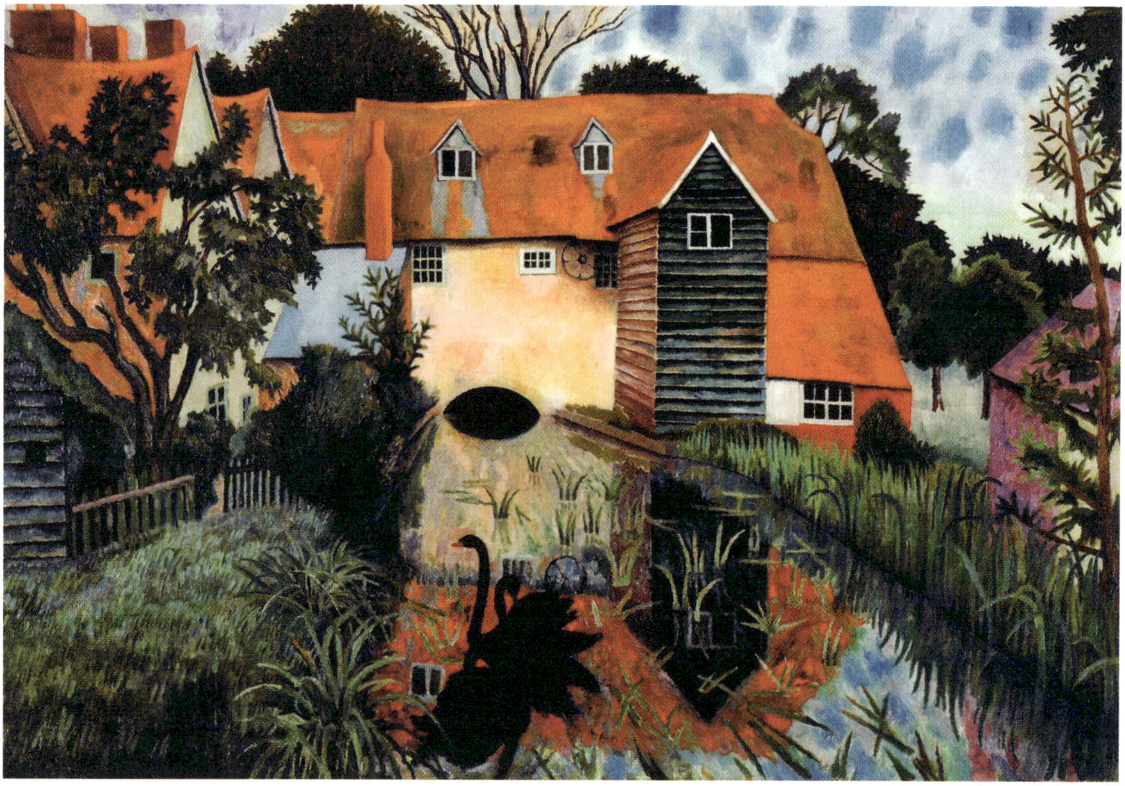

Dora Carrington, *Tidmarsh Mill*,
oil on canvas, *c.* 1918.

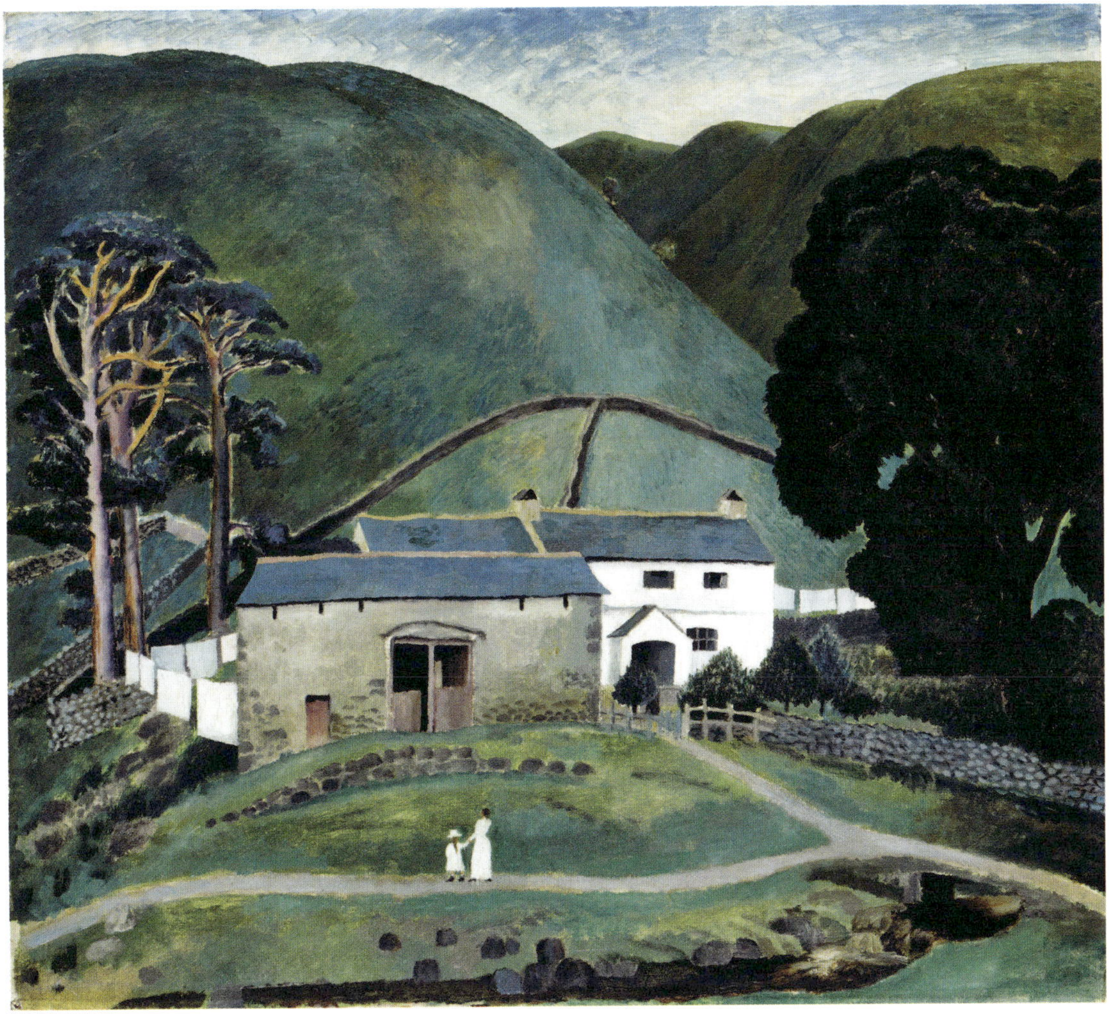

Dora Carrington, *Farm at Watendlath*,
oil on canvas, 1921.

CHAPTER 5

BEGINNING AGAIN

The exceptional slowness with which Ben Nicholson's career began was first noted by John Summerson in 1948. His slim volume on Nicholson in the Penguin Modern Painters series bluntly states: 'The unproductiveness of the early period is remarkable.'[1]

Nicholson's training at the Slade School of Art had lasted only a year, 1910–11, and made little impact. Looking back in 1963 on his time as an art student, his sole recollection was 'my daily pineapple lunch with Paul Nash at Schoolbred', costing a shilling, 'or 1s 3d if you had cream', and the billiards they played afterwards at the Gower Hotel round the corner.[2] But whereas Nash, by the mid-1920s, had achieved fame through his war paintings and with his revival of the English landscape tradition in modern terms, Nicholson was talking in that same period about his need to start afresh as a painter and go back to beginnings.

After the Slade he had travelled in Europe, spending a year in Tours learning French and another in Milan learning Italian, and considered becoming a writer rather than a painter. As he was asthmatic, he was exempted from military service during the war. In 1917 he travelled to Pasadena, spending time in California to improve his health. His decision to return to painting seems to have been made in response to the news that his mother had died – a loss that must have hit hard, as he never forgot her strength of character and 'Scotch purpose' or the way her 'vitality and busting up of conventions' offset his father's 'brilliance and elegance'.[3]

He returned home in June 1918 and, in 1919, showed his determination to paint by finishing *The Red Necklace*, a picture he had begun three years earlier. That same year he painted *Blue Bowl in Shadow*, in which one side of the bowl is in such deep shadow that it disappears into the black background, while its other side casts a shadow on a nearby object that appears to be a small framed mirror. Both are placed on a black mantelpiece or ledge. This sombre work, neatly signed with Ben's initials, reflects his father William Nicholson's liking for sparse subjects treated with an economy of means and acute perception. Ben's style had hardly changed since 1911, when he

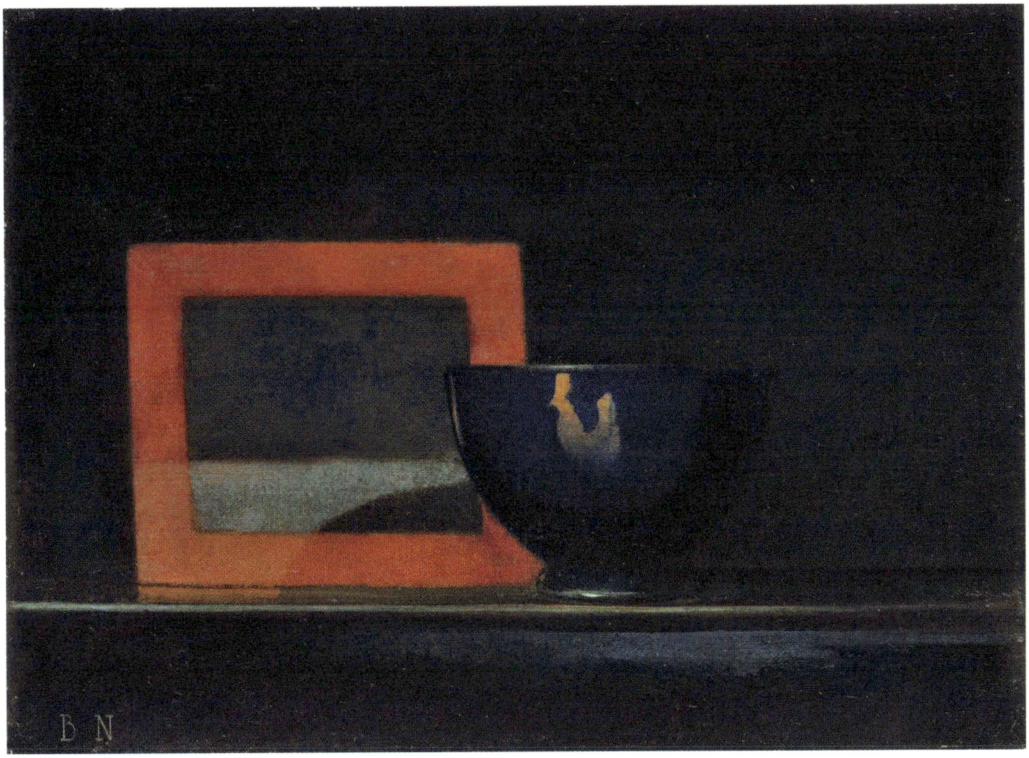

Ben Nicholson, *Blue Bowl in Shadow*, oil on canvas, 1919.

had painted his first oil on canvas, making as his subject one of the striped jugs in his father's collection.[4] This work is reproduced in two 1948 books: Summerson's aforementioned Modern Painters title, and a monograph on Ben Nicholson published by Lund Humphries. *Blue Bowl in Shadow* again affirms his debt to his father's art and to the old master tradition, noticeably in the finely positioned highlight on the foot of the blue bowl. Stillness is a recurrent feature in interwar painting, as will be shown, but it is precisely this kind of perfectionism against which Ben Nicholson would eventually rebel when he decided to 'bust up the sophistication all around me'.[5] After that point, he made a patient advance towards abstraction – an advance which he regarded as a move towards, not away from, reality.

Had it been asked in 1919 whether the next leader of the avant-garde would be Ben Nicholson or the fiercely bellicose Wyndham Lewis, former leader of the vorticists, all bets would surely have been on the latter. That year, Lewis published *The Caliph's Design*, a collection of squibs and short essays showing how up to date he was with what was happening in art in both London and Paris. At the start of the book he announces that a section of modern painting is incompatible with the 'constructive tendency' required by a revolutionary epoch, and that this incompatibility exposes a fatigue at the heart of modern painting. *The Caliph's Design* engages the reader in thinking about the future of the arts; it is also a diatribe against much contemporary architecture, painting and sculpture. Lewis admits the vigour and conviction of Picasso, Matisse, Derain and Balla, but for him the great vitality of these and other artists merely points up 'a very serious scepticism and discouragement in the use of that vitality'.[6] He regrets that in this 'shallow, tired and uncertain time' there is no 'great communal or personal force in the Western World of to-day, unless some new political hegemony supply it, for art to build on and to which to relate itself'.[7] Instead he notes that intellectual exhaustion is the order of the day 'and the work most likely to find acceptance...is that work that most vigorously and plainly announces the general bankruptcy and its own perdition'.[8] The book, if hastily put together, was surely a bid for leadership; and there was much in Lewis's past to uphold that bid.

In the pre-1914 period, he could rightly have laid claim to a more advanced knowledge of avant-garde art in Europe than any of his English colleagues. He had risen to a position of leadership on the back of his semi-cubist drawings based on Shakespeare's bitter tragedy *Timon of Athens*, after which he moved through further stylization into near abstraction. The group of rebel artists who gathered around him initially called themselves 'English cubists'. Unlike their French counterparts, they were not interested in dissolving forms into a spatial continuum, but dealt more in brittle images that rested firmly on the picture's surface. The term 'vorticism' did not come into being until 1914, by which time Lewis had learnt much from Marinetti's assertive methods of publicity, as became evident in the short-lived magazine *Blast*. Lewis conceived of the vorticist as a detached observer at the centre of the vortex of modern life. In his own art, this was to be conveyed through his startlingly original drawings and paintings of a metropolis, based on his experience of skyscrapers in Manhattan. These became key images within the vorticist movement, which had only just begun when war broke out.

Lewis himself enlisted in the army in March 1916 and received a commission as second lieutenant in the Royal Garrison Artillery, which required him to serve in direct contact with some of the most destructive weaponry of the war. In December 1917, after experiencing the Third Battle of Ypres, he was appointed official war artist by both the Canadian and British governments. In 1918 the British War Memorials Committee commissioned *A Battery Shelled* (1919), which drew on his experience of the Western Front and depicted an artillery gun battery under attack from shell fire. The severe, clipped stylization associated with vorticism dominates the centre field, where gunners, who have been moving shells and are indistinguishable one from another, leave the cannon unmanned and run for cover in their dugouts, while on the left-hand side three men – presumably officers, fleshed out in a more human form – stand watch, seemingly still and unmoving in the face of danger, one with a pipe still in his hand. This splitting of the picture into two modes, the active and the contemplative, invites the viewer to experience a sense of danger and also to reflect on the nature of war. Alun Munton has connected this pictorial division with that found in Piero della Francesca's *Allegory with the Flagellation*, where a seemingly dispassionate exchange is taking place between three men in the foreground on the right side of the picture while further back on the left side Christ is undergoing flagellation.[9] In Lewis's painting, the two different modes of representation also voice a clash between the human and the inhuman activity of war, in which even the spirals of smoke from exploded shells take on a machine-like appearance.

After finishing this picture in 1919, Lewis, like many other artists, seemed uncertain as to how he should proceed. He hopped between styles with great dexterity and pursued his love of eccentric subject matter and arcane imagery, using abstract and cubist ingredients to crush and contain the human figure. But his autobiography

Wyndham Lewis, *A Battery Shelled*, oil on canvas, 1919.

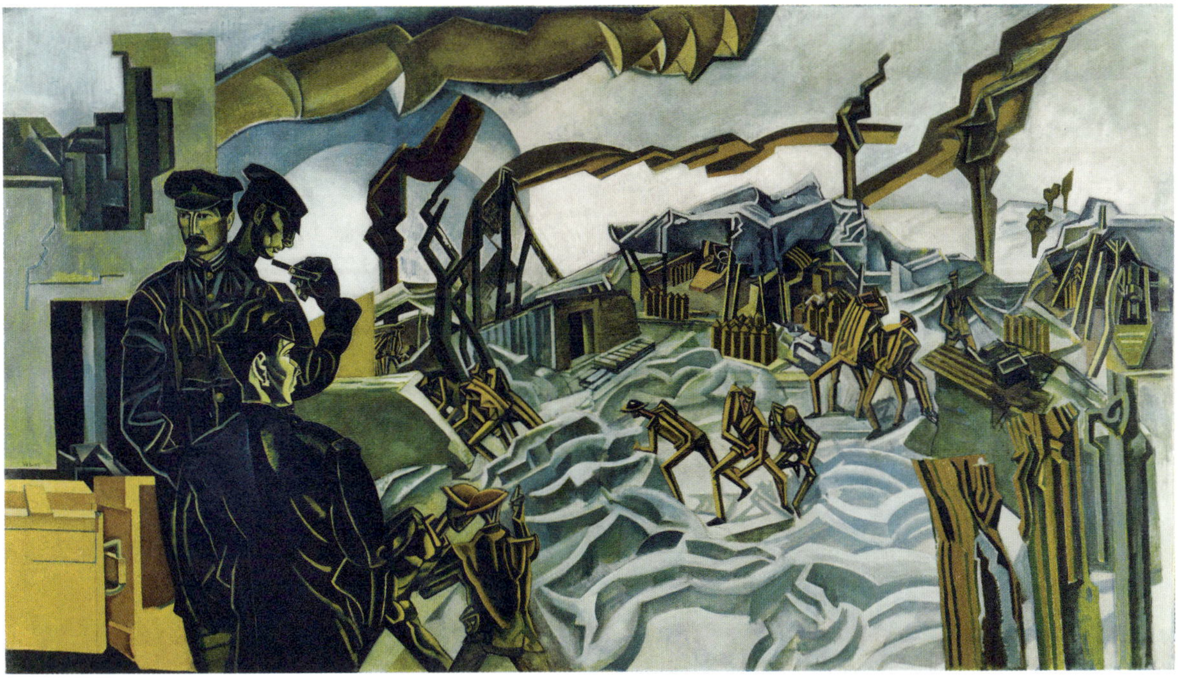

records a change of heart: 'The geometrics which interested me so exclusively before, I now found bleak and empty. They wanted *filling*. They were still as much present in my mind as ever, but submerged in the coloured vegetation, the flesh and blood, that is life.'[10] He returned to drawing the female nude in the 1920s, making shapes succinct through the use of emphatic linear emphasis and thereby creating a sense of compressed energy. It was almost as if he was mocking the practice of life drawing as taught to him at the Slade under the professorship of Henry Tonks.

Professor Tonks had insisted that his Slade pupils not only draw from the nude model but also copy old master drawings in the Prints and Drawings Department of the British Museum. To reach this department, when he used the back entrance, Lewis had to walk through rooms called the Ethnographic Galleries, filled mostly with Oceanic or Polynesian artefacts. 'We have here in the British Museum some very fine collections of New Ireland masks, Easter island monoliths and other varieties of Pacific and S. America [*sic*] stuff,' Lewis later explained to the American James Thrall Soby. 'Even when at the Slade School I was directed to go to the Print Room at the Museum and study the drawings of Raphael and Michelangelo I had always to pass cases full of more savage symbols on my way to the shrines of cinquecento.'[11] It is as if, in the early 1920s, with academicism warring with non-Western influences in his work, Lewis was experiencing a momentary nostalgia for the Slade, from which he had been ejected after little more than a year owing to his poor attendance and rebellious attitude.

Although the war had robbed Lewis of his role as leader, he had kept a close eye on the London Group. This important exhibiting society had held its first show in 1914. The following year, it had managed to absorb what remained of the earlier Camden Town Group and its realist mission (as developed by Harold Gilman and Charles Ginner)[12] along with the vorticists, thereby creating a diverse membership. Lewis would have been aware in February 1919 of the hiatus caused by the death of Gilman, its president, from Spanish flu at the age of forty-three. He died in a hospital on Shaftesbury Avenue, having spent the previous two weeks successfully nursing Charles Ginner back to health from the same illness. In October 1919 a memorial exhibition of Gilman's work went on show at the Leicester Galleries, its catalogue containing Ginner's appreciation of Gilman as an artist whom he ranked with 'Hogarth, Rowlandson and the great English tradition of realism'.[13] Lewis also wanted to write an appreciation, for though he and Gilman were very different as artists, Gilman had been for Lewis a loyal friend and supporter. Joining forces with Louis F. Fergusson, a civil servant and friend and patron of Gilman who also wished to pay tribute, Lewis persuaded Chatto & Windus to publish *Harold Gilman: An Appreciation*. Fergusson praised Gilman's interest in interiors, his handling of paint and his love of teapots: 'a Gilman teapot is of gusto and tactile values all compact'.[14] Lewis commented on Gilman's honesty, perhaps wanting to revive and amend Clive Bell's 1917 remark about Camden Town painting: 'Theirs is no vulgar provincialism, but, in its lack of receptivity, its too willing aloofness from foreign influences, its tendency to concentrate on a mediocre and rather middle-class ideal of honesty, it is, I suspect, typically British.'[15] Lewis concurred with the idea of honesty in paint, and connected it with the fact that Gilman had been the son of a vicar: 'There was a parsonic honesty in his painting; a moral rectitude in his pursuit of pictorial truth, as he understood it. He showed indulgence for dishonourable painters.... But there was a very frigid Anglican core to his make-up as a painter that came into full and useful play in his functionings as President of a Group.' Nevertheless, Lewis added that Gilman was 'one of the most amusing, genuine, equable, sensitive individuals I have met'.[16]

Two years before Gilman died, Roger Fry had been elected to the London Group and joined both the jury and hanging committees. His arrival came to be associated with an increase in the number of artists influenced by French art, and in particular by the more constructive aspect of post-impressionism as exemplified by Cézanne. This was resented by some, while a more open quarrel was Fry's disagreement with C. R. W. Nevinson, who, in his role as social secretary, had gone through a copy of *Who's Who* for names of people to invite to private views. In terms of sales this may have been a canny ploy, but Fry, with his Quaker background, disliked the attempt to turn the London Group's annual exhibition into a high-society event. After further complaints, Fry resigned his official positions within the London Group and suggested that in future its jury should be drawn by lot. This suggestion was seized on and Fry played no part in the making of the next two exhibitions, but incompetent hanging and consequent loss of sales eventually led to him being asked back. In the wake of Gilman's death, Lewis feared that he would take on the presidency, but Fry refused it and the position went to Bernard Adeney. The critic Frank Rutter described Adeney as 'a blameless echoer in biscuit and pale green tints of Cézanne's less successful nudes and landscapes' but noted astutely of the London Group that Fry 'remained the power behind the throne'.[17]

Now that peace had returned, however, Fry wanted to rid himself of financial burdens and responsibilities so that he could travel and spend long periods painting in France. In 1919 he closed down the Omega Workshops, where excitement over post-impressionist colour and rhythms had spilled out of the frame and into the decorative arts, in the course of a creative venture that turned out to be a commercial failure. He also stripped Durbins, the house he had designed outside Guildford, so that it could be held in trust and occupied by a series of residents, and took a large house with his sister Margery at 7 Dalmeny Avenue in an insalubrious part of Camden.[18] Finally, he resigned his position as joint editor of the *Burlington Magazine*, identifying Aldous Huxley as a potential successor and inviting him down to Durbins to offer him the post. Afterwards, Huxley wrote to his brother: 'I went last week to stay with old Roger Fry, who for a man of fifty is far the youngest person I have ever seen. I am not sure that he isn't really younger than oneself. So susceptible to new ideas, so much interested in things, so disliking the old – it is wonderful.'[19] As to the editorship, Huxley refused it on the justifiable grounds that he knew nothing whatever about art. These alterations suggest that Fry wanted freedom, not power. But what did give him lasting influence was the unexpected success of *Vision and Design*, his book of essays first published in 1920 and continuously reprinted in the years to come.

Lewis, predicting a further increase in Fry's influence, seceded from the London Group in 1920. The previous year, he and others had founded Group X and mounted an exhibition in March at the Mansard Gallery in Heal's, Tottenham Court Road. It consisted of work by ten artists, one of whom was the realist Ginner and four of whom – Jessica Dismorr, William Roberts, Edward Wadsworth and Lewis himself – were former vorticists. Although Lewis's foreword in the catalogue insisted that 'experiments undertaken all over Europe during the last ten years should be utilized directly and developed, and not be lightly abandoned or the effort allowed to relax', the anonymous group title and the lack of any obvious unity among the artists exhibiting meant that it did not promote a strong purpose or character. Group X disbanded after its first and last exhibition. David Peters Corbett concludes that Lewis 'had to recognise that there was no longer any possibility of asserting a homogeneous and committed radical modernism'.[20]

Yet modernism, if no longer able to strike a homogeneous chord, did inspire some outstanding work in the immediate aftermath of the First World War. As we have seen, it remained one of several styles used by the poster artist Edward McKnight Kauffer; and a frankly modernist approach informs Winifred Knights's *The Deluge*, a large canvas measuring 5' × 6' (150 × 180 cm). In 1920, this work made Knights the first woman to win the Rome Scholarship in Decorative Painting, thereby gaining a prestigious scholarship as well as the material benefit of £250 per annum during her three-year period at the British School in Rome. 'Decorative painting' was a term used for large-scale narrative painting capable of holding its place on a wall within an architectural setting – and for many years *The Deluge* did just that, asserting a disconcerting presence at Tate Britain, quite out of key with its neighbours.

Knights had been put forward with seven other students at the Slade for the scholarship. In February 1920 she learnt she had got through the first stage, but she had to wait until July to find out the conditions surrounding the second stage, when the subject and size of the painting would be announced. After that, she had just eight weeks in which to produce the finished work. Her first response to the subject of the Deluge was conventional: she produced a watercolour showing a line of figures and animals making their way towards the ark. More original was her handling of the background, where those doomed to die were clustered together on the tops of two hillsides, already turned into islands by the flood water. But in subsequent drawings the mood of the scene darkens. There are no longer any animals, nor any offer of safety or hint of future salvation. Instead the focus is entirely on the people who are doomed to die; Knights's subject is the panic and terror experienced by those fleeing from the advancing flood.

Knights was no stranger to traumatic experience. Sacha Llewellyn, in her ground-breaking book on this artist, reminds us that there had been a gap of almost a year during her training at the Slade. It followed an episode that took place on 19 January 1917, when, sitting in the upstairs part of a tram car crossing Blackfriars Bridge, Knights witnessed from a distance the detonation of Messrs Brunner Mond Ltd's TNT factory in Silvertown, East Ham. This incident killed 73 people, injured 400 and flattened 600 houses; it is said to have been the largest explosion on British soil during the First World War. Given that London had become a target for aerial warfare in May 1915, the horror Knights experienced on the bus would have had an ongoing resonance. However, in *The Deluge* the agonies and immediacies of the flood are not ostensibly to the fore: the tragedy has been formalized into a central gathering of upraised arms and fleeing figures, in such a way as to still action and enhance the finality of the design. This formality does not destroy the emotive nature of the scene, but it changes its register. It appears as a beautifully choreographed, tragic dance,[21] paused in action and held still more firmly in position by the silent background with its stark, anonymous buildings, hills, water and sky, all enfolded in shades of grey. The grey gives way to grey-blue in some of the clothing and in turn is offset by small, graded touches of maroon. Such delicacy and exacting precision hones the composition and keeps panic, hysteria and suffering at bay.

Similarly Jacob Kramer, in 1919, made dramatic use of modernist simplification in his *Day of Atonement* (1919) in order to bring out the communal identity of the congregants as they stand in silent prayer on Yom Kippur, the holiest day in the Jewish calendar, a day of expiation and introspection. Kramer had an obsession with the spirit of Judaism, and in *Day of Atonement* he arrived at a formalization that gives voice to silent prayer, to Jewish identity and suffering. As David Manson has remarked, in this painting 'the structural tensions in the composition perfectly reflect the emotional content of the picture'.[22]

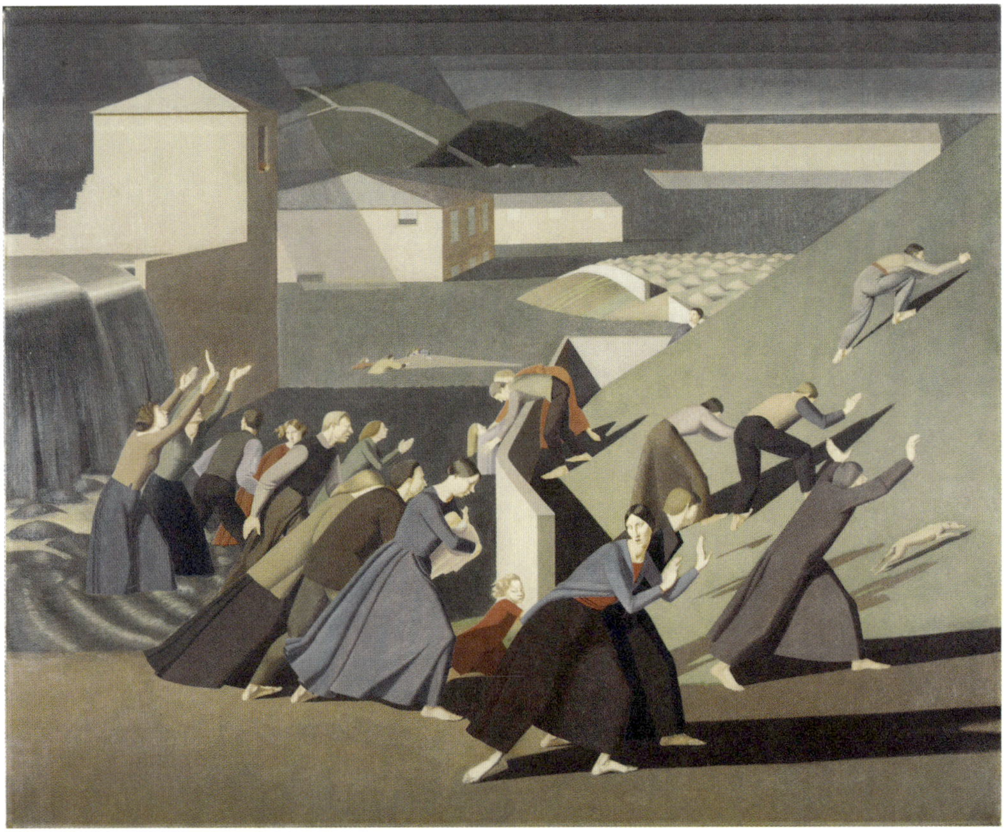

Winifred Knights, *The Deluge*,
oil on canvas, 1920.

Born in Ukraine, Kramer (like David Bomberg and Mark Gertler) had come to England as a Jewish immigrant. He arrived in 1900, aged eight. Financial assistance from the Jewish Educational Aid Society enabled him to study for a year at the Slade School of Art but, unlike Gertler, he did not gain from it socially. Invited to exhibit with the vorticists, he showed four works with them at the Doré Gallery, London, in 1915; yet he receives no mention in Richard Cork's two-volume monograph on this subject. The experience of living in London and then in Leeds, amid an alien culture, seems only to have intensified his awareness of his racial and national origins. Kramer was not, although his mother was Orthodox, a practising Jew – at least not during the second half of his life – but his best-known paintings are of Jewish subjects: tense, haunting images, strange and compelling. In an art world all too often vitiated by English politeness and decorum, he introduced a largeness and simplicity of design and a robust energy, while remaining a peripheral figure.

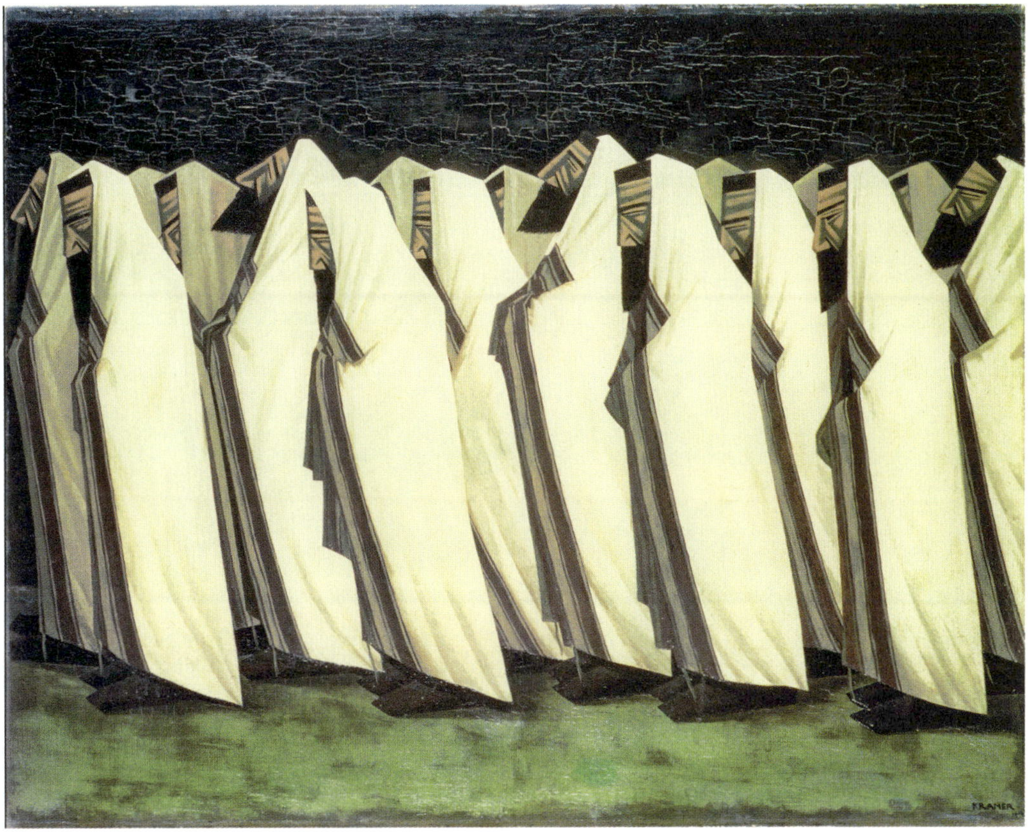

Jacob Kramer, *Day of Atonement*,
oil on canvas, 1919.

Lewis, after leaving the London Group, did not immediately abandon a radical stance. In April 1921 he mounted at the Leicester Galleries a richly satirical exhibition titled 'Tyros and Portraits'. Two of these grinning figures cackle with laughter as they pore over Ovid's handbook on seduction in the largest and most significant of the 'Tyro' paintings, *A Reading of Ovid* (1920–1). But at what, or whom, is the satire intended? 'Tyro' means 'beginner' or 'novice'. When conceiving these Tyros, Lewis said he wanted to convey 'a new type of human animal...[a] new and sufficiently elastic form or "mould" into which one can translate the satirical observations that are from time to time awakened by one's race'.[23] Many suggestions have been made as to what might be the targets for this satire: dominant figures or theories in the current art world; post-war racketeering; or the stagnation and decay of post-war European culture. It is possible that the aggressive delineation of the figures, which edges towards caricature, may also mock modernist stylization. 'His keynote, however,'

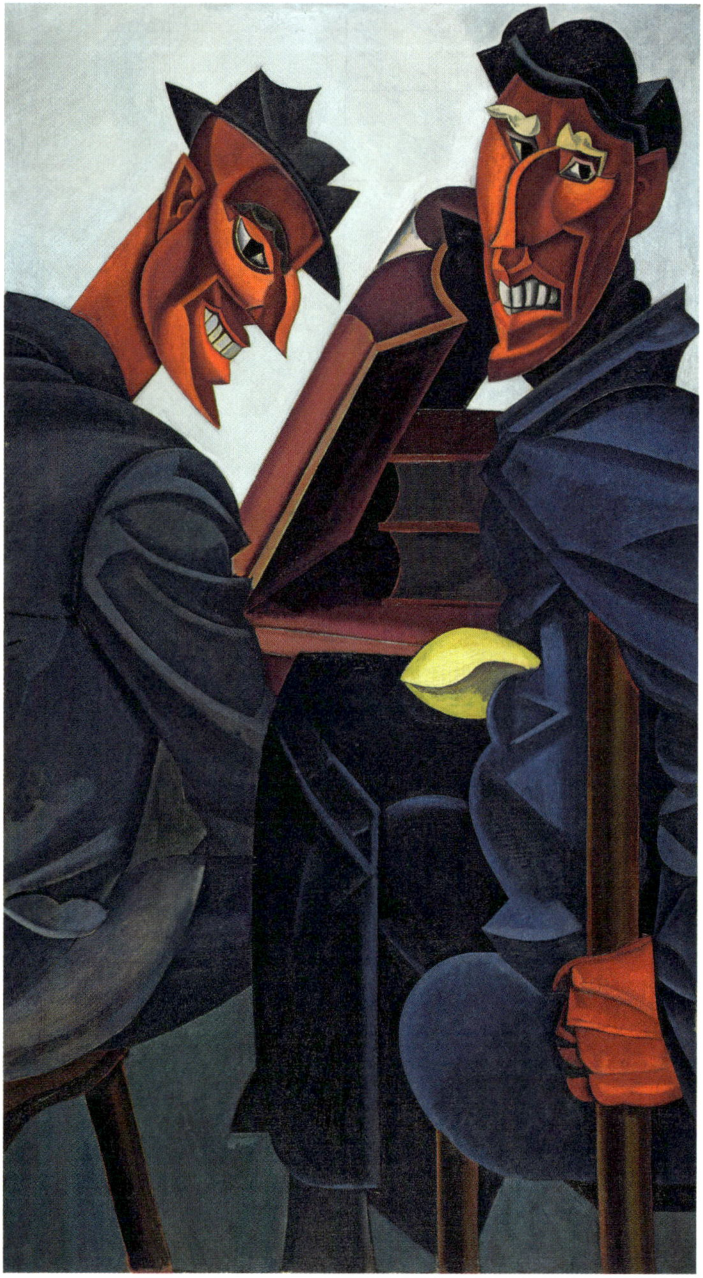

Wyndham Lewis, *A Reading of Ovid*,
oil on canvas, 1920–1.

Lewis wrote of 'The Tyro', 'is vacuity; he is an animated but artificial puppet, a "novice" to real life.'[24] Picking up on this, Robin Gibson suggests that in *A Reading of Ovid* 'these vacuous creations, grinning lewdly over Ovid, are Lewis's symbols for the intellectual dishonesty he sensed among his contemporaries'.[25] Even the elegant lemon-yellow handkerchief that flares out of the top pocket of one of the two tyros seems a form of mockery. But whatever shifts in meaning can be discerned, these cynical portraits, once seen, haunt the mind as a curious and definite period statement; yet they failed to achieve for Lewis the success and publicity he needed. As an artist he then slipped out of sight for a period, and almost eleven years passed before his next solo exhibition. His writing appears to have taken over, and between 1920 and 1939 he wrote twenty-three books.

In his non-fiction he frequently returned to the anger and disappointment first vented in *The Caliph's Design*. He became a forceful voice of protest against the corruption and decadence of post-war culture, and blamed the First World War for causing artistic expression to slip back into 'political propaganda and romance'.[26] His obsession with the damage done by the Great War led on to anger with the machinations of post-war culture; and it was almost certainly his understanding of post-Versailles Germany as underdog and victim that led to his brief flirtation with Nazism and his book *Adolf Hitler* (1931), in which he tried to persuade the British public of the virtues of Hitler and the National Socialist Party. This and his second political treatise, *Left Wings over Europe: or, How to Make a War About Nothing* (1936), undermined his reputation, and he afterwards tried to ameliorate his position in two subsequent books, both published in 1939: *The Jews, Are They Human?*, an attack on anti-semitism, and *The Hitler Cult – and how it will end*, a contract for the latter being signed with Dent & Sons on 20 August 1939. Both books have been judged to offer 'discomfortingly half-hearted recantations'.[27] Less often criticized is Lewis's recurrent and often damaging use of hyperbole and polemic. The critic John Russell once observed of him: 'all that I have read seems to me sham-tough writing and destructionism. Despite all the surface noise, flak and so forth there is rarely any genuine penetration of the subject.'[28]

Yet despite his melodramatic leanings, his misogyny, violent anti-communism and self-obsession, Lewis had the capacity to attract and retain loyal friends: Harold Gilman, Augustus John, the Tate director John Rothenstein and the young Michael Ayrton among them. Even Ben Nicholson allowed Lewis's influence to shape his portrait of Edith Stuart-Wortley, painted in 1917. More importantly, Nicholson came to share Lewis's belief that much post-war art was inherently decadent and that painting needed to be refreshed and renewed. 'Listlessness, dilettantism is the mark of studio art,' Lewis had instructed readers of *The Caliph's Design*: '*You must get Painting, Sculpture, and Design out of the studio and into life somehow or other*, if you are not going to see this new vitality desiccated in a pocket of inorganic experimentation.'[29]

In 1919, the same year that Lewis's Group X held its first and last exhibition, another group of artists founded an exhibiting society. Initially its membership consisted of seven painters and five sculptors, and this gave rise to its title, the Seven and Five Society. But when in 1920 it mounted its first exhibition at Walker's Galleries in London, its membership had risen to eighteen. Few of the artists involved at that time are remembered today, but the leading figures behind its creation are thought to have been the painter Ivon Hitchens and the sculptor Leon Underwood. The introduction to the exhibition catalogue amounted to a manifesto, and of its six short statements, the most pertinent are the following:

> The 'SEVEN & FIVE' are grateful to the pioneers, but feel that there has been of late too much pioneering along too many lines in altogether too much of a hurry, and themselves desire the pursuit of their own calling rather than the confusion of conflict.
>
> The object of the 'SEVEN & FIVE' is merely to express what they feel in terms that shall be intelligible, and not to demonstrate a theory nor to attack a tradition.
>
> Individual members have their own theories of Art, but as a group the 'SEVEN & FIVE' has none.

This sounds like an avant-garde in retreat. Compared with the radical ferocity of the Vorticist Manifesto, this 'pathetic little document', in Charles Harrison's words, vividly evokes what he called 'the prevailing mood of the early post-war years'. He castigates the Seven and Five Society for its timidity, provincialism and conservatism, and is irritated by its 'vaunting of principles of tolerance in the absence of theory' and offering only 'laissez-faire within narrow limits'.[30] Such condemnation seems fair, but when this complaint extends into the mainstream of English art in the 1920s, it is noticeable that Harrison overlooks the possibility of competing forms of modernism. And if we follow Lewis's directive and move out of the studio into life, then it is necessary to admit that artists embraced broader, more diverse ways in which to express modernity.

Undeterred by discouraging reviews, the Seven and Five Society did not fold after its first show but continued to mount exhibitions annually for almost all of the next fifteen years, the exception being 1930. However, like Group X, it had difficulty establishing a clear identity. The painter Mary Attenborough (who became Mary Potter after her marriage) was taken out to lunch by Ivon Hitchens in 1922, soon after she had left the Slade, and invited to become a member. Two years later she resigned, partly because she disliked belonging to groups but also because she was still uncertain as to what the Seven and Five represented. Admittedly the list of members whose work appeared in the first four exhibitions is fairly nondescript.[31] Change began with the arrival of Ben and Winifred Nicholson, in 1925 and 1926 respectively; in their wake came Cedric Morris and Christopher Wood, and afterwards David Jones, Frances Hodgkins, Barbara Hepworth, Henry Moore, John Piper and the ceramicist W. Staite Murray. By 1927 a more pronounced character had clearly emerged, identifying the Society with innovation and a refreshing directness in the handling of paint. Ben Nicholson, when he eventually became president, introduced numerals into the Society's name, and it became the 7 & 5 Society – until 1935, when he got rid of the word 'Society', finding it old-fashioned, after which it was simply called the 7 & 5. But it was Winifred Nicholson, with her robust character, who initially helped bring to the fore a more cohesive identity.

The Seven and Five Society had no fixed venue for its annual exhibitions, but in 1931 it settled for the next three years at the well-known Leicester Galleries. One of its strengths can be identified with a rule in its constitution: after every exhibition an election was held at which only those members, existing or newly proposed, whose 'ayes' exceeded their 'noes' were elected. This system forestalled stagnation and, instead of trailing reactionary chains of members, the group's membership changed each year and its vitality was renewed. Harrison admits that it became 'the principal platform for the only significant group movement in English painting during the 1920s', and where, in the 1930s, developments were encouraged which countered England's isolation.[32]

The success of the Seven and Five Society in the late 1920s owed much to the progress achieved by Ben and Winifred Nicholson during their sojourn in the Swiss canton of Ticino in the early part of this decade. While there, Ben gave Winifred a pot of *mughetti* – lilies of the valley – wrapped in white tissue paper. When placed, still wrapped, on a windowsill, the opaque folds of paper caught and refracted the light bouncing off the snow-covered landscape outside. A few pencil marks, still visible in Winifred's final painting of the scene, establish the bones of the composition but evidently did not delay her for long: the pot, flowers and background landscape are painted in an urgent, harsh, almost offhand manner that condenses her idea of

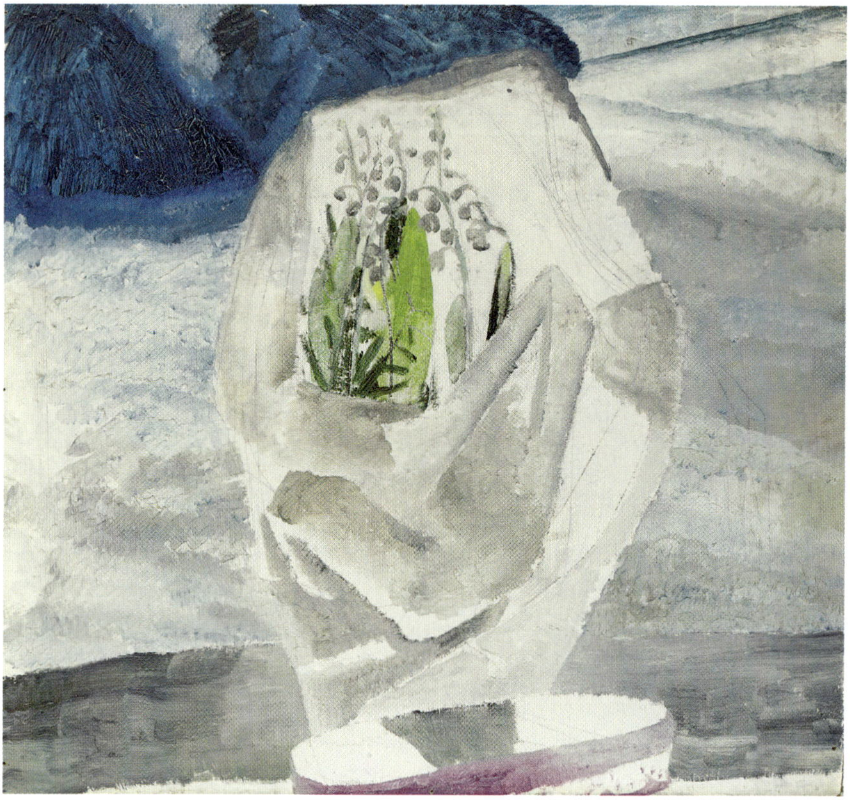

Winifred Nicholson, *Mughetti*,
oil and pencil on board, c. 1921–2.

the real into a powerful, vibrant image. It was the first of many paintings in which she linked inside with outside by means of potted plants or flowers in some form of receptacle placed on a windowsill.

The results of the Nicholsons' time in the Ticino went on show in 1923, in a joint exhibition at London's Paterson Gallery. It was Winifred, not Ben, who enjoyed a knock-out success: the money she earned contributed towards the acquisition of Banks Head, a Cumbrian farmhouse with a garden offering a panoramic view of distant fells. She would retain the house to the end of her life and it became woven into her way of life and her art.

While Ivon Hitchens was staying at Banks Head in 1925, his paintings began to resemble Winifred's in both style and subject matter. It is also said that her father-in-law William Nicholson and Paul Nash both lightened their palettes under her influence. Within the Seven and Five Society her stance as an artist affected the young sophisticate Christopher Wood, fresh from Paris and the company of Jean

Cocteau, Picasso and others. By 1927, the art critic P. G. Konody reckoned that Winifred probably had 'no equal among modern British painters as a colourist of the most exquisite refinement'.[33] More importantly, she made colours more real and more active in the making of a picture. Her aim, as she once said, was 'to paint pictures than can call down colours, so that a picture can be a lamp in one's room, not merely a window.'[34]

Winifred Nicholson was among the first artists in England in the 1920s to understand that painting, to be modern, did not necessarily need new subject matter, but instead a change in approach to the medium. She surpassed other artists of her generation in her insight into the nature of colours. Her strength of mind and character owed much to her family heritage and to the freedom she had enjoyed in childhood, much of it spent in grand surroundings. A summary of her background therefore deepens understanding of her role within the interwar period, for although her work nowadays attracts a great deal of appreciation, the measure of her achievement is only beginning to be fully recognized.

Much of her childhood was spent in the home of her grandfather George Howard, 9th Earl of Carlisle, at Castle Howard in Yorkshire: one of England's greatest baroque monuments, designed by Vanbrugh. In keeping with the Grand Tour tradition, three generations of earls had travelled extensively in Europe, bringing back Italian Renaissance masterpieces and other treasures to hang in the staterooms. Castle Howard also commanded such an extensive estate that for a hundred years it had its own railway station. The earl and his wife Rosalind, known as 'the Radical Countess' owing to her interest in liberalism, temperance and woman's suffrage, had eleven children, one of whom, Lady Cecilia, became a liberal activist and a gifted watercolour painter. She married Charles Henry Roberts, a fellow of Exeter College, Oxford, where Winifred, their eldest child, was born in 1893. Two years later, Charles gave up teaching in favour of a political career. In 1905 he became MP for Lincoln and later Derby. Because his mother-in-law offered to pay his electoral and home expenses, the family spent much time either at Castle Howard or at another family house, Naworth Castle in Cumberland, a former border stronghold surrounded by wooded glens.

Painting ran deep in Winifred's background. Her great-grandmother Mary Parke – George Howard's mother – had studied under Peter de Wint and produced a wealth of topographical watercolours. She had, however, died young, fourteen days after the birth of George, to whom she bequeathed (so it seemed to Winifred) her own ardent desire to paint. He had studied painting under Alphonse Legros and in the 1850s became a member of the Etruscan School, led by Giovanni Costa, who encouraged British artists working in Rome to paint outdoors in the *campagna*, thereby achieving a fresh and distinctive style of landscape painting. Back in England George moved easily in artistic circles, commissioning Philip Webb to design a London house for him, befriending Burne-Jones and patronizing William Morris's decorative ventures. At a time when aristocrats were still regarded as the principal custodians of culture, he served for thirty years as a trustee of London's National Gallery.

Lord Carlisle, as he became known, travelled widely even after his marriage to Rosalind Stanley in 1864 and the birth of their eleven children. The couple initially preferred Naworth Castle to Castle Howard, and in 1879 the earl became a Liberal MP for East Cumberland. He was never as radical as his wife and eventually they fell out irretrievably over the issue of home rule in Ireland, which divided the Liberal Party. Rosalind's passion for political reform and her management of their vast family estates increasingly required her to spend most of her time at Castle Howard, while George remained at Naworth, where he concentrated on painting and his commitments in Cumberland. By then, little united the couple other than their shared dislike of alcohol.

Her grandfather's love of painting and of nature had a formative influence on Winifred. Her memories of him were intimately connected with Naworth Castle and its surroundings.

> Walking in the high glen with my Grandfather under the beeches, and the leaves just coming out – my Grandfather said that Dante said that the colour of angels' wings was the colour of young beech leaves. After we walked in the wet mud and the moss, we went back to the library with its smell of old bound books and that great fire of logs, and read Froissart. And Madge [the children's nurse] said, 'They walk hand in hand, like lovers, not like a grandfather and his granddaughter.' Then I was shy and did not hold his hand until we got into the high woods. He called for me every day after painting, when it grew dusk, and we walked beside the beck. There were ferns, I don't remember any flowers. When I had been younger we read the *Water Babies*, that was in the Drawing Room, I would sit on the Morris carpet. He read it seven times to me from beginning to end. It was very dark and very frightening running to bed, through the great hall and along the wainscoted passages....I had a white muslin frock for going down into the drawing room after tea and a blue silk sash. High up above the books, there were Tudor pictures in the drawing room, that looked down on us as we read, their faces were like eggs inside their ruffs.[35]

Also prevalent in her memories were moments of light, especially when it took on a colour she called 'celestial amber' owing to its crystal clarity and rich colouring. It is entirely in keeping with Winifred's spiritual bent that she experienced this colour in 1911 in Cumberland on the morning her grandfather died. While sitting on a low brick wall, she watched a break in the sky – 'and I beheld the heaven open to receive him'.[36]

As a young woman Winifred was not only securely positioned in society but also rooted in life by her strong feelings and intuition. After her grandfather died, she enrolled at the Byam Shaw Art School in London. Like many other female pupils, she was in awe of Byam Shaw owing to his reputation as a latter-day Pre-Raphaelite and history painter. But when he criticized her painting of a mother-of-pearl shell by saying 'You are seeing too many colours, Roberts,'[37] she had sufficient self-confidence to withstand his objection. His words reminded her of the time when her grandfather had introduced her to the elderly Holman Hunt, whose pale blue eyes simultaneously gave her the impression that he could no longer see very well and that his eyes 'had seen all that was needed to see'.[38]

Nevertheless, her obedience to Byam Shaw's teaching led to her first public success. In 1914, her watercolour painting *Lincoln Cathedral (Prior Wimbush's Tomb)*[39] was included in the Royal Academy's Summer Exhibition. Using correct perspective, it shows a view through the pillars of the canopy over Wimbush's tomb to the medieval stained-glass window beyond. The picture is predominantly dusky grey and brown, but it was the light coming in through the stained glass that sustained her attention. She may have shared her interest in stained glass at the Byam Shaw with a young Irishwoman, Evie Hone, who was to make her reputation first as an abstract artist and then with her outstanding designs for stained glass. Owing to a bout of polio suffered shortly before her twelfth birthday, Evie had difficulty moving; Winifred noticed that she was unable to stand at her easel during life drawing classes, and had to be brought to art school and collected. Although this cut her off from some aspects of student life, it proved no bar to friendship with Winifred, who recalled: 'We saw each other often and talked of colour and of Ireland.'[40]

Colour was much to the fore in Winifred's thinking about painting. Her resentment of Byam Shaw's observation that she was 'seeing too many colours' led Christopher Andreae to conclude that she had become wary of 'punctilious exactitude', of anything that constrained or limited colour.[41] Later in life, looking back on the incident, she realized that she had been trying to catch the shell's iridescence, something that is not always visible to others 'because colours hide, they will only show themselves under the right conditions, and only to certain eyes at certain times'.[42] Of critical importance to her understanding of colour and light was a trip made in the company of her father to Ceylon, India and Burma in 1919–20, although most of their time was spent in India. Not only did the exoticism and atmosphere of the subcontinent jolt her expectations of landscape, but she realized that Eastern art used lilac to create sunlight. She subsequently began to find lilac in many places, such as rooftops, foliage or dried earth, and throughout her life would often use it in her pictures to counteract yellow.

If Winifred was already turning her back on art school conventions and instead searching for what she called 'the New Vision in painting', she nevertheless identified 'promise and accomplishment' with 1923.[43] This was the year in which she and Ben finally returned to London after three extended periods in the Ticino. While there, they had lived at Villa Capriccio in the village of Castagnola, five kilometres from Lugano and on the northern shore of its lake.

Winifred had met Ben Nicholson soon after her return from India, at her Aunt Norah Howard's house at Boar's Hill, Oxford. Winifred, in the drawing room, heard Ben talking with her aunt in the hallway and, although she had not then seen him, knew instantly that she would marry him.[44] They married in November 1920 at St-Martin-in-the-Fields, Trafalgar Square. In Winifred's memory of the event, Ben had chosen for her wedding dress a dark brown woollen gown rather like a monk's habit, wholly devoid of ornament of any kind. This did not offend her, although it shocked some members of her family; but his choice of flowers did, for she did not much like the red roses he gave her, tied up very tight with navy blue ribbon. One of the last things said to her by her beloved grandfather before his death had been 'Finish your daffodils.' And although that actual painting never did get finished, George's love of flowers stayed with her always, and flowers, mostly modest, seasonal or wild, remained a recurrent feature of her art.

How much Winifred knew about Ben before they met is not clear. If unfamiliar with his background she would soon have learnt that his father, William Nicholson, had first made his name producing prints and posters with James Pryde under the joint pseudonym 'J. & W. Beggarstaff'. He had then gone on to excel at portraits and still lifes, becoming one of the most admired painters of the Edwardian period. Winifred must also have been told that Ben's mother, Mabel Pryde – a painter, and the sister of James – had died of the Spanish flu in July 1918, and that soon afterwards Ben's brother Anthony had been killed in the war a few weeks before it ended. Then, too, there was another painful family incident: William Nicholson had recently stolen away Ben's fiancée, Edith Stuart-Wortley, and married her, Ben afterwards flinging a ring she had given him into the Thames.

Ben's quick-wittedness and jaunty humour may have masked some of these knocks, but his need of emotional stability must nevertheless have been paramount. Winifred recalled: 'He was thin and tense and ill – but very active – his breathing troubled him.'[45] Their decision to winter abroad was made chiefly for health reasons. After a travelling honeymoon in which they raced round major sites in Italy, gaining only limited pleasure from what they saw, they ended up in Lugano, which Ben had previously visited and liked. Winifred had noticed that whenever Ben got a cold, he became asthmatic; but in Lugano, where the mountains were covered with snow and the lake, sky and air, as Winifred claimed, were all blue, he was free of colds. And when two or three years later he did catch a cold, no asthma followed.[46]

Their three winters in Castagnola became the seedbed for new ideas about art. They were mercifully free from the need to earn money: Winifred's father secured the Villa Capriccio by buying it and initially renting it to the young couple for £150 a year. The allowance of £500 per annum which Rosalind Howard had settled on her granddaughter when she began to study at the Byam Shaw continued, for she believed, as she told Winifred, that 'small painters were as worthwhile as great painters'.[47] So the Nicholsons had ample funds to cover living expenses and travel costs. They furnished the house inexpensively with peasant furniture, plates and cups and decorated its white walls with reproductions of Gauguin's work and others by the Douanier Rousseau. They made a trip to Milan to see the 'primitives' – in this case, the work of artists from the early Italian Renaissance in the Brera – but Sebastiano Barassi has also suggested that they may have sought out examples of *pittura metafisica* by artists representative of the Italian post-war 'call to order'.[48] Mostly, however, they picked up ideas about modern and contemporary art in Paris, where they always stopped for a few days en route to or from England. They spent summers with their parents in London or Cumberland, abandoning Lugano when the lake turned hot and thundery and not returning until autumn.

Much of their first winter at the Villa Capriccio had been spent making the house liveable while they digested what they had seen or heard in Paris, brooding on the city's creative energy, on Cézanne's legacy and on that of cubism with regard to the handling of forms and space. They were living in what Winifred called 'the free space of mountain and sky',[49] at a distance from the London and Paris art worlds; the house was large enough for each of them to have their own studio, and they worked hard. The climate made it possible to watch the sun coming up over the mountains while they ate breakfast on the balcony of their bedroom, and also to watch the stars come out at night. The absence of friends, family or visitors meant there was nothing to disturb what Winifred called 'the tranquillity of painting', and they took long walks in the hills or beside the lake.[50] 'There was harmony – I never remember wanting anything.'[51]

Winifred's contentment made any rivalry between them impossible even when they sat down together and painted more or less the same scene. Yet there is one painting in which Ben appears to strike out in a manner very different to his wife's: *Cortivallo, Lugano* (retitled *1921–c. 1923 (Cortivallo, Lugano)* in the 1960s, when Nicholson decided that all his picture titles should begin with their date) is a coolly analytical work, more conceptual than expressive. It uses the minimum of ingredients to construct space and form and to hold the picture together. At a time when he was learning much from Winifred's bold use of colour and the invigorating immediacy that she brought to her handling of trees, flowers and landscape, he produced this work in a very different register – partly, perhaps, to explore what he had learnt from Cézanne, and partly out of a need to balance their shared interest in 'primitivism' with other intellectual concerns.

For Winifred, a starting point had been the tissue-wrapped pot of *mughetti* gifted her by Ben in 1921–2. The use of tissue paper wrapped round potted plants recurs in her work, notably in *Cyclamen and Primula* (Kettle's Yard, Cambridge), where the various lights in the paper – transparent, opaque or reflected – help mediate

Ben Nicholson, *1921–c. 1923 (Cortivallo, Lugano)*,
oil and graphite on canvas, c. 1921–3.

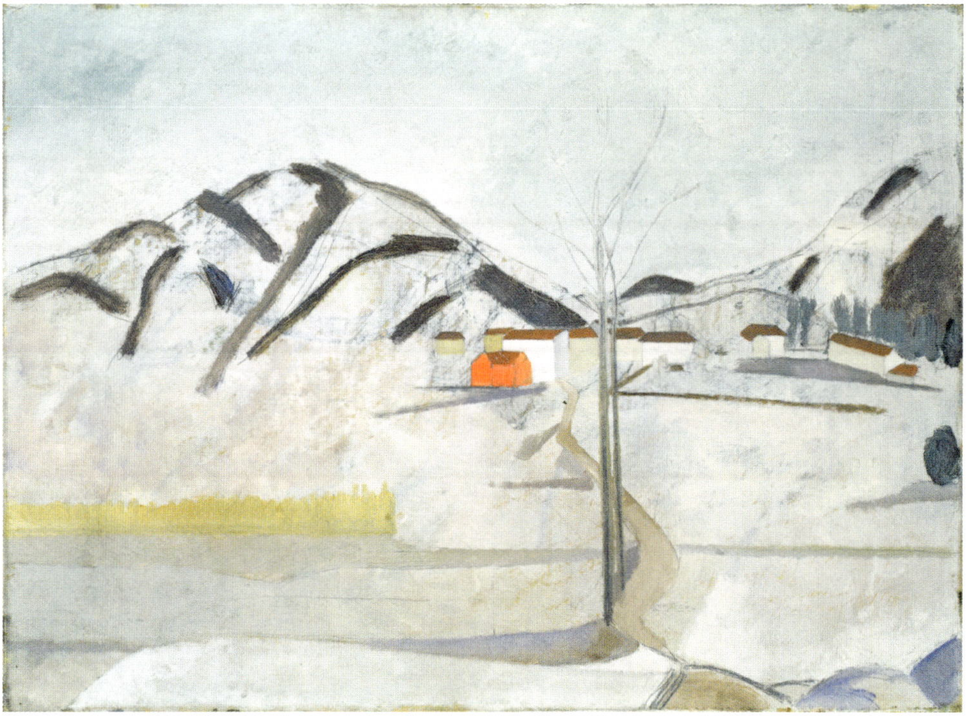

between the plants and their setting. The distant mountains, the windowsill and the paper all play a part in the construction of the whole.

Before leaving Lugano in 1923 they began making preparations for their joint exhibition. Winifred later remembered this as having taken place at a Bloomsbury bookshop, but in fact the venue was the Paterson Gallery at 5 Old Bond Street. She was, however, correct in saying that all her paintings of flowers on a windowsill sold, but not one of Ben's portraits or landscapes. His pictures, she insisted, represented 'masterpieces and forerunners of all that was to come',[52] but no one at the time understood them. Yet they must have stirred interest: a year later, in 1924, Ben was elected a member of the Seven and Five Society and was also given a solo exhibition by London's XXI Gallery. By then, as Winifred rightly said: 'Ben was exploring the New Vision in every direction.'[53]

Some years later, when further change was again in the air, Ben and Winifred visited William Nicholson and his wife Edie at their home, the White House, at Sutton Veny near Warminster in Wiltshire. The upset between father and son over Edie was a thing of the past, and the evening was relaxed. The four of them ate in a small, intimate parlour and the occasion was full of sparkle and jokes. All present were artists,[54] and inevitably painting became part of the conversation. William Nicholson claimed that yellow ochre made an excellent highlight. He looked to Winifred for approval. She replied: 'I use it for my dark.'[55]

Her father-in-law's face momentarily wrinkled with confusion. She, meanwhile, suddenly realized that the doors of the world which he and his art represented were closing. 'With his still lifes he was at ease, and free to express the shine on the scales of the fish on his dish, the shine on the knife, the texture of the crust of the loaf of bread, the glister of the silver teapot,' she acknowledges, in her memory of this event; but 'his impact with an object, even those he admired, never went below the surface of it'. She continues:

> He was painting the same themes as he had painted in the Edwardian security of pre-First World War, the same themes but an octave higher in key. His was more English and had less echo of that Spanish echo of Velasquez that lurks in the gloom of his earlier work. He became as English as Hogarth and reaches a high point of excellence. The doors are shut on Cubism, on Guernica, on Post-Impressionism even. He is painting still lifes at the same time as that other still life painter across the Channel, Braque – and the doors are closed between them....William Nicholson was painting behind the barrier of the surface and no one could pour out of his silver teapot except William Nicholson himself.[56]

Yet, with her far-seeing honesty, Winifred also recognized that in time such barriers would become less troublesome and respect would revive for William's ability to stay close to what he saw in front of him, his handling of colour, and above all the way 'his hand knew what it could do'. She concluded, 'we shall value the contribution of England in 1930 which William Nicholson has given us'.[57]

By the late 1920s, a small circle of supporters had formed around the Nicholsons. Two key figures now emerged in close association with each other and with Ben: the collector Helen Sutherland, his most significant early patron and lasting friend, who by 1948 owned thirty-two examples of his art and would also become Winifred's most important collector;[58] and Jim Ede, then a curator at the Tate Gallery, frustrated by its conservatism and whose love of the metaphysical poets fed into his interest in spiritual ideas. Ede and his wife (also called Helen) lived in part of a large house in Hampstead and, owing to Ede's love of people, they regularly entertained. It was at the Edes' house that Ben Nicholson would have supper with Braque in July 1934, and it was their parties that expanded Helen Sutherland's acquaintance with the art world during the 1920s – although by the time she got to know Jim Ede she had already met Nicholson at the London home of another mutual friend, the painter Constance Lane.

By 1925, Nicholson had reached a point where he wanted to strip back his painting to an elemental stage. Before leaving Lugano he had announced his desire to paint a white cup and saucer. He returned from a visit to Milan with a book on Braque with very good reproductions and admitted to Cecilia Roberts, his mother-in-law: 'The more I think and see of painting the more the abstract stuff interests me to the exclusion of all else.'[59] He himself experimented in this vein during 1923–4, but only three of the abstracts produced at this time remain extant today. Well known is the one in the Tate, *1924 (first abstract painting – Chelsea)*; but it is *1924 (Trout)* that best demonstrates his fascination with the way in which flat geometric shapes, overlapping with each other and even in some places suggesting areas of shadow, can penetrate pictorial space with the suggestion of layering. This was an interest he was to pursue in pictures such as *1932 (Au Chat Botté)* (Manchester Art Gallery), in which hints at representation jostle with abstraction, and later this spatial exploration of layering would become a key ingredient in his mid-1930s white reliefs.

Far from being a false start, Nicholson's two early abstract paintings were a new beginning, although they were put aside at the time for further explorations with other new beginnings, notably his obsession with how to paint a goblet. With this series, he stripped back his painting to the essentials in art. Twenty years later, Ben described how he had told Laura Riding 'that I painted a goblet because it was the

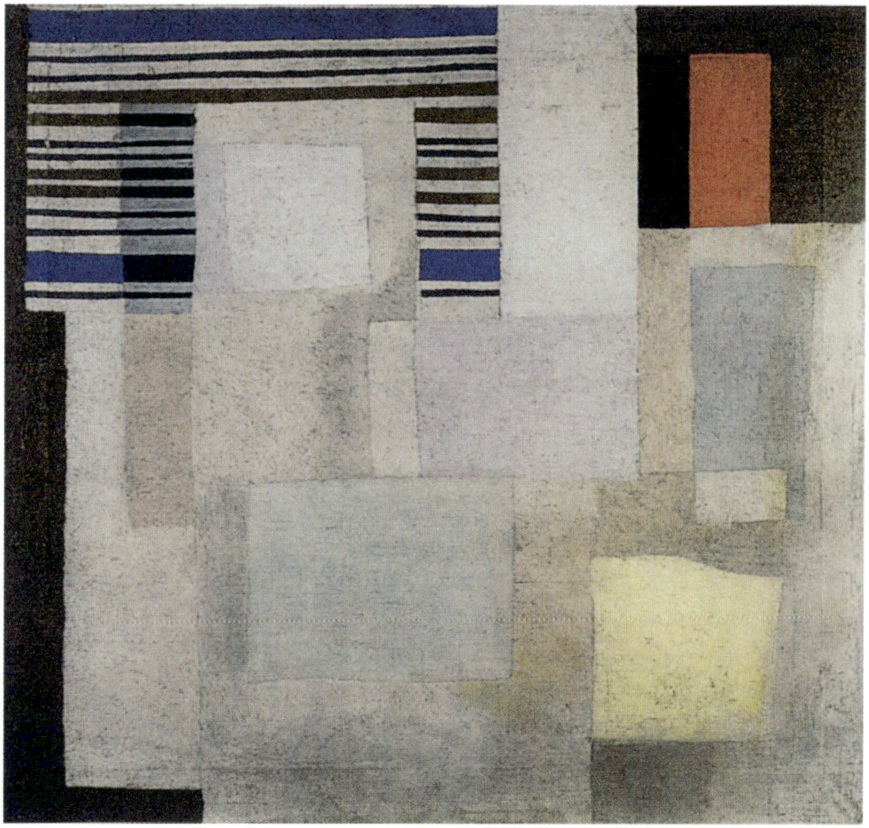

Ben Nicholson, *1924 (Trout)*,
oil on canvas, 1924.

object with the simplest form and that after many years one could perhaps take the next step – a mug – the addition of the handle being a big event, and the next step being a jug with the addition of a spout.'[60] Both Helen Sutherland and Jim Ede owned goblet pictures, this development culminating with *Apples and Pears* (1927: Kettle's Yard, Cambridge), in which the insistence on the autonomy of colour and mark seems to war against their representational role. The previous year, 1926, Ben had told Winifred that Ede thought his painting of a black goblet and two pears the best painting in this vein he had done so far. Ben added: 'It is a little over simple.... But the ideas are getting fuller and the air suddenly swishes well round behind the objects – which is a stage towards a complete conception.'[61] Later, he would state the issue more concisely: 'A painting or a carving is quite simply the expression of an idea. No one can pretend that the early Italians or the negroes[62] by whom some of the most lovely ideas have been expressed through painting and through carving, have tried to "give a faithful picture of natural objects".'[63]

At the time of her meeting with the Nicholsons Helen Sutherland had recently moved into a house in Belgravia, in Lowndes Square (since demolished). She had begun to frequent exhibitions and to purchase art, mostly in Paris. Winifred and Ben, then living in Chelsea but shortly to move to 20 Dulwich Common, brought about a change in direction of her looking. Her first letters to Ben are missing, but they appear to have begun soon after their first meeting. In a letter dated 24 February 1926, Nicholson is still addressing her as 'Miss Sutherland', yet it is apparent that they have established a raft of shared interests. Evidently a drawing or small painting accompanied the letter.

> Dear Miss Sutherland,
> Would this wish you many happy returns? If it would I would like you so much to have it? If it wouldn't I would like you so much to choose one sometime that would?
>
> Of all those paintings we saw I find the Picasso-Prima remains with me. It forebodes a most exciting new thing. It is very amused at finding itself there in all that company.
>
> I enjoyed my time with you today and yesterday ever so much. It will be great fun when you come to stay with us or we with you. It makes a good design in 3 I feel – rather like the Duccio or the Rafael [*sic*] Three Graces.
> Yrs always Ben.[64]

Their correspondence reveals much about the evolution of Nicholson's career, which Helen followed, imaginatively entering into his creative life. 'I do appreciate it', she wrote, 'when you tell me about some idea which is a living one to you, and so it becomes to me gradually.'[65]

The year before meeting Helen Sutherland, the Nicholsons had spent their first summer at Banks Head, the old farmhouse Winifred had purchased following her success with their joint 1923 exhibition. They had discovered it was for sale during a walk in Cumberland while staying with Winifred's parents, outside the village of Banks near Carlisle.[66] In order to make it suit their needs they had employed builders to remove any Victorian ornamentation and return the house to its original simplicity. They also wanted more light. The builders, following local custom formed by cold winter winds, wanted to insert narrow, upright windows with narrow, upright panes in symmetrical formation. The Nicholsons insisted on wide, squat windows with square and not necessarily symmetrical panes. Fairly near the start of their friendship with Helen, they wanted her to see it, and she made her first visit while staying in her summer apartment at Bamburgh Castle.

Helen, who never learnt to drive, arrived in her Rolls-Royce with her chauffeur, Mills. Ben insisted that Mills, who usually ate apart, should sit down to lunch with them all in democratic fashion. The contrast between life at Banks Head and life at Lowndes Square must have been very great. Deliberately so; Ben was in revolt against the 'studied elegance' of his father's way of life at Sutton Veny.[67] The contrasting austerity of Banks Head may have reminded Helen of the frugality and order she had experienced in the course of her education at the Convent of the Assumption in Paris, for she was not discomforted by Banks Head. She admired both her hosts. 'She [Winifred] was very beautiful and accompanied everywhere by a beautiful Cumbrian sheep-dog. Ben was very remarkable; potently individual (potent was a favourite word of his) but at the same time eagerly, extraordinarily responsive too. He was utterly absorbed in the adventure both of painting and living – he insisted that painting and living must be one thing.'[68] At Banks Head Helen noted the gentleness, understanding and generous love shown to babies, children, animals, country people, farmers, friends and strangers who lived in or passed through the house, something that is also felt in Winifred Nicholson's painting *The Warwick Family*. To Ben, Helen afterwards wrote of a feeling that at Banks Head, 'the world of the imagination really reaches and touches and lights up and enfranchises the ordinary human life so that it is lived in all its beauty & promise & fullness'.[69] Their exchange of letters continued, peppered with discussion of pictures, books, music, the beauty of winter and its clarity of light. Four years after they first met, Ben wrote to Helen: 'I am so pleased you like our life.'[70]

Helen Sutherland's support of the Nicholsons was at its most valuable and intensive from 1925 to 1935. In 1929 she sold her house in London and moved to Rock,

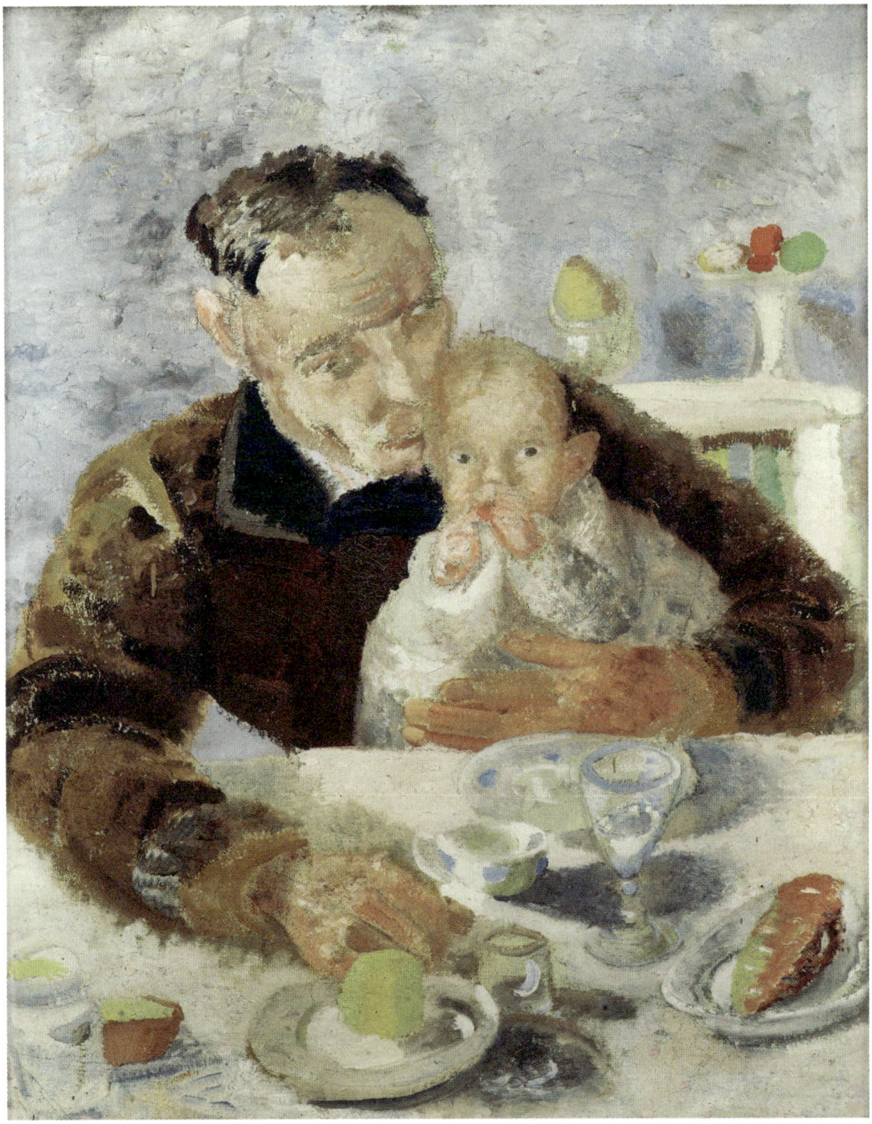

Winifred Nicholson, *Father and Son*,
oil on canvas, 1927.

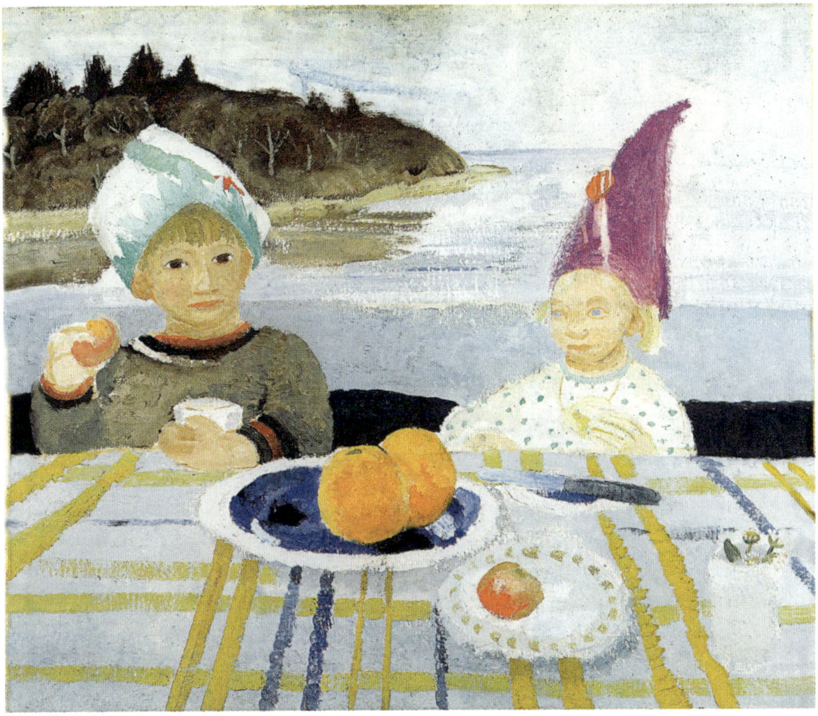

Winifred Nicholson, *Jake and Kate on the Isle of Wight*,
oil on canvas, 1931.

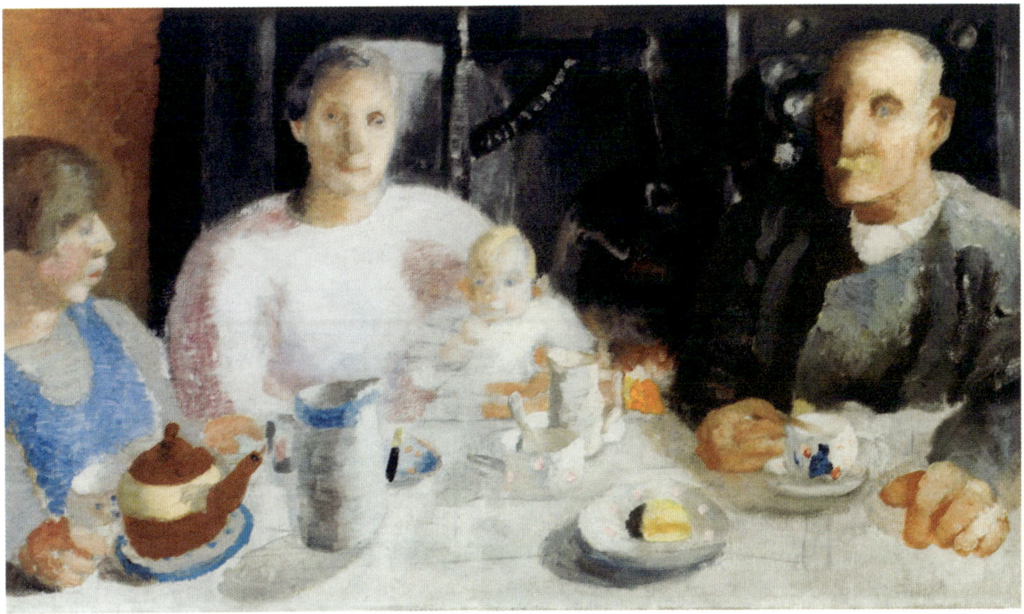

Winifred Nicholson, *The Warwick Family*,
oil on canvas, c. 1926.

a tiny hamlet not far from Alnwick in Northumberland. Here she rented Rock Hall, the core of which is a pele tower and castle. In the 18th century a fire had reduced its east wing to an uninhabitable shell. It has been described as a 'mishmash of crenellations, fortified tower, blocked windows and doors, medieval gables, thickened walls, gunloops and bay windows'.[71]

Viewing the building today, in the wake of subsequent residents including a youth hostel and a school, it is hard to see how Sutherland, with her exquisite taste, imposed order upon it. But in 1929, soon after she moved in, it became an intensely romantic setting for her collection of contemporary art. On its walls hung work by Winifred Nicholson, David Jones, Alfred Wallis and Christopher Wood as well as several Ben Nicholsons, including two of his most romantic pictures: *1928 (Porthmeor Beach, St Ives)* and *Porthmeor Window*. All of these artists belonged to, or had work shown by, the Seven and Five Society. After Ben was made its chair in 1926, he had helped to transform it into a leading, progressive artists' exhibiting society. English art was once again discovering that it had an avant-garde.

Ben Nicholson, *1928 (Porthmeor Beach, St Ives)*, oil on canvas, 1928.

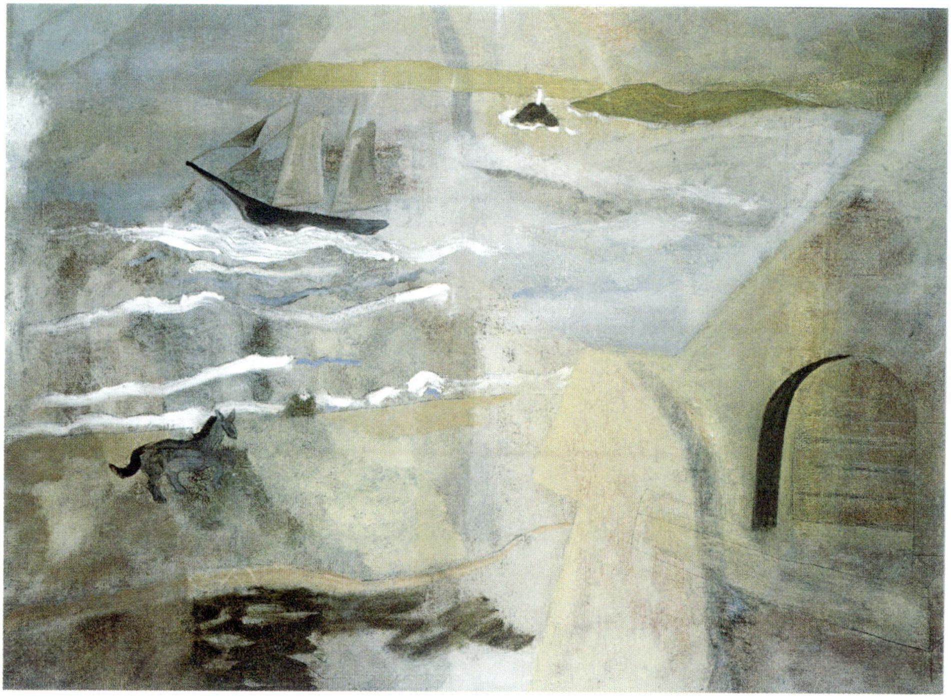

CHAPTER 6

'WHAT HO! GIOTTO': STANLEY SPENCER AT BURGHCLERE

Stanley Spencer is a familiar figure within the history of British art. We can follow what he looked like at many stages of his life through his self-portraits, beginning with the almost bruisingly intense pencil-and-ink drawing of 1913 and continuing with a series of oil paintings in which, at irregular intervals, he took stock of himself. 'I don't want to lose sight of myself for a second,' he once announced.[1] This might suggest overweening egocentricity, but his art is deeply rooted in affection not only for self but also for community. And if viewed from another perspective the remark conveys determination, as a sensory being, to remain alert to everything around him: to Cookham, the village where he grew up, as well as to people, activities, ideas, nature, music, associations and memories.

Spencer's early letters, with their misspellings and grammatical errors, reveal the limitations of his home education, for he was let off lessons he found difficult and allowed to draw or amble around the village on his own. To gain entrance by means of a scholarship to the Slade School of Art he had to sit a general knowledge exam and was afterwards told that he had got in by the skin of his teeth, which suggests allowances had been made. But his love of reading had begun before he arrived at the Slade, and while there, from 1908 to 1912, he mixed with others from very different backgrounds and began to develop new interests.

Gwen Darwin (the granddaughter of Charles Darwin), for instance, befriended him, paid for him to go to the dentist and lent him a copy of John Donne's sermons. Out of this came his small gem of a painting, *John Donne Arriving in Heaven* (1911), which takes place on Widbrook Common in Cookham and is inspired by Donne's belief that heaven is inchoate here on earth, to be found in many directions, and with much coming and going between the two. The Frenchman Jacques Raverat, a fellow student at the Slade, paid Spencer six guineas for this picture and gifted it to Gwen shortly before he married her. Spencer was excited by their union and Jacques

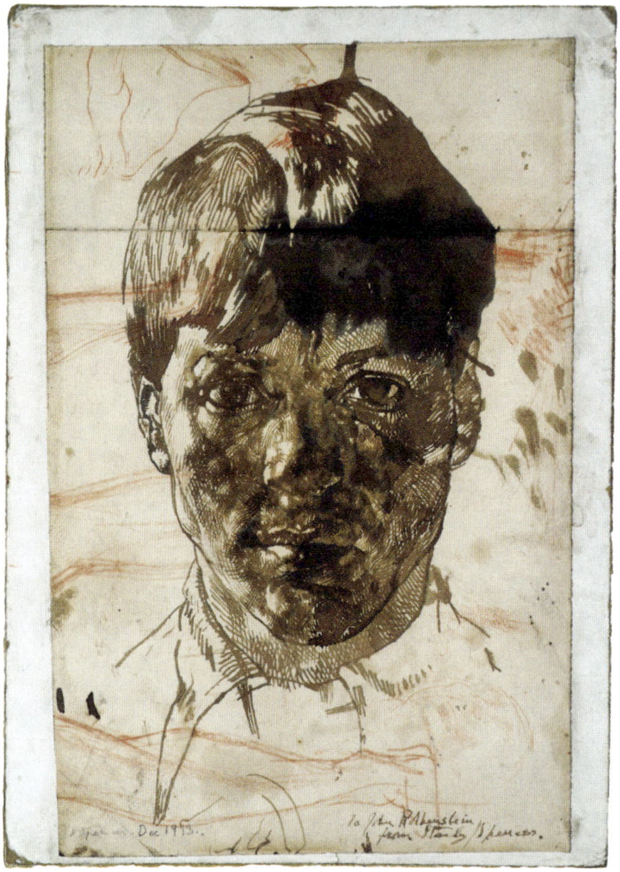

Stanley Spencer,
Self-Portrait,
December 1913,
pencil and ink
on paper, 1913.

and Gwen remained important presences in his life, even though after leaving the Slade he saw them only intermittently. His love of Milton was sparked by Jacques's habit of reading aloud in a great voice from an ancient copy of *Paradise Lost*, as Spencer recalled,[2] leaving forever imprinted on his mind the passage where Satan is

> Hurled headlong flaming from th' ethereal sky
> With hideous ruin and combustion down
> To bottomless perdition, there to dwell
> In adamantine chains and penal fire...

The Raverats also shared with Spencer their collection of art books and reproductions, and these, combined with his visits to the National Gallery, furthered his interest in Renaissance art. A reproduction of a portrait of Christ by one of Leonardo's followers, Bernardino Luini, is said to have triggered Spencer's first self-portrait

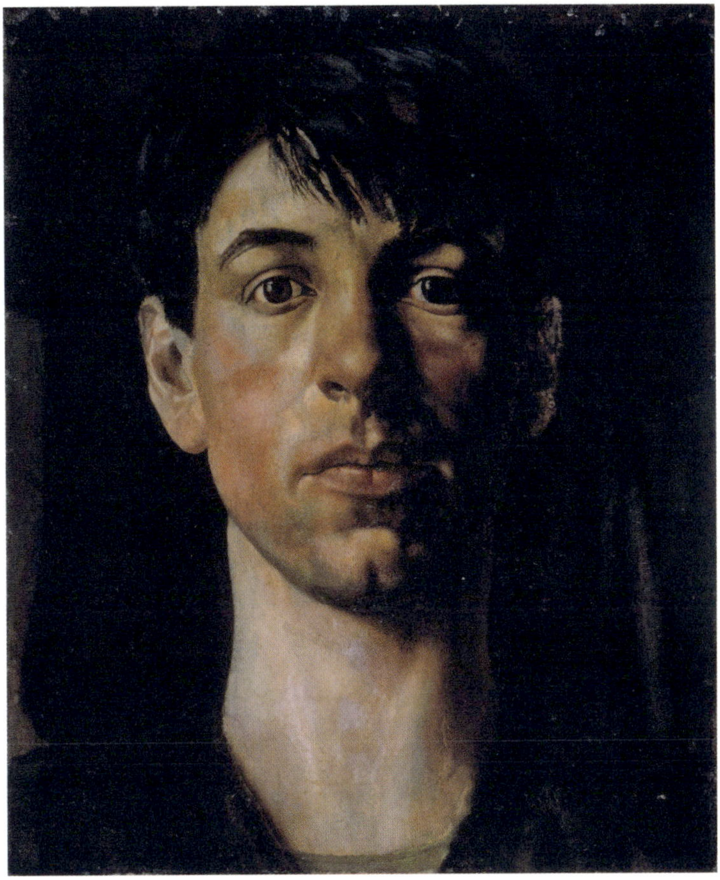

Stanley Spencer,
Self-Portrait,
oil on canvas,
c. 1914.

in oils.[3] He struggled with this picture over several months and was still painting it when war broke out on 4 August 1914. It was bought that same year for £18 by the civil servant and collector Edward Marsh, who was astonished by its compelling effect, Spencer's larger-than-life-size face gripping attention as it looms out from the kind of dark background that Professor Tonks often urged his pupils to employ.

Exhibitions, books, articles and documentary films, including one chiefly based on memorable interviews with his two daughters,[4] have brought Stanley Spencer closer to us. Yet despite all the information available, the matrix of ideas on which his work rests has only been lightly investigated. His mind, fed by his reading, teemed with thoughts and observations. He could be exhaustingly loquacious, talking so much about Cookham on arriving at the Slade that he was soon nicknamed 'Cookham'. He also became an extensive letter-writer. He admitted to his first wife Hilda (née Carline) that he wanted his letters to her to form his autobiography, despite his sporadic attempts to compose an autonomous account of his life. He went

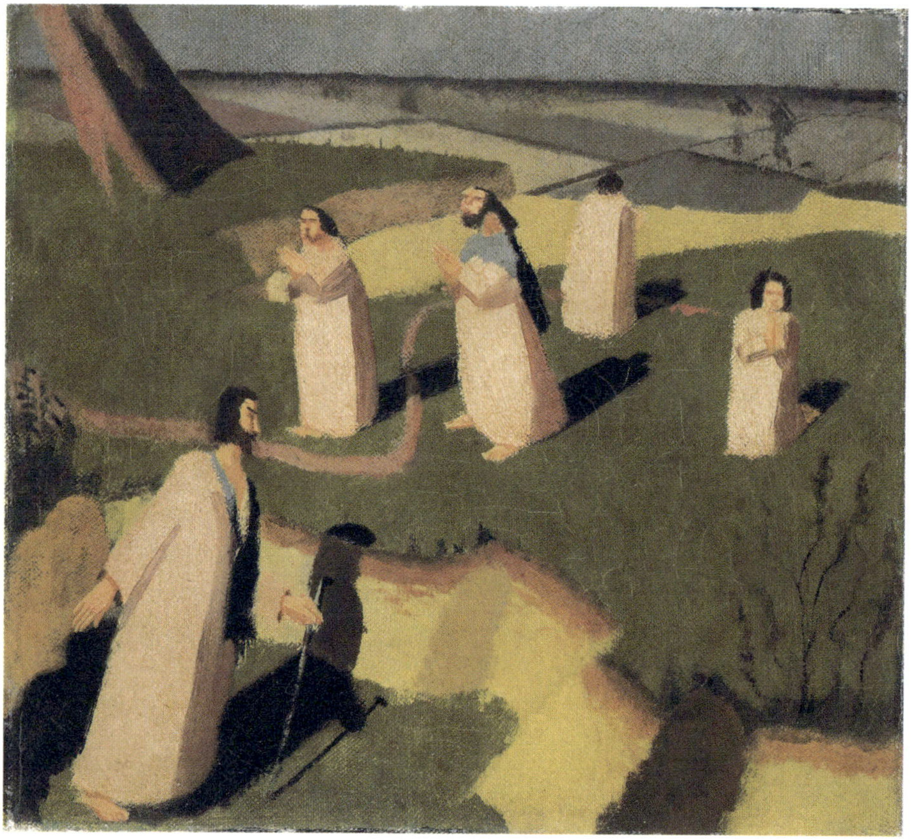

Stanley Spencer, *John Donne Arriving in Heaven*,
oil on canvas, 1911.

on writing to Hilda after their divorce, and some nine of his letters were written to her after she died. There were moments when his eccentricity suggested mental imbalance and sexual frustration, the latter caused by his unhappy alliance with Patricia Preece, his second wife. His work, too, underwent a less happy alteration when a drier method of handling paint gave to his pursuit of pattern and texture an arid quality. Similarly, his use of distortion for expressive purposes became less felt than deliberately manipulative. But during the late 1920s, when given the opportunity to memorialize the Great War, he produced a complete set of wall paintings for the Sandham Memorial Chapel at Burghclere in which imaginative conceptions joined hands with a bedrock of reality, resting on mature thought and personal experience. As a result, the decorative scheme at Burghclere, near Newbury in Berkshire, offers one of the most profound reflections on the human and moral dilemma created by war.

Sandham Memorial Chapel is from the outside an unprepossessing building. The two almshouses, attached to the chapel on either side, were added at the request of two donors who were worried about building a private chapel in a parish that already had two churches and in a village some distance from their own home. But if the chapel looks outwardly dull, inside it often startles the first-time visitor with the busy figurative scenes covering three of its four walls. One detail that readily catches the eye on the lower level shows the backside of a hospital orderly on his knees, scrubbing the floor between two baths. Such prosaic activities, rarely depicted in a religious building, here take their place as part of a sustained imaginative feat that produced a living memorial and a spectacular example of public art.

Spencer gave the architect Lionel Pearson a small-scale drawing of the shape he wanted for the chapel. It was based on Giotto's Arena Chapel, otherwise known as the Scrovegni Chapel, at Padua. Both buildings are architecturally little more than viewing boxes for wall decorations. At Padua, the light comes from a set of windows down the north side of the nave. At Burghclere, light enters from above the entrance door, through a tall high window. Now that the chapel belongs to the National Trust, a transparent blind covers this window and on sunny days a second is added to it. Spencer would surely have objected to this, as it dims some of the scenes and can make viewing difficult; hence the relief when the main panels were removed from the walls for temporary exhibition at London's Somerset House, where they were seen in far better light.

After leaving the Slade, Spencer had continued to make new friends, among them Henry Lamb, who had originally undergone medical training before turning to painting. They met in 1913, each making a strong impression on the other: Lamb

Sandham Memorial Chapel.

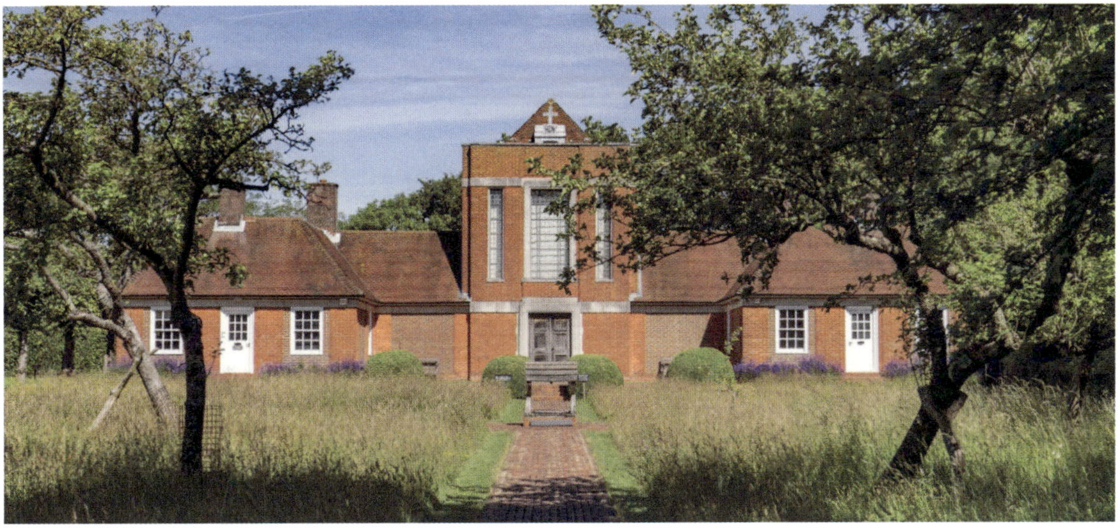

admiring Spencer's character and work, Spencer admiring Lamb's piano playing and discernment, for he recognized in Lamb a person on whom he could try out his ideas. They kept in touch during the war and renewed their friendship when it ended. In 1923, while staying in Dorset with Lamb, Spencer was invited to show some of his drawings to two visitors, Mr and Mrs J. L. Behrend, whom he had met once before. For some time he had wanted to put his wartime experiences to use in the decoration of a chapel or a House of Remembrance. He had begun producing drawings towards this end, even though he had no receptacle for them and seemingly no possibility of finding one.

These two art patrons, with a fortune that came from cotton seed and shipping, had recently begun to support young or relatively unknown artists. There was also an unexpected link between Mrs Behrend and Spencer. Her brother, Lieutenant Henry Willoughby Sandham, had died in 1919 from an illness contracted while fighting in Macedonia, where Spencer had himself served, first with the Royal Army Medical Corps (RAMC) and then as a soldier. This coincidence may have played a part in the Behrends' decision to commission a memorial chapel decorated by Spencer.

After further discussion about the nature of the commission, it became evident that the Behrends did not wish to interfere with his choice of subjects – however, they did insist that the chapel should be situated not at Cookham, but nearer to where they lived. To make such a major commission viable the Behrends had a house built for Spencer in Burghclere so that he, his wife and their two young children could live there while he worked on the chapel decorations. These occupied him for some five years, between 1927 and 1932. Although dedicated to Mary Behrend's brother, the chapel was always intended to be a memorial to all the

Stanley Spencer, *Washing Lockers* (detail), Sandham Memorial Chapel.

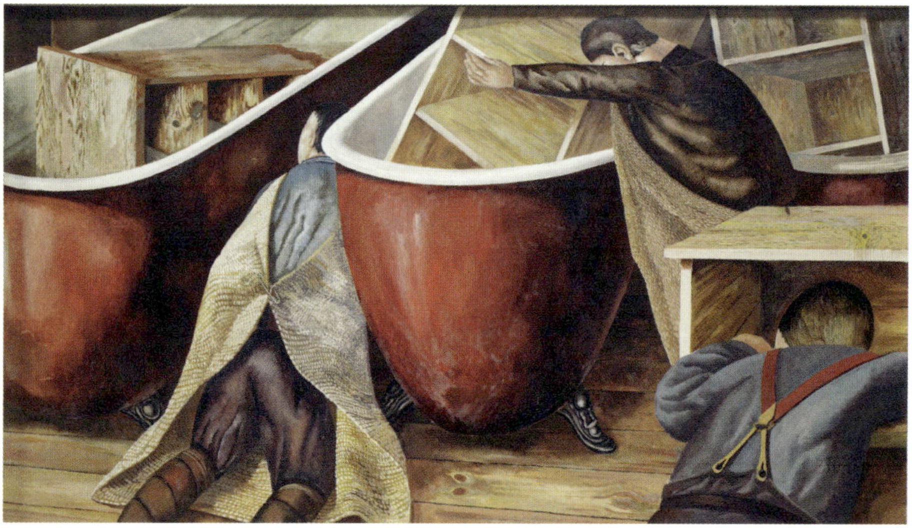

fallen. It was dedicated as an Oratory of All Souls by the Bishop of Guildford on 25 March 1927 – coincidentally, the same day of the year that the Arena Chapel in Padua had been consecrated six centuries earlier.

Spencer never visited Padua except imaginatively, through the eyes and words of John Ruskin. Alongside his collection of reproductions of old masters and Gowans & Gray art books (one of which focused on Giotto's work at Assisi), he cherished Ruskin's book *Giotto and His Works at Padua*, which had been gifted him in 1911 by the Raverats. Almost certainly this would have been the edition published by George Allen in 1900 and 1905, with plentiful photographic reproductions.[5] But the text also infiltrated the Slade after it had been reprinted in 1906, in the 24th volume of E. T. Cook and Alexander Wedderburn's *The Works of John Ruskin*. It helped bring about a shift in taste, for Ruskin emphasized the spareness and simplicity of Giotto's designs and their consequent dramatic intensity. He praised Giotto's 'bold and somewhat heavy touch', his broad rendering of drapery and his tendency to portray 'plain, masculine kind of people'. He emphasized Giotto's refusal to be distracted from the essential drama by unnecessary detail: 'There is no filling of the landscape with a variety of scenery, architecture or incident, no wealth of jewellery and gold spent on the dresses of the figures. The background is never more than a few gloomy masses of rocks.'[6]

Roger Fry also drew attention to Giotto after he accepted in 1909 a position as lecturer at the Slade, which committed him to giving a series of six-week courses twice a year during the first two terms of the academic year. These were free to Slade students but also open to the public for a fee. Spencer mentions the lectures in a letter to Gwen, but we do not know how many or which he attended. The generic title of Fry's course of lectures, during 1909–10, was 'Monumental Art'. He took his listeners from 5th-century Greece through to the present day. Caroline Elam has observed that the hero of this course was Giotto, to whom two lectures were devoted. She also notes that Fry placed much emphasis on 'the importance of drama and the expression of emotion and how these are achieved, not by accuracy of representation and naturalistic tricks but by composition, spacing, gesture and line'.[7] Through his lectures and writings, Fry enhanced the growing awareness of the 'sincerity and intensity of feeling' to be found in early Renaissance art, which now seemed to offer an alternative to what Sue Malvern has called 'the bombast and rhetorical pretension of sixteenth-century art'.[8] Spencer's great shout – 'What ho! Giotto' – on learning that he had gained the commission to decorate the chapel at Burghclere demonstrated his understanding of Giotto's achievement. It also asserted his desire to share in this artist's search for what Fry in his lectures had called 'the large human outlook' and shared communal values.

This major project brought into focus some of the ideas and ambitions that had previously shaped Spencer's life and art. Growing up in Cookham, in easy reach of the river and walking as a child alongside high garden walls, he had imagined the Bible stories, which his father daily read aloud to the family, taking place just the other side of these walls – hidden from sight, but in close proximity to his daily life. This led to the merging in his mind of the sacred with the profane, the transcendent with the quotidian. 'My feeling for things being holy was very strong at that time,' he later recalled.[9] Cookham took on, for him, a religious significance, and there were some mornings, after he had swum in the river, that he seemed to be living in an earthly Paradise and experienced 'visitations'. What exactly he meant by this word is not clear,[10] but it may relate to his gift for linking places with ideas for his pictures. As he put it, 'I liked to take my thoughts for a walk and marry them to some place in Cookham.'[11]

The idea of decorating a chapel had been in the air before the war began, after Jacques Raverat returned from a visit to France filled with admiration for the great churches at Auxerre and Vézelay. Gwen, meanwhile, although her Darwin family was largely atheistical, had been reading Dostoyevsky, whose work opened her mind to religious thoughts. And both Raverats had become friendly with the sculptor and letter-carver Eric Gill, who shared Jacques's passionate interest in medieval art. The relation of art to religion was much discussed. 'The artist is an instrument of God,' Jacques told Spencer at this time, hurriedly adding that by 'God' he did not mean an old man with a beard, 'but simply that force, those forces, not ourselves, which drive us, blindly and irresistibly'.[12] Early in 1912, amid talk about plans for another post-impressionist exhibition in London, Jacques, partly in reaction to this news, dreamt up the idea of a temple or church which he, Gwen, Spencer and Gill could all decorate. This group ambition was, however, soon replaced by a more viable option: namely that they should all work together on an illustrated Bible, an idea that retracted still further when the decision was taken to decorate just the Four Gospels. A meeting to decide the way forward was held at the Raverats' home in March 1913. Only a month before, Gill had converted to Roman Catholicism, and now, with the fanaticism of a new convert, he declared that the project could not be done 'merely in relation to our private sentiments on the subject but must be done in relation to dogmatic Christianity – and the only dogmatic Christianity for us is that of Rome'.[13] For Gill this meant that their source must be the Rheims version of the Bible, authorized by Rome. His views horrified Gwen and Spencer, as Jacques mentions in a letter to his friend Katherine Cox: 'like the good sentimental protestant English they are...they cannot bear the thought of any but the English authorised version'.[14] An uproar of protest uncovered differences – of creed and opinion, as well as in their work – and before long, it was clear that their plan to work collaboratively on a religious theme was impossible. It momentarily revived in 1915, when Gill wrote to Jacques asking if he would fund the building of a chapel onto the side of his house at Ditchling, and Jacques once again began dreaming of what kind of frescoes he, Gwen, Spencer and Gill might create to fill its interior.

This dream also faded, but Jacques and Gwen retained a desire to take up fresco painting. Almost certainly, their knowledge of this medium came through lectures on fresco technique given at the Slade by Mary Sargant Florence, to which Gwen drew Spencer's attention. In 1914 Jacques and Gwen each executed a fresco in an old granary attached to Gwen's mother's house in Cambridge (now Darwin College). And in 1915, they filled the back wall of what was then an open verandah attached to the house in Cambridge belonging to Francis and Frances Cornford (the latter being Gwen's cousin) with a Mediterranean landscape, again using the fresco method of painting on wet plaster. Later, when he began to conceive of the Burghclere Chapel decorations, Spencer initially thought of using fresco – perhaps fired by Jacques and Gwen's enthusiasm for it, but also because it was the medium that Giotto had used.

Eight days after the war began, Spencer knew that he wanted to enlist. 'If I go to war I go on one condition: I can have Giotto, The Basilica of Assissi…& Fra Angelico in one pocket, and Masaccio, Masolino and Giorgione in the other.'[15] He and his brother Gilbert joined the Maidenhead Branch of the Civic Guard in a local park, where they demonstrated their martial zeal by rushing about clutching wooden rifles. Being only 5'2" in height and weighing just under seven stone at the time, Stanley was below the physical standard required for the army, though, later, as the need for new recruits grew urgent, these requirements were changed. While side-lined, he began to feel crushed by the knowledge of what was happening elsewhere owing to the war, and this made it impossible for him to go on painting at Cookham and to take pleasure in his surroundings. On his mother's advice, he and Gilbert sought enlistment in the Home Hospital Service of the RAMC and both became medical or 'nursing' orderlies. Gilbert disappeared first, but Stanley managed to delay taking up work until July 1915 in order to finish some of his paintings. When he followed Gilbert into the role of medical orderly it was to the same hospital – Beaufort War Hospital, near Bristol – but a different ward. He was to continue working in this field, with the 68th and 66th Field Ambulances in Macedonia, before taking up active service on the front line with the 7th Battalion of the Royal Berkshire Regiment. But it was at Beaufort that he had a transformative experience which would later have a profound influence on his decoration of the chapel at Burghclere.

The War Hospital, formerly a lunatic asylum, was a grim building on the outskirts of the city. In the course of three months it had been transformed into a hospital capable of receiving 1,500 patients. It terrified Spencer on his arrival and he was repeatedly shocked by the harsh treatment often meted out to the patients, the autocratic commands and the petty regime under which the hospital functioned. Many patients who were cured looked on it almost as a relief to be sent back to the Front. Meanwhile, convoys of wounded men kept on arriving as the enormity of the war began to make itself felt. Spencer spent most of his time indoors and longed for fresh air and exercise. He continued to experience 'innumerable, unanalysable mental shocks', hated the 'utterly selfish spirit' of his fellow orderlies,[16] and generally found the place vile and degrading. He was given mostly menial, repetitive and physically exhausting jobs and his inner equilibrium was completely shattered. Yet he retained what he called 'some kind of homing instinct', so that, as he said: 'I am always finding spiritual nesting places.'[17]

By late autumn, however, he was trying to escape by applying for overseas service. He worked ten, sometimes fifteen hours a day, with much time spent on the back-breaking task of scrubbing floors. He wrote to the Raverats, telling them that he had decided to volunteer for overseas work as he was getting impatient at Beaufort, although he thought it had done him good. He was proud of the sheer number of men he had bathed. 'Every Wednesday morning I had to bathe patients, about 6 I did in an hour and a half. When I am ready for the Kingdom of Heaven, I shall tell God to take into consideration the number of men I have cleaned & the amount of *floors* I have *scrubbed*, as well as the excellence of my pictures so as to get him to let me in...'[18] He was in fact scrubbing a floor early in 1916 when he became aware that, 'like a Christ visiting Hell',[19] someone was walking down the stone passage towards him. That person was a young intellectual named Desmond Chute.

Without knowing it, Spencer had suddenly acquired fame. His 'big picture' – as he referred to *The Centurion's Servant*, one of the pictures he had been determined to finish before leaving for Bristol – had been selected by Professor Tonks for inclusion in the New English Art Club autumn exhibition for 1915, and the *Times* art critic had praised it highly. This caught the attention of some of the people he worked with in the hospital, who now looked quizzically at this person they had formerly regarded as an insignificant orderly. The review had also caught the attention of Chute, then living with his family in Bristol, who knew of Spencer's work and was astonished to learn that the artist was currently working at Beaufort.

Chute belonged to a high-profile, well-connected theatrical family. His own interests were in art, music and literature. He had enrolled at the Slade in 1913, but his studies had been interrupted by ill health and war. Unable to fight owing to medical problems, he had returned to Bristol. He was still only twenty, whereas Spencer was four years older; yet, in terms of cultivation, knowledge and sensitivity, Chute had much to offer Spencer, who immediately recognized an affinity between them. From then on, he spent his monthly thirty-six hours' leave in Chute's company. They went on long walks during which Chute uncovered Bristol for Spencer: showing him places, taking him to concerts and to the houses of people he knew, and bringing him to his family home, where they spent hours talking and reading. Chute was making a translation of the *Odyssey* and would give Spencer relevant passages from this while he read aloud the original. It was not just that Chute was 'terribly good and kind to me and appreciated the mental suffering that I was going through',[20] as Spencer later recalled, but that the contrast between the harshness and misery of his work and the cure he now experienced was so great. 'I used to sit looking out of the wide-open window & listen to him translating Homer's Odyssey & Iliad.... Our evenings were so satisfying.'[21]

As well as introducing Spencer to these classic texts, Chute also gave him St Augustine's *Confessions*, initially lending him the book to read and later copying out specific passages for him to keep. One of these was from Book I, Chapter 4, in which the performances of God are described by a series of paradoxes, such as 'Ever busy, yet ever at rest'. The whole chapter, with its emphasis on the creativity of God, moved Spencer deeply, transforming his attitude to the unrewarding and relentless round of menial, tedious, onerous physical tasks he faced on a daily basis at the War Hospital.

> What art Thou then, my God?...Highest, best, most powerful, most omnipotent; most merciful and most just; most deeply hidden and yet most near. Fairest, yet strongest; steadfast, yet unseizable [incomprehensible]; unchangeable, yet changing all things; never new, yet never old....Ever busy, yet ever at rest; gathering, yet needing not; bearing, filling, guarding; creating, nourishing, and perfecting; seeking, though Thou hast no wants.... What can we say, my God, my life, my holy joy? or what can anyone say who speaks of Thee?[22]

After reading St Augustine, Spencer regarded everything he had to do at Beaufort Hospital, whether it was replacing dressings, carrying heavy tea urns or scrubbing floors, as part of a divine performance, everything falling into place as part of the unity within variety. St Augustine's *Confessions* transfigured his daily life. He frequently referred back to the lines *Ever busy, yet ever at rest; gathering, yet needing not; bearing, filling, guarding; creating, nourishing, and perfecting; seeking, though Thou hast no wants* – which became a key source of inspiration. He took from these words an understanding that God is served and glorified by the smallest of tasks, even the sewing on of a button, and that rest is paradoxically related to work, as giving is to receiving. In other words, St Augustine's *Confessions* gave back to him some of the mental freedoms he associated with peacetime. He wrote to a friend: 'After my day's work at Beaufort, I have wanted to draw a picture of everything I have done. But why...I could not say.' At the same time he no longer felt that 'a great clammy death seemed to be sitting or squatting on all my desires and hopes'.[23] Jacques Raverat's possibly teasing remark that the artist had to become a servant of God had found a practitioner.

Spencer did finally receive an invitation to go for training in field ambulance work at Tweseldown Camp near Aldershot before being shipped out to the Eastern Mediterranean, to Salonika. There, in Macedonia, latterly as an infantryman and where he was often in the front line, he had further experiences which, like his work at the War Hospital, eventually fed into his decoration of the Sandham Memorial Chapel. During his two and a half years in Macedonia, attempts were made, led by his lifelong patron and supporter Muirhead Bone, to get Spencer released from the army so that he could take up an appointment as a war artist. His former teacher, Professor Tonks, knew well that he was unlikely to be of much use as a soldier and referred to him as 'a genius pitched in the mud'.[24] Applications for his release were made in May 1918 and continued at intervals until November, but it was not until he was invalided home with malaria in December 1918 that Spencer was able to take up the Ministry of Information appointment.

In January 1919 he began work on his large canvas *Travoys Arriving with Wounded at a Dressing-Station at Smol, Macedonia, September 1916*. It drew on his memory of an attack made by the 22nd Division on Machine Gun Hill in the Doiran-Vardar Sector in September 1916, which continued for several days. During this period the wounded passed through the dressing stations in a constant stream, by means of mountain ambulance transport – in other words, mules and stretchers, as shown by Spencer in this picture.

Later, at Burghclere, Spencer's memories of war were to fill not only two long landscapes at the top of the side walls, which are about twenty-eight feet in length, but also eight large lunette scenes. Below these are eight predella-like scenes based on his experience of working as an orderly at Beaufort. It is often remarked that nowhere in the chapel does the visitor encounter the horrors of trench warfare. Although Spencer did not deliberately censor his art in any way, his overall intention was not to portray the destruction and darkness of war but to redeem it. Some notes by Spencer exist, transcribed by his brother-in-law Richard Carline, which are thought to relate to a lecture he delivered in Oxford in 1922. These notes put forward the belief that what any artist is seeking is some kind of redemption, 'redemption from ugliness, meaningless....Nothing is real until its physical and spiritual revelations are both apparent....No one loves anything until he can exactly express what it is he loves.'[25]

Spencer, who knew much about the boredom and tedium of war, at Burghclere deliberately sought to depict scenes that are busy and alive with positive acts: soldiers filling up water bottles at a stream, laying out their kit for inspection or map-reading, or washing clothes on the rocks of the riverbed at Todorova. In the hospital scenes he draws on his memory of small details such as the buttering of vast quantities of bread, the filling of tea urns or the making of a bed while the patient keeps warm, wrapped in an eiderdown and standing on a hot-water bottle.

The visual narrative that unwinds at Burghclere climaxes in the end wall, behind the altar. Spencer did not immediately arrive at a single unified scene for this wall,

Stanley Spencer, *Travoys Arriving with Wounded at a Dressing-Station at Smol, Macedonia, September 1916*, oil on canvas, 1919.

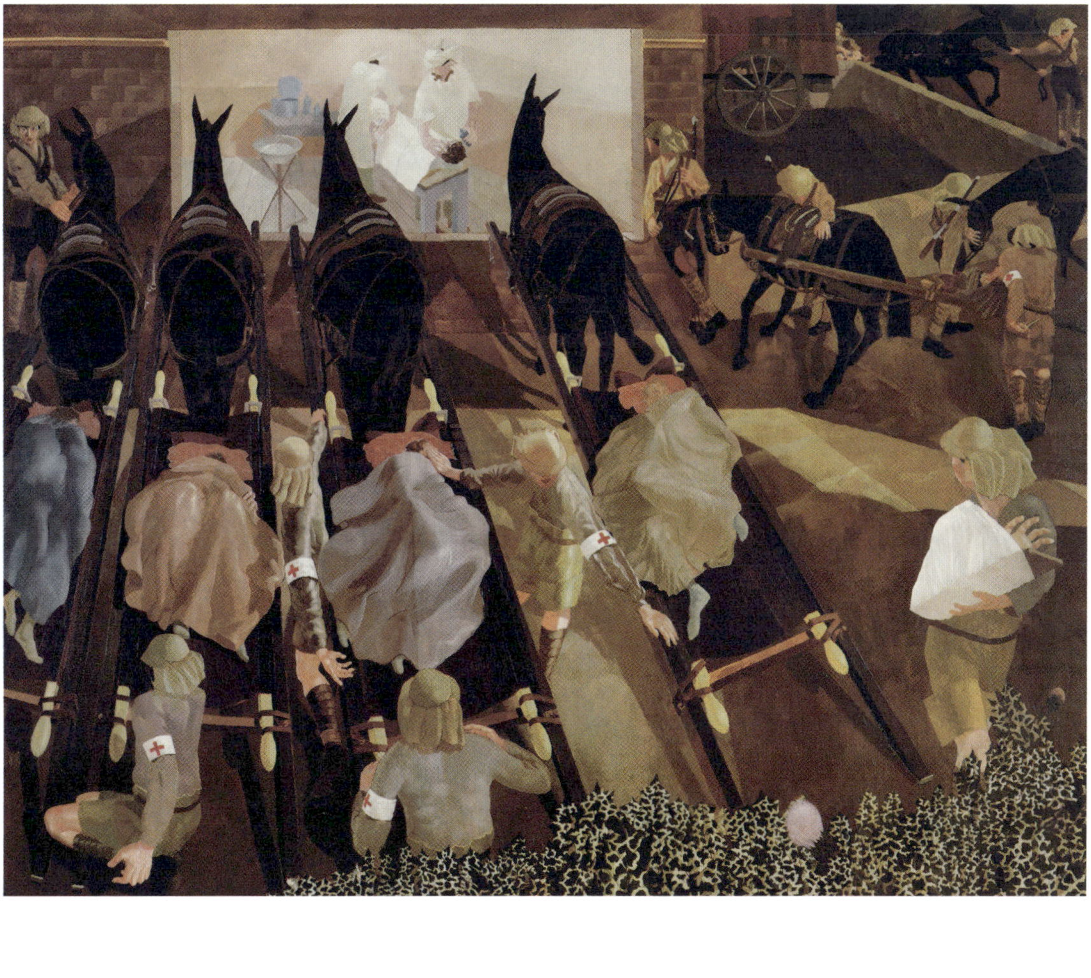

over 5 metres wide and 8 metres tall, but he recognized early on that its pictorial message would be critical to the altar and to the chapel as a whole. Unfortunately, the absence of any cross on the altar in recent years has removed one of Spencer's stated intentions: 'It is therefore...imperative that the top of the altar should be slightly above the bottom of the big picture so as to enable the cross on the altar to be in relationship to the whole uninterrupted mass of the canvas at the back.'[26] Nevertheless, as Keith Bell has pointed out, the foreground crowd of soldiers and crosses, which appear immediately behind the altar, are painted almost life-size and therefore create a slightly trompe l'oeil effect owing to the sense that they occupy the same space as the viewer, 'thus engaging the congregation directly in the experience of the Resurrection'.[27]

The Resurrection of the Soldiers, as this end wall is titled, depicts a scene outside the walled village of Kalinova in Macedonia. Unlike Spencer's earlier *Resurrection at Cookham* (1924–7), a mural-size canvas in the Tate collection, it does not show the soldiers rising up out of their graves. Instead they are shown quietly engaged with daily tasks: cutting wire, polishing epaulettes or removing puttees, then part of the standard-issue army uniform. In his design of the picture Spencer's intention was to create, by means of the white crosses and the intimate spaces between them, a series of waves receding upwards and backwards. In the first wave, on the lower part of the wall, the men greet each other, shake hands and seem to be gradually gaining awareness of a new state of consciousness. Things are the same and yet different, and the mood seems benign. Belongings are returned. In the lower right corner, to the left of the door, a soldier takes out a red pocket book. Spencer identified it as 'a little red leather covered Bible', given to a soldier by his sister but which he had lost. 'Being the resurrection,' Spencer explains, matter-of-factly, 'I find it.'[28] In the next wave a more reflective stage emerges. Here, too, there are passages of touching simplicity, such as the soldier reaching out to stroke the tortoise – a reminder, perhaps, that each regiment in the Greek army had its own pet tortoise. In this segment there is also a sense of rest and remembrance: crosses are to be leant against or reflected on, as one figure does lying on his stomach, just above the two central mules.

These mules seem to be rising up, as if they too are shaking off old burdens and are curving their necks to see the Christ figure, higher up but hardly distinguishable. Finally, the soldiers hand in their standard-issue crosses to Christ, who sits near the top of the wall. The crosses are being returned to Christ much in the same way that, after the Armistice, army equipment was handed in; and it is almost as if the Armistice has been transposed to a heavenly register.

This way of thinking about the Resurrection is idiosyncratic, but not blasphemous. New life here means handing in your cross. From whichever side these soldiers came, they had carried a cross on behalf of their nation. Each man's cross was not just the suffering of trench life, their fear and their wounds; it was the fact that they were doing something on behalf of others. They were carrying out orders they may not have liked or understood; they were put in the position of killing their fellow human beings in hand-to-hand combat; their desperate desire to survive could sometimes only be fulfilled by looking into the eyes of another and shooting or stabbing him. And they did this because their nations and their leaders had somehow willed it, and they had been led into this conflict. Their crosses may not have been very noble. They may have acted cruelly or selfishly, but each of them also carried a burden that was not their own sole responsibility. And so Spencer paints their resurrection as a handing in of their crosses to the man who first carried *the* cross. In doing this, they hand back to him the whole bloody mess of their lives. Although the figure of Christ is pushed far into the background and is visually muted and indistinct, it is nevertheless his presence that translates this crudely physical vision of crowds of morally compromised soldiers into a Resurrection scene. Their crosses become symbols of burdens carried in all ages, amid the confusion and the moral chaos of the world in which we live.

The passage in St Augustine's *Confessions* that had caught Spencer's attention – *Ever busy, yet ever at rest; gathering, yet needing not; bearing, filling, guarding; creating, nourishing, and perfecting; seeking, though Thou hast no wants* – gives to the performances of God a rhythmic beat. Despite the many and varied scenes depicted elsewhere in this chapel, it is here, in the Resurrection, that a similar pulse is best conveyed.

Alan Wilkinson, in his masterly study *The Church of England and the First World War*, notes that despite the readiness to believe in supernatural deliverances, in superstition and fatalism, the troops mostly had little time for Christianity. To many of the soldiers it seemed that God, if there at all, was distant and helpless. Meanwhile the war threw into prominence for churchmen urgent questions about death and future life. Spencer confronts these concerns in his Resurrection; he envisages the afterlife mostly by holding up a mirror to life and, in so doing, delivers an understanding of divine intervention and the sacredness of human life. The suggestion in this Resurrection scene and, indeed, in every scene in the chapel at Burghclere, is that the activity of God is to be glimpsed in and through humanity in all its multifariousness; and that St Augustine's glorifying and performing God requires of us simply to be there, attentive in quiet moments, as well as to routine and possibly menial tasks – even amid the wasted theatre of a world war.

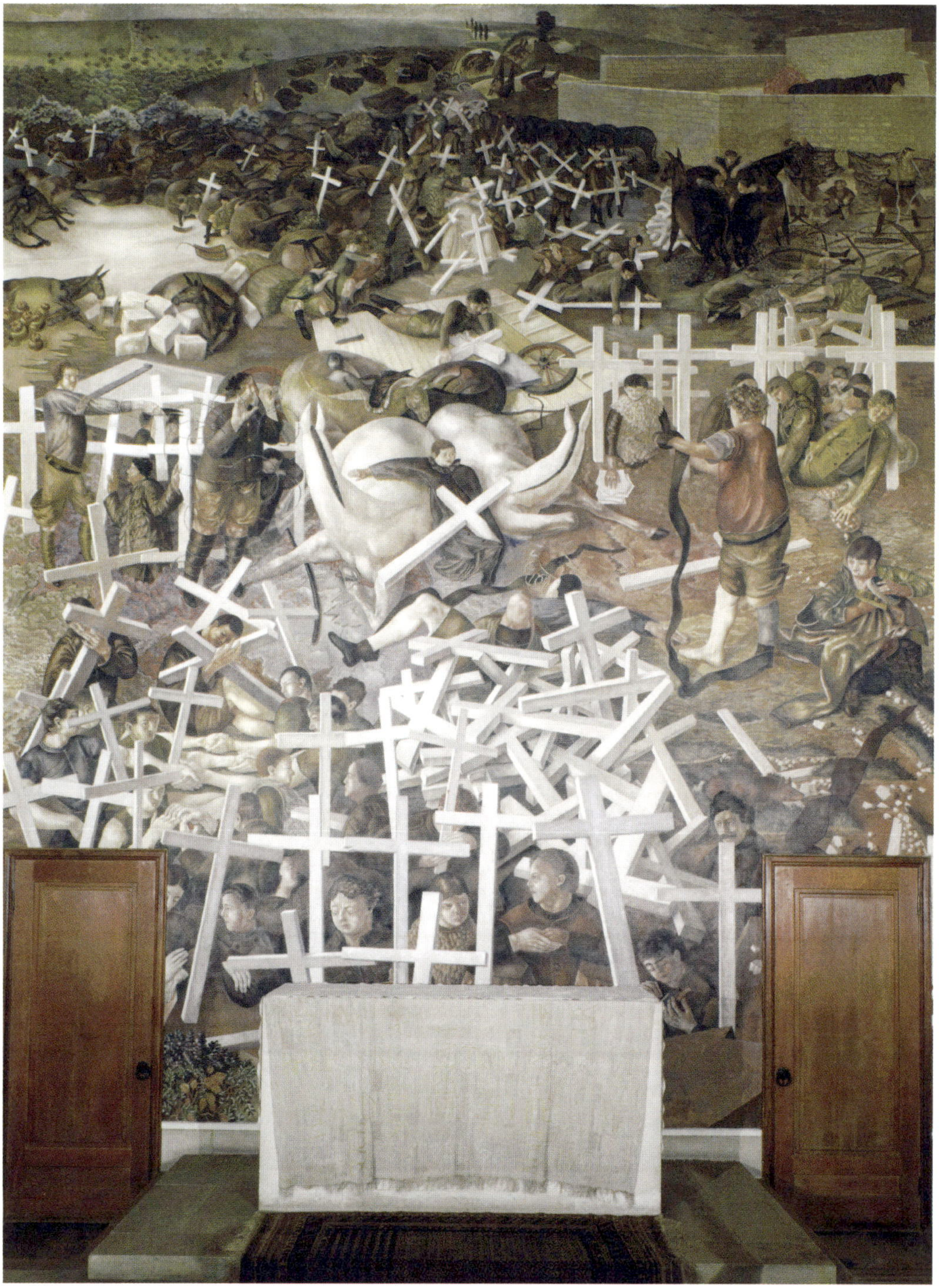

The altar in Sandham Memorial Chapel.

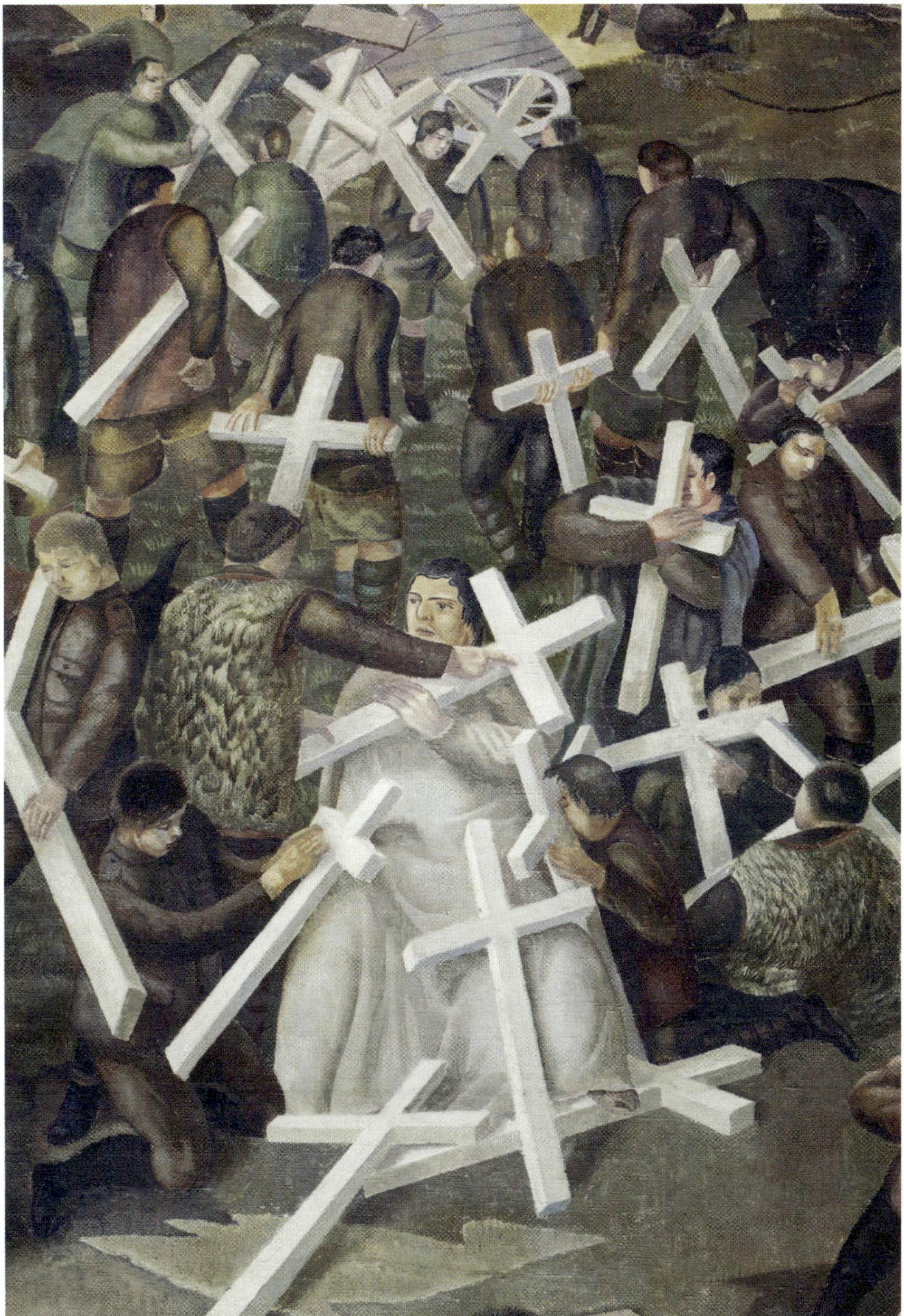

The Resurrection of the Soldiers (detail), Sandham Memorial Chapel.

CHAPTER 7

EXPANDING THE WESTERN EUROPEAN TRADITION

In a 1937 talk for radio, afterwards reproduced in the pages of the *Listener*, Virginia Woolf reminded her listeners of the promiscuity of words. She said: 'Words, English words, are full of echoes, of memories, of associations – naturally. They have been out and about, on people's lips, in their houses, in the streets, in the fields for so many centuries. And that is one of the chief difficulties in writing about them today – that they are stored with meanings, with memories, that they have contracted so many famous marriages. The splendid word "incarnadine", for example, who can use it without remembering also "multitudinous seas"...'[1]

A similar malleability applies to British art: time and again it has opened itself up to unexpected alliances with foreign artists. One notable example is the 17th-century Flemish artist Anthony van Dyck, whose influence on British society portraiture has resonated down the centuries. In the 1920s, this openness to influences from abroad became a readiness to engage with cultures distant in time or place and outside the Western European tradition. The artists whose practice developed in this way were expanding the language of art. This was most noticeable in the field of sculpture, where a return to 'direct carving' went hand in hand with the study of ancient and 'primitive' cultures. The term 'primitive' was in frequent use at the time by archaeologists, art historians and critics, often within an evolutionary conceptual framework. Italian artists, for example, before and after Giotto and up to the later Quattrocento were referred to as 'primitives', owing to their position within the Italian Renaissance. Nevertheless, this term could also carry derogatory associations of 'savagery' and 'barbarism', qualities then regarded as anterior to civilization. It is therefore a troubling label and will be used here within inverted commas.

In order to track the challenge offered by an expanded canon, we need to look back to the period before 1914. Jacob Epstein began investigating pre-classical non-Western sculpture in the Louvre while studying at the Académie Julian, but after experiencing the British Museum during a visit from Paris, he decided to settle in London in 1905. His skill at making portrait busts, modelled in clay and then cast in bronze, soon earned him a reputation; meanwhile his visits to the British Museum and the Victoria and Albert Museum, often made in the company of Eric Gill, developed his interest in carving. Both Epstein and Gill initially looked hard at Indian and Egyptian art. It has also been suggested that Assyrian art, in particular the human-headed winged bulls from the palace of Sargon II at Khorsabad (721–705 BC) in the British Museum, inspired Epstein's 1912 design for the tomb of Oscar Wilde in the Père Lachaise cemetery in Paris. Here a horizontal wing mass is aligned with the flying figure in such a way that it seems to be pushing it forward, creating the impression not of a monument to the past, but of a messenger being sent out into the future. Funded by an anonymous donor, Epstein chose to carve the entire work out of a single block, and a twenty-ton piece of Derbyshire limestone had to be dragged to his Chelsea studio by twelve horses.

The British Museum, Rupert Arrowsmith reminds us, was at this time 'the most dynamic, the most diverse, and in many cases the most dubiously acquired international sculpture collection on Earth'.[2] Eric Gill's diary records that on 11 November 1910 he and Epstein viewed the recently opened 'Manet and the Post-Impressionists' exhibition together, after which they headed off to the British Museum. The aesthetic challenge of the former would only have been enhanced by a visit to the latter. If they chose the main entrance they would have crossed the forecourt and climbed the steps leading into a building overwhelmingly modelled on a Greek temple, its imposing scale making itself additionally felt by monumental pillars ornamented with severe Ionic capitals, eight of which uphold a tympanum over the main entrance. The figurative relief inside this had been modelled by the Royal Academician Richard Westmacott, who studied under the neoclassical sculptor Canova, and its theme was 'The Progress of Civilization'. Figures, suggesting the infancy of culture, crouch into the tight corners at both ends of the tympanum amid fauna and flora then alien to Europe such as banana plants, elephants and lions; as the eye moves towards the apex of the tympanum, the figures straighten up and become Greek-like allegorical representations of the humanities and the sciences. Today this seems a crudely risible piece of cultural propaganda, but at the time its Eurocentric narrative was further encoded, as Arrowsmith suggests, by the positioning of two sculptures from Rapa Nui (Easter Island), the enormous *Hoa Hakananai'a* and the slightly smaller *Moai Hava*, beneath the tympanum, where they sat for some seventy years in the shadowy spaces between the gigantic columns upholding the portico. Their presence was almost certainly intended to offer a deliberate contrast to the smoothly carved, 'soap-bar' classicism of the central figures in the tympanum above. Inside the building, this narrative was further embodied in the display on the ground floor. The west side of the building privileged European exhibits and its holy of holies, the Parthenon marbles, were housed in the 'Elgin Saloon' and were soon to be further reified by new galleries, paid for by Sir Joseph Duveen. But a greater part of the fascination of the British Museum for Epstein, Henri Gaudier-Brzeska and Henry Moore were the artworks that did not depend on Greek canons of beauty and which were, Arrowsmith notes, 'positioned far from this sacred precinct and presented as valuable only in terms of their anthropological or theological significance'.[3]

Henri Gaudier arrived in London in 1911. He was accompanied by Sophie Brzeska, a woman twenty years older than him, whom he had met in Paris. To make their cohabitation respectable, they conjoined their surnames and presented themselves as brother and sister. Between March 1911 and July 1913, Henri Gaudier-Brzeska, while working as a foreign-language clerk for a timber importer in the City of London, spent his spare moments in the Cast Courts of the Victoria and Albert Museum or in the British Museum. Epstein kick-started him into stone carving by asking him at their first meeting if he cut stone. 'Most certainly,' Gaudier-Brzeska replied, eager for approval, and hurried off to find the necessary stone that, once carved, would make this true.[4]

Friendship with Epstein deepened Gaudier-Brzeska's passion for the British Museum. Another of his colleagues, Horace Brodsky, recalled: 'The British Museum was always a great stimulus, and he would rush back to his studio with a new idea formed in his mind: then he would go straight to his bench and get paper and pencil, if he had not stone, and roughly draw some design the visit had suggested.'[5] Brodsky also saw how impressionable the young man was, readily exhilarated by his surroundings and intensely receptive to all impressions. As well as studying Polynesian, Chinese, Assyrian and Egyptian art in the British Museum, Gaudier-Brzeska also admired Michelangelo, Rodin and Brancusi. In a very short space of time he abandoned Rodinesque naturalism for a more abstract and rhythmic handling of form. This huge leap forward is best seen in his *Red Stone Dancer* (*c.* 1913). The astonishing sure-footedness with which he moved from a 19th-century aesthetic into a visual language that pioneered a modern approach gave him a catalytic role in the development of modernist sculpture in Britain between the wars. He remained a haunting influence even after he was killed by a bullet through the head, aged twenty-three, during a battle in Neuville-Saint-Vaast at Artois on 5 June 1915.

Ezra Pound identified Gaudier-Brzeska's death as the gravest individual loss sustained by the arts during the war. Pound also wrote a memoir of him, which, when published in 1916, included his writings and some of his letters. Henry Moore was to find this book 'a great help and excitement',[6] and it is probable that the opening line of 'Vortex', Gaudier-Brzeska's manifesto for sculpture – 'Sculptural energy is the mountain' – helped bring to the fore Moore's analogy of the human figure with hills, caves and landscape. While reviewing Pound's book, Roger Fry saw clearly that Gaudier-Brzeska had sought 'to create a classic art, one of purely formal expressiveness',[7] an achievement shared with the Romanian sculptor Constantin Brancusi. It was chiefly through Gaudier-Brzeska, and to a lesser extent Epstein, that Brancusi's influence came to England. Gaudier-Brzeska met Brancusi only once, in 1913 at the Albert Hall,[8] shortly before the opening of the Allied Artists Association's annual London salon, in which the Romanian showed three sculpted heads. In this same exhibition Gaudier-Brzeska exhibited his own work for the first time, showing six plasters and one bronze.

Pound's memoir attributes to Gaudier-Brzeska that which was central to Brancusi's aesthetic: 'that the beauty of sculpture is inseparable from its material and that it inheres in the material'.[9] This led to the doctrine of 'truth to materials' which became a catchphrase among sculptors in the 1920s and attendant on a belief in carving. Brancusi committed himself wholeheartedly to carving and sought to portray the essential rather than the particular in his art, thereby giving rise to a sophisticated and profound form of simplification. His art and ideas were to be hugely influential on modernist sculpture, on Gaudier-Brzeska as well as on Moore and Barbara Hepworth; Brancusi's desire to combine the vitality of 'primitive' art with the idealization of classical art identified a union that was to become a central challenge for Moore. Both Moore and Hepworth visited Brancusi's studio during the 1920s.

A memorial exhibition of Gaudier-Brzeska's sculptures, pastels and drawings was mounted at the Leicester Galleries before the war ended, in May/June 1918. *The Times* pronounced that it showed him to have been 'one of the most remarkable artists of our time'.[10] It attracted the attention of discerning collectors, although many of the sculptures on show were already in private hands. The beautiful way in which the mother and child are folded together in *Maternity* (1913), which had been lent by Roger Fry and is now in the collection of the Musée National d'Art Moderne, Paris, may have stimulated Frank Dobson's *The Man Child*, produced in 1921. Dobson was another artist who frequented the British Museum and is said to have been especially interested in art from the Congo. The compact arrangement in *The Man Child*, with its two women pressed up close against a male child, must have had a strong emotional appeal in 1921 after the decimation of male servicemen during the war. Eagerness for topicality may explain why Dobson was willing to exhibit it unfinished, and it was only completed many years later. At its first showing, it demonstrated a move away from the set of ideal standards of human proportion

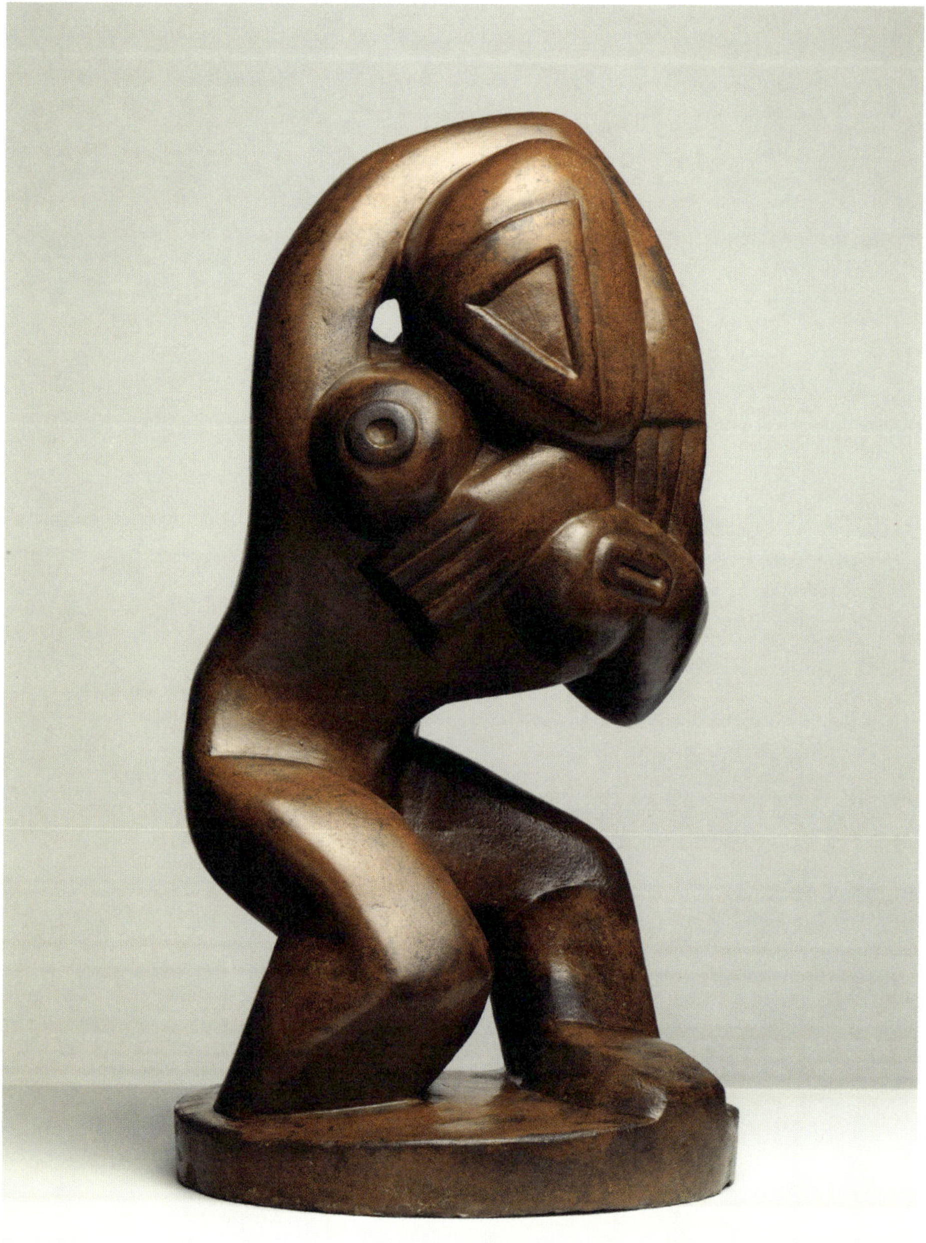

Henri Gaudier-Brzeska, *Red Stone Dancer*,
Mansfield stone, *c.* 1913.

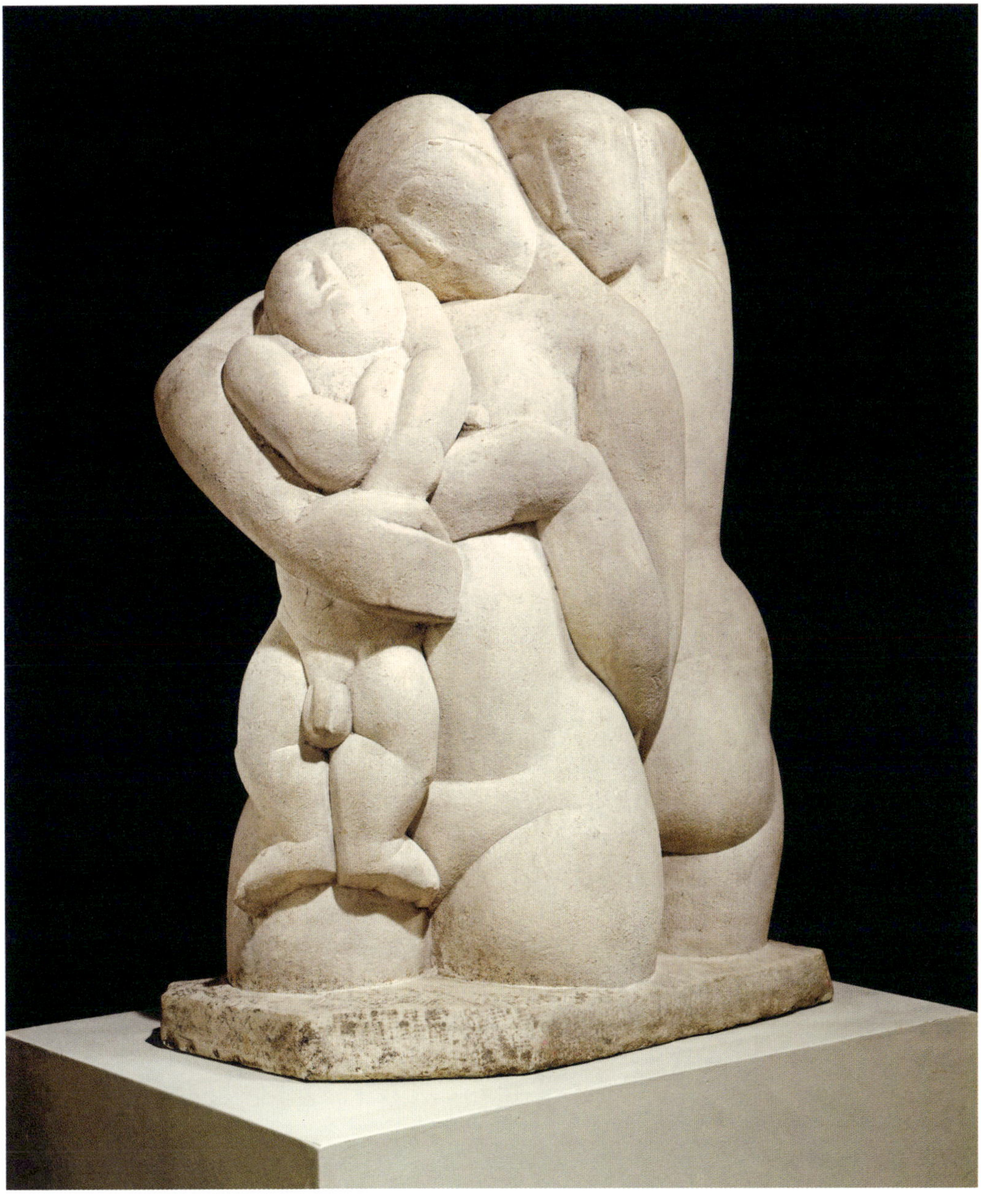

Frank Dobson, *The Man Child*,
Portland stone, 1921.

and beauty that the Greco-Roman tradition and the Italian Renaissance had created, a hegemony which Epstein and Gaudier-Brzeska had also successfully challenged.

Much less would be known today about Gaudier-Brzeska had not Jim Ede acted decisively on discovering that the boardroom at the Tate Gallery – which doubled as Ede's office – had become the repository of Gaudier-Brzeska's artistic estate in late June 1926. The story behind this development has been explored by Roger Cole in the second of his two books on Gaudier-Brzeska,[11] but is hardly noticed elsewhere. Likewise, Sophie Brzeska's part in the narrative is rarely considered.

Sophie inherited Gaudier's estate by means of an inter vivos gift. It is never easy being tasked with the role of artist's widow, and she had been deeply affected by the loss of Gaudier. T. E. Hulme, a key theorist within the vorticist group who was himself shortly to lose his life in the war, had asked Stanisława de Karlowska, the Polish wife of the artist Robert Bevan, to break the news of Henri's death to Sophie. When together, the Gaudier-Brzeskas had frequently lived on the edge of poverty. Now, badly in need of funds, Sophie could have sold some of the best sculptures and drawings in her possession; but she did not do so, in the hope that at a future date some would be acquired for the nation. Ede later claimed that the comprehensive nature of the memorial exhibition at the Leicester Galleries owed much to her 'indefatigable energy', and that although she thought Pound's memoir 'mostly about himself', she also welcomed it as something from which further enquiry would spring, thereby affirming that Gaudier's name would not be lost to history.[12] This may be true, but Sophie's mental health was less stable than Ede suggests. Oliver Brown, who ran the Leicester Galleries with Cecil Phillips, recorded in his memoirs that it was the Bevans who first came to him with the idea for a memorial and that towards the end of the exhibition, Sophie, looking very ill, wanted to take everything away and leave the country, as she felt she was being persecuted. She left pacified, having been given a folder of drawings.[13]

Soon afterwards Sophie moved to Wotton-under-Edge in Gloucestershire, to 3 Wortley Terrace, one in a row of tiny cottages that no longer exists. The money she received from sales at the 1918 memorial exhibition, 'while considerable, was not sufficient to bear interest upon which she could live',[14] so she had to use capital, which gradually diminished. The threat of poverty and noisy neighbours further agitated her mental instability. She made visits to London, often staying with de Karlowska, and developed the habit of haunting places where she and Gaudier had shared their life together. Brodsky describes her at this time as 'a forlorn creature, dragging herself around, wretchedly dressed and shod – a most pitiable spectacle'.[15] In 1922 she was removed from her cottage and incarcerated as a 'pauper lunatic' in Gloucester's County Mental Hospital.

Sophie died in 1925, aged fifty-three, intestate and almost certainly penniless. Yet her estate contained Gaudier-Brzeska's sculptures, pastels and drawings, his letters to her and her own literary manuscripts, which alone filled three trunks and five packing cases and included many drafts for her unfinished autobiographical novel, a journal, short stories and accounts of her relationship with Gaudier. All was valued at £545. As happens when someone dies intestate and there appear to be no known heirs, the state took over. Her estate was eventually transferred to the Treasury Solicitor, whose duty it was to establish whether there were any next of kin or other claimants. Advertisements were placed in four English newspapers. But, as nothing was posted in any French or Polish newspapers, no appearances were entered and grant of administration was made on 20 April 1926, following which the sculptures and drawings had to be offered to a national collection. Hence the arrival of the entire estate at the Tate Gallery, with the expectation that the work would be shown to the board of trustees for consideration. The gallery's director, Charles Aitken, did not think Gaudier-Brzeska's art would arouse much interest.

Nothing happened for some months. In the meantime, the critic R. H. Wilenski was asked to value the entire estate. He took into account the cost price of a work of art before it reaches a dealer, and the fact that when works of art appear on the market in large quantities their value is diminished. In his objective and considered opinion the entire estate was worth £250. Soon afterwards the Leicester Galleries, whom the Treasury identified with Gaudier-Brzeska owing to the memorial show, were invited to mount an exhibition from the work available or to make their best offer. They came back with the latter – almost certainly having got wind of Wilenski's estimate, as it came in a little below, at £220.

Then, in November 1926, after several months' delay, the Tate trustees surprised Aitken by selecting three sculptures and seventeen drawings, on the understanding that the Treasury was prepared to offer these as a permanent loan. A further three sculptures and eighteen drawings were accepted by the Contemporary Art Society, of which Ede was then secretary. Although some of the best things were now spoken for, this still left nineteen sculptures, thirteen oils or pastels and 1,595 drawings. Ede had been privy to discussions with the Leicester Galleries, and he had also been given full responsibility by Aitken for dealing with the correspondence concerning the estate. Knowing that the Treasury was hoping to receive £220, he persuaded the collector C. Frank Stoop to pay £160 for the Tate acquisitions, which, as was agreed, Stoop gifted back to the Tate through the CAS in 1930. And after much thought over several months, Ede finally wrote to the Treasury, pointing out that it was unlikely the Leicester Galleries would come up with their offer as the monetary value of the estate had been diminished by the loss of choice items. Mindful that

£60 was still needed if the Treasury was to receive the amount formerly offered by the Leicester Galleries, he himself now offered to pay this sum for the remaining items. His offer was accepted, but there was one drawback: as a Tate employee, he was a civil servant, and there was a Treasury rule that government property could not be sold to civil servants without sanction. Ede therefore arranged for his friend Edward McKnight Kauffer to act as his front and put up the money. This process was repeated when Ede discovered that, for an extra five guineas, he could also gain such rights as the Crown had in the copyright on Sophie Brzeska's papers and those of Gaudier-Brzeska. In this way he achieved a terrific coup, at a stroke becoming far and away the largest owner of Gaudier-Brzeska's work as well as the copyright owner of the mass of papers related to his work. Copyright ownership also gave him the right to make casts of some of the sculptures. This last benefit later helped make possible Ede's creation of Kettle's Yard in Cambridge, a place that would act as a monument to the aesthetic Brancusi had done so much to inspire, and where an attic room, filled with drawings, would always be kept as a kind of shrine to Gaudier-Brzeska.

In the immediate aftermath of his negotiations with the Treasury, Ede, while still working at the Tate, started his *Life of Henri Gaudier-Brzeska*, first published in 1930. In 1931 a cheaper edition appeared under a different title, which the American publisher Knopf preferred: *Savage Messiah*. One of the book's eccentricities is that it reads like a biographical novel, the relationship between Henri and Sophie taking precedent over discussion of Gaudier-Brzeska's art. But perhaps this could have been predicted. Sophie Brzeska, writing in her journal three years after Henri's death, opined: 'It is inconceivable that our story won't live on, that it won't move those who only know base physical passion. Our story will become a legend.'[16]

By the mid-1930s, further developments within modern art had given rise to the term 'international modernism'. This referred to artists, architects and designers, mostly living in Paris, who were committed to the 'modern movement' and bound together by a set of ideals, which, if applied universally, would override the boundaries associated with national identity. This was at a time when museum collections were often categorized by national 'schools' – English, French, Italian or Spanish, for example. Nowadays, museums are beginning to acknowledge that nationhood need not necessarily be the prime characteristic by which an object is categorized; and in a global world it is more readily appreciated that the work of artists can have more fluidity than the emphasis on national identity suggests. In England, Roger Fry, with his generalizing philosophical bent, led the way in the search for aesthetic principles that could be applied to the art of many countries. This interest had begun, early in his career, in 1905, when he produced an edition of Sir Joshua Reynolds's *Discourses* and noted Reynolds's interest in the concept of unity within the arts. In 1932 Fry was appointed Slade Professor at Cambridge and began to devise a series of lectures that would survey the history of world arts. His sudden death in 1934 meant that he did not complete these lectures,[17] nevertheless in the course of his life he had done much to broaden the public's interest in art. Henry Moore took up Fry's interest in aesthetic unity and came to the conclusion that it was above all 'primitive art' that 'shows art to be a universal continuous activity, with no separation between past and present', producing what he called a 'common world-language of form'.[18]

A great deal has been written about Henry Moore, but the focus here is on his role in the expansion of the canon or the breakdown of the dominance of the Western European tradition. Ironically, all the originary motivating experiences of this far-seeing radical sculptor were sourced by localism. The seventh of eight children, he grew up in a family that never went on holiday. Home was Castleford, a small town with five coal mines, chemical works and potteries all within a mile and a half of its centre. Yet the proximity of industry did not cut him off from nature, as the nearby countryside was still being farmed, leaving him keenly aware of the sharp contrasts in his surroundings.

Moore always stressed his rootedness in the area around Castleford and all his life proudly declared that he was a Yorkshireman. His interest in sculpture began not with his discovery of Donatello or any other great sculptor but with the anonymous craftsmen who carved the animals and grotesque heads for the corbels on the porch at St Oswald's Church, Methley, where he was taken on a visit as a schoolboy. Inside the church he was astonished by two funerary alabaster effigies showing Lionel, Lord Welles and his wife, lying side by side. He later came to associate their compelling stillness with Egyptian art. They were, he said, 'the first real sculptures' that he remembered.[19]

Moore left school at the age of fifteen, already wanting to become a sculptor. His father steered him towards teaching as a more reliable source of income. War made other decisions more pressing and in 1917, having turned eighteen, Moore opted to volunteer rather than wait for conscription. He joined the Civil Service Rifles in February and did his military training in Winchester. It has been mistakenly claimed that on visits to London from Winchester he enjoyed his first experience of the National Gallery and the British Museum. He may have seen the buildings, and possibly the 'Picture of the Month' in the National Gallery, but by this date both museums had sent their collections away for safekeeping. The British Museum had closed to the public in March 1916 and did not fully reopen for almost three years; the significance of its collections did not properly begin to make an impact on Moore until 1921–2. Instead, in 1917 he fought in the Battle of Cambrai, experienced trench warfare and mustard gas poisoning, and was marked by the human suffering he had witnessed. After the war ended, an ex-serviceman's grant made it possible for him to continue his education, and in September 1919 he gave up his commitment to teaching and enrolled at Leeds School of Art.

Technical demonstrations and academic methods that upheld the classical past governed the classes at Leeds. Imagine therefore the surprise Moore had when, early in 1921, he discovered in the Leeds Art Reference Library a copy of Roger Fry's *Vision and Design* and read the opening paragraphs of an essay on African carving:

> What a comfortable mental furniture the generalizations of a century ago must have afforded! What a right little, tight little, round little world it was then when Greece was the only source of culture, when Greek art, even in Roman copies was the only indisputable art, except for some Renaissance repetitions! Philosophy, the love of truth, drama, and for all we know music – all these were the fruits of a special kind of life....Consequently if we could only learn the Greek lessons of political freedom and intellectual self-consciousness all the rest would be added unto us.
>
> And now, in the last sixty years, knowledge and perception have poured upon us so fast that the whole well-ordered system has been blown away, and we stand bare to the blast, scarcely able to snatch a hasty generalization or two to cover our nakedness for a moment.[20]

Moore came to regard this book as 'the most lucky discovery'.[21] Its wide-ranging essays on 'The Art of the Bushmen', 'Ancient American Art' and 'Mohammedan Art' opened his mind to new things. But the essay which made the most powerful impact on him was one Fry had hustled into the book at the last moment under the title of the Chelsea Book Club exhibition 'Negro Sculpture', which he had reviewed for the *Atheneaum*. This title would be unacceptable today, but at that time it was commonly used to describe African carvings. As it proceeded, the essay transformed Moore's understanding as to what sculpture should do and be. Fry pointed out that all archaic European sculpture, such as Greek and Romanesque, for instance,

> approaches plasticity from the point of view of bas-relief. The statue bears traces of having been conceived as the combination of front, back and side bas-relief. And this continues to make itself felt almost until the final development of the tradition. Complete plastic freedom with us seems only

> to come at the end of a long period, when the art has attained a high degree of representational skill and when it is generally already decadent from the point of view of imaginative significance.

In contrast with this tradition, Fry notes that the plastic sense of the African artist 'leads him to give its utmost amplitude and relief to all the protuberant parts of the body, and to get thereby an extraordinarily emphatic and impressive sequence of planes. So far from clinging to two dimensions, as we tend to do, he actually underlines, as it were, the three-dimensionalness of his forms.'

Aware that he was writing at a time when the received view in England was that African art offered only ethnographic interest, Fry trumpeted, loud and clear, his conclusion:

> We have the habit of thinking that the power to create expressive plastic form is one of the greatest human achievements, and the names of the great sculptors are handed down from generation to generation, so that it seems unfair to be forced to admit that certain nameless savages have possessed this power not only in a higher degree than we at this moment but than we as a nation have ever possessed it....some of these things are great sculpture – greater, I think, than anything we produced even in the Middle Ages. Certainly they have the special qualities of sculpture in a higher degree. They have indeed complete plastic freedom; that is to say these African artists really conceive of form in three dimensions. Now this is rare in sculpture.[22]

We hear an echo of Fry in Moore's mature reflection, written for a book published in 1981: 'True full sculptural expression is through sculpture completely in the round.'[23] But at the time he first read Fry's book, his dominant awareness was that it opened the way to other books, to new ways of seeing and above all to the British Museum. 'That was really the beginning,' Moore said of *Vision and Design*.[24] African art had been collected and discussed by artists working in Paris before the 1914–18 war. By the early 1920s, Jacob Epstein had acquired a large collection of African and Oceanic carvings. Henry Moore, after moving from Leeds to the Royal College of Art in the autumn of 1921, got to know Epstein and was invited to see his collection, which was housed in his bedroom. The room was so stuffed with carvings that Moore wondered how Epstein managed to get into bed without knocking something over. At a time when a good example of so-called 'primitive' carving could be picked up at the Caledonian Market for £10, Moore himself would also have liked to collect, but as his scholarship to the Royal College of Art amounted to £90 for the entire year, he was not able to do so.

In England, African and Oceanic art was aesthetically underrated prior to the 1920s. A rare reference to it in art is the black and white beaded African arrow bag, then in Roger Fry's possession, which he placed in the background to his painting *Lilies* (1917), now in Bristol Art Gallery, to offset the lilies and the Chinese figurine. This same year he had taken active steps to obtain more information on African sculpture. In 1917, while still joint editor of the *Burlington Magazine*, he had

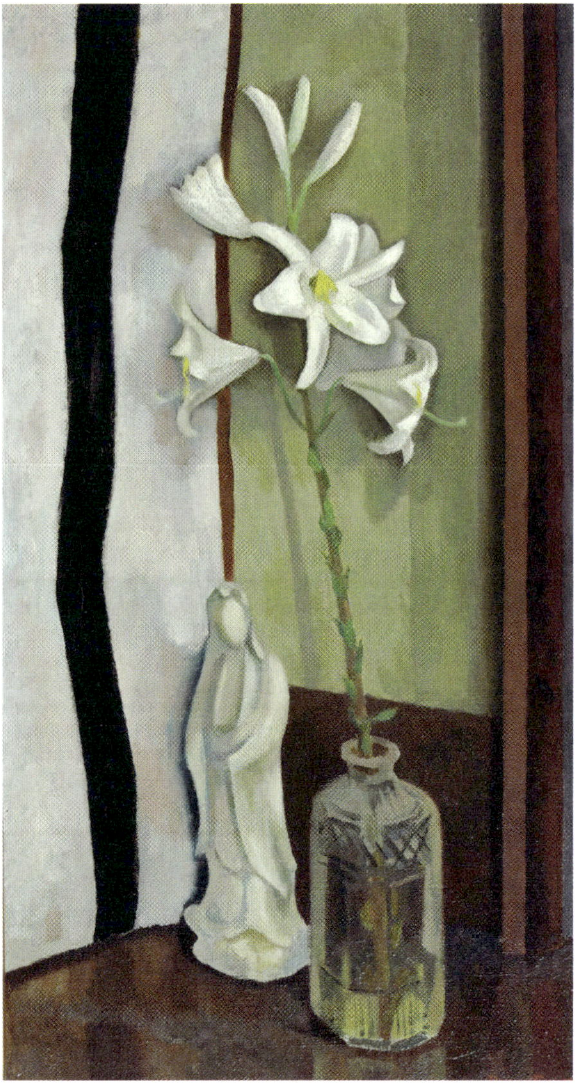

Roger Fry, *Lilies*, oil on canvas, 1917.

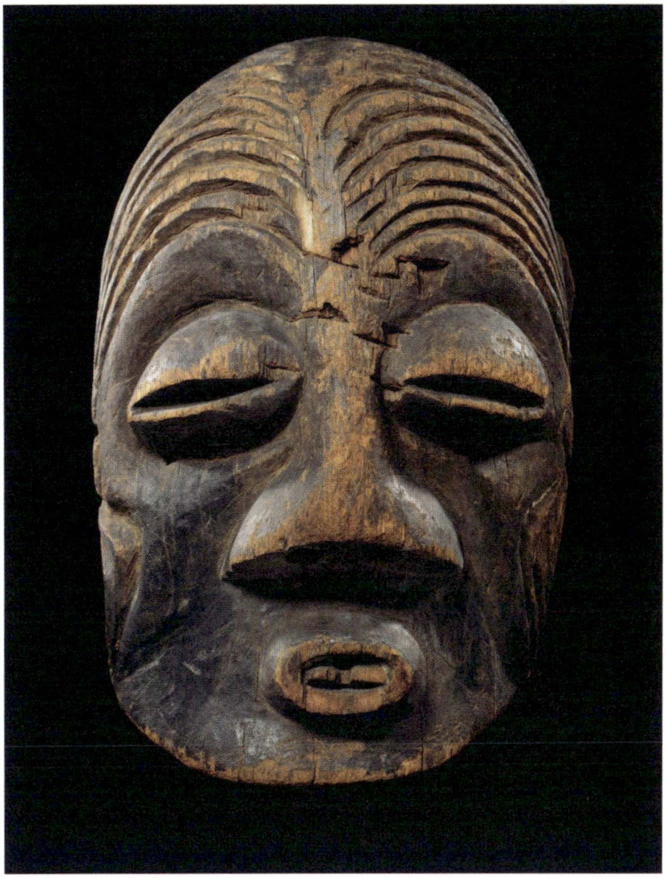

African dancing mask
from Uvira,
Lake Tanganyika.

written to the dealer Rose Vildrac in Paris, asking if she or her husband Charles knew of someone who could write on African art for the magazine. Soon after the war, he travelled to Paris and visited the Vildracs, the Louvre and Paul Guillaume, who in 1917 had published *Sculptures nègres*, the first book in France to focus on African and Oceanic carvings as art. Fry not only studied Guillaume's collection of African sculpture but also that in the possession of artist André Derain. This is recorded in a letter he sent to Vanessa Bell, where he reports on Derain's stated desire to get rid of 'quality in painting'. Fry adds: 'I think I know what he means. He wants the vision to be communicated directly so that one is quite unconscious of the medium through which it is given'[25] – an aim that may have been inspired by Derain's interest in African art. A few years later, in 1924, Fry acquired in Paris an African dancing mask originating from Uvira, Lake Tanganyika, Zaire (now the Democratic Republic of the Congo).[26] Its powerful presence demonstrates some of the qualities he admired in African carvings, notably the emphatic three-dimensionality, a 'disconcerting vitality' and, in the figures, 'an inner life of their own'.[27] His review of the Chelsea Book Club exhibition, when republished in *Vision and Design*, marked a turning point in the appreciation of African art in England.

Only a small handful of collectors and curators had Fry's breadth of interest in art. But it was above all his communicative skills, the freshness and accessibility of his observations and ideas, that earned *Vision and Design* a wide audience. Since 1920, the book has almost never been out of print. After studying natural sciences at Cambridge Fry had trained as a painter, and he continued to paint whenever possible all his life, in the hope that he would leave the most important imprint of his mind in paint. But early on he had been easily derailed, partly for financial reasons, by his ability to lecture on art and to produce art journalism. While simultaneously becoming a connoisseur of Italian art, he had been invited by the poet Henry Newbolt to write for *Pilot* magazine, but then moved on to the *Athenaeum*, where he replaced F. G. Stephens, one of the original members of the Pre-Raphaelite Brotherhood, as its main art critic. His productivity with book and exhibition reviews, as well as series of articles in a more art historical vein, enhanced his reputation, as did his association with an international network of scholars and dealers in Italian art.

In 1903 he became one of the founders of the *Burlington Magazine* and in 1906 he began working for the Metropolitan Museum of Art in New York, initially as curator and then as European Adviser.[28] This was an intensely difficult period for him, not least because, now married with two children, he was aware that his wife, the artist Helen Coombe, was beginning to show signs of mental illness. Strains on his position at the Metropolitan became noticeable and early in 1910 a disagreement with the chairman, J. Pierpont Morgan, terminated his appointment. Later that year he was faced with the need to have Helen certified and placed in an asylum. After this he turned his back on the establishment and completely altered the focus of his career by placing his entrepreneurial skills at the service of modern art, mounting his two seminal post-impressionist exhibitions in 1910 and 1912 and becoming something of an entrepreneur, opening the Omega Workshops in 1913.

When in 1919 he presented Chatto & Windus with a set of essays on artists from within the Western art tradition as well as other topics from cultures outside that tradition, the publishers did not at first recognize the originality of what was on offer. Assuming it would only appeal to an educated elite, they opted for a handsome volume, slightly larger than quarto, printed on thick high-quality paper. Its full-page black and white illustrations were printed on art paper and interleaved with protective tissue. The cover price was fixed at a guinea but, when published, the book sold for 25 shillings, owing to the high cost of paper in the immediate aftermath of war. Fry complained at its high price to his friend Marie Mauron: 'I wanted every student to have it – and the poorest people.'[29] Frances Hodgkins, quick to recognize the importance of *Vision and Design*, recommended it to her students, but warned them of its high price. Soon after, however, as has been mentioned, it was followed by smaller and less expensive editions and much reprinting. By 1937 it was available for sixpence as a Pelican paperback, owing to the arrival in the publishing world of Allen Lane and Penguin Books.

Fry's essays overturned establishment opinion. He showed that the Greco-Roman Renaissance tradition, with its emphasis on mimetic representation, could be regarded as an anomaly among the great civilizations of the world – something that Henry Moore also came to recognize. In its quarto format, the first edition of *Vision and Design* carried a frontispiece illustrating a portion of a Maya sculpture from Piedras Negras, remains that date from about AD 50–200. The image relates to the chapter on ancient American Art; Fry chose it because it illustrated the 'extreme richness of decorative effects' achieved in Maya art, but it must have baffled many readers. Sam Rose has argued that, owing to his wide-ranging interest in world art and his fascination with aesthetics, Fry had begun to construct 'a whole system of thought about how the humanly made visual world was meaningful'.[30] It is, however, difficult to pin Fry down to any particular role within the history of aesthetics owing to his openness to re-evaluations of art and aesthetics. He adopted, as Christopher Reed rightly noted, 'a methodology of doubt';[31] and although he can be associated with a predominantly formalist stance during the second decade of the 20th century, no monolithic ideology guided his thinking and writing about art. When the Courtauld Institute in London came into existence in 1930, dedicated to the study of art history, Fry wrote a letter to the editor of the *Burlington Magazine*, his main hope being that, whatever specialisms were to be on offer, 'there should be a considerable period of study in which the student is led to contemplate typical works of art of all periods and all countries' in the spirit of 'perceptive enquiry'.[32]

Vision and Design cut through barriers that had previously shut out wider appreciation of other cultures. Fry's directive, as previously mentioned, was simply to look at form. Its narrow focus excludes much, but in Fry's day it had a liberating, democratizing influence, not only opening up access to other cultures but also slicing through the seemingly tangled confusion then surrounding modern art. Fry's name is often linked with Clive Bell's, but Fry's formalism is different to that of Bell as expounded in *Art* (1914), a short book in which, for the sake of polemic, Bell simplifies Fry's ideas and removes subtlety and nuance. Bell coined the phrase 'significant form' as that which gives rise to aesthetic experience; Fry, in his review of *Art*, argued that something always has to be *added* to form to give it significance.

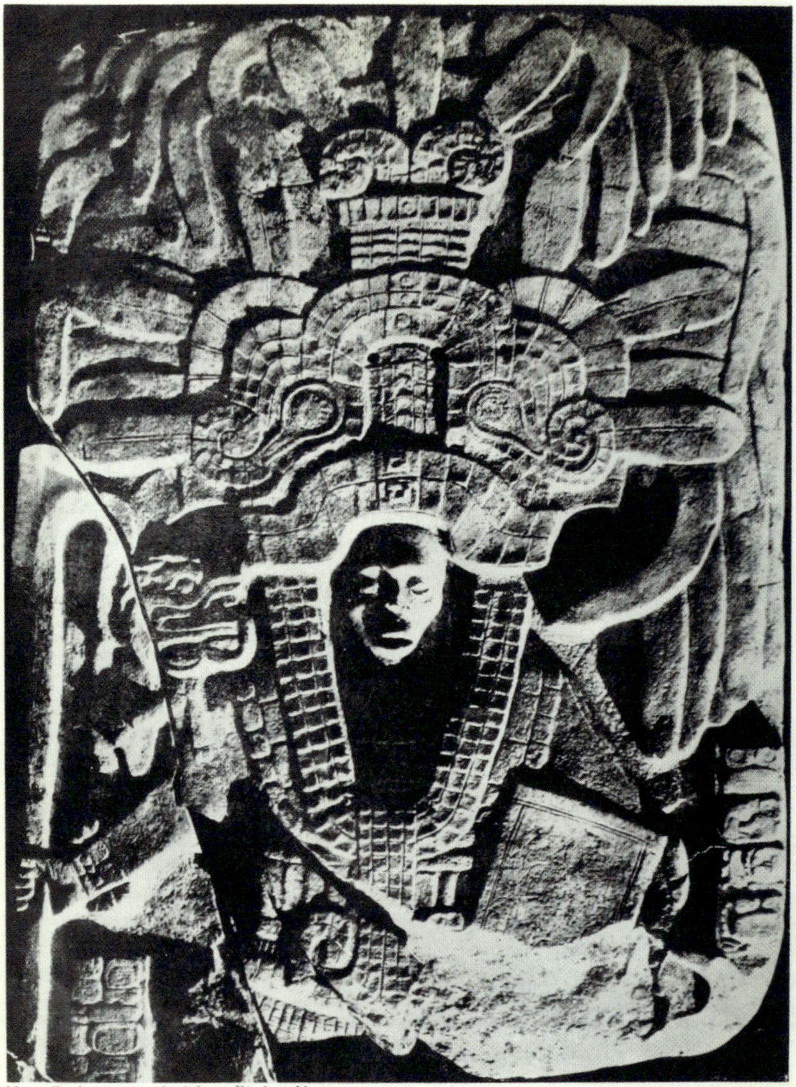
Maya Sculpture (portion) from Piedras Negras
Frontispiece

Frontispiece to Roger Fry's *Vision and Design*, 1920.

In his own writings and lectures on art, Fry often showed how formal interests are used to pursue expressive and poetical ends. His approach to art was never cut off from life but remained alert to its expressive, communicative and intentional vitality. For the young Henry Moore, reading *Vision and Design* in Leeds Art Reference Library, Fry's essays on African art and ancient American art had immediate relevance. 'Once you'd read Roger Fry', he later admitted, 'the whole thing was there.'[33]

The fact that the ancient past has come down to us primarily in the more durable materials of wood or stone perhaps explains why it is mostly sculptors who gained inspiration and fresh strength by looking beyond the Western European tradition, at cultures different and distant to their own. One exception is Matisse, who visited the British Museum in October and again in November 1919, as is recorded in the visitors' book for that period.[34] His main purpose was to view the Chinese collections. He later told a friend: 'A poet showed me all the splendours of the Chinese masters: it was a revelation of a new world to me. All the barriers of race and time collapsed before me, since I was forced to realize that these Chinese a thousand years ago had already seen our problems and had resolved them more or less in the same way we have today.'[35] The poet in question is thought to have been Matthew Stewart Prichard, a friend of Matisse who had made a study of Chinese art. But the fact that this epiphany took place in the British Museum and among its Chinese collections makes it much more likely that it was Laurence Binyon, who had set up a near autonomous sub-department within the British Museum's Prints and Drawings Department and did much to help expand the Museum's Chinese, Japancsc and Indian art collections.

Also interesting is the fact that Roger Fry, whose own interest in Chinese art led him to imitate Chinese examples in the pottery he made for the Omega Workshops and who later wrote about Chinese bronzes, appears to have recognized the Chinese ingredient in Matisse's work before Matisse himself did. In his catalogue introduction to the Second Post-Impressionist Exhibition in 1912, Fry argued: 'Matisse aims at convincing us of the reality of his forms by the continuity and flow of his rhythmic line, by the logic of his space relations, and, above all, by an entirely new use of colour. In this, as in his markedly rhythmic design, he approaches more than any other European to the ideals of Chinese art. His work has to an extraordinary degree that decorative unity of design which distinguishes all the artists of this school.'[36]

When Moore began his art school training, sculpture was very little regarded. After completing the two-year drawing course at Leeds in one year, he had opted to concentrate on sculpture, and the School of Art had to set up a sculpture department to cater for his needs. At the Royal College, too, he found that the sculpture department was tiny, inhabited by only six or seven students. The dimness that surrounded sculpture in the early 1920s partly explains why his discovery of the British Museum caused him such excitement. Even before encountering *Vision and Design* he had begun keeping a 'History of Sculpture' notebook, with facts about Chaldea, Babylonia, Assyria and Mesopotamia and the sculpture associated with these regions.

It is also evident from some of his early carvings, made at Leeds, that Moore had already begun looking at examples of ethnographic art in the collection of Sir Michael Sadler, the vice-chancellor of the University of Leeds, who opened his home and collection to students with an interest in art. Here Moore also had the opportunity to view works in Sadler's possession by famous post-impressionists: artists such as Kandinsky, Matisse and Picasso 'opened up a world that was other than the Victorian, academic, art-school world'.[37] Sadler evidently thought highly of Moore: he became a long-term supporter, bought a number of his works and made possible the Museum of Modern Art, New York's acquisition of Moore's *Two Forms*, a 1935 piece in pyinkado wood.

At the Royal College of Art in September 1921, where Derwent Wood headed up the sculpture department and Barry Hart taught stone carving, the main emphasis of the teaching was on classical art, against which Moore soon wanted to rebel. He took life drawing classes under Leon Underwood, whose passion for African, Aztec and Native American sculpture would have chimed with the first stirrings of Moore's own interest in the 'primitive', archaic and tribal. When Underwood left the Royal College in 1923, Moore and another Yorkshireman, Raymond Coxon, persuaded him to give them private tuition at his studio-based Brook Green School of Art in Hammersmith. Nevertheless it was chiefly Fry's *Vision and Design* that sent Moore to the British Museum in 1922. Once inside the Museum, he felt like 'a starved man having Selfridges' grocery department all to himself'.[38]

He worked his way systematically, section by section, around the Museum, making notes and sketches as to the ground covered. 'Got as far as Easter Island,' Notebook 3 records in July 1922, and then, a few days later, 'reached N.W. Coast'. Moore was seeking a comprehensive knowledge of non-Western art. He recalled: 'The existence of such varied traditions outside European art was a great revelation and stimulus.'[39] Hence his repeated visits, for two or three hours at a time, twice or more each week. 'One room after another caught my enthusiasm,' he explained. 'The wonderful thing about the British Museum is that everything is stretched out before you and you are free to make your own discoveries....In my most formative years, nine-tenths of my understanding and learning about sculpture came from the British Museum.'[40] To James Johnson Sweeney, he later admitted: 'The Royal

College of Art meant nothing in comparison. Every Wednesday, Saturday and Sunday I would go to the British Museum. But not till after three months did things begin to settle into any pattern of reality for me. Till then everything was wonderful – a new world at every turn.'[41]

One area of the Museum that he first discovered on his second visit, an hour before closing time, was the Ethnographic Galleries, packed with cases overflowing with objects from Asia, Africa, America and Oceania, including Benin bronzes. He described it as 'overcrowded and jumbled together like junk in a marine stores so that after hundreds of visits I would still find carvings not discovered there before'.[42]

Moore said that he chose sculpture over painting because it was 'more real to me – it is actual reality'.[43] His study of objects in the British Museum enabled him to find ways through which he could enhance or strengthen the expressive reality of his art. His distrust of attempts to show movement in sculpture made him especially appreciative of the stillness and timelessness of the poses in Egyptian art and the grandeur that results from this. Looking at the statue of Horemheb and one of his wives seated on chairs with lion-paw feet, he noticed how 'a superb sense of repose and serenity' was conveyed by their arms. It was memories like these that inflected his own work, and an echo of Egyptian sculpture can be felt in his handling of shoulders, arms and hands in a series from the early 1930s that employs the motif of interlocking hands. This is most clearly felt in *Girl with Clasped Hands* (1930), where the tension between face and hands is similar to that which he observed in a 22-centimetre-high alabaster Sumerian carving in the British Museum (*c.* 3000 BC). The way in which the figure clasps her tiny hands in front of her led Moore to observe: 'It is as though the head and the hands were the two focal points – one cannot look at the head without being also conscious of the hands.'[44] Yet although a Sumerian precursor exists for this and other works by Moore,[45] the style of figuration in *Girl with Clasped Hands* is most definitely sourced by a blending of cultures.

Another work that made a lasting impact on Moore in the British Museum was his first sighting of Amenhotep II's enormous, 18-foot-long red granite arm, terminating in a clenched fist. This giant fragment made him realize how monumental and impressive sculpture could be. But it was not just size that enabled Moore to discover in other Egyptian pieces 'a monumentality of vision'. He explained: 'The Egyptians in their sculpture wanted to show that life had a greater significance than the ordinary daily routine of living. They managed to imbue a grandeur, a permanence, and some sort of religious meaning into their sculptures. I admire works of art which have this more-than-everyday feeling. When Cézanne paints two men playing cards, somehow they take on a nobility that raises everyday life to a height that gives a new faith in it, a new importance.'[46]

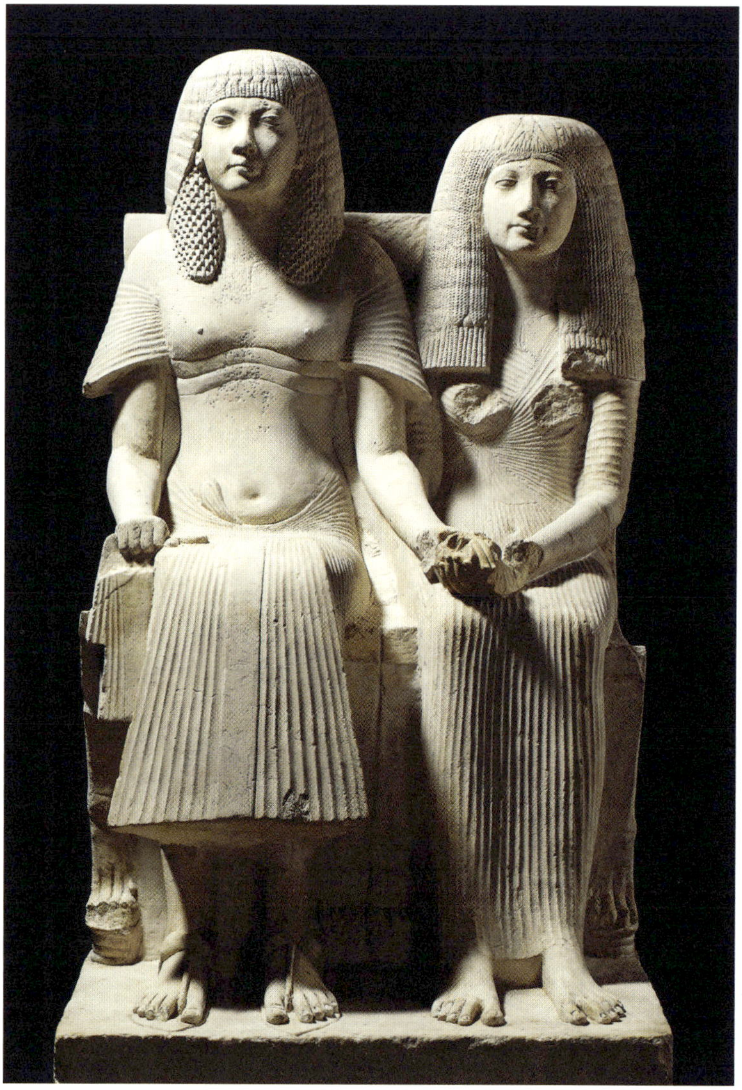

Horemheb and one of his wives,
limestone, from the Egyptian collection of the British Museum.

Moore graduated from the Royal College of Art in 1924 and was awarded a six-month travelling fellowship, but he did not take this up until early the following year. Instead, in the autumn of 1924 he joined the staff of the RCA, becoming assistant to the new professor of sculpture, Ernest Cole. Teaching occupied two days of his week, leaving ample time for him to pursue his own artistic interests and giving him financial security.

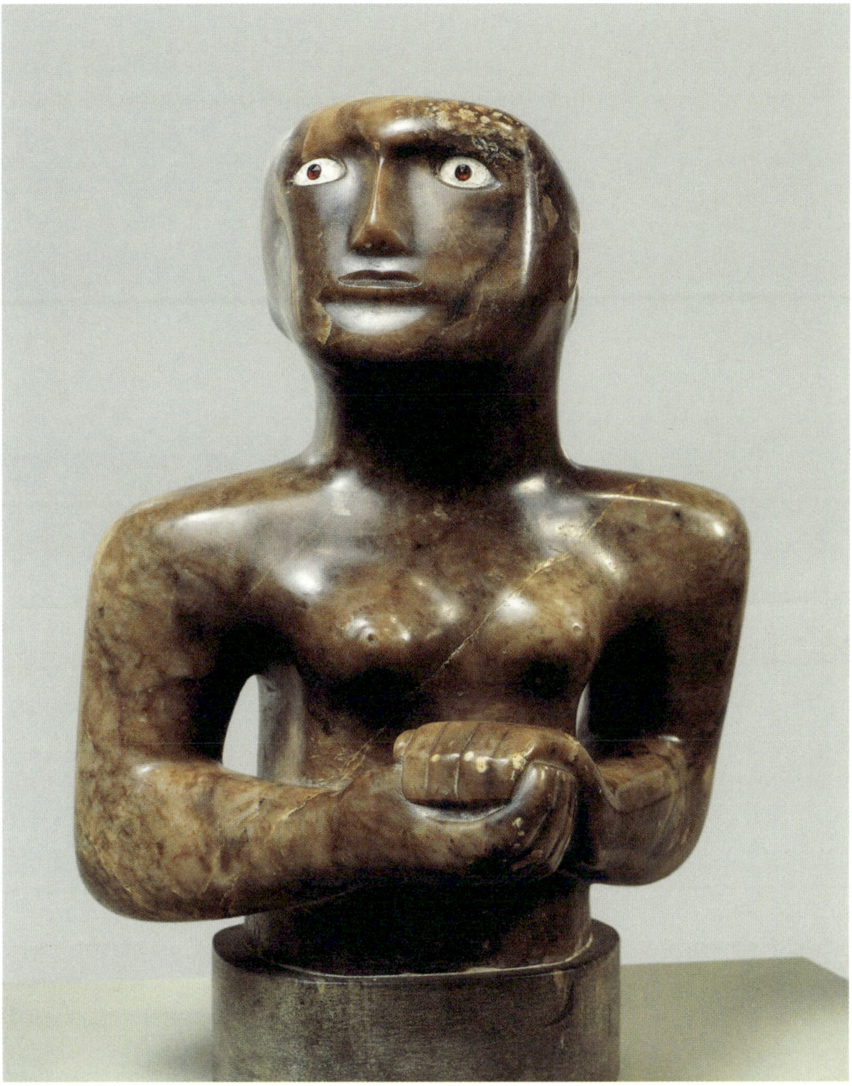

Henry Moore, *Girl with Clasped Hands*,
Cumberland alabaster, 1930.

During the early 1920s Moore had also read Ezra Pound's memoir of Gaudier-Brzeska, whose own study of non-European art had led him to simplify natural forms into an expressive language of near-abstract shapes. The examples of Epstein and Gaudier-Brzeska helped Moore to grow increasingly confident in his assimilation of non-Western idioms and his mastery of direct carving. But an extensive tour of Italy undertaken in 1925 unsettled him, for it returned him to the Renaissance canon from which he had been trying to break free. Only with hindsight would he come to see that Italy had brought to the fore creative tensions within him that would eventually enrich his work, making possible negotiations and sometimes marriages between aspects of the classical or Renaissance tradition and the tough vigour of pre-Columbian art, which by the mid-1920s had become the dominant influence in his work. Nevertheless, wide-ranging interests continued to shape his art. In the front of his 1926 notebook he wrote: 'Keep ever prominent the world tradition/ the big view of sculpture.'[47]

One thing he had kept in mind since 1922, when he first saw a reproduction of it at Anton Zwemmer's bookshop in London, was a Chacmool figure in the Museo Nacional de Antropología in Mexico City. He found this image in Walter Lehmann's *Altmexikanische Kunstgeschichte*, which had been published in Berlin in 1922. 'It was the pose that struck me', he later said, '– this idea of a figure being on its back and turned upwards to the sky instead of lying on its side, which is a different sort of idea from the Renaissance or Greek reclining figure, which is usually on its side.'[48] Three years later, he saw a plaster cast of the figure in the Musée du Trocadéro in Paris. This may have had its limitations, but its three-dimensionality would have reinforced the tension created by the decisive sideways turn of the head to one side, which is in such dramatic contrast to the severe, symmetrical pose of the arms and legs. It triggered in Moore's imagination all sorts of possibilities. He first made

Toltec-Maya Chacmool,
limestone, c. 900–1224

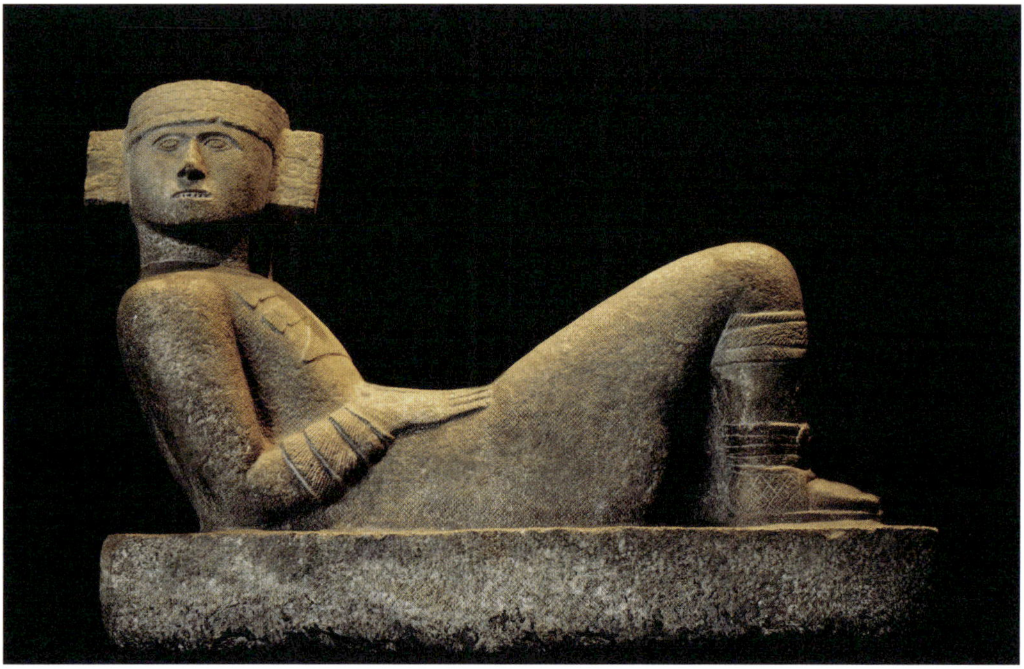

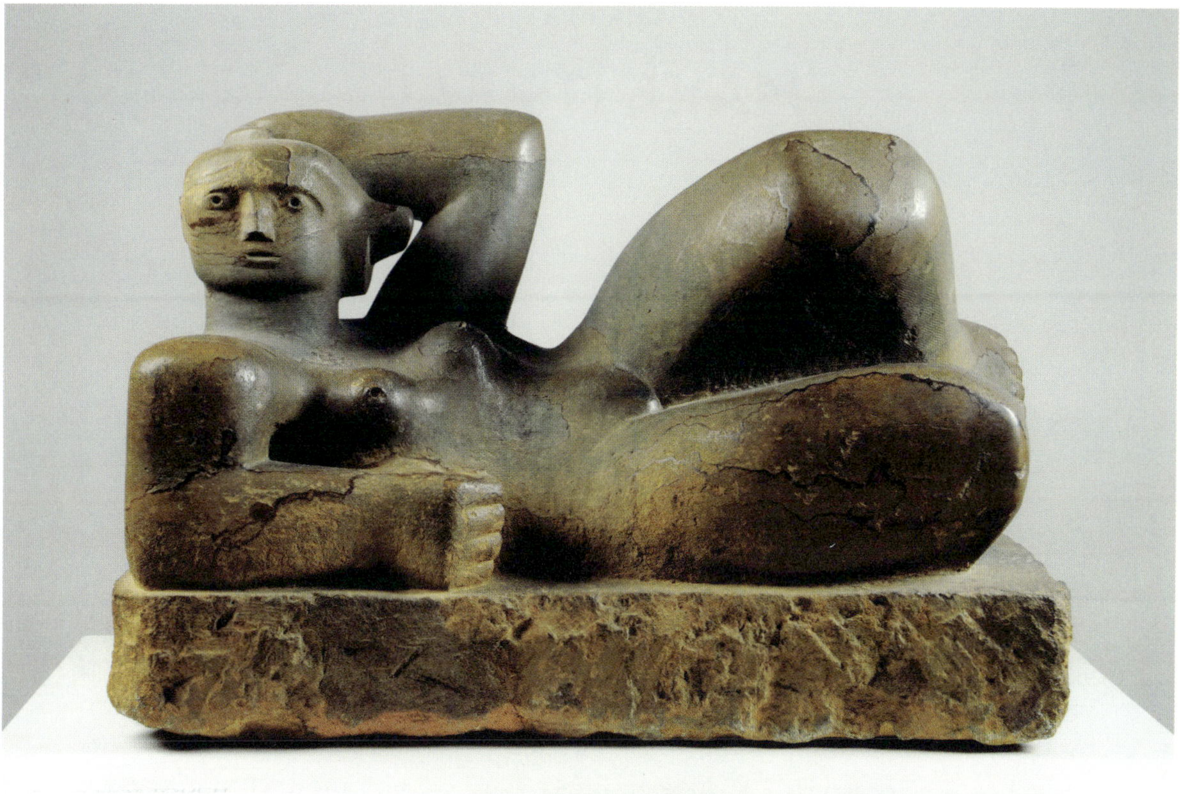

Henry Moore, *Reclining Figure*,
brown Horton stone, 1929.

his own reclining figure (now lost) in 1924–5, and at least seven others followed before he arrived at his *Reclining Figure*, 1929, in brown Hornton stone. As with many of his reclining figures, this one is full of echoes, memories and associations that come from more than one culture and country. Above all it upholds an appropriate respect for the physical properties of the material out of which it is made. For some fifty years the reclining figure remained one of Moore's principal motifs: he explored it in stone, wood, lead, plaster and string on wood block, with far-reaching imaginative power. Abstraction and surrealism at different times informed his approach, enabling the forms to play various roles, evoking sensations of landscape or creating long willowy outlines or breaking into rugged fragments. All this surging creativity stemmed from his first sight of a small illustration of the Mexican rain goddess. When asked, in 1977, why the Chacmool had such tremendous impact on him, Moore mentioned 'its stillness and readiness'; then added, 'and the legs coming down like columns'.[49]

CHAPTER 8

MAKE IT REAL

'Make it new' is often regarded as a modernist imperative. The phrase came into popular use after 1 January 1934, when Faber & Faber published, under this title, a book of essays by Ezra Pound. But the suggestion that newness should be the guiding ingredient in any form of modern expression, be it art or poetry, is not the message that Pound's essays convey. His stance is slightly different, for he wanted to prove the contemporaneity of the past by connecting the work of Provençal troubadours, Elizabethan classicists and translators of Greek with present-day values and ideals. Among these ideals, as he saw it, was the need for clarity in the handling of words – a characteristic associated with the Imagists, a group of poets to which Pound belonged.

The geneaology behind the expression 'Make it new' has been much discussed by Pound scholars.[1] It goes back a very long way, to an inscription that Ch'eng T'ang, first king of the Shang dynasty (1766–1753 BC), had inscribed on his washbasin. Pound learnt of this historical anecdote through two neo-Confucian sources, in English and French translations, after he began studying Confucius in October 1913. In the late 1920s he began making his own translation of one of these sources, the *Da Xue*, and in the retelling of this anecdote he used 'renovate' as the critical term, but in a lengthy footnote he arrives at 'make it new' when retranslating from the French. Still more years had to pass, however, before it became a catchphrase for an aesthetic which, in Pound's view, achieves modernity not at the expense of the past, but by means of a return to the past for the purposes of renewal, recycling or quotation; in other words, by means of a process not unlike that of the cultural rediscovery and rebirth associated with the Italian Renaissance. But, as used by the many commentators on modernism, this catchy slogan became ever more imprecise and removed from the meaning that Pound had originally intended.

It has also been pointed out that Pound may have first encountered the phrase when reading his friend Laurence Binyon's *The Art of Botticelli: An Essay in Pictorial*

Criticism (1913).[2] The passage in which it occurs evokes precisely the kind of aesthetic that Pound later envisaged: a looking backwards, not in a form of yearning for the past, but so as to fortify the next forward move.

> There are always those who cry that to be honestly ourselves we should accept the tendencies of our time, that we are the products of our age and should reflect its current ideas and nothing more. The voice of experience rejects this shallowness. We are made up not only of what circumstances force upon us, but of wants, desires, rebellions; and it is these which are the most vital and motive parts of ourselves....We cannot discard the past; we cannot throw away our heritage, but we must remould it in the fire of our necessities, we must make it new and our own.[3]

The need to remould the past in 'the fire of our necessities' fostered the revivalism that is a prominent feature of the interwar period. It is the subject of the next chapter. In advance of this it is necessary to bring to the fore another imperative, not so much to 'make it new' but instead to communicate 'the real'. This term is discerned differently according to the artist's interests and subjectivity. It is often felt by the viewer when an image becomes replete with sensation, colour or narrative interest. It is sensed, for instance, in Harold Harvey's *The Critics* (1922), where the scene is gradually intensified by the handling of light and space, the relations of the figures to each other and to the room, and by means of the objects scattered across the table, all of which bring the narrative to a stilled moment in which a sheet of paper, its content hidden from the viewer's gaze, is held up for contemplation. Here and in other pictures discussed in this chapter it is noticeable that artists in the 1920s, instead of chasing after transient effects of light like the impressionists or the expressionism licensed by post-impressionism, cherished stillness. It was this same quality that drew Henry Moore to Egyptian art in the British Museum, where, in the limestone figure of the chamberlain Inyotef, son of Senet, from around 1950 BC, he recognized, especially when the figure was viewed from the back, 'a stillness of waiting, not of death'.[4] It is often in stillness that the real is found. In 1935, Moore argued that 'once a good piece of sculpture has been produced, even if it was made like the palaeolithic "Venuses" 20,000 years ago, it is *real* and a part of life, here and now, to those sensitive and open enough to feel and perceive it' (emphasis added).[5]

With stillness comes stability. Standing still and looking hard at what was in front of you was perhaps a way of staying in the present, resisting the shadow cast by the memory of war as well as that which came later, the growing certainty of further

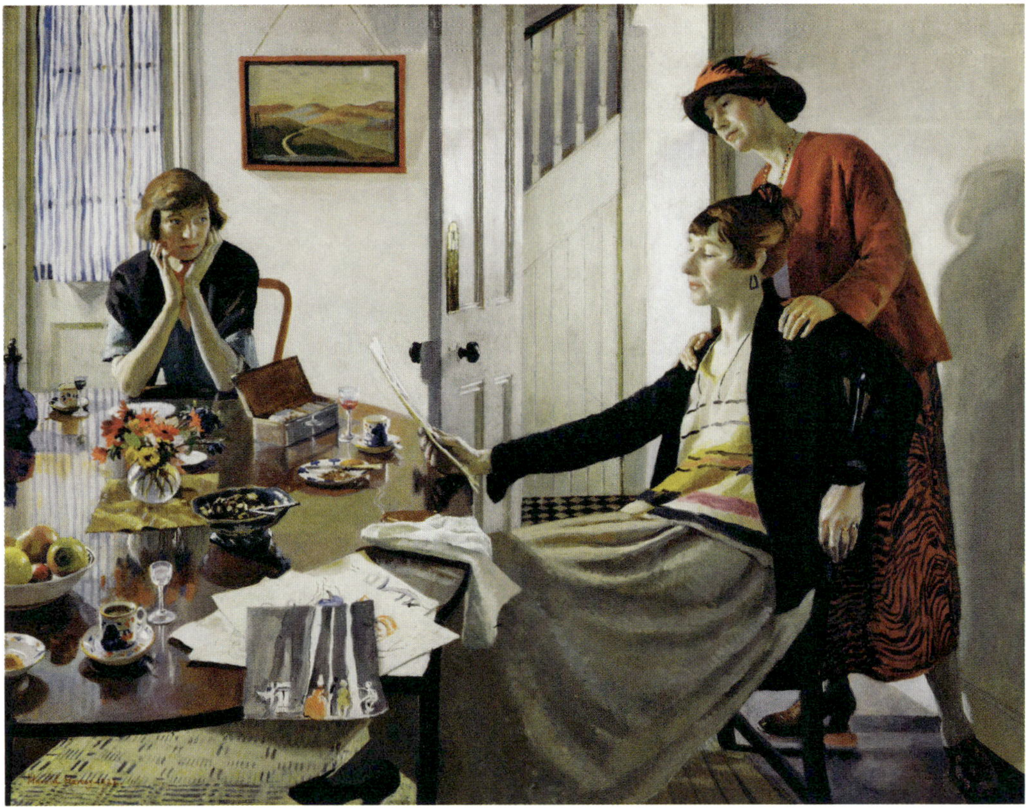

Harold Harvey, *The Critics*,
oil on canvas, 1922.

conflict. A need to rediscover the peace and sense of permanence offered by nature lies behind Rex Whistler's staging of *The Vale of Aylesbury* (1920: National Trust, Upton House) in a style that looks back to the 18th century. By contrast, Evelyn Dunbar's more intimate *Winter Garden* captures the colours that emerge under winter light. The scene represents her parents' garden in Strood, near Rochester. It was begun in 1929, while she was studying at Rochester School of Art, soon after which she left for London to study further at the Chelsea School of Art and then at the Royal College of Art. The painting was completed in 1937. It breathes a gentleness as its bare trees and empty beds unfold across a broad format. Quietly romantic, it evokes what John Piper called the 'shaping force' of nature. He explains: 'As a race we have always been conscious of the soft atmosphere and the changeable climate of our sea-washed country, where the air is never quite free from mist, where the light of the sun is more often pale and pearly than it is fiery. This atmosphere has sunk into our souls.'[6]

On emerging from the RCA in the late 1920s, Dunbar became part of a gang of artists who took their activities as plantsmen and plantswomen as seriously as their art. They made gardens, swapped seedlings by post and got involved in illustrating books on plants. Dunbar herself both wrote and illustrated *Gardener's Choice* with some participation from Charles Mahoney, her tutor at the Royal College of Art, a fine landscape painter and admirer of Samuel Palmer. Together they visited Edward and Charlotte Bawden at Brick House, the garden of which benefited greatly from the work Mahoney put into it. Mahoney had been asked by William Rothenstein at the Royal College to put together a small team to undertake some wall decorations based on fables for a school in Brockley. Dunbar was the first person he approached, and together, over the next three years, they did most of the work, revelling in the opportunity this gave for rural scenes.

Mahoney remains a rather silent, enigmatic figure. Our knowledge of their short love affair, which coincided with the Brockley murals and the production of *Gardener's Choice*, is one-sided, as her letters to him still exist but not his to her. In relation to landscape Dunbar's interests extended further than his owing to her deep affection for the Kent landscape, which had begun in childhood. In 1940, when offering her services as an artist to the War Artists' Advisory Committee (WAAC), she asked if there were opportunities to make a record of 'women's agricultural or horticultural work, anything connected with the land' and added: 'I feel I could do this with keen understanding.'[7] This was no idle boast. Her finest painting is perhaps *A Land Girl and the Bail Bull* (1945), painted for the WAAC, in which the necessary chain and snap-link is held behind the young woman's back as she approaches the bull. He looks up warily but is perhaps already smelling the contents of the bucket held in her other hand, which would have contained cattle-feed pellets laced with liquorice or molasses. Lured by that irresistible scent, he will eventually put his snout into the bucket, and the Land Girl will deftly attach the snap-link to the ring through his nose. Meanwhile, dawn has broken and a beautiful mackerel sky hovers over the distant view, as if in acknowledgment of the ending of war and the promise of things to come.

Dunbar had grown up with the *Christian Science Monitor*, which in her parents' house arrived daily. Her commitment to Christian Science remained with her all her life, and in the opinion of her biographer Christopher Campbell-Howes it became the 'foundation' of her work. He explains that 'the Christian Scientist trains the mind to exclude anything that gives a distorted or mistaken view of the divine universe', in order to focus on the sinlessness 'symbolised in the Judaeo-Christian tradition by Adam and Eve before the Fall'.[8] Dunbar's personal mission, therefore, would have been an attempt to return to the sanctity of the Garden of Eden; but with this

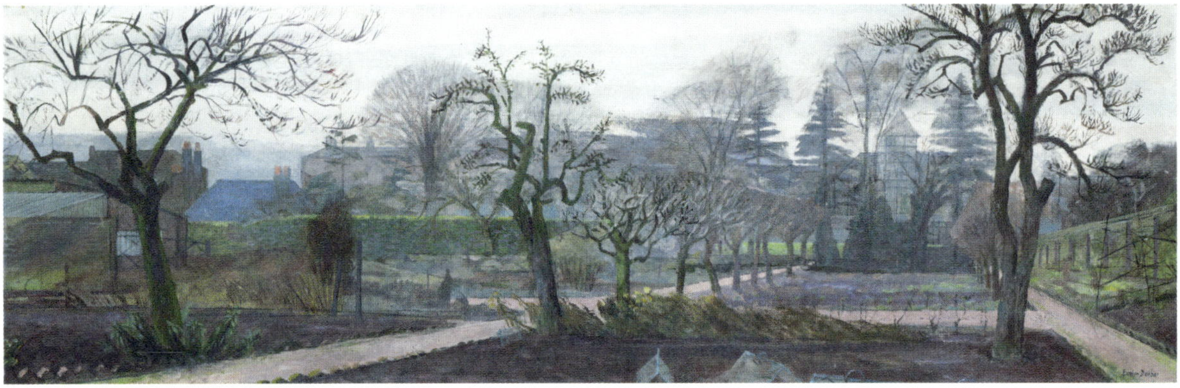

Evelyn Dunbar, *Winter Garden*,
oil on canvas, c. 1929–37.

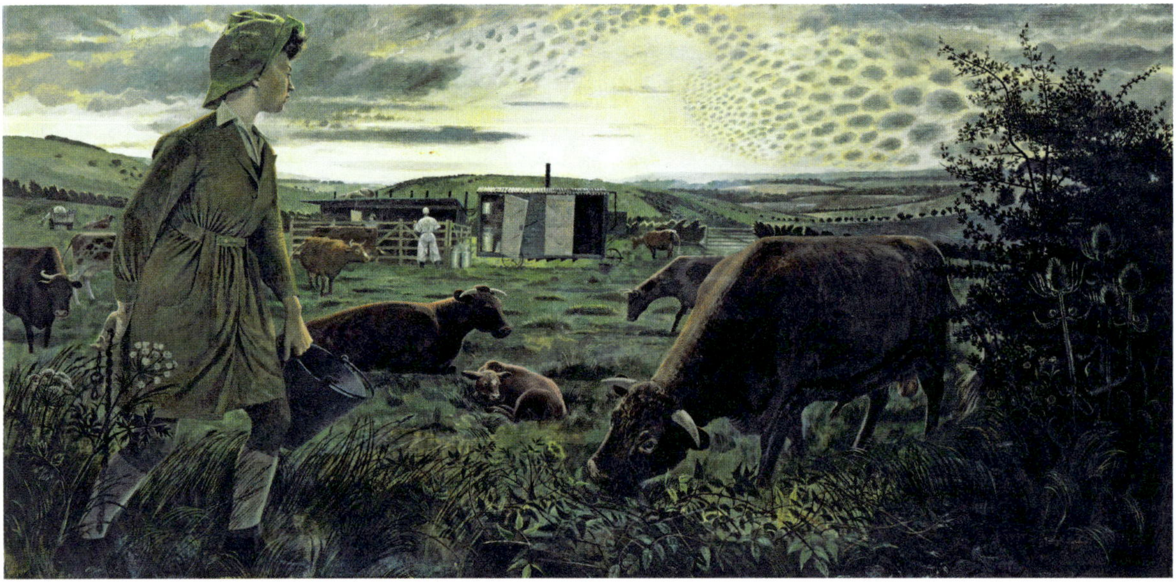

Evelyn Dunbar, *A Land Girl and the Bail Bull*,
oil on canvas, 1945.

aim came a duty to look after the world around her with devotion, intelligence and hard work. Campbell-Howes argues that, in her art, ploughed fields are recurrent symbols of promise.

A transformative stillness can also be found in etchings made by F. L. Griggs, owing to his habit of stepping outside time and imaginatively re-entering the medieval world. As an illustrator he had from the start been driven by an antiquarian love of old buildings, which he initially found in forgotten corners of small towns. Illustrations by him filled twelve of the series of late Victorian and Edwardian guidebooks called *Highways and Byways*, where they distil the charm of a scene. But his work took on more serious intent after he moved in 1903 to Chipping Camden in Gloucestershire, where C. R. Ashbee, the architect, designer and leader of the arts and crafts movement, had set up his Guild of Handicraft only the year before, and where Griggs converted to Catholicism in 1912. By the early 1920s, now a member of the Royal Society of Painter-Etchers and Engravers, he was producing composite etchings of Gothic buildings in which towers, spires and turrets, deliberately archaic, voice the symbolic and emotional grandeur of the past in a deliberate contrast with the poverty of the present. *Anglia Perdita* (1921–5), the title of one of his prints, typically evokes a lost world of spiritual beauty. Like others disillusioned with post-war society, he shared in the contemporary revival of interest in medievalism, his work becoming a form of protest against industrialism. But when viewed through the eyes of a Roman Catholic, as in Griggs's case, there was a further reason for a sense of loss, for he associated medieval times with a period before the break with Rome, when, so he believed, there had been unity, purity and strength within these shores.

This sense of loss also informs his etching *Owlpen Manor*, created in 1930, by which time England had moved still more firmly into the twentieth century. This Tudor house, built between 1450 and 1616, with its seven hanging terraces in the garden, sits at the foot of the Gloucestershire hills. Griggs first heard about it through a garden enthusiast and mentioned it to his friend and colleague, the architect and craftsman Norman Jewson, with whom he had shared occasional projects to buy and repair ancient buildings in and around Chipping Camden. Jewson went to see Owlpen. Much of the house was shuttered and abandoned, having been left in a state of dereliction for seventy years, but a gardener was still being paid to maintain the yews in the state they had first achieved in Queen Anne's day. Jewson found in the kitchen wing a resident caretaker who was still showing visitors a few of the rooms and the treasures they held. He noticed that 'one of the main roof trusses had given way, the great stone bay window had become almost detached from the wall and huge roots of ivy had grown right across some of the floors'.[9] Soon afterwards, in November 1924, Griggs made his first visit to Owlpen and was

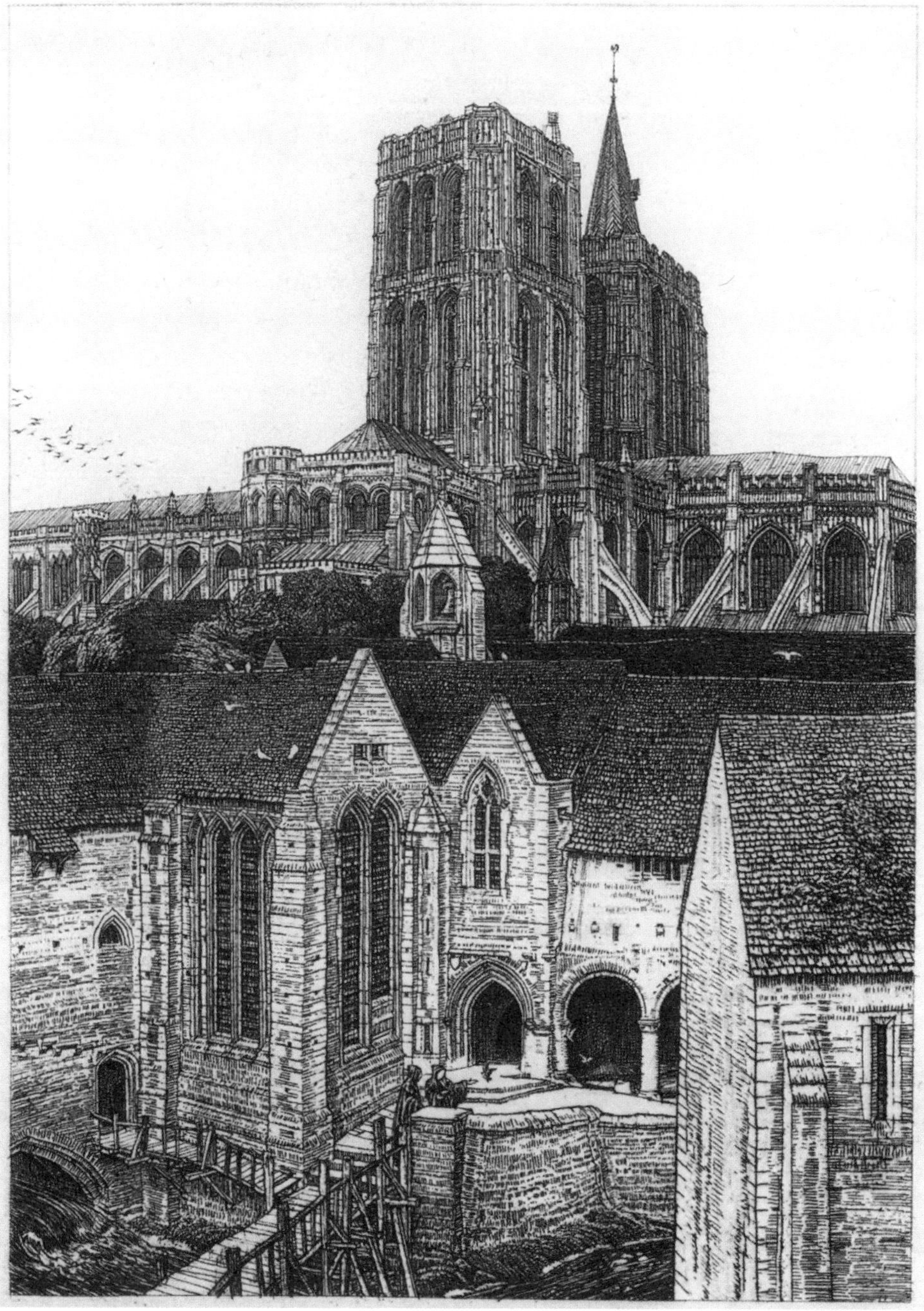

F. L. Griggs, *Anglia Perdita*,
etching, 1921–5.

completely smitten. Far from being disturbed by its decay, he described the house to a friend as a Sleeping Beauty and quoted Tennyson:

> Softer than sleep, all things in order stored,
> A haunt of ancient peace.

He also admitted to dreaming about the house and wanted to render it in a way 'that might capture some of that wonderful wistfulness and beauty'.[10] He made further drawings of it, but it was not until 1930 that he made his famous etching of Owlpen. It was a tribute to Jewson, who in 1925 had succeeded in buying and restoring the house at his own cost, seeking out the best traditional materials and using a team of Cotswold craftsmen as his labourers to achieve the kind of detail in the fashioning and repairs that was in accord with the age of the house. Ancient houses of this kind were for Jewson symbols of 'the accumulated experience of the past'.[11]

F. L. Griggs, *Owlpen Manor*,
etching, 1930.

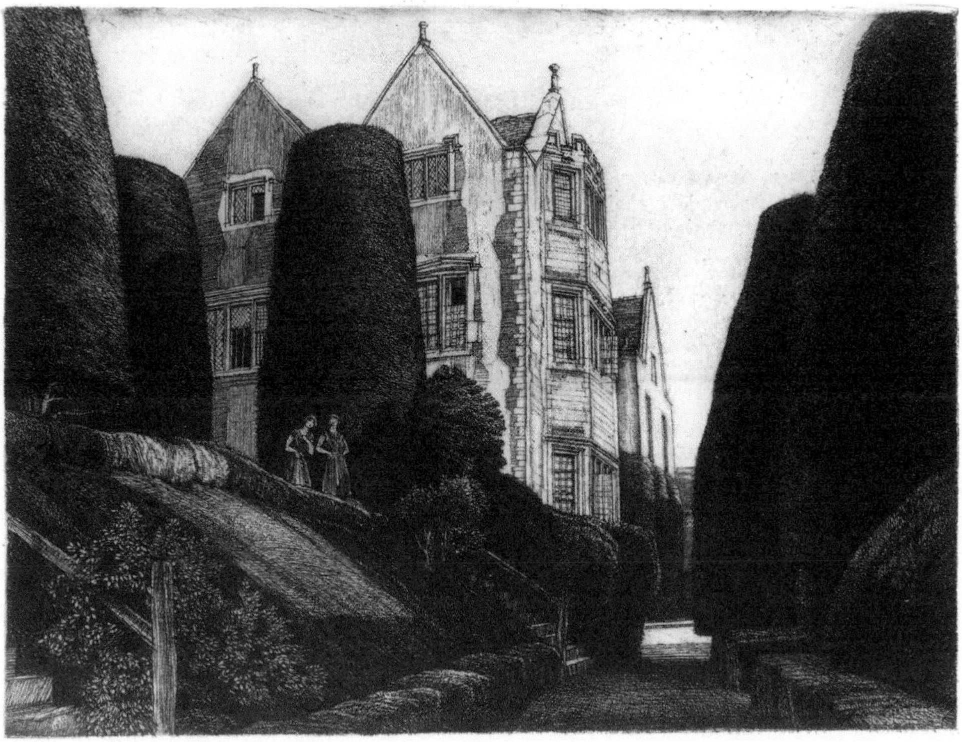

Work was completed in 1926 and Jewson, having achieved his aim of salvaging the house, immediately had to sell it to reduce his debts. During the previous period, when the owner had wished neither to repair nor sell it, it had been left in what Jerrold Northrop Moore calls 'a sort of living mortmain', a reference to an ancient act which, before the Settled Land Act, had safeguarded the perpetual, inalienable ownership of real estate. Hence the reference to 'alien hands' in the inscription Griggs added to his *Owlpen Manor* etching: 'To my friend Norman Jewson, who with only one purpose, and at his own cost and loss, possessed himself of the demesne of Owlpen, when for the first time in seven hundred year it passed into alien hands; he with great care and skill, saved this ancient house from ruin.'

What we see in this print is the dreamy beauty of Owlpen after Jewson had brought it into the present – 'modestly restyled as the Gentleman's Residence of the interwar years, with the servant's hall, capacious domestic offices, a flower room, two bathrooms, its own water-driven electric plant (in the Grist Mill) and a new-fangled patent heating system'[12] – while simultaneously returning the manor to its past, but in much better form: taking the visitor out of time, into another world, akin to Griggs's world of prelapsarian beauty. It almost justifies Griggs's resistance to foreign influence and his deep regret at the arrival of French post-impressionism in Britain and the modern ideas it had spawned. All these, he thought, worked against national identity and native traditions.

An almost eerie quality of stillness inhabits Winifred Knights' *Edge of Abruzzi: Boat with Three People on a Lake* (1924–30). This painting was begun soon after Knights had married the artist Tom Monnington in 1924. Both were then working at the British School in Rome and, to escape the city in high summer, had taken an apartment in Piediluco, overlooking a lake. Stillness does not come easily: Knights worked on this painting at intervals over a period of six years. *Edge of Abruzzi* achieves a sense of timelessness beyond human reach. Stillness can be disturbing and for this reason it appealed also to the surrealists, who used it to express the uncanny.

Tristram Hillier, who trained at the Slade and then in Paris under the renowned teacher, artist and theoretician of cubism André Lhote, first began to show an interest in surrealism in the early 1930s. A hint of this can be found in his carefully staged *Pylons* (1933: Tate Collection), in which these symbols of modernity carry the warning 'Danger' and lead out across the sands to the thin black line of the sea. In the late 1930s, Hillier returned to more realistic subject matter and began using tempera, a combination that ironically made his work more surreal owing to an even sharper focus on stillness. This transfixing quality can be found in his paintings of French landscapes, such as *La Route des Alpes* (1937: Tate Collection), in which the pylons are significantly updated. He and his second wife, Leda Hardcastle, settled

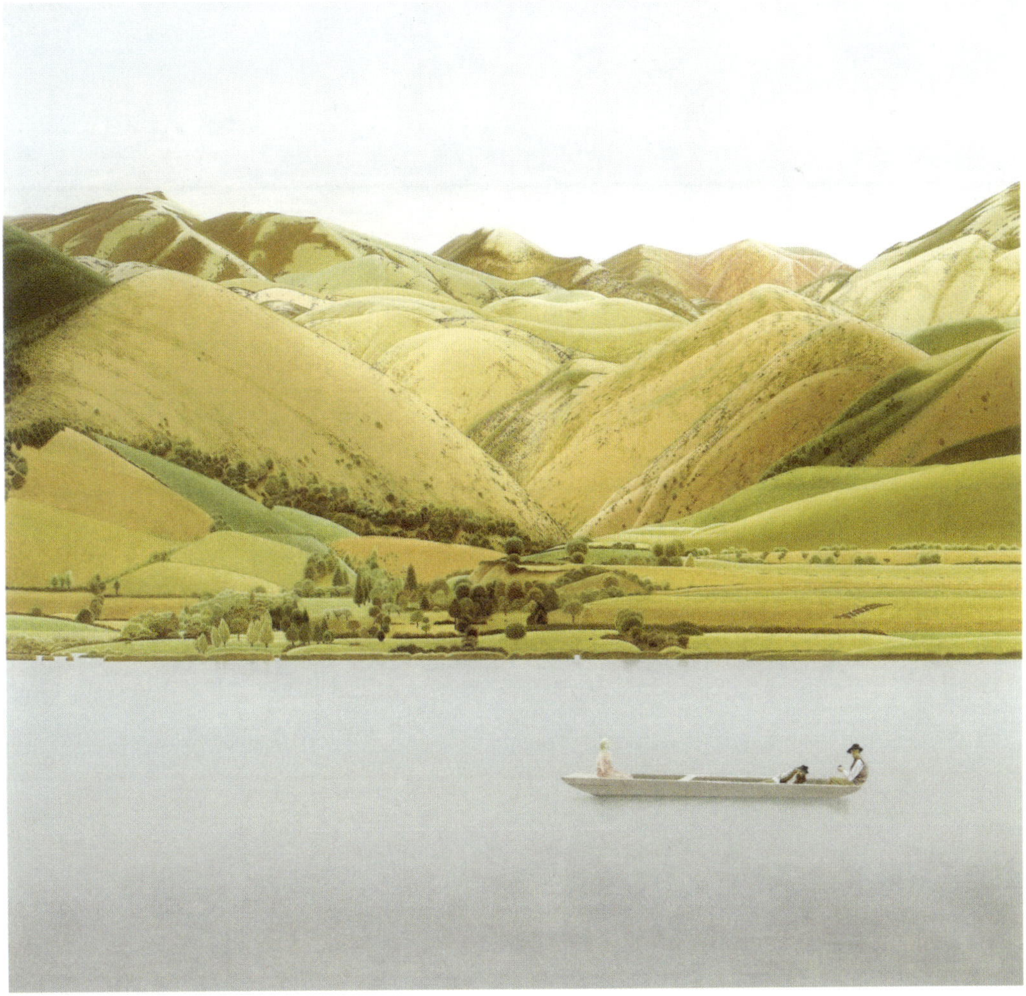

Winifred Knights, *Edge of Abruzzi: Boat with Three People on a Lake*, oil on canvas, 1924–30.

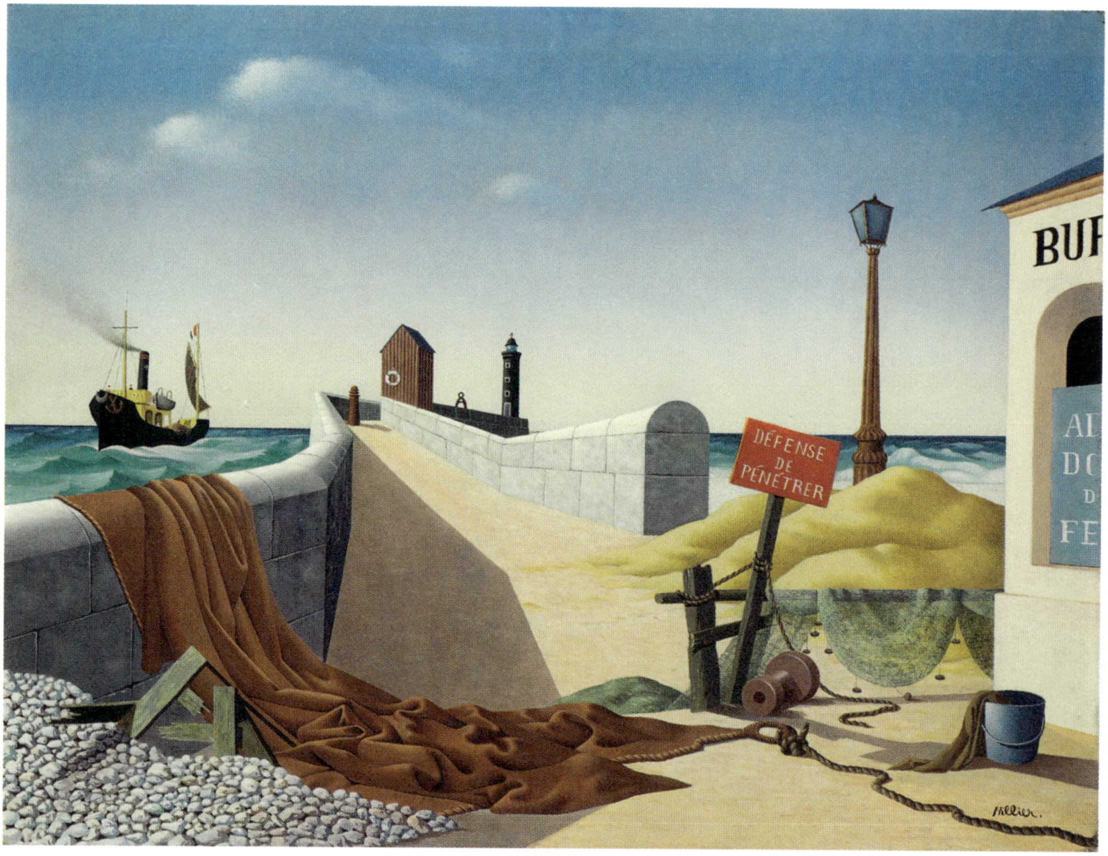

Tristram Hillier, *The Lighthouse*,
oil on canvas, 1939.

that year at Etretat in Normandy, near Le Havre, where Edward Wadsworth often stayed with them, both men enjoying painting harbour scenes made surreal by their extreme stillness. Wadsworth also made many visits to Vence, near where he kept a large boat.

Stillness in interwar art denied any return to impressionism. The light that blazes over Hillier's harbour scene *The Lighthouse* is bright and creates sharp shadows, but the scene appears more stage-lit than sunlit. In the hands of those artists who helped set the mood for a classical revival, stillness contributed to a cool perfectionism, as found in Meredith Frampton's still lifes filled with classical urns, broken pillars, vases and ruins. In his portraits, such as *Frederick Gowland Hopkins*, painted in 1938 and today in the collection of the Royal Society, the surrounding paraphernalia points to his professional life as a biochemist and lepidopterist. Here and in other portraits, Frampton gives to every detail the same evenness of attention, with the result that, like a mirror reflection, the portrait is fully present yet at the same time infinitely remote. The style is deliberately emotionless and simultaneously weirdly compelling.

A more aggressive use of hyper-realism, Gerald Brockhurst's *By the Hills* (1939), presents the viewer with a vivid recreation of the glamorous Lady Marguerite Strickland, posed like the Mona Lisa against a distant view of hills. She is known to have featured in advertisements for shampoo, Pond's cream and cigarettes, and even in this portrait adopts a promotional manner. The Ferens Art Gallery in Hull paid the costly sum of 850 guineas (£892) for it in 1939.

A different, more interior kind of stillness can be found in Gwen John's paintings from the 1920s. If we compare one of her early masterpieces, *Chloë Boughton-Leigh* (1904–8), with *Young Woman Holding a Black Cat*, currently dated *c.* 1920–5, it can be seen that in the later painting all the compositional subtleties of the earlier work have been removed. In the Boughton-Leigh portrait, the subject's head is tilted to the right to offset the slope of her shoulders to the left. Every detail – from the picture on the wall behind to her pearl earrings, necklace, the buttons on her dress and its patterned fabric as well as the reading matter in her hand – is beautifully positioned within the composition as a whole; but each also carries connotations as to the personhood of the sitter, hinting at narrative potential. Look now at *Young Woman Holding a Black Cat*, where everything extraneous to the subject, as defined by its simple title, has been shorn away. No subtle tilting of head or body is needed. Instead a greater degree of stillness is conveyed by the stability of the young woman's position and by the cat seated upright on her lap. Neither is going anywhere; they are here to stay.

There are two other versions of this subject in which a young woman holds a cat and others in which the sitter, in a similar pose, holds a book or some sewing. Likewise, some ten versions exist of John's *The Convalescent*, most of which were again painted in the 1920s. She used the same model for both series and this same young woman posed in all for some forty to fifty of her oil paintings, more than a quarter of John's entire oeuvre in this medium. 'Just a neighbour,' John says of her in one letter,[13] thereby preserving her anonymity and upholding the suppression of personhood in these paintings. Admittedly a sense of mute inwardness is felt in *Young Woman Holding a Black Cat*, but equal attention has also been given to the tonal alteration needed to convey the fall of light on black fur.

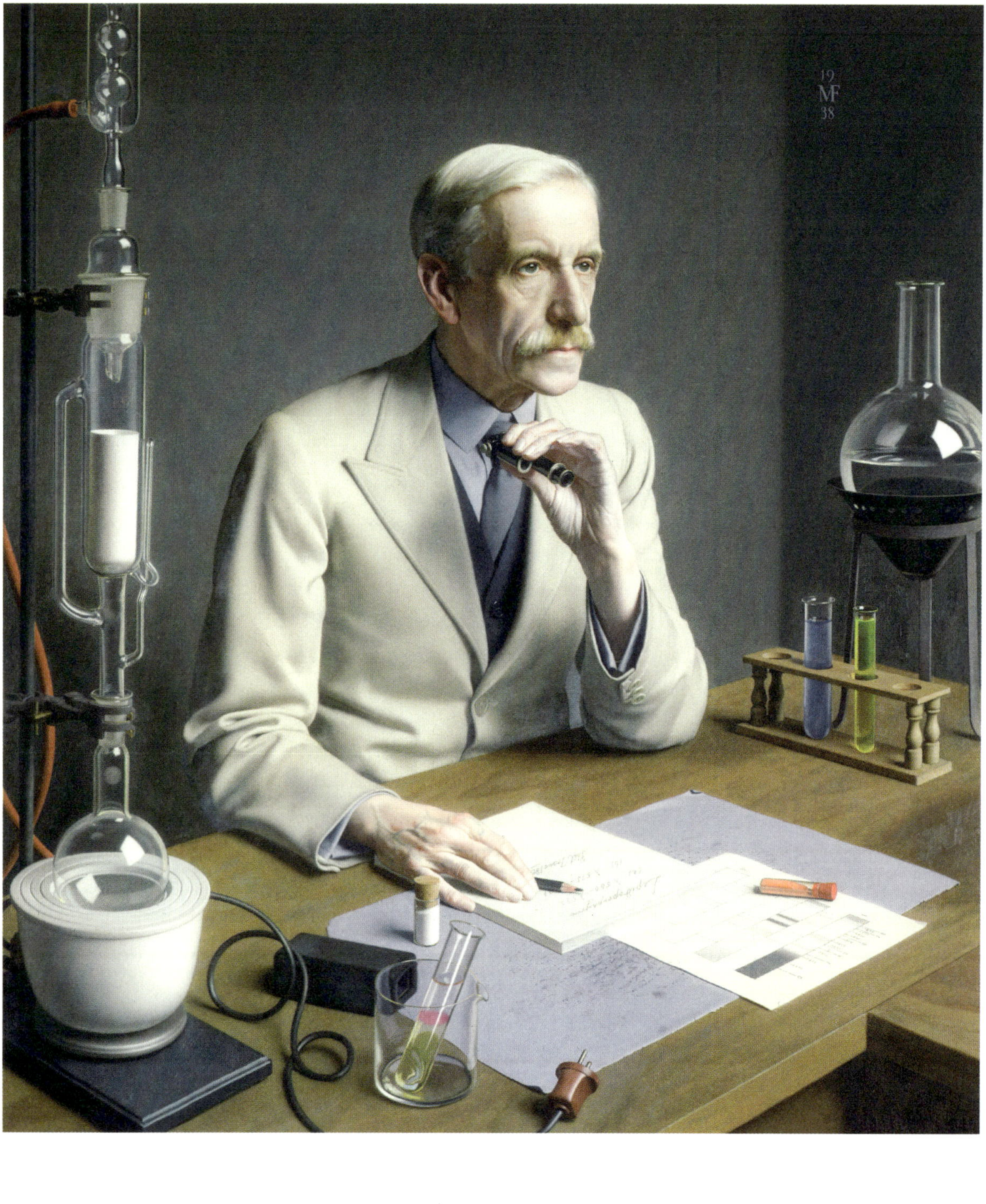

Meredith Frampton, *Frederick Gowland Hopkins*, oil on canvas, 1938.

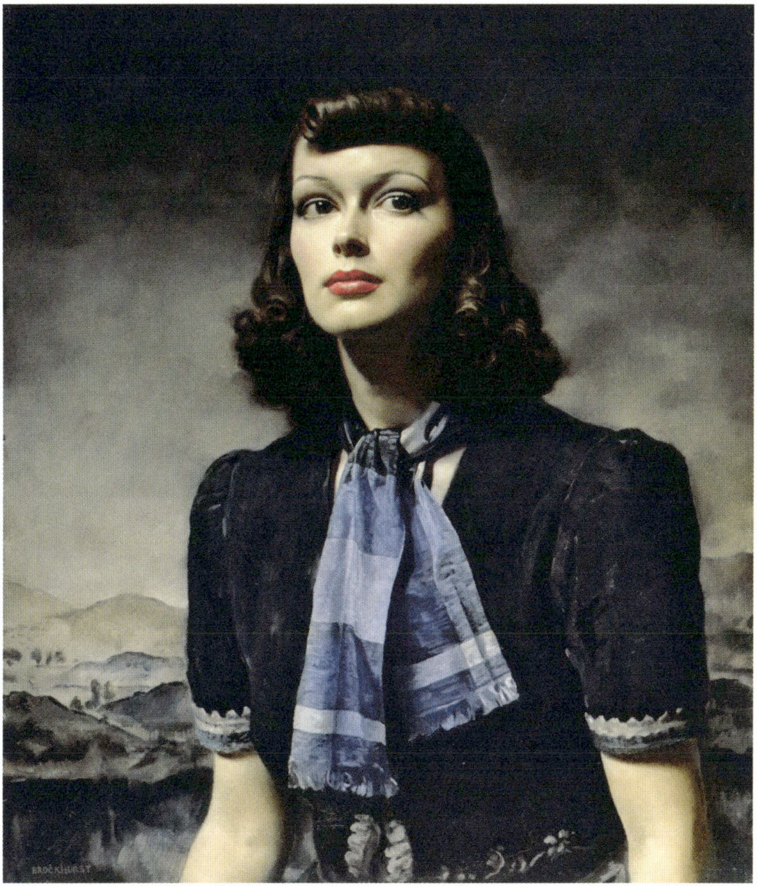

Gerald Brockhurst, *By the Hills*,
oil on canvas, 1939.

John's interest in working through a series of pictures on the same subject, with minor alterations in some of the details, is a habit that appears to have been stimulated by the commission she received around 1913 to paint a portrait of Mère Marie Poussepin (1653–1744), foundress of the Soeurs de Charité de la Sainte Vierge de Tours. This picture was to be based on the reproduction, used on prayer cards, of a portrait thought to have been made in Mère Poussepin's lifetime. Soon after John began work on this commission, the nuns at Meudon decided they wanted not just one portrait but several, presumably for the other main rooms in their convent. John began working on several at once, in this way attaining an evenness of style,

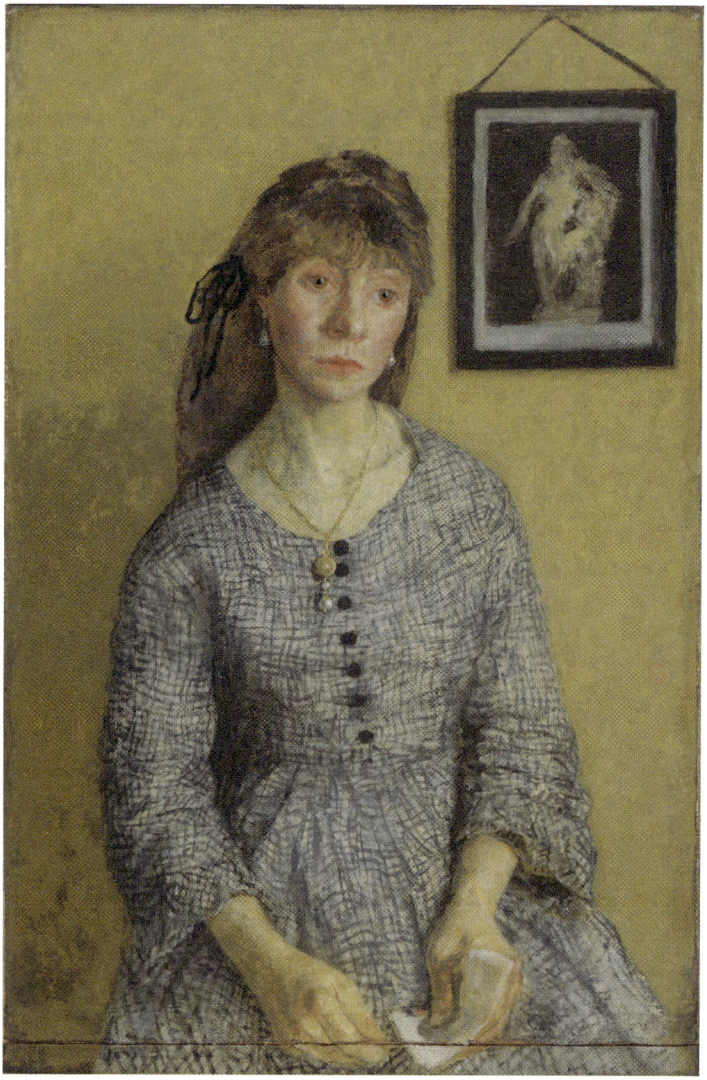

Gwen John, *Chloë Boughton-Leigh*,
oil on canvas, 1904–8.

method and a degree of similarity. The result was that she got very behind with the commission. But the fact that she began taking instruction in the Catholic faith in Meudon in 1912, and was received into the Catholic Church the following year, may also have affected what she now sought for in her art.

Another factor in John's formation as an artist, possibly at times in conflict with her new-found Catholic faith, was her friendship with the Austrian poet and novelist Rainer Maria Rilke, whom she met around 1906. He had initially come to Paris in

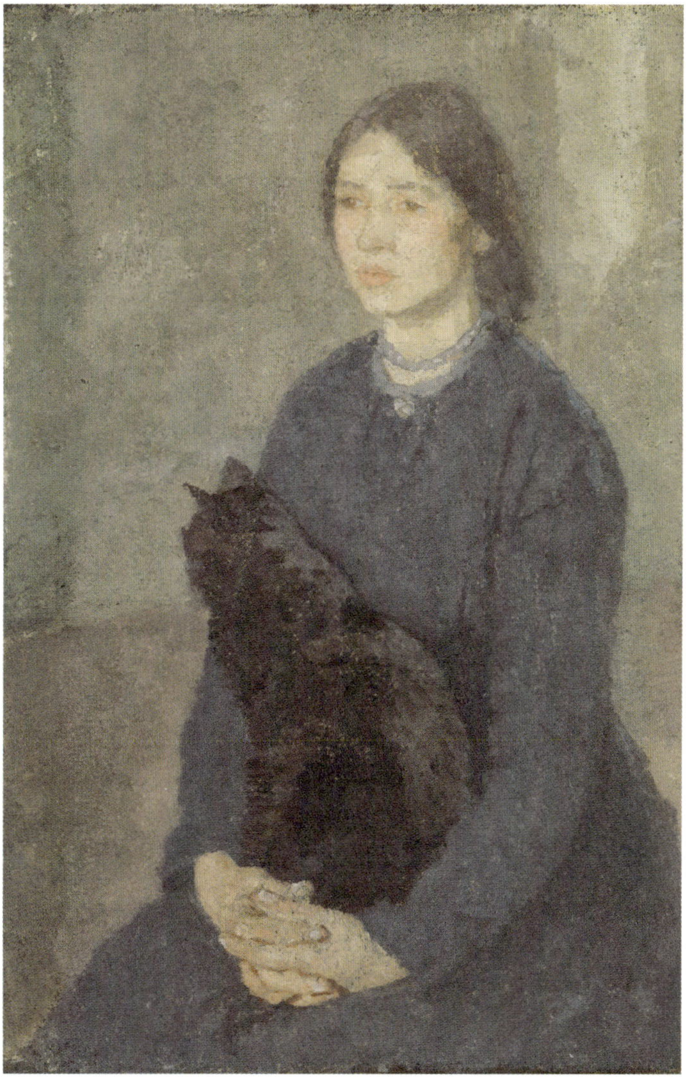

Gwen John, *Young Woman Holding a Black Cat*, oil on canvas, c. 1920–5.

1902 to write a book on Rodin and in 1905 had been shoehorned into a position as the great sculptor's secretary – a move effected by Clara Westhoff, also a sculptor and a former pupil of Rodin and to whom Rilke was unhappily married. While living in Paris, he studied the animals in the zoo at the Jardin des Plantes as well as the Cézannes in two rooms devoted to a memorial display of his work in the 1907 Salon d'Automne. 'All reality is on his side,' he noted. '...Objects have a quality of necessity with him...how great and incorruptible is his gaze.'[14] As if searching for a similar form of objective expression in his poetry, Rilke began writing 'thing-poems' (*Dinggedichte*), which Michael Hofmann has described as poems about things, but also poems that are 'a thing', not a mood or an atmosphere.[15] In turn, this paring down may have influenced John's painting. She would also have been aware of Rilke's striving for a breakthrough in his creativity, an alteration connected in his mind with that 'for which I yearn so strongly: to be a real person among real things'.[16]

Rilke and Gwen John were alike in having regular contact with Rodin and witnessing his massive productivity; Gwen was also an occasional model for Rodin and one of his lovers. She and Rilke were aware that his central philosophy was simply 'toujours travailler'. Rilke, however, was also convinced of the artist's need for solitude. What he wrote at this time to Clara, who retained her association with the artists' colony at Worpswede in Germany, might also have been said to Gwen: 'Everyone must find in his work the centre of life and thence be able to grow out radially as far as may be.'[17] Sadly, what Gwen John gained from her friendship with Rilke in terms of ideas and instruction will probably never be fully understood, as only four of his letters to her exist and, over time, their friendship was limited by Rilke's love of travel and his habit of moving about with no fixed abode. Nevertheless her emotional and spiritual dependence on Rilke is plain to see in a note among her papers, written in 1927, the year after he died: 'I accept to suffer always, but Rilke! Hold my hand! You must hold me by the hand!/Teach me, inspire me, make me know what to do. Take care of me when my mind is asleep, you began to help me, you must continue.'[18]

Gwen John's debt to Rilke, the steadying influence of her Catholic faith and the obsessive concern with picture-making that lies behind her repetitions of the same subject, all suggest that she had moved into a position where she wanted to engage not with surface detail and objective reality but with perceptive observation, similar to that which drove Cézanne's desire to realize his 'petite sensation'. His famous remark was in her mind when she wrote to Ursula Tyrwhitt in 1936, 'I'm tired of not knowing how to "realise" my little paintings ("realise" is Cézanne).' In the same letter she offers to lend her friend 'a little book I have about Cézanne....It is *very* precious to me so please send it back or bring it in October.'[19] It is interesting that at this relatively late stage in her life she took herself off to classes with André Lhote, even though in 1927 she claimed to have reached a stage where she was confident in her grasp of technique. Near the start of her career, James McNeill Whistler had taught her the importance of tonal values, but Lhote's example seems to have shown her the need for *passage*, the movement from dark to light. Otherwise he appears simply to have confirmed a belief at which she had already arrived: that painting was primarily an *affaire* of *volumes*.[20]

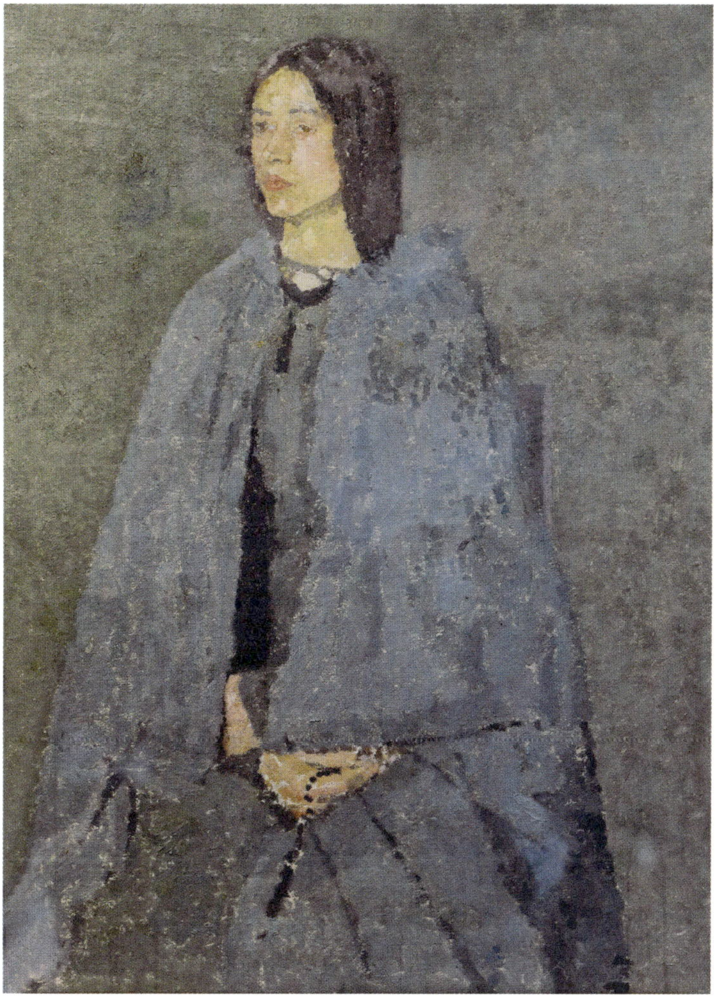

Gwen John, *Portrait of a Girl in Grey*,
oil on canvas, c. 1918–23.

Portraits of solitary young women dominate Gwen John's work of the 1920s. Some convey, usually through the face, a vital hint of the sitter's personality. But the majority remain unknowable, for the search, as in Cézanne's portraits, seems to be for something deeper and more impersonal. These young women, as we have seen, are shown holding a cat, or reading a book or letter, or simply seated; being rather than doing, with hands folded or holding a rosary, as in *Portrait of a Girl in Grey* (*c*. 1918–23), where the young woman's bodily presence is flattened by a grey cloak. With their quiet intensity, they incite the viewer's awareness of interior life, its obscurities hinting at the ultimate loneliness of the human condition. From another perspective, it can be argued that paintings celebrating the quietness of the female domain uphold a radical alternative to narratives of modernism that privilege speed and movement. But it is unlikely John thought of them in this way, for, like Agnes Martin, she too painted 'with her back to the world'.[21] Unlike some of the earlier examples of her work, these portraits say little or nothing about fashion, class or social milieu and instead insist on a more hidden meaning. It is as if John is remembering the dictum of Sir Joshua Reynolds, which, as a student at the Slade, she had noted down: 'Art in its perception is not ostentatious; it lies hid, and works its effects, itself unseen.'[22] Each repetition of the same subject was Gwen John's way of demanding from the medium of paint new ways of apprehending the mystery of human existence.

These paintings can be aligned with the interwar search for 'the real', something that goes beyond surface appearances and may be a point of arrival, a moment of satisfaction, of stillness, acceptance, understanding or a further challenge. Gwen John searched for this in her studio at Meudon; Ben Nicholson found it when he walked into a small upstairs room in Paul Rosenberg's gallery in Paris and encountered a cubist Picasso.

> It must have been a 1915 painting – it was what seemed to me then completely abstract. And in the centre there was an absolutely miraculous *green* – very deep, very potent and absolutely real. In fact, none of the actual events in one's life have been more real than that, and it still remains a standard by which I judge any reality in my own work...[23]

Nicholson's remark makes evident how powerful the sense of the real can be; how it can call, as Laurence Binyon suggested, to our 'wants, desires, rebellions; and to... the most vital and motive parts of ourselves'. Another occasion when Ben Nicholson encountered 'the real' was in the summer of 1928 when he and Christopher Wood, while staying nearby in Cornwall, made a day visit to St Ives and chanced upon paintings, mostly on irregularly shaped pieces of card or board, by Alfred Wallis, a fisherman who had taken up painting at the age of seventy. The authentic nature of his naivety, together with its abundant expressiveness, excited them. This proved to be no passing fad. Fourteen years later, on the day that Wallis died, Nicholson wrote to Jim Ede: 'I don't think a good Wallis is representational, it is simply REAL.'[24]

Alfred Wallis, a former mariner born in 1855, was self-taught as an artist. He had much to say about the sea, boats, lighthouses, harbours and the environs of St Ives. His intuitive feeling for the placement of his subjects was unencumbered by any academic teaching, while his dependence on memory gave his art depth of feeling and force as well as formal ingenuity. In recent years, his outsider art has increasingly come to be seen not as a side issue in the history of modernism but as a significant catalyst in the formation of the avant-garde in England during the late 1920s.

Prior to his meeting with Wallis, Ben Nicholson had moved on from his obsession with goblets. Gradually other objects had crept back into his paintings, but there was still a fierce resistance to any form of easy or slick representation. In his drawings and in his paintings he wanted his imagery to be in dialogue with the materiality of his ground, be it paper, canvas or board. He frequently textured the ground used for his oils, and in his drawings of landscape knew how to focus on very few things in such a way that the empty passages of white paper became charged with pictorial space. Yet for all their boldness, his pictures still had the air of searching experiments, an uncertainty that was rarely, if ever, seen in his behaviour. He was a recognized leader and in 1926 was made the first ever president of the Seven and Five Society.

Christopher Wood, on the other hand, had been immersed for some five years, since the age of twenty, in a cosmopolitan life in Paris. He had spent much of that time in the company of wealthy men: first the financier and collector Alphonse Kahn and then José Antonio de Gandarillas, who was socially well connected owing to his role as a diplomat at the Chilean embassy and who owned a house in London as well as in Paris. In his company Wood travelled widely in Europe, also visiting the Balkans and North Africa. Instead of studying at an art school, Wood gained an understanding of painting through mingling with the elite. Augustus John gave him encouragement; Picasso, whom he first met in 1923, gave him advice about drawing; and Moïse Kisling, a Polish painter living in Paris, became a close friend. Wood and Gandarillas formed an immediate friendship with Jean Cocteau in the south of France and drove back to London with him to be present at the opening night of the Ballets Russes's *Le Train bleu*, a one-act ballet for which Cocteau had written the libretto. After this, Wood shared his Parisian studio for some months in 1924 with Cocteau, from whom he acquired, if he had not already begun it, the habit of taking opium.

But beneath the worldly sophistication of his social and urban life Wood was searching, as an artist, for an innocence of vision. During much travelling in 1922 he had read Van Gogh's letters, which greatly moved him, and thereafter he often successfully adopted the Dutchman's manner when painting flowers. This same year he wrote a letter to his mother in which he asked: 'Do you know that all the great modern painters...are not trying to see things and paint them through the eyes of a man of forty or fifty or whatever they may be, but through the eyes of the smallest child who sees nothing except those things that would strike him as being the most important? To the childish drawing they add the beauty and refinement of their own experience – this is the explanation of modern painting.'[25] But the compound was less easy to achieve than this suggests. Wood's paintings show him stumbling through the legacy of cubism, paying homage to Cézanne, imitating Rousseau and striving for the simple and direct, with varying degrees of success, in recognition of the cult of primitivism.

While in London in 1925, Wood had been persuaded by the sculptor Frank Dobson to send in work to the London Group's annual exhibition. The following year, two pieces by him were accepted by the London Group and went on show in the Mansard Gallery. After this Wood divided his time between London and Paris, his recent success encouraging his desire to develop a network of artist-friends in England. Towards the end of 1926, he met the Nicholsons. An immediate rapport is conveyed by the fact that the day after they showed Wood their work, he in turn showed them his. He was working at this time in Gandarillas's house in Cheyne Walk, in a small bedroom on the top storey filled with an array of canvases. One of the pictures he showed the Nicholsons was *Red Dogs*, as Winifred referred to it, although today it is known as *China Dogs in a St Ives Window*; this had been painted during or soon after his first visit to Cornwall, in 1926. Wood and Gandarillas had gone to the Scilly Isles before moving to St Ives, where Gandarillas made his departure, thereby giving Wood a welcome period of solitude in which he did constructive work. On this first visit to St Ives some of the pictures he made appear a little forced and overcrowded, whereas he seems to have arrived at the *China Dogs* painting with consummate ease, the orange-red of the winged chair complementing the mid-blue of the sea. This and other paintings seen for the first time in a small bedroom in Cheyne Walk made an unforgettable impression on Winifred Nicholson's mind: 'He produced masterpiece upon masterpiece....We walked home in high skies. Here was England's first painter. His vision is true, his grasp is real, his power is life itself.'[26]

Ben proposed and Winifred seconded Wood for membership of the Seven and Five Society in December 1926. Cedric Morris, who had exhibited with the Seven and Five in January, also found himself voted in as a member of the society at the same meeting and by the same proposers, only in reverse order. He was on terms of friendship with the Nicholsons and Wood, but it was nevertheless Wood they asked to exhibit with them and the potter William Staite Murray at the Beaux Arts Gallery, London, in April and May 1927; and Wood was also invited to stay with them at Banks Head the following year.

It was then, in the spring of 1928, two to three months before their meeting with Wallis, that the real bonding between the Nicholsons and Christopher Wood occurred. Winifred recalled: 'His arrival was like a meteor....We all three painted and thought of nothing else. Inspiration ran high and flew backwards and forwards from one to the other.'[27] Wood, who had begun to fall in love with women, was pleased to be at a distance from Paris and enjoyed the plain, white-painted rooms at Banks Head, from which everything Victorian had been removed. He was unaccustomed to painting outdoors in front of nature, having previously worked from drawings and memory. He was also very intrigued by Ben's method of working by means of omission, extracting from the scene in front of him only a few necessary ingredients and then reproducing them with minimal fuss, rendering trees with a few wriggling strokes of the brush, as if wishing to reduce representation to a sign language. One of the subjects they all painted, though not necessarily at the same time, is Northrigg Hill. Winifred used the fullest brush, pushing thick paint around to suggest an unsettled sky and the changing light on the fields and distant mountains. Ben's handling is more concise and closely tied to his conception of the scene, and Kit (as Wood's friends called him) produced uneven and slightly scratchy landscapes, perhaps because, though seduced by the Cumbrian landscape, he was hindered by awareness that if he embraced it too fully Ben would tell him that he should have left more out. Wood afterwards admitted to having grasped 'a certain way of execution' during this stay, with reference to the Nicholsons' emphasis on selection and simplification. He also recognized a certain completeness at Banks Head, but added sadly that it was 'complete without me, therefore is not mine'.[28] Their exchange of ideas about painting was resumed in August, when Wood joined the Nicholsons in Cornwall, where they had taken a house at Feock overlooking Pill Creek. It was from here that Ben Nicholson and Wood set out on a day visit to St Ives.

The story of their discovery of Wallis is well known. Less frequently mentioned is that it happened in the wake of Ben Nicholson's attempt to strip down painting to its essentials, as well as Christopher Wood's experiments with modernism as part of his search for an innocent vision. Both were already intensely interested in 'primitivism' as a means of ridding art of its staleness and decadence. But Wallis's pictures, with their characterful naivety, their directness, subtlety and depth of experience, refocused their ambitions.

Through the open door of Wallis's house, they saw his paintings, pinned or nailed to the walls of his front parlour. They knocked on the door and inside found Wallis seated at a kitchen table, where most of his painting was done. Afterwards Wood conveyed the momentousness of this encounter and their exchange by saying that it had been like meeting Cézanne. The attraction of St Ives and Wallis caused the visiting party to relocate, the Nicholson family moving into lodgings overlooking the quay and Wood taking Meadow Cottage, which overlooked Porthmeor Beach, for himself and Frosca Munster, a Russian émigré and wife of a Polish count, who had first joined the party at Feock. After the Nicholsons left St Ives around the second week of October, Wood stayed on until December, seeing Wallis daily and observing his methods and the paints he used. 'I am more and more influenced by Alfred Wallis', he wrote, '– not a bad master though: he and Picasso both mix their colours on box lids!'[29]

Had this chance meeting not happened, much of Wallis's art and his reputation might not have survived. Although St Ives was then full of painters, many of them sharing his interest in the sea, he was nevertheless regarded as an eccentric figure. He had taken up painting 'for company' in his seventies, after his wife died, producing pictures mostly on card or board obtained from the local grocer and using house paint or that left in the tin after most of it had been applied to the hull of a ship. One of his early pictures, now in the Kettle's Yard collection, is signed in capital letters with the 'S' in his surname written back to front. Lack of schooling had left him near illiterate, although his claim that he had first gone to sea as a cabin boy at the age of nine is unproven.

He first appears, listed in a census in 1871, as an apprentice basketmaker. Most of his life was spent working on deep-sea fishing boats. Shipping records show that he crossed the Atlantic on at least two occasions, once as part of the crew aboard *Pride of the West*, which landed at St John's, the capital of Newfoundland, where he saw icebergs off the coast that later reappeared in some of his paintings. He returned on another West Country schooner, *Belle Aventure* of Brixham, the journey lasting three months. According to Robert Jones, to be profitable these ships sailed with a minimum of crew, 'perhaps four or five men, who had to be available day or night to make sail adjustments, pump ship, take their turn at the wheel of the tiller',[30] and they frequently encountered terrible weather conditions. In later life Wallis worked as a marine scrap merchant, but his memories of his earlier years remained powerful. He often placed some of his pictures in the street outside his house so that he could explain to passers-by the nature of the ships, weather conditions and historical matter. He was a well-known figure in the town but as an artist he was unknown outside of his locality to anyone, except perhaps to the artist Cedric Morris.

But after 1928 and his meeting with Nicholson and Wood, two metropolitan sophisticates, things changed. Wallis soon found himself in communication with Jim Ede, in his role as curator at the Tate Gallery. Ede encouraged Wallis to send regular bundles of his paintings to him at the Tate, where he hung some in his office and sold others to artists, writers and collectors, thereby gaining for Wallis a discerning audience among supporters of the avant-garde: Margaret Gardiner, Geoffrey

Grigson, Herbert Read, Adrian Stokes, John Summerson and Helen Sutherland. Wallis sent regular shipments between 1929 and 1939, accompanied by short notes. In total Ede himself acquired over ninety-three works by Wallis, although he never made the journey to St Ives to meet the artist. The only dealer who did was Lucy Wertheim, herself something of an outsider in the London art world and firmly committed to outsider art. She showed twenty of Wallis's pictures in her London gallery in 1931.

The pleasure Wallis's art gives is readily felt. He delights in the shapes of sails and masts, and the details associated with different kinds of ship. He also likes to show how boats sit in the water or lean against tall waves. Although ships of all kind can be found in his art, he wanted primarily to paint, as he several times told Ede, 'what used to be', hence his fascination with schooners and brigantines. Often, if painting on card, he cut off two or three of the sharp corners so that the eye continues round the composition instead of stopping abruptly at the edge. His vision is untrammelled by academic correctness but it is nevertheless canny: among the abrupt messages slipped into his parcels to Ede is one that reads: 'I do not To put Collers what Do Not belong I Think I spoils The pictures Their have Been a lot of paintins spoiled By putin collers where They do not Blong.'[31] In his early works, such as *White Houses – Hales Down, near St Ives*, in the Kettle's Yard collection, he initially mapped out the composition in pencil, then worked with paint, and finally returned to pencil, fiercely adding, in this case, multiple chimneys. But any stylistic development is not easy to perceive: he appears to have changed his approach according to his choice of subject and what materials were available to him. The atmosphere his paintings emit stems primarily from his choice of colours, which Nicholson itemized as 'lovely dark browns, fierce greys, strange whites and a particularly pungent Cornish green'.[32] However, in his paintings of the wreck of the *Alba* – a Panamanian freighter that in January 1938 ran aground on the rocks of the Island, a stretch of land jutting into the sea at one end of St Ives Bay – he adopted a more painterly approach and, here and elsewhere, began mixing his colours to create a moody yellow or burnt orange. He also made use of abrupt alterations in scale, permitting small, intense details to offset rough and scrubby treatment of the picture surface, a technique that Nicholson now added to his habit of texturing his backgrounds.

The impact of Wallis on Nicholson is best seen in the latter's *1928 (Pill Creek)*, in which the sweeping movement within the surface texture carries the eye into and around the picture while also suggesting the wind moving through the trees, giving vitality and a sense of mystery to this moonlit scene. Although its subject was inspired by the place where Nicholson was staying before he met Wallis, it is right to assume,

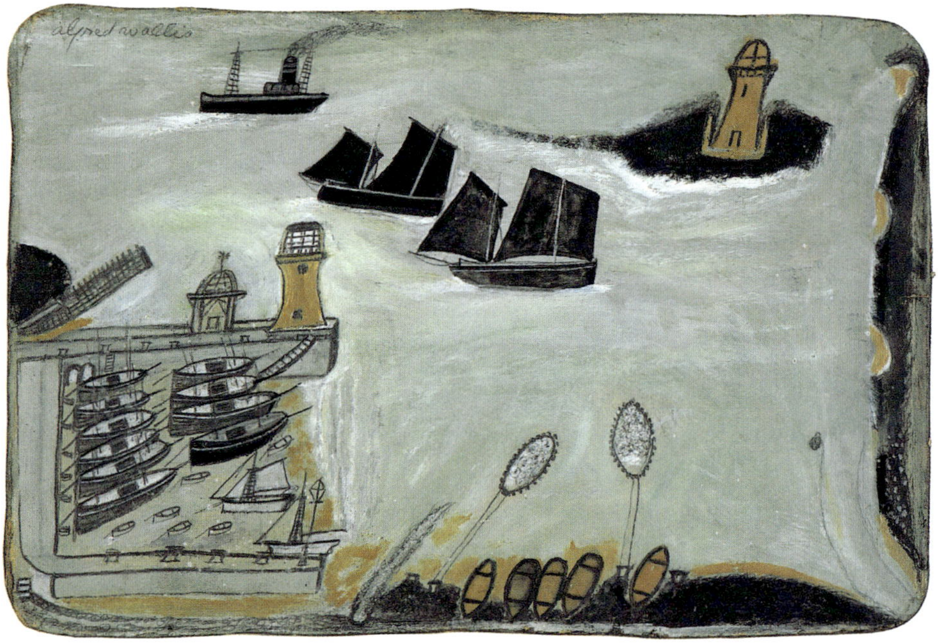

Alfred Wallis, *Three Ships and Lighthouse*,
oil and pencil on card, *c.* 1934–8.

as others have done, that this painting was very likely produced in London, largely from memory, and therefore post-dates his meeting with Wallis. Its evident sophistication far exceeds Wallis's practice, but nevertheless it is Wallis's pictorial freedom that has licensed Nicholson's leap into a more imaginative use of composition. Its lyricism is matched by that also found in Nicholson's *1928 (Porthmeor Beach, St Ives)*, later described by him in a letter to John Summerson as 'a 1928 very large, very romantic ptg of a wild seashore with a wild horse prancing & a sailing ship, white lighthouse on a rock and a sky down in amongst it all & a Victorian urinoir in the foreground', a conjunction of sources that evidently amused him.[33]

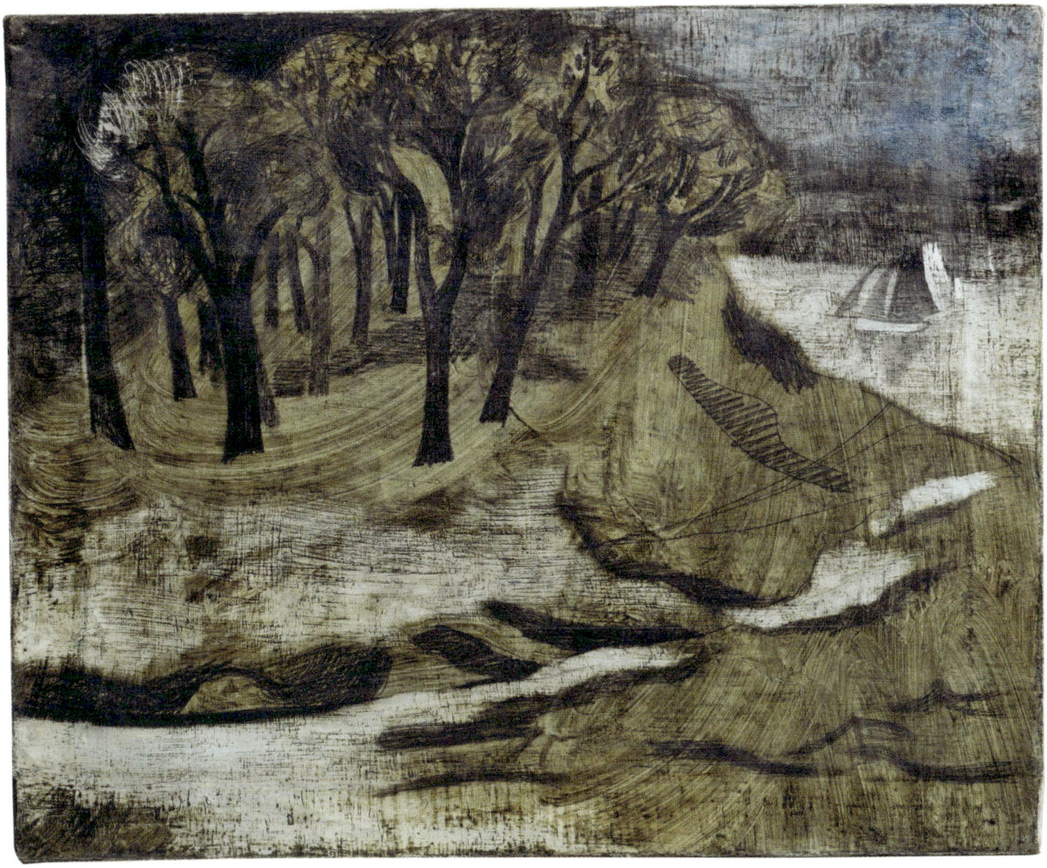

Ben Nicholson, *1928 (Pill Creek)*,
gesso, oil and pencil on canvas, 1928.

Wallis's influence on Wood was equally powerful and prepared him for his experience of Brittany the following summer. After a hectic time in Paris, Wood travelled to Dinard, then moved on to Douarnenez in Finistère, the most western edge of France, in the company of the French artist, illustrator and stage designer Christian Bérard. Both rented rooms in the Hotel du Commerçants in the rue Jean Jaurès. Wood told his mother that he and Bérard spent 'most of the day together and work enormously',[34] but when the painter Francis Rose arrived in late August he noticed that Bérard had withdrawn to his room and 'spent days on end smoking opium'.[35] By then Wood had moved out to be with Frosca Munster in a villa on the edge of the sea in the tiny village of Tréboul, just around the bay from Douarnenez. Wood had gained the use of a rowing boat from which he painted other boats, and in this way may have discovered the whitewashed villa where, with Frosca, he found it possible in September to look 'quietly at all the things I love the most',[36] among them fishing boats with huge brown sails and the way boats from the port at Douarnenez passed the bottom of the garden before sailing across the bay. The following year, he returned to Tréboul, and there painted *Le Phare*. Many years later, after Ede had constructed the Kettle's Yard house out of four tiny cottages, he demonstrated the affinity between Wood and Wallis by placing a large Wallis underneath Wood's *Le Phare*. Its title picks up on the newspaper in the painting, the title of which, in translation, is *The Lighthouse*, thereby pointing up a link with Cornwall and Wallis's many paintings of lighthouses. Here again is an unleashing of romanticism in the dark tones of the black and grey sea, contrasting with the sudden whites elsewhere and the deep brown of the fishing boat's sails. The previous year, when Frosca Munster was with him, she had often liked to play bridge with friends after dinner, but the cards shown in *Le Phare* have been identified as tarot cards, offering a prediction of emotional or financial hardship. Ede thought this one of Wood's best paintings: 'The mystery of his life is in it.'[37]

Some of Wallis's most ambitious paintings are harbour scenes where he adopts an aerial view to show the placing of ships, or takes the viewer on a journey along the coast and past lighthouses, as in *Two Ships and a Steamer Sailing past a Port* (Kettle's Yard, Cambridge). Ede played an undeniably important role in Wallis's career, although the only Wallis he succeeded in getting into the Tate collection had to be gifted by him. Others joined it later as more gifts arrived, among them two Wallises from Ben Nicholson, another from Barbara Hepworth and two from the critic and painter Adrian Stokes. Ben Nicholson also assisted in the dissemination of Wallis's work, giving a superb example, *St Ives Harbour*, to MoMA in New York, and Winifred Nicholson also became a significant patron. But it was Ede who did most to secure his reputation. In keeping with Ede's regulations, a generous showing of Wallis's art has always to be on public display in Kettle's Yard. It points up the interconnectedness in Ede's collection. The high point represented here is the momentary climax in the late 1920s when Wallis's vision triggered a new surge of energy, giving Wood the confidence to look 'quietly at all the things I love the most', and encouraging the use of a painterly lyricism, real feeling and a romantic kick.

One of the most pervasive influences on the search for 'the real' in English painting between the wars was Paul Cézanne. His example, more than that of any other French artist, sat on the shoulders of many English artists at this time, even though, as we shall see, English national museums initially gave his art a frosty welcome.

One of Cézanne's dictums – 'I have not tried to reproduce nature: I have represented it' – is quoted by Herbert Read in his book *Art Now* (1933). For Read, who was very interested in psychoanalysis at this time, this remark suggested a metaphysical conception of painting: 'a notion that there existed in the sense-data of the painter, a "real" vision independent of the intellect and beyond, at the back of the emotions: a raw material underlying experience'.[38] More usually a sense of the real is identified with Cézanne's integrity; with the evident struggle that lay behind his art; with his attempt to pin down a particular kind of light, or to convey space and atmosphere while leaving visible the building blocks of the underlying design. Then too there is the richness and density of his colours, his love of warm–cool colour contrasts and subtle gradations, for there are many reasons to admire Cézanne. Time and again, English artists in the interwar period acknowledged a debt to him. Christopher Wood, for example, made a copy of a version of his *Cardplayers* in 1923; Paul Nash looked to Cézanne in order to gain in his own landscapes more stability and structure; and Ben Nicholson, like many other artists, studied Cézanne for ways in which to resolve the relationship between flatness and depth.

Spatial ambiguity, the struggle to express depth and distance without denying the reality of the picture surface, is a major concern for any painter. Cézanne solved it in some of his pictures by working with patches of colour, conveying depth and form through changes in tone and hue. His artistic strategies, and his apprehension of the difficulties in translating looking into art, made him the father or patron saint of modern art in many countries; but in England the art establishment, blind to the anguish that lay behind his desire for fixity, for a long time distrusted his work, finding it unskilful and clumsy. The resistance to him among museum and gallery curators meant that his art crept slowly into Britain. From another perspective, this resistance can be interpreted as an acknowledgment of his difficulties and subversiveness, his break with convention, his strangeness and the disturbing coldness and impersonal nature of some of his portraits. In 1910, at 'Manet and the Post-Impressionists',

Roger Fry's first post-impressionist exhibition, the chief response to Cézanne had been protective laughter. 'Fine ladies', Desmond MacCarthy recalled, 'went into silvery trills of artificial laughter,' and one man laughed so loudly in front of one of Cézanne's portraits of his wife that he had to be taken outside and walked up and down in the fresh air for five minutes.[39]

Yet it needs to be remembered that the increasingly reclusive Cézanne, in the early 1890s, was largely unheard of even in Paris until Ambroise Vollard gave him his first one-man show in 1895. William Rothenstein, a contemporary of Roger Fry, had seen his work at Vollard's and other dealers before 1895 and admitted: 'It never occurred to me, nor to anyone else at that time, that Cézanne would become an idol to be worshipped.'[40] Even Fry himself, who became the chief spokesman for this artist in Britain and whose working relationship with Italian art historians could have gained him access to Cézannes in private collections in Florence, was slow to recognize his stature.

In 1905 the French dealer Durand-Ruel brought to London an exhibition of French impressionism in which there were ten Cézannes. They made no distinctive impact on Roger Fry, who saw this show – perhaps because all the paintings within it came from the 1873–7 period, and Cézanne's work may not have stood out dramatically from the rest. But in 1906, at an International Society Exhibition in London, Fry was stalled by two Cézannes. At this time he was particularly disappointed by much contemporary English art owing to its weak imitation of impressionism and its lack of *disegno*, an Italian term referring not just to the design of a drawing or painting but also to the intellectual concept behind it. But looking at these two Cézannes – a still life and a landscape – in 1906, Fry suddenly felt that here was a contemporary artist whose work fully satisfied his demand for an architectonic sense of underlying design. Here at last was also the solution to a problem that had obsessed him for over a decade: 'how to use the modern vision with the constructive design of the older masters'.[41]

One of the two paintings that convinced him of Cézanne's 'peculiar genius' was the outwardly bleak landscape *Le bassin du Jas de Bouffan* (*c.* 1876), which yet had an extraordinary feeling for light. Fry wrote: 'The sky and the reflections in the pool are rendered as never before in landscape art, with an absolute illusion of the planes of illumination. The sky recedes miraculously behind the hill-side, answered by the concavity of lighted air in the pool. And this is effected without any chiaroscuro – merely by a perfect instinct for the expressive quality of tonal values.'[42] Two years later, in 1908, Fry affirmed, in a letter published in the *Burlington Magazine*, that Cézanne's 'position is already assured'.[43] And when making arrangements for 'Manet and the Post-Impressionists' in 1910, he confidently included twenty-one

Cézannes. It is very unlikely that he had time to examine these works fully before they arrived in London. But while the critics broke out in fury at the threat to long-cherished standards of beauty that Van Gogh, Gauguin, Cézanne, Matisse and Picasso seemed to challenge, Fry realized that post-impressionism demanded a reconsideration of the very purpose and aims of pictorial art. His decision to show the Cézannes alongside the paintings by Manet at the start of the exhibition, as Anna Gruetzner Robins has argued, showed that he already saw Cézanne as Manet's successor. But by the time the exhibition ended, Fry was convinced that all the new directions explored by post-impressionists derived in some measure from the great originator of the whole idea, Cézanne.

To prepare his audience for Cézanne, Fry had published in the January 1910 issue of the *Burlington Magazine* the first of a two-part essay on Cézanne by Maurice Denis, which Fry himself had translated and introduced. This may have been the first time that Cézanne's famous statement, made during the last few months of his life, was made known in English: that he wanted to 'make of impressionism something solid and durable, like the art of the museums'. Denis's essay and Fry's introduction amounted to a trumpet blast for Cézanne in England, Fry arguing that from this artist stemmed a whole set of new tendencies in French art: 'a new ambition, a new concept of the purpose and methods of painting...new courage to attempt in painting that direct expression of imagined states of consciousness which has for long been relegated to music and poetry'.[44]

Looking back at the 1910 exhibition in the catalogue introduction to his Second Post-Impressionist Exhibition in 1912, Fry wrote: 'It was not surprising that a public, which had come to admire above everything in a picture the skill with which the artist produced illusion, should have resented an art in which such skill was completely subordinated to the direct expression of feeling.'[45] Fry's discussion of post-impressionism shifted the emphasis formerly placed on literary, moral or representational matter onto aesthetic content and the aesthetic experience it aroused. 'These artists', he wrote in the catalogue, 'do not seek to give what can, after all, be but a pale reflex of reality. They do not seek to imitate form, but to create form; not to imitate life, but to create life.'[46]

Fry put on record that in the First Post-Impressionist Exhibition, Cézanne drew down the most violent denunciation from critics and public alike. Two years later, at the Second Post-Impressionist Exhibition, he noticed that Cézanne was now the one artist exempted from abuse. Fry himself had done much to promote a better understanding of Cézanne during the first exhibition. He had opened the eyes of the collector and educationalist Sir Michael Sadler, who, as a result, bought a Cézanne in 1911, the same year in which he became vice-chancellor of Leeds University. He was the first Briton to own one. Soon afterwards he was joined by Gwendoline Davies, one of the two wealthy sisters whose Welsh grandfather, a coal and railway magnate, had set up the Ocean Coal Company. She acquired two Cézannes in Paris during the First World War while the city was under heavy bombardment. The National Gallery's director, C. J. Holmes, also travelled to Paris while the German artillery was still bombarding the city in 1918, to attend the sale of Degas's private collection, dispersed at auction over six days. He refused to buy anything later than Boudin and returned home with some of the special government grant unspent. This left his companion John Maynard Keynes, who had persuaded the Treasury to put up this acquisition money, free to use his own money to acquire a small painting of apples by Cézanne that today hangs in the Fitzwilliam Museum, Cambridge.

The Tate Gallery was equally nervous about Cézanne. In 1921 it turned down Gwendoline Davies's offer to lend her two Cézannes. The following year, it rejected a portrait of Madame Cézanne offered at a price of £8,000 and declined it again a few months later when the price had been reduced to £7,000. Admittedly the Tate's annual purchase grant at this date was very small, but the minutes for the trustees board meeting held on 16 November 1921 record that Sir Joseph Duveen was willing to provide the money for the purchase of a Cézanne. Ironically, it turned out that the Tate became the first public gallery in England to own a Cézanne outright when, in 1933, two oils entered its collection via a bequest from C. Frank Stoop: *The Gardener Vallier* (1905–6), a fine example of Cézanne's late style, and *Still Life with Water Jug*, from the 1890s. Stoop, a Dutchman and stockbroker, had lived in London and permitted Jim Ede to smuggle into the Tate one of his Picassos while the director of the Gallery, J. B. Manson, was away. As this was the first Picasso to hang in the Tate, Ede wrote excitedly to Ben Nicholson: 'Great fun the press view to the Wilson Steer exhibition. I took all the Press to see the Picasso!'[47]

The story of Cézanne's arrival in England would have been still more dire if Samuel Courtauld had not taken steps to improve the Tate's holding in French art after Duveen agreed to pay for additional galleries in which to house 'modern foreign art'. In 1923, Courtauld transferred £50,000 into a trust for the purchase of such work, on the following conditions: that the trust would be named the Courtauld Fund; that it would be administered by its own trustees; and that purchases would be confined to a specific list of French artists. This went into immediate action and after just over three years, all the money had been spent. Two Cézannes were among these acquisitions: a self-portrait from 1880–1, and *Hillside in Provence*. As a unit, the acquisitions went on display in the winter of 1925–6 at the Tate before being merged with the rest of the collection, and received very full and favourable notices in the press. All of this contributed significantly to the success of the new modern foreign art galleries. But the works paid for by Courtauld did not belong to the Tate: they were housed there initially but owned by the Courtauld Fund, for, as the deed of gift made clear, the paintings bought with this benefaction were ultimately destined for the National Gallery.

Courtauld had a long-term involvement with this gallery, serving for two mandates on its board of trustees and twice holding the role of chairman. He also sat on the Tate Gallery's board of trustees and in this way was very aware that in both museums the arrival of modern French art was 'triggering fertile art historical connections'. The French impressionists and their immediate followers gradually came to be seen as heirs of the old masters, thereby helping to break down the former divide between the old and the modern.[48] This was perfectly in line with his adviser Roger Fry's understanding of Cézanne's importance.

In her biography of Fry, Virginia Woolf writes: 'It is difficult in 1939, when a great hospital is benefiting from a centenary exhibition of Cézanne's works, and the gallery is daily crowded with devout and submissive worshippers, to realise what violent emotions these pictures excited less than thirty years ago.'[49] This centenary exhibition was mounted by gallery owners Paul Rosenberg and Jacques Helft, and the income from it was to aid the Rebuilding Fund for St George's Hospital. Two months later the Wildenstein Gallery in New Bond Street also mounted a retrospective of Cézanne's art, together with a selection of autograph letters by him and some of his personal objects. Yet resistance to this artist had not completely vanished. The artist and critic Patrick Heron was studying at the Slade School of Art in the late 1930s and, as he recollects in a later interview, there 'wasn't a single member of the Slade staff at that date who didn't assert that Cézanne suffered from astigmatic vision. Picasso they hadn't heard of. I cannot tell you', he concludes, 'how benighted England was then.'[50]

CHAPTER 9

REVIVALISM

Whereas the Italian futurists had wanted to turn their backs on the past, to abandon it or destroy it, much English art between the wars was motivated by a wholly different attitude, by a desire to raid the past for ideas, subjects and methods that would challenge and enrich the present. This took many forms, but behind them all can be heard an echo of Laurence Binyon's words, which, although written in 1913, have direct relevance to interwar revivalism: 'We cannot discard the past...we must remould it in the fire of our necessities, we must make it new and our own.'[1]

One of the most arresting landscape artists to emerge in the late 1920s was Algernon Newton. In his art he blends past practice with a modern sensibility, and the real with the romantic. He was born in 1880 into a prosperous Victorian family. His grandfather, Henry Charles Newton, himself an amateur painter, had founded with William Winsor, in 1832, the firm Winsor & Newton, which rapidly became a leader among colourmen owing to the firm's commitment to quality and innovation. Algernon's father also painted for many years, but he himself was a delicate child who was bullied at school. As a result, he took himself off to Sandow's School of Physical Culture to gain a better physique. He went up to Cambridge but left after a year, uncertain what to do next but knowing vaguely that he wanted to become an artist. He married young, at the age of twenty-three, and brought up four children during the years in which he learnt painting from various teachers and embarked on an unsatisfactory start to his career. 'We never seemed able to stay in any place more than three years,' he wrote of himself and his wife in his memoir.[2] They decided to try living in Switzerland for the benefit of their children, then aged between six and twelve, but once there Newton felt shut in by the mountains. He was so evidently a failure as an artist that his brother encouraged him to move with his family to British Columbia, where he worked on a sheep ranch before moving back to England and to Cornwall.

When war broke out Newton volunteered for the army, joining the Royal 1st Division Yeomanry. He was invalided out in 1916 with double pneumonia, from which he nearly died. In 1918 the family moved again from Cornwall to Theale in Berkshire, so as to be near Reading, where the children went to school. Having established for his family a degree of stability, Newton made sure they were well provided for and then removed himself from what had become an unhappy marriage.

Back in London, he took a small studio in Chelsea and, finding himself in a precarious financial position, scraped a living as a pavement artist. He met the woman who eventually became his second wife, and together they managed to survive on her income until the sale of one of his paintings for £30 bought him time to study the pictures in the National Gallery. It was there that he became fixated on Canaletto, studying one of his Venetian scenes for weeks on end. With the help of a magnifying glass, he managed to analyse Canaletto's technique and identify the exact colours in his duochrome underpainting, which not only gave a unity to the whole but also had a defining influence on the subsequent glazes delineating the lights and shadows that run through his paintings. While studying Canaletto, Newton began applying a similar analysis to the colours created by the sunlight and shadows in London's streets as he walked every day between Chelsea and the National Gallery. He came to the conclusion that Canaletto's method was no artificial construct, but based on accurate observation of visual phenomena.

Canaletto's example left Newton aware that he needed to develop his visual memory. Instead of painting what he saw, he began walking around London with a sketchbook and pencil in his pocket, drawing scenes and making use of a numbered system to identify which colours went where. He became especially fond of the Regent's Canal. 'I liked walking along the towing path of the Regent's Canal and seeing London as it were, from the wings in a theatre. Walking along the towing path one seemed to lose all sense of locality, there was nothing to indicate the district one was passing through. Occasionally a cream-coloured Regency house would cast its trembling reflection into the dark water of the canal...'[3]

The sensations Newton wanted his paintings to arouse were not those experienced *in medias res* but those which exist at a deeper and more contemplative level. At an early stage he had felt discontented with the loosely impressionist styles used by British artists in the early part of the twentieth century. Even before his in-depth study of Canaletto he was employing painting methods more akin to those used in the 18th century which left the picture surface perfectly smooth, its meticulousness untroubled by any expression of the artist's personality. His *In Kensington* (1923: York Art Gallery) could at first glance be attributed to Paul Sandby. He also found a mentor in Richard Wilson, but he was nevertheless a slow developer.

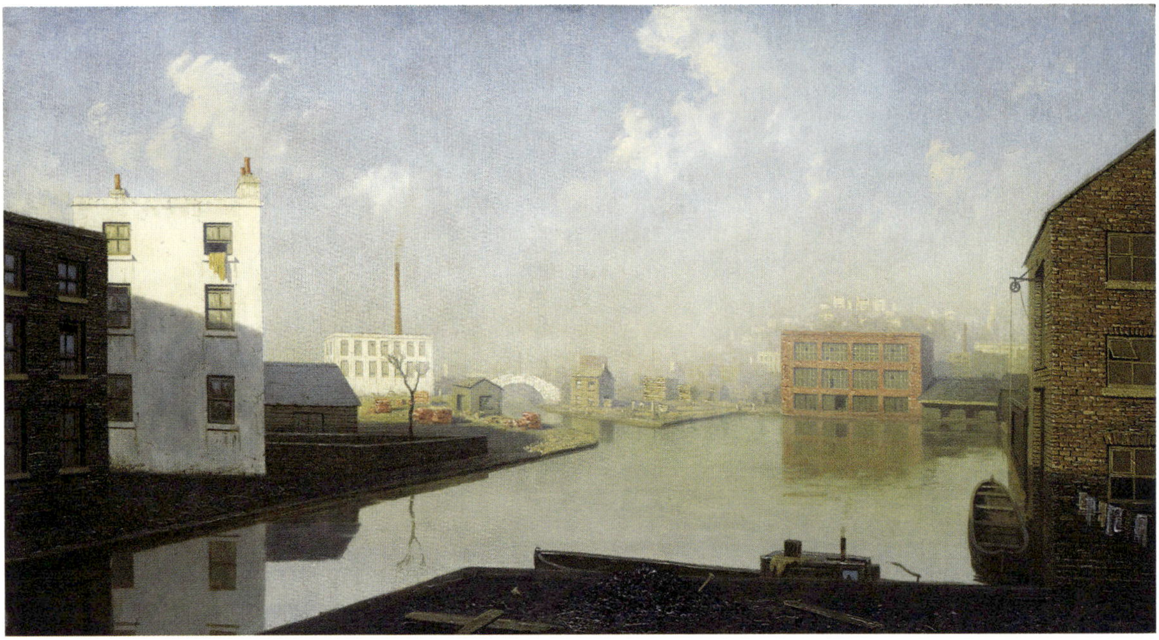

Algernon Newton, *Canal Basin*,
gesso, oil on canvas, 1929.

Having begun to exhibit in the Royal Academy Summer Exhibitions in 1923, he did not have his first solo exhibition until 1931, by which time he was fifty-one. He was particularly taken with canals, perhaps because the flatness of the water satisfied his need for stillness. Topographical accuracy was not his primary aim; what he wanted was 'a mood, a mental atmosphere, a sentiment'. He said of *Canal Basin* (1929): 'I remember trying hard to absorb the sentiment I saw in the rather dirty neglected-looking white house standing by the dark water of the canal in a dim half-light. It seemed to me that I wanted to express the ghostly presence of its past fading into the night. I began to realise for the first time the importance of sentiment in art.'[4]

Although Newton made many pencil sketches on the spot, he sometimes blended observational matter with memory and imagination, creating an architectural setting that had only a generalized link with a specific place. *Outskirts of Cheltenham* (1932) may be one of these, as considerable artifice lies behind such a magisterial scene.

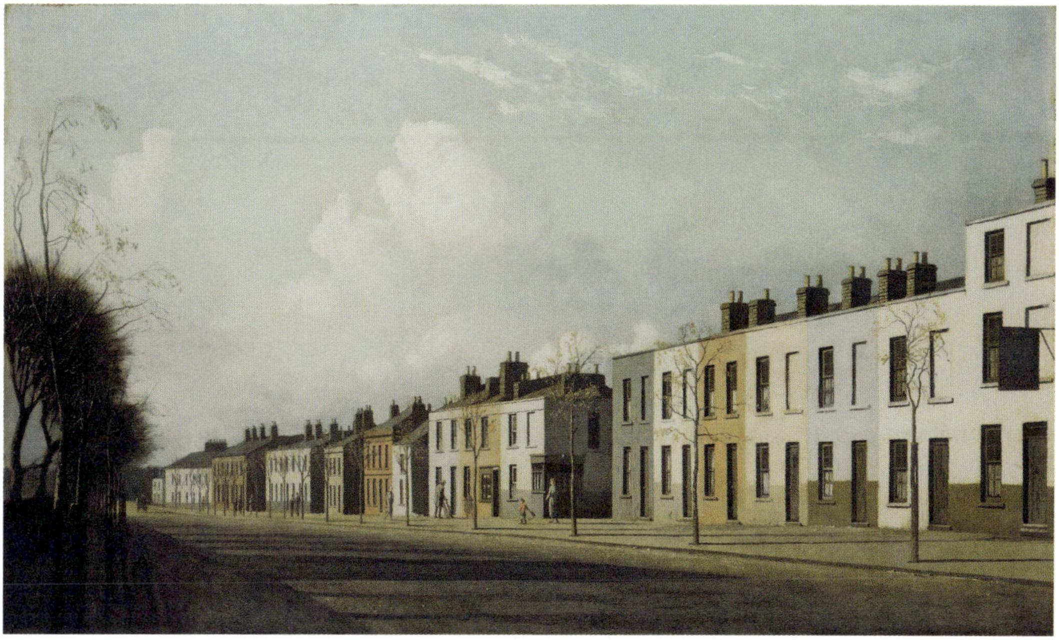

Algernon Newton, *Outskirts of Cheltenham*, oil on canvas, 1932.

It was exhibited in the British Pavilion at the 1934 Venice Biennale. It is hard to pin down its exact mood, but its stillness is disquieting. Newton was very much a man of his times, despite his allegiance to old master methods, and he understood that modernity could display a grave melancholy and worn look. His experience of the First World War had left him a committed pacifist, and the sorrowfulness that seems to inhabit his scenes may in part relate to tensions within him. Figures, when they do appear, as in *Outskirts of Cheltenham*, are barely noticeable and do not interrupt the overall mood. Andrew Graham-Dixon suggests that 'he could not bear the tranquillity of his scenes to be disturbed by human restlessness'.[5] Yet buried into his preferred subjects – canal scenes, run-down inner suburbia and anonymous terraced houses or back views of the same, mostly found in Bayswater, Paddington, Camden and Kentish Town – is a deep humanity. He noted:

> There always seemed to be a warm haze enveloping everything, even the sky....I was chiefly attracted to the poorer districts and the slums. They seemed to me so much more beautiful than the west end of London, there was more of the individual character of London there, far more mental atmosphere and a certain sadness made up of human associations hung over the sordid streets and backwaters of London...[6]

A desire to transcend time is not difficult to discern in art and literature of the interwar years. It becomes an unspoken command of Mrs Ramsay in Virginia Woolf's novel *To the Lighthouse* (1927), during a dinner party that begins badly owing to tension and discontent among the family and its guests. The mood suddenly alters when the succulent *boeuf en daube* arrives and gives off its aromatic fragrance after the lid is removed from the pot. Tension gives way to a sense of pleasurable ease and well-being, to such an extent that Mrs Ramsay finds herself saying silently: 'Life stand still here.' Stillness can enhance poetry, drama or the perfection found within classical beauty; but it can also invite nostalgia or hint at the uncanny and disturbing. At its most compelling, as in Algernon Newton's canal scenes, it seems to override time and movement, evoking something similar to T. S. Eliot's 'still point of the turning world', a place 'where past and future are gathered'.[7]

English revivalism in the interwar years reactivated a variety of earlier styles, methods and traditions. At a time when there was a growing interest in the early Italian Renaissance, the method of egg tempera painting was revived. Revivalism also gave new life to etching, wood engraving and watercolour painting. One way or another, it can be found in more pockets of interwar art than it is possible to explore here. But there is no doubt that the need to conserve and reanimate the past, and then to return to the present and to modernity, became, in some hands, a part of the progressive diversity of this period.

A significant aspect of English revivalism was a return to classicism. This was happening not just in Britain but across Europe in the aftermath of the Great War. Owing to the fact that Picasso in art and Stravinsky in music became prime exponents of this shift in style, classicism became intertwined with the trajectory of modernism, which is why the 'classical turn' cannot simply be described as conservative and reactionary. The infiltration of classicism into English art first received serious attention in 2017, when Pallant House Gallery in Chichester mounted the exhibition 'The Mythic Method: Classicism in British Art 1920–1950' and published a book of the same title by Simon Martin. His preface began with a useful reminder: 'Although the history of modern art is often characterised as a relentless dash towards the future...the truth is usually more complicated and less linear, with artists looking back as they look forward.'[8]

Both exhibition and book pointed out abundant references to the mythology, art and architecture of ancient Greece and Rome. Allusions to ideal beauty permeated not just the art of this period but also advertising, film and fashion, with Grecian-style clothes designed by Parisian couturiers Madame Vionnet or Madame Grès appearing in the pages of *Vogue*. References to poses drawn from Greek statuary can be spotted in surprising places, such as William Roberts's proletarian scene *Sunbathers*, where the male figure in the top right corner references the river god on the Parthenon frieze. The British Museum had long been regarded as a major hub of classicism, its importance recognized by the fact that since 1900 a nearby tube station had been named after it. (This closed in 1933 after another Underground station, Holborn, opened less than a hundred yards away.) In 1926

William Roberts, *Sunbathers*,
gesso, oil on canvas, 1936.

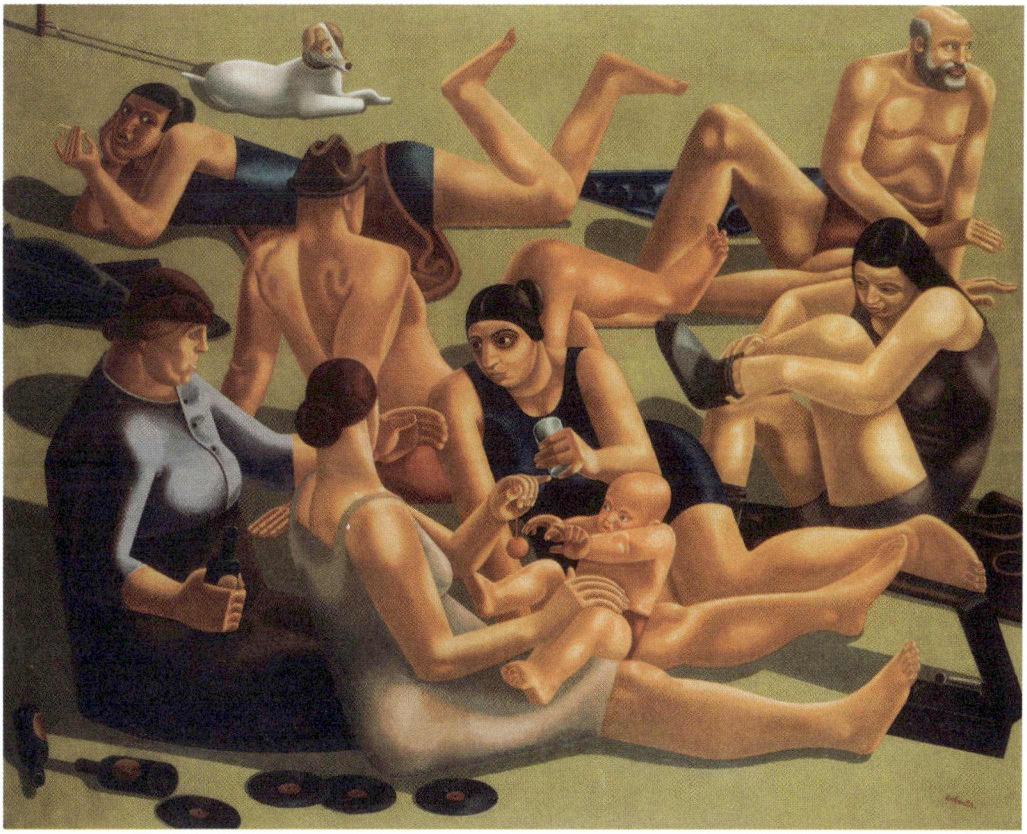

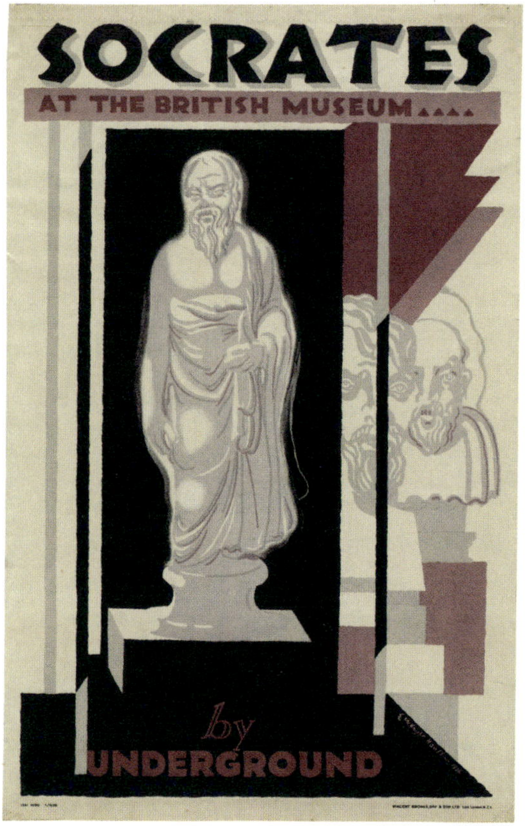

Edward McKnight Kauffer,
Socrates at the British Museum,
lithograph, 1926.

Edward McKnight Kauffer celebrated the Museum's recent acquisition of a small marble figurine of Socrates in a London Underground poster, its lettering reading 'Socrates at the British Museum...by Underground'. Much press coverage had been given to this small sculpture when it was gifted in 1925, presumably because the Athenian philosopher is regarded as the intellectual father of Western philosophy. Today, however, enthusiasm for it has dimmed, the catalogue entry admitting to uncertainty as to what it is – a Hellenistic original from the second century BC or a Roman copy – and where it was excavated. It may no longer rate as one of the Museum's best-loved treasures, but for a time it helped to sustain the all-embracing vogue for classicism.

Wyndham Lewis identified classicism as 'anything which is nobly defined and exact, as opposed to that which is fluid'.[9] This view was almost certainly shaped by his friend T. E. Hulme's interpretation of classicism as 'finite and fixed', a mode of expression in deliberate opposition to the infinite possibilities of the Romantic vision. But a more modern view of 'the classical' immediately recognizes that it is neither fixed nor past but 'the cumulative effect of reiteration, an ever-shifting reflection of the present that harkens back to a distant, if elusive past'.[10] It has also been suggested that one reason why classicism had such a call on the attention of artists at this time was a conscious or half-conscious awareness that although Victorian values were thought to be out of date, nothing obvious had emerged to replace them in British society. Classicism, to some extent, filled this moral vacuum by offering a stability that chimed with the period interest in stillness.

Piecemeal this admiration of the classical past may have been, but it had a particular purpose: after the First World War and the immense trauma left in its wake, there was a need for stillness, calm, discipline, order and self-possession. 'These fragments I have shored against my ruin,' T. S. Eliot famously wrote in *The Waste Land*. It is a line that springs to mind in connection with the art of the period, even before a fascination with ruins, ancient and new, began to develop and took on new meaning owing to the threat and eventual onset of another world war. Eliot is also responsible for coining the phrase 'the mythic method' while praising James Joyce's *Ulysses* for its dependence on Homer's great narrative. In Eliot's view, Joyce had lifted appropriate styles and symbols from the *Odyssey* as 'a way of controlling, of ordering, of giving a shape and a significance to the immense panorama and anarchy which is contemporary history'.[11] There are many moments during the interwar period when art shows a similar tension between shaping modernity and respect for tradition.

The first to reintroduce a classical element into wall paintings were Vanessa Bell and Duncan Grant. In the summer of 1920 the economist John Maynard Keynes – having resigned from the Treasury, and flush with the unexpected international success of his hastily written book *The Economic Consequences of the Peace* (1919), which predicted that economic chaos and political repercussions would follow the harsh war reparations imposed on Germany – decided to commission his Bloomsbury friends to decorate a wood-panelled room. It was the largest in his set of rooms inside Webb's Court at King's College, Cambridge. Bell and Grant designed a series of allegorical figures representing the muses for eight academic disciplines: Science, Political Economy, Music, Classics, Law, Mathematics, Philosophy and History. These were to cover eight panels, four either side of the entrance door, running almost the full length of the room. They were to be harmonized with the rest of the room by colouring the remaining wood panelling a cool mid-blue and maroon. In addition, Bell designed appliqued semi-transparent curtains to modify the light entering through large, round-arched windows at each end of the room. So complete was the overall effect that *Vogue* magazine ran an illustrated article on the room in early March 1925.

A complete set of studies for the eight figures was made in 1920, which no doubt helped to gain college approval for this decorative project. In these, the use of a book and three loincloths give respectability to the male nudes. In the finished paintings, however, the loincloths were removed and the naked men alternate with four classically draped female figures, each holding an object associated with one of the eight subjects. The life-size figures rise up in their panels like statuary in a niche, their heads touching the upper border. The ground behind them is filled with mottled paint, and a band of gold forms a border around each. The scale of the figures in relation to the size of the panel signals a possible debt to Natalia Goncharova's *The Evangelists*, which had arrived late in London in 1912 for the Second Post-Impressionist Exhibition. The Russian artist's use of the four evangelists' hands and an unfurled scroll to create movement and drama may have encouraged Bell and Grant to make similar use of hands and the scroll motif, with rhythmic effect.

The intention behind this commission was to heighten the impact made by the room and to give it a more purposive unity. To achieve this an earlier, smaller mural by Grant had to be covered up, a decision Grant himself must have accepted. It is a bold work, showing grape harvesters and dancers, but its scale in relation to the wall space available is less satisfactory. Christopher Reed, who has written

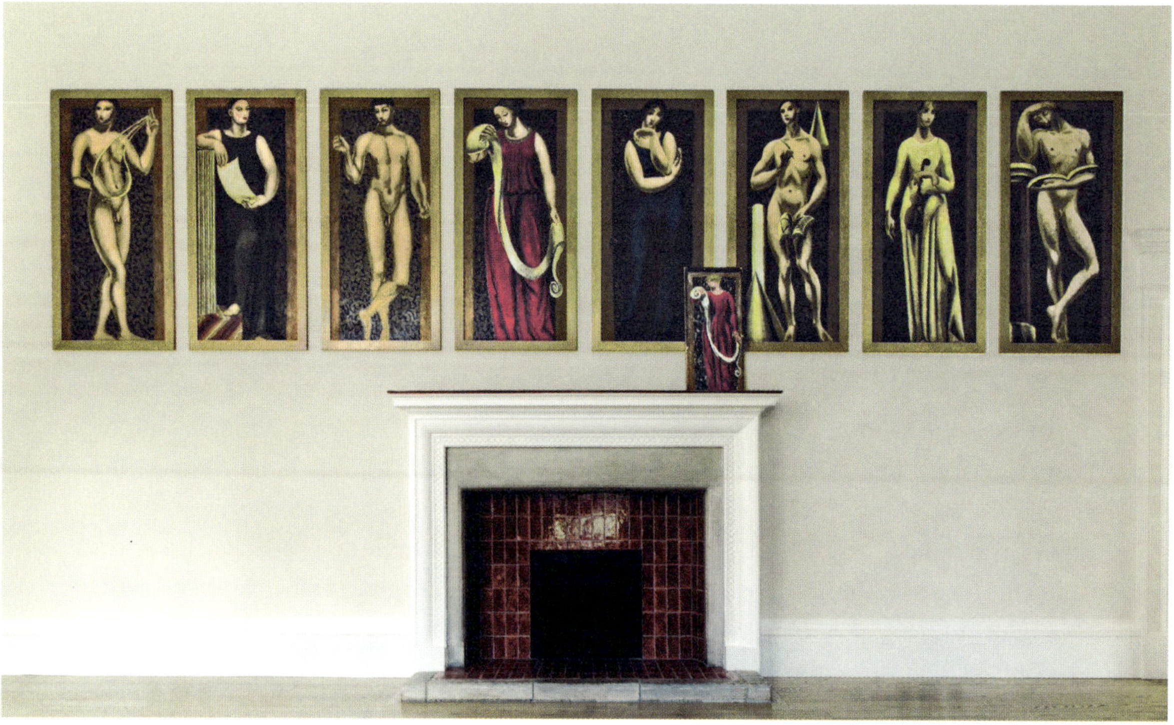

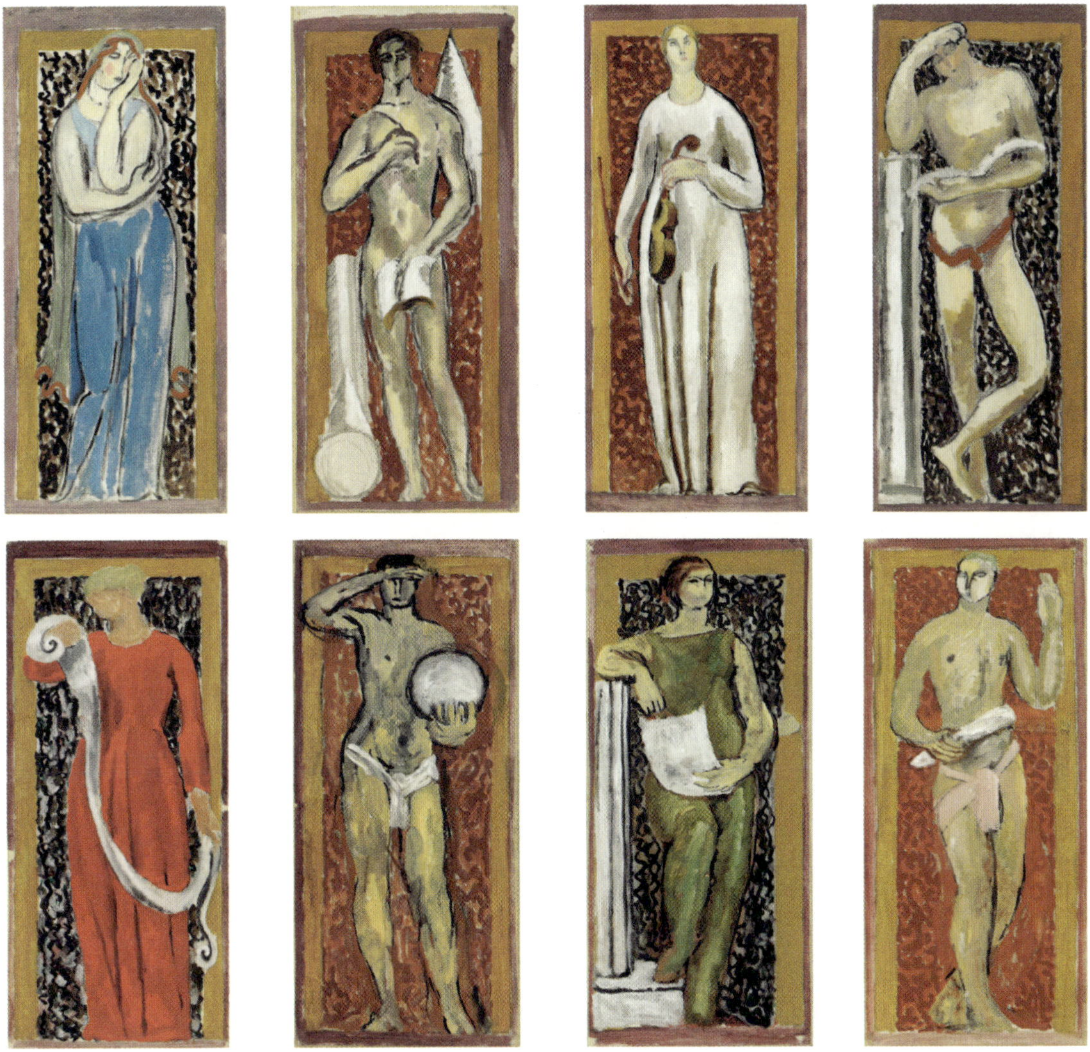

ABOVE
Vanessa Bell and Duncan Grant, studies for eight allegorical figures, representing the Arts and Sciences, commissioned by Maynard Keynes in 1920 for one of his panelled rooms in Webb's Court, King's College, Cambridge.

LEFT
The finished wall decorations, which, after some ninety years, were removed from their chosen setting and hung in another part of King's College.

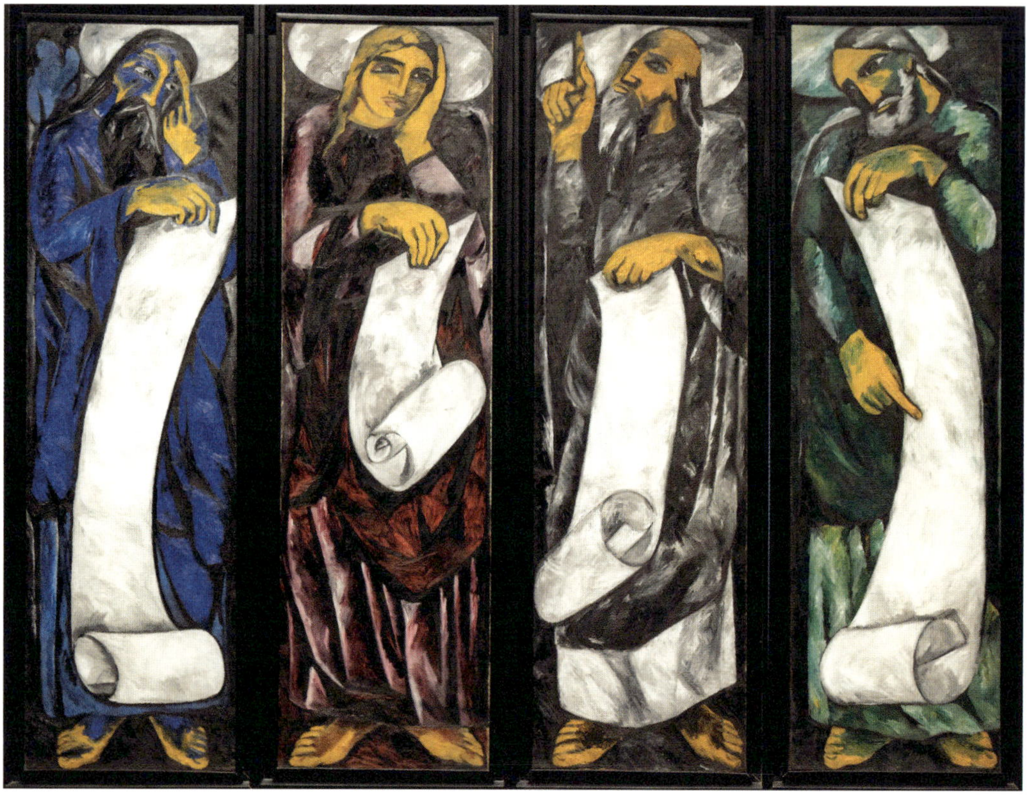

Natalia Goncharova, *The Evangelists*, oil on canvas, 1911.

ingeniously about the significance of Bloomsbury decorative art, argues that Keynes's recent success had turned him into a public figure and this, combined with his homosexuality, made it necessary to hide the provocative sensuality of Grant's earlier bacchanalian mural so that the room could become 'a setting suited in style and subject to a public figure who might be expected to receive dignitaries and reporters'.[12] But the eight figures are surely far more confrontational than the earlier mural – not only because three of the panels contain full frontal male nudity, but because the reference to the classical past is gently mocking, offhand, amusing, free and easy, and this in a college and university where much of the academic teaching and administrative practices had their foundations in that past. Bell and Grant, in their handling of the figures, gambolled playfully with the Greco-Roman and Italian Renaissance traditions and, when it came to the allegorical content, frequently got muddled as to which objects belonged to which figure. Even Reed himself admits that some visitors 'were shocked at what was still a very unconventional environment' created by these eight figures, clothed or naked.[13] Sadly, more orthodox views and the less permissive 21st century have brought about the removal of the panels to another college building, thereby detaching them from the context for which they were designed and weakening their impact. The commission had taken two years in all to complete, and Bell and Grant were evidently encouraged by the result. At Christmas 1922 they sent round a handmade advertisement seeking further commissions, which read: 'Vanessa Bell Duncan Grant decorations domestic ecclesiastical theatrical 8 Fitzroy St, W.1'.[14]

No stable style, mood or subject characterizes Duncan Grant's work in the aftermath of the war. Instead his art demonstrates flexibility, a willingness to mutate according to the needs of the subject and of the moment. This adaptability gives it added resonance. Shortly before the wall decorations for Keynes, Grant had referenced classicism in his *Venus and Adonis* of 1919, a subject most readily associated with the story found in Book 10 of Ovid's *Metamorphoses*, where Venus, the goddess of love, falls deeply for the human Adonis, a young hunter who accidentally dies after being attacked by a wild boar. Grant's source, however, is more likely to have been Shakespeare's long comic poem of the same title. It departs from Ovid's version by making Adonis unwilling to respond to Venus's repeated attempts to seduce the young man, as his heart is more set on hunting. In Grant's picture the enormous foreground figure of the reclining Venus is contrasted with the tiny figure of Adonis out hunting in the background. The picture at first seems joyously exuberant and witty, full of the 'delicate and half-humorous fantasy' that Roger Fry admired in Grant's work.[15] Yet it may have had an additional purpose, as a gently teasing reminder that his relations with Vanessa Bell had changed. It was painted after the birth of Bell and Grant's daughter, Angelica, born on Christmas Day 1918, and during a period when Grant felt it necessary to re-establish their relations on a non-sexual basis. Bell had long been aware of Grant's homosexuality, but this did not curb her love for him, and the parallel suggested between the imbalance in their relationship and that conveyed by Grant's amusing interpretation of Shakespeare's *Venus and Adonis* would not have escaped her notice. 'All I feel I can do in this case', Grant decided, 'is to build slowly for her a completely strong affection on which she can lean her weary self.'[16] This he succeeded in doing, and the result was a lifelong working partnership as well as much domestic stability and happiness.

Grant was very much alive to all that was going on in 1919. He greatly enjoyed the return of the Russian Ballet, especially Sergei Diaghilev's production of *La Boutique fantasque*, especially its sets and costumes, which had been designed by André Derain. Excited by these, Grant claimed he had never seen sets designed by an artist. 'It's quite a different thing', he wrote to Bell, 'and adds to the triumph

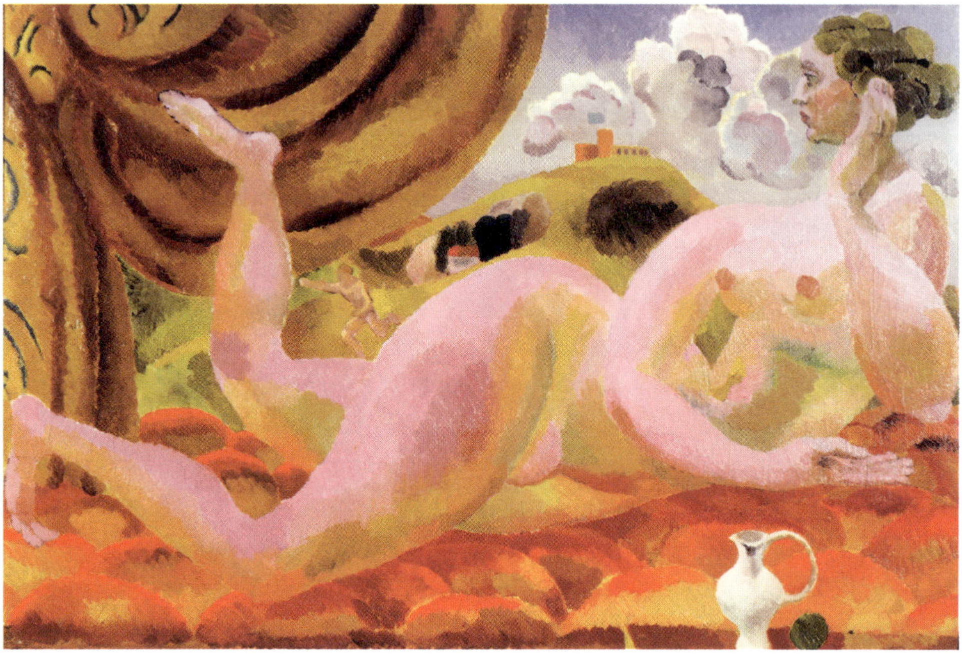

Duncan Grant, *Venus and Adonis*, oil on canvas, 1919.

of modern art much to the discomfiture of the upper and cultural classes.' In this same letter he mentions meeting Picasso and Derain (with both of whom he was on friendly terms) while they were in London that summer. 'Derain said that with my gifts I ought to attack "des grandes problèmes" but I don't really understand what that means.'[17]

Grant was painting hard that summer, partly to make up for time lost during the war but also because London's Carfax Gallery had offered him a solo exhibition to be held in February 1920. His vigorous sensibility was stimulated by many things: not just the pleasures and interest that came through the eye, but also his enjoyment of books. In the summer of 1920, as he told Bunny Garnett, he was 'ravished by Beyle's [Stendhal's] correspondence in four volumes'.[18] In August 1919, he had turned again to Delacroix's *Journal*, where he would have been reminded of this artist's view that in a painter it is the imagination that speaks before all else. In the autumn he paid a visit to his parents near Dartford in Kent, where he took great delight in a visiting circus. 'It was all enchantingly traditional with clowns and exquisite horses and jugglers. The audience was perfect and one felt hundreds of miles away from the world of culture.'[19] This entertainment seems to have provoked his *Juggler and Tightrope Walker*, with its clever and imaginative use of distortion, giving to the composition, like the tightrope walker, a delightful poise. It is a confident and original painting, but Derain's suggestion that he should be more ambitious and tackle 'des grandes problèmes' may have been to the fore of Grant's mind when he and Vanessa Bell called on Picasso in Paris, after a trip to Italy in 1920.

Picasso readily showed them his recent work. There were paintings in which the language of cubism was still dominant, as well as others that revealed he had embarked on a neoclassical phase. Not only in Picasso's studio, but during the lively exchanges Bell and Grant had with other artists in Paris, Grant would have noticed a move towards greater stability in the modelling of form; this was part of the French *rappel à l'ordre*. He himself began painting still lifes in a more solid manner, jettisoning his former fluency with the flow of colour across form in favour of greater emphasis on the shape and weight of still life objects and the relationships between them. Even his highlights in the reflections found in glasses or on table-tops are now more rigidly in place. At some point he merged this new manner with the 'classical turn' by painting *Still Life with Classical Bust* (1922), as it is now called, although the plaster bust shown, admittedly in a classical style, is by the French sculptor Marcel Gimond. This and a tight cluster of dim-coloured flowers in a small pot offset the architecture of the bare surroundings. Grant has suppressed any hint of his more customary use of calligraphic brushwork, and his use of close tones and dark colours makes for a sombre palette similar to that found in his *Still Life*

Duncan Grant, *Still Life with Classical Bust*, oil on canvas, 1922.

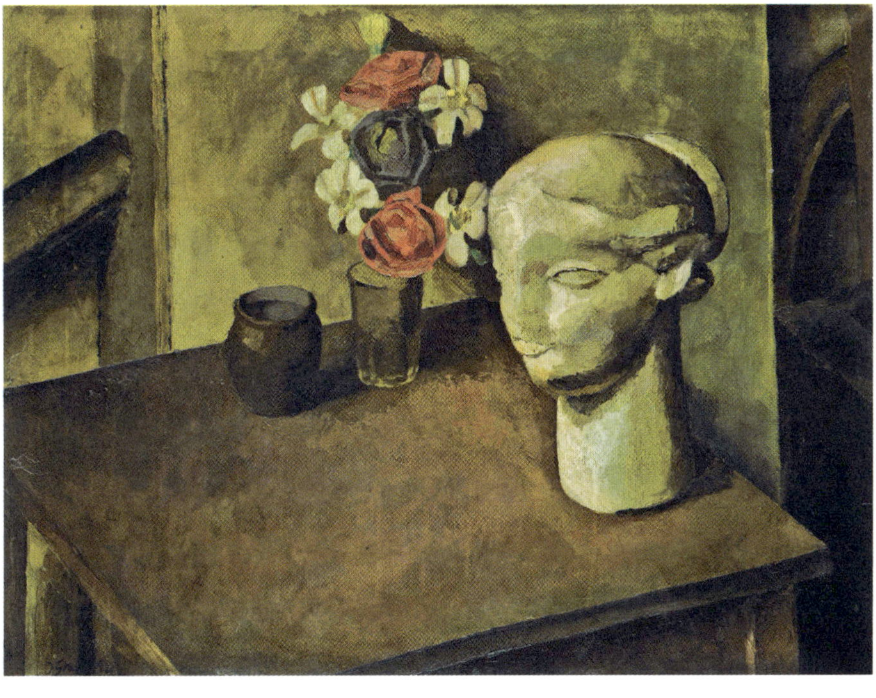

with Carrots, painted that same year and sold to the collector Sir Edward Marsh, who bequeathed it to the Tate. Admittedly, much in *Still Life with Classical Bust* has been learnt from Cézanne, but both pictures in their quiet but compelling realism uphold the interwar need to turn back, *recueillir*, to arrive at a profound stillness, an absolute fixity that nevertheless also conveys awareness of transience and mortality.

Much revivalism was light-hearted and romantic. It led to the use of slightly self-mocking historical pastiche, as can be found in Rex Whistler's murals for the Tate Refreshment Room. These, in turn, encouraged Edward Bawden and Eric Ravilious's free play with medievalism in their murals for the Refreshment Room at Morley College, formerly the Samuel Morley Memorial College for Working Men and Women. This institution had begun life as a progamme of lectures held in the Royal Victoria Hall and Coffee Tavern (better known as 'the Old Vic'), but it had moved out in 1912 to a Georgian house in Lambeth, thereby making way for Lilian Baylis at the Old Vic to begin in 1914 a long series of Shakespearean productions. The fame of these plays became associated with the area, and this influenced Bawden and Ravilious's decision to base their murals on Shakespeare, old English dramas, miracle plays and pantomime, in a spirit of free fantasy and without any logical or chronological sequence. Sadly these latter murals no longer exist, but like Rex Whistler's mural at the Tate, they transformed a gloomy basement room into a sensation – to such an extent that Queen Mary commanded a private viewing with the two artists in attendance.

The decision to decorate the Tate Gallery's Tea Room, as the space was originally called, was initiated by Joseph Duveen, who pledged £500 for the purpose. He had previously provided funds for two Slade students to brighten up the Boys' Highway Club in Shadwell with a mural, a task that Professor Henry Tonks gave to Rex Whistler and Mary Adshead. Tonks also sat on the committee formed in connection with the Tate commission, by which time twenty-one-year-old Rex Whistler had left the Slade, where he had been one of Tonks's star pupils. Not only had he shown no interest in post-impressionism or any of the other avant-garde techniques that Tonks deplored, but his work, with its correct perspective, elegance of design and restrained colour, was always beautifully finished. The only thing that Tonks regretted in his pupil was that Whistler was 'incurably unobservant',[20] preferring to work from imagination or memory. This may be why, as Anna Thomasson has observed, Tonks nudged Whistler, while he was still a student, towards decoration by giving him the task of improving the School's main staircase before the King and Queen's visit for tea at the Slade on the occasion of its centenary.[21] Whistler rigged up palms, hydrangeas and red curtains with gold tassels and fringes to make the entrance duly ceremonious, but it was the staircase itself that greatly amused the King and Queen, as it had been made to look like solid gold.

Whistler's inventiveness and readiness to engage with hard work made him acceptable to the Tate's director, Charles Aitken. What Tonks primarily admired was Whistler's gaiety and originality. 'I have never met anyone like him,' Tonks told a friend. 'He amuses me because he has a certain gift of humour, I can not describe it, very subtle, that touches some recesses in my mind, all hidden under a most respectful (and really respectful) manner.'[22]

Whistler's idea was to wrap the sixty-foot-long Tea Room in a continuous, fantasy classical landscape, in a manner associated with the picturesque and the Regency period. It was to be very different from the bucolic village scene with Gypsies dancing in front of a half-timbered inn that he and Adshead had produced in the Boys' Highway Club. Instead the new mural was to retreat from realism into a dreamlike echo of the past, while its immersive takeover of the entire room – even the doorways had been incorporated into the fantasy – was to make it unlike anything London had seen before.

Two years earlier, a strong friendship had sprung up between the nineteen-year-old Whistler and fifty-two-year-old Edith Olivier, who lived in a cottage on the Wilton estate in Wiltshire. References to both the great house and estate had already begun to appear in Whistler's art, and more would appear in the Tate mural. Olivier had a passionate interest in places, especially Wiltshire, which was bound up with her interest in folklore, history, literature and anecdote. With a similar mixture of fact and fantasy, Whistler traces in his mural the imaginary journey of a hunting party, first seen leaving a palace in one corner of the room and then riding through various countries: hunting for truffles in the oak woods of France, spearing sturgeon and meeting strange beasts, including a unicorn and a ghost. On the wall pierced by windows, the party passes through China, with its Great Wall, then Peru, before ending in a classical landscape reminiscent of Claude Lorrain.

We can be certain that the initial idea for this subject was Whistler's. He and Edith Olivier met at the Tate Gallery on 25 March 1926 so that he could show her the Tea Room, after which she recorded in her diary: 'he means to have a coach and four going on a journey all [a]round the room, passing all over the world and collecting the things eaten in the Tea Room'.[23] But almost certainly, Olivier had a role in the unfurling of Whistler's initial conception. She seems also to have provided the title, *In Pursuit of Rare Meats*, as this is also the title of the children's story she wrote based on the mural. The story supplies a fantasy narrative that connects with many passages and details in the mural but also contains incidents that do not appear on the Tate's walls.

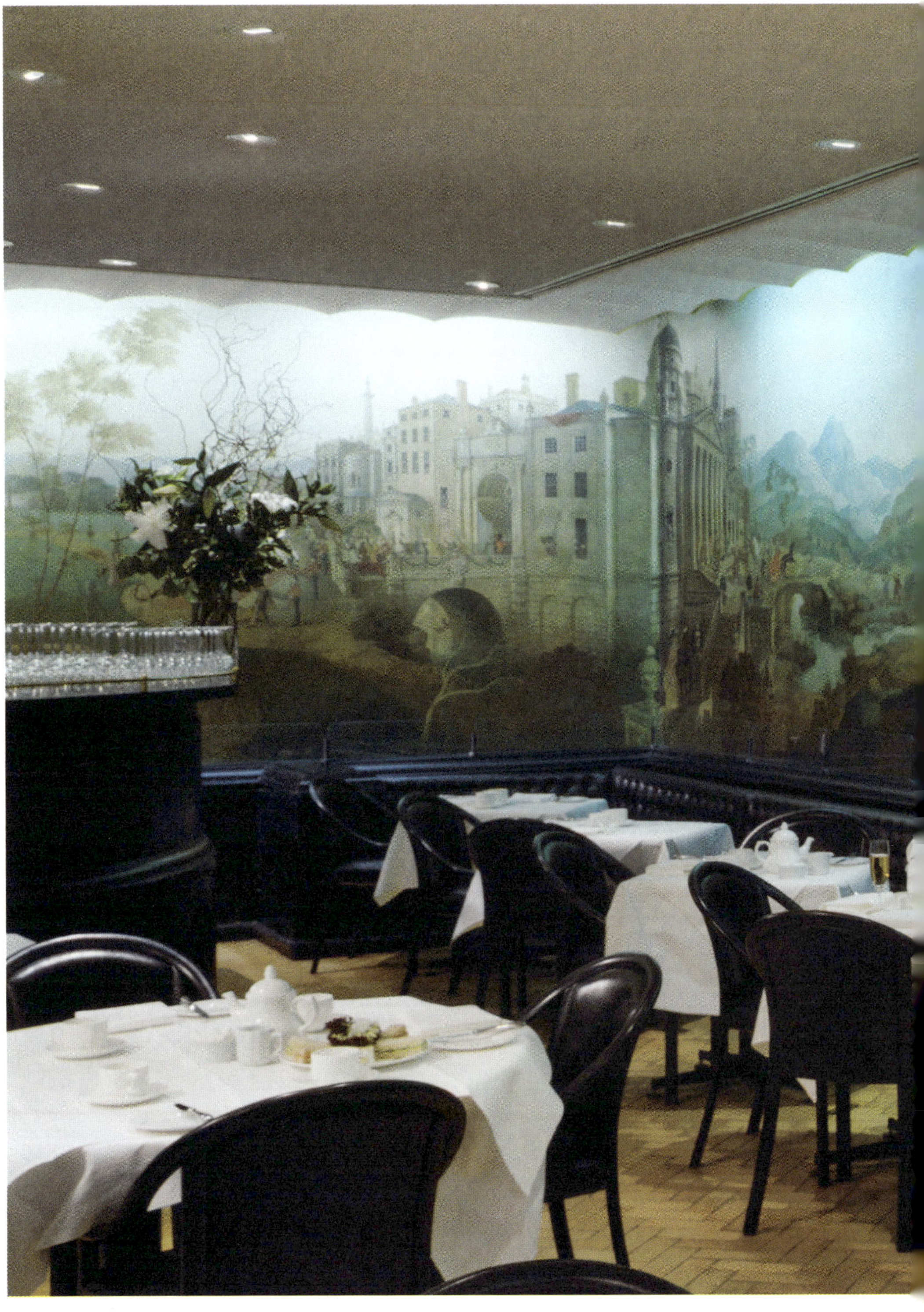

Rex Whistler, *The Expedition in Pursuit of Rare Meats*, 1926–7,
mural decoration in the Tate Tea Room.

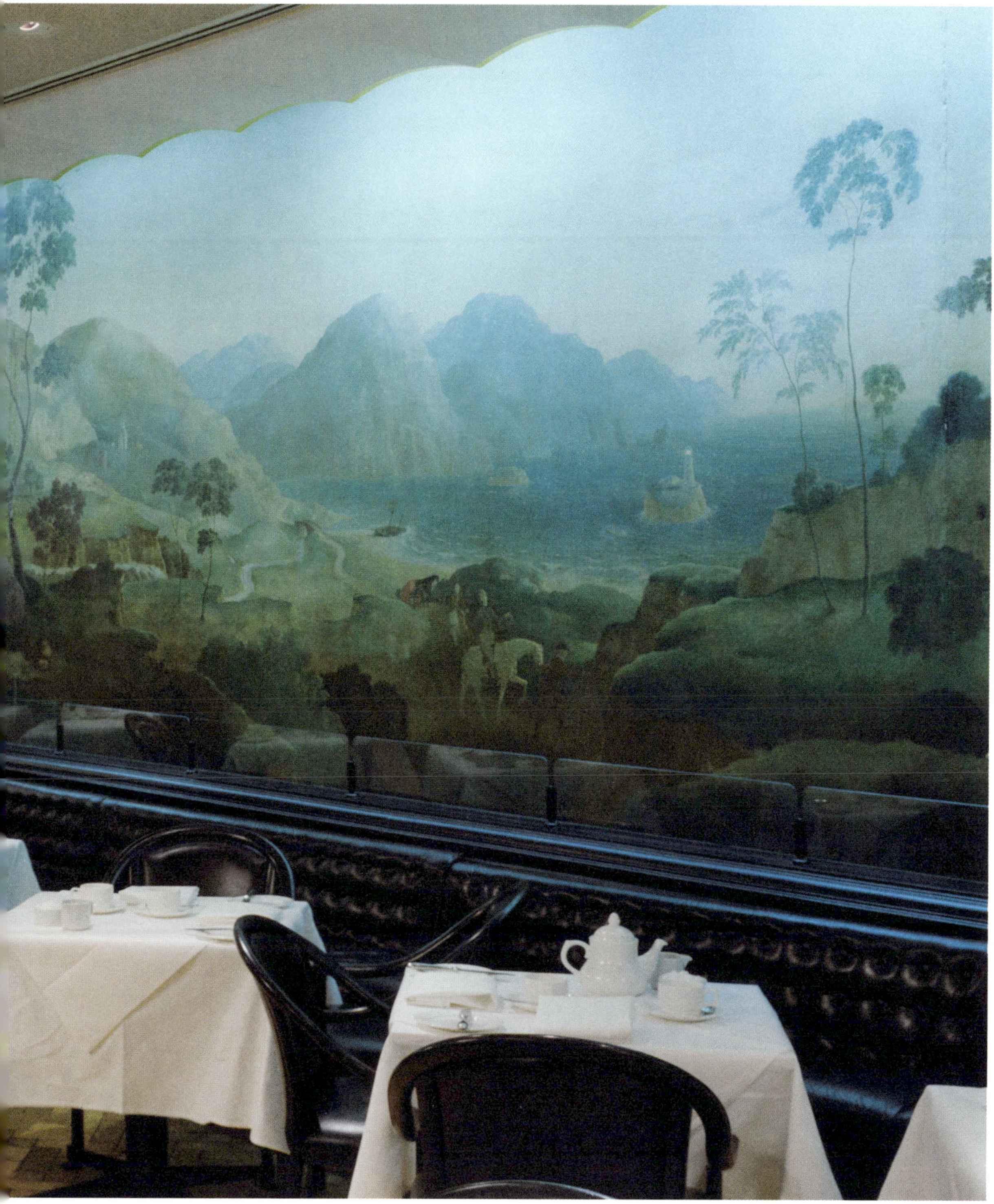

Whistler never properly finished the mural in the way that he intended, and some details may have suffered from the great flood in 1928 that caused the Embankment wall in front of the Tate to be breached. This resulted in water sweeping across the road and roaring into the Tate's basement, unhinging doors, pushing aside masonry and covering Whistler's mural to a height of eight feet. The mural survived (probably owing to the wax and oil which Whistler had mixed into his colours) but it is possible that some details were diminished. At the time of the salvage operation, prime attention was given to Turner's watercolours, which had sat for some hours in solander boxes in four wooden presses covered with mud.

Whistler's move from realism into fantasy may have been influenced by his liking for the poet and anthologist Walter de la Mare. After an abortive attempt to study at the RA Schools, where he lasted only a term, Whistler had moved to the Slade, where he and Stephen Tennant became friends after discovering they both had a dislike of the life-room. Tennant has put on record their fondness for poetry and 'fairy tales, mythology, legends containing magic spells', adding, 'and we found a strong reciprocal bond in the passionate vividness of our imaginations'.[24]

Walter de la Mare's novel *Henry Brocken* was one of Whistler's favourite books. His admiration for de la Mare would almost certainly have led him to his popular anthology *Come Hither: A Collection of Rhymes & Poems for the Young of all Ages* (first published in 1923, a revised and expanded version appearing in 1928), into which he had poured his wide reading and expert knowledge of rhymes, nursery jingles, ballads and legends. His selection of 483 poems was more demotic in its range than that found in Palgrave's *Golden Treasury*, for it included more ancient and anonymous poems and more ballads, and enjoyed immediate and lasting success. It may have encouraged Whistler's decision to compile and illustrate his own anthology, which included more poems by de la Mare than by any other poet. According to Laurence Whistler, who wrote a biography of his older brother Rex, Walter de la Mare was for Rex 'the supreme romantic of the modern age, creating a world of his own by transfiguring with strangeness what was familiar or at hand'.[25]

Come Hither and Whistler's Tate mural are cultural indicators of the need for fantasy in a period squeezed between two wars. Both artists knew how to play upon the imagination of others, thereby carrying the reader or viewer into the past or into a different world. When the Tate mural first went on public show on 30 November 1927 in the newly decorated Refreshment Room, as it was renamed (later becoming the Tate Restaurant), its great sweep and bucolic mood raised the Tate's profile, brought Whistler renown and enhanced the reputation of the Slade. When, in 1968, talk arose of the need to expand or move the existing restaurant, letters of protest on behalf of the mural reached *The Times*, one from David Cecil who saw that Whistler's 'romantic irony' turns the whole mural into subversive mockery of the picturesque.[26] Yet, at the time of writing, the Tate Restaurant in Tate Britain remains closed after concerns were raised in the press and online about racist details in Whistler's mural. Figures depicted in the work include an enslaved Black boy with a rope around his neck, having been captured by the Princess's maid to help with the hunt. Other panels feature caricatured depictions of Chinese people. In response to the criticisms, the Tate has acknowledged the presence of offensive and unacceptable content and its relationship to racist and imperialist attitudes of the 1920s. The work forms part of a Grade I-listed historic interior, but its future is uncertain.

In the late 1920s, the fashion for wall decoration spread into private houses. In 1925 the architect Professor Charles Reilly in Liverpool had commissioned Mary Adshead to decorate his dining room, and her three wall decorations, titled *A Tropical Fantasy*, were exhibited at the Royal Institute of British Architects in 1926 before being installed in his house.[27] Wall decorations made possible further play with classical motifs, often married with an art deco style. In this way the painter John Armstrong attracted a roster of wealthy patrons, among them Samuel Courtauld, who, in need of somewhere to hang his collection of impressionists and post-impressionists, had moved in 1926 into Home House, a great Robert Adam mansion in London's Portman Square. In fact it was Courtauld's wife Lillian who commissioned murals from Armstrong for her studio, while in her bathroom an outline line drawing of acrobats and jugglers travelled over the ceiling as well as the walls. Armstrong's imaginative interest in classical motifs not only fed into his paintings but also his poster designs for Shell and the General Post Office. In a slightly later phase of his career his awareness of surrealism, combined with his response to the Spanish Civil War and other aspects of the deteriorating international scene, took his work to a different level of achievement. An example is *The Heaviness of Sleep* (1938), where acute and exact treatment of nature is combined with a composition that hints at the power of dreams and the unconscious.

Another trigger for revivalism was the switch in interest from the giants of the High Renaissance – Michelangelo, Leonardo and Raphael – to a more pronounced interest in the early Italian Renaissance, which in the interwar years came to be regarded as a period of greater purity and simplicity of expression. This alteration in taste brought with it a desire to revive ancient mediums and methods, in particular the use of egg tempera. This was a medium that had been almost entirely forgotten in England until, in 1899, Christiana Herringham brought out her translation into English of Cennino Cennini's *Il libro dell'arte o trattato della pittura*, with valuable explanatory notes. Evidence of this ignorance about tempera is proved by the fact that Ruskin thought Botticelli and all the Italian primitives, as they were then called, painted in oils, until he encountered Mrs Herringham making a tempera copy of a picture in the National Gallery and asked her what she was doing. It was the desire to revive the medium as a practical one for artists that led Herringham and others in 1901 to establish the Society of Painters in Tempera. Its early exhibitions were held at the Carfax Gallery in St James's, and among its founder members was the artist Joseph Southall.

The medium of tempera requires precise and meticulous treatment. Dry powdered colours are mixed with the yolk of an egg, slightly thinned with acetic acid or water, instead of oil, varnish or turpentine, as in oil painting. The ground used is habitually either a wooden panel or a silk stretched over a wooden frame, to both of which polished layers of gesso have been added. The chief difficulty in using tempera is that it dries so rapidly, almost as soon as it has been laid on the ground. This makes it necessary to work with a preconceived design and clear outlines. There can be no blurring or mixing of colours except by means of careful hatching, one colour on top of another, or by the use of thin glazes gradually built up. It is hardly surprising that the pristine quality associated with the medium can result in subjects that look a little stiff or rigid, but the restraining element in egg tempera can also release a jewel-like perfection.

Southall had learnt tempera painting in Italy and brought it home to Birmingham School of Art, where he became a leading figure in the tempera revival and one of the foremost painters in tempera in this country. After a long engagement, he married his cousin, Anna Elizabeth (Bessie) Baker in 1903, when both were in their forties. They had always been determined to marry and had held back from doing so until she had passed child-bearing age, on the understanding that the basis of their marriage would be kinship, intimacy and a close working partnership. It was Bessie who built up the gesso grounds for Joseph's tempera paintings, often giving them as many as eight layers of gesso, which were then smoothed to an ivory finish and sealed with two layers of size. She also gessoed and gilded some of the frames for his paintings. He worked in watercolour as well as tempera, and his paintings were exhibited widely, in Britain, France, Italy, Belgium and the United States. He was elected to membership of various bodies, including the Art Worker's Guild. Interest in tempera painting underwent a further revival in 1930 owing to the enormous success that year of the Royal Academy's Winter Exhibition of Italian art, which not only contained examples of tempera painting but also amounted to the largest selection of Italian Renaissance art ever shown in this country.

During the Southalls' thirty-four-year marriage most of their summers were spent in Suffolk, at Southwold, which boasted a small fishing industry. Many of Joseph's

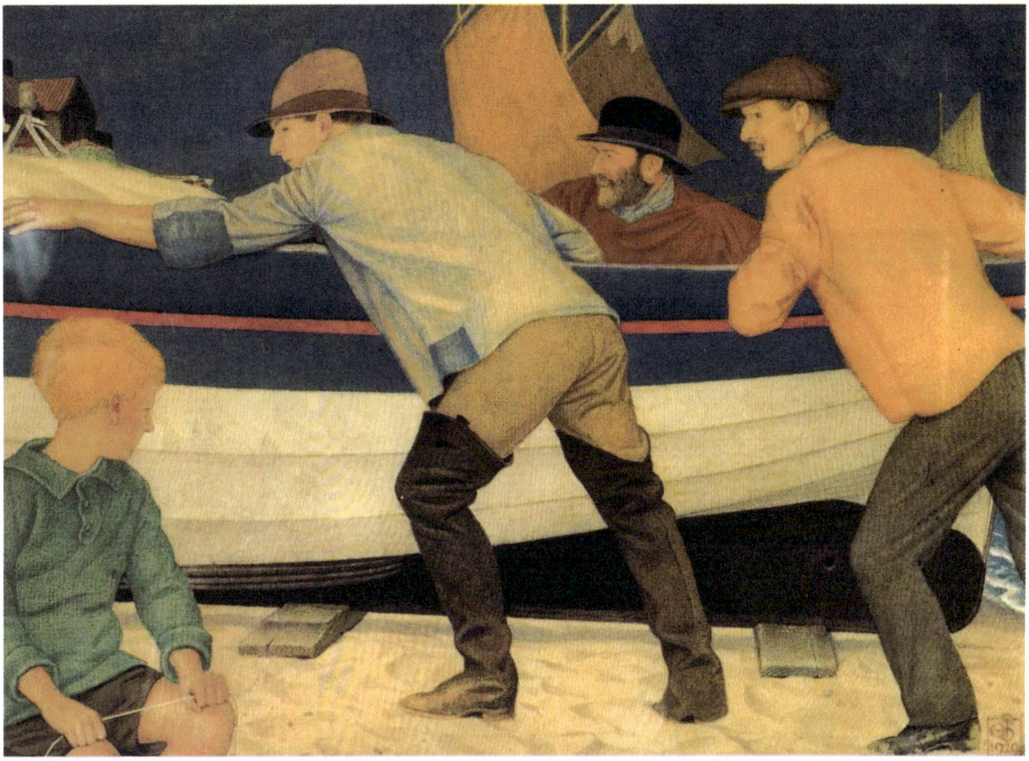

Joseph Southall, *Up from the Sea*,
tempera on fabric, 1920.

best pictures were done here. His romantic nature and love of precision can be observed in his painting of old-fashioned schooners as well as in his fascination with the latest in female fashions which came to the fore in the early 1930s, as in *Fishermen and Visitors* (1931) and other scenes. His earlier pictures focus more on his admiration for the labour of fishermen. In *Up from the Sea* (1920), for example, the picture is cropped like a modern snapshot yet is crafted with nostalgia, in tribute to three generations of Suffolk fishermen. A sense of the real inhabits the forward thrust created by pushing a boat ashore up a pathway of planks, and it finds an echo in the shape of the background sails.

Another part of Southall's life was given over to politics: he became a member of the Independent Labour Party and a strong advocate of pacifism. His interests have been neatly entwined in George Breeze's summary in the *Dictionary of*

National Biography: 'In his life Southall brought together the gathered stillness of a Quaker meeting, the jewelled calm of tempera painting, and the peace sought by pacifism.'[28]

Mention has previously been made of the turn to the linocut as a refreshing print medium in the late 1920s. The print market in general remained buoyant throughout most of the decade until the Wall Street crash of 1929 and the following depression. Much attention has been given to the revival of wood engraving, fostered by a return of interest in Thomas Bewick (1753–1828) and in Dürer, ballads and chapbooks, with the result that, having formerly been used as a reproductive medium, it once again became an art form expressive in its own right. A swelling of interest led to the founding of the Society of Wood Engravers in 1920. It was troubled by disagreements and in 1925 Leon Underwood, Blair Hughes-Stanton and Gertrude Hermes seceded, forming the Wood Engraving Society. Much of the work done in this medium was directed towards private presses. One of the most famous was the Golden Cockerel Press, under Robert Gibbings. He enlisted Eric Gill as his chief collaborator but also gave work to the young Eric Ravilious, who worked for private presses as well as more commercial printing houses, in a highly sophisticated vein.

Less had been written about the etching revival but, like wood-engraving, it too became a route for talented students to modern fame. It played a significant role in the career of Graham Sutherland, for instance. As a student in the etching department at Goldsmith's, he studied Rembrandt and James McNeill Whistler, as is apparent from his early etchings. Between 1922 and 1938 he produced forty etchings that made a significant contribution to the history of print-making, and it was through this work that he first attracted public attention.

That Sutherland became very skilful in this medium in a short space of time can be seen from the sureness, delicacy and balance found in his etching *The Black Rabbit* (1923), of which there are two states. The setting is Arundel Park, Sussex, and the title refers to the pub in the centre of the composition. The following year, shortly before his twenty-first birthday, Sutherland held his first solo exhibition at the XXI Gallery in the Adelphi. At around this time, another Goldsmith's student found a copy of Samuel Palmer's etching *The Herdsman's Cottage* in the Charing Cross Road and brought it to show his peers. Since his death in 1881, Palmer's work had been ignored. This dark, overbitten print, owing to excessive use of acid, had an electrifying impact on Sutherland, Paul Drury and others, partly because Palmer's handling of the medium broke many of the rules about etching as taught at Goldsmith's and elsewhere. A sudden change in Sutherland's method can be seen in *Village* and *Pecken Wood*, two of six pastoral etchings he produced between 1925

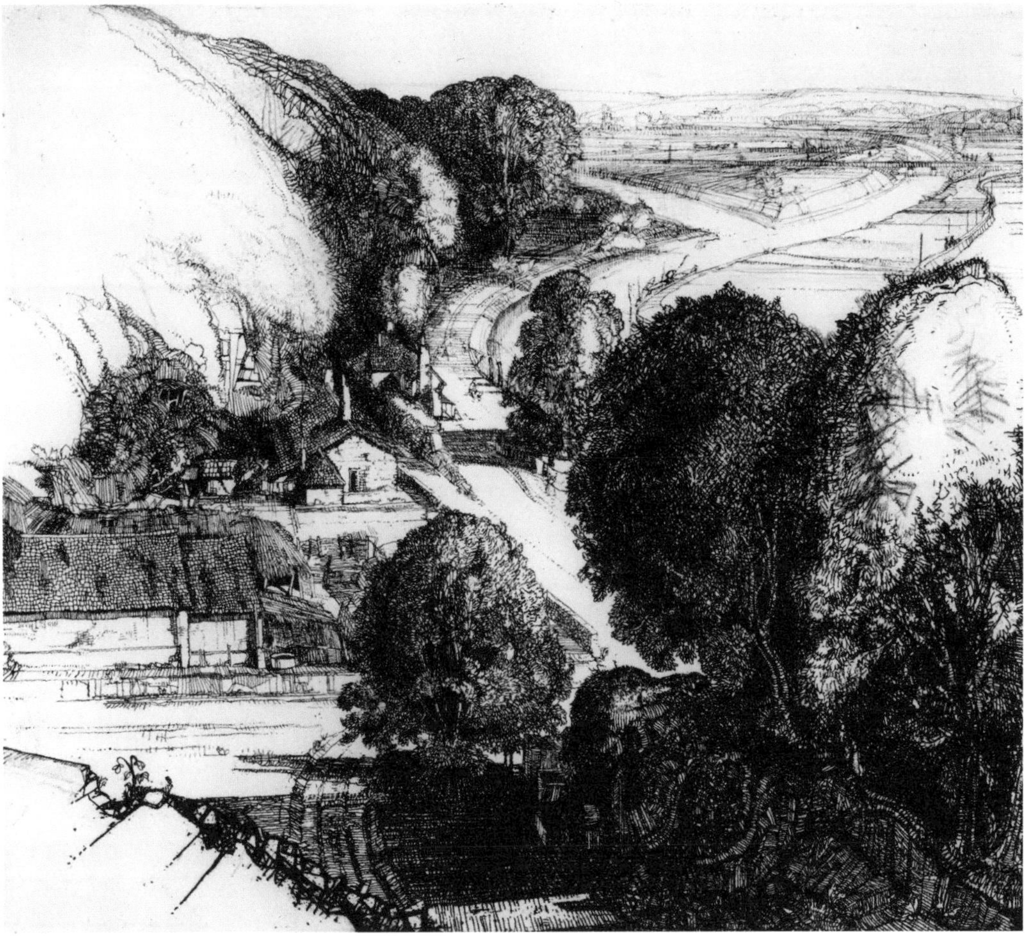

Graham Sutherland, *The Black Rabbit*,
etching, 1923.

and 1927, but perhaps the best of this group is *St Mary Hatch* (1926) in its first state, before the plate was cut down. It comes closest to the visionary mood which Palmer achieved for seven years while living at Shoreham in Kent. Before being cut down, it carried an inscription along the bottom of the plate in Latin taken from Psalm 15, possibly as a homage to Palmer: 'Lord, who shall abide in thy tabernacle? Who shall dwell in thy holy hill? He that walketh uprightly, and worketh righteousness.' This work also shows how pastoralism, boosted by the rediscovery of Palmer at an exhibition mounted in the Victoria and Albert Museum in 1926, became a vehicle for ideology, for a growing appreciation of those who work on the land, and for the traditions that surround and reinforce this way of life.

A return to etching also played a role during the 1920s in the career of Augustus John, whose flamboyant dress and character, together with his love of Gypsies and their way of life, had made him a larger-than-life figure in the art world. As a young man in the autumn of 1898 he had been persuaded by two friends from the Slade, Benjamin Evans and Ambrose McEvoy, to go with them to Amsterdam to see a Rembrandt exhibition at the recently opened Stedelijk Museum. Many works came from abroad, as once Queen Victoria had agreed to lend two Rembrandts, other private collectors and institutions fell in line. This is said to have been the first 'blockbuster' exhibition: it included 120 paintings and 350 drawings, and was insured for the massive sum of £4 million sterling. Rembrandt's etchings formed another concurrent exhibition at the nearby Rijksmuseum. A reduced version of the Stedelijk exhibition travelled to London in 1899 as the Royal Academy's Winter Exhibition, at which 102 paintings were shown in four rooms and the fifth was devoted to his drawings.

The impact made by Rembrandt on artists in England deepened in 1902 owing to the appearance of a pocket-sized book by Auguste Bréal. The modest scale of this book encouraged Bréal to concentrate not on Rembrandt's oil paintings but on the intimacy of his etchings and drawings. It was made additionally attractive by Bréal's insights into Rembrandt's humanity, his compassion and sympathy with the people he represented. Although small, the book had a powerful influence.

John had initially taken up etching at the suggestion of Benjamin Evans. His first was a head and shoulders self-portrait, made in 1901. It is just over three inches tall and three inches wide (82 × 76 cm). The self-portrait was a theme that Rembrandt had explored all through his life, often in etchings on a similarly small scale. In Campbell Dodgson's *A Catalogue of Etchings by Augustus John*, published in 1920, in which the numbering of the etchings is preceded by Dodgson's initials, the first ten images are all self-portraits owing to the author's decision to present the images not in chronological order, but according to theme. They reveal John's investigative use of this medium. In the case of his first self-portrait, only two states exist. In the second of these we find that he has pulled out the lapel of his coat to enhance its shape and filled it with a heavy black shadow, while also giving more finish to the face. This increase in the use of blacks stabilizes the image and enables the head to sit more comfortably on the body. Effects of shadow, light, density and weight in subsequent self-portraits are variously achieved, often by retouching with drypoint, although John would also burnish out accents and shading that he felt had become too dominant. His etched portrait of his friend Benjamin Evans (CD 89) went through four states and ended as a smorgasbord of technical experiments.

Like Sutherland, John mastered the medium quickly. Two years after his first self-portrait, he etched a portrait of Wyndham Lewis in which the lights and darks are finely balanced and the sitter's firmness of character is well conveyed. Some of his freshest etchings, such as his deft likeness of William Rothenstein (CD 21), appear to have been caught at one sitting. His etching of Yeats, together with variants of it, dates back to 1907, when Yeats was revising his collected works and wanted an etching for its frontispiece. Lady Gregory supplied the commission and John went to Galway, where he painted Yeats's portrait and made numerous other studies in preparation for the etching. Yeats was by then forty-four and no longer a youthful romantic poet; John registered his maturity, but this did not please Lady Gregory. In the end a Sargent drawing took the place of John's etching in the new edition of Yeats's collected works, but in subsequent printings there has been a return to one or other of John's portraits. There is no doubting the empathy with his sitters that John achieved, whether they were young or old, rich or poor, famous or anonymous. Portraiture remained always at the heart of his career.

Etching invites a more reflective approach than is found in John's drawings and oil paintings, and it gave him the opportunity to work in a less flamboyant register. The generosity of his flung line, which made his drawings so bold and dashing, is here constrained. The etched line, less quickly drawn than that executed in charcoal, crayon or pencil, makes speed of execution difficult. The intimacy of these etchings suggests we are encountering John in a more private mood, exploring his gift for the steady build-up of certainty, as is found in the sixth state of *The Serving Maid* (CD 41). It is not possible to know what the young woman is thinking or feeling or what has caused her slightly backward look. But her momentary pose, after many trials and much reworking, is fixed in such a way that once seen it is hard to forget. It is no wonder that Campbell Dodgson, in his catalogue of John's etchings, proudly boasted that the most complete private collection of them belonged to 'the author'. His catalogue was fully subscribed prior to publication in 1920. Its appearance was timed to coincide with a second exhibition of John's etchings at the Chenil Gallery in Chelsea, which was a phenomenal success and raised £7,000 in sales.

Dodgson is a significant figure within the history of John's etchings. He spent his entire working life in the British Museum's Prints and Drawings Department, first as Assistant Keeper from 1893 and then as Keeper from 1912 until his retirement in 1932, helping to make the department what it now is – one of the jewels in the Museum's crown. However, up until 1949, the Museum would not permit the use of public funds for contemporary material and would only include acquisitions of this kind if they were gifted. It seems that, near the start of his career, Dodgson – who had private means, as he came from a family of stockbrokers – was determined to build up a collection that would complement the holdings of the Museum. Among other prize acquisitons, he sought out Käthe Kollwitz prints in Germany, and probably bought some directly from the artist. He also collected the work of two artists in toto, Muirhead Bone and Augustus John. Not only did he gift some items to the Museum during his lifetime, but the rest of the 5,000 items in his collection arrived as a bequest to the Prints and Drawings Department after his death. The combination of Dodgson's catalogue and the 1920 Chenil Gallery show of his etchings appears to have led to John's 1921 election to the Royal Academy as an ARA.

It would seem that the habit of letting the past return encouraged a wider reconsideration of the history of English art. One of the first to see a connection between native traditions and modernist endeavour was Herbert Read. In 1922, as a young man and poet, he entered the Victoria and Albert Museum as a curator of ceramics and glass. In this great museum he had the opportunity to become familiar with a large sweep of English art. He may have been the lesser co-author when he worked with the pottery expert Bernard Rackham on a major historical catalogue, *English Pottery: Its Development from Early Times to the End of the Eighteenth Century* (1924), but two years later he published a weighty folio-sized book on *English Stained Glass* which revealed his great passion for the medieval period.

Both books acknowledge the relevance of national identity to the arts; Read's thoughts on this subject prefigure Nikolaus Pevsner's famous Reith lectures on 'The Englishness of English Art'. In 1933, when Read took over as editor of the *Burlington Magazine*, then Britain's most prestigious art journal, he wrote a lengthy piece in support of a forthcoming survey of British art that was to form the Royal Academy's Winter Exhibition, opening in January 1934. The article, 'English Art', attempted to define essential characteristics of English art and style. For Read, as later for Pevsner, a key ingredient was a certain graphic or linear freedom – that which Blake identified as 'the bounding line and its infinite inflections and movements' – which, as Kate Aspinall has pointed out, becomes for Read 'the basic linear signature of our race' in Anglo-Saxon times, and which he found in 'the clarity and the brilliance of our medieval illuminators'.[29] This linear signature he even finds in Gainsborough's late style, in 'his thin brush strokes, deft and dexterous, fearless in their lightness – what do they express but a joy in linear rhythms, a desire for clarity and concision, for the determinative and the definite?'[30] His essay pursues many fascinating links and comparisons between artists from medieval times up to 1860, the period covered by the exhibition's survey.

At one point Read suggests that it is possible to regard the English school of watercolour painting as a return to 'the grace, the clarity and the brilliance of medieval illustrations'.[31] He signs off his long essay with the following observation:

> I do not wish to end this essay on a banal note of prophecy; but the conjunction in our time of a final emancipation from puritan inhibitions of the sensibility, and of a general return to a type of art which, whatever its content, employs the definite line and the clear colour of our earliest and purest tradition, makes a situation of extraordinary interest and most unforeseen possibilities.[32]

As Read had earlier that year moved in to 3 Mall Studios off Tasker Road in Hampstead, which had been found for him by Barbara Hepworth and Ben Nicholson, then living at No. 7, it may seem likely that their work and that of Paul Nash, another of his friends, was foremost in his mind. But his prophecy is also relevant to what was happening simultaneously in watercolour painting.

In the hierarchy of values surrounding art, watercolour has often been regarded as a lesser medium than oil. This may be one reason why the work of Eric Ravilious receives no mention in Charles Harrison's landmark book *English Art and Modernism 1900–1939*, first published in 1981, and where the name of Edward Bawden is only mentioned in an appendix listing the members of the Seven and Five Society. At that time, it must have seemed impossible to regard a watercolourist as also a modernist. But the revival of watercolour painting is an important ingredient in interwar art. and another outlet for the modern sensibility in pursuit of the real and the romantic.

Bawden and Ravilious first met in the autumn of 1922, on entering the RCA as students in the Design School. They became friends and rivals, developing what might be called a working partnership, in that their interests were closely allied and they both operated successfully across the fine art/commercial art divide. But at the RCA it was Bawden whose talent first caught the attention of his tutor Robert Anning Bell, who remarked: 'Exceptionally good student...shows marked originality in design flavoured with a little of the exaggeration and grotesquerie so popular now.'[33] This awareness of what was fashionable and, above all, of the need to be light and amusing, contributed to both Bawden's and Ravilious's success as designers. Together with Ravilious's interest in wood engraving and their mutual involvement with mural decorations at Morley College, it meant that it was some time before watercolour painting began to figure significantly in their careers. Their work in watercolours only properly took off after they found and rented Brick House in Great Bardfield in 1930 and began to explore the Essex landscape. They continued to make this property their base even after both of them had married; the house by then belonged to Bawden, whose father had helped make its acquisition possible at the time of Edward's marriage to Charlotte Epton.

According to Andy Friend, there is no record of Ravilious doing any watercolour painting during his first year at the RCA;[34] yet his interest in this medium had begun earlier, at Eastbourne School of Art, where he first studied. There he had made friends with a fellow student, Donald Towner, who was greatly interested in the English watercolour tradition and drew Ravilious's attention to Alfred Rich's book *Water Colour Painting*, published in 1918. Chiefly a technical introduction to this medium, and laced with commonsensical advice, it daringly suggested that telegraph poles did not need to be excluded from a landscape as they could help give the necessary balance to the composition. This advice may have encouraged Ravilious's inclusion in his mature work of barbed wire, lines of which do indeed play a part in the design of his compositions. His earliest extant watercolours suggest that he learnt much from Alfred Rich regarding contemporary practice in the medium. An early work, *Warehouses by the River*,[35] if it did not bear Ravilious's signature, could be attributed to several minor watercolourists working at this time. However, in the summer of 1923 Ravilious painted *Wannock Dew Pond* and appears to have taken a step back, towards a more antiquated style. The poor quality of the paper used has probably damaged the tonal balance between the sky and the landscape, but what is chiefly noticeable in this quietly intense work is its scholarly understanding of the pictorial values associated with the true school of watercolour painting, that of the late 18th and early 19th centuries.

It becomes evident that Ravilious made very good use of the RCA's close relationship with the Victoria and Albert Museum, as the two institutions were then adjacent. He had only to go through a doorway and down a flight of steps to find himself close to the Prints and Drawings Department, where he could call up solander boxes of watercolours and sit in intimate relationship with choice examples of work by William Alexander, J. R. Cozens, Thomas Girtin, John Sell Cotman, Francis Towne and Samuel Palmer, all artists he admired. The knowledge he acquired through the study of these works would have brought him into contact with Martin Hardie, the Keeper of Painting, Engraving and Illustration. At a post-vacation Sketch Club show in the autumn of 1923 at which Ravilious showed eight or nine watercolours, Hardie bought *Wannock Dew Pond*, which must have given Ravilious a sense of the older man's approval of the direction in which he was moving.

Ravilious also had access to the British Museum's Prints and Drawings collection, and came to admire greatly John Cotman's *Greta Bridge*. Here, too, he would almost certainly have encountered Laurence Binyon, one of whose daughters, Helen, was in the same year as Ravilious at the RCA. The friendship between Helen and Ravilious was slow to form, Ravilious later recalling that at first they were only on 'hat raising terms';[36] but not only did a close friendship develop, it also led on,

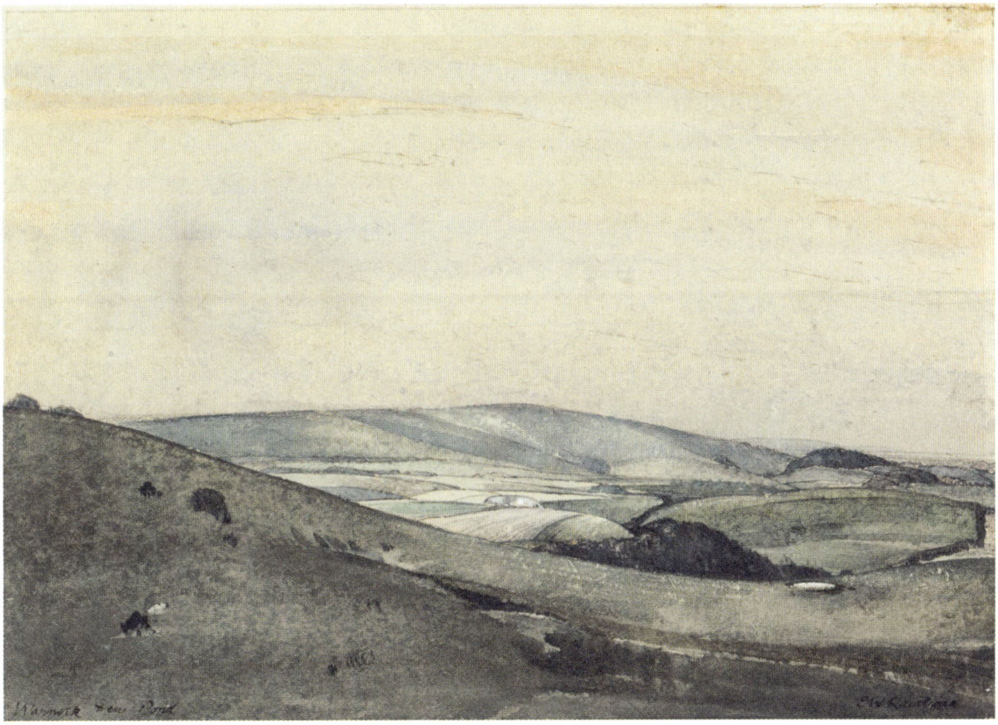

Eric Ravilious, *Wannock Dew Pond*,
watercolour and ink, 1923.

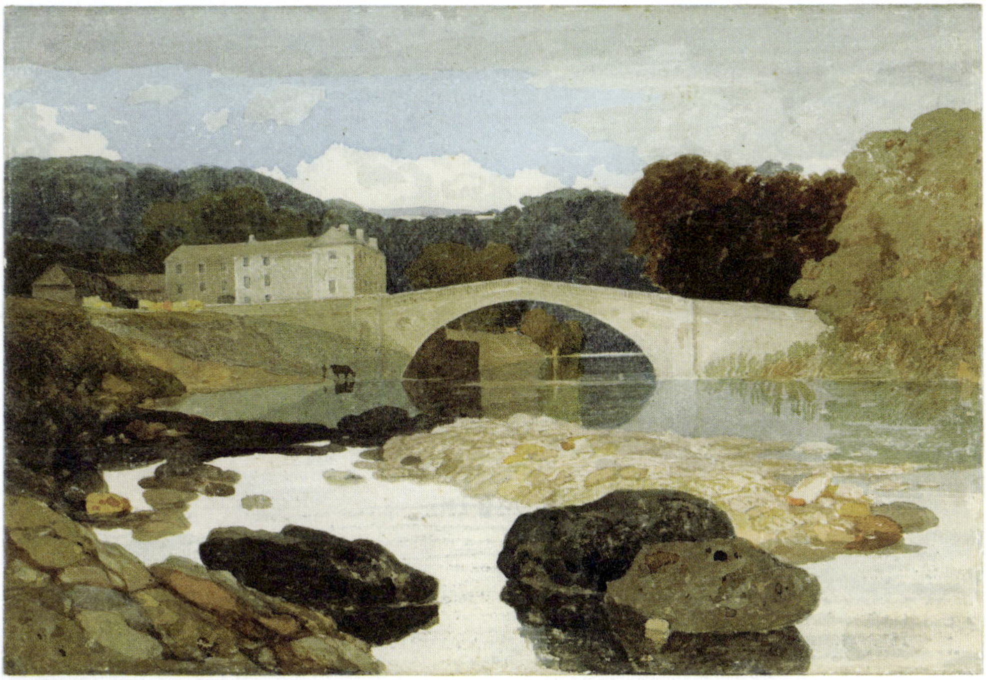

John Sell Cotman, *Greta Bridge*,
watercolour, *c.* 1805.

after Ravilious had married Tirzah Garwood, to an affair that proved painful to everyone concerned. During their student days, however, it may have been Helen who encouraged Ravilious to sign the visitors' book in the Prints and Drawings Department and access its collection, as she had done even before she joined the RCA.[37] Ravilious must also have been aware that Helen's father was actively involved in promoting a revival of interest in watercolour painting.

Laurence Binyon, as has been mentioned, is a recurrent figure within the history of British art. He spent forty years of his life working for the British Museum. Initially, he had been pipped at the post by Campbell Dodgson for a position in the Prints and Drawings Department and was instead assigned to the Department of Books. However, after two years, he moved into Prints and Drawings and embarked on a four-volume catalogue of all the watercolours in the collection by British artists or by foreign artists who worked in Britain. In 1909 he was made Assistant Keeper and in 1913, he became Keeper of Oriental Prints and Drawings, a sub-department within the Prints and Drawings Department. This he had begun amassing two years before, at the instigation of the Keeper Sidney Colvin, who was aware of Binyon's interest in Chinese and Japanese art. His knowledge of Eastern art and literature was generously shared with others, to the extent that Ezra Pound affectionately nicknamed him 'Bin Bin'. And it was almost certainly Binyon who showed Matisse the Museum's Chinese treasures in 1919. He was aided in his work by his protégé Arthur Waley, a shyer but equally formidable scholar who managed to teach himself both Chinese and Japanese languages simultaneously.

In addition to the duality of his professional interests, Binyon the curator was also a poet, verse dramatist and translator as well as being socially very active in London's artistic and literary world. He allowed much of his writing on art to be informed by a poet's sensibility, as Ravilious would have discovered when reading either Binyon's essays on Crome, Cotman, Girtin and Towne, or his two popular books, *Landscape in English Art and Poetry* (1931) and *English Watercolours* (1933). Whereas previous writers on watercolour painting had followed the traditional art historical concern with the evolution of style and technique, Binyon, influenced by Eastern art, was more interested in an understanding of watercolours as a form of spiritual and emotional expression.[38] He was also very aware that the golden age of English watercolour painting was contemporaneous with the great period of Romantic poetry, and that it had initiated a forward movement in landscape painting that vitally influenced the art of the 19th century – a period in which, as he remarked, 'English landscape...led the world.'[39]

One watercolourist whom Ravilious particularly admired was Francis Towne, who painted in Wales and in the Lake District and in 1780 went to Rome, where he made many drawings of the city and its surroundings. His style is instantly recognizable owing to his habit of designing landscape in solid masses. His simplification of colour into flat shapes looks forward to modernist techniques in that it promotes a vigorous grasp of essentials. The results can be bare and austere, yet his work still belongs to the pictureseque tradition, an aesthetic which valued variety, intricacy, balance and surprise. Christopher Hussey, whose 1927 book *The Picturesque* reawakened interest in this topic, argues that the use of artifice in the making of the picturesque marked the first step towards abstract aesthetic values, and therefore towards modernism.

In Laurence Binyon's opinion, the watercolour artist who best demonstrated proto-modern ingredients was John Sell Cotman. It needs an eye attuned to abstract composition and formal values to understand why Cotman decided to paint in one of his pictures a seemingly nondescript drop-gate. Binyon observes that Cotman is never interested in merely portraying the facts of a scene or a place; it is the design potential in any scene which he seeks out, in which shadows also play a part. Even in his gentle *Duncombe Park* (1805), showing little more than part of a stream, a sand bank and trees in the distance, there is a sense of pattern underlying the seemingly haphazard ingredients as well as a delicate but persistent attentiveness to the beauty of nature. Constable once asserted that a landscape could be constructed around an old post, and there has been a long tradition in English art of focusing on the humble or disregarded, which includes both Cotman and Ravilious.

In 1933 Ravilious's admiration for Cotman's *Greta Bridge* took him in search of the actual scene, while he and his wife Tirzah were painting murals at Morecambe Bay, in the LMS Railway Hotel in Lancashire. With them was the architectural historian and editor J. M. Richards, who recollected: 'We took off one day, hiring a car and asking the hotel for a picnic lunch. Eric had discovered from the map that the place where Cotman had painted a picture of which he was especially fond – Greta Bridge – was not far away and conceived an ambition to see what it was like now. We found the way with some difficulty. The bridge was easily recognizable. The search for it took us through some beautiful Pennine scenery. It rained, but the outing refreshed us all.'[40]

One reason why *Greta Bridge* is so satisfying is that the single arch of the bridge is placed in the centre of the design, thereby creating a resting point for the eyes. The light of the sky and its clouds are reflected in the foreground of the river, which not only helps enhance the solid rocks in the foreground but also balances and unifies the scene. Every part seems conjoined to the whole at the level of design or composition, quite aside from its representational role, and this also makes it a forerunner of modernism.

Ravilious wanted to bring to watercolour painting a modern sentiment. He had been tutored during his final year at the RCA by Paul Nash, a leading figure in the revival of wood engraving, who had given him useful advice in relation to this medium. He also gradually became aware of the watercolour technique employed by Paul and John Nash. Both allowed the white of the paper to play a part in the composition, as did Cézanne. Both also made use of the starved brush and avoided the more usual habit, regarding this medium, of using water plentifully to create transparent or opaque washes of flat colour, or the wet on wet technique. Ravilious himself adopted the use of the starved brush when creating hatching or cross-hatching, as it allows the white of the paper to show through and suggests the sparkle of the light. With an increase in his technical ability came a new desire. He returned in 1925 to Eastbourne School of Art to undertake some teaching, and there admitted that one of his greatest ambitions was to revive the English tradition of watercolour painting.[41]

Not until the 1930s did watercolour painting come to play a dominant role in his career. But if *Wannock Dew Pond* is compared with *Chalk Paths* (1935), it is immediately apparent how far he has travelled; the latter makes the former look tired and out of date. In *Chalk Paths* every part of the picture has become an active ingredient in the whole, bringing out the freshness and drama of the scene. It is presented with such clarity, deftness and precision that the landscape seems to spring to life before our eyes. Downland walks can be exhilarating owing to the bareness of the downs and their subtle declivities. These are hard to grasp even with the eye, let alone on paper with brush and watercolour, and in order to do so Ravilious has simplified and exaggerated without losing a sense of authenticity in his communication of the sense of place associated with these downs.

Chalk Paths has been painted from a high vantage point. This gives the scene a dynamic that encourages the eye to travel in and through the landscape. Instead of remaining a passive observer, the spectator is invited to become actively involved in experiencing this terrain, with the tilt of the slopes and the full reach and stretch of the paths. The barbed-wire fence makes a modern intrusion into the landscape. Other artists might have ignored it, but Ravilious uses it to explore the tension within his picture, bringing the wire fence right down into the bottom right-hand corner and also letting it continue into the far distance. It enhances perspective yet also contributes to the structure of the composition and to the surface patterning that gives a decorative unity to the work.

Unlike Bawden, who found enough subjects for his purpose in the north-west Essex village where he lived, Ravilious thrived on a sense of displacement. He produced his best watercolours far from home and was fascinated by the intrusion of

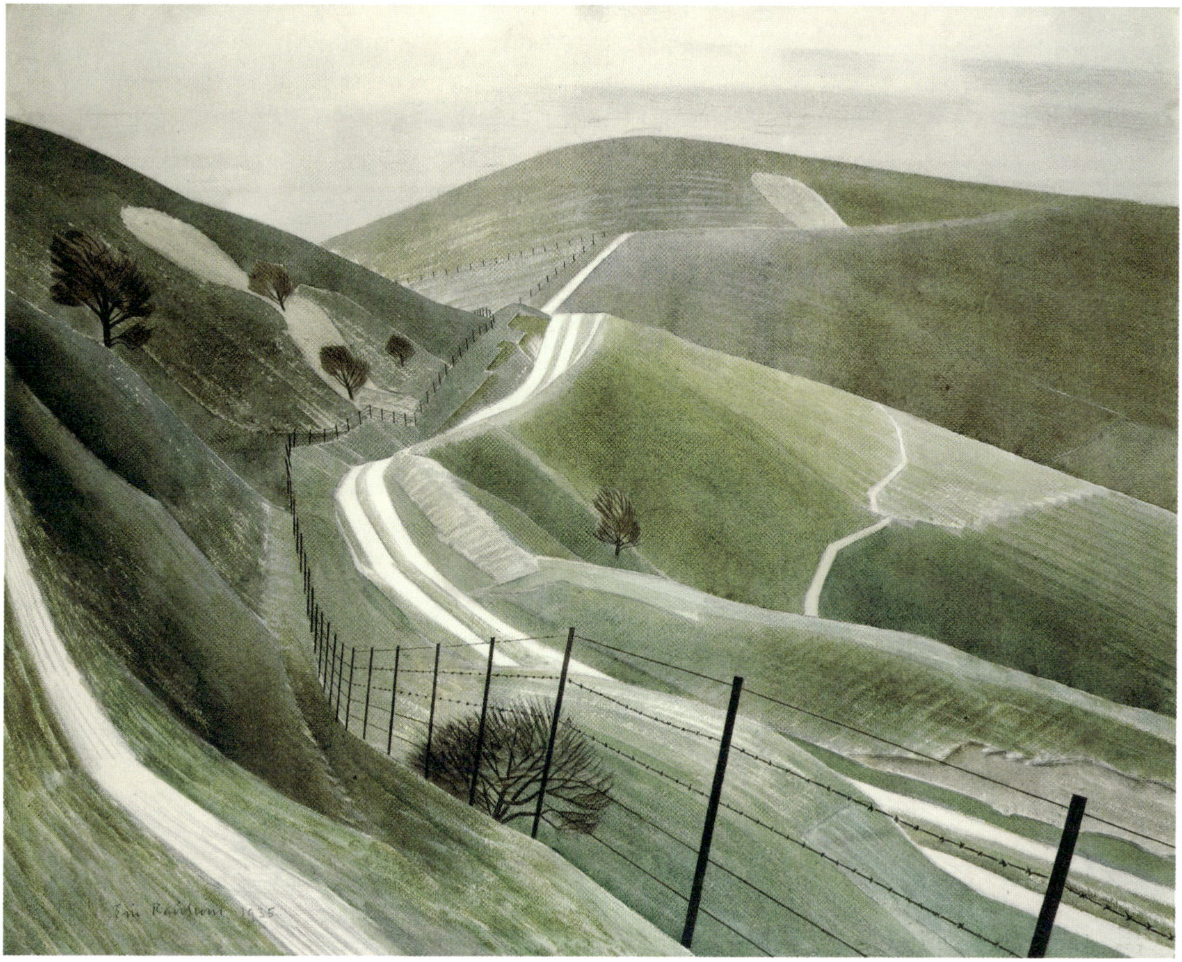

Eric Ravilious, *Chalk Paths*,
watercolour and pencil, 1935.

machines, unexpectedly beached in rural places. His view of England may be selective but he is never cosy or complacent. His landscapes are mostly seen under a chilly, grey sky, and when the sun does appear in one corner it rarely warms the scene. An understated melancholy imbues many of the interiors he painted, which, like his landscapes, make use of angular recession that leaves his designs taut and strained. Even when he sets out to charm, as in his wood engravings for the Kynoch Press, his vignettes, which imitate those by Thomas Bewick, lack the fullness and earthiness they celebrate. Far from being bucolic, they convey a brittle tension which is modern.

Ravilious frequently drives his brush across the paper in a manner not unlike that of an engraver using his tools to create hatching. He creates the clods of earth in a recently ploughed field in *Downs in Winter* by means of a scudding brush. Ravilious's father, before becoming a coachman to a wealthy individual and, later on, the owner of an antiques shop, had originally begun work as an agricultural labourer. Alan Powers has suggested that Ravilious, despite being very socially adept, retained a sense of identification with the farming or artisan class from which he came.[42] His work suggests that he was stimulated by a nostalgia for rural values, for a way of life dominated by the cycle of the farming year and the crafts associated with it – all of which were in danger of disappearing owing to changing methods of agriculture and, in the 1930s, the depressed state of arable farming. There are other watercolours, notably *Cuckmere Haven* (1939), where Ravilious achieves a kind of pristine quality, as if the world has been seen afresh. It is not surprising that one of his favourite authors was Thomas Traherne, the 17th-century mystic whose words and lyrical, religious fervour make radiant the natural world.

Because much of his subject matter falls within the English landscape tradition and his preferred medium was watercolour, Ravilious was for many years ignored by modernist art historians. Today he is recognized as one of the 'romantic moderns'[43] and his reputation has soared. This would not have surprised Paul Nash, who never despised watercolour but instead, in 1937, extolled Girtin and Cotman's 'architectural' use of watercolour paint as a true standard of English taste.[44] Ravilious closed the circle, reviving the English watercolour tradition in modern terms and at the same time bringing to fulfilment the complex emotions that his own watercolours, with their stillness and nostalgia, so beautifully convey.

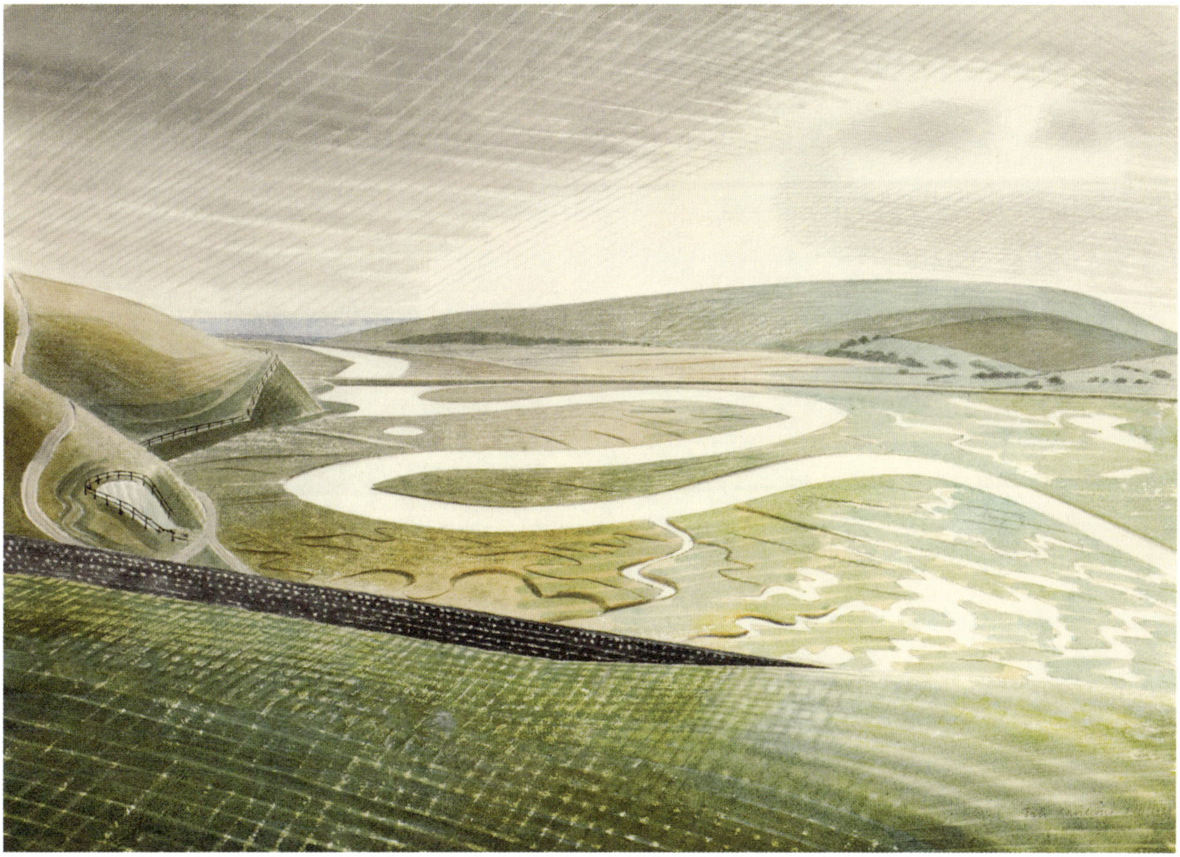

Eric Ravilious, *Cuckmere Haven*,
pencil and watercolour, 1939.

CHAPTER 10

MODERN ART IN A PHILISTINE WORLD

'Lucy, have you never heard of Picasso?' remarked Edward Wadsworth's wife, Fanny, teasingly, after seeing their friend Lucy Wertheim's collection of pictures.[1] Wertheim was the wife of Mari Paul Johan Wertheim, a shipping magnate and Dutch consul in Manchester, who had been born in the Netherlands but had taken British citizenship. By the late 1920s, she had formed a collection of 19th- and early 20th-century French and British paintings which was respectable but evidently not modern or daring enough to meet with Fanny Wadsworth's sophisticated approval. The remark stung and its note of 'faint disdain' was not forgotten.

Picasso's name acted as a litmus test in England well into the 1930s, exposing philistinism in unexpected places. The first comprehensive exhibition of his art in Britain was mounted by the Leicester Galleries in 1921. Although seventy-two paintings were on show, only a few drawings and prints sold and what should have been a wild success proved a financial disaster, bringing in £92. In the press, negative reviews exceeded positive comments. A significant part of the exhibition had been the cubist works lent by Léonce Rosenberg. When the gallery owners suggested his prices were too high, he replied:

> I know that London is, at present, a very bad market for archaic and advanced modern art, and that *very small* places on the continent are very much better markets than the huge old town of London. But I am not prepared to sell under value things because your people are not up-to-date. Never mind if you do not sell anything. I can sell my Picassos on the Continent and in America very much better. If the London people are not prepared to pay the necessary prices well, let them go....They forget that Picasso is the greatest artist living since Cézanne.[2]

Ten years later, when Alex. Reid & Lefevre prepared to mount an exhibition of his work, they still doubted whether London was ready for Picasso. However, this show, titled 'Thirty Years of Pablo Picasso', did make some headway, beginning a market for Picasso's work in London and convincing the *Observer* critic that Picasso was 'the dominating, the most significant and most inspiring figure in the twentieth century'.[3] Yet although his reputation in Britain increased during the 1930s, information on him was still not easy to come by, as it mostly appeared in leading Parisian magazines such as *Cahiers d'Art*, *Minotaure* and *Documents*, on sale in London at Zwemmer's bookshop but hard to find elsewhere. At the Slade School of Art in the late 1930s, Patrick Heron, while a student there, noticed that most of the staff had barely heard of Picasso; as a result, his name rarely entered art school discussions. His work had been denied entrance into public collections in England until late 1933, when the Tate Gallery was obliged to accept three Picassos and two Matisses from the bequest of the stockbroker C. Frank Stoop.

One of these paintings had in fact hung in the Tate before this point. Jim Ede had managed to infiltrate one of Stoop's Picassos as a loan in 1929, while other staff were away. Ede himself had arrived at the Tate in 1921, following a year at the Slade and another as a lecturer at the National Gallery; at the Tate he was made assistant, along with James Bolivar Manson, to the gallery's director, Charles Aitken. He quickly realized that the institution had no clear idea as to what professional duties he should perform. 'What shall we give Ede to do?' he heard his superiors saying, after a few minor jobs had been found. At one point he was sent on estate duty office business to Paris, where he discovered that Picasso and other artists were willing to see him owing to his association with the Tate.

'It is amazing the interest which is taken here in painting,' he wrote to Aitken. 'I am seeing pictures from 8 am till sometimes midnight.'[4] On his return he was disappointed to discover that Manson took no interest in the artists he had seen, nor the lists of pictures he had brought back. Manson, first and foremost a painter, took his responsibilities at the Tate lightly while continuing to exhibit regularly with the London Group and the Monarro Group. In 1928, two years before he became director of the Tate, he was evidently considering a return to painting full time, as he asked Roger Fry if it was financially viable as a way of life. His chief asset was personal charm; he had scant interest in French art after impressionism. Further evidence of the philistinism at the Tate was his remark that no Henry Moore would ever enter the gallery while he was its director. His eight years in this position, from 1930 to 1938, proved disastrous.

Unlike Manson, Edward and Fanny Wadsworth took an interest in things that the Tate ignored. Since teaming up with Wyndham Lewis, first at the Rebel Art Centre in

1914 and then as a vorticist, Edward had followed Picasso's career. The Wadsworths were related to the Wertheim family through marriage – Lucy Wertheim's younger sister had married Walter Wadsworth, a cousin of Edward's – but more binding was the fact that the two families shared an interest in modern art. After visiting the Wertheims in Manchester in the late 1920s, Edward and Fanny invited Lucy to stay with them in London.

Lucy did not greatly like Edward Wadsworth's paintings, which at that time concentrated on landscape, still life and maritime subjects, sharply delineated and always woven into a masterly design. To her they seemed too intellectual. Likewise, when Myfanwy Evans and John Piper visited the Wadsworths in 1934 to raise support for the magazine *Axis*, the bright amorphous shapes in Edward's abstracts and his 'near hard-edged romanticisations of industrialised scenes' aroused antipathy in Myfanwy, who thought they looked like a journalist's idea of modern art.[5]

Edward Wadsworth, *Bright Intervals*,
tempera on canvas laid on panel, 1928.

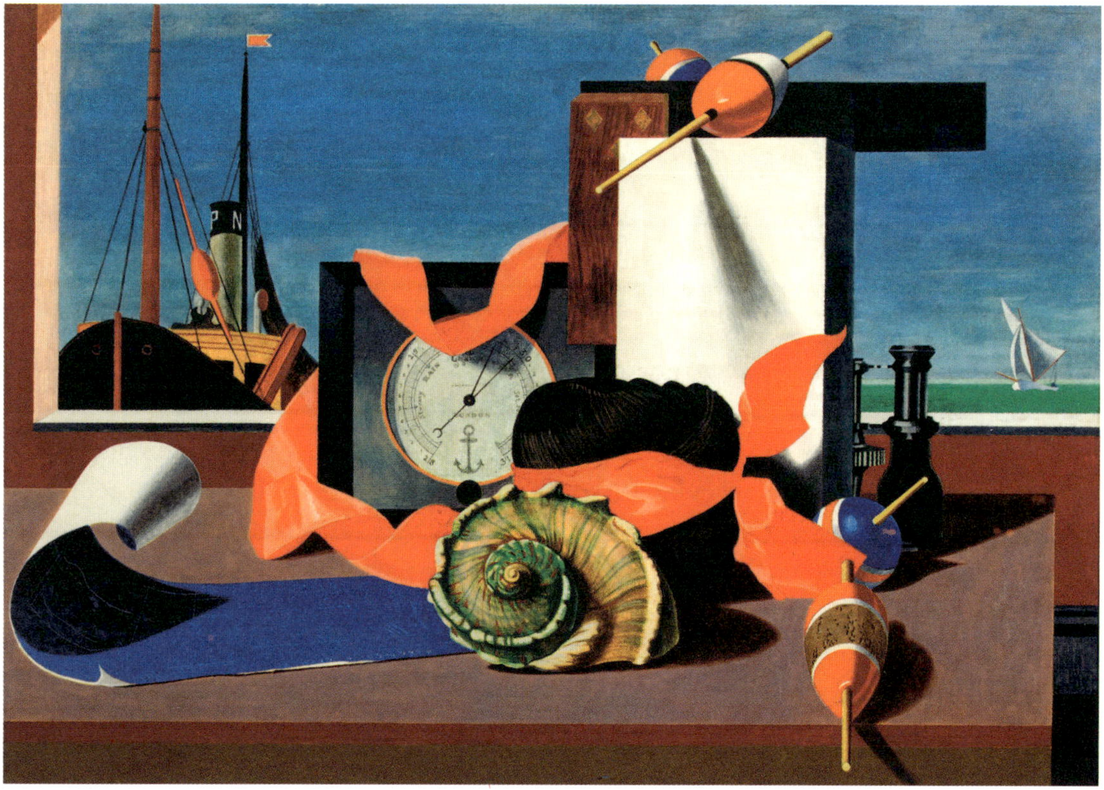

Nevertheless, Lucy Wertheim's visits to the Wadsworths in Kensington jolted her out of what she now recognized to be 'a decidedly complacent outlook on art in general'.[6] How could they not? One room, known as Edward's 'den', was entirely filled with pictures by Wyndham Lewis. Elsewhere in his collection were two unsettling paintings by Fernand Léger. These and other works that seemed to Lucy Wertheim 'ultra-modern' advanced her perception of modern art. 'No more really restful pictures for me in the future! I craved exhilaration and stimulation! Picasso had triumphed!'[7]

This left her better prepared for her future role as an influential gallerist in the heart of London's West End, then the main centre for the commercial art world. It was made possible by her husband's offer to guarantee the cost of the gallery's rent for the first three years, on the condition that she avoid commitments in the school holidays so as to be available for her family. She already had a well-developed gift for befriending artists and for showing enthusiastic appreciation of their work. In 1925, while Frances Hodgkins was working as designer and adviser for the Calico Printers' Association in Manchester, she and Lucy Wertheim met during a small gathering in a private home and chatted over tea. 'What an odd little creature!' Wertheim's companion remarked of Hodgkins after they left, but Wertheim's experience had been very different. She recalled: 'I remember the immediate *sympathie* between us: her wit, the charm of her warm voice, her felicity of expression. I felt that I had made a friend.'[8]

Not long afterwards, again over afternoon tea and among friends, Lucy expatiated on the charms of a watercolour by Hodgkins that she had recently bought. Hodgkins, overhearing what was being said, turned to Lucy's husband and said: 'Your wife should open a gallery for us poor artists: her enthusiasm would make it a success.'[9] Although these words were spoken half in jest, they lodged in Wertheim's mind, forming the germ of an idea to which she would later return. She was fortunate in having for her four children an excellent nanny, who had arrived soon after the birth of the first child. The nanny and her husband's generosity allowed Wertheim much freedom of movement. She went often to London, where they had a flat in Regent's Park, and, while keeping an eye out for additions to her own collection, she had noticed how under-promoted modern English art was by the few galleries that took an interest in this field.

She arrived early one morning, in the spring of 1929, at Tooth's in Bond Street, which was holding a private-view day for a Christopher Wood exhibition. There she bought a small canvas of a purple crocus in a pot. It filled her mind all day long, to such an extent that a couple of days later she returned to the gallery to reassure herself of its existence. She recalled: 'I remember that it seemed incredible to me that so much joy could be mine for the mere transference of twelve guineas to the coffers of Messrs. Tooth.'[10] While she feasted her eyes on the picture, a gallery assistant came up to her to explain that the young artist who had painted it was present and wished to be introduced.

In this way Lucy Wertheim met Christopher Wood, one of the foremost romantics of the day, who over the next two summers was to produce some of his best work in Cornouaille, a historic region on the west coast of Brittany that had strong links with Cornwall and was at one time regarded as a British colony. Here, at Douarnenez and also at nearby Tréboul, Wood was again to enjoy association with a working fishing community, with its fetes, songs, drinks and local traditions as well as its sturdy white houses, white beaches and its Catholic churches, rising up against sea and sky as stark reminders of the Christian faith. Although he was to find in Douarnenez friends from Paris, he nevertheless felt sufficiently released from London and Paris to gain the necessary freedom in which to develop his art. By the summer of 1930, on his second visit to this area, he noted that it had become 'composed and reflective, not so wildly poetic, but sounder and more subtle' than his previous work, including that he had produced at St Ives.

At Tooth's, Lucy Wertheim had been immediately struck by Wood's 'great charm of manner' and the 'grace with which he moved' despite a slight limp caused by an affliction to his knee, as well as the 'extraordinary intelligence of his face'.[11] It seemed to her that their friendship began from the moment of introduction. But because visitors to the exhibition kept interrupting their conversation with questions about his pictures, she eventually suggested they should retire to the flat in Regent's Park for lunch. She had the advantage of knowing that sustenance could be readily supplied. 'My husband was in London at that time and I knew that my woman according to custom had left the table laid and a lunch just ready for the finishing touches should either or both of us turn up for a mid-day meal. My husband did not return that particular morning, somewhat to my relief as the subject of modern art frankly bored him, and Christopher and I were still talking twenty to the dozen on this fascinating subject when he put in an appearance towards tea-time.'[12]

Soon afterwards she called on Wood at the small Chelsea house in Minton Place, off Bury Street, that had been gifted him by José Antonio de Gandarillas. Wood had recently spent time in Dieppe with Frosca Munster, painting, and when Wertheim left she carried with her a picture of Dieppe. Wood sold it to her for £45, admitting that it was a high price (his oil paintings were then selling for around £30), but with the observation that he thought it the best painting he had so far produced. Then, in August of that year, he disappeared on his first visit to Brittany, settling at Douarnenez and then moving to nearby Tréboul, where Frosca again joined him.

There was relatively little contact between Wood and Lucy Wertheim for the rest of the year but, with two of his paintings in her possession, their friendship remained firm. The bond of sympathy between them immediately revived in their correspondence the following spring.

The paintings Wood made in Tréboul in 1929 achieved a new freedom and greater physicality. In his *Boat in Harbour, Brittany* (1929), the inky black sea pushes the boat forward, while the composition positions the viewer very close to the edge of the harbour wall on which stand two women in Brittany costumes, watching as the men attend to the ship's anchor and sails. The urgency conveyed is as much felt in the pictorial means as in the subject, with the foremost taut brown sail cutting across a view of the old buildings climbing up the hill behind. Even the delineation of the planks in the deck of the boat and the stones in the harbour wall have an insistent immediacy that contributes to the animation of the whole. It is not surprising that some of Wood's Tréboul paintings caught the attention of a leading French gallerist, Georges Bernheim, who invited him to hold a solo exhibition at his Paris gallery in May 1930. Wood was all too aware that very few English artists received offers of this kind and that, if successful, it would greatly enhance his reputation.

He immediately informed his close friends, the Nicholsons. Worried by the sheer size of Bernheim's gallery, he also mooted the idea that Ben Nicholson should share the exhibition with him. This was agreed but, from Wood's point of view, it may have been a mistake: Nicholson's art, very much at this time under the influence of Braque, was closer to the French taste for modernism. Whereas the freedoms in Wood's art were put to the service of a poetic vein – albeit a sea-shanty vein, contributing towards what Gwen Raverat described, in her role as art critic for *Time and Tide*, as a 'fashionable clumsiness'.

In March 1930, a month before his Paris show was due to open, Wood spent a short time in Cornwall again, in Mousehole near Penzance, where he claimed to be 'working at enormous pace and absolutely deliriously happy painting'.[13] However, the pictures that resulted from this short trip are characterized by darkness and much use of black. If one of these works, *PZ134, Cornwall* (1930) is compared with *Boat in Harbour, Brittany*, the former appears much more sombre, less vigorous and something of a retreat to a more conventional manner. It is possible that this quieter, less explosive mood connects with Wood's attempt at around this time to terminate his dependency on opium. How far his addiction affected his painting is hard to say, but it may explain certain oddities in his pictures such as the upside-down figure on the sand in *La Plage, Hotel Ty-Mad, Tréboul*, or the oversized boy, out of scale with the rest of the picture, in *The Jumping Boy* (both belonging to Sheffield Museums Trust). It may also have contributed to his financial difficulties, the pressures of

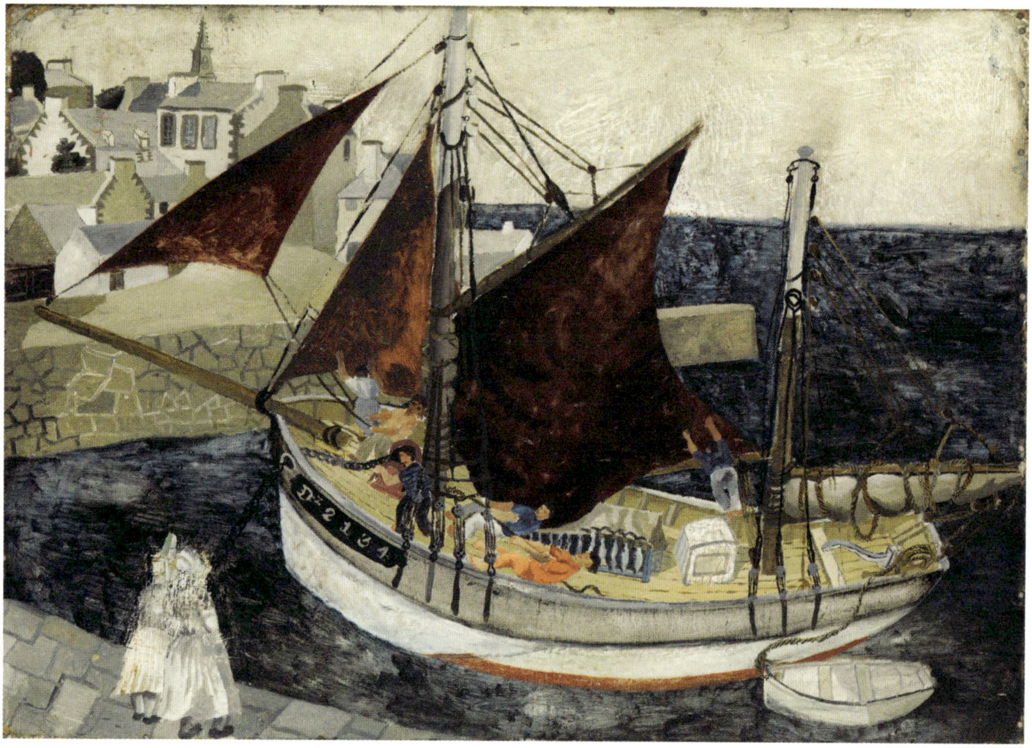

Christopher Wood, *Boat in Harbour, Brittany*,
oil on board, 1929.

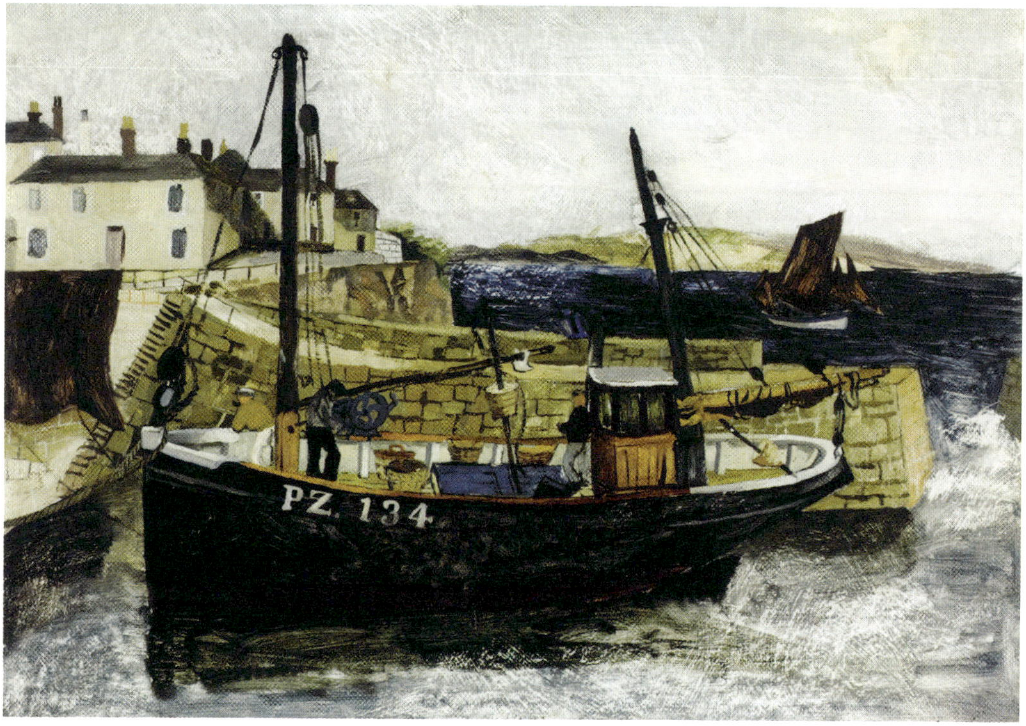

Christopher Wood, *PZ134*, *Cornwall*,
oil on board, 1930.

which sometimes prompted him to make unrealistic demands for money or to act out of character, as Lucy Wertheim noted. His anxiety over the forthcoming show in Paris was almost certainly related to his desperate need to earn money.

It meant much to him that Wertheim came to Paris shortly before the exhibition opened, and he was there to meet her at the station when she got off the train. She had by now taken over the supportive role that Winifred Nicholson had formerly filled in his life; this was further demonstrated when the exhibition opened, for she bought five of his paintings. Much of her stay in Paris was spent in his company, and when the exhibition closed she acquired five more paintings, as nothing further had sold other than a couple of small works. 'Pour moi c'est trop anglais,' she had heard one man say to another at the *vernissage*. But even the London art establishment at this time regarded Wood with suspicion, the Tate Gallery having recently turned down one of his paintings offered as a gift by the renowned collector Edward Marsh. Wertheim's acquisitions were an expression of her confidence in him, and all she had bought, she insisted, were for her own collection.

Towards the end of May, Wood, now back in London, had arranged to take his mother to the annual Cochran Revue at the London Palladium, the first night of which was always a major social occasion, as Charles B. Cochran's ability to spot and attract talent made theatrical news. That year's programme included a short ballet, *Luna Park*, for which Wood had designed costumes and the set. At the last moment he had to pull out of the plan, so instead Wertheim accompanied his mother to the revue and afterwards put her up for the night in the Regent's Park flat. This further affirmed her loyalty to Wood, as well as earning her the lasting friendship of his mother.

The following morning, Wertheim again visited Wood at Minton Place and bought, for £35, *The Yellow Man* – one of his most haunting paintings, partly made so by the absence of any key to its obscure symbolism. Soon afterwards, he dined with her at the flat. He agreed to reappear again for dinner two days later, but never did; nor did any explanation arrive until ten in the evening, when a friend rang to say he was indisposed. In addition to his unpredictability, there were moments when Wood seemed to be in a trance, oblivious to the fact that he might be in a public place or in the company of others. At one moment he confessed to Wertheim 'his terror of being left alone when a certain mood that he had come to dread descended on him'.[14]

Despite these intimations of his inner distress, Wertheim greatly admired Wood's show at the Georges Bernheim Gallery. It made her determined to proceed with the idea of setting up a gallery of her own, with the primary intention of promoting young English artists. When she informed Wood of this, he was immediately excited by the possibilities it offered. Wertheim's warm enthusiasm for art and her good judgment regarding pictures left him convinced that she would succeed. 'I shall become great through you!' he declared.

'Indeed', Wertheim recalled, 'from the moment the idea was mooted he assumed that it was a settled thing and would never refer to it as a possibility. It was always "when we have our gallery," for from the beginning he intended to take an active part in its affairs.'[15]

Looking back on her life in her autobiography *Adventure in Art* – mostly written in 1938–9, but then laid aside and completed during the war years before its publication in 1947 – Lucy Wertheim recalled the difficulties she had faced in 1930: '...it must be remembered that in the days when I opened my gallery there was no British Council, no council for the Encouragement of Music and the Arts, no British Institute for Adult Education and no BBC talks on Modern Art. In 1930 it was a pioneering job to sponsor the unknown British artist.'[16] She began looking for suitable premises and considered a house in Berkeley Square, but was advised by an art world habitué to 'dig myself in' within one hundred yards of Bond Street, owing to the critics' dislike of going farther afield. She therefore opted for a large room on the mezzanine floor in 3–5 Burlington Gardens and, owing to its size, furnished it with comfortable chairs to give it an elegant but homely atmosphere. The opening date was to be 7 October 1930, and the first exhibition would be a one-man show of works by Christopher Wood.

That summer the Wertheim family spent part of the school holidays in a little house in Sussex. On the day that her son Michael drove into Worthing to do some shopping, Lucy was expecting to hear from Wood with the hope that he might join them there. Her son returned with an evening newspaper and showed it to his mother with a grave face. In the 'Stop Press' column was news of Christopher Wood's death earlier that day. He had fallen under a train at Salisbury Station.

Although it has been suggested that drugs may have caused Wood to fall accidentally, suicide remains the accepted conclusion. Numbed by the news of his death, Wertheim at first decided to cancel all the plans for her gallery. What point had it, now that he was gone? She also recognized 'how much I had come to count on Christopher's co-operation and the éclat of his work to make good in the eyes of the world my claim for the English Painter of Today'.[17] On the day after his funeral she spent some hours with his mother, who pressed her to continue with the gallery and with a show of his paintings. Aware that his recent death would colour the reception of his work, Wertheim begged to defer the exhibition until the following year; but in the end, the gallery did open as planned, with a mixed exhibition. Wertheim mounted a show of her own collection of Wood's paintings the following February. Her gallery continued to be regarded as a shrine to his art, as there was usually something by him on show, or work that could be brought out on request.

The Seven and Five exhibition in 1931 included many of Wood's paintings, as a kind of memorial. The first major retrospective of his work was mounted in 1938, by Rex Nan Kivell of the Redfern Gallery in the New Burlington Galleries. It was accompanied by a book-size catalogue with an essay by Eric Newton. In the eight years since his death modern art had moved on considerably, and Wood's style must by then have looked outmoded. But 50,000 visitors attended the exhibition – far more than the numbers who came to see the exhibition of Picasso's *Guernica* and studies for it, which opened in the New Burlington Galleries and then transferred to the Whitechapel Gallery later that year. The Christopher Wood retrospective made a lasting impression, ensuring that Wood's death went down in history as one of the major artistic losses of the interwar years.

Many artists took inspiration from the way Wood painted, among them Richard Eurich. Rex Nan Kivell, knowing that Eurich admired the childlike clarity of Wood's paintings and how hard up he was at the time, sent him £5 so that he and his wife could come to London to see the show. For Eurich it was a 'never to be forgotten' exhibition. 'After his death', Eurich recalled, 'his prodigious output was revealed and his outlook had a profound effect on my work; for here was a young man who had tried out all manner of fashionable styles before emerging perfectly free and uninhibited to paint what he loved.'[18] He admired how Wood painted 'with freshness and inevitability, like a folk song', and later told his growing family that Wood had painted 'like a bird sings'.[19]

In spring 1933 the philistinism aroused by the mere mention of Picasso's name came to the fore in the pages of the *Listener*, then the forum in which social and cultural issues were given the widest airing. On 31 May the magazine carried an illustration of a head in profile painted by Picasso which was on view at the Mayor Gallery in a mixed show, with the announcement that several artists (unnamed) were keen to have it bought by the Contemporary Art Society so that this artist could be represented in a public gallery. At that time no Picasso had entered the permanent collection of any museum or gallery in England, although Stoop's bequest to the Tate would soon alter this situation. The Mayor Gallery, recently opened by Freddy Mayor and Douglas Cooper, would have been pleased to read in the *Listener* the welcome given to this proposal by the critic Edward Crankshaw, who claimed that Picasso united contemporary consciousness with age-old principles and that 'the astonishing *Profile* of Picasso...sets the heart beating as few modern things can. It is difficult to speak of this painting in moderate terms.'[20] An irate response from a Mr G. Faulkner Armitage in the 'Letters' section began a debate that ran for weeks. Picasso and his admirers were accused of seeking to destroy beauty, truth and good craftsmanship. The artist John Piper came to his defence. He had been an admirer of Picasso for some time; early in his career, at a time when no monographs on Picasso were available, he had compiled his own, filling a scrapbook with his copies of Picasso's work or reproductions culled from magazines such as *Cahiers d'Art*, which he bought at Zwemmer's bookshop in the Charing Cross Road. His letter begins:

> Some of your correspondents demand an *explanation* of the painting by Picasso reproduced in your columns a few weeks ago. May I ask why? Does 'Philistine' [as one letter had been signed] demand an explanation when confronted by a beech tree on the South Downs, or a sunset over the Mediterranean a Aboukir (whence he writes)....Why an explanation? And what would Mr Faulkner Armitage say if I wrote to *The Listener* demanding an explanation of the fact that a grove of beech trees had been purchased by the National Trust and preserved for the nation? A beech tree and a Picasso may be beautiful or they may not: everybody has to make the decision for himself in the end; but surely neither needs any more *explanation* than a nice cut of roast beef...[21]

This gave additional stir to the debate and further protests irrupted. In August, Ben Nicholson joined the fray:

> I am very much surprised to see that one or two people who have written letters to *The Listener* in connection with the 'Profile' painting by Picasso, do not know that there is a large section of responsible opinion in Europe and in America which regards Picasso as one of the vital painters, not merely at present alive, but in the history of painting.
>
> Those people who do not yet understand Picasso's work or who think that they do and dislike it, can quite safely concede this fact. I suggest that, when they understand this, instead of dismissing the discovery of this new world (which has an almost exact parallel in the world created by Einstein) as of no importance, they should reserve their opinion and try to find out something of the opinions and ideas of those who hold a contrary view.[22]

A week later, on 9 August 1933, the editor, having allowed the controversy to run for nearly three months, declared it closed. However, owing to the interest and passion it had aroused, he appended a list of books containing information on Picasso, for readers who 'may wish to get at the root of the matter for themselves'. He also gave space to one final letter, from Piper. It ends:

> There is no explanation of a work of art of any period. The merit of a picture is unalterable from the moment it is painted: it is unaffected by praise or abuse or even explanation. The most a critic can do is to describe the technical method of an artist, which may be uninteresting, or write about his own reactions to a work of art, which may be unrepresentative. It is to be hoped that your correspondents when they look at a Raphael feel the beauty of what they see, and do not admire it because they have been told to by generations of critics. If they would be enriched by the experience of Picasso they must look at his work for themselves.... And do not let them be put off by Mr English who diagnoses a 'subconscious inferiority complex' in the modern artist, and, having seen some modern advertisement, decides that 'modern art is propagandist'. All good art is propagandist, whether it wants to be or not. But Byzantine art is not made futile by the existence of the Albert Memorial.

Piper's confident, sprightly tone may have caught Ben Nicholson's attention,[23] as it did others. The young Myfanwy Evans first encountered John Piper, her future husband, in the pages of the *New Statesman and Nation*, where she admired his 'stylish, undidactic writing, relaxed jokes and perceptive eye'.[24] He was at this time dividing his energies between painting and writing, undertaking art criticism to bring in some necessary money. The same year, 1933, he wrote two articles entitled 'Younger English Painters' for the *Listener* at the request of critic Janet Adam Smith, then its assistant editor. 'Twenty years ago artistic London was a long way behind Paris,' he opined: 'today the distance between the two capitals is small indeed.' As an example of good contemporary English art he references a Ben Nicholson still life, titled *January 27, 1933*,[25] praising the way in which 'he alludes to the objects on the café table without any insistence on their physical reality – there is no imitative comment on their solidity and colour, for instance; and by means of a few simple forms and subtle colours he has stated an experience which has authority while painting a picture which has a fine unity and rhythm'. He concludes: 'This is a painting which is both decorative and expressive, and expressive of the artist and the age.'[26]

Although he was versed in the writings of Roger Fry, Clive Bell and R. H. Wilenski, Piper's interests already extended beyond a narrowly formalist approach to art. Given his later ideological disagreement with Nicholson, it is interesting to note that even in the early 1930s he was alert to the importance of native traditions. 'Landscape has always played a large part in English art,' he writes,[27] arguing here and elsewhere that, owing to the Englishman's partiality for his native land and for the sea, these two things remain powerful emotive agents in English art. But, as he admits in the second of his two articles on 'Younger English Painters': 'French art has been the means, the liberating force, for the emotion. And this is the crux of the matter of French influence. English painting is not less English today because it has made use of this liberating force: a force which has freed it from making dull and sentimental records of natural and human phenomena, and producing pictures which had very little to do with nature and humanity, and nothing at all to do with art.'[28]

Piper's views, and especially his praise of French influence, would have been welcomed by Ben Nicholson. It was in 1933 that the influence of Braque on Nicholson was replaced by that of Picasso. On 15 March and again on 18 or 19 April Nicholson had visited Picasso in Paris, on the second occasion in the company of Barbara Hepworth, who later recalled that he showed them a succession of 'miraculous paintings'.[29] This same year Nicholson and Hepworth joined Abstraction-Création, an exclusive non-figurative group formed by Jean Hélion after the demise of its predecessor, Cercle et Carré (Circle and Square).

While Nicholson was making connections in Paris with artists, dealers and publishers, Piper was exploring ideas about abstract art in his reviews. 'We do not hear enough of Kandinsky in London, in spite of *The Art of Spiritual Harmony*, now twenty years old, which has proved prophetic and still makes lively reading,'[30] he wrote after seeing four Kandinskys in a Mayor Gallery exhibition. This same month he praised Edward Wadsworth's abstract compositions, likening them to clocks and revolvers because 'they are composed of carefully selected and unerringly arranged parts that make a working whole'. Part of their attraction for him was their coastal origin, the sea having been, he claimed, 'the prompting emotion and the controlling factor'.[31]

At a time when Nicholson was increasingly moving towards abstraction, this article caught this attention. Piper was already much in his mind as, in August 1933 while staying at Seahouses, Northumberland, he had spent time examining photographs of Piper's work. These would have demonstrated, notably through his use of collage, Piper's interest in Picasso, Braque and post-cubist methods of picture-making. As Nicholson had recently become president of the Seven and Five Society, he was vetting Piper for membership. And by the spring of 1934 not only had Piper been elected to membership, he had also been given the role of secretary and chairman of the hanging committee. Piper's ambition to be an artist first and a writer second is not in doubt; but he only achieved prominence as a painter once he joined the Seven and Five. Nicholson's interest, it seems, was both timely and determinative.

It was soon after Piper became affiliated that the Society demonstrated its progressiveness by replacing the nouns in its title with numerical digits. Its continued vitality was ensured by the rule in its consititution that enabled it each year to refresh its membership. At its annual exhibition in March 1934, Piper showed five paintings, all based on seaside subjects.[32] But at a meeting held soon afterwards Nicholson put forward a motion, which was agreed, that at the next annual show all exhibits should be 'non-representational'.[33] Some non-representational paintings had already been included in the 1934 exhibition, by artists whom Paul Nash nicknamed 'Ben's boys' – Francis Butterfield, Arthur Jackson and John Cecil Stephenson, this last residing in one of the Mall Studios in Hampstead, where Nicholson was now living with Barbara Hepworth. During this same meeting, the membership underwent its annual purge, leaving just eleven artists: Ivon Hitchens, Frances Hodgkins, Ben Nicholson, Winifred Nicholson, David Jones, W. Staite Murray, Barbara Hepworth, Henry Moore, Francis Butterfield, Arthur Jackson and John Piper. However, Hodgkins, unwilling to go abstract, resigned over Nicholson's motion. Piper read out her letter of resignation at a General Meeting on 3 May 1934 and afterwards reported the regret expressed by all those present.[34]

It was no small feat for Piper to find himself occupying a significant role within England's most avant-garde exhibiting society, and at a period which the art historian Andrew Causey has described as 'a moment of ambition, energy and uncertainty in British art'.[35] But it must also have been a source of anxiety, for Nicholson's motion would have made Piper very aware that he had not yet produced any abstract work. His mentor at this time was Braque, whose work he studied in issues of *Cahiers d'Art*. But when Nicholson headed off to Paris in April 1934, Piper felt a need to do the same, having now learnt that Paris was not only the cultural capital of Europe but also a centre of international modernism and non-figurative art.

As if torn between England and France, Piper sent Nicholson a postcard of Beachy Head lighthouse which read: 'Paris must be interesting now. We are going in June.'[36] Later that month, he and his first wife, the artist Eileen Holding, set out with an introduction from Nicholson to Jean Hélion (a key figure and networker within the Parisian avant-garde) and to other artists, almost certainly including César Domela, then giving lessons on abstract art to Ben's estranged wife, Winifred Nicholson.

In Paris Piper encountered, among other things, Domela's shallow reliefs, crisp arrangements of modern materials which banished quotidian muddle and mess. This art inspired Piper to break up and diversify the picture surface, and began his interest in the making of painted reliefs incorporating synthetic materials.[37] The impact of Paris on Holding was to turn her attention to the making of painted wooden constructions, in a style indebted to the De Stijl artist Georges Vantongerloo.

We glimpse them both at work later that summer in a letter Piper sent to Myfanwy Evans, whom he had met soon after their return from France. 'Eileen has [taken] to Constructivist art, with awful consequences of sawings, chisellings, stacks of wood about the place, squares and wet towels on the head. I confine myself to [cleaning?] strips from a wireless shop and a little perforated zinc and dainty pots of enamel.'[38]

In their personal lives at this time both Nicholson and Piper were undergoing momentous events. In the summer of 1934, Nicholson's new partner Barbara Hepworth was expecting a child (which turned out to be triplets), while the Pipers' unhappy marriage was moving towards an agreed separation. The catalyst was John Piper's meeting with Myfanwy Evans at a house party organized by Ivon Hitchens at Sizewell. Talk about art and artists became a bonding ingredient, and it was to her that he wrote excitedly about his meeting with Braque in July 1934 at the home of Jim Ede, in the company of Nicholson and Hepworth.[39] By the end of the year Piper and Evans had established a partnership which would be ratified by marriage in 1937, when his divorce came through.

In August 1934 Myfanwy Evans also went to Paris, having been given £20 by an aunt – enough to cover a stay of one month. She, too, took with her introductions to Hélion from both Nicholson and Piper, and while there, visited the studios of Mondrian, Brancusi, Kandinsky, Domela, Giacometti and others. It was Hélion who persuaded her to found and edit a magazine in England promoting the abstract cause. John Piper, on hearing of this, immediately rallied behind the idea. 'I have masses of titles for the new magazine,' he wrote, while Myfanwy was still in Paris, 'and have filled the first 12 numbers with super ideas....*The Studio* will be crying for help in a fortnight. What a sensible man Jean Hélion is, hitting on the right idea straight away.' He wondered whether to tell Nicholson and 'get him all excited and on the hop about the new and only art magazine', and he also dismissed the doubts Myfanwy had about her credentials. 'Holes in knowledge be damned. Knowledge is not a bit of Gruyere cheese, what is needed is grit....Hurry home and be at it.'[40] Together they worked on the magazine *Axis* (1935–7), which proved to be of no small significance to the Nicholson/Piper alliance.[41]

Much of the autumn was spent raising support for *Axis*. Nicholson was kept informed of its progress. In October, Piper wrote to him: 'Myfanwy Evans's magazine is going forward – she has seen [Michael] Sadler (as well as Read and [Geoffrey] Grigson) with fairly encouraging results.'[42] Nicholson and Hepworth, Evans and Piper were united at this time in their recognition of the prejudice against abstract art. Oliver Brown at the Leicester Galleries, for instance, had terminated his association with the 7 & 5 Society on learning that its 1935 exhibition was to be entirely non-figurative. He had written to Piper explaining that such an exhibition had insufficient chance of success to justify his usual allocation of two large rooms to the 7 & 5. As a result, the 1935 exhibition took place elsewhere, in the gallery Anton Zwemmer had opened in 1929 at 26 Litchfield Street, a side street almost adjacent to his bookshop. With justification, Myfanwy later identified with *Axis* a single clear intent: 'We thought there was a voice behind abstract work and it was a good thing to have it heard – that's all.'[43]

While in France, she had become aware that Nicholson and Hepworth had preceded her in their visits to the city. Listening to the complex debates about abstraction, she began to understand better the goal of purity in their art, for in 1934 Ben Nicholson had begun making his white reliefs. *Axis* was to devote considerable space to his work and that of Hepworth: both had examples of their work illustrated in the first issue, while the second carried two essays on Ben Nicholson's white reliefs, Herbert Read remarking in one that these were 'integral with light and precision, with economy and cleanliness – with all the virtues of modern sensibility'.[44] And the third issue, which focused on sculpture, carried a well-illustrated article on Hepworth's recent work. But despite this evidence of solidarity, there was a part of Myfanwy that, from the start, was willing to acknowledge the limitations inherent in abstract art.

Ben Nicholson, *1935 (White Relief)*,
oil on carved Pavatex relief, 1935.

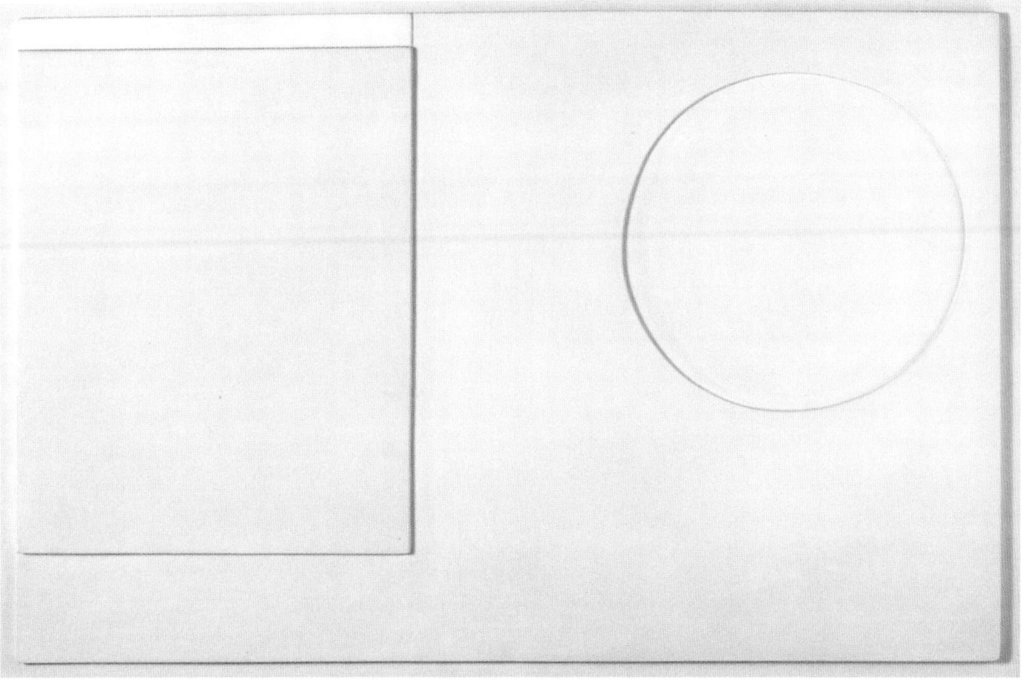

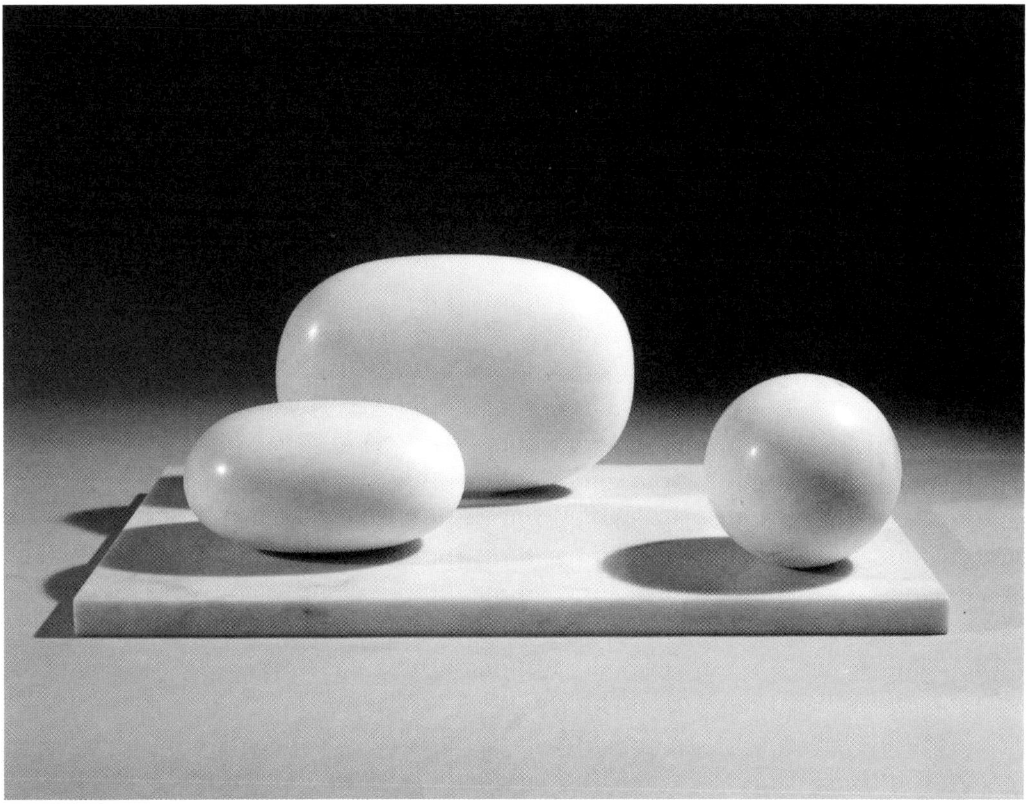

Barbara Hepworth, *Three Forms, 1935,*
Seravezza marble on marble base, 1935.

A careful reader of *Axis* would have detected this ambivalence in its first issue. The cover, designed by Piper, is strikingly modern, with its bold, uncluttered design, sans serif lettering and crisp delivery, in style close to the work of the former Bauhaus tutor Jan Tschichold. But the impact made by this cover was not matched by Myfanwy's first editorial, which betrays her struggle to extract a cogent argument out of the conflicting opinions surrounding abstract art. Its heading – 'Dead or alive?' – signals equivocation. In the magazine's subtitle – 'a Quarterly Review of Contemporary "Abstract" Painting and Sculpture' – she had deliberately clothed the term 'abstract' with inverted commas, for she was all too aware that it was applied haphazardly to work that was non-naturalistic or surrealist or merely decorative, and that as a label it was inadequate and sometimes misleading. 'It suggests certain limits rather than defines them and is not in itself a criterion,' she observes. Overall, the impact of her first editorial is less compelling than that of *Axis 1* taken as a whole, for its illustrations alone, showing the work of Arp, Calder, Domela, Giacometti, Julio González, Hélion, Hepworth, Arthur Jackson, Paul Nash, Nicholson, Miró, Moore, Picasso, Piper, Ceri Richards and Wadsworth, heralded a new stage in the recognition and appreciation of modern art in England.

'It is a kind of discipline which opposes itself to the degenerations of the Royal Academy,' wrote Jim Ede of abstract art, 'and out of it will spring a clearer conception of the nature of art.'[45] But alongside positive statements of this kind, the first issue of *Axis* also contained articles by Geoffrey Grigson and Paul Nash which displayed reservations about this art. Admittedly Nash had expressed doubts to Myfanwy about his eligibility for inclusion in a magazine devoted to non-figurative art, but she had assured him that exploration of his differences was perfectly acceptable. In a memorable passage, he explained his need to secede from pure abstraction: 'I discern among natural phenomena a thousand forms which might, with advantage, be dissolved in the crucible of abstract transfiguration; but the hard cold stone, the rasping grass, the intricate architecture of trees and waves, or the brittle sculpture of a dead leaf – I cannot translate altogether beyond their own image, without suffering in spirit.'[46]

Nash's article is said to have angered Nicholson and Hepworth. They rightly detected that *Axis*, which had set out to promote non-figurative art, contained from the start seeds of rebellion and dissent. Geoffrey Grigson, reviewing the English paintings and sculptures reproduced in *Axis 1*, wrote freely of a reductiveness, a means of creating order 'by leaving out, by negation', resulting in work that represented 'a small history of English ideas, English hesitancy, English error and English performance'. He went on to detail his reaction to every artist in turn, with corrosive honesty. On Ben Nicholson's recent white reliefs, he wrote: 'An image of infinity,

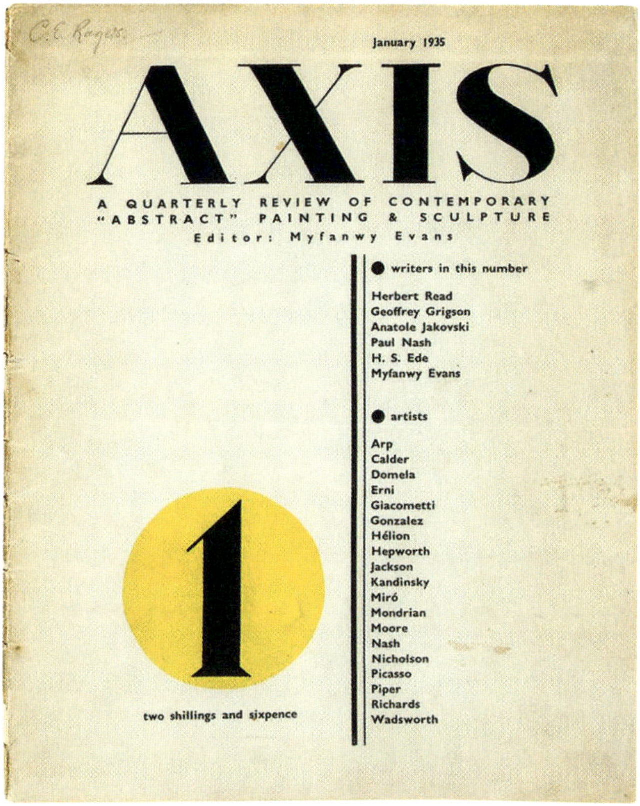

The cover of the first issue of *Axis*, published 1935.

ordered by saying "no" rather than "yes"....Admirable in technical qualities, in taste, in severe self-expurgation, but too much "art itself", floating and disinfected.' John Piper, a friend of Grigson, fared no better. 'Domela somewhat vivified,' Grigson observed. 'An attempt to advance in biomorphic abstraction, though irresolute here and there in form.'[47] The best that can be said for these dispiriting appraisals is that they demonstrated the magazine's willingness to acknowledge differing points of view, to explore issues concerning the social role of art and to re-examine the direction in which art was moving. *Axis*, although it had an overriding purpose, would always remain a broad church.

While *Axis* encouraged debate, Nicholson and Piper often exhibited together as representatives of abstract art, for the latter had begun to develop, in paintings and relief, a very decisive non-figurative style. They were, for instance, both part of the exhibition of abstract art in January 1935 at 59 Finchley Road, the headquarters of

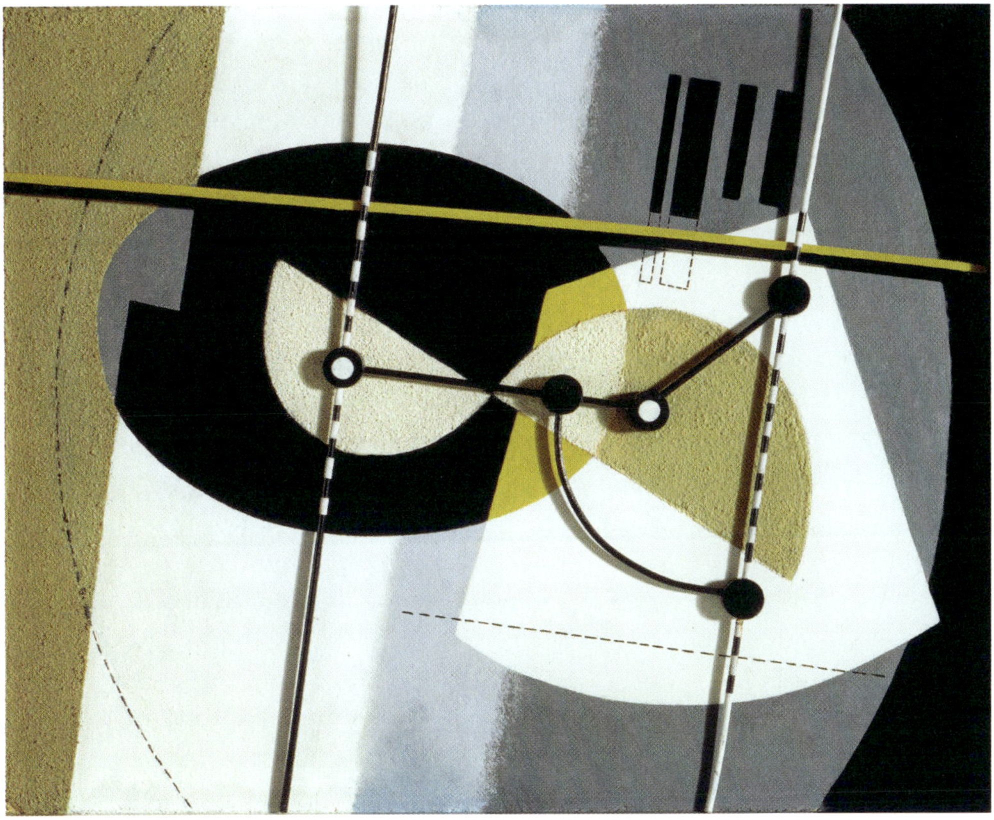

John Piper, *Abstract Construction*,
oil with sand on wood, 1934.

the Experimental Theatre Company, where Piper for the first time showed his constructed reliefs. 'My first totally abstract pictures', he later told Richard Ingrams, 'were constructions, with straight and bent rods and discs on a different plane from, but near to, the surface of the picture, which in itself was often varied in its own surface (for instance, smooth enamelled areas were neighboured by coarse sandpaper areas).' They reminded one critic of 'UndergrounD [*sic*] wiring diagrams, or nightmare relief maps such as a neat and gifted electrician might improvise in sleep'.[48]

This same year the young Sydney John Woods, a painter and arts journalist recently back from a productive visit to Paris, began contributing book and exhibition reviews to the monthly magazine *Decoration*, a high-class glossy periodical with a strong commitment to modern interior design. Whenever possible, he promoted abstract art. The January 1936 issue carried his article 'Why Abstract?', which contained illustrations of work by Moore, Holding, Jackson, Piper and Nicholson among others, all shown in domestic settings to underline the fertile dialogue between architecture and sculpture and painting. Woods argued that all three arts had assimilated 'the Machine' and now had a common foundation in their use of space, light and precision. 'From this starting point', he enthused, 'our culture could be raised to great heights...'[49]

An angry riposte was published the following month. In *Decoration,* Herman Schrijver dismissed Woods's article as 'clear nonsense'. Piper came to his defence in the March issue. He objected to Schrijver's claim that 'art like religion is a subject which means something different to each person'. 'Art, like religion,' Piper insisted, 'is at its best – indeed classical art only exists at all – under the strictest control. When the control slackens art – and religion – become (in strict relation) vague and rudderless.' Further on, his letter reveals how passionately he had embraced the modernist belief in the need for an art that transcended personality and nationality in its search for a universal language: 'Neither art nor religion is an *individual* quality, except in the most petty sense. Each is unworthy of its name unless it is a code, and a recognizable code, within which an individual can function, and can earn the right to be considered as an individual. And the only painting and sculpture to-day which has any code, that is to say any humility or order, is of the type touched on by Mr. Woods. And it is so because it is practised by the only artists who are humble enough to submit to an ideology dictated by, and characteristic of, the times: artists who thereby allow themselves a chance of finding themselves as individuals.'[50]

Though soon to lose faith in just the kind of ideology he here espouses, Piper, in March 1936, fully supported Woods's missionary zeal. Wanting to extend the audience for modern art, Woods curated three exhibitions in non-art venues, and work by Nicholson and Piper appeared in all of them. The first, in November 1935, took place in the Everyman Cinema and Theatre at Hampstead, in tandem with showings of two abstract films by the Fischinger brothers in their 'Lichtertanz' series, created by the play of light on abstract mobiles placed against a black background. Copies of *Axis* were on sale in the foyer, together with a brochure by Woods containing a defence and explanation of abstract art. The two subsequent exhibitions, organized by Woods, promoted abstract art as the ally of modern architecture and design.

The first of these – 'Modern Pictures for Modern Rooms' – Woods cleverly placed in the Duncan Miller Showrooms, Lower Grosvenor Place, London, in April 1936. Here paintings and sculpture mingled with furniture by Marcel Breuer, a radiogram by Wells Coates, and rugs and textiles by Ashley Havinden, among other items. 'If you travel by car or tube or aeroplane, live in glass and concrete, move in a world where speed and space, light and precision are elements of importance', began Woods's introduction, 'you expect an art arising out of this...'[51] The result was an impressive line-up: Naum Gabo, Brancusi, Giacometti, Hélion, Arthur Jackson, Miró, Moholy-Nagy, Hepworth, Mondrian, Moore, Ben Nicholson, Wolfgang Paalen, Piper, Eileen Holding and Woods himself. There were twenty-one works in all, and the entire collection could have been bought for £653 1s – but, owing to the lack of public interest in abstract art, not a single work sold.

The idea was repeated on a less ambitious scale in November 1936, when abstract art was shown in room situations at Bowman's,[52] a popular furniture shop in Camden Town where good modern furniture could be acquired at economical prices. Woods kept no record of the artists he included in this show, but a photograph exists showing a large John Piper abstract hanging on one wall. A readiness to link art with design made both Nicholson and Piper willing to engage with advertising at this time. Both applied their skills with abstraction to the making of promotional material for Imperial Airways at the request of Marcus Brumwell, patron and friend of Nicholson and Hepworth. Nevertheless, by 1937, the forms in some of Piper's abstract paintings had begun to cluster together against an atmospheric ground which, in its suggestiveness of sky or sea, conveys the feeling that the outside world is trying to break in.

With hindsight, a high-water mark in the history of modernism had been reached the year before, in the spring of 1936, with the 'Abstract and Concrete' exhibition organized by Nicolete Gray. Formerly Nicolette [*sic*] Binyon, and a friend of Myfanwy's at Oxford, she had set up a contemporary art loan scheme in an attempt to foster wider appreciation of modern artists. She also occasionally wrote art criticism for *Life and Letters*. When *Axis* appeared, she had been intrigued to find illustrated in its pages art that could not be seen in London. Wanting to bring a representative selection of this new work to England, she sought help from Myfanwy, who supplied her with artists' addresses and found venues for the exhibition. Ben Nicholson chipped in with advice and two of his patrons – Helen Sutherland, who was also a friend of Nicolete Gray's, and Marcus Brumwell – agreed to help finance the venture.

Further discussion of this exhibition and Nicolete Gray's role within it can be found in the next chapter. One detail in the course of its making troubled John Piper's relationship with Ben Nicholson. Piper offered to design a poster. Whether driving a car or wrapping a parcel, he had an innate craftsmanship. He had succesfully created a colour reproduction for *Axis* of a Picasso painting by means of a paramat block. For the poster, John and Myfanwy bought stencils and printing sets in a pet shop in Reading and he set to work, adding lettering to a line block of a black and white Mondrian. 'Ben would write more to us from Paris if he suspected we were using Mondrian's picture like an advertisement for a gas cooker,'[53] Myfanwy wrote in her diary. Soon afterwards a vehement protest did indeed reach them through Barbara Hepworth and the poster had to be altered. Good relations must have been restored by 15 February 1936, the day on which the week-long show opened at 41 St Giles, Oxford, as two days later John and Myfanwy had tea with Ben and Barbara.

Piper did all he could to make this exhibition a success. In an attempt to interest the Lefevre Gallery in taking the show, he invited the dealer Duncan Macdonald to Fawley Bottom to meet Nicolete. 'Macdonald came,' Myfanwy's diary records, '– snorted and scoffed and talked big and small was sincere charming deferential and obstreperous and rather humiliating. Shot off with the superior office boy in the Rolls without having come to any consensual conclusion.'[54] In order to pursue the matter, Piper went to London the next day to see Macdonald, with the result that 'Abstract and Concrete', after touring Oxford, Liverpool and Cambridge, was shown, in expanded form and better hung,[55] at the Lefevre in May 1936. During this tour, very few works sold, but among them were a couple of Pipers.

Piper had good reason to be pleased that at last his abstracts were beginning to sell. Among the five works he exhibited in 'Abstract and Concrete' was his five-by-six-foot *Forms on Dark Blue*, which chimed well with the overall mood of highbrow seriousness. He had directed much of his time, energy and goodwill towards the abstract cause over the previous months, encouraging others in his role as secretary of the 7 & 5. 'We both feel,' he wrote to Winifred Nicholson in 1935, of an abstract gouache she had shown in the Society's 1935 exhibition, 'that it is one of the most interesting things in the show. It has a direct connection with your older work and with the present movement.'[56] But in May 1936 he began to resent what seemed to him the hardening of an association into a party line. To Ben Nicholson he explained:

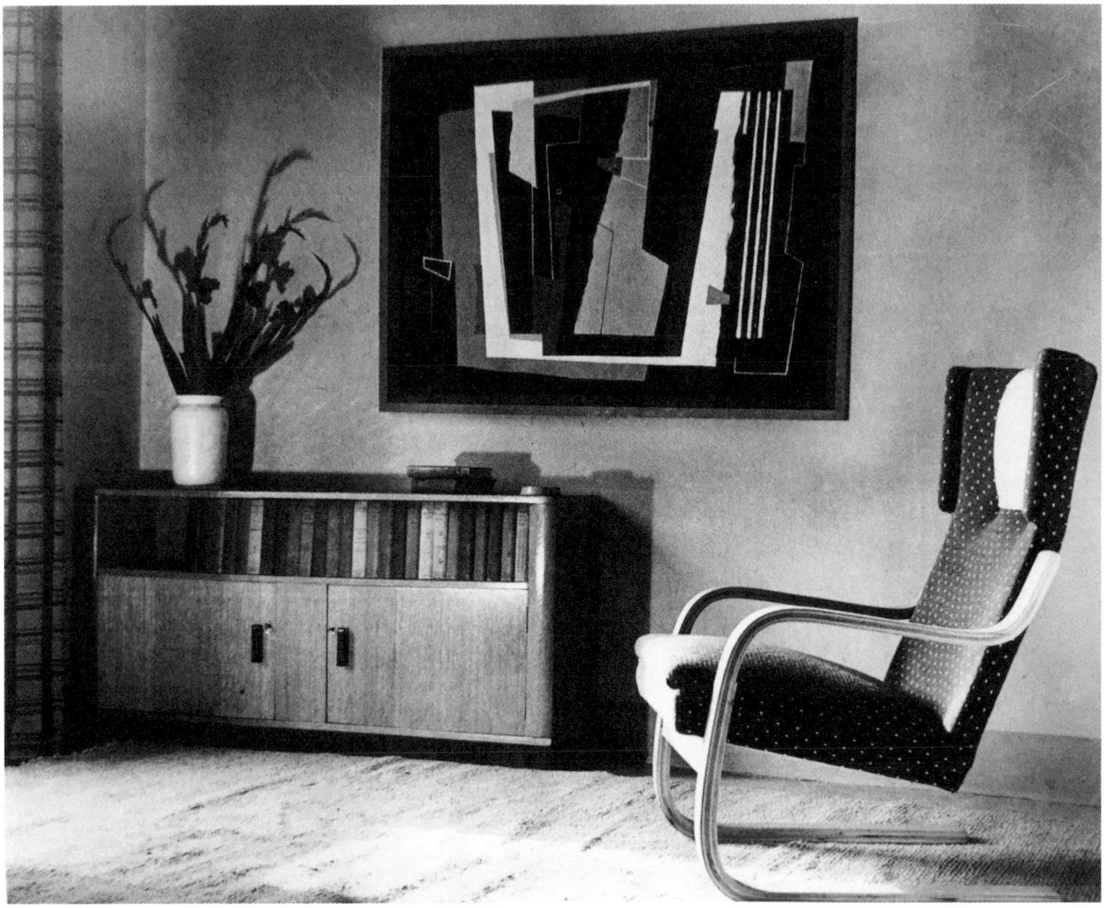

John Piper's *Forms on Dark Blue* hanging in Bowman's furniture shop, Camden Town, 1936.

> There is nobody I'd rather be associated with than you (and Barbara and [Arthur] Jackson) in any continent – but with you and Barbara and Jackson as individuals – as artists – and not as part of a movement. I persist in thinking this very important. I believe that movements are only discovered afterwards. That forcing them at the time of their progress is to kill the artists in them...[57]

A tighter ideological focus worried him. Having witnessed the way in which the 7 & 5 had evolved, changing and refreshing its membership at regular intervals, he favoured organic growth. His above-quoted letter to Nicholson is adamant that history cannot be made, only recognized later, and that the single most important ingredient should remain the artists themselves: 'They must agree to show with one another kick one another out without sentiment when they want to and propose new exhibitors whose work they like, on the grounds of that alone (not because it fits in with a theory). That is bound to make a movement that will be recognised as of GREAT HISTORIC SIGNIFICANCE.' This letter made it evident that he was determined to stand apart if need be. Nicholson and Hepworth, perhaps sensing as much, made a visit to Fawley Bottom a few days later, on 13 May 1936. Myfanwy's diary simply records: 'Ben and Barbara. Hell.'[58]

With Winifred Nicholson now living in Paris, the 7 & 5 no longer benefitted from her energy and strength of character. Her absence seems to be a factor in the parting of ways between Hepworth and Nicholson and the Pipers. But another factor in the shifting scene had been the arrival in London of Naum Gabo, the Russian constructivist, whose ideas would find an important outlet in *Circle*,[59] an international survey of constructive art that was in the planning stage during the summer of 1936. Gabo, Nicholson and the architect Leslie Martin were to act as the book's three editors. Although Gabo had been a significant figure within the Parisian avant-garde, he first met Piper, Hepworth and Nicholson in 1936, on his visit to the 'Abstract and Concrete' exhibition,[60] Nicolete Gray having generously paid for his fare and obtained the visa that enabled him to get into England on a Soviet passport. Soon afterwards, Gabo had settled in London, where his presence strengthened the abstract cause. In July 1936 Nicholson and Hepworth sent curt notes resigning from the 7 & 5,[61] perhaps having heard of Piper's rebellion against the 7 & 5's 'non-figurative' rule, which he now felt was pointless.[62] In their eyes, he had become a betrayer of the modernist cause. Almost fifty years later Piper recollected, with some feeling, the 'belligerence and antagonism' that he had encountered at this time,[63] remarking also to Peter Cannon-Brookes that Herbert Read had been among those who regarded him as 'an apostate'.[64]

Behind his and Myfanwy's renegade stance lay their awareness of the worsening political situation in Europe. As the emphasis on pure abstraction hardened into an ideology, it began to betray an affinity with totalitarianism, which, Tzvetan Todorov argues, became the great innovation of the twentieth century precisely because it played so successfully to people's need for an absolute.[65] No fellow traveller, Piper's letter to Nicholson shows that he was not prepared to sacrifice the present to a historical concept; nor was he willing to sacrifice art to a cause. Two years earlier, Roger Fry, voicing a similar stance, had argued in his book *Reflections on British Painting* that 'the spread on the Continent of an intolerance of opinion, an intolerance which we used to think had passed with the Middle Ages, has given us an enhanced sense of the value of our national distaste for coercion in matters of opinion'.[66]

One reason why the abstract contingent had decided to close ranks was because of the challenge presented by the surrealists. On 11 June 1936, immediately after the 'Abstract and Concrete' exhibition closed, the International Surrealist Exhibition opened at the New Burlington Galleries in London. Its various publicity stunts drew attention to this art which emphasized the disordered and irrational, with results that were very far removed from the abstract artists' search for clarity, harmony and order. Myfawny, keeping her finger on the pulse, had devoted *Axis 5* entirely to the 'Abstract and Concrete' exhibition, giving the editorial to Herbert Read; however, in recognition of a forthcoming event, she had also commissioned from Roland Penrose a review of David Gascoyne's *A Short Survey of Surrealism*.

'Order, order!' rapped out *Axis 6* in the summer of 1936, its cover asking 'Abstraction? Surrealism?' Myfanwy's irritation with the politics of art and the consequent aesthetic mayhem is apparent in her editorial. Both she and Piper were intensely conscious of changes that had recently taken place both in the art world and on the wider political front. In November 1935, after Mussolini's invasion of Abyssinia, Piper had contributed to the exhibition 'Artists Against Fascism and War' organized by the Artists International Association (AIA) in a house in Grosvenor Square. In March 1936, Hitler had sent troops into the demilitarized Rhineland. And, while this summer issue had been in progress, the violence in Spain had increased as it sat on the brink of a civil war. In such a climate, Myfanwy found herself feeling impatient with both abstractionists and surrealists. In her editorial she admitted her disinclination to support either those who used art to promote a utopian ideal of precision, light and clarity, or those for whom art created a bridge between dream-life and reality, the conscious and the unconscious. Instead, her interest now lay with art which irresistibly bound her to the present; with those artists who felt it 'right to alter according to their inclination and nature, and not according to a group-programme'.[67]

Picasso was evidently one of these. John Piper's contribution to *Axis 6* was an article titled 'Picasso belongs where?' It pointed out that Picasso was a 'shocking manifesto-follower', in that, although his work betrayed affinities with both abstraction and surrealism, he could not properly be assigned to either camp. Alan Powers suggests that Piper is here offering Picasso as a paradigm for '*Axis*'s desire to escape from art politics into a greater imaginative reality'.[68] Ben Nicholson, on the other hand, saw in this article and other content in this issue, a personal attack, on himself and his attempts to influence the direction art should take. Piper hastened to disabuse him of this, as his letter to Winifred Nicholson makes clear:

> I don't agree about the 'personal attack' on Ben in *Axis* – nobody has expressed such an opinion except Ben and you to us. Myfanwy and I both have a great opinion of Ben, and think his contribution of vital importance – but it seems to me that Myfanwy's article (and John Woods') were perfectly justified personal statements of their attitudes – and very genuine attempts to clear the ground and find where they stood. I personally admire Ben so much that I feel entitled to criticize his attitude to myself occasionally as well as praising him continually.[69]

Yet Nicholson may also have been surprised to find in *Axis 6* a lenghty article by Jean Hélion promoting Poussin and Seurat as the two artists against which all modern art should be assessed. Still more bitter to his ears would have been S. J. Woods's essay, 'Time to Forget Ourselves', in which he seemed to turn his back on all that Nicholson had achieved. 'It is time we forgot Art and Abstract, time the "movement" ceased and manifestos were burned, time we cut our beards, ceased to be artists and became men and painters. Art has chased out life, and now life must come back if art is to remain.'[70]

CHAPTER 11

THE AUSTERE, THE VIOLENT OR THE STRANGE

If English art during the 1920s owed much to individual endeavour, the 1930s witnessed a greater interest in communal effort. We encounter in this chapter the making of Paul Nash's progressive group, Unit One, and the making of the International Surrealist Exhibition. The magazine *Axis* likewise owed much to the collaborative spirit which it inspired. As we have seen, in the middle of this decade Myfanwy Evans had found herself editor of *Axis*, in which role she sought to encourage discussion of abstract art while also allowing Paul Nash to express reservations on the subject and Geoffrey Grigson to be downright rude about certain artists. Her stance as an editor was always broad church and her policy, over time, open to reconsideration.

In her late teens Myfanwy had spent empty, wintry Sunday afternoons in the Tate Gallery, enjoying the French pictures recently acquired by the Courtauld Fund and displayed in newly built rooms dedicated to modern European art. Later she realized that her lack of knowledge about any kind of art from before the impressionists was a positive help, as no set of ideas as to what art should do or be intervened between her eyes and the painting or sculpture at which she was looking. But on entering the art world she became one of its most astute observers, immediately sensing that it was a bellicose place. 'There were two sets of enemies for artists: those who hated all art since Manet and those who blindly idolized the École de Paris. The latter were the most dangerous: "You don't want to look at that stuff," said Mr McDonald [*sic*] of the Lefevre Gallery at their exhibition of Ivon Hitchens. "Come up and see my Derains".'[1] Myfanwy was equally irritated by the way people used the phrase 'significant form' when talking about art, taking an easy pleasure in its association with aesthetic emotion, but without any awareness of the 'urgency and necessity that produced it and without really relating it to the tougher developments of the movement – the austere, the violent or the strange'.[2] It seemed to her that instead many English painters seemed satisfied with producing 'stale and etiolated versions of the Fauves'.[3]

What made Myfanwy's observation of the art world so acute was the fact that during her 1934 visit to Paris, when she was lent a flat and survived for a month on the £20 given her by her aunt, she for the first time looked at art not from the outside but from the inside, through the eyes of artists she met and through their lives and thoughts. Among these artists were Brancusi, Domela, Giacometti, Kandinsky, Mondrian, Jean Arp and Sophie Taeuber-Arp. She later wrote: 'All the artists I visited that summer had the same quality of private, active intensity in the midst of an indifferent world – a world that, all the same, like a selfish parent, had produced the very life that it rejected or was bored by.'[4] From Jean Hélion, in particular, she received 'an upsurge of belief in the actual activity of painting then'.[5] This awareness of its relevance to the moment in which she was living removed any need for aesthetic or moral judgment, as it seemed beside the point. 'This was the way it [painting] was being done. What mattered was the capacity to be in it at the moment of its existence.'[6] But this switch from the position of an outside observer to that of an actual participant, especially when work on *Axis* began, brought home the complexity of this fast-changing decade.

Another person equally immersed in the world of artists was the art historian, poet and critic Herbert Read, who had left the Victoria and Albert Museum in 1931 to take up the Watson Gordon Chair of Fine Art at the University of Edinburgh. Two years earlier, he had published an essay on 'The Meaning of Art' in the *Listener*. With regard to art, this magazine aimed at a combination of 'catholicity of outlook with popularity of style'.[7] Read's essay evidently satisfied this remit as one of the editors, R. S. Lambert, afterwards invited him to submit a weekly column on any art topic he thought fit. After fifty-four of these contributions, Read modified them slightly and shuffled them into a book titled *The Meaning of Art*, which came out in 1931. 'It is to the diversity of the human spirit, and with the realisation that this diversity can be diversely expressed, that we must look for an explanation of the vitality and of the validity of modern art,'[8] he told his readers, also freeing them from a need for realism by suggesting that abstraction made it possible for artists to explore anew the making of symbols.

One of the essays in the *Listener* had resulted from an introduction received from Eric Maclagan, then director of the Victoria and Albert Museum, to Henry Moore. When the essay appeared in April 1931, Read's claim that Moore, 'in virtue of his sureness and consistency, springs straight to the head of the modern movement in England'[9] must have startled many. But it was his next book, *Art Now* (1933), that made Read the acknowledged champion of modern art, the person to go to for support or for catalogue introductions. In this instance his starting point was not articles for the *Listener* but lectures delivered at Bangor, at the newly created

Courtauld Institute and at Armstrong College, Newcastle-upon-Tyne, where one of these lectures formed the annual Charlton Lecture, still in existence today at Newcastle University.

Art Now was itself a very modern creation. It was one of the first books to use sans serif lettering throughout and, in its revised edition of 1936, the pencil-thin white and red lines (or white and blue, in an alternative edition) in its hardback binding made it look like a piece of constructivist design from post-revolutionary Russia. It carried 128 black and white illustrations of recent European paintings and sculpture, which Douglas Cooper, then partnering Freddy Mayor at the Mayor Gallery, helped bring together and which were updated for the 1936 revision. However, few of these illustrations are mentioned in the text, let alone discussed in any detail, for the content of the book is more accurately described by its subtitle, 'An Introduction to the Theory of Modern Painting and Sculpture'. And it was this concern with abstract ideas, intellectual concepts, artistic doctrines and the philosophy behind art that made Read a new voice in the field of art criticism, as well as the informed insights that he brought to a wide view of modern art.

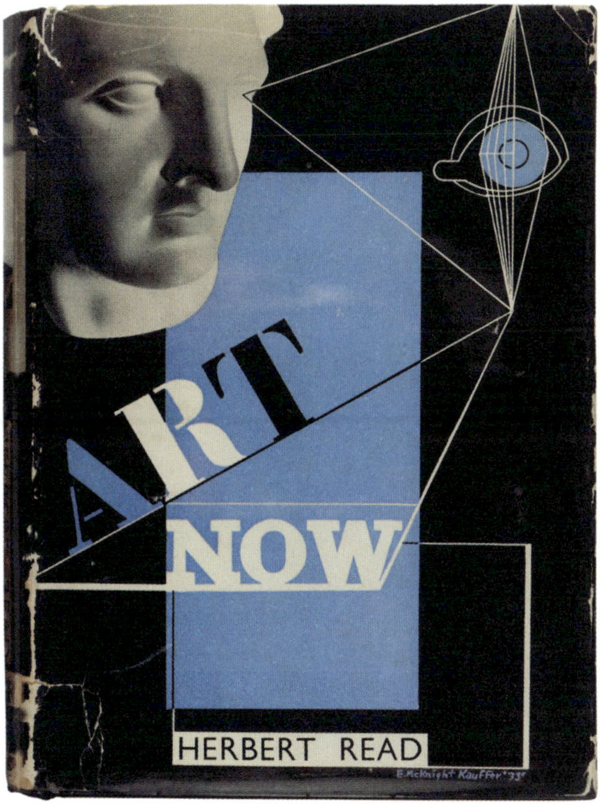

Edward McKnight Kauffer, jacket design for Herbert Read's *Art Now*, 1933.

Among these is his explanation that 'primitive' art – like that of Alfred Wallis, whose work he illustrated – is not the result of special feeling or thought but of expression and objectification; that Matisse's integral vision is achieved by 'holding on to a fixed focus, a single line of sight, and painting passionately, intensely, swiftly what the eye in this immediate act perceives',[10] with colour harmonies often derived from remote sources; and that Edvard Munch's return, in the wake of post-impressionism, to 'a mode of expression more consonant with the Nordic genius' enabled him to pass on to German expressionism the emphasis on emotional unity in art.[11] Where relevant, as in his concise analysis of Die Neue Sachlichkeit, with its relentless, sardonic realism, Read puts his finger not only on the pulse of the modern but also on its relation to the political situation in Europe. He slips into his preface mention of the sacking in Germany of artists from art schools and museum directors from their posts. Since Hitler had become chancellor in January 1933, giving greater power to the Nazis, dictatorship had replaced democracy, the removal of modernist art from public view becoming part of the 'cleansing' of all things 'unGerman'.

The reader also senses in *Art Today* Read's desire to acknowledge Roger Fry as his mentor, but also to depose him by means of a broader vision. He seizes on an article Fry wrote for the *Listener* on 'Sensibility versus Mechanism' and argues that it reveals Fry's lack of appreciation of geometric abstraction; whereas Fry's chief complaint against 'Mechanism' was the way mechanical reproduction in the decorative arts can deaden the expression of sensibility. In any event Fry was no obstacle to Read's continued rise to fame, as he died unexpectedly, after a fall, on 9 September 1934. However, in May of that year he had reviewed *Art Now* in the *Burlington Magazine*. His appreciation of the book was greatly hindered by his strong prejudice against German art and by his dislike of the surrealists and what he characterized as their dependence on 'unreasonable levels of unconscious life'.[12] It is, however, understandable that, having witnessed his wife's irreversible mental decline, Fry preferred to cling to reason and sanity rather than meddle with dreams and the subconscious. Two years later, a political cause brought Virginia Woolf, among others, to dine with Read at 3 Mall Studios. Later, he was to praise her biography of Fry, but used his review of it to vent bitter, malignant criticism of Fry himself.

After Read resigned from his professorship at Edinburgh in June 1933, he left behind his wife and son and eloped to London with one of the Music Faculty, Margaret Ludwig (better known as 'Ludo'), who became his second wife after his divorce came through. They lodged briefly in Henry Moore's studio flat at 11a Parkhill Road while Moore and his wife Irina were spending time in Kent. Living on this road – 'on the frontier that divides the two worlds of Hampstead and Camden Town',[13] as Read neatly observed – placed him in easy reach of the Mall Studios, a short, terraced row of studio houses reached by a path off Tasker Road. Read discovered that he could rent No. 3 Mall Studios, and in doing so he became a neighbour of Barbara Hepworth and Ben Nicholson, who had moved into No. 7 with Hepworth after her first husband, John Skeaping, left.

Next to them was the artist John Cecil Stephenson, a northerner from Bishop Auckland, who on Walter Sickert's advice had taken over No. 6 back in 1919. Like Hepworth and Moore, Stephenson had trained at Leeds School of Art and at the RCA. In 1922 he had become Head of Art at the School of Surveying and Building in the Northern Polytechnic, Holloway Road, where he remained for the rest of his career. His interest in architecture shaped his use of abstraction when, under the influence of his studio neighbours, he broke with figuration in 1933 and became a very fine abstract artist. His work attracted Mondrian's admiration, and was illustrated in *Circle*.[14] Also present in Read's 'nest of gentle artists' (a phrase he later used as the title of an article describing this period)[15] was Paul Nash, who from 1936 lived nearby in Eldon Road, on the other side of Haverstock Hill.

'For five years', Read recalled, 'I lived in friendly and intimate association with this group of artists, visiting their studios almost daily and watching the progress of their work.'[16] It was, he claimed, the happiest period of his life. Between 1933 and 1939 he was the spokesperson for the avant-garde while also editor of the *Burlington Magazine*, which meant he was grooming texts on old masters while lauding the austerity and purity of mid-1930s abstraction and delivering verbal fireworks in praise of surrealism's assault on the mind and senses.

John Cecil Stephenson, *Abstract Painting*, egg tempera on canvas on board, 1935.

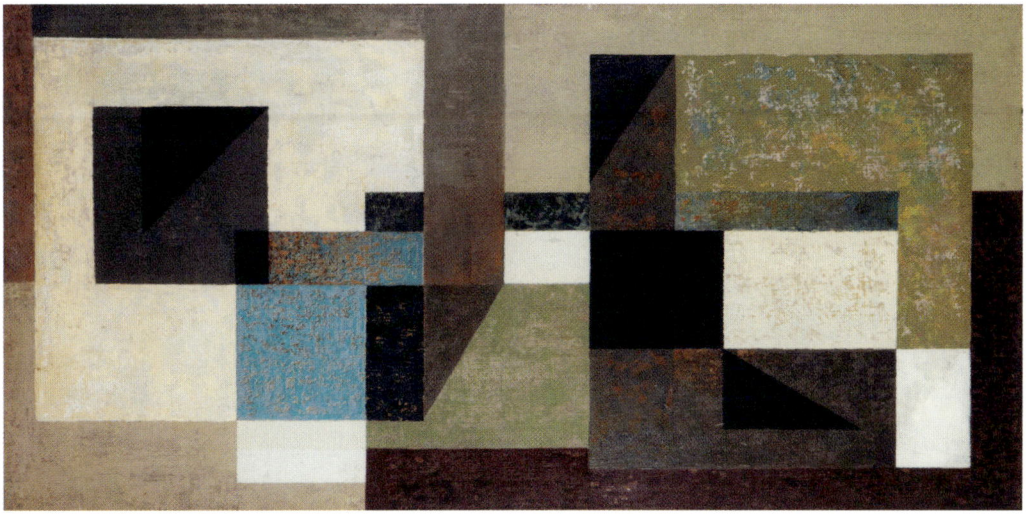

Read's nest, however, was to be enlarged by its sympathy with what was happening in nearby Lawn Road. Here Jack Pritchard, a marketing director for the Venesta Plywood Company, had bought a plot of land after his marriage in 1924 on which he intended to build a family house. Pritchard is said to have had 'an instinctive feeling for the fusion of technology with art'.[17] He became known as 'Plywood Pritchard' as he was always seeking new uses for plywood, which he regarded as an important material for the modern world, especially after advances in bent plywood made it a structural material. When it came to finding an architect for his family house, it is not surprising that Pritchard chose Wells Coates, who had used plywood extensively for the shop interiors he designed for Cresta Silks.

Jack Pritchard and his wife Molly had met at Cambridge and both were progressives. Owing to their interest in non-traditional methods of education, they set up a nursery in Hampstead, which was managed by Beatrix Tudor-Hart. In 1930 Pritchard and Coates visited the Weissenhof in Stuttgart, a housing estate built for the Deutscher Werkbund in 1927 as a kind of showcase for modernist design and involving seventeen architects, including Le Corbusier and Mies van der Rohe. This same year Pritchard commissioned Corbusier, Pierre Jeanneret and Charlotte Perriand to design the Venesta stand at the Building Trade Exhibition. After this he found himself increasingly drawn into the world of modernist design, while in London he became a founder member of the think tank Political and Economic Planning, formed in 1931 with a commitment to the physical and economic reconstruction of Britain and to long-term planning. In this way he made good friends with Julian Huxley, an influential biologist and pioneer of X-ray crystallography.

Meanwhile, interest in the Bauhaus had begun to percolate through to magazines in Britain. In 1931 Pritchard again visited Germany in the company of Coates and another architect, Serge Chermayeff, partly to experience the Bauhaus at Dessau. Although Walter Gropius had resigned in 1928 at a time of growing political hostility, the factory-like glass, metal and concrete building that he had designed for the art school remained an eloquent symbol of the 'true architectonic spirit' that Gropius thought all Bauhaus students should imbibe. This and other factors, including his interest in Continental experiments in modern communal living, decided Pritchard that his plot of land on Lawn Road would accommodate not a house, nor even a pair of houses, as had at one point been suggested, but instead a block of flats which could become just such an experiment.

Molly Pritchard drew up the brief for Coates and, while the design was being refined by means of compact planning, simplicity of form and the identification of modern materials, Jack formed, in December 1931, the Isokon Furniture Company – primarily for the making of plywood furniture, but also to develop these flats. It was assumed that in the modern urban world, professional men and women with very few possessions needed only minimal facilities for sleeping, cooking and clothes storage, and the target audience was defined as 'businessmen and women who have no time for domestic troubles'.[18] The five-storey building was composed of twenty-two 'Minimum Flats', each containing a bed-sitting room, a dressing room linked to a bathroom, and a kitchenette. In addition there were four two-room flats with sliding partitions, three studio flats, and a large penthouse on the fifth floor, where the Pritchards lived. The success of the scheme for the Lawn Road Flats seemed assured when a prototype of the 'Minimum Flat' was shown at the Exhibition of Industrial Art in the Home in June 1933. The project was completed in 1934, a date that is often associated with the ending of a transitional period of modernism in art and design that had begun around 1928. At the time it was one of the few domestic buildings in London to make use of reinforced concrete, and it was initially painted a dazzling white. At the opening ceremony in July 1934, Molly Pritchard announced: 'This building is perhaps the most modern building in England. It is not only modern as an architectural piece – it expresses a revolutionary idea for living.'[19]

Shortly after the flats became available, the Pritchards began welcoming refugees from Nazi Europe. At Dessau, the Bauhaus building had been taken over by stormtroopers in 1932; the School managed to recreate itself in Berlin under the directorship of Mies van der Rohe, only to be terminated by the Nazis in 1933. Its existence had lasted only fourteen years, yet its influence was to spread far and wide. The first Bauhaus members to settle into the Lawn Road Flats, in October 1934, were Walter and Ise Gropius. They did so on the encouragement of several British modernists who promised help and a guarantee of employment, but it was Pritchard who offered them a place to live,[20] and, after their arrival, helped Gropius find a job with the architect Maxwell Fry. Gropius had arrived with a huge reputation as the visionary founder of the Bauhaus, but in coming to England he was cut off from his roots, his culture and his contacts. Despite what must have seemed very cramped accommodation if compared with houses he and his wife had lived in before, he wrote to Marcel Breuer soon after arriving, urging him to join them. He found in Herbert Read 'a kindred soul' and came to regard Henry Moore as 'the best of the living English artists';[21] but aside from this 'gentle nest' he often felt frustrated by the slowness, cluelessness and philistinism that he encountered in Britain. A visit to Cambridge 'convinced him that the fundamentally conservative attitude of Englishmen made it impossible for them to appreciate anything new'.[22] Nevertheless, he and Ise remained in the Lawn Road Flats until 1937, when Gropius accepted an invitation from Harvard University to take over as chair of the architecture department in the Graduate School of Design.

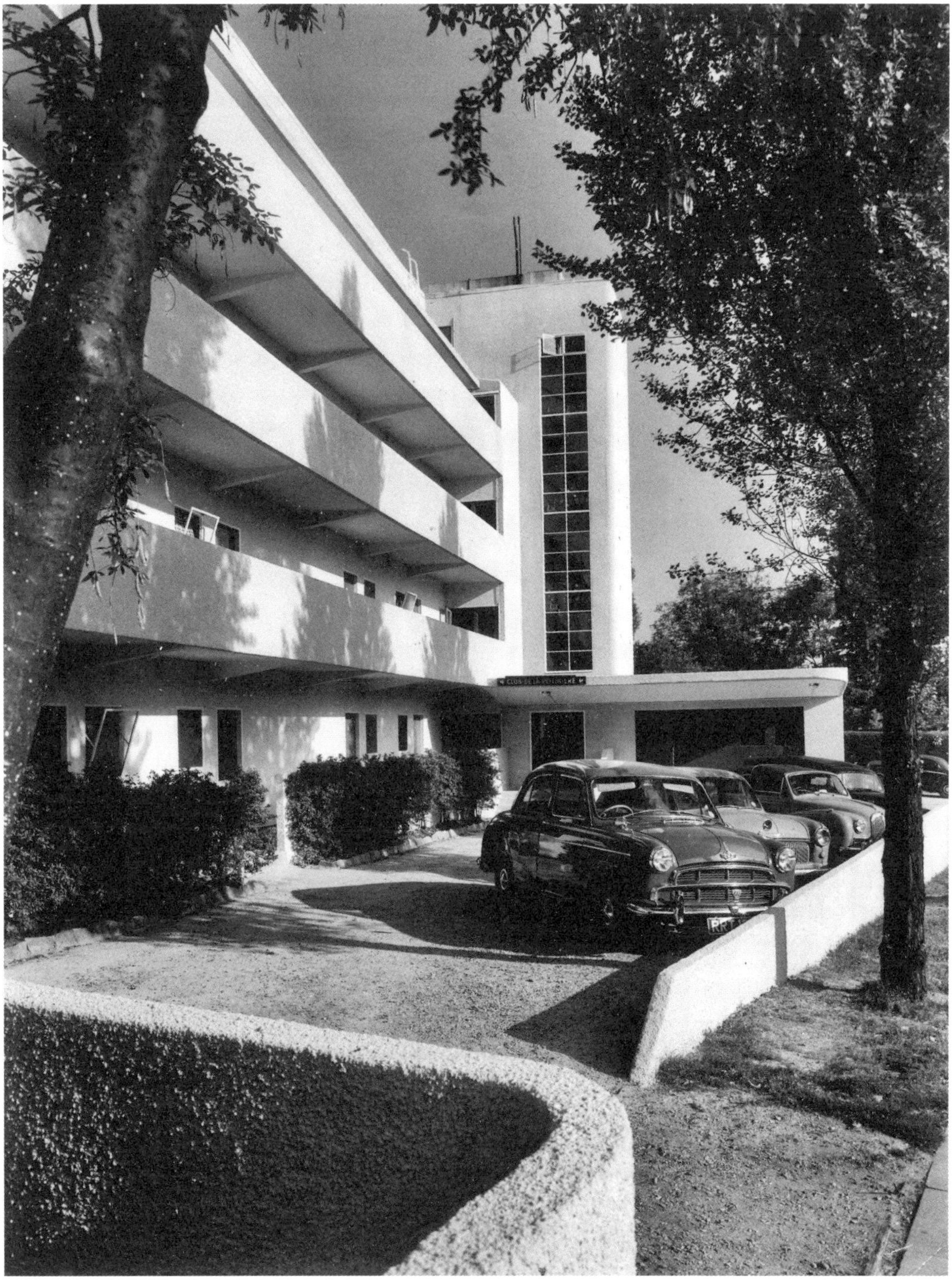

Wells Coates's Lawn Road Flats following post-war repair
and renovation, *c.* 1950.

Other Bauhaus residents stayed only for limited periods in the flats, among them Breuer, even though he became the lead furniture designer for Isokon, making innovative, elegant use of the new advances in bent plywood in his design for the famous Isokon Long Chair and other pieces of furniture. He was also to design the Isobar restaurant in 1937, at a time when some alteration to the accommodation enabled Pritchard to incorporate the venue that gave the Lawn Road Flats a social hub. Another short-term refugee resident, László Moholy-Nagy, wholeheartedly acknowledged the benefits he gained from connections made through Pritchard and the Hampstead circuit. He collaborated with Julian Huxley on the film *London Zoo* and, following an introduction from Ashley Havinden, gained a position with the traditional men's outfitters Simpsons of Piccadilly, designing its shop windows. A pioneer graphic designer, photographer, maker of films and constructivist artist who regarded light as raw material for art and design and saw both as one practice, Moholy-Nagy enjoyed a highly fertile period while living in London between 1935 and 1937. Herbert Read, who had first met him on his exploratory visit to England in 1933, two years later voiced the opinion that he was 'one of the most creative intelligences of our time'; by this time, they had become close friends and advocates.[23]

Moholy-Nagy too eventually left for America after being appointed director of a new design school in Chicago which he named The New Bauhaus. But as Sibyl Moholy-Nagy, his second wife, recalled, for the first time since his Bauhaus days he had found in London men and women with whom he could discuss his work. She wrote: 'The unique English capacity for friendship, an objective, unemotional association which warmed and stimulated without obligation, seemed particularly strong among London artists and intellectuals.... By and by a close circle developed – Herbert Read, Henry Moore, Jack Pritchard, Jim Crowther,[24] Julian Huxley, Barbara Hepworth and Ben Nicholson.... And we all benefitted from Jack Pritchard, manufacturer of Marcel Breuer's plywood furniture and generous host to many a Continental refugee in his ever-open Lawn Road Flats.'[25] In this way, a particular corner of North London came to harbour, if only for a short while, a formidable array of talent that turned England, temporarily, into a lighthouse for international modernism.

A task that had fallen to Read soon after his return to London was the takeover of responsibility for Unit One. This group attracted the attention of Gropius because, as described by Paul Nash in his founding letter, published in *The Times* in June 1933, it sought as the Bauhaus had done to do away with the division between artists and architects, the common bond being 'the expression of a truly contemporary spirit'. This Nash wanted to infuse into English art, as well as a more rigorous sense of 'structural design'. Initially he had not included Ben Nicholson in the group, explaining in a letter to Henry Moore that he thought his old friend's judgment was 'not entirely sound'.[26]

Nicholson himself had earlier sensed that a breakthrough was imminent. A letter he sent in February 1933 to Winifred Nicholson, then living with their children in Paris, stated: 'There is a feeling over here as if in the painting world everyone realizes we are all on the brink of a new discovery – it is rather lovely – (even the dealers are all smiles & full of beans as if they have sensed some form of life).'[27] In November, while plans for a Unit One exhibition were under way, Paul Nash, acting under doctor's orders, removed himself to the French Riviera owing to an attack of bronchitis agitated by asthma, to which he had been prone ever since being gassed during the war. Read took up both the Unit One exhibition and the accompanying book, which he modelled on the annual Abstraction-Création brochure, bringing together artists' statements and photographs of their work. He sent round a questionnaire to obtain what he needed from all those involved, among whom he included Ben Nicholson.

The exhibition opened in 1934 at the Mayor Gallery and afterwards travelled to Liverpool, Rusholme and Hanley. The eleven members of the group were sculptors Barbara Hepworth and Henry Moore; painters John Armstrong, John Bigge, Edward Burra, Tristram Hillier, Paul Nash, Ben Nicholson and Edward Wadsworth; and architects Wells Coates and Colin Lucas. A book, also titled *Unit One*, was published to coincide with the exhibition, and each artist or architect contributed a short essay about their work. An awareness of social needs underpins much that is said. Wells Coates writes about the role of the architect employing new technology: 'The work of integrating, unifying and synthesizing a multitude of these new material details, processes and conditions, and of giving to the whole design a formal aspect of order and significance, calls for the utmost precision, vigilance, sincerity and clarity of vision on the part of the architect, who is, it must be remembered, not only the *composer*, but also the *conductor* of the many executants of his work.'[28] All were pulling together in this book to show in their work true contemporary expression.

This was an interesting moment in the history of English art. Nicholson had taken his recent Braque-inspired experiments with a linear fluidity further, first incising his lines into the surface of his paintings and then moving on to the making of his white reliefs, the first of which he completed early in 1934. They were to figure later that year in the Unit One exhibition and then again in his solo exhibition, also held at the Mayor Gallery in 1935. Using mostly the circle and the rectangle, together with subtle alterations in low relief, they bring into play, when lit from the side, sharp contrasts of light and shadow, but ultimately depend on the unifying whiteness of the whole. Nicholson created this by covering his reliefs with three coats of Coverine (a quick-drying substitute for gesso), then a coat of Flake White and finally one of Titanium, thereby achieving what he called 'a marvellous deep silvery white', while admitting it took a long time to do.[29] His use of white aligned him with the International Style in architecture and art, particularly with Corbusier's white-painted villas and with the white grounds used by Mondrian for his paintings.

Instrumental in Nicholson's development was his never-to-be-forgotten first visit to Mondrian's studio apartment, on 5 April 1934. The narrow, sparsely furnished flat was far from silent, as it was next door to a dancing school and looked out over the railway lines that brought trains in and out of the Gare Montparnasse. Although Nicholson acknowledged he did not fully understand Mondrian's abstraction at first sight, he registered the studio as a place made sacred by the activity that went on within it, comparing it to 'those hermits' caves where lions used to go to have thorns taken out of their paws'.[30] Nicholson's gift with words also produced a memorable statement in the Unit One book: that when a work of art reaches completion and 'form, depth and colour' are at their most satisfying, it becomes 'a living thing as nice as a poodle with 2 shining black eyes'.[31] This description perfectly fits his own *Gouache 1936* – the year he reintroduced colour into a series of severely abstract paintings in which the influence of Mondrian is immediately felt. The colour of each geometric unit in this picture has a very precise hue, tone, weight and density, as they lock together around the red square. Two years later, Nicholson gifted this work to the Reads, inscribing it 'for Herbert and Ludo Xmas 1938'.

The person chiefly responsible for bringing the achievement of abstract art to wide notice in 1936 was Nicolete Gray. It was she who, at a time when abstract art was still incomprehensible to many, stepped forward and promoted an extreme form of modernism through 'Abstract and Concrete: an international exhibition of abstract painting and sculpture'. She brought to this task an open mind and an unprejudiced eye, as well as confidence in her own judgment. Her inner certainty owed much to her decision, during her first year at Oxford, to place herself under instruction for reception into the Catholic Church. Her parents, Laurence and Cicely Binyon, asked her to wait a year before taking this step, which she did, even staying away from Father Martin D'Arcy's weekly 'at homes' at Campion Hall, without however damaging the close friendship she enjoyed with him over many years. After a year had passed, she became a Catholic convert.

Also relevant to her understanding of art was the fact that her father had not only moved with his family into one of the six houses that then formed part of the British Museum, but during the forty years of his life spent working for the Department of Prints and Drawings, had become a leading authority on the art of India, Persia,

China and Japan. He spent his Saturday mornings and Sunday afternoons visiting museums and art exhibitions. Nicolette (as she was known in childhood) often accompanied him, and it is probable that her father's interest in non-Western art helped free her from conventional prejudices concerning art. She herself took lessons in Persian while recuperating from appendicitis and in 1931, at the age of nineteen, reviewed the Persian exhibition held at the Royal Academy. In this review she made unexpected connections between Persian art, Stanley Spencer's Sandham Memorial Chapel and Ben Nicholson's *Christmas Night* (1930), one of his most romantic pictures, which she had recently seen in the Leicester Galleries. 'All these pictures achieve a concentration which I thought was beyond the function of painting,' she admitted.[32] By the age of twenty-four she, like Ben Nicholson, asserted her desire for 'the real' and stated very simply the basis of her approach to art: 'I am interested in everything that seems to me to be a true expression of a real feeling or a true statement of a real thing.'[33]

Nicolete had by then married Basil Gray, an Assistant Keeper in the British Museum's Prints and Drawings Department and later Head of Oriental Prints, Drawings and Paintings. The first of their five children appeared when she was twenty-three. She could not, with the onset of a family, take on a full-time job, but nor could she live an entirely domesticated life, and so she began writing art criticism for *Life and Letters*. As she began to be more involved with contemporary art she noticed how precarious the financial situation was for many artists, and so devised a loan scheme. She wrote to artists whom she believed to be doing good and important work and asked them to lend her examples of their work, as well as photographs of further examples, so that she might display in her own home as up-to-date a selection of contemporary art as could be found anywhere in London, for potential clients to see. She had a good response from the artists she contacted, and Ben Nicholson suggested she might advertise her 'enterprising scheme' in Myfanwy Evans's *Axis*.

Nicolete acted on his advice and contacted Myfanwy, whom she had known at Oxford. She was not overly impressed by *Axis*, finding some of its articles 'pretentious rubbish', but her association with Myfanwy appears to have crystallized her interest in abstract art just at the time when Nicholson and Hepworth were pursuing an austere purity sustained by idealism. Both believed that the liberation of form and colour achieved by abstract art paralleled, or was linked to, other forms of freedom. Far from representing a retreat from reality, abstract art, like good design, offered a vision of order and was therefore a potential agent for change. Possibly owing to their influence, Nicolete began to claim that abstract art was 'an index to present day life' and had become 'by far the most significant of all painting and sculpture that is being produced'.[34] This remark appears in the circular she sent out asking for contributions towards 'Abstract and Concrete', to be developed in association with *Axis*, and for which they needed to raise £50 to cover expenses.

Her aim now was to mount an international exhibition of abstract art – the first in Britain – which would comprise work by artists of nine different nationalities. The final roll call included Alexander Calder, César Domela, Hans Erni, Naum Gabo, Alberto Giacometti, Jean Hélion, Barbara Hepworth, Eileen Holding, Arthur Jackson, Wassily Kandinsky, László Moholy-Nagy, Joan Miró, Piet Mondrian, Henry Moore, Ben Nicholson and John Piper. It was an astonishing list. As Gray proudly pointed out in her foreword to the catalogue, of the sixteen artists, 'only one is a Frenchman'; and, moreover, 'for the first time since the eighteenth century England is making a real contribution to an international art'.[35]

Of course, not everyone saw it in this light. 'Art Show Shocks', announced the *Sunday Pictorial*,[36] while the *Daily Mail* dismissed it as 'a jolly leg pull'.[37] Christie's

The 'Abstract and Concrete' exhibition, 1936.

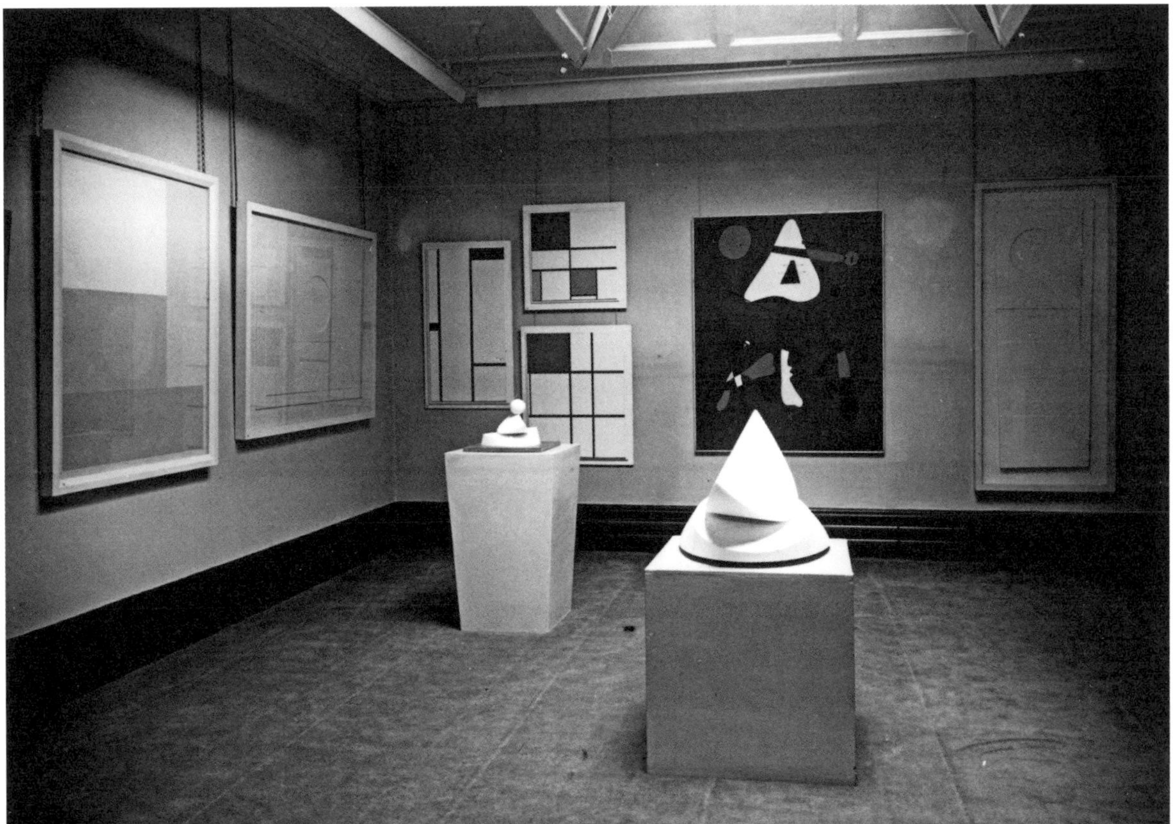

was prepared to testify, for the purposes of customs and insurance, that the exhibits were almost worthless in terms of monetary value. The three Mondrians were for sale at £50 each, but neither the Tate nor the Contemporary Art Society showed any interest – making it possible for Helen Sutherland and Nicolete Gray to acquire one each. It is also of interest that the philosopher R. G. Collingwood helped Gray with the unpacking and assembling of the exhibition when it opened at Oxford and was afterwards seen having a long discussion of the works of art with his colleagues – a fact that suggests the exhibition influenced the thinking behind his book *The Principles of Art* (1937), in which he set out to rid aesthetic discussion of 'moribund theory' and to 'contribute in my own way...to the new movement in the arts'.[38] Further on in his Preface, he claims: 'Everything written in this book has been written in the belief that it has a practical bearing, direct or indirect, upon the condition of art in England in 1937.'[39]

The 'Abstract and Concrete' exhibition remains a significant landmark in the history of British art, even though abstract art afterwards quickly slipped into a pronounced dichotomy with surrealism once the International Surrealist Exhibition had opened in London in June 1936. This rapid alteration left scant room for the formation of a new group identity, which is why Unit One folded after its first and last exhibition. Yet for a short period John Piper and Ben Nicholson had such confidence in the relevance of abstract art to the historical moment that they began to incorporate the year of execution into the titles of their pictures; Piper labelled some of his 1935 abstracts simply 'Painting 1935', thereby implying that these pictures were exactly what painting should look like at that moment in time. Herbert Read expressed awareness of fluidity when revising *Art Now* in 1936, adding a short piece titled 'Epilogue 1936' which concludes: 'Art is in transition: that is one certain fact. And it is more than one reason why it would be vain to attempt anything in the nature of a pontifical judgement on its immediate manifestations. We should be content with the fact that art is alive – more vital and experimental than at any time since the Renaissance.'[40]

The International Surrealist Exhibition arrived hard and fast on the heels of 'Abstract and Concrete', opening on 11 June 1936. Its emphasis on the dreamlike, the disturbing and the irrational must have felt like the return of the repressed after the careful deliberation and pursuit of pure form that had governed the making of the works shown in the preceding exhibition. As mentioned, Myfanwy had shown considerable diplomacy in inviting Roland Penrose to review David Gascoyne's *A Short Survey of Surrealism*, which acted as a foil to the rest of *Axis 5* which was entirely devoted to 'Abstract and Concrete'.

Penrose had met Gascoyne by chance in 1935, while living in Paris. Together they conceived of the International Surrealist Exhibition, but Penrose was the lead partner, owing to his silver-spoon heritage: 'I was born in a cloud smelling strongly of oil paint, honest banking and piety,' he admitted,[41] referring to his father, James Doyle Penrose, Quaker and popular academic painter, and his mother, Josephine Peckover, descended from the Peckovers of Wisbech, who had set up a bank and were also devout Quakers.[42] And so, like Roger Fry, also from a Quaker background, Penrose expanded the public understanding of art in England, having a confidence that stemmed from a legacy of dissent, both men having a readiness to stand apart from mass opinion and trust the evidence of their own experiences. It was in fact Fry who persuaded the young Penrose that he should take up art and study in Paris, which eventually he did, after a stint at the tail end of the First World War as an ambulance driver and after completing his studies at Cambridge (first in history, then architecture).

After a puritanical upbringing, Paris proved liberating. Penrose left behind 'the well-ordered life, soft carpets, fat woolly cats, porridge, roast beef for Sunday lunch and family prayers' and 'with a small allowance in my pocket I was born again'.[43] He studied under André Lhote and met the artist Janko Varda, who introduced him to Cassis. There, in 1923, he bought a boat and a house – the Villa des Mimosas – and constructed a studio in its garden. Very organized in everything he did, he was less confident in his management of personal relationships. He lost his inhibitions in relation to women after Varda took him to a brothel, and then met the beautiful and mysterious poet Valentine Boué, with whom he became infatuated. They soon married but were not entirely happy, and they later became estranged. In appearance Penrose, in photograph after photograph, seems a model of conventional English reserve; yet he made friends with other artists easily, and through his friendship with Max Ernst moved swiftly into the dangerous heart of the surrealist movement.

In preparation for the International Surrealist Exhibition, Gascoyne and Penrose returned to England to identify a nucleus of interested people. They also needed to set up an organizing committee, as well an advisory committee in France. There was certainly evidence of surrealist activity in England before the 1936 exhibition took place. John Banting had shared an exhibition with John Bigge at Lucy Wertheim's gallery in 1931 in which some of Banting's figures were made surreal by blood-red veins running across the surface of their skin. In 1932 Paul Nash had begun painting *Harbour and Room*, which was later included in the International Surrealist Exhibition: it yoked together the image of the sea and a boat entering harbour with a view of a room, its striped wallpaper asserting a control and order about to be subverted by the sea and boat. Nash, with Eileen Agar, had also been on

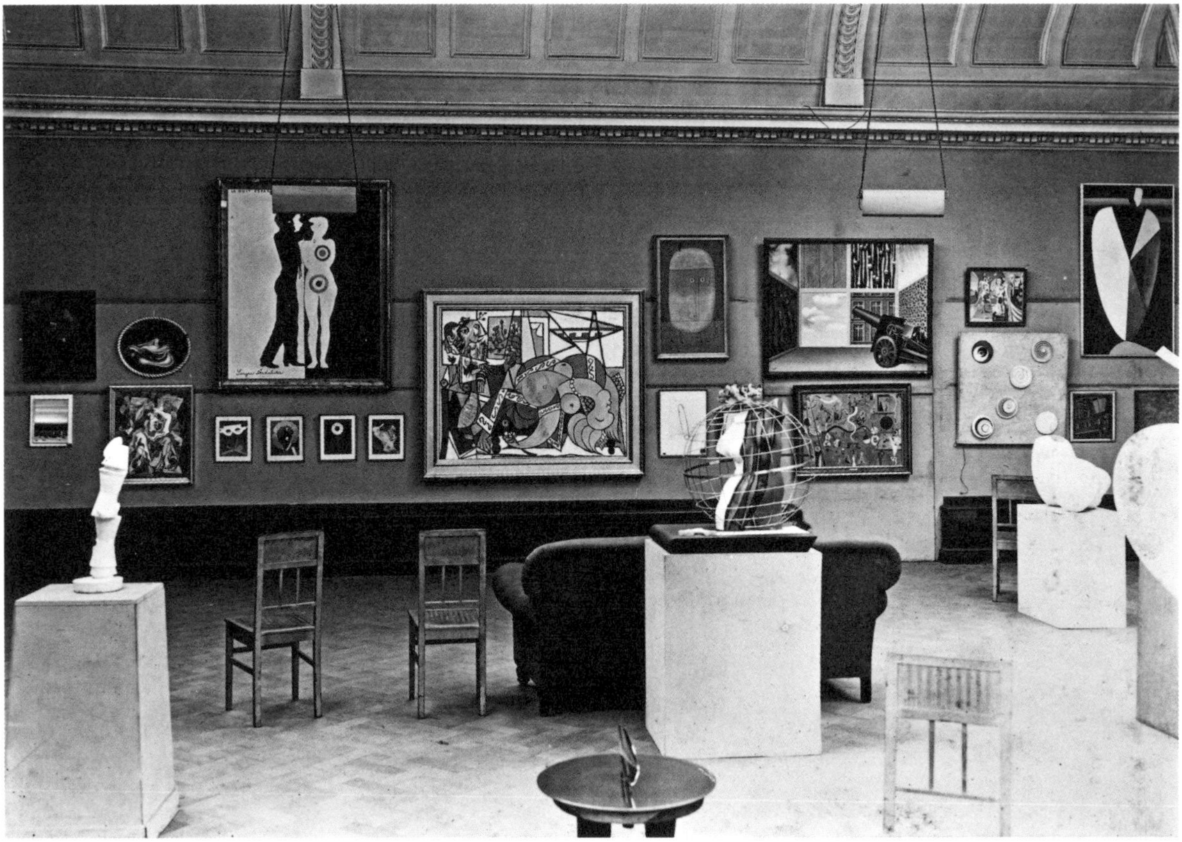

The International Surrealist Exhibition, 1936.

the lookout for 'strange' objects, much admired by surrealists, whose emphasis on dreams and dreaming had been noted in literary form by Humphrey Jennings and Julian Trevelyan while working on a magazine titled *Experiment.*

Penrose and Gascoyne chose as the venue for the exhibition the New Burlington Galleries in Burlington Gardens, off Bond Street. It was in the heart of the West End and it was available to rent; however, it was not a place that figured largely in the mind of the public. Its two large rooms were on the third floor of the building and had to be reached by means of a lift; Penrose soon concluded that the rooms were more often frequented by cats than by people.

A false rumour that the exhibition would only last nine days may explain in part why it received a thousand visitors a day and on the opening night caused traffic jams in Bond Street and Piccadilly. A crowd of 1,150 people squeezed into the galleries to hear the spokesperson for surrealism, André Breton, give the opening speech. Minor distractions included Dylan Thomas offering boiled string in teacups and enquiring whether visitors wanted it weak or strong, while a 'Surrealist phantom' (Sheila Legge) wandered through the crowd in a long white satin gown, her face obscured by a veil of roses, clutching a dummy leg in one hand and a raw pork chop in the other. Best known of all is the story of Salvador Dalí, who, with the help of the wealthy aesthete and collector Edward James, had gone to Seibe Gorman & Co. to acquire a diving suit with a very old-fashioned and heavy bubble helmet that had to be screwed down to keep it in place. He arrived at the exhibition wearing this, with two borzois on a leash in one hand and a billiard cue in the other. This last may have saved his life, as it soon became apparent that Dalí was about to expire from too much heat and too little air. While someone went urgently to look for a spanner, Edward James managed to prise open the helmet's front port with the billiard cue.

Chiefly what made the event memorable was a spectacular display of surrealist painting and sculpture together with Oceanic, African and American objects, amounting to 392 items in all. The walls were hung in places two or three rows deep. A huge Man Ray painting of a pair of red lips floating over a landscape surmounted one doorway, and everywhere there were works of art which to a greater or lesser degree demonstrated the surrealists' ability to jar the mind and set it dreaming. T. S. Eliot toured the exhibition in the company of Read and became obsessed with Meret Oppenheim's teacup, saucer and spoon, objects normally associated with refreshment but here found lined with fur. Eileen Agar's *Angel of Anarchy*, a head made up of composite materials and blinded by the bandanna covering its face, also upset rational expectations and released the imagination.

Agar, who shared with Paul Nash a fascination with found objects, claimed she had not thought of herself as a surrealist until invited to take part in this exhibition, although she had lived in Paris during part of the 1920s and was familiar with aspects of surrealism. She was certainly drawn into the surrealist world by the exhibition and continued to explore its imaginative power, but at the time she thought its intensity and brilliance impossible to sustain.

Despite the mockery and protest it aroused, the exhibition firmly established surrealism in the public mind and attracted new artists into its fold. Nevertheless, ferocious arguments abounded, especially after Herbert Read and Hugh Sykes Davies promoted surrealism as a reaffirmation of the romantic principle in art and claimed Coleridge and Wordsworth as its ancestors, to which even a surrealist supporter, Humphrey Jennings, objected. The works themselves offered dialogic play on both the real and the romantic and gave rise to Read's deliberately sensational speech, which began: 'The work of art is to be judged, in the first place, not by its physique, but by its imaginative scope, its intimate revelations, its surprising incoherence, its super-reality.' Then came a warning: 'Do not judge this movement kindly. It is not just another amusing stunt. It is defiant – the desperate act of men too profoundly convinced of the rottenness of our civilisation to want to save a shred of its respectability.'[44] English critics, with their habitual dislike of foreign importations, took Read's command literally and damned the show, amid widespread public suspicion that surrealism was in fact less desperate than romantic.

David Gascoyne in the introduction to his *Short History of Surrealism*, published the same year, proved a helpful guide: 'It is the avowed aim of the Surrealist movement to reduce and finally dispose altogether of the flagrant contradictions that exist between dream and waking life, the "unreal" and the "real", the unconscious and the conscious, and thus to make of what has hitherto been regarded as the special domain of poets, the acknowledged common property of us all.'[45] Gascoyne himself had been deeply impressed by the writings and theories of André Breton, and he had joined the surrealist movement on England's behalf even before he and Penrose met on a pavement in Paris. Eileen Agar, while living in Paris, had initially thought the surrealists to be a 'proud, elegant and unforgettable group'.[46] But in London in 1936, while listening to Breton's speech, she was moved by the conviction with which he claimed surrealism to be an international organism with the potential to become the absolute core of a world consciousness. She also noticed that he tended to regard painting as 'a lamentable expedient',[47] a secondary means of communicating surrealist ideas which were best expressed in poetry.

If the French surrealists were more concerned with philosophy, psychology and politics than with the visual arts, in England the situation was reversed, with its visual impact rated more highly than the political manoeuvrings of Breton and his group. Yet Breton was convinced that the London exhibition of 1936 marked the

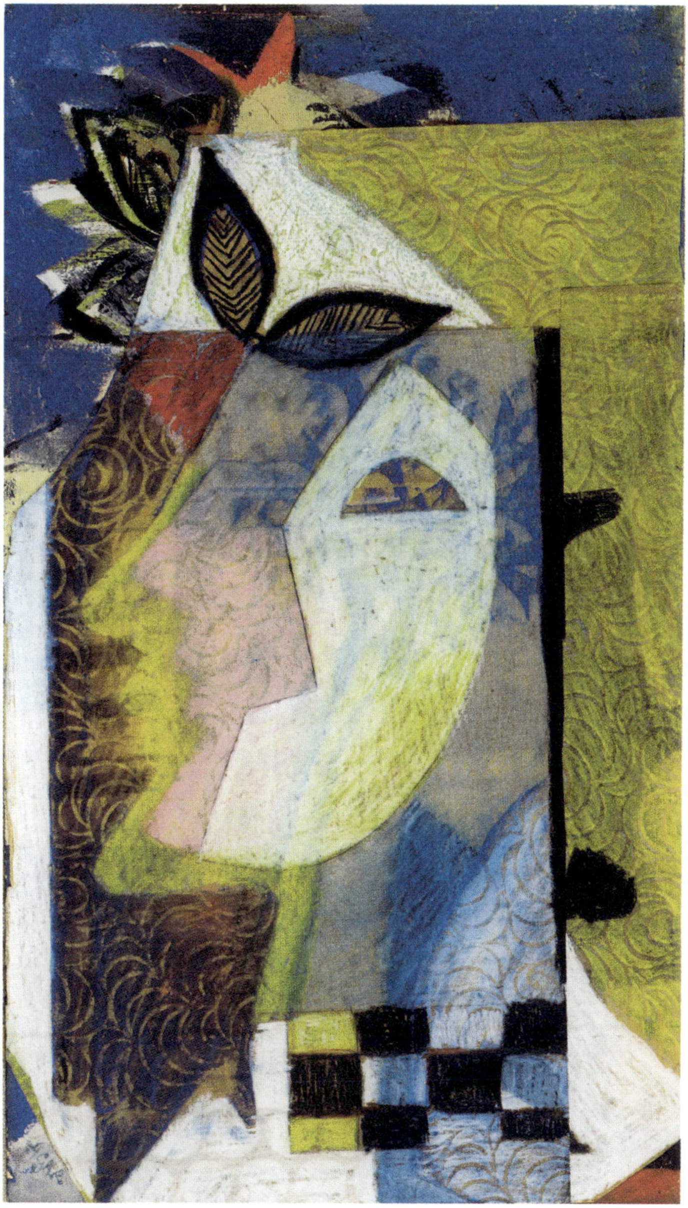

Eileen Agar, *Guardian of Memories*,
oil, crayon and collage on board, 1938.

high point of surrealist influence, and he held up England as the great future hope – the launching pad of world enlightenment. In an imperfect world, Breton thought England the country that came nearest to disinterested truth and justice; yet surrealism in England remained always more of a social grouping than a unifying belief, in Paul Nash's words, 'a state of being and behaviour'.[48]

Valentine Penrose was not entirely taken with the surrealists when Roland, initially through his friendship with Paul Eluard and Max Ernst, began to draw her into the group. She hated the sadism behind a story that Ernst told about a seal thrown into boiling water so that its reactions could be observed. With hindsight, it seems that Valentine had not only gynaecological problems but also psychological difficulties. When she and Roland joined a party of artists, which included Picasso, at Mougins in the Riviera, where sunbathing and beachcombing were the order of the day, Roland felt himself to be inside 'a unforgettable dream of marvels';[49] but in the photographs, Valentine looks pained. Eventually their marriage was dissolved on the grounds of non-consummation. A year or two later Penrose met an American with a remarkable zest for life, Lee Miller.

With this 'Hellenic beauty...full of *élan vital*', in Eileen Agar's words, Penrose again stepped onto an emotional rollercoaster. His immediate infatuation with Miller's beauty suggests that he may have bought into a surrealist ideal of woman that prevented their relationship from deepening. A belief in the need for sexual freedom, which led to a great deal of wife-swapping among the surrealists, seemed necessary to both but undeniably troubled their marriage. Nevertheless, Penrose cared for Miller deeply.

He cared also for Picasso, who, Penrose once observed, seemed to charge everyone's emotional batteries. Although Penrose had by the 1930s become a competent artist in a surrealist vein, he also had a very sharp eye for the work of others. After seeing a reproduction of Picasso's *Femme nue couché au soleil sur la plage*, he was left with a 'longing to see and if possible own the original'.[50] Accompanied by Eluard, he went to see the artist in Paris to ask if he could buy it. Picasso agreed, but said they would have to fetch it from Boisgeloup, his country property in Normandy. Within a few minutes the artist's chauffeur had been summoned and all present, including Picasso and his son, set off.

The picture was smaller than Penrose had expected, but it remained his 'dream painting' and marked his first acquisition of a work by this great artist. The experience appears to have started him on a new wave of buying: James King claims that within a short space of time Penrose assembled the most important collection of cubist and surrealist paintings in England, among them two masterpieces now in the Tate collection – Max Ernst's *Célèbes* and Picasso's *The Weeping Woman*. He continued to do a great deal to promote modern art, becoming in the late 1940s a formative influence behind the creation of the Institute of Contemporary Arts (ICA), and also bringing to the attention of the Tate's trustees Henri Matisse's collage *The Snail*, which the Gallery acquired in 1962..

But it could be argued that Penrose's major achievement is the way he reconciled England to Picasso. It was he who arranged for *Guernica* to be brought to Britain in 1938. For the ICA's second exhibition, '40,000 Years of Modern Art: A Comparison of Primitive and Modern', held in 1948, he persuaded Alfred Barr at MoMA, New York, to loan *Les Demoiselles d'Avignon*. This Barr did out of gratitude to Penrose for lending some of his own Picassos to MoMA during the war. Much concern was expressed as to how such an outstandingly important work should travel, shipping being chosen over the potential loss or damage if it travelled by air. But when this enormous painting reached the exhibition venue (the Academy Cinema in Oxford Street) it turned out that Penrose had miscalculated the width of its curved concrete staircase. Fortunately a bomb crater still existed outside a corner of the building, which was below ground. This made possible the removal of a strip of bricks to create an emergency entrance for *Les Demoiselles*.

Penrose's friendship with Picasso enabled him to embark in the 1950s on the first biography of this artist. *Picasso: Life and Work* came out in 1958, to great éclat. It was followed by the first full-length retrospective of Picasso's work, curated by Penrose for the Tate Gallery, in 1960. 'The effect is stunning: it is as if we had never seen him at all,' wrote Lawrence Gowing.[51] Four years later Penrose negotiated with Picasso, on behalf of the Tate Gallery, the acquisition of his *Three Dancers*, which, with Matisse's *The Snail*, was the most important modern purchase by an English national museum since Seurat's *Bathers, Asnières*. Formerly the butt of jokes and snide reviews in England, Picasso had now fully arrived, his fame, if still contentious, now unassailable.

CHAPTER 12

THE SPANISH CIVIL WAR, MONDRIAN IN LONDON AND NEO-ROMANTICISM

In July 1936, shortly after the International Surrealist Exhibition had opened, the *Left Review* published a satirical drawing by James Boswell showing well-to-do visitors emerging from the lift at the New Burlington Galleries to see this strange, disturbing exhibition. Across the advancing figures is juxtaposed a fragment of type, reminding viewers of Herbert Read's warning speech at the opening event. In this and other drawings for the *Left Review*, Boswell's socialist stance is underscored by his awareness of George Grosz's graphic style, used to attack German political and military elites. One of these, showing a single male member of Britain's ruling class, achieves a biting indictment of this class enemy even before you notice the brief caption underneath: 'Six-figure income'.[1]

Although the *Left Review* lasted only four years (1934–8), it enjoyed a close association with the Artists International Association (AIA). All three of the *Review*'s main illustrators – Boswell, James Fitton and James Holland – were present at Misha Black's Charlotte Street studio in 1933 for the first official meeting of the AIA (originally known as 'Artists International'). The early history of this group is slightly blurred by differing accounts of its formation and the influences upon it, but its commitment to activism was visible from the start. Although its overarching aim, as stated in 1934, was 'The International Unity of Artists against Imperialist War on the Soviet Union, Fascism and Colonial Oppression', its immediate activities concerned issues of the day, strikes, elections, unemployment and the Hunger Marches. Much talent and energy lay behind the making of cartoons, posters, banners and mimeographed newspapers, many of which were produced during evening classes in lithography taught by Fitton at the Central School of Arts and Crafts in

Southampton Row. In this early period there were also fortnightly discussions on 'Communism and Art' fortified by the first-hand experiences of Cliff Rower and Pearl Binder, two members who had worked in Russia – the latter having been greatly impressed by the sheer amount of work available there for the graphic artist and the encouragement given to women artists.

But what initially might have seemed a youthful left-wing protest group, firmly committed to the working-class movement and enjoying links with the Marx Library and the Marxist Club of London University, soon began to attract a wider audience and membership owing to problems at home and abroad. For instance, in October 1932 the National Unemployed Workers' Movement had organized a Hunger March that brought a 150,000-strong meeting to Trafalgar Square. A speech was made demanding the abolition of the means test on unemployment benefits and an end to the restriction on pay to sailors, soldiers and policemen. The government hit back by passing the Incitement to Disaffection Act of 1934, which in turn led to mass protest among the liberal intelligentsia and the founding of the National Council for Civil Liberties. In the unfolding of this development, the AIA's first publication, a cyclostyled book titled *Hunger Marches* (1934) containing satirical drawings by Boswell, Fitton and Holland, played its part.

The year 1935 saw an alteration to the organization's title, the introduction of the word 'Association' suggesting a broader and less specific political stance. It also simplified its mission statement – 'The AIA stands for Unity of Artists against Fascism and War and the Suppression of Culture' – which touched more readily an existing nerve, owing to the advancing threat of fascism in Europe. In this way the AIA followed what was happening in other places on the Continent, the move towards a Popular Front. When the AIA launched an exhibition titled 'Artists against Fascism and War' this same year, it pulled in work by a range of prominent artists: Eric Gill, Augustus John, Laura Knight and Charles Cundall (who contributed a painting of the Durham Miners' Gala) as well as Hepworth, Nicholson, Piper and Moholy-Nagy, among others. Further contributions came from artists living in France, Poland, Holland and Russia, and six thousand visitors paid three pence each to see what was on show. One section, devoted to photographs of working-class life, included the work of Edith Tudor-Hart, an Austrian–British photographer who had trained at the Bauhaus and had a knack for getting inside impoverished lives without patronizing or sentimentalizing her subjects. Socially engaged subjects also figured prominently among the prints and drawings in the exhibition and inevitably, the AIA's cultural and social interests reignited interest in realism. This same year James Holland sent a letter to the Foreign Committee of the Moscow Union of Soviet Artists, explaining his art: 'I want to show something of the real life of this

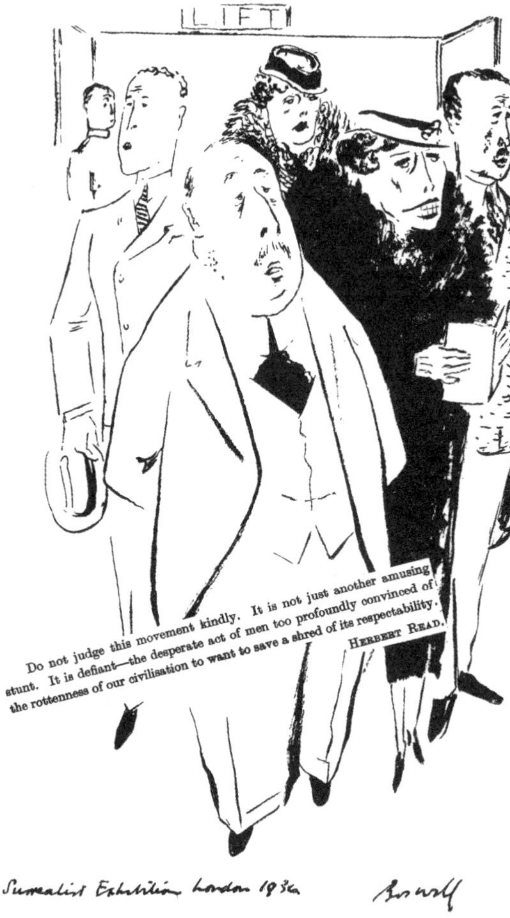

James Boswell, satirical drawing for the *Left Review*, July 1936.

country which goes on in the city suburbs, industrial towns, factories, shipyards, coalfields, shops and offices. This unfashionable material has only been used when falsified by a spurious romanticism. The English tradition of realism has been lost for more than a century. I want to show the chaotic life under an inadequate and decaying social structure.'[2]

On 18 July 1936, soon after the International Surrealism Exhibition ended, the right-wing Nationalist insurgents led by Franco executed a coup against Spain's left-wing, democratically elected Republican government. At the time, many in Britain saw this as an unmistakeable war about fascism versus democracy. George Orwell recollected in *Homage to Catalonia*: 'When the fighting broke out on 18 July it is probable that every anti-Fascist in Europe felt a thrill of hope'[3] – but disappointment followed, first with the Non-Intervention Agreement signed in August 1936, and then with the realization that the war, being faction-driven and full of opposing

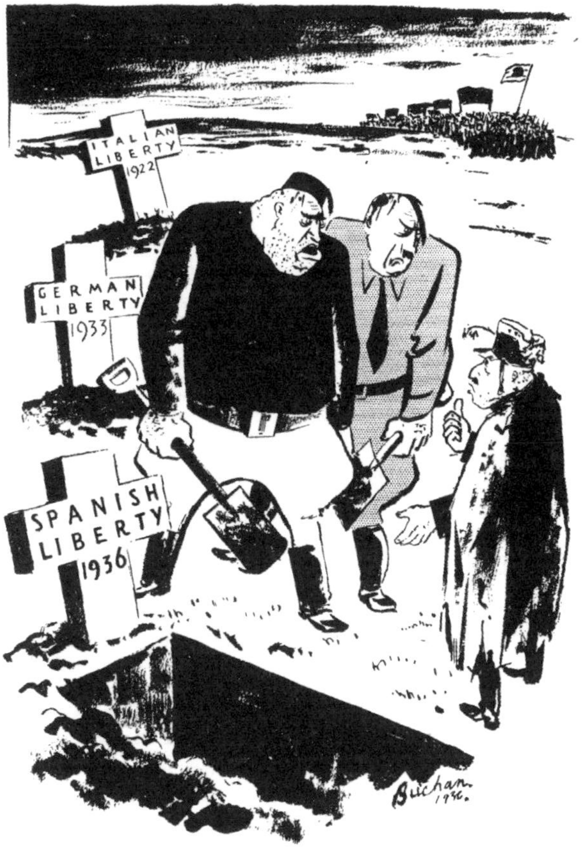

'What! Not murdered the Spanish workers yet?' BUCHAN

Buchan (James Boswell), satirical drawing for the *Left Review*, September 1936.

ideologies, could not sustain grand ideals. However, in 1936 its link with the rise of fascism was very much to the fore in people's minds. Boswell encapsulated this in another satirical drawing for the *Left Review*, signed 'Buchan' (an abbreviation of his middle name, Buchanan, more usually used when he did cartoons for the *Daily Worker*). It shows three graves, marked 'Italian Liberty 1922', 'German Liberty 1933' and 'Spanish Liberty 1936'. The last is still open, and a diminutive Franco addresses the grave-diggers Hitler and Mussolini with the words, 'What! Not Murdered the Spanish Workers Yet!'

It is estimated that some 500 British people went out to Spain to fight in the Civil War. Among them were members of the AIA, including Maro Rowley and Christopher Caudwell, both of whom were killed, as well as Clive Branson and Hugh Slater. Another member, Felicia Browne, was already in Spain when the fighting began. Having recently taken a course in self-defence, she went into a communist militia office and demanded to be enlisted to fight on the Saragossa front, on the grounds that she was a member of the London Communist Party and could fight as well as any man. After joining a communist militia in August 1936, she was one of a party sent to blow up a rebel munitions train. When they came under fire from the Nationalists she went forward to aid a wounded Italian. The rebels turned their fire on the two of them and Browne was killed outright. Her comrades had to leave her body behind, but retrieved what possessions were on her person; these included a sketchbook filled with drawings of her companions in the militia, which eventually formed a significant part of her memorial exhibition held in Frith Street in London. Duncan Grant wrote a foreword to the catalogue based on his responses to her drawings.

Money gained from the sale of works in this exhibition, and from a memorial book of Browne's drawings published by Lawrence & Wishart, was given to Spanish Relief and Spanish Medical Aid. Her death prompted one of her friends, Nan Youngman, to join the AIA, and this may be true of others too, for in memory Browne became, as Simon Martin notes, 'a potent symbol of the fight against Fascism'.[4] This would have helped spur on the AIA's many fundraising activities on behalf of Spain. Its most memorable event was that held in June 1937 at the Albert Hall to raise funds for Basque children, many of whom had been orphaned by the war. The programme cover carried a drawing by Picasso, made in preparation for *Guernica*. One highlight of the evening was to be a live recording of Paul Robeson from Moscow, but at the last moment he telegraphed the impresario C. B. Cochran that he was flying back, 'and he appeared in person to a tumultuous reception'.[5]

There was also a picture auction in which was sold a Picasso drawing of a weeping woman that Vanessa Bell's younger son, Quentin, had managed to obtain from the artist. Three weeks later, Quentin's brother Julian Bell was killed by shrapnel while working as an ambulance driver in Spain; when his mother received this news by telephone, she let out a cry which the workman who heard it never forgot. Another cry can be found in Virginia Woolf's *Three Guineas*, published in 1938. Bemused by multiple opinions on politics and on war, and troubled by the photographs of dead children that arrived in her post as propaganda against the Nationalists before the attack on Madrid, Woolf makes the narrator say: 'As we listen to the voices we seem to hear an infant crying in the night, the black night that now covers Europe, and with no language but a cry, Ay, ay, ay, ay.... But it is not a new cry, it is a very old cry.'[6] This cry became in Picasso's *Guernica* a howl of protest and rage at the total warfare that destroyed Guernica in broad daylight on a market day, when women and children had come into town clutching animals and produce. Looking at this painting in 1937, Myfanwy Piper observed that Picasso had reset the artistic agenda by 'purging into formality' a difficult subject and demonstrating that 'unbearably violent emotion' could become 'a formal symbol for art to-day'.[7]

Guernica was brought to England in the autumn of 1938, along with over sixty of Picasso's preparatory drawings for it. It was shown first in the West End, at the New Burlington Galleries, and then at the Whitechapel Art Gallery in the East End, where it attracted a larger audience and came under the auspices of the Stepney Trades Council and the local Labour Party. At the opening on 31 December 1938, the leader of the Labour opposition, Clement Attlee, sat with others on the platform immediately in front of Picasso's great painting. A scrap of film exists showing him making a speech in which the painting is claimed as an image of the coming struggle – which Britain could not avoid – against the forces of fascism. By then, it was clear that the painting had come to signify far more than the bombing of a specific Basque town, and indeed Picasso, while gaining imaginative energy from specific texts and images about its ruination, had made no attempt to depict the actual bombing or the actual place. Instead his memorialization of the event aims at something very different. Herbert Read realized this when he wrote in the *London Bulletin* in October 1938: 'Not only Guernica, but Spain; not only Spain, but Europe, is symbolised in this allegory.'[8] It seems that even before the start of the Second World War, Picasso's *Guernica* had become an international symbol of protest against oppression and destruction. A group of patrons helped make *Guernica*'s arrival in London possible; a list of their names, including that of Virginia Woolf, can be seen down the right-hand side of the poster advertising the event.

For many years, cultural perspectives on the Spanish Civil War focused mostly on the politics of engagement among writers. Stephen Spender even went so far as to refer to it as 'the poets' war'.[9] Aside from *Guernica*, shown in London and Manchester in 1938–9, images associated with this conflict received scant attention before 2014, when the Pallant House Gallery mounted the exhibition 'Conscience and Conflict: British Artists and the Spanish Civil War'. This revealed how the war and the humanitarian disaster it created aroused a deep and widespread response on the part of artists. Even Sir Frank Brangwyn, RA, from the safety of his Ditchling studios in Sussex, worked his way through various studies of dispossessed women and children, trying out various compositions before arriving at a touchingly dense image of children pressing up against a Madonna-like figure with a toddler in her arms. He used the white line method to allow the woman to form a beacon of light amid the surrounding darkness and turned to the scraperboard technique to achieve this. It was afterwards converted into a lithographic poster, advertising the non-political and impartial General Relief Fund for Women and Children in Spain. More modern in appearance and minimal in the means used is Edward McKnight Kauffer's

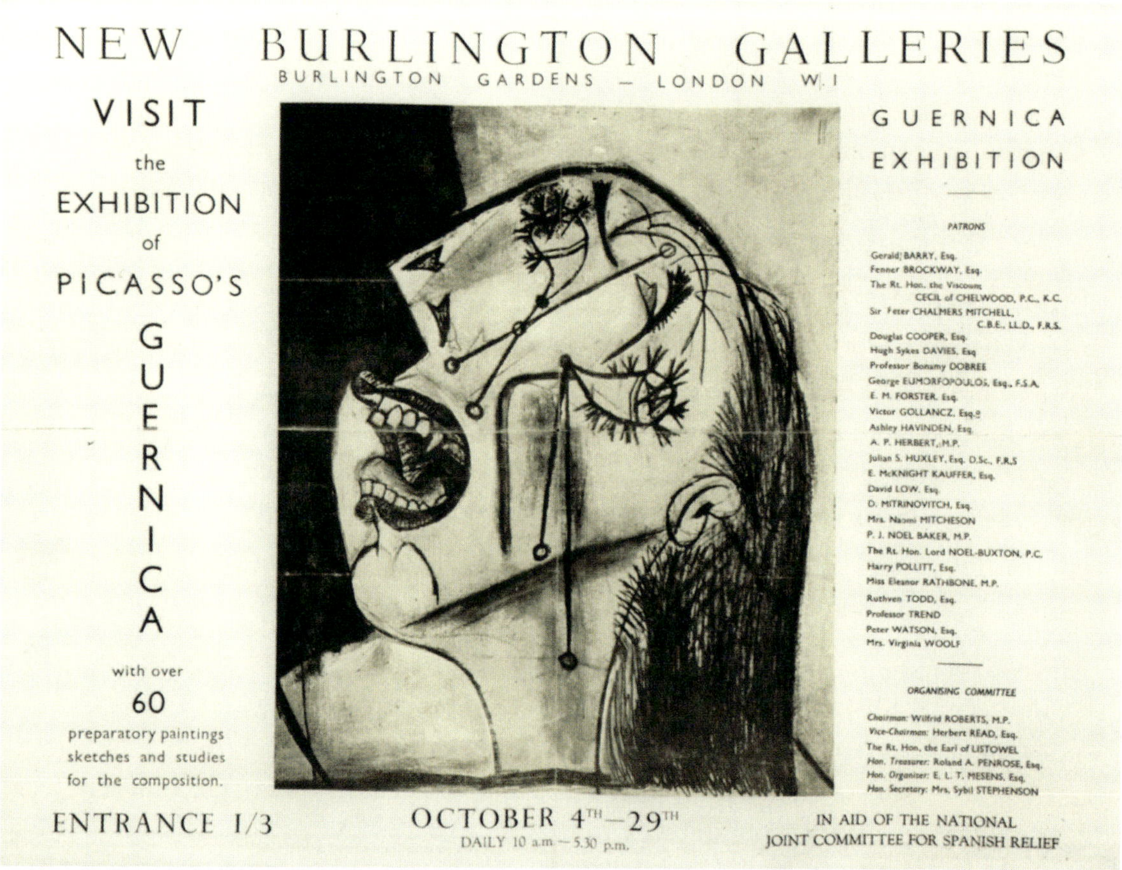

Poster for the exhibition of Picasso's *Guernica* at the New Burlington Galleries, 1938.

poster *Help Wounded Human Beings: Help to Send Medical Aid to Spain*; although the man's head in this image is based on El Greco's *Self-Portrait as St Luke* (*c.* 1604) in the Sacristy of Toledo Cathedral, its pathos chimes well with the command 'Help Wounded Human Beings'.

Another name associated with posters for the Spanish Civil War is that of Felicity Ashbee, whose more garish style gave such fierce urgency to the message in her designs that the London Passenger Transport Board refused to display her posters, regarding them as too political, even though they were intended to benefit the non-partisan National Joint Committee for Spanish Relief. Ashbee's roots lay in the arts and crafts movement, for she was the daughter of C. R. Ashbee, founder of the Guild of Handicraft, which he moved out of East London to Chipping Camden in Gloucestershire. She herself became an art teacher and graphic artist as well as an ardent supporter of the Communist Party.

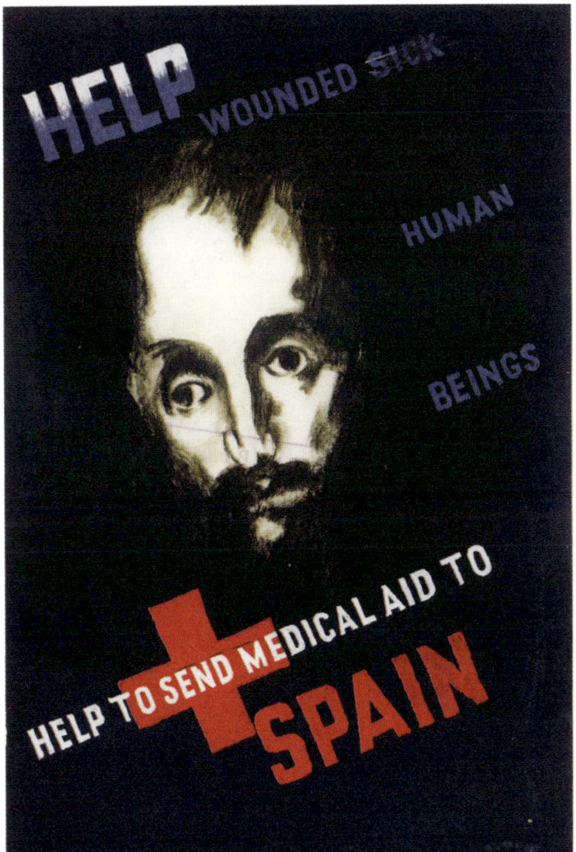

Edward McKnight Kauffer, *Help Wounded Human Beings: Help to Send Medical Aid to Spain*, bodycolour, 1937.

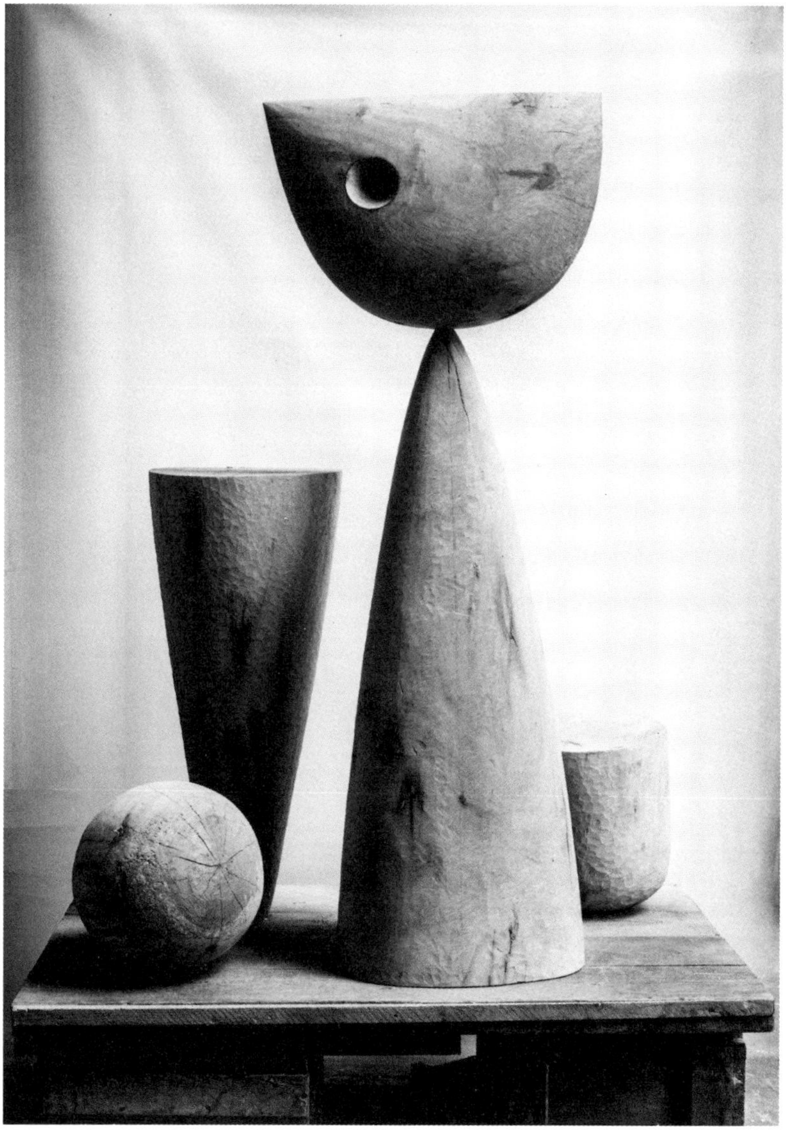

Barbara Hepworth, *Project: Monument to the Spanish War*, 1938–9 (unfinished).

Artists also found an outlet for their response to the Spanish Civil War by hand-painting messages and images onto empty billboards, often attracting a crowd of watchers as they did so. Much of this work was inevitably ephemeral. Nevertheless, the Spanish Civil War is today regarded as a high point for the making of protest or propaganda art in England. Not all artists, of course, were on the side of the Republicans; supporters of the Nationalists, as Simon Martin argues, were often both artistically and politically conservative – 'suspicious not only of avant-garde art, but also concerned by the spread of communism from Russia and by reports of anti-Catholic violence and destruction of historic artworks and churches by left-wing anarchists'.[10]

Among the range of artefacts produced is Barbara Hepworth's subtly affecting *Project: Monument to the Spanish War* (1938–9). It presents a group of five carved wooden objects, left bare and unpolished, with the mark of the chisel still visible here and there on their mottled surfaces. A falling and rising movement is suggested by the way one near-cylindrical shape narrows towards its base while nearby a similar form begins with a broad base and tapers sharply as it rises to a point, on which balances a smaller oblong shape, like a half-filled pocket. Into this has been carved a hole that acts like an all-seeing, symbolic eye, holding all five forms in tension.

One of the most important experiences in Hepworth's formation as a sculptor had been her visit, while in Paris with Nicholson in 1932, to Brancusi's studio. Huge millstones sat on the floor and served as plinths for his sculptures: a head, a fish or a bird in flight, made in marble, brass or wood. Each work depended on complete unity between idea, form and material in order to express Brancusi's conceptions. Hepworth later recollected: 'To me, bred in a more northern climate, where the approach to sculpture has appeared fettered by the gravity of monuments to the dead – it was a special revelation to see this work which belonged to the living joy of spontaneous, active and elemental forms of sculpture.'[11] Her own *Project: Monument to the Spanish War* achieves the gravity of monuments, but with simple elemental forms. It never proceeded beyond the maquette, yet it expresses her faith in art's agency, the belief that the language of shape and form can cool and calm, as well as excite, the senses, producing an equipoise that keeps hatred and violence at bay. Hepworth was not apolitical, but no hint of partisan politics enters this carved maquette. Instead, the sculpture seems to act as a homage to Spain, rather than loyalty to one warring side or the other. Sadly, the work was lost during the Second World War.

One artist greatly stimulated by the Spanish Civil War was Edward Burra (1905–76). Having a great love of Spain, he learnt its language so that he could read Spanish poets and novelists in the original. He especially admired the morbidity in Spanish painting as found in the work of Zurbarán, Velázquez, El Greco and especially Goya, but also in the art of José Gutiérrez-Solana, who, although well funded by his father, specialized in misery. As a young man at art school in Madrid, Solana had haunted the slums and watched the behaviour of the crowds that flocked to El Rastro, the city's flea market. He made frequent trips to Andalucia and other places, making sketches of the carnivals he saw and the hospitals, cemeteries and bordellos he visited. After settling in Madrid in 1917 he became a notable figure within artistic, literary and intellectual circles, gaining widespread fame with his epic scenes of grief and horror painted in a harsh, abrupt, expressive manner.

Burra's enthusiasm for Solana and his dark subjects encouraged his own tendency towards an exaggerated mode of expression. He was also aware that contemporary Spanish writers saw in Goya's art a reflection of Spain's fundamental leaning towards violence and fantasy. Soon after Mario Praz's *The Romantic Agony* (1933) came out, Burra read it, engaging with its forceful argument that erotic sensibility, as well as the cult of devil worship and witchcraft, are key influences within the history of Romantic literature.

John Rothenstein, author of the first book on Burra, was astonished to discover that most of this artist's pictures, often full of menace and intimations of conflict, had been painted in a solid mid-Victorian house in which all the furniture was comfortable and reassuring and the drawing room was hung with Victorian watercolours. Edward had been born in South Kensington, but his father, a solicitor, had retired early and moved the family to Playden outside Rye; this remained Edward's home base for much of his life. His education had been cut short at the age of thirteen when severe arthritis and pernicious anaemia set in. Later in life he also suffered from a hereditary affliction, an enlarged spleen. He lived with almost constant pain and could not stand for long periods of time; when painting, he used mostly watercolour or gouache and only very rarely oil, his twisted hands making it difficult for him to hold a brush.

Burra often pasted together sheets of fine Whatman watercolour paper in order to create large-scale works in watercolours, and he appears to have had the entire painting in his mind's eye right from the start. He worked with his paper placed flat on a table or sometimes the floor, up in an attic room that had nothing of the ordered composure found elsewhere in the house. Here he huddled down amid piles of books, magazines and novels in several languages as well as photographs, reproductions, Victorian scrapbooks, newspaper cuttings and a gramophone, as if to demonstrate Nietzsche's famous saying: 'One must still have chaos within oneself to be able to give birth to a dancing star.' In this way he introduced a new breadth into watercolour painting, while also bringing to his work a high degree of finish and a miniaturist's love of detail.

Burra's primary interest, as Andrew Causey has observed, was 'human energy and style'.[12] He loved the world outside his own body and was able to forget about pain while working with wit and imagination (and sometimes help from magazine illustrations) on pictures that mingled satire with fantasy. He was also a visual raconteur, noticing sly looks as well as the excrescences of fashion, his eye hungrily enjoying street scenes and the inhabitants of snack bars, dance halls, restaurants and sleazy cafés, or the coagulation of types in and around Minuit Chanson in Paris, where for 25 centimes you could listen through a tube to a song of your choosing. Burra found subjects wherever he went, whether to Bordighera with his mother in 1925 or Toulon and Marseilles with Paul Nash in 1930. Nash, impressed by Burra's breadth of observation, included him in Unit One and called him the modern Hogarth, but noted his refusal to engage in the preaching that informs Hogarth's 'modern moral subject'.[13]

Wyndham Lewis was, directly or indirectly, a shaping influence: Burra bought most of his books soon after they came out. Both men tested themselves against the surface of things rather than hidden meanings, and when Lewis announced in 1930 'the only thing that interests me is *the shell*',[14] Burra, despite his interest in literary associations, might well have agreed. Nothing, however, was beyond his imagination, its liberation encouraged by the example of surrealism. Above all, Causey explains, 'Burra liked life on the margins...natural vitality unawed by social conventions...the dandy and the tramp, both displaced types far from the centre of everyday acceptability.'[15]

Although to an extent cut off from life by his illnesses or sequestered in his attic studio, he created a tumultuous world and was not by nature a recluse. At Chelsea Polytechnic (later Chelsea College of Art), where he had studied (1921–3) before moving on to the Royal College of Art (1923–5), he gained a small gang of loyal friends. Among them were the dancer and choreographer William (Billie) Chappell and Clover de Pertinez, with whom Burra visited Spain in 1935. Another close friend was Barbara Ker-Seymer, who paired up with Olivia Wyndham, a society photographer and central figure within the 'wild young things' of the 1920s. From Wyndham, Ker-Seymer caught an interest in photography. She obtained a portable Baby Box camera, which enabled her to take impromptu shots from unexpected angles, thereby introducing a new informality and fluidity into photojournalism. She took hundreds of photographs, many in the company of Burra while they went round London together, and her use of the camera almost certainly encouraged his pleasure in the unexpected viewpoint when his personal style began to emerge

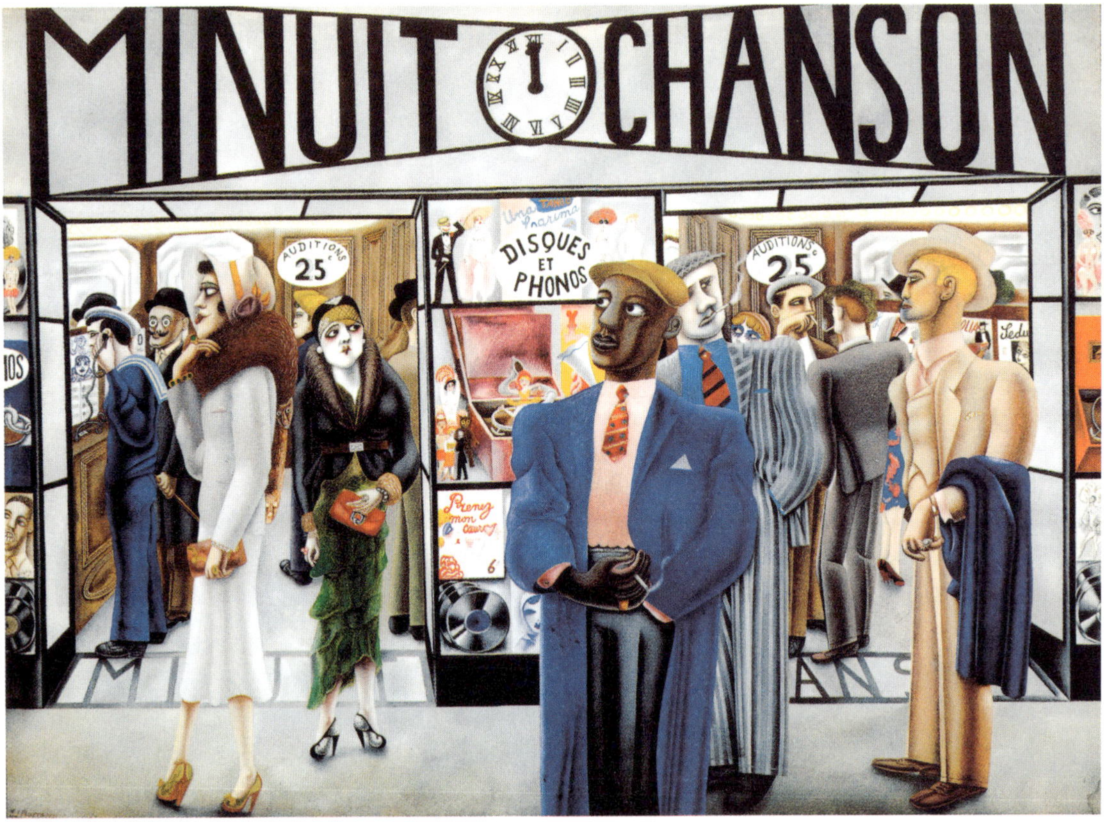

Edward Burra, *Minuit Chanson*,
watercolour heightened with bodycolour, 1931.

in the late 1920s.[16] Further affirmation of their affinity is found in Burra's painting *Minuit Chanson* (1931), its precision and brilliance comparable with medieval book illustration. It belonged to Ker-Seymer, and remained with her for many years.

Burra had made his first visit to Spain in 1933. It coincided with an outbreak of church-burning, part of an eruption of anti-clerical violence that had come about in the wake of the recent abolition of the monarchy. More life-enhancing that year had been his sudden departure for America, where he stayed for five months. He travelled with the theatre designer Sophie Fedorovich and Olivia Wyndham, the latter arranging for him to stay in Harlem for the first part of his visit with the famous African American actress Edna Lloyd Thomas. Burra had left for America without informing his parents where he was going or for how long; his stable home base had, paradoxically, enabled him to develop a liking for raffish parties and an anarchic lifestyle. But for someone who had been collecting jazz records since his student days, it was still more exciting to find himself living in the place where the Harlem Renaissance had begun in the 1920s, giving to African Americans a new sense of pride and identity. It was here that, for the first time, Black experience had entered the realm of American cultural history. Burra's keen responsiveness to what he saw and experienced resulted in pictures of Harlem that make him one of the first English artists to engage deeply with the lives of Black people. Some of the erotic excitements he encountered are glimpsed in a letter he sent to Billie Chappell, after being taken to a nightclub at which the chief cabaret attraction was a Black male impersonator of Gloria Swanson.[17]

One of Burra's 1934 paintings shows a Black couple dancing. He used almost the same setting for *Dancing Skeletons* (1934), except that gallows appear in the background of the latter and the moon has a crudely drawn, mirthful face. Despite the replacement skeletons and the garish colours, this is not a particularly bitter painting, even if it acts as a reminder that the dance of life ends in death. But the hint of menace found in some of his work from the late 1920s gradually became more sinister, his interest in morbidity helping to explain Causey's claim that 'Spain dominated Burra's art in the late thirties'.[18]

His second visit to Spain, in 1935, took him to Madrid and Barcelona. In both places he frequented unsafe nightclubs and music halls: 'Like an insect or a small nocturnal creature, he possessed – or could assume – protective colouring, and settle unremarked in any kind of background.' So William Chappell observes, noting also his love of the *paso dobles*, flamenco singing and the rattle of heel boots and castanets, 'as well as the divine melancholy of the chords falling like golden rain from beneath the fingers of the guitarists, "A sound", Edward said, "to bring tears to your eyes, it's so beautiful."'[19] He returned to England in August owing to his father having

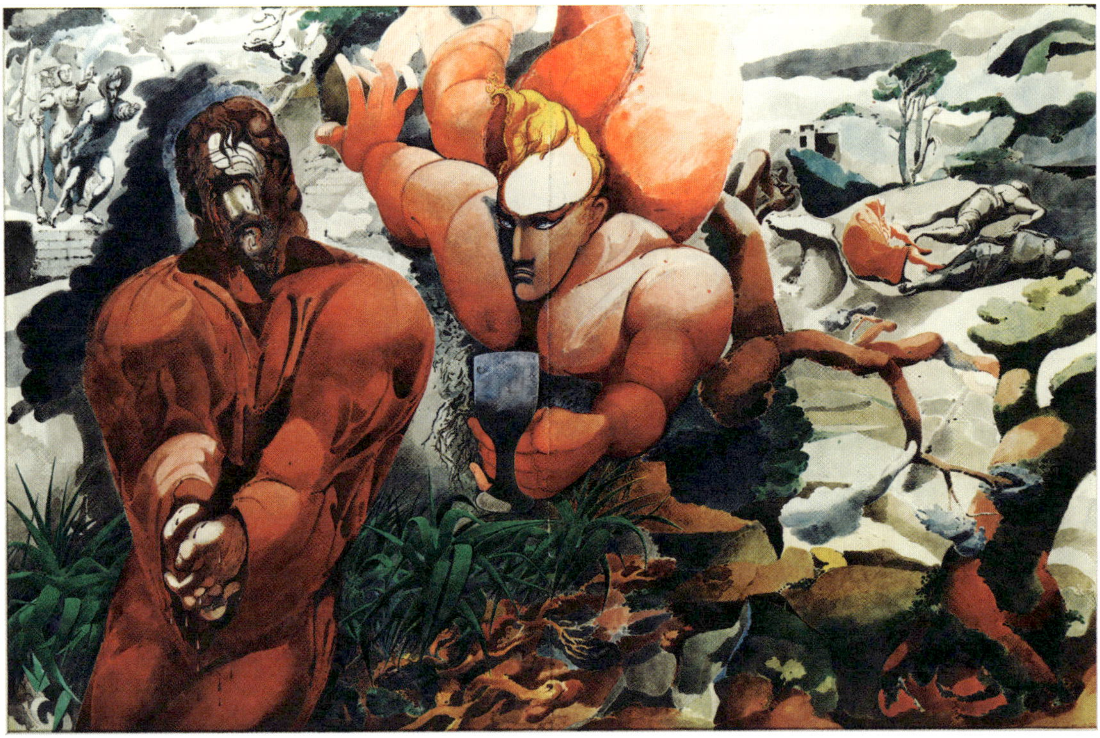

Edward Burra, *Agony in the Garden*,
watercolour, 1939.

fallen ill but resumed his colloquy in Spain in the spring of the following year, in search of further raw and vivid sensations; although he left it three months later owing to the increasing violence that preceded the Civil War.

Although Burra did not witness at first hand the war in Spain, it is very much an absent presence in his art for the next two to three years, the cruelty and destruction obliquely conveyed by soldiers and ruins, by a spectre or a watcher, a Beelzebub or, as he titles one painting, *A Prisoner of Fate*. After experiencing the baroque churches of Mexico City during a visit to Mexico in the first half of 1937, his own paintings begin to burgeon with baroque energy and a more manipulative handling of light, thereby conveying extreme emotion. Nowhere is this more clearly felt than in his *Agony in the Garden* (1938), an apocalyptic scene expressive of heightened drama. Almost certainly Burra would have known the two contemplative versions of this same subject, by Andrea Mantegna and Giovanni Bellini, in London's National Gallery. In contrast with these, his interpretation is more visceral, as well as innovative in the amount of attention given to the angel: it almost balances in visual importance the figure of Christ, whose eyes and hands sweat drops of blood in keeping with the description found in Luke 22:43–4: 'And there appeared an angel unto him from heaven, strengthening him. And being in an agony he prayed more earnestly: and his sweat was as it were great drops of blood falling down to the ground.' Although Burra painted several religious subjects in the late 1930s and again in the early 1950s, he had no religious affiliation and was by nature unlikely to submit himself to any institution or doctrinal belief. Instead, Christ's prayerful suffering makes eloquent the historical moment, already filled with an abundant awareness of the destructiveness of war and a presentiment of what was yet to come.

Clover de Pertinez tells us that Burra's main reason for wanting to travel to Spain in 1935 was to escape King George and Queen Mary's Silver Jubilee in May of that year. On boarding the night ferry at Newhaven, they were almost the only passengers, as everyone that spring seemed to be travelling in the opposite direction. This suited Burra. 'A la minoría siempre' was his motto, taken from the Andalusian poet Juan Ramón Jiménez.[20]

Walter Sickert took a different view of the Jubilee. He contributed to the event by painting a portrait of the King, basing it either on a press photograph that formed a *Daily Express* newsvendor's poster or an almost identical photographic image found in the *Star* on 8 May 1935.[21] In these, the King is shown dressed in the uniform of an admiral of the fleet. Rebecca Daniels has identified the photograph as having been taken on 7 May 1935, the day after the actual Jubilee, when the King and Queen made a short drive to St James's Palace in connection with a thanksgiving speech given by the King to the 'great family', as he referred to the British Empire.[22] Sickert adjusted the image, pushing the Queen further forward so that our view of her is cropped by the frame of the car window and the focus is predominantly on the King. Also pertinent to Sickert's needs was the angle of vision offered by the photograph, which positions the viewer in the street outside the car, as part of the anonymous crowd lining the streets in the hope of glimpsing royalty.

Although based on an image created by the mechanical eye of the camera, this portrait is treated by Sickert with great affection. His ability to make expressive use of paint at this late stage in his career had behind it 'the knowledge of a lifetime' – the winning phrase used by Whistler in the Whistler vs Ruskin trial, when challenged to explain why he had asked 200 guineas for a picture that had taken little more than a day and a half to paint. Sickert likewise, from 1927 onwards, while basing many of his paintings on photographs or using line engravings of works by Victorian illustrators for a series he named 'Echoes', opened himself to similar misunderstandings with regard to his purpose and his handling of paint. The dealer and writer Lillian Browse, a leading promoter of his art, observed a 'tragic deterioration' in his work after 1930; Clive Bell described the Echoes as 'ridiculously feeble', and as late as 1960 Michael Ayrton dismissed them as 'sad squeaks'.[23] But in the case of Sickert's 1935 portrait of George V he not only deftly edits the source

Walter Sickert, *King George V and Queen Mary*, oil on canvas, 1935.

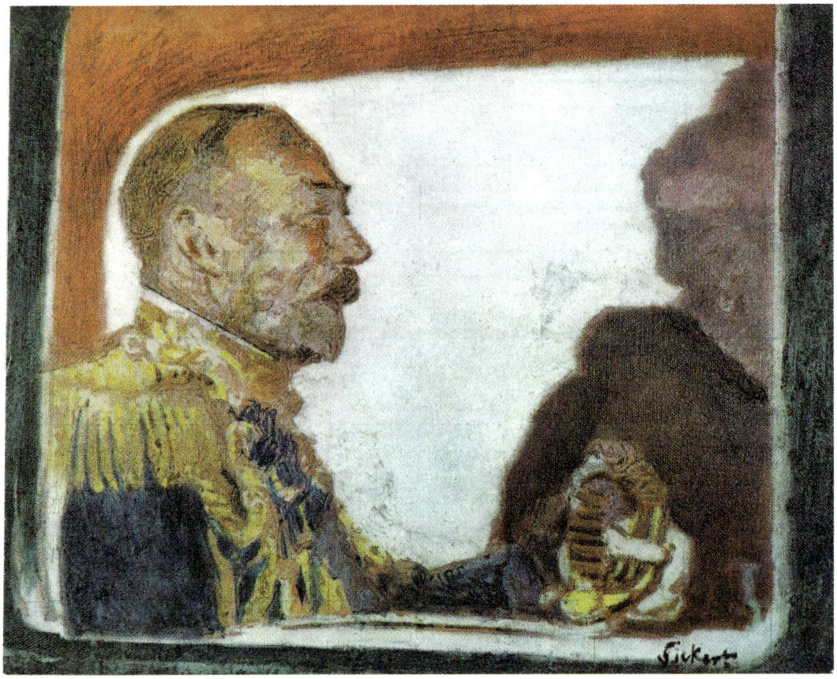

image, as we have seen; he also uses paint to intensify it. In all his paintings based on photographic images, he never seeks to disguise or obliterate his source material. On the contrary, the photographic nature of the source material continues to inhabit the material presence of the work of art and, in the case of this 1935 portrait of the King, asserts the importance within the work of a photograph's capacity to carry common knowledge and common appeal.

Any doubt as to Sickert's affection for the King is banished by the letter he sent to the *Daily Telegraph* in September 1936, after the King had died and discussion had begun as to what form a monument to him should take. Sickert immediately waded in: 'It must be our aim to present him as he appeared to us, and to that extent we are sacred holders of a trust.' He wanted George V to be shown in civil dress, as he was mostly seen, and on a pedestal roughly nine steps in height. He continued: 'Let us have no inflation and no numismatic euphemisms, but the man we loved and saw as he received his guests in the garden. The well-cut clothes should reveal the athletic and active figure that we knew aboard his yacht or on horseback – the country gentleman and the sportsman. The sculptor must give the note of gaiety which characterised a man who was often laughing, and the eyes bright.'[24]

Sickert had earlier painted a portrait of George V based on a photograph of the King and his racing manager, Major F. H. W. Fetherstonhaugh, at Aintree racecourse.

Walter Sickert, *King George V and his Racing Manager*, oil on canvas, 1929–30.

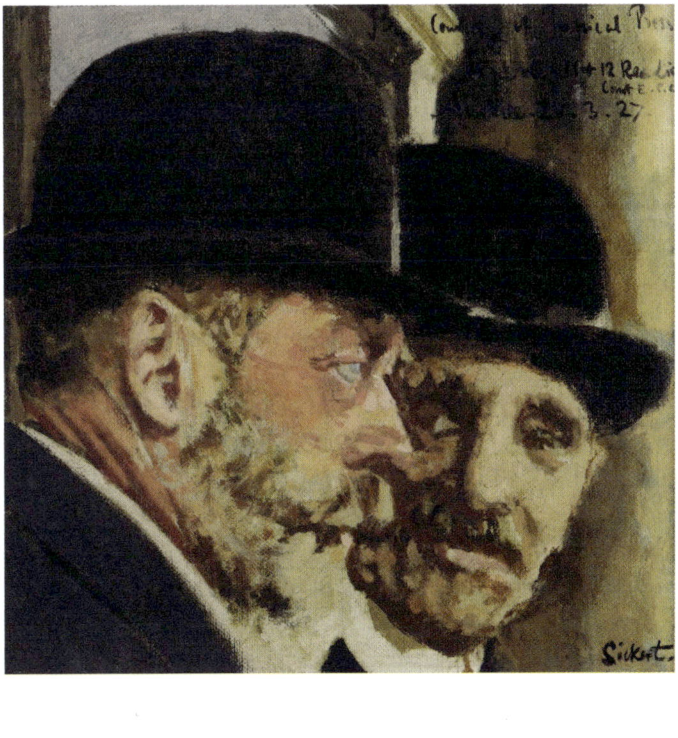

Both men had been wholly unaware of the photographer when the picture was taken. It was published in the *New Chronicle* on 25 March 1927, as Sickert duly acknowledged in the painted inscription which he added to the top right-hand corner of his painting. Far from being ashamed of using a non-art source for this portrait, he valued the insights and information that an instantaneous photograph had given him. In this case, he was fascinated by the expression on the racing manager's face: 'There was a sort of affectionate deference which showed you something about his attitude to the king.'[25] A certain sense of complicity between the two men is also suggested by the way the photograph jams their faces together and almost merges into one unit the dark mass created by their identical bowler hats. Above all, what is so unusual about this portrait of a king is that it has no false formality. In the same way that Burra in his *Agony in the Garden* had made real the sense of human suffering pushed to its limits, Sickert likewise, by means of his uninhibited procedures, transforms a haphazard find into something more real than what is achieved by most royal commissions.

During the late 1930s a multiplicity of styles, all competing against each other, made for a lively confusion in the art world. The rumpus created by the International Surrealist Exhibition in 1936 had dismayed supporters of abstract art. Margaret Gardiner tells how, after visiting the exhibition, Hepworth, Nicholson and Gabo had sought to restore themselves at an ABC tea shop and there decided that some form of robust alternative had to be found. What finally emerged in June 1937, in the wake of many discussions, was the book *Circle: International Survey of Constructive Art*, edited by Nicholson, Gabo and the architect Leslie Martin. Hepworth records that she and Martin's wife, Sadie Speight, took charge of production and layout.[26] The cover, with its columns of names in sans serif lettering, echoed the design of *Axis*, but inside was a major compendium on modern art, design and architecture with asides on town planning, art education and the state, biotechnics, and choreography. Its four main sections – painting, sculpture, architecture, art and life – were all intended to bear witness to Gabo's essay, born out of his association with Russian constructivism, titled 'The Constructive Idea in Art'. This idea, he argued, was as readily to be found in the engineering of a bridge as in a work of art. His use of the phrase alluded to generalities as well as to the particular: on the one hand 'the constructive idea' was a 'general concept of the world, or better, a spiritual state of generation, an ideology caused by life, bound up with it and directed to influence its course'. But it also offered an entirely new approach to art by refusing to separate content and form: 'The thought that Form could have one designation and Content another cannot be incorporated in the concept of the Constructive idea.

In a work of art they have to live and work as a unity, proceed in the same direction and produce the same effect.'[27] For a short period, the term 'constructive' replaced 'abstract' in talk about non-representational art. The book's contributors came from ten different countries. Gardiner thought it a dazzling achievement; but Myfanwy Piper, in a tape-recorded conversation with Margaret Garlake, later admitted to irritation with its 'priggish' missionary belief that serenely beautiful abstraction would act as a catalyst for the improvement of society.[28] Her riposte to *Circle* was her anthology *The Painter's Object* (1937), the first book in England to reproduce Picasso's *Guernica*. In her introduction, Myfanwy argues that Picasso's 'whole practice as an artist has been to make a formal virtue out of chaos, to exploit the incredible ruin and inconsequence and purposelessness of the world today'.[29]

No artist in England could match the intensity of Picasso's vision, and for those seeking an alternative to abstract or constructive art and to surrealism in 1937, one way forward was a return to realism. William Coldstream has vividly described how confusing it was in the early 1930s for young painters to discern what and how they should paint: all the intelligent books on art which he and his friends read taught them 'to regard subject matter as merely an excuse for good painting'[30] – by which he meant modernist experimentation or abstraction. It was difficult to establish a career as a professional painter with inconsistent and immature paintings in the wake of the 1930 slump, which made him more aware of social problems. He became convinced that art needed to be redirected towards a wider public, and so around 1935 he gave up painting and started work with the documentary film-maker John Grierson, co-operating with W. H. Auden and others on the film *Coal Face*.

Grierson's documentaries were made not in the studio but on site, and employed not actors but ordinary people, dramatizing and interpreting the narrative to avoid naive realism. When Coldstream returned to painting in 1937, he did so convinced that art had to be 'humanly' as well as 'artistically' interesting. He now took his subjects direct from life and painted them 'straight', without any abstraction or modernist treatment. That year he, Graham Bell, Victor Pasmore and Claude Rogers opened the Euston Road School; it did not seek to impose a style on its pupils but encouraged a measured, deliberately unrhetorical appraisal of the material world, without bombast or unnecessary display. Inspiration was drawn from Sickert's willingness to extract subjects from everyday scenes, from Degas's artistic probity and from Cézanne's searching analysis. The result was a lyrical realism, socially inspired but aesthetically conceived.

Painting became still more satisfactorily married to social convictions when the anthropologist Tom Harrison, who was to found Mass Observation with the poet and journalist Charles Madge, invited Bell and Coldstream to join him and others in Bolton, in making an experimental scientific record of working-class behaviour and views on everyday life and current affairs. The aim was to see how much at variance these were with the dominant views reported on radio and in the press. While other researchers picked up information on the street or by eavesdropping on conversations heard on buses, Bell and Coldstream climbed onto the roof of Bolton Art Gallery and spent almost three weeks in a position of elevated seclusion, producing soft townscapes, their realism gently blurred by the smoking chimneys then riddling Bolton (or 'Worktown', as Harrison called it), deliberately giving it an 'everyman' gloss.

The fact that the surrealists shared in the Euston Road School's interest in the documentary approach contributed to a slight blurring of the stylistic boundaries separating one style from another. At an AIA event on 16 March 1938, two of the British surrealists, Humphrey Jennings and Julian Trevelyan, together with Roland Penrose, challenged Bell, Coldstream and the sculptor Peter Peri on the relative merits of surrealism versus those of realism. But Jennings and Trevelyan soon after joined forces with Mass Observation and, like Bell and Coldstream, followed Harrison in Bolton. Still further confusion was caused in 1939, when the London Gallery mounted an exhibition titled 'Living Art in England' and asked all the exhibitors to define themselves as either 'constructivist', 'surrealist' or 'independent'. Irritated by these labels, Piper sent in 'Coast in Wales', a small painting that hovered between representation and abstraction, and labelled himself as 'a cubist, abstract, constructivist, surrealist independent'.[31]

By 1938, John Piper had abandoned abstraction. The previous year, he had spent much time between May and October travelling around Oxfordshire, filling half a dozen sketchbooks with annotated landscape and architectural drawings and taking hundreds of photographs for his *Shell Guide to Oxfordshire*. This seems to have reignited his love of travel, as he and J. M. Richards, who worked for the *Architectural Review*, began touring parts of Britain by car, gathering ideas for articles and finding interest in things and places mostly regarded as commonplace. One outcome of this journeying was 'Black and White: An Introductory Study of a National Design Idiom', in which the use of black and white surface decoration, a workaday idiom found on Belisha beacons, chequered kerbs, road signs and bollards, is traced back to a nautical tradition for the decoration of boats, lighthouses and quayside paraphernalia.[32] This article acted as a prequel to the visual culture perspective employed in 'The Nautical Style', written and illustrated by Piper and published in the January 1938 issue of the *Architectural Review*. A razor-sharp essay praising not high modernism but the demotic, it found 'coastal gaiety' in an array of maritime items, even in the bay window, which at the seaside 'blossoms and riots...in the

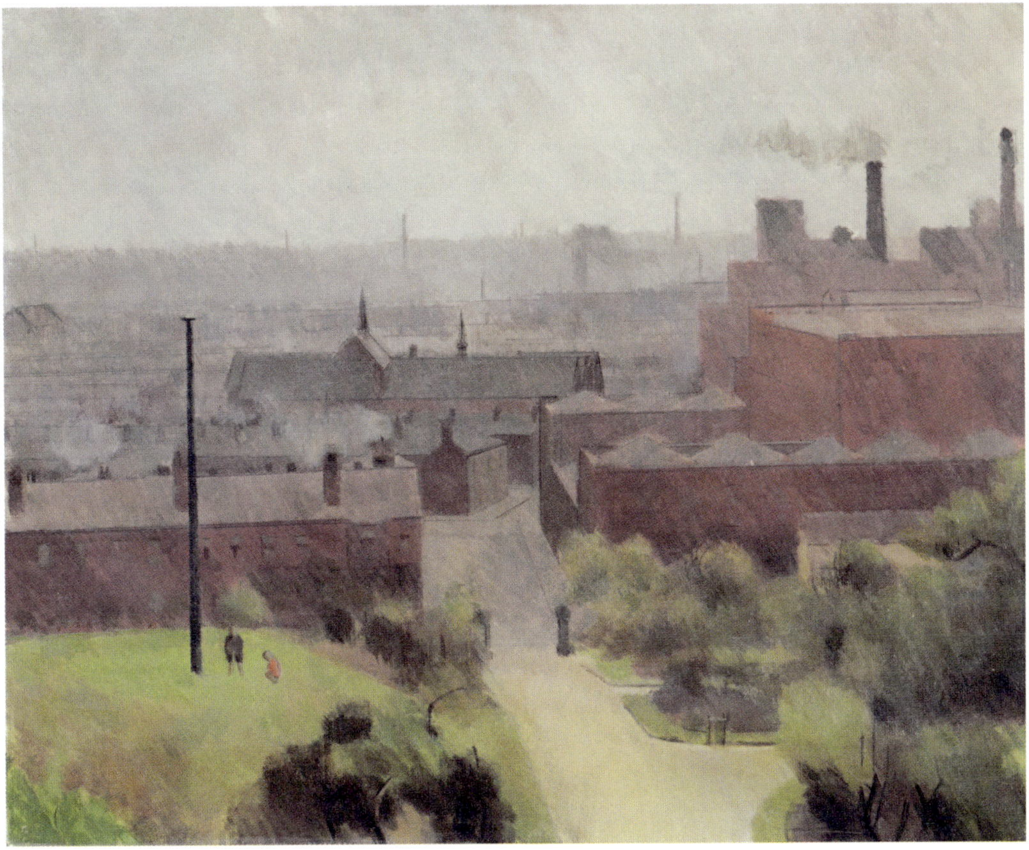

Graham Bell, *Thomasen Park, Bolton*,
oil on canvas, 1938.

spirit of a Rowlandson print'.[33] 'No one,' comments Timothy Mowl, 'had written from such an anarchic, wonderfully persuasive viewpoint before.'[34]

Late in 1938, Piper and Richards visited Brighton, where Piper found so much potential in the town's abundance of architectural styles that he decided to make a series of aquatints recording its streets and buildings, in imitation of the style adopted by travel books from the late 18th and early 19th centuries. *Brighton Aquatints* was published later the following year and received a full-page review by Osbert Sitwell in the pages of the *Listener*.

Another who now looked askance at abstraction was the elderly New Zealander Frances Hodgkins. As ever, she was fearful of any form of intimacy that would impede concentration on her work, but she accepted invitations to stay with the Pipers at

Fawley Bottom Farmhouse. On her visits she would walk down the road to a small farmyard whose owner, believing that once the war began, bartering would become the chief means of exchange, had collected anything he could lay his hands on: old doors, sheds, lavatory basins and all kinds of objects. Here Hodgkins would sit and stare, draw and paint, as if paying witness to the tokens of a past civilization, not only enjoying such a characterful mess but also making something of it. She did something similar on her visits to the strange and near deserted Purbeck Island, as John Piper noticed when reviewing her solo exhibition at the Lefevre Gallery in 1940: 'she has found in the much quarried, much disturbed ground...subjects that are symbolic enough: railed-in areas, concentration camps, of rusting milk cans, farm implements in disuse or dereliction, a man plucking a fowl in an outhouse. Described, these subjects are apt to sound simply "modern". In fact, they are of the times and timeless. They are powerful and extraordinary and are about humanity and its fate.'[35]

Where were the paparazzi in September 1938? By today's standards, they should have been thick on the ground when Piet Mondrian arrived in London, moving into No. 60 Parkhill Road after spending a few nights at the Ormonde Hotel, Belsize Park.

While living in Paris, Mondrian had come to be regarded as a heroic figure among the international modernists, owing to his dedication to his work. Not only had he rigorously subjected his art to a process of geometric simplification, but his aesthetic and theoretical ideas had become allied with a desire for spiritual purification, a commitment that grew out of his complex religious beliefs. He had grown up in a devout Dutch Calvinist home and, while studying in Amsterdam at the Academy of Fine Art, encountered neo-Calvinist thinking and the influential theologian and politician Abraham Kuyper. But in 1900, at the age of twenty-eight, he appears to have undergone a deep crisis of faith and gradually withdrew from the Reformed community. In 1909, a year after he attended lectures by Rudolf Steiner, he joined the Dutch chapter of the Theosophical Society. The influence of theosophy on his theoretical thinking about art is an established fact, but only recently has it been pointed out that his painting and writing 'also demonstrate significant *continuities* with his Reformed roots'.[36]

Few would deny that among his peers, Mondrian went furthest in his search for universal truth in art, driven in part by his religious background. Yet, outside of the Mall Studios, where he enjoyed friendships with Nicholson, Hepworth and John Cecil Stephenson, his influence on British art had little immediate effect, his chief admirer being Marlow Moss, a London-born painter who spent most of her life living in Continental Europe, developed her own version of neo-plasticism, and became a founder member of the Abstraction-Création group in Paris, where she established a friendship with Mondrian. In London, Mondrian remained an outsider. He had arrived later than other influential émigrés, and, with hindsight, it can seem that his presence did not crown the achievement of international modernism here as it had done in Paris. Interests had moved on, and the classical purity of high modernist abstract art began to seem out of touch with the needs of a darkening period in European history. By 1939, even Ben Nicholson was beginning to allow representation to creep back into his work.

Nevertheless, for two years this sixty-six-year-old man, who lacked adequate support from collectors and dealers and was very impoverished, made his home in London, in Hampstead, then a cosmopolitan area and not yet at the mercy of property developers. No. 60 Parkhill Road was a boarding house with a communal bathroom on the first floor. Ben Nicholson, who had arranged for Mondrian to take a room on the ground floor, had been guided by the need to find a cheap rent. A redeeming feature was a three-pane, double-height sash window. It overlooked a garden, which might also be thought advantageous. Mondrian grumbled: 'Too many trees.' Self-parody, perhaps, because of his renowned hatred of the colour green, which for many years he had banned from his palette; he limited himself to white, greys, black and the three primary colours, in keeping with the laws of neo-plasticism that he and Theo van Doesburg had first explored in the Netherlands.

Mondrian decorated his London room in the same way he had treated the two studios he had occupied, one after the other, in Paris. He painted it white and furnished it with squares or oblongs painted in the colours of his restricted palette, so that the room and his pictures formed a unity. Miriam Gabo, wife of Naum Gabo, whom Mondrian had known in Paris, helped him to shop in Camden Town for cheap kitchen furniture, which he made pristine with several layers of white paint. Orange boxes, similarly treated, also helped to furnish the room. Soon it was transformed into a sanctuary for work. As before, everything visible would have upheld his aesthetic, while anything personal would have been hidden or destroyed. This erasure of individuality links Mondrian with the bare, anonymous surfaces of architecture's international style and Le Corbusier's promotion of an impersonal 'machine' aesthetic. But it also connects with his ambition to arrive through his art at a universal language and what he called 'pure reality'. He restated his theoretical principles in 'Plastic Art and Pure Plastic Art', an essay first published in *Circle* in 1937 and therefore written specifically for a British audience. One of these principles was to represent reality objectively, not subjectively, for the latter in his view 'must of necessity result in an individual expression which veils the pure representation of beauty'.[37]

Paintings by Mondrian had begun to infiltrate Britain after three of his pictures hung in the 'Abstract and Concrete' exhibition. Winifred Nicholson, who had bought a Mondrian in Paris before 1936, was one of the first people in England to own his work. Another owner was her sister-in-law, Nan Roberts. Nan was married to Wilfrid Roberts, MP, who had been instrumental in warning Winifred that war was coming and encouraging her, and Mondrian, to leave Paris in the summer of 1938.

Around 1937 Winifred had arranged for both her own Mondrian and Nan Roberts's to be hung in the front kitchen at Banks Head in Cumberland. Her own – *Composition with Double Line and Yellow* – was hung near the old cast-iron range, on a wall facing the window opposite. Nan's painting, *Composition with Blue and Yellow* (1935), was at the other end of the room above an old wooden settle resting on the stone-flagged floor. (Both now belong to major museums, the Scottish National Gallery of Modern Art and the Hirshhorn Museum in Washington, DC respectively.)[38] Recognizing that a

Piet Mondrian, *Composition with Double Line and Yellow*, oil on canvas, 1932.

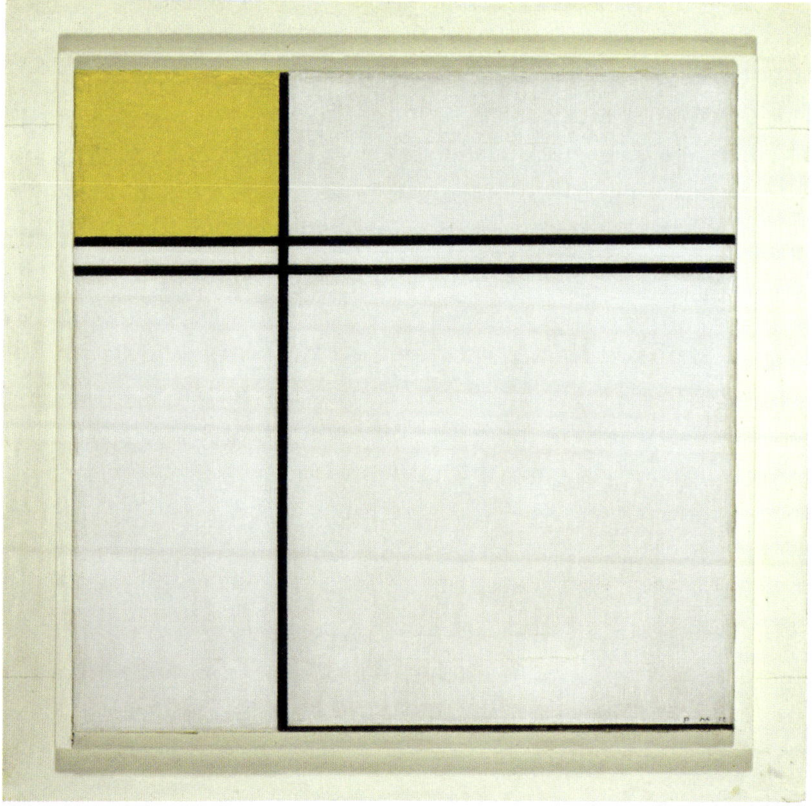

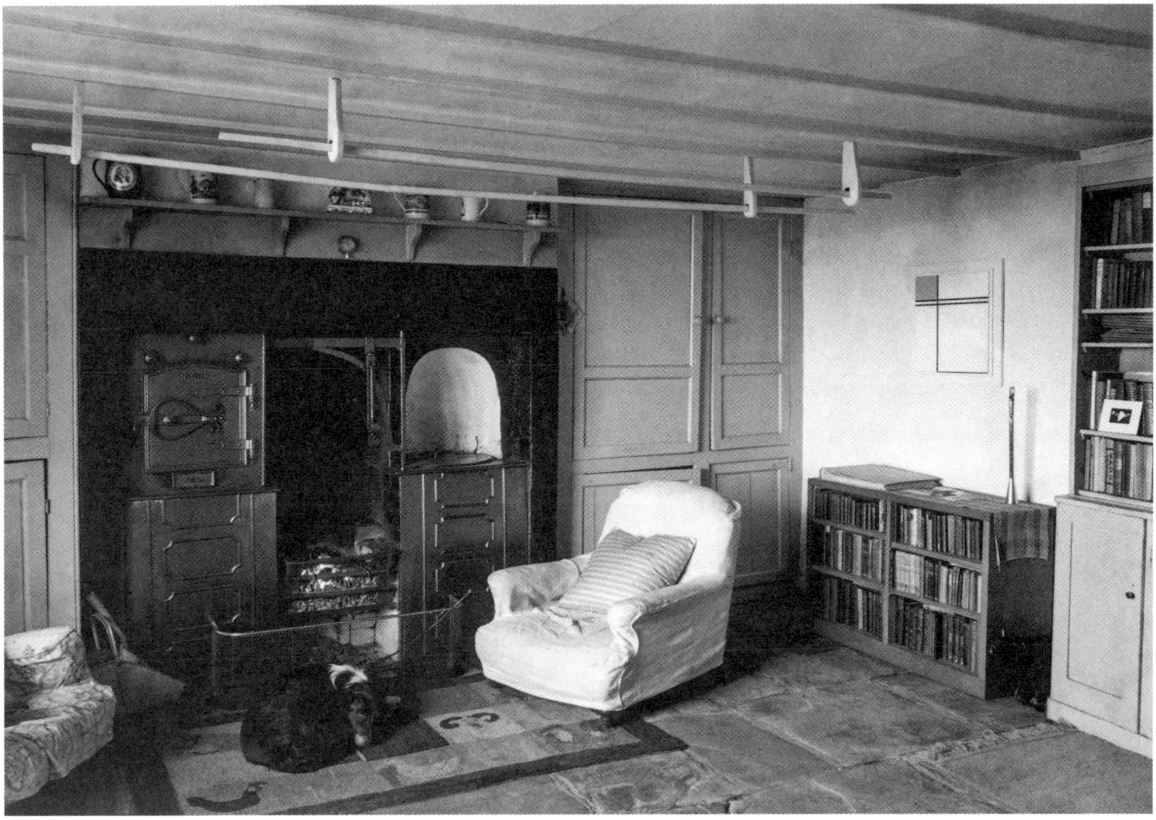

The front kitchen at Banks Head, showing a Mondrian in place.

Mondrian could help promote a sense of the modern, Winifred lent the second picture in 1938 to Alastair Morton, who lived five miles away at Brampton in Brakenfell, a house designed by Leslie Martin. He needed a publicity photograph, as he had recently taken over from his father as design director of Edinburgh Weavers and had set up a line in 'constructivist fabrics', fusing textile design with modern art. The Mondrian is very much to the fore in Morton's publicity image, which gave rise to the mistaken assumption that he owned it.[39]

Photographs of both Mondrians at Banks Head were taken by Arthur Jackson, a pupil of Ben Nicholson and cousin of Barbara Hepworth. Looking at the photograph of *Composition with Double Line and Yellow* in situ, it is at first surprising to see such a rarefied work hanging in this modest rural farmhouse, which sits in an outlying spot on the line of Hadrian's Wall, far removed from the French capital where it was painted. Yet both picture and room share a sparseness, a clarity and a precision. Winifred had come to know Mondrian well while living in Paris in the mid-1930s, and at one point she told him: 'You are the first person who has ever painted yellow, pure lemon yellow like the sun.' Initially Mondrian rejected this remark, but the next time they met, he said: 'I have thought about it, and it is so, but it is merely because cadmium yellow has been invented.'[40]

In 1954, Winifred wrote about *Composition with Double Line and Yellow* in an article for the *Christian Science Monitor*: 'I now have a Mondrian on my wall – merely a contrast of horizontal against vertical lines crossing white spaces, and one poised yellow square. I have known busy politicians who cared nothing for art, come and write their speeches in this room where the Mondrian lives. That small canvas expresses the still order behind turmoil.'[41]

Mondrian's closest ally while in London was Ben Nicholson. Their association lasted, in all, seven years. It was the subject of a small, illuminating exhibition, 'Mondrian/Nicholson', at the Courtauld Gallery in 2012, showing how powerful, elegant yet also visceral abstract art can be. Owing to their play with asymmetry, both artists achieved what Mondrian called a dynamic equilibrium. They regularly exchanged photographs of their work, Mondrian also taking an interest in Hepworth's sculptures. It was therefore a blow to him when, for the safety of their children, Nicholson and Hepworth moved to St Ives at the invitation of Adrian Stokes two weeks before war broke out. They begged Mondrian to go with them, but he declined. He had found London conducive to work but he had also, even before leaving France, resolved that America would be his final destination.

It was not the war that decided him on his next move, but the fall of France in June 1940, followed by the onset of bombing in London in August. Most of the Lawn Road Flats were now empty. The Blitz began in earnest on 7 September 1940, and two nights later Mondrian's windows at Parkhill Road were blown in. His decision to leave was not so much to do with self-protection as the need to protect his paintings. The fall of Holland in May meant that he no longer needed a visa to enter America. On 13 September, having sent his pictures on in advance, he moved with his suitcases to the Ormonde Hotel and for eight days and nights sat bolt upright, fully dressed, in the hotel's shelter. Finally a ticket was booked and a friend drove him to Liverpool, where he boarded a White Star liner. On 23 September 1940, after a two-day delay in departure, he sailed for New York.[42] He left England as quietly as he had arrived.

The final outbreak of the romantic in English art between the wars took place in Paris in 1939. Chamberlain's announcement of 'Peace in our time' on his return from Munich in September 1938 had assuaged anxiety over the possibility of war. However, in March 1939 Hitler entered Prague, and the following month Mussolini invaded Albania. With Britain and France pledging support to Poland, Hitler's next objective, war became increasingly inevitable.

This did not, however, prevent the young Michael Ayrton from arriving in April 1939 in Paris, where a small bevy of former art students from St John's Wood Art School could already be found. Among them was John Minton. Ayrton and Minton had first become friends during a student trip to Paris in 1938 arranged by Pat Millard, principal of the Art School, which Ayrton had joined the year before. He was four years younger than Minton, red-cheeked, cocksure and already familiar with Paris, having studied there independently as a teenager in 1936 after giving up formal education at the age of fourteen. While in Paris, he had been fired with pro-Republican feeling in relation to Spain and shot off there, hoping to involve himself in the Civil War. Learning of this, his mother, Barbara Ayrton, chair of the Labour Party and MP for North Hendon, had arranged his return and subsequently sent him to relatives in Vienna, where he had moved among the Viennese intelligentsia and met Sigmund Freud. Ayrton's bright talk about painters and painting and his own experiences had impressed Minton. While in Paris in 1938, they both agreed that on leaving art school they would return there promptly.

There was an additional motivation behind this decision. Ayrton, before arriving at St John's Wood Art School, had studied briefly at Heatherley's, where he made friends with another student, Michael Middleton, whom he introduced to Minton. The three young men formed a triumvirate and become passionately interested in the French neo-romantics after reading James Thrall Soby's *After Picasso*. This book had been published in America in 1935 and was hard to come by; its rarity gave it additional resonance and, in Middleton's words, it 'hit us in the midriff and became our Bible'.[43]

One of the central aims of the book was to acknowledge the importance of Picasso but also to dislodge him. Soby explains:

> In calling this book *After Picasso*, I have meant to imply two things: that in Paris certain painters younger than Picasso have already produced enough important work so that they, and not he, must stand for the latest developments in modern art; second, that much in the work of these younger painters was originally derived from Picasso.[44]

Soby demoted Picasso from his role as 'a great contemporary artist' to 'an old master of modern painting'. Having been in awe of Picasso, this must have had a liberating effect on the young Minton and on his friends: no longer did they need to look askance at representation, or experiment with cubism or abstraction. Soby's book went on to document reactions to Picasso as found in the work of the Paris-based neo-romantics and the surrealists. Pertinent here is a remark by Gertrude Stein, a supporter of Picasso, whose comparison of his vision with that of the surrealists may have been stimulated by her reading of Soby. She is on record as saying in 1938: 'The Surrealists still see things as everyone sees them, they complicate them in a different way but the vision is that of everyone else, in short the complication is the complication of the twentieth century but the vision is that of the nineteenth century.'[45] It is a telling insight and perhaps one reason why Ayrton, Minton and Middleton, when reading Soby's book, paid relatively little attention to the surrealists and much more to the neo-romantics.

Soby's exposition of French neo-romanticism gave particular attention to the work of two Russians based in Paris, Eugène Berman and Pavel Tchelitchew, as well as to that of the Frenchman Christian Bérard, then better known as a stage designer than as a painter. It soon became evident in their work that what attracted these three young Englishmen was the neo-romantics' emotive visual language and an almost adolescent sense of disenchantment. Soby neatly opined: 'Theirs is a quiet intelligence rather than an enforced intellectuality.' He noticed also a 'disturbing sadness', a prevalent use of deep monochrome blue and a gloomy atmosphere reminiscent of Picasso's Blue period. They filled their canvases, he claimed, with '*unashamed* poignancy'.[46]

Of the three friends, Minton had arrived first in Paris, where his romantic inclinations led him straight to the Delacroix paintings in the Louvre. While an art student in London he had developed a passion for the ballet and had made several friends among the Sadler's Wells corps de ballet. After Ayrton reached Paris in April the two went regularly to the ballet, theatre, films and exhibitions, keeping an eye out for sightings of their neo-romantic mentors. For Minton, his most memorable theatrical experience was seeing Jean Giraudoux's play *Ondine* with sets by Tchelitchew. In his painting he explored various influences and had earlier fallen under the spell of de Chirico, but in Paris he admired Berman's use of broken columns and arches, blasted trees and ruined palaces to create imaginary scenes for waifs and strays, clinging lovers and mournful adolescents, while all around the ground is strewn with stones or small rocks to enhance the sense of arid desolation. 'I know I am a little unhinged about Berman,' Minton admitted while in Paris, 'but his tense, theatrical melancholy impresses me very much.'[47]

On hearing that Berman had been affected by his visits to Les Baux in Provence, an ancient, ruined town on top of a rocky outcrop, Minton and Ayrton in the summer of 1939 followed in his footsteps. Prior to this, Minton had been meandering around, trying out various subjects and making what he called 'flashy paraphrases of better-known masters'.[48] Les Baux immediately changed his focus of attention. 'Les Baux is an extraordinary place,' he wrote, after the first of his two visits to the area, '– once the capital of Provence, there are now eight inhabitants, and the rest is in fantastic ruins with enormous rocks strewn about in curious positions. The whole atmosphere is charged with romantic desolation. I did a lot of paintings and crowds of drawings.'[49] He and Ayrton interrupted their visit to Les Baux to make a return to Paris, where they sat through six performances by Léonide Massine at the Palais de Chaillot. On their return, they had Middleton in tow. All three friends rated Les Baux highly, and its scorched and barren terrain continued to provided Minton with rock-strewn settings for his neo-romantic compositions for several more months.

In late August 1939, Minton was advised to leave Paris immediately; Ayrton was elsewhere, so it was left to Minton to pack up and empty their shared studio. He left books, paintboxes and easels at their hotel. What canvases he could carry he took with him, along with his registered luggage.

Back in London, Minton began the habit of wandering the streets at night, often visiting the Docklands where he found he could pick up sailors, about whom he had developed an obsession. Meanwhile his paintings began to achieve recognition. Throughout much of 1941, he and Ayrton worked on designs for John Gielgud's production of *Macbeth*. Then when the Blitz began in earnest in the spring of 1941 he found the East London dockland scene transformed into the kind of ruined landscape which had haunted his mind since his discovery of Les Baux. His favourite area, Poplar, was particularly hard hit. Using pen and ink, he produced scenes, some drawn as if from above, in which destruction is translated into a theatre of the soul, an arena in which to explore feelings of wretchedness, guilt and alienation. A hint of this can be found in an earlier ink and wash drawing, *The Desolate Stage* (1939), in which a scatter of ingredients creates a tense theatrical scene under a darkening sky, evoking uncertainty and fear. The precise narrative is unclear, although the decision to subvert the norm and portray the isolated reclining nude in the lower left corner as male rather than female almost certainly relates to Minton's exploration of his still hidden homosexuality. But personal content, dreams or fantasies do not occlude the way this drawing also catches the mood of the day fostered by the imminence of war.

One of Minton's earliest patrons was Lucy Wertheim. She had begun to include his work in her group exhibitions and had bought a work by him for her own collection.[50] In 1924 she had moved her London gallery down the road to rooms in Albany, at 8 Burlington Gardens, where she increasingly struggled to make her 'adventure in art' financially viable. It was the finality of war that ended her association with the West End art world. She had kept the gallery going by the skin of its teeth, reducing her personal expenditure to make this possible. Instead of convivial luncheons at the Berkeley or Savoy, she came to know 'how excellent a meal of herring roes (served piping hot) could taste at the quiet A.B.C. deserted after office hours, round the corner'.[51] In June 1939 she formed an agreement with Fred Uhlman to let the gallery to the Society of Refugee Artists on a commission basis. The show did well and to some extent re-established her finances, enabling her to take a holiday.

On 1 September 1939 she hung an exhibition of drawings by a New Zealand artist. Two days later, war was declared. Shortly afterwards, Wertheim was told that a regulation now forbade more than twelve people to congregate in one room. On 5 September, she was further warned that the authorities were taking over the gallery premises for use as an air-raid shelter. She removed all her belongings and sent notices to the personal columns in *The Times* and the *Daily Telegraph*, requesting artists to collect their pictures. Her gallery was no more. The restlessness and disquiet of war began.

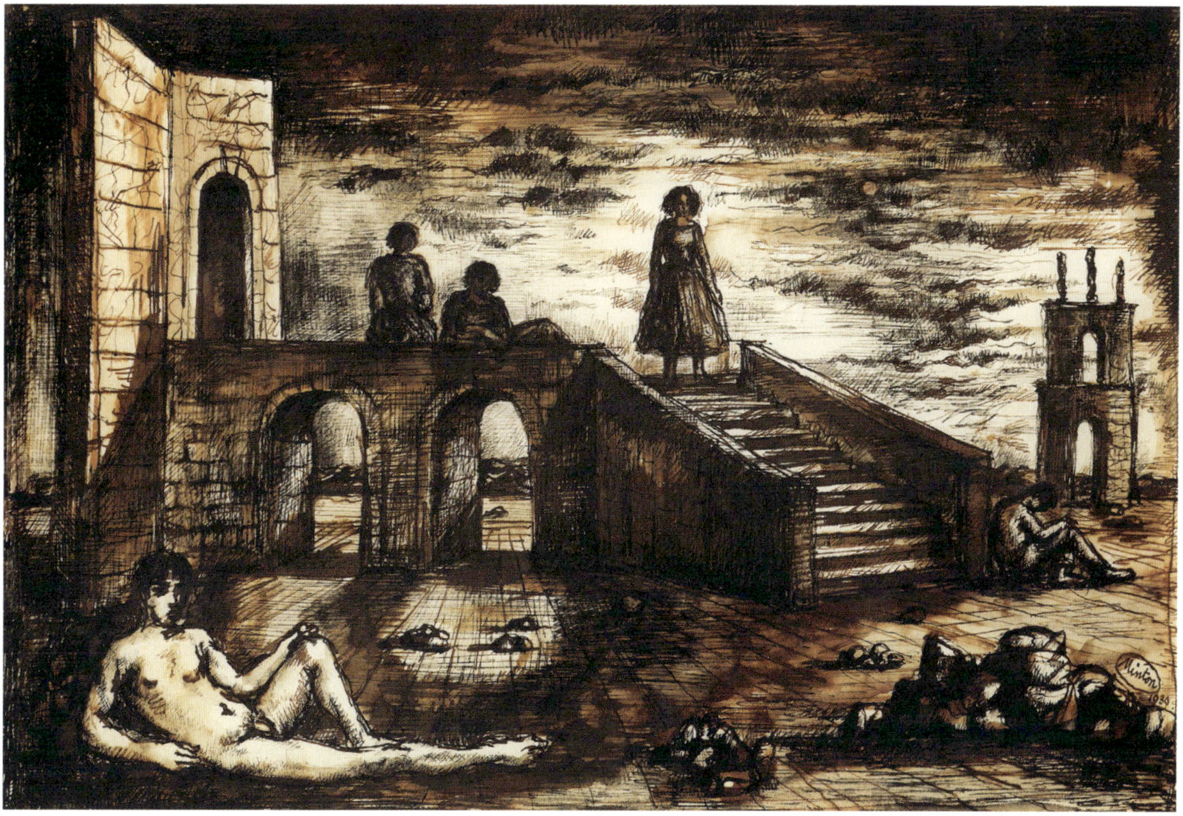

John Minton, *The Desolate Stage*,
pen, ink and wash, 1939.

NOTES

INTRODUCTION

1 Charles Harrison, *English Art and Modernism 1900–1939* (Allen Lane/Penguin, 1981), p. 203.
2 Richard Morphet, 'Le Réalisme Anglais entre les deux Guerres', *Cahiers du musée national d'art moderne* 7/8 (1981), pp. 322–45. This essay was written in English, and here and elsewhere in this book I quote from Morphet's typescript of his original text.
3 David Peters Corbett, *The Modernity of English Art 1914–30* (Manchester University Press, 1997), p. 16. The tenacity of Peters Corbett's argument in this book has been a major stimulus, even in those places where I chose to disagree.
4 Ibid. pp. 10–11.
5 M. Berman, *All That is Solid Melts into Air: The Experience of Modernity* (Verso, 1983), p. 15.
6 Bridget Riley, *The Eye's Mind: Bridget Riley, Collected Writings 1965–1999* (Thames & Hudson, 1999), p. 128.
7 Myfanwy Evans, 'Abstract Art: Collecting the Fragments', *New Oxford Outlook* (22 November 1935), p. 260.
8 Ibid.
9 I am grateful for the opportunity to read Stuart Sillars's forthcoming book, *Picturing England between the Wars: Word and Image 1918–1940*, in advance of its publication and for this period detail which nicely affirms the democratization of art. The Tudor Walters Report received full affirmation in the Addison Act of 1919. This stipulated that local authorities had a duty to provide housing and that the recommendations of the Report were to be followed in their siting and construction.
10 Caroline Elam, *Roger Fry and Italian Art* (Ad Ilissum in association with the *Burlington Magazine*, 2019), p. 76.
11 See Katy Deepwell, *Women Artists between the Wars: 'A fair field and no favour'* (Manchester University Press, 2010), pp. 194–7. Deepwell is here referring to the Society of Women Artists, the Women's International Art Club, the Glasgow Society of Women Artists and the Scottish Society of Women Artists. She observes: 'These groups are rarely mentioned in histories of British art and their histories are not widely known.' This situation is then rectified in the pages that immediately follow.
12 Wyndham Lewis, *The Caliph's Design: Architects! Where is your Vortex?*, ed. Paul Edwards (Black Sparrow, 1986), p. 87.

CHAPTER 1

1 C. R. W. Nevinson, interview in the *Daily Express*, 25 February 1915.
2 Wyndham Lewis, *Rude Assignment* (Hutchinson & Co., 1950), p. 129.
3 Further insult emerged in April 2021 when the Commonwealth War Graves Commission admitted that at least 116,000 – and potentially up to 350,000 – predominantly African and Middle Eastern First World War casualties may not be commemorated by name at all.
4 The War Office had banned the exhumation of bodies for reburial in Britain in 1915.
5 Paul Gough, 'Imagery of Emptiness and Re-appearance on the Battlefields', in Avril Maddrell and James Sidaway, *Deathscapes: New Spaces for Death, Dying and Bereavement* (Ashgate, 2010), p. 275.
6 It has been pointed out that whereas rival museums such as the Munich Glyptothek and Schinkel's Altes Museum were designed around collections, Smirke's British Museum, which was still in the process of being built, grew by accretion in a vain attempt to keep pace with its growing collections. See Ian Jenkins, *Archaeologists and Aesthetes in the Sculpture Galleries of the British Museum 1800–1939* (British Museum Press, 1992), p. 57.
7 Ibid. p. 140.
8 See https://c20society.org.uk/war-memorials/London-royal-artillery-memorials.
9 James Fox, *British Art and the First World War 1914–1924* (Cambridge University Press, 2015), pp. 89–90.
10 The history of First World War Art in Britain has been well documented. For leading authorities on art, see Meirion and Susie Harries, *The War Artists: British Official War Art of the Twentieth Century* (Michael Joseph, 1983); Sue Malvern, *Modern Art, Britain and the Great War* (Yale University Press, 2004); Paul Gough, *A Terrible Beauty: British Artists in the First World War* (Sansom & Co., 2010); Paul Edwards, *Wyndham Lewis: Art and War* (Lund Humphries, 1992); and James Fox, *British Art and the First World War, 1914–1924* (Cambridge University Press, 2015).
11 Quoted in G. Kavanagh, *Museums and the First World War: A Social History* (Leicester University Press, 1991), p. 130.
12 Anna Airy to Robert Ross, June 1918 (IWM Archives: ART/WA1/031).
13 Gough, 'Imagery of Emptiness', p. 270.
14 Paul Nash to Gordon Bottomley, 16 July 1918, quoted in Claude Colleer Abbott and Anthony Bertram (eds), *Poet and Painter: Being the Correspondence between Gordon Bottomley and Paul Nash, 1910–1946* (Oxford University Press, 1955), p. 99.
15 Paul Nash to Margaret Nash, 13 November 1917: TGA 8313/1/1/166.
16 Simon Grant, 'A Landscape of Mortality', *Tate Magazine* 6,

https://www.tate.org.uk/art/artists/paul-nash-1690/landscape-mortality.

17 Andrew Causey, *Paul Nash: Landscape and the Life of Objects* (Lund Humphries, 2013), p. 47.

18 Gough, 'Imagery of Emptiness', p. 271.

19 The Hon. Evan Charteris, *John Sargent* (William Heinemann, 1927), p. 214.

20 Malvern, *Modern Art*, p. 87.

21 Wolfgang Kemp, quoted in Malvern, *Modern Art*, p. 87.

22 In both instances Dodd produced competent but unexciting work. Yet when disappointment was expressed it was usually over some slight inaccuracy in the handling of facial features. Behind these criticisms lay a deeper disappointment: that the heroism of war had been overlooked in favour of a banal naturalism, the superficially real trumping the romantic.

23 John Piper's remark comes from notes he supplied to accompany his aquatint of the Brighton Pavilion in *Brighton Aquatints* (1939, n.p.).

24 This was added in 1919, after the closure of the BWMC scheme, and was paid for by IWM funds.

25 A copy of this catalogue is included in Royal Academy of Arts, *Imperial War Museum: The Nation's War Paintings and Other Records* (HM Stationer's, 1919).

26 See Harries, *The War Artists*, p. 136.

27 Quoted in Harries, *The War Artists*, p. 141.

28 Yockney's report is lodged with the IWM and is quoted in Harries, *The War Artists*, p. 149.

CHAPTER 2

1 Margaret Nash, 'Memoirs of Paul Nash', published in abridged form in Paul Nash, *Outline: an Autobiography* (Lund Humphries, 2016), p. 198.

2 *The Times*, 13 November 1918, p. 9.

3 David Reynolds, *The Long Shadow: The Legacies of the Great War in the Twentieth Century* (W. W. Norton & Co., 2014), p. 142.

4 Ibid.

5 David Cannadine in his 'Pictures across the Pond', in Inge Reist (ed.), *British Models of Collecting and the American Response* (Ashgate, 2014), p. 17, gives a succinct account of America's rise in economic power, its plutocracy and vast wealth, as well as the use to which this would be put with regard to British art.

6 Samuel Hynes, *A War Imagined: The First World War and English Culture* (Bodley Head, 1990), p. 310.

7 See the 2016 edition of Nash, *Outline*, p. 152.

8 Paul Nash, 'The Arts League of Service', *New Witness* (23 May 1919), p. 72. A fuller discussion of the League and its relation to the period can be found in James Fox, *British Art and the First World War 1914–1924* (Cambridge University Press, 2015), pp. 149–51.

9 See Fox, *British Art*, p. 134.

10 Cannadine, 'Pictures across the Pond', p. 15.

11 Ibid. p. 17.

12 S. N. Behrman, *Duveen* (Hamish Hamilton, 1952), p. 1.

13 The price officially given today is £182,200 ($728,800). However, Gerald Reitlinger in *The Economics of Taste: The Rise and Fall of Picture Prices 1760–1960* (Barrie and Rockcliff, 1961), p. 322, gives £148,000 as the price.

14 Roberson Archive, Hamilton Kerr Institute, Cambridge: HKI MS 865-1993, 169, 317; and letter-book 1939–40, HKI MS 866-1993, 47. Quoted in Sally Ann Woodcock, 'Charles Roberson, London Colourman, and the trade in artists' materials 1820–1939', PhD thesis, University of Cambridge, 2019.

15 These unfinished chapters in note form are included in Nash, *Outline*, both in the original edition and in the new edition published by Lund Humphries in 2016. See note 1.

16 Roger Fry to Jean Marchand, 8 September 1919, in *The Letters of Roger Fry: Vol. 2*, ed. Denys Sutton (Chatto & Windus, 1972), pp. 455–6.

17 This remark, made by Nicholson in a recollection of this period, appears in a letter to John Summerson (3 January 1944) and is quoted in Jeremy Lewison (ed.), *Ben Nicholson: The Years of Experiment 1919–1939*, exh. cat. (Kettle's Yard, 1983), p. 12.

18 Nicolete Gray, *The Paintings of David Jones* (John Taylor/Lund Humphries in association with The Tate Gallery, 1989), p. 28.

19 Quoted in *The Times*, 22 July 1897.

20 This passage from the Curzon Report also caught the attention of Ronald Alley, who quotes it in his *Catalogue of the Tate Gallery's Collection of Modern Art* (Tate Gallery, 1981), pp. viii–xix. For a more detailed account of the Tate Gallery during the interwar years, see Frances Spalding, *The Tate: A History* (Tate Gallery Publishing, 1998).

21 The phrase 'death-scattering' was used by Lewis-Hind in his description of this painting in the *Daily Chronicle*: '[Nevinson] has seen the crew of the mitrailleuse crouched in their pit (one dead), angular, implacable, machine-brains of destruction, the men like the gun, the gun like the men.' C. Lewis-Hind, 'Four Pictures: Developments in Modern Art', *Daily Chronicle* (9 March 1916). The full quote can be found in Michael J. K. Walsh, *C. R. W. Nevinson: This Cult of Violence* (Yale University Press, for the Paul Mellon Centre for Studies in British Art, 2002), p. 146.

22 See David Peters Corbett, *The Modernity of English Art*

1914–1930 (Manchester University Press, 1997), p. 46.

23 *Blast 2*, 1915, p. 23. Lewis appears to have forgotten, or not known, that Leighton was shortly before his death raised to the peerage.

24 *Horizon* 10: 56 (August 1944), p. 146.

25 Frank Rutter, *Art in My Time* (Rich & Cowan, 1933), p. 89.

26 Augustus John to Laura Knight, 9 April 1938. Quoted in Michael Holroyd, *Augustus John, Vol. 2: The Years of Experience* (William Heinemann, 1975), p. 107.

27 The ARA was for many years regarded as the initial stage in the move towards full membership as an RA. It is now a defunct category.

28 See Andrew Stephenson's article on the 1924 RA Summer Exhibition in *Chronicle* 250 and online celebration made by the Paul Mellon Centre of the RA's 250th year, https://chronicle250.com/1924.

29 Ebenezer Wake Cook, *Retrogression in Art and the Suicide of the Royal Academy* (Hutchinson, 1924), p. 174.

30 Timothy Wilcox, writing about the Summer Exhibition in 1928 for *The Royal Academy Summer Exhibition: A Chronicle 1769–2018*, chronicle250.com/1928.

31 This scheme had been set up in recognition of the Canadian contribution to the war. At a time when Canadians were still British citizens, 700,000 men had fought against the Germans in Flanders.

32 'The Keeper's Report', *Annual Report of the Royal Academy of Arts*, 1922. A copy of this is held in the Royal Academy Archive.

33 Tate online catalogue entry on Charles Sims's *I Am the Abyss and I Am Light*, https://www.tate.org.uk/art/artworks/sims-i-am-the-abyss-and-i-am-light-n04396.

34 See Wilcox, *Royal Academy Summer Exhibition*.

35 From the Charles Sims file, Royal Academy Archive. See information provided by Terry Riggs in October 1997, quoted in Tate online collection catalogue entry for *I Am the Abyss and I Am Light*.

CHAPTER 3

1 'Smith, Sir Matthew Arnold Bracy', *Oxford Dictionary of National Biography*, https://doi.org/10.1093/ref:odnb/36152.

2 Matthew Smith to Francis Halliday, *c.* 1950, quoted in Malcolm Yorke, *Matthew Smith: His Life and Reputation* (Faber & Faber, 1997), p. 62.

3 Matthew Smith to John Lyman, 28 February 1915, quoted in Yorke, *Matthew Smith*, p. 88.

4 A fuller description of his war experience is given in Yorke, *Matthew Smith*, pp. 100–3.

5 Quoted at greater length in Yorke, *Matthew Smith*, p. 105.

6 Ibid. p. 105. See also Alice Keene in *Matthew Smith*, exh. cat. (Barbican Art Gallery, 1983), p. 22.

7 *Eugène Delacroix: Selected Letters 1813–1863*, ed. and trans. Jean Stewart (Eyre & Spottiswoode, 1971), p. 125. The production Delacroix attended was titled *Faustus* and had been adapted from Goethe's poem by George Sonane and Daniel Terry with music by Bishop, Horn and Cooke. It opened at the Drury Lane Theatre on 16 May 1825.

8 *The Journal of Eugène Delacroix*, trans. Walter Pach (Crown Publishers, 1948), p. 476.

9 Ibid. p. 64.

10 Ibid. p. 52.

11 *Delacroix: Selected Letters 1813–1863*, pp. 102–3.

12 Yorke, *Matthew Smith*, p. 114. This phrase which Yorke uses seems accurate, but it is worth noting that no document by Matthew Smith is used to uphold the claim.

13 Richard Cork, review of a Matthew Smith exhibition at the Crane Kalman Gallery, *Financial Times*, 5 June 2020.

14 Francis Bacon, quoted in *Matthew Smith*, exh. cat., p. 42.

15 Her description of it is given in a letter to Ursula Tyrwhitt. See *Gwen John: Letters and Notebooks*, ed. Ceridwen Lloyd-Morgan (Tate Publishing in association with the National Library of Wales, 2004), p. 62.

16 Claude Flight, 'The Art of To-day', *Colour* 2: 4 (April 1926), p. 8. Quoted in Stephen Coppel, *Linocuts of the Machine Age: Claude Flight and the Grosvenor School* (Scolar Press, 1995), p. 17.

17 Quoted in Sydney D. Kitson, *The Life of Cotman* (Faber & Faber, 1937), p. 307.

18 S. Uwins, *Memoir of Thomas Uwins, R. A.*, vol. 1 (Longman, Brown, Green, Longmans and Roberts, 1858), p. 143.

19 According to James Russell in *Ravilious in Pictures: Sussex and the Downs* (Mainstone Press, 2009), the discovery that the white horse is collaged over an image of the Wilmington Giant was first revealed by restorers. Russell also mentions that Ravilious made two versions of this picture, and his wife Tirzah cut them up and spliced together the best parts of each in order to make this final work. Ravilious's great love of chalk figures on the downs led him to suggest a picture book on this subject for children to Noel Carrington, then editor of Puffin Picture Books for Penguin. The book was unfinished at the time of Ravilious's death.

20 Frank Rutter, 'The Galleries: Women's International Art Club', *Sunday Times*, March 1919; MS-Papers-5599-12, Press clippings, Alexander Turnbull Library, Wellington. Quoted by Joanne Drayton, *Frances Hodgkins: A Private Viewing* (Random House NZ, 2005), p. 172.

21 Frances Hodgkins to Rachel Hodgkins, 20 December 1918, in *Letters of Frances Hodgkins*, ed. Linda Gill (Auckland University Press, 1993), p. 338.

22 A. G. Stephens, 'Frances Hodgkins', Supplement to the *Bookfellow* (Sydney), 1 May 1913, pp. ix–x. Quoted in Iain Buchanan, Michael Dunn and Elizabeth Eastmond, *Frances Hodgkins: Paintings and Drawings* (Thames & Hudson, 1995), p. 16.
23 Frances Hodgkins to Rachel Hodgkins, 19 April 1901, in *Letters of Frances Hodgkins*, p. 83.
24 Frances Hodgkins to Rachel Hodgkins, 26 August 1901, in *Letters of Frances Hodgkins*, pp. 95 and 97.
25 Quoted in Stephens, 'Frances Hodgkins', p. x; and in Buchanan et al., *Frances Hodgkins: Paintings and Drawings*, p. 16.
26 Myfanwy Evans, *Frances Hodgkins* (Penguin, 1948), p. 10.
27 Gill, *Letters of Frances Hodgkins*, p. 577.
28 Frances Hodgkins to Rachel Hodgkins, 4–5 October 1924, *Letters of Frances Hodgkins*, p. 383.
29 Ibid. p. 123.
30 Ibid. p. 303.
31 Ibid. p. 339.
32 E. H. McCormick, *Portrait of Frances Hodgkins* (Auckland University Press, 1981), p. 91.
33 Linda Gill, in *Letters of Frances Hodgkins*, p. 295, claims that Hodgkins first met Cedric Morris in 1917; and there is a very early watercolour of Hodgkins by Morris in the Tate collection, thought to be painted in 1917, at which time Morris was living for a year in Zennor, Cornwall, and painting insects and plants.
34 Iain Buchanan states that Morris saw these paintings of children in Hodgkins's St Ives studio. See Buchanan et al., *Frances Hodgkins: Paintings and Drawings*, p. 33. But in the transcript of an interview made in 1969 for a documentary on Hodgkins in the Tate Archives (TGA 8317.6.4.12), it is clear he is referring to the London studio in Eldon Road.
35 The suggestion that these two titled works are probably one and the same was first made by Iain Buchanan in Buchanan et al., *Frances Hodgkins: Paintings and Drawings*, p. 32.
36 Arthur Lett-Haines, transcript of an interview about Hodgkins for a documentary, 1969 (Tate Archives: TGA 8317.6.4.11).
37 Ibid.
38 Cedric Morris, typescript of a recording made in connection with a documentary on Frances Hodgkins, 1969 (Tate Archives: TGA 8317.6.4.12).
39 Frances Hodgkins to Arthur Lett-Haines, 30 January 1928, Martigues (Tate Archives: TGA 8317.1.1.2060).
40 Evans, *Frances Hodgkins*, p. 11.
41 Quoted by Andrew Lambirth in *Cedric Morris: Artist Plantsman* (Garden Museum, 2018), p. 29.
42 The words are Marinetti's as remembered by Hodgkins, and quoted in Stephens, 'Frances Hodgkins', pp. ix–x. A more extensive quotation from this source can be found in Drayton, *Frances Hodgkins*, pp. 135–6.
43 See Hannah Segal, 'A Psycho-analytical Approach to Aesthetics', in Melanie Klein, Paula Heimann and R. E. Money-Kyrle (eds), *New Directions in Psycho-analysis: the significance of infant conflict in the pattern of adult behaviour* (Tavistock Publications, 1971), p. 390.
44 See Joyce H. Townsend and Sarah Hilary, 'A Lively Parrot: Frances Hodgkins's *Wings over Water*', Tate Papers 5 (Spring 2006), n.p., https://www.tate.org.uk/research/publications/tate-papers/05.
45 John Piper, *British Romantic Artists* (Collins, 1942), p. 47.
46 Gill, *Letters of Frances Hodgkins*.
47 Myfanwy Evans, 'Round the Exhibitions', *Listener*, 18 April 1940, p. 778.
48 Quoted in Richard Cork, *David Bomberg* (Yale University Press, 1987), p. 140.
49 Sarah MacDougall and Rachel Dickson, *Bomberg* (Ben Uri Gallery and Museum, 2017), p. 103.
50 Ibid. p. 104.
51 Ibid.
52 Bomberg's dismissive remark was expressed privately and then reported by Lilian Bomberg to Richard Cork. See Cork, *Bomberg*, pp. 173–4; also n. 56, p. 329.
53 Ibid. pp. 180 and 181.

CHAPTER 4

1 Richard Morphet, as found in the original English-language text for 'Le Réalisme Anglais entre les deux Guerres', *Cahiers du musée national d'art moderne* 7/8 (1981), pp. 322–45.
2 The catalogue to the East London Art Club exhibition, held at the Whitechapel Art Gallery, 1928, can be found in the Whitechapel Archives.
3 Walter Richard Sickert, 'Idealism', *Art News*, 12 May 1910, p. 217.
4 *Daily Mail*, n.d. (December 1928), n.p.
5 Virginia Woolf, *To the Lighthouse* (Penguin, 2000), p. 141.
6 Quoted in David Buckman, *From Bow to Biennale: Artists of the East London Group* (Francis Boutle Publishers, 2012), pp. 74–5.
7 Buckman, *From Bow to Biennale*; The Gentle Author, *East End Vernacular: Artists Who Painted London's East End Streets in the Twentieth Century* (Spitalfields Life Books, 2017).
8 The book is undated, but was published in either 1927 or 1928.
9 Edric Holmes, *London's Countryside* (Robert Scott, n.d.), p. 330.
10 Ibid. p. 13.
11 Henry Morton, quoted by Sarah Fill in her essay 'Paul Nash, Surrealism and Prehistoric Dorset', in Emma Chambers (ed.), *Paul Nash*, exh. cat. (Tate Publishing, 2017), p. 49.
12 Paul Nash, *The Shell Guide*

to Dorset (Architectural Press, 1936), p. 7.

13 Fill, 'Paul Nash, Surrealism and Prehistoric Dorset', p. 49.

14 Quoted from an Ordnance Survey circular of 8 April 1909, in Richard Oliver, *Ordnance Survey Maps: A Concise Guide for Historians* (Charles Close Society, 2005), p. 47.

15 Holmes, *London's Countryside*, p. 329.

16 See Stuart Sillars, *Picturing England between the Wars* (Oxford University Press, forthcoming).

17 Adrian Bell, *Men and the Fields* (B. J. Batsford, 1939), p. 59.

18 Clough Williams-Ellis, *Britain and the Beast* (J. M. Dent, 1937), p. 97.

19 Gerard Manley Hopkins, 'Binsey Poplars', in *Poems of Gerard Manley Hopkins* (Oxford University Press, 1931), p. 39.

20 Nash, *The Shell Guide to Dorset*, n.p.

21 John Piper, *British Romantic Artists* (Collins, 1942), p. 7.

22 See Paul Nash, *Outline: an Autobiography* (Lund Humphries, 2016), p. 218.

23 Ibid.

24 Ibid.

25 Paul Nash to William Rothenstein, 16 May 1921; transcript made by Nash's first biographer, Anthony Bertram (Victoria and Albert Museum Archives). Quoted by Claire Colvin in *Paul Nash Places*, exh. cat. (The South Bank Centre, 1989), p. 38.

26 Nash, *Outline*, p. 219.

27 Anthony Bertram, *Paul Nash: The Portrait of an Artist* (Faber & Faber, 1955), p. 111.

28 Nash, *Outline*, p. 219.

29 Margaret Nash, 'Memoirs of Paul Nash, 1913–1946', in Nash, *Outline*, p. 207.

30 Emma Chambers, 'Introduction', in Chambers, *Paul Nash*, p. 13.

31 Andrew Causey, *Paul Nash* (Clarendon Press, 1980), p. 112. His later, more summary thoughts on Nash's work at Dymchurch can be found in Andrew Causey, *Paul Nash: Landscape and the Life of Objects* (Lund Humphries, 2013).

32 Owing to difficulties at this time in buying works by contemporary artists for the British Museum, Campbell Dodgson, descended from a family of stockbrokers, built up a large private collection of prints and drawings which he bequeathed to the Museum.

33 Andrew Causey refers to this interview with William Gaunt (*Design and Drawing*, October 1926) in *Paul Nash: Paintings and Watercolours*, exh. cat. (Tate Gallery, 1975), p. 25. The entry on this watercolour in Causey's 1980 monograph on Nash reveals that John Carter bought the painting on Nash's behalf.

34 Percy Bysshe Shelley, 'Time', in *The Complete Poetical Works of Percy Bysshe Shelley* (Oxford University Press, 1905), p. 174.

35 Causey, *Paul Nash* (1980), pp. 112–13.

36 Christopher Neve, *Unquiet Landscape: Place and Ideas in 20th-Century British Painting* (Faber & Faber, 1990), p. 5.

37 Claude Colleer Abbott, 'Introduction', in Gordon Bottomley, *Poems and Plays* (The Bodley Head, 1953), p. 11.

38 Ibid. p. 12.

39 Paul Nash, quoted in the introduction to Claude Colleer Abbott and Anthony Bertram (eds), *Poet and Painter: Being the Correspondence between Gordon Bottomley and Paul Nash, 1910–1946* (Oxford University Press, 1955), p. xviii.

40 Once, after received a packed letter from Nash, Bottomley wrote: 'it was very nice to be pulled up to date with regard to your doings and plans, and we marched through all you sent rapidly and rapaciously and with large enjoyment.' Ibid. p. 114.

41 Quoted in Causey, *Paul Nash* (1980), p. 120.

42 See Paul Nash to Gordon Bottomley, 7 January 1924, in Abbott and Bertram, *Poet and Painter*, p. 175.

43 Quoted in Causey, *Paul Nash* (1980), p. 122.

44 Ibid.

45 St Augustine's *Confessions*, X, 8, in Pusey's translation, quoted in Frances A. Yates, *The Art of Memory* (Routledge, Kegan Paul, 1966), p. 46.

46 Paul Nash, 'Photography and Modern Art', *Listener*, 27 July 1932, p. 130.

47 Causey, *Paul Nash* (1980), p. 185.

48 Nash's 'Unit One' letter to *The Times* can be found in its entirety in Andrew Causey (ed.), *Paul Nash: Writings on Art* (Oxford University Press, 2000), pp. 97–9.

49 Quoted in Causey, *Paul Nash* (1980), p. 112.

50 The frequently repeated statement that Gilbert Spencer also acted as best man for John Nash is scotched by Andy Friend in *John Nash: The Landscape of Love and Solace* (Thames & Hudson, 2020), p. 315, n. 2.

51 Andrew Lambirth, *John Nash: Artist and Countryman* (Norwich: Unicorn Press, 2019) and Friend, *John Nash*. It would be wrong to suggest that before this John Nash had been ignored. Several publications had previously investigated particular aspects of his work. His supporters include Sir John Rothenstein, who published a short monograph on him in 1983, and Ronald Blythe, whose *First Friends* (1999) focused on the Nash brothers during their student days, war years and courtships. Here the main emphasis is on relationships, but, as Blythe observes, 'The real passion which emerges is that for landscape.' None of the previously published books on John Nash had presented

such a complete overview as is now offered by Lambirth's monograph and Friend's biography.

52 Naomi Lightman, in an unpublished paper delivered in January 2016 on 'Eyes, and No Eyes', found in the fourth volume of *Evening at Home*, points out that the lack of sectarian ethos in the book as a whole allowed children from different religious groups to respond to this particular story or chapter.

53 The author of the tale is Dr John Aikin, not his sister, Mrs Barbauld. *Evenings at Home, or The Juvenile Budget Opened*, corrected and revised edition (George Routledge & Sons, n.d.), p. 281.

54 John Nash, quoted in Ronald Blythe, *John Nash at Wormingford* (Aldgate Press, n.d.), p. 24.

55 Friend, *John Nash*, p. 309.

56 Sir John Rothenstein, *John Nash* (Macdonald & Co., 1983), p. 11.

57 Ibid. p. 20.

58 Edward Marsh, *A Number of People* (William Heinemann, 1939), p. 360.

59 Ibid. p. 355.

60 Rothenstein, *John Nash*, p. 55.

61 Friend, *John Nash*, p. 21.

62 Ibid. p. 16.

63 Quoted in ibid. p. 113.

64 John Nash, quoted in Blythe, *John Nash at Wormingford*, p. 22.

65 Charles Ginner, 'Neo-Realism', in *New Age*, 1 January 1914. Reprinted as a preface to the catalogue for a Harold Gilman and Charles Ginner exhibition at London's Goupil Gallery, April–May 1914.

66 Blythe, *John Nash at Wormingford*, p. 8.

67 Dora Carrington to John Nash, n.d. [*c*. 1914–15], in Anne Chisholm (ed.), *Carrington's Letters: Her Art, Her Loves, Her Friendships* (Chatto & Windus, 2017), p. 14.

68 Dora Carrington to John Nash, n.d. [1913], in Chisholm, *Carrington's Letters*, p. 9.

69 Chisholm, *Carrington's Letters*, p. 178.

70 Tate Archives, as yet uncatalogued.

CHAPTER 5

1 John Summerson, *Ben Nicholson* (Penguin, 1948), p. 7.

2 'The red ivory ball and the two whites, one with a spot and one without, and the clink of their relationships became an "experience" far more related to art than anything they taught me at the Slade.' *Ben Nicholson: Writings and Ideas*, ed. Lee Beard (Lund Humphries, 2019), p. 16. First published as 'The Life and Opinions of an English Modern' in the *Sunday Times*, 28 April 1963. Shoolbred's was a large department store in Tottenham Court Road.

3 Ibid. pp. 15 and 16.

4 It was evidently a homage to his father and was probably gifted to William, as it was in his possession in 1948.

5 Nicholson recollects this ambition in a letter to John Summerson (3 January 1944), quoted in J. Lewison (ed.), *Ben Nicholson: The Years of Experiment 1919–1939*, exh. cat. (Kettle's Yard), 1983.

6 Wyndham Lewis, *The Caliph's Design: Architects! Where is your Vortex?*, ed. Paul Edwards (Black Sparrow Press, 1986), p. 9. This book follows that of the first edition published by the *Egoist* in 1919, and indicates in the notes where substantive alterations were made in 1939 when preparing for its re-publication.

7 Ibid. p. 120.

8 Ibid.

9 Alun Munton, 'Wyndham Lewis: War and Agression', in David Peters Corbett (ed.), *Wyndham Lewis and the Art of Modern War* (Cambridge University Press, 1998), p. 21.

10 Wyndham Lewis, *Rude Assignment: An Intellectual Autobiography* (Hutchinson & Co., 1950), p. 129.

11 Wyndham Lewis to James Thrall Soby, 9 April 1947, in *The Letters of Wyndham Lewis*, ed. W. K. Rose (Methuen, 1963), p. 407.

12 Gilman and Ginner called themselves 'neo-realists' when exhibiting in 1913, first at the Allied Artists Association in the summer and then at the Goupil Salon in the autumn. The following year, they shared an exhibition in April at the Goupil Gallery and in the catalogue reprinted Ginner's manifesto 'Neo-Realism', which had first been published in the *New Age* on 1 January 1914. The three objectives behind neo-realism as identified by Ginner were a) personal research, b) love of the medium and c) objective transposition of nature. It is possible that this manifesto gave Lewis the idea for his Vorticist Manifesto.

13 Charles Ginner, 'Harold Gilman: An Appreciation', in *Memorial Exhibition of Works by the late Harold Gilman*, exh. cat. (Leicester Galleries, 1919), p. 5.

14 Wyndham Lewis and Louis Fergusson, *Harold Gilman: An Appreciation* (Chatto & Windus, 1919), p. 31.

15 Clive Bell, 'Contemporary Art in England', *Burlington Magazine*, July 1917, p. 36. Quoted in Richard Thomson's essay 'Gilman's Subjects, Some Observations' in exh. cat. to the Arts Council touring exhibition 'Harold Gilman 1876–1919' (1981–2).

16 Lewis and Fergusson, *Harold Gilman*, p. 14.

17 Frank Rutter, *Art in My Time* (Rich & Cowan, 1933), p. 187.

18 Previously it was always thought Durbins had been sold at this time, but Louise Campbell in *Studio Lives: Architect, Art and Artist in 20th-Century Britain* (Lund Humphries, 2019), p. 66, corrects this error.

19 *Letters of Aldous Huxley* (Chatto & Windus, 1969), p. 169.

20 David Peters Corbett, *The Modernity of English Art 1914–30* (Manchester University Press, 1997), pp. 74–5.
21 For an extended discussion of the role of dance within *The Deluge*, see Ayla Lepine's article 'Dance, Theatre and Performance', in 'Tate Papers, In Focus – *The Deluge*, 1920, by Winifred Knights', http://www.tate.org.uk/research/publications/in-focus/the-deluge/dance-theatre-performance.
22 David Manson, *Jacob Kramer: Creativity and Loss* (Sansom & Co., 2006), p. 101.
23 'Dean Swift with a Brush – The Tyroist explains his art', *Daily Express*, 11 April 1921, n.p.
24 Ibid.
25 Quoted in Joanna Skipwith (ed.), *The Sitwells and the Arts of the 1920s and 1930s*, exh. cat. (National Portrait Gallery, 1994), p. 104.
26 Wyndham Lewis, *Blasting and Bombardiering* (Eyre & Spottiswoode, 1937), pp. 252–3.
27 See Lara Trubowitz, 'Wyndham Lewis: Jewish Antisemites and Tolerant Britain in the Era of the Jewish Refugee', in *Civil Antisemitism, Modernism and British Culture 1902–1939* (Palgrave Macmillan, 2012), pp. 145–79.
28 John Russell to John Piper, 29 May 1942 (Tate Archives: TGA 200410/1/1/3587).
29 Lewis, *The Caliph's Design* (1986 ed.), p. 12; emphasis original.
30 Charles Harrison, *English Art and Modernism 1900–1939* (Allen Lane and Indiana University Press, 1981), p. 165.
31 Historically useful is Harrison's chart of the Seven and Five Society's membership in *English Art and Modernism*, pp. 346–7.
32 Harrison, *English Art and Modernism*, p. 165.
33 P. G. Konody, 'Advanced Art at the Beaux Arts Gallery', *Observer*, 24 April 1927. Quoted in Jovan Nicholson and Julian Stair, *Art and Life: Ben Nicholson, Winifred Nicholson, Christopher Wood, Alfred Wallis, William Staite Murray, 1920–1931* (Philip Wilson Publishers, 2013), p. 106.
34 Quoted in Andrew Nicholson (ed.), *Unknown Colour: Paintings, Letters, Writings by Winifred Nicholson* (Faber & Faber, 1987), p. 24.
35 Ibid. p. 28.
36 Ibid. p. 32.
37 Ibid. p. 30.
38 Ibid.
39 Illustrated in Christopher Andreae, *Winifred Nicholson* (Lund Humphries, 2009), p. 38.
40 Nicholson, *Unknown Colour*, p. 75.
41 Andreae, *Winifred Nicholson*, p. 44.
42 Nicholson, *Unknown Colour*, p. 23.
43 Ibid. p. 38.
44 Ibid. p. 32.
45 Ibid. p. 32.
46 Ibid. p. 33.
47 Ibid. Winifred Nicholson's memory is here so specific in its details that I have stayed with this story, but her grandson Jovan Nicholson suggests that the £500 allowance was in fact part of her marriage allowance rather than coming entirely from Rosalind Howard.
48 Sebastiano Barassi, 'The Allure of the South: The Nicholsons in Italy and Switzerland, 1920–23', in Nicholson and Stair, *Art and Life*, p. 17. Barassi also suggests that a reason why the Nicholsons eventually left Lugano may have been the rise to power of fascism in Italy and the ongoing unrest in the Balkans, as this would have restricted their travel in southern Europe. However, the main cause of their departure was the prospect of a joint exhibition at the Paterson Gallery. This altered their status as artists and within the London art world.
49 Nicholson, *Unknown Colour*, p. 36.
50 Ibid. p. 35.
51 Ibid. p. 36.
52 Ibid. p. 39.
53 Ibid.
54 Edie, William's second wife, painted under the name Elizabeth Drury and for six years, between 1926 and 1932, exhibited with the Seven and Five Society. She destroyed most of her paintings after she and William separated.
55 Nicholson, *Unknown Colour*, p. 77.
56 Ibid. p. 79.
57 Ibid. p. 80.
58 *Ben Nicholson, paintings, reliefs, drawings* (Lund Humphries, 1948) includes a list of owners. Helen Sutherland owned the most, with thirty-two; next came Leslie and Sandy Martin with twenty-nine; third was Ede with seventeen. By the time of her death in 1965, Sutherland had close to fifty works by Ben Nicholson in her possession and had given away a handful to public art galleries and to friends.
59 Beard, *Ben Nicholson: Writings and Ideas*, p. 20.
60 Ben Nicholson to John Summerson, 25 April [1944], quoted in Beard, *Ben Nicholson: Writings and Ideas*, p. 23.
61 Ben Nicholson to Winifred Nicholson, n.d. [*c.* June 1926], quoted in Beard, *Ben Nicholson: Writings and Ideas*, p. 23.
62 This term, unacceptable today, was then in everyday parlance.
63 Ben Nicholson, 'The Aim of the Modern Artist', *Studio* 104 (December 1932); quoted in Beard, *Ben Nicholson: Writings and Ideas*, pp. 23–5.
64 Ben Nicholson to Helen Sutherland, 24 February 1926, private collection, on loan to Tate Archives.
65 Helen Sutherland to Ben Nicholson, n.d. [1931] (Tate Archives: TGA 8717.1.2.4707).
66 Winifred described it as 'a grey farmstead, a little house built out of the Roman Wall stones,

a byre and a barn, on the line of the Roman Wall overlooking the valley of the Irthing river, and over towards the blue-grey fells' (Nicholson, *Unknown Colour*, p. 43).

67 Campbell, *Studio Lives*, p. 150.

68 Helen Sutherland in *Paintings and Drawings from the private collection of Miss Helen Sutherland*, exh. cat. (Scottish National Gallery of Modern Art, 1962), n.p.

69 Helen Sutherland to Ben Nicholson, n.d. (Tate Archives: TGA 8717.1.2.4712).

70 Ben Nicholson to Helen Sutherland, 30 September 1929, private collection, on loan to Tate Archives.

71 T. Baker, 'A Kind of Prolonged Retreat: Helen Sutherland at Rock', *Northern Review* 14 (2004), pp. 79–94.

CHAPTER 6

1 Quoted in Maurice Collis, *Stanley Spencer* (Harvill Press, 1962), p. 203.

2 Recollected in a letter to Desmond Chute; see Paul Gough (ed.), *Your Loving Friend, Stanley: The Great War Correspondence between Stanley Spencer and Desmond Chute* (Sansom & Co., 2011), p. 120.

3 This may be the head of Christ in the National Gallery, London, now said to be 'after Bernandino Luini' and a copy of the central figure in Luini's *Christ Among the Doctors*.

4 *Arena: Stanley and His Daughters* (BBC Four, 2018).

5 The text had, however, originally been published by the Arundel Society in 1854 with woodcut illustrations. For further analysis of the significance of Ruskin's interpretation of Giotto for Spencer, see Duncan Robinson, *Stanley Spencer: Visions of a Berkshire Village* (Phaidon Press, 1979), p. 14; Caroline Leder, 'Influences in the Early Work of Stanley Spencer', in *Stanley Spencer*, ed. Duncan Robinson, exh. cat. (Arts Council of Great Britain, 1976); and Susannah Avery Quash, 'Valuable Assistance: Stanley Spencer's Friendship with Gwen and Jacques Raverat', *Apollo* CL: 451 (October 1999), pp. 3–11.

6 John Ruskin, *Giotto and His Works in Padua* (George Allen, 1905), p. 46.

7 Caroline Elam, 'From Giotto to the Bushmen: Roger Fry at the Slade 1909–1913', *Burlington Magazine* 160: 1386 (September 2018), p. 729.

8 Fry's remark is quoted in Sue Malvern, *Modern Art, Britain and the Great War: Witnessing, Testimony and Remembrance* (Yale University Press, 2004), p. 87.

9 This recollection by Spencer is quoted in Keith Bell, *Stanley Spencer: A Complete Catalogue of the Paintings* (Phaidon, 1980), p. 39.

10 The closest that Spencer comes to an explanation of this experience is in a memoir of his life at Cookham sent from Salonika to Chute in March 1917: 'During the morning I am visited and walk about being in that visitation. How at this time everything seems more definite and to put on a new meaning and freshness you never before noticed. In the afternoon I set my work out and begin the picture. I leave off at dusk feeling delighted with the spiritual labour I have done.' See Gough, *Your Loving Friend, Stanley*, p. 113.

11 This remark is frequently quoted in the literature on Spencer and most recently has been used online, somewhat inappropriately, by the National Trust to advertise the Sandham Memorial Chapel. See https://www.nationaltrust.org.uk/maidenhead-and-cookham-commons/features/stanley-spencer-and-cookham-common.

12 Jacques Raverat to Stanley Spencer, n.d. [*c*. 1912–13], private collection. Quoted in Frances Spalding, '"Working for an Imaginary Temple": Stanley Spencer, Eric Gill, Jacques and Gwen Raverat', *Burlington Magazine* 143: 1178 (May 2001), p. 291.

13 Eric Gill to Jacques Raverat, 19 March 1913; William Andrews Clark Library, UCLA.

14 Quoted in Spalding, '"Working for an Imaginary Temple"', p. 294.

15 Stanley Spencer to Henry Lamb, 12 August 1914, in *Stanley Spencer: Letters and Writings*, ed. Adrian Glew (Tate Publishing, 2001), p. 50.

16 Quoted in Gough, *Your Loving Friend, Stanley*, p. 19. I am grateful to Gough for his excellent description of the hospital and Spencer's state of mind during his time there, and for a fuller account of Desmond Chute than it is possible to include here.

17 Stanley Spencer, notebook, Feb. 1938–43. Quoted in Glew, *Stanley Spencer*, pp. 13 and 31.

18 Stanley Spencer to Jacques and Gwen Raverat, Glew, *Stanley Spencer*, p. 65.

19 Stanley Spencer, quoted in Collis, *Stanley Spencer*, pp. 49–51 and 67–8.

20 Quoted in Gough, *Your Loving Friend, Stanley*, p. 26.

21 Quoted in ibid. p. 28.

22 It is difficult to establish which translation Spencer was given, and it seems that the passages which Chute copied out for Spencer, some of which he learnt by heart, may have been compiled by Chute from differing texts. He had been educated at Downside, was at this time translating the *Odyssey* and was later to become a priest.

23 Stanley Spencer, 'Reminiscences', Glasgow, 1944: TGA 733.3.8; quoted in Richard Carline, *Stanley Spencer at War* (Faber & Faber, 1978), p. 202.

24 Henry Tonks to Alfred Yockney, 12 October 1918; quoted in Meirion and Susie Harries, *The War Artists: British Official War Art of the Twentieth Century* (Michael Joseph, 1983), p. 110.
25 Stanley Spencer, untitled MSS, possibly part of a lecture delivered in Oxford (1922). See Glew, *Stanley Spencer*, p. 120.
26 Stanley Spencer to Richard Carline, n.d., Tate Archives, Box 825; quoted in Bell, *Stanley Spencer*, p. 422.
27 Ibid.
28 Quoted in Kitty Hauser, *Stanley Spencer* (Tate Publishing, 2001), p. 153.

CHAPTER 7

1 This famous conjoining of words is gifted by Shakespeare to Macbeth after he has murdered Duncan: 'Will all great Neptune's ocean wash this blood/Clean from my hand? No, this my hand will rather/The multitudinous seas incarnadine/Making the green one red.' Not only is this association richly imaginative, it is also the first time that the word 'incarnadine' was made to act as a verb. Woolf's essay in *Listener* was published on 5 May 1937 and is reproduced in *The Essays of Virginia Woolf, Vol. 6*, ed. Stuart N. Clarke (Chatto & Windus, 2012), p. 95.
2 Rupert Richard Arrowsmith, *Modernism and the Museum: Asian, African, and Pacific Art and the London Avant-Garde* (Oxford University Press, 2011), p. 4.
3 Ibid.
4 The full story of Gaudier's meeting with Epstein can be found in H. S. [Jim] Ede, *Savage Messiah*, ed. Sebastiano Barassi and Jon Wood (Kettle's Yard and Henry Moore Institute, 2011), p. 31.
5 Horace Brodsky, *Henri Gaudier-Brzeska 1891–1915* (Faber & Faber, 1933), p. 64.
6 Henry Moore in conversation with Huw Wheldon in Alan Wilkinson (ed.), *Henry Moore: Writings and Conversations* (Lund Humphries, 2002), p. 151.
7 Roger Fry, 'Gaudier-Brzeska', *Burlington Magazine* 29: 161 (August 1916), p. 209.
8 Gaudier's meeting with Brancusi is recorded in Brodsky, *Henri Gaudier-Brzeska*, p. 94.
9 See Harriet Zines, *Ezra Pound and the Visual Arts* (New Directions, 1980), p. 212. Pound's influence on the development of sculpture in the 1920s was through his *Gaudier-Brzeska: A Memoir* (John Lane/The Bodley Head, 1916) and his article 'Brancusi' in the *Little Review* (New York, Autumn 1921).
10 'Art at the Front'. The review appeared in *The Times*, 25 May 1918. It is quoted in full in Roger Cole, *Gaudier-Brzeska: Artist and Myth* (Sansom & Co., 1995), pp. 163–4.
11 See Cole, *Gaudier-Brzeska*.
12 As stated in Ede's essay 'The Odd Woman', originally conceived as a foreword or postscript to *Savage Messiah.* He decided against its inclusion and it remained unpublished until the 2011 edition of *Savage Messiah*, published by Kettle's Yard and the Henry Moore Institute, where it forms part of Appendix 1, p. 275.
13 See Oliver Brown, *Exhibition: The Memoirs of Oliver Brown* (Evelyn, Adams and McKay, 1968).
14 See Brodsky, *Henri Gaudier-Brzeska*, p. 153.
15 Ibid. p. 160.
16 Sophie Brzeska, *Journal*, 5 June 1918, held in the Special Collections department of the Albert Sloman Library, University of Essex. A fuller citation can be found in Evelyn Silber, *Gaudier-Brzeska: Life and Art* (Thames & Hudson, 1996), p. 64, n. 59.
17 Those lectures that had been completed were introduced and edited by Kenneth Clark in Roger Fry, *Last Lectures* (Cambridge University Press, 1939).
18 Henry Moore, 'Primitive Art', *Listener* (24 April 1941), p. 598.
19 Henry Moore and John Hedgecoe, *Henry Moore: My Ideas, Inspiration and Life As an Artist* (Ebury Press, 1986), p. 26.
20 Ibid. p. 86.
21 Henry Moore quoted in J. J. Sweeney, 'Henry Moore', *Partisan Review*, March–April 1947, p. 182. Also quoted in Sebastiano Barassi et al., *Becoming Henry Moore* (Henry Moore Foundation, 2017), p. 27.
22 This quotation and the two above all come from the 'Negro Sculpture' section in Roger Fry's *Vision and Design* (Chatto & Windus, 1920).
23 Henry Moore, *Henry Moore at the British Museum* (Harry N. Abrams, Inc., 1981), p. 8.
24 Ibid.; Barassi et al., *Becoming Henry Moore*, p. 29.
25 *The Letters of Roger Fry: Vol. 2*, ed. Denys Sutton (Chatto & Windus, 1972), p. 458.
26 This item forms part of the Roger Fry Collection, donated after his death in 1934 by his sister Margery Fry, as one of the executors of his will, to the Courtauld Gallery.
27 Fry, *Vision and Design*, pp. 65–6.
28 A detailed, balanced account of his involvement with the Metropolitan Museum and the acquisitions that he helped make possible can be found in Caroline Elam, *Roger Fry and Italian Art* (Ad Ilissum in association with the *Burlington Magazine*, 2019), pp. 35–71.
29 Sutton, *The Letters of Roger Fry, Vol. 2*, p. 489. Also quoted in Elam, *Roger Fry and Italian Art*, p. 76.
30 Sam Rose, *Art and Form: From Roger Fry to Global Modernism* (Pennsylvania State University Press, 2019), p. 5.
31 Christopher Reed, *A Roger Fry Reader* (The University of Chicago Press, 1996), p. 309.

32 Roger Fry, 'The Courtauld Institute of Art', *Burlington Magazine* 57 (December 1930), pp. 317–18.

33 *Henry Moore on Sculpture*, ed. Philip James (Macdonald, 1966), p. 33.

34 From the visitors' books we know that Matisse stayed at the Savoy Hotel and visited the British Museum on 28, 29 and 30 October, and again on 27 November.

35 Henri Matisse to Frank Harris, 1922, quoted in *Matisse in the Studio*, exh. cat. (Royal Academy of Arts, 2017), p. 34.

36 Fry, *Vision and Design*, p. 158.

37 Barassi et al., *Becoming Henry Moore*, p. 31.

38 Henry Moore, unpublished notes for Unit One, 1934. Quoted in Wilkinson, *Henry Moore: Writings and Conversations*, p. 44.

39 Moore, *Henry Moore at the British Museum*, p. 11.

40 Ibid. p. 7.

41 Wilkinson, *Henry Moore: Writings and Conversations*, p. 45.

42 Henry Moore, 'Primitive Art', *Listener*, 24 August 1941. See Wilkinson, *Henry Moore: Writings and Conversations*, p. 104. For a period the Ethnographic Collection, as it was then called, was removed to the Museum of Mankind in Burlington Gardens.

43 Moore, *Henry Moore at the British Museum*, p. 8.

44 Henry Moore, 'Mesopotamian Art', *Listener*, 5 June 1935, p. 944. This piece was in part a review of Christian Zervos's *L'Art de la Mésopotamie* (1936) and in part Moore's own assessment of Sumerian sculpture's most compelling characteristics.

45 See Jon Wood's essay, 'Inner Experience: *Gudea*, Sumerian sculpture and Henry Moore', in Barassi et al., *Becoming Henry Moore*, pp. 93–117.

46 Moore, *Henry Moore at the British Museum*, p. 8.

47 Notebook No. 6, reproduced in *Henry Moore: Complete Drawings, Vol. 1, 1916–29*, ed. Ann Garrould (Lund Humphries in association with the Henry Moore Foundation, 1996), p. 139.

48 Wilkinson, *Henry Moore: Writings and Conversations*, p. 98.

49 Ibid.

CHAPTER 8

1 A helpful summary as well as further insight is found in Michael North's 'The Making of "Make It New"', *Guernica*, 15 August 2013, https://www.guernicamag.com/the-making-of-making-it-new/.

2 See David Peters Corbett, '"Make It New": Laurence Binyon, Pound and Vorticism', *Paideuma: Modern and Contemporary Poetry and Poetics* 26: 2/3 (Fall & Winter 1997), pp. 183–94, where this passage is quoted.

3 Laurence Binyon, *The Art of Botticelli: An Essay in Pictorial Criticism* (Macmillan & Co., 1913), p. 17.

4 Henry Moore, *Henry Moore at the British Museum* (Harry N. Abrams, Inc.), p. 35, ill. p. 73.

5 Henry Moore, 'Mesopotamian Art', *Listener*, 5 June 1935, pp. 944–6.

6 John Piper, *British Romantic Artists* (Collins, 1942), p. 7.

7 Quoted in Christopher Campbell-Howes, *Evelyn Dunbar: A Life in Painting* (Romarin, 2016), p. 246.

8 See Campbell-Howes, *Evelyn Dunbar*, pp. 31–2.

9 Quoted in Jerrold Northrop Moore, *F. L. Griggs: The Architecture of Dreams* (Clarendon Press, 1999), p. 166.

10 Ibid.

11 Norman Jewson, *A Little Book of Architecture* (Oxford University Press, 1940), p. 75.

12 Nicholas Mander, 'Norman Jewson, Architect', https://owlpen.com/arts/norman-jewson.

13 See Mary Taubman, *Gwen John* (Scolar Press, 1985), p. 126, n. 37.

14 See *Looking is a marvellous thing: From Rainer Maria Rilke's letters to his wife Clara, on looking at Cezanne's pictures in the Salon d'Automne, Paris, October 1907* (Pickpockets, *c.* 1992), n.p. For a fuller account of Rilke's intense absorption in the work of Cézanne, see *Selected Letters of Rainer Maria Rilke 1902–1926* (Macmillan & Co., 1946), pp. 189–208.

15 Michael Hofmann, 'Slashed, Red and Dead', *London Review of Books*, 21 January 2021, p. 31.

16 Rainer Maria Rilke and Lou Andreas-Salomé, *Rilke and Andreas Salomé: A Love Story in Letters*, trans. Edward Snow and Michael Winkler (W. W. Norton, 2008), p. 92.

17 Quoted in 'Chronicle 1903–1908', in Rainer Maria Rilke, *Letters to a Young Poet*, trans. M. D. Herter Norton (W. W. Norton & Company, 1934), pp. 101–2.

18 Gwen John, MS dated 19 April 1927, held in the National Library of Wales: NLW MS 22277A, f. 9.

19 Gwen John to Ursula Tyrwhitt, 30 August 1936, quoted in *Gwen John: Letters and Notebooks*, ed. Ceridwen Lloyd-Morgan (Tate Publishing in association with the National Library of Wales, 2004), p. 185. It is difficult to identify this book with any certainty, but it is possible it was the 1926 reissued edition of Joachim Gasquet's *Cézanne*.

20 Lloyd-Morgan, *Gwen John: Letters and Notebooks*, p. 184.

21 A phrase used by Agnes Martin to express her position and that of her art in relation to the outside world, and which formed part of the title to an exhibition of her work held at MoMA, New York, in 1997.

22 See Sue Roe, *Gwen John: A Life* (Chatto & Windus, 2001), p. 41.

23 Ben Nicholson quoted in John Summerson, *Ben Nicholson* (Penguin Books, 1948), p. 7.

24 Ben Nicholson to Jim Ede,

29 August 1942, Kettle's Yard Archive.

25 Christopher Wood to his mother, 28 July 1922 (Tate Archives: TGA 773.2).

26 Andrew Nicholson (ed.), *Unknown Colour: Paintings, Letters, Writings by Winifred Nicholson* (Faber & Faber, 1987), p. 83.

27 Ibid. p. 86.

28 Christopher Wood quoted in Richard Ingleby, *Christopher Wood: An English Painter* (Allison & Busby, 1995), pp. 185–6.

29 Quoted in Elizabeth Fisher and Andrew Nairne (eds), *Alfred Wallis: Ships and Boats* (Kettle's Yard, 2012), p. 12.

30 Robert Jones, *Alfred Wallis: Artist and Mariner* (Halsgrove, 2001), p. 132.

31 Alfred Wallis to Jim Ede, 30 November 1935, Kettle's Yard Archive, University of Cambridge: AW 21.

32 Quoted in Fisher and Nairne, *Alfred Wallis*, p. 14.

33 Ben Nicholson letter to John Summerson, TGA 20048.1.72.2. Jovan Nicholson and Julian Stair, *Art and Life: Ben Nicholson, Winifred Nicholson, Christopher Wood, Alfred Wallis, William Staite Murray, 1920–1931* (Philip Wilson Publishers, 2013), p. 131.

34 Quoted in Ingleby, *Christopher Wood*, p. 217.

35 Francis Rose, quoted in ibid. p. 218.

36 Christopher Wood, quoted in ibid. p. 219.

37 Jim Ede, quoted in ibid. p.249.

38 Herbert Read, *Art Now*, rev. ed. (Faber & Faber, [1933] 1938), pp. 67 and 70.

39 Desmond MacCarthy's recollection of this landmark exhibition is quoted in Virginia Woolf, *Roger Fry: A Biography* (Hogarth Press, 1940), p. 154.

40 William Rothenstein, *Men and Memories*, vol. 2 (Rose and Crown Library, [1931] 1934), p. 123.

41 Roger Fry, *Vision and Design* (Chatto & Windus, 1920), p. 191.

42 Roger Fry, 'The New Gallery', *Athenaeum*, 13 January 1906, pp. 56–7.

43 *The Letters of Roger Fry, Vol. 1*, ed. Denys Sutton (Chatto & Windus, 1972), p. 300.

44 Roger Fry, Introduction to 'Cézanne – 1' by Maurice Denis, *Burlington Magazine* 16: 82 (January 1910), p. 207.

45 Roger Fry, 'The French Post-Impressionists', in *Vision and Design*, p. 156.

46 Ibid.

47 H. S. [Jim] Ede to Ben Nicholson, 18 April 1929 (Tate Archives: TGA 8717.1.2.853).

48 See Anne Robbins, 'Courtauld and the National Gallery: "An assault on a big scale"', in *Courtauld Impressionists: From Manet to Cézanne*, exh. cat. (National Gallery, 2018), p. 33.

49 Woolf, *Roger Fry*, p. 153.

50 In David Sylvester (ed.), *Patrick Heron*, exh. cat. (Tate Gallery, 1998), p. 21.

CHAPTER 9

1 See Chapter 8, n. 3.

2 Algernon Newton, 'Thoughts about Art and Life', autograph typescript (Tate Archives: TGA TAM 32). Much that follows on Newton is based on this as yet unpublished autobiographical memoir.

3 Ibid.

4 Quoted in Patrick Elliott, *True to Life: British Realist Painting in the 1920s and 1930s* (National Galleries of Scotland, 2017), p. 112.

5 See *The Peculiarity of Algernon Newton RA (1880–1968)*, with an essay by Andrew Graham-Dixon, exh. cat. (Daniel Katz Gallery, 2012), p. 6.

6 Newton, 'Thoughts about Art and Life'. Quoted in *Algernon Newton, RA, 1880–1968*, exh. cat. (Sheffield City Art Galleries, 1980), n.p., and in *The Peculiarity of Algernon Newton RA (1880–1968)*, p. 8.

7 From T. S. Eliot's 'Burnt Norton', in *Four Quartets*.

8 Simon Martin, *The Mythic Method: Classicism in British Art 1920–1950* (Pallant House Gallery, 2017), p. 7.

9 Wyndham Lewis, *Paleface* (Chatto & Windus, 1929), p. 255.

10 Isabelle Loring Wallace, 'Classicism and Contemporary Art', *Burlington Contemporary* (28 February 2019), http://contemporary.burlington.org.uk/reviews/reviews/classicism-and-contemporary-art.

11 From T. S. Eliot, 'Ulysses, Order and Myth', *Dial* (November 1923), pp. 177–8.

12 Christopher Reed, *Bloomsbury Rooms: Modernism, Subculture, and Domesticity* (Yale University Press, 2004), p. 220.

13 Ibid. p. 222.

14 This hand-painted advertisement can be found in the Mortimer Rare Book Library, Smith College. Reproduced in Frances Spalding, *Virginia Woolf: Art, Life* (National Portrait Gallery, 2014), p. 116.

15 See *The Letters of Roger Fry, Vol. 2*, ed. Denys Sutton (Chatto & Windus, 1972), p. 438.

16 An analysis of their relationship at this time and a fuller quotation from Grant's diary can be found in Frances Spalding, *Duncan Grant: A Biography* (Chatto & Windus, 1997), pp. 200–1.

17 Grant's letter is quoted in Simon Watney, *The Art of Duncan Grant* (John Murray, 1990), p. 47.

18 Ibid. p. 231.

19 Duncan Grant to Vanessa Bell, October 1919. Quoted in Watney, *The Art of Duncan Grant*, p. 47.

20 Henry Tonks to Augustus Daniel, quoted in Laurence Whistler, *The Laughter and the Urn: The Life of Rex Whistler* (Weidenfeld & Nicolson, 1985), p. 61.

21 Anna Thomasson, *A Curious Friendship: The Story of a Bluestocking and a Bright Young Thing* (Macmillan, 2015), p. 58.

22 Whistler, *The Laughter and the Urn*, p. 92. Also quoted in Thomasson, *A Curious Friendship*, p. 60.
23 Thomasson, *A Curious Friendship*, p. 60.
24 Stephen Tennant, essay on Rex Whistler (1948), quoted in Thomasson, *A Curious Friendship*, p. 27.
25 Whistler, *The Laughter and the Urn*, p. 66.
26 David Cecil, letter to *The Times*, 20 August 1968, p. 7. This letter was written at a time when the Tate Gallery was considering the need to enlarge the restaurant and to remove Rex Whistler's murals. Another letter published in *The Times* on the same day, from Laurence Whistler (brother of Rex), refers to the murals as being 'eloquent of the 1920s, having much in common with the work of Edith Sitwell and William Walton. They are eloquent, witty, mocking, romantic. Such qualities may not be valued now by sophisticated people, but they will be.'
27 The decorations still exist and now hang in Liverpool University's Victoria Art Gallery and Museum.
28 'Joseph Southall', *Oxford Dictionary of National Biography*, https://doi.org/10.1093/ref:odnb/64535.
29 Herbert Read, 'English Art', *Burlington Magazine* 63: 369 (December 1933), pp. 243–76. See also Kate Aspinall, 'Signature of Our Race: Herbert Read and the Line that links Medieval Illumination and 1930s British Modernism', *Visual Resources* 32: 1–2 (1916).
30 Read, 'English Art', p. 259.
31 Ibid. p. 269.
32 Ibid. p. 277.
33 Quoted in Andy Friend, *Ravilious & Co.: The Pattern of Friendship* (Thames & Hudson, 2017), p. 34.
34 Ibid. p. 36.
35 Reproduced in Alan Powers, *Ravilious: Artist and Designer* (Lund Humphries, 2015), p. 70.
36 Quoted in Friend, *Ravilious & Co.*, p. 31.
37 Helen Binyon's name, and that of her sister Nicolete, can be found in the Prints and Drawings Visitors' Book on 4 February 1922, and Helen's name appears again on 4 March 1922 – the same day that Paul Nash also visited the department, giving his address as Dymchurch, Kent.
38 On Binyon's departure from the British Museum, a short article in the *Burlington Magazine* (62: 361 [April 1933], p. 153) stated: 'He has proved himself a master of routine, but has added to that mastership "a spiritual rhythm passing into and acting upon material things".'
39 Laurence Binyon, *English Watercolours* (Batsford, 1939), p. 5.
40 J. M. Richards, *Memories of an Unjust Fella* (Weidenfeld & Nicolson, 1980), p. 100.
41 Helen Binyon, *Eric Ravilious: Memoir of an Artist* (Lutterworth Press, 1983), p. 43.
42 Powers, *Ravilious*, p. 9.
43 See Alexandra Harris, *Romantic Moderns: English Writers, Artists and the Imagination from Virginia Woolf to John Piper* (Thames & Hudson, 2010).
44 Paul Nash, 'A Characteristic', in *Paul Nash: Writings on Art*, ed. Andrew Causey (Oxford University Press, 2000), p. 236. First published in *Architectural Record*, March 1937.

CHAPTER 10

1 Quoted in Lucy Carrington Wertheim, *Adventure in Art* (Nicholson and Watson, 1947), p. 3.
2 Quoted in James Beechey, Patrick Elliott, Helen Little and Chris Stephens, 'Picasso in Britain 1920–1939', in *Picasso and Modern British Art*, exh. cat. (Tate Publishing, 2012), p. 105.
3 Ibid.
4 H. S. [Jim] Ede to Charles Aitken, 28 October 1927 (National Gallery Archives, 215.4).
5 Myfanwy Piper, 'Back in the 1930s', *Art and Literature: An International Review* (Winter 1965), p. 145.
6 Wertheim, *Adventure in Art*, p. 3.
7 Ibid. p. 4.
8 Ibid. p. 2.
9 Ibid.
10 Ibid. p. 8.
11 Ibid.
12 Ibid. p. 9.
13 Christopher Wood to Ben Nicholson, postcard, 12 March 1930 (Tate Archives: TGA 8618.71). Quoted in Virginia Button, *Christopher Wood* (Tate Publishing, 2003), p. 50.
14 Wertheim, *Adventure in Art*, p. 14.
15 Ibid. pp. 11 and 12.
16 Ibid. from 'Author's Note', n.p.
17 Ibid. p. 19.
18 Andrew Lambirth, *The Art of Richard Eurich* (Lund Humphries, 2020), p. 31.
19 As recalled by Eurich's daughter Philippa Bambach in a Zoom discussion about her father Richard Eurich, recorded by Lund Humphries to celebrate the publication of Andrew Lambirth's monograph on Eurich in 2020.
20 Quoted by Piper, 'Back in the 1930s', p. 141.
21 John Piper in 'Letters', *Listener*, 5 July 1933, pp. 36–7.
22 Ben Nicholson in 'Letters', *Listener*, 2 August 1933, p. 174.
23 In his artist's statement for Unit One the following year, Nicholson echoed Piper by likewise using Raphael as his touchstone for aesthetic experience.
24 Myfanwy Piper, introduction to *John Piper: A Retrospective* (Waddington Galleries in association with James Kirkman, 1994).
25 See Norbert Lynton, *Ben Nicholson* (Phaidon, 1993), ill. 82.

26 John Piper, 'Younger English Painters – I', *Listener*, 22 March 1933, p. 455.
27 John Piper, 'Younger English Painters – II', *Listener*, 29 March 1933, p. 490.
28 Ibid. p. 492.
29 See Christopher Green, 'Ben Nicholson and Picasso', in *Picasso & Modern British Art*, exh. cat. (Tate Publishing, 2012), p. 42.
30 John Piper, 'December Galleries', *New Statesman & Nation*, 16 December 1933, p. 809.
31 John Piper, 'Recent Paintings by Edward Wadsworth', *Apollo* 18: 108 (December 1933), p. 387.
32 The titles of the works he exhibited are *Breakwaters*, *English Coast*, *String Solo*, *Sand and Shingle* and *Seaweed*.
33 The disparate artists within the 7 & 5, even after the purge, were not all equally committed to abstract art, but must have accepted the decision recorded in the minutes book: 'The exact definition of "non-representational" is left to the discretion of the hanging committee, but as a general guiding principle a work will be excluded if it possesses any element dictated only by natural appearances' (Minutes of the 7 & 5 Society, Tate Archives: TGA 849).
34 See Iain Buchanan, Michael Dunn and Elizabeth Eastmond, *Frances Hodgkins: Paintings and Drawings* (Thames & Hudson, 1995), p. 83, n. 73.
35 Andrew Causey, *Paul Nash: Writings on Art* (Oxford University Press, 2000), p. 2.
36 John Piper to Ben Nicholson, 9 April 1934 (Tate Archives: TGA 8717.2.3402).
37 When asked by R. Myerscough-Walker in an interview for the *Artist* (May 1944) whether or not his abstracts represented any particular subjects, Piper replied: 'They were related to the painting I had done immediately before. Since I had been painting a good deal at the seaside – at Dungeness and in Dorset – the abstract paintings were influenced by forms and colours on the beach and cliff, but only vaguely.' It is possible that some of his shapes and colours were distilled from nautical objects – buoys, staysails, the masts and hulls of boats. Almost certainly, his abstracts, in their organization and use of interval, rhythm, harmony and proportion, owe much to his love of music. Myfanwy Piper recollected on radio that when she first got to know Piper, he and an organist friend had a passion for Handel's Second Concerto for Organ and Strings, which they played over and over again, by turns, on the piano. Piper himself, in an essay, likened a Henry Moore drawing to one of Bach's 'engine-rhythms', by which, as he explains, he meant the following: 'Balance, separation, silence, precision, sternness, nakedness, delicacy, rigour: all the words one might find helpful in attempting to describe the nature of a Bach fugue' ('Aspects of Modern Drawing', *Signature* 7 [November 1937]).
38 John Piper to Myfanwy Evans, 26 July 1934 (Tate Archives: TGA 200410/9).
39 John Piper to Myfanwy Evans, 13 July 1934 (Tate Archives). There is some confusion in the literature on Piper as to the date that he first met Braque, owing to the fact that Piper, towards the end of his life, told certain art historians that he had met Braque in 1927 at Ede's house. Braque had come to London in 1927, but there is no reference among the guest lists kept by Ede that either Braque or John Piper visited his house that year. Braque came to London again in October 1933, but had Piper met him then, he might have not written so excitedly to Myfanwy about their meeting in July 1934, when Ede gave a supper at his house for Braque, and Nicholson, Hepworth, Gallatin and Hélion, and 'Mr and Mrs Piper' joined them after dinner (Ede's pocket diary for 6 July 1934, Kettle's Yard, Cambridge).
40 John Piper to Myfanwy Evans, 5 September [1934] (Tate Archives: TGA 200410/9).
41 An earlier short-lived attempt at an avant-garde magazine had been undertaken by Sidney Hunt, a painter, poet, designer and member of the Seven and Five Society (1926 to 1933). He produced two issues of *Ray* (1926–7), which asserted an international focus with an emphasis on dada and constructivism. The magazine, wide-ranging in outlook, was nevertheless very much the product of a one-man band. It was virtually forgotten before Iria Candela published '"The only English periodical of the avant-garde": Sidney Hunt and the Journal "Ray"', *Burlington Magazine* 152 (April 2010), pp. 239–44.
42 John Piper to Ben Nicholson, 2 October 1934 (Tate Archives: TGA 8717.1.2.3402).
43 Myfanwy Piper, tape-recorded conversation with Margaret Garlake made on 21 November 1994 as part of the National Life Stories series: British Library, C466/251/01-03.
44 Herbert Read, 'Ben Nicholson's Recent Work', *Axis 2* (April 1935), p. 16.
45 H.S. [Jim] Ede, *Axis 1* (January 1935), p. 23.
46 Paul Nash, *Axis 1* (January 1935), p. 26.
47 Geoffrey Grigson, *Axis 1* (January 1935), p. 10.
48 Hugh Gordon Porteus, 'Exhibition of Abstract Painting at the Experimental Theatre', *Axis 1* (January 1935), p. 27.
49 The illustrations that he used for

these five artists were the same as those later used in the book Woods published with Roger Smithells, *The Modern Home: Its Decoration, Furnishing, and Equipment* (F. Lewis Ltd, 1936).

50 *Decoration* 11 (March 1936), p. 44.

51 S. J. Woods, 'Introduction', in *Modern Pictures for Modern Rooms*, exh. cat, Duncan Miller Showrooms (April 1936), n.p.

52 The ground floor of what once was Bowman's is now divided into three retail outfits, but on the floor above, just beneath the curved arches of each window, can still be seen the lettering advertising the shop's wares: Drapery, Curtains, Furniture, Carpets, Bedsteads, Bedding.

53 Myfanwy Evans, unpublished diary, 6 January 1936 (courtesy of Clarissa Lewis).

54 Myfanwy Evans, unpublished diary, 1 February 1936 (courtesy of Clarissa Lewis).

55 J. M. Richards, after visiting the exhibition at the Lefevre Gallery, wrote to Peggy Angus saying that it was 'the London equivalent of the one that was at Oxford, but much better; better pictures, more of them and far better hung. Really a very good show.' Richards to Angus, n.d. [April 1936] (East Sussex Record Office).

56 John Piper to Winifred Nicholson, n.d. [summer/autumn 1935] (courtesy of Andrew Nicholson). Later this year, in November 1935, this particular abstract was illustrated in *Axis 4*.

57 John Piper to Ben Nicholson, 5 May 1936 (Tate Archives: TA 8717:1.2.3403).

58 Myfanwy Evans, unpublished diary for 1936 (courtesy of Clarissa Lewis).

59 According to Margaret Gardiner, this idea was 'born in an ABC tea shop' after the three artists had viewed the International Surrealist Exhibition in June 1936 (Margaret Gardiner, *Barbara Hepworth: A Memoir* [Lund Humphries, 1994], p. 46). A formal meeting to pursue the idea took place on 20 June 1936 (Martin Hammer and Christina Lodder, *Constructing Modernity: The Art and Career of Naum Gabo* [Yale University Press, 2000], p. 236).

60 See Hammer and Lodder, *Constructing Modernity*, p. 492, n. 20.

61 This fact is recorded by Myfanwy in her diary, 3 July 1936 (courtesy of Clarissa Lewis).

62 John Piper voiced this opinion two months later in a letter to Winifred Nicholson, 6 September 1936 (courtesy of Andrew Nicholson).

63 John Piper to Rachel Billington, interview transcript, 1983 (Tate Archives: TGA 8318.27).

64 John Piper to Peter Cannon-Brookes; reported by him to the author in conversation, 30 October 2003.

65 See Tzvetan Todorov, *Hope and Memory*, trans. David Bellos (Atlantic, 2004).

66 Roger Fry, *Reflections on British Painting* (Faber & Faber, 1934), pp. 17–18.

67 Myfanwy Evans, 'Introduction', *Axis* 6 (Summer 1936), p. 8.

68 Alan Powers, *Ravilious: Artist and Designer* (Lund Humphries, 2015), p. 256.

69 John Piper to Winifred Nicholson, 6 September 1936 (courtesy of Andrew Nicholson).

70 S. J. Woods, 'Time to Forget Ourselves', *Axis* 6 (Summer 1936), p. 21.

CHAPTER 11

1 Myfanwy Piper, 'Back in the 1930s', *Art and Literature: An International Review* (Winter 1965), p. 148.

2 Ibid. p. 137.

3 Ibid.

4 Ibid. p. 139.

5 Ibid.

6 Ibid.

7 R. S. Lambert, introduction to *Art in England* (Penguin Books, 1938), p. 5.

8 Herbert Read, *Art Now*, rev. ed. (Faber & Faber, [1933] 1938), p. 60.

9 'Henry Moore', *Listener*, 22 April 1931, p. 688.

10 Read, *Art Now*, p. 79.

11 Ibid. pp. 84 and 86.

12 *Burlington Magazine* 64 (May 1934), p. 245.

13 Herbert Read, 'A Nest of Gentle Artists', first published in *Apollo* 76: 7 (September 1962). It was reprinted in *Herbert Read: A British Vision of World Art* (Leeds City Art Galleries in association with the Henry Moore Foundation and Lund Humphries, 1993), pp. 59–61.

14 *Circle: International Survey of Constructive Art* (Faber & Faber, 1937), plate 29.

15 Read, 'A Nest of Gentle Artists'.

16 Ibid.

17 Fiona MacCarthy, *Walter Gropius: Visionary Founder of the Bauhaus* (Faber & Faber, 2019), p. 279.

18 John Allan et al., *Isokon Gallery: The Story of a New Vision for Urban Living* (Isokon Gallery Trust, 2016), p. 28.

19 Ibid. p. 36.

20 More accurately, Pritchard offered Gropius a place to live and reserved for him a single-person 'Minimum Flat', not realizing, until Ise stepped out of the train with him at Victoria Station, where a welcome party was waiting to receive them, that Gropius was a married man. He hastily telephoned through to the Flats, asking for arrangements to be changed so that a two-room flat would await them, and then drove them very slowly through London so that there was time for the necessary alterations to be made. See MacCarthy, *Walter Gropius*, pp. 292–3.

21 Ibid. p. 301.

22 Ibid. p. 308.

23 Herbert Read, 'A New Humanism', *Architectural Review*,

October 1935, p. 151. Quoted in Valeria Carullo, *Moholy-Nagy in Britain 1935–1937* (Lund Humphries, 2019), p. 14.

24 J. G. Crowther was Moholy-Nagy's first English client; he designed a book cover for Crowther's *An Outline of the Universe* in 1930.

25 Sibyl Moholy-Nagy, *Moholy-Nagy: Experiment in Totality* (MIT Press, 1969), pp. 135–7.

26 See Sarah Jane Checkland, *Ben Nicholson: The Vicious Circles of his Life & Art* (John Murray, 2000), p. 121.

27 Ben Nicholson to Winifred Nicholson, 22 February [1933], quoted in Lee Beard (ed.), *Ben Nicholson: Writings and Ideas* (Lund Humphries, 2019), p. 25.

28 Herbert Read (ed.), *Unit One: The Modern Movement in English Architecture, Painting and Sculpture* (Cassell and Co. Ltd, 1934), p. 109.

29 Ben Nicholson to Winifred Nicholson, 29 June [1935], quoted in Beard, *Ben Nicholson*, p. 33.

30 Ben Nicholson to John Summerson, 3 January 1944, quoted in Checkland, *Ben Nicholson*, p. 132.

31 See Beard, *Ben Nicholson*, p. 31.

32 Nicolete Binyon, 'Nets', *Fritillary*, 14 February 1931.

33 Nicolete Gray, 'An Open Letter to Miss Grier', the principal of Lady Margaret Hall, Oxford, concerning a lending scheme to bring together contemporary artists and patrons (Nicolete Gray Archive).

34 Nicolete Gray, circular written in connection with the 'Abstract and Concrete' exhibition (Nicolete Gray Archive).

35 Nicolete Gray, 'Foreword' to 'Abstract and Concrete' exh. cat., 1936.

36 'Art Show Shocks', *Sunday Pictorial*, 18 April 1936, n.p.

37 *Daily Mail*, 17 April 1936, n.p.

38 R. G. Collingwood, *The Principles of Art* (Clarendon Press, 1938), pp. iv–v.

39 Ibid. p. vi.

40 Read, *Art Now*, p. 153.

41 Quoted in James King, *Roland Penrose: The Life of a Surrealist* (Edinburgh University Press, 2016), p. 1.

42 The Peckovers eventually went into partnership with the Gurneys of Norfolk and in 1896, along with nineteen other banks, merged with Barclay's.

43 Roland Penrose, *Scrap Book, 1900–1981* (Thames & Hudson, 1981), p. 28.

44 Quoted in Charles Harrison, *English Art and Modernism 1900–1939* (Allen Lane and Indiana University Press, 1981), p. 312.

45 David Gascoyne, *A Short Survey of Surrealism* (Cobden-Sanderson, 1935), p. x.

46 Eileen Agar, typescript of a lecture on surrealism, TGA.

47 Ibid.

48 Paul Nash, 'A New Poetry', in *News Chronicle*, 7 June 1937, p. 10. See Andrew Causey, *Paul Nash: Writings on Art* (Oxford University Press, 2000), p. 140.

49 From an undated letter [mid-October 1936] from Penrose to Picasso, MS, Roland Penrose Archive; quoted in King, *Roland Penrose*, p. 140.

50 Penrose, *Scrap Book*, p. 80.

51 Lawrence Gowing, 'Light, Love and Picasso', *Observer*, 10 July 1960, p. 21.

CHAPTER 12

1 Illustrated in the *Left Review*, June 1937, p. 260.

2 James Holland to the Foreign Committee of the Union of Artists, 1935; quoted in Lynda Morris and Robert Radford, *The Story of the Artists International Association, 1933–1953* (The Museum of Modern Art, 1983), p. 20.

3 George Orwell, *Homage to Catalonia* (Penguin, 2000), p. 189.

4 Simon Martin, *Conscience and Conflict: British Artists and the Spanish Civil War* (Pallant House Gallery, 2014), p. 37.

5 As recollected by Yvonne Kapp, one of the organizers. See Morris and Radford, *The Story of the Artists International Association*, p. 33.

6 Virginia Woolf, *A Room of One's Own and Three Guineas* (Penguin Books, 2000), p. 269.

7 Myfanwy Evans, 'The Painter's Object' in Myfanwy Evans (ed.), *The Painter's Object* (Gerald Howe, 1937), pp. 8 and 9.

8 Herbert Read in 'Picasso's "Guernica"', *London Bulletin* 6 (October 1938), p. 6.

9 Quoted in Richard Crossman (ed.), *The God that Failed* (Harper and Brothers, 1950), p. 244.

10 Martin, *Conscience and Conflict*, p. 57.

11 Sophie Bowness (ed.), *Barbara Hepworth: Writings and Conversations* (Tate Publishing, 2015), p. 29.

12 Andrew Causey, *Edward Burra: Complete Catalogue* (Phaidon, 1985), p. 9.

13 The 'modern moral subject' is a term first employed by William Hogarth (1697–1764) for satire on the manners and morals of the day.

14 Jeffery Myers, *The Enemy: A Biography of Wyndham Lewis* (Routledge and Kegan Paul, 1980), p. 159. Also quoted in Causey, *Edward Burra*, p. 23.

15 Causey, *Edward Burra*, p. 9.

16 Burra disliked exhibiting, but his reputation appears to have been made early on by two exhibitions he had at Leicester Galleries in April 1929 and May 1932, and later by an exhibition at the Redfern Gallery in November and December 1942.

17 See *Well, Dearie! The Letters of Edward Burra*, ed. Wiliam Chappell (Gordon Fraser, 1985), p. 79.

18 Causey, *Edward Burra*, p. 59.

19 *Well, Dearie!*, p. 92.

20 See Clover de Pertinez, 'Edward in Spain', in William Chappell (ed.), *Edward Burra: A Painter*

Remembered by His Friends (Andre Deutsch in association with the Lefevre Gallery, 1985), p. 75.

21 Wendy Baron, *Sickert: Paintings and Drawings* (New Haven and London: Yale University Press, 2006), p. 537. Sickert was a great reader of newspapers, sometimes running to six a day.

22 Rebecca Daniels, 'Press Art: The Late Oeuvre of Walter Richard Sickert', *Apollo* 156 (October 2002), p. 31.

23 All three criticisms are referred to, and footnoted, by Richard Morphet in his seminal essay 'Late Sickert, then and now', in *Late Sickert: Paintings 1927 to 1942*, exh. cat. (Arts Council, 1981), p. 8.

24 *Walter Sickert: The Complete Writings on Art*, ed. Anna Gruetzner Robins (Oxford University Press, 2000), p. 686.

25 This remark was made in one of six lectures delivered by Sickert to Thanet School of Art during October and November 1934; see Robins, *Walter Sickert: The Complete Writings*, p. 652, and also Baron, *Sickert: Paintings and Drawings*, p. 527.

26 See *Barbara Hepworth: Writings and Conversations*, ed. Sophie Bowness (Tate Publishing, 2015), p. 64. Hepworth also claims that the idea of publishing this book was born in 1935, a mistake corrected by Bowness, who affirms it was conceived in 1936. Not all permissions were obtained for the illustrations, John Piper being annoyed that two of his abstracts were included without his permission.

27 Naum Gabo, 'The Constructive Idea in Art', in Leslie Martin, Ben Nicholson and Naum Gabo (eds), *Circle: International Survey of Constructive Art* (Faber & Faber, 1937), p. 6. A slightly shortened version can be found in Charles Harrison and Paul Wood (eds), *Art in Theory, 1900–2000: An Anthology of Changing Ideas* (Blackwell Publishing, 2003), pp. 385–7. The relation between content and form appears on p. 6 in the original and on p. 385 in *Art in Theory*.

28 Myfanwy Piper in conversation with Margaret Garlake, 21 November 1994, as part of the National Life Stories series (British Library, C466/251/01-03).

29 Evans, *The Painter's Object*, p. 9.

30 See William Coldstream, 'Painting', in R. S. Lambert (ed.), *Art in England* (Penguin Books, 1938), p. 100.

31 See *London Bulletin* 8–9 (January–February 1939), n.p.

32 J. M. Richards, 'Black and White: An Introductory Study of a National Design Idiom', *Architectural Review*, November 1937.

33 John Piper, 'The Nautical Style', *Architectural Review* 83 (January 1938), pp. 1–14. This essay is reissued, revised and extended in John Piper, *Buildings and Prospects* (Architectural Press, 1948).

34 Timothy Mowl, *Stylistic Cold Wars: Betjeman versus Pevsner* (John Murray, 2000), p. 50.

35 John Piper, review in *Horizon* 4: 24 (December 1941), pp. 415–16.

36 Jonathan Anderson and William A. Dyrness, *Modern Art and the Life of Culture: the Religious Impulses of Modernism* (InterVarsity Press, 2016), p. 177.

37 Piet Mondrian, 'Plastic Art and Pure Plastic Art', in Harrison and Wood, *Art in Theory*, p. 388.

38 The Hirshhorn catalogue on *Composition with Blue and Yellow* gives pride of place to Nan Roberts in the provenance for this painting, but later on mentions Winifred Nicholson as its original owner. Almost certainly, at the time of the transaction, Winifred was acting on behalf of her sister-in-law.

39 This assumption is corrected by Lesley Jackson in her book *Alastair Morton and Edinburgh Weavers: Visionary Textiles and Modern Art* (V&A Publishing, 2012), pp. 109–10 and p. 377, n. 21.

40 This conversation is reported in Andrew Nicholson (ed.), *Unknown Colour: Paintings, Letters, Writings by Winifred Nicholson* (Faber & Faber, 1987), p. 109.

41 Winifred Nicholson, 'I Like to Have A Picture In My Room', in *Unknown Colour*, p. 234. First published in the *Christian Science Monitor*, 1954.

42 Charles Darwent, *Mondrian in London: How British Art Nearly Became Modern* (Double-Barrelled Books, 2012), p. 86.

43 Conversation between the author and Michael Middleton, quoted in Frances Spalding, *John Minton: Dance till the Stars Come Down* (John Curtis in association with Hodder & Stoughton, 1991), p. 26.

44 James Thrall Soby, *After Picasso* (Edwin Valentine Mitchell; Dodd, Mead & Co., 1935), p. xi.

45 Gertrude Stein, *Picasso* (Batsford, 1938), p. 43.

46 Soby, *After Picasso*, p. 8.

47 John Minton to Robin Treffgarne, 12 June 1940, quoted in Spalding, *John Minton*, p. 40.

48 John Minton to Edie Lamont, 4-5-6 1939, quoted in Spalding, *John Minton*, p. 32.

49 Ibid.

50 An early landscape by Minton, dating from the late 1930s, was acquired by Wertheim for her own collection and gifted to Worthing Museum and Art Gallery in 1973.

51 Lucy Carrington Wertheim, *Adventure in Art* (Nicholson and Watson, 1947), p. 85.

ACKNOWLEDGMENTS

My thanks go first to Jamie Camplin for commissioning this book then to Sophy Thompson for keeping it in Thames & Hudson's fold when interruptions caused delays. I am deeply grateful for her patience and for the encouragement given me by the editor Julia MacKenzie, shortly before her retirement. Camilla Rockwood, the copy-editor allocated to my book, was an absolute gift and a pleasure to work with, as was Maria Ranauro, the art editor, who worked tirelessly on the complicated relationship between images to text. I am also indebted to Rowena Alsey for her handsome design of this book, and to Poppy David, who took such care over the quality of the pictures.

Writing is often thought to be a solitary business, and indeed long days spent working alone are necessary. Yet an immensely sociable world surrounds the study of art history. Having been part of it for some time, it is difficult for me to separate earlier debts from those incurred more recently in connection with this book, as together they have formed a continuum of help, information, and ideas. Nevertheless, in more recent times I would like to thank Rupert Arrowsmith, Ariane Bankes, Wendy Baron, James Beechey, Jonathan Black, Peter and Cordelia Bourne, David Boyd Haycock, Frances Christie of Sotheby's, Rebecca Daniels, Charlotte Edwards, Donato Esposito, Hugh Fowler Wright, David Fraser Jenkins, Andy Friend, Philippe Garner, Anne Goodchild, Paul Gough, Edmund Gray, Michael Grist of MacConnal-Mason, Anna Gruetzner Robins, Rachel Boyd Hall, Philip Harley of Christie's, Alexandra Harris, Ayla Lepine, Clarissa Lewis, Paul Liss, Sacha Llewellyn, the late Richard Luckett, Tom Marks, Simon Martin, Laura Moffatt, Richard Morphet, Jovan Nicholson, Alan Powers, Ingram Reid of Bonham's, James Scott, Peyton Skipwith, Jennifer Sliwka, the Rev. Stephen Tucker, Nigel and Iris Weaver.

I am grateful to Jovan Nicholson for permission to quote from Winifred Nicholson's writings; to Philippe Garner for quotations from Lucy Wertheim's *Adventure in Art* and her correspondence with Christopher Wood; to Clarissa Lewis for John Piper's writings and to the Tate Archives for an exchange of letters between Ben Nicholson and Helen Sutherland. Adrian Glew and his staff in the Tate Archives have been unfailingly helpful with small details. I am also indebted to several libraries: the Tate Library, the London Library, the British Library and, in the late stages of this book, to Cambridge University Library, where speed of access to material has been incredibly helpful. My thanks go also to my literary agent Zoë Waldie for her support and encouragement, and to friends for the refreshment gained through the pleasure of good company, discussion, shared meals, and music – Peter and Liza Miller, Sophie MacCarthy, Robert Anderson, Julia Hedgecoe, Dame Gillian Beer, Patrick Hemmerle, Geoffrey Howard, Jules Lubbock and Maggie Iversen, Lucy Gent, Lauro Martines. This book is dedicated to Leanna Spalding, who directed my attention to tiny snails, hungry spiders, the tiniest of worms hiding in the compost, and who insisted on using my pockets as depositories for small stones, dandelion stems, and daisies. Precious cargo, gone but not forgotten.

SOURCES OF ILLUSTRATIONS

a = above; **b** = below, **l** = left; **r** = right

2 Pallant House Gallery, Chichester, on loan from a private collection. **11** Russell-Cotes Art Gallery & Museum, Bournemouth. Photo Artepics/Alamy Stock Photo. **14** © Tate. **17** Photo Topical Press Agency/Hulton Archive/Getty Images. **19** Private collection. © The Estate of Stanley Spencer/ Bridgeman. **20** Hyde Park Corner, London. **22** National Gallery London. Photo Heritage Image Partnership Ltd/Alamy Stock Photo. **26** © Imperial War Museum (Art.IWM ART 1931). **27** © Imperial War Museum (Art.IWM ART 2243). **29** © Imperial War Museum (Art. IWM ART 2242). **31** © Imperial War Museum (Art.IWM ART 2705). **33a** © Imperial War Museum (Art. IWM ART 1921). **33b** © Imperial War Museum (Art.IWM ART 2626). **36–37** © Imperial War Museum (Art.IWM ART 1460). **40** © Imperial War Museum (Art.IWM ART 323). **41** Imperial War Museum (Art.IWM ART 2266). © The Estate of Gilbert Spencer. All Rights Reserved, DACS 2022. **46l** Museum of Modern Art, New York. Dept. Architecture and Design. Gift of the artist (438.1939). Digital image, The Museum of Modern Art, New York/ Scala, Firenze. © Simon Rendall. **46r** Cooper Hewitt, Smithsonian Design Museum. Gift of Mrs. E. McKnight Kauffer. © Simon Rendall. **47** Courtesy Cheffins, Cambridge. **50a**, **50b** Courtesy the Huntington Library, Art Museum, and Botanical Gardens, San Marino, California. **53** Samuel Courtauld Trust, The Courtauld Gallery, London. © The Estate of Vanessa Bell. All rights reserved, DACS 2022. **54** Leeds Museums and Galleries. Centre for the Study of Sculpture. © The Estate of Sir Jacob Epstein/Tate, London 2022. **55** Tate, London. © The Estate of Sir Jacob Epstein/Tate, London 2022. **66** Beaverbrook Collection of War Art, Canadian War Museum, Fredericton. **69** Tate, London. Photo 916 collection/Alamy Stock Photo. **72** Tate, London. © Tate. **77** Tate, London. © The Estate of Sir Matthew Smith. **80a** Redfern Art Gallery, London. **80b**, **81a** Courtesy Osborne Samuel Gallery, London. **81b** Private collection, courtesy Bonhams London. **84** Tate, London. **86** Aberdeen Art Gallery and Museums. Photo History and Art Collection/Alamy Stock Photo. **87** National Railway Museum York. Photo SSPL/Getty Images. © The Estate of Leonard Campbell Taylor/ Bridgeman Images. **92** Collection of Christchurch Art Gallery Te Puna o Waiwhetū, purchased with the assistance of the National Art Collections Fund, London, 1980. **94** National Museum of Wales, Cardiff. Purchase with assistance of Knapping Fund, 1973. © The Estate of Sir Cedric Morris/Bridgeman Images. **95** Courtesy MacConnal-Mason Gallery, London. © The Estate of Sir Cedric Morris/ Bridgeman Images. **96** Auckland Art Gallery Toi o Tāmaki, purchased with funds from the William James Jobson Trust, 1954. ©The Estate of Sir Cedric Morris/Bridgeman Images. **97** Auckland Art Gallery Toi o Tāmaki. **98** Tate, London. **102** Sheffield Galleries and Museums Trust. Photo Museums Sheffield/ Bridgeman Images. © The Estate of David Bomberg. All Rights Reserved, DACS 2022. **105** Private collection. Courtesy the Estate of the Artist. **107** Private collection. © The Estate of Elwin Hawthorne. **111** Laing Art Gallery, Newcastle-upon-Tyne. Tyne & Wear Archives & Museums/Bridgeman Images. **115a** Lady Margaret Hall, Oxford. **115b** British Museum, London. **116a** Private collection. Courtesy Piano Nobile, Robert Travers (Works of Art) Ltd. **116b** Dudley Council Museum Collection (1954/17). **118a** The Whitworth, The University of Manchester/ Bridgeman Images. **118b** Private collection. Photo The Fine Art Society, London/Bridgeman Images. **121a** The Higgins Art Gallery & Museum/Bridgeman Images. **121b** Private collection. Photo James Austin/Bridgeman Images. © Angela Verren Taunt. All rights reserved, DACS 2022. **124a** Collection of the McNay Art Museum, Gift of The Tobin Endowment. **124b** from *English Review, Theatre-craft Supplement*, August 1922. **125** Tate, London. **127** Pallant House Gallery, Chichester. Karley Bequest through the Art Fund 1989. **132** Courtesy the ING UK Art Collection. © The Estate of John Nash. All rights reserved 2019/Bridgeman Images. **135** Leicester Arts and Museums Service. Purchased by the Friends of the Museum Fund from the artist through the Art Exhibitions Bureau, 1941/Bridgeman Images. © The Estate of John Nash. All rights reserved 2019/Bridgeman Images. **138** Private collection. **139** Tate, London. **141** Private collection. © Angela Verren Taunt. All rights reserved, DACS 2022. **143** © Imperial War Museum (Art.IWM ART 2747). **148** Tate, London. **149** Leeds Museums and Galleries/ Bridgeman Images. The Estate of John David Roberts. By permission of the Treasury Solicitor. **150** National Galleries of Scotland, Edinburgh. © by kind permission of the Wyndham Lewis Memorial Trust (a registered charity)/Bridgeman Images. **154** Private collection. © Trustees of Winifred Nicholson. **160** Tate, London. © Angela Verren Taunt. All rights reserved, DACS 2022. **163** Private collection. © Angela Verren Taunt. All rights reserved, DACS 2022. **166** Patrick Bourne & Co., London. © The Trustees of Winifred Nicholson. **167a** Bristol Museum and Art Gallery. © The Trustees of Winifred Nicholson. **167b** Courtesy Piano Nobile, Robert Travers (Works of Art) Ltd. © The Trustees of Winifred Nicholson. **168** Private collection. © Angela Verren Taunt. All rights reserved, DACS 2022. **170**, **171** Tate, London. © The Estate of Stanley

Spencer. All rights reserved, 2022/ Bridgeman Images. **172** Fitzwilliam Museum, University of Cambridge. © The Estate of Stanley Spencer. All rights reserved, 2022/Bridgeman Images. **173** Photo courtesy the author. **174** National Trust Images/ John Hammond/Bridgeman Images. © The Estate of Stanley Spencer. All rights reserved, 2022/ Bridgeman Images. **181** © Imperial War Museum (IWM ART 2268). **184** National Trust Photographic Library/A C Cooper/Bridgeman Images. © The Estate of Stanley Spencer/Bridgeman. **185** National Trust Images/John Hammond/ Bridgeman Images. © The Estate of Stanley Spencer/Bridgeman. **190** Tate, London. **191** Tate, London. © The Estate of Frank Dobson. **198** Bristol Museums, Galleries & Archives. **199** Roger Fry Collection, Courtauld Gallery, London/ Bridgeman Images. **202** Roger Fry, *Vision and Design* (Chatto & Windus, 1920). **206** British Museum, London. **207** British Council Collection. Reproduced by permission of The Henry Moore Foundation. **208** Museo Nacional de Antropologia, Mexico. Photo Peter Horree/Alamy Stock Photo. **209** Leeds Museums and Galleries/ Bridgeman Images. Reproduced by permission of The Henry Moore Foundation. **212** Birmingham Museums and Art Gallery/ Bridgeman Images. **214a** © Tate, London. **214b** Tate, London. **216** Ashmolean Museum, Oxford. **217** British Museum, London. **219** Private collection. **220** Courtesy MacConnal-Mason Gallery, London. © The Estate of Tristram Hillier. All Rights Reserved 2022/ Bridgeman Images. **222** The Royal Society, London/Bridgeman Images. © The Trustees of the Meredith Frampton Estate. **223** Ferens Art Gallery, Hull Museums, Hull. © Richard Woodward/Bridgeman Images. **224**, **225** Tate, London. **227** Scottish National Gallery of Modern Art. Purchased with assistance from the Henry and Sula Walton Fund and Art Fund, 2020 (GMA 5648). Photo Peter Barritt/Alamy Stock Photo. **234** Courtesy the Pier Art Centre, Stromness, Orkney. Photo Alistair Peebles. **235** Private collection, courtesy Bonhams London. © Angela Verren Taunt. All rights reserved, DACS 2022. **244** Private collection, UK. Photo courtesy Daniel Katz Ltd, London. © The Estate of Algernon Cecil Newton RA. **245** Private collection, Belgium. Photo courtesy Daniel Katz Ltd, London. © The Estate of Algernon Cecil Newton RA. **247** Private collection. Photo Christie's Images/Bridgeman Images. The Estate of John David Roberts. By permission of the Treasury Solicitor. **248** Museum of Modern Art, New York. Poster Gift of the artist (388.1939)/Scala, Florence. © Simon Rendall. **250** By permission of the Provost and Scholars of King's College, Cambridge. Originally published in 'The Bloomsbury Set', *World of Interiors*, June 2017. Photo Antony Crolla © The Condé Nast Publications Limited. Artwork © The Estate of Duncan Grant. All rights reserved, DACS 2022 and © The Estate of Vanessa Bell. All rights reserved, DACS 2022. **251** Private collection. Christie's Images/Bridgeman Images. © The Estate of Duncan Grant. All rights reserved, DACS 2022 and © The Estate of Vanessa Bell. All rights reserved, DACS 2022. **252** State Hermitage Museum, St Petersburg/ Bridgeman Images. Natalia Goncharova © UPRAVIS/DACS 2022. **254** Tate, London. © The Estate of Duncan Grant. All rights reserved, DACS 2022. **255** Private collection. © The Estate of Duncan Grant. All rights reserved, DACS 2022. **258–259** Tate, London. **263** Nottingham City Museums & Galleries/Bridgeman Images. **265** Private collection/Bridgeman Images. By permission of the Estate of Graham Sutherland. **271a**, **271b** British Museum, London. **275** Private collection/Bridgeman Images. **277** Towner Art Gallery, Eastbourne/Bridgeman Images. **280** Swindon Museum and Art Gallery. Purchased with the assistance of the Victoria and Albert Museum Purchase Grant Fund, 1967 (AG166). **284a** Tate, London. **284b** Towner Art Gallery, Eastbourne. Acquired through the Lucy Carrington Wertheim Bequest. **293** Private collection/Bridgeman Images. © Angela Verren Taunt. All rights reserved, DACS 2022. **294** Tate, London. Barbara Hepworth © Bowness. **296** Courtesy Bloomsbury Auctions. **297** Whitworth Art Gallery, University of Manchester/Bridgeman Images. © The Piper Estate/DACS 2022. **301** © The Piper Estate/DACS 2022. **307** Collection of Bran Webb. © Simon Rendall. **309** Private collection. © The Estate of John Cecil Stephenson. **312** Pritchard Papers, University of East Anglia. Photograph taken by John Maltby © Pyrok Ltd. **317** Tate, London. **320** National Galleries of Scotland, Edinburgh. **323** Government Art Collection. © The Estate of Eileen Agar/Bridgeman Images. **328**, **329** © The Estate of James Boswell. **332** The Sherwin Collection, Leeds. © Succession Picasso/DACS, London 2022. **333** Victoria and Albert Museum, London. © Simon Rendall. **334** Photo Barbara Hepworth. Collection Bowness. Barbara Hepworth © Bowness. **338** Private collection. Photo Lefevre Fine Art Ltd, London/ Bridgeman Images. Edward Burra © The Estate of the Artist, c/o Lefevre Fine Art Ltd, London. **340** Birmingham Museum and Art Gallery. Edward Burra © The Estate of the Artist, c/o Lefevre Fine Art Ltd, London. **342** Private collection. **343** Royal Collection, London. **347** Yale Center for British Art, Paul Mellon Fund/Bridgeman Images. **350** National Galleries of Scotland, Edinburgh. **351** Tate, London. **357** Courtesy Zuleika Gallery. © The Estate of John Minton/Bridgeman Images

INDEX

Pages in *italic* refer to images